# Hurricane Michael

## A Storm of Corruption

Margo Deal Anderson

# DEDICATION

This book is dedicated to my friend and co-defendant, James Finch, who was indicted because he stood by me as I exposed the corruption in the City of Lynn Haven after Hurricane Michael, thwarting the plans of those who set me up, those who wanted to make sure that not only would I no longer be the Mayor, but that I would not be able to pursue the seat in Congress for which I was ready to pursue. James has stood by me not only in friendship, but financially, with our combined legal fees more than five million dollars; he has been my friend through the darkest days imaginable, and our goal now is to expose the corrupt justice system that did this to us, as the Bay County Florida Sheriff, Tommy Ford, and his corrupt investigative team provided the initial false information to the FBI which led to our indictment. Hopefully, our story could be the beginning of reform for the Federal Grand Jury system... where anyone can be accused and indicted by ruthless prosecutors, when conviction becomes more important than truth. Less than 1% of Federal grand jury transcripts are ever unsealed; Judge Mark Walker of the Northern District of Florida took that almost unprecedented step in our case, a step which revealed that the FBI Agent and the Assistant U.S. Attorney made false statements to the Grand Jury, resulting in the removal from office and indictment of Margo Anderson, and six months later, multi-millionaire, James Finch. If it happened to us, it could happen to anyone.

# *Foreword*

## *by*

# *Guy Lewis*

### *Former U.S. Attorney and Fox News Contributor*

My law partner, Jeff Forman, and I walked into a large conference room in the U.S. Attorney's Office in Tallahassee. The acting U.S. Attorney, four federal prosecutors, including the chief and deputy chief of the criminal division, and multiple FBI agents and supervisors were there waiting. With few exchanged cordialities, we argued for well over an hour as to why James Finch, the single most successful and colorful businessman in Lynn Haven, Florida, should not be indicted on federal corruption charges. I reminded the group that James had produced hundreds of thousands of pages of records, including his tax returns to the Grand Jury. I indicated that James would sit for a no holds barred interview with the FBI and prosecutors. I offered to allow the FBI to polygraph James. We had nothing to hide.

Having participated in hundreds of these types of make-or-break presentations, both as a prosecutor and a defense attorney, ours was a powerful argument based on the facts and the law. I ended the presentation stating in no uncertain terms that James Finch and Margo Anderson were innocent. The lead prosecutor walked us to the elevator, telling us that he was interested in James' cooperation, but stated that James would have to plead guilty and admit his criminal conduct. I told the prosecutor that James would be happy to answer any of the government's questions, but that James did not bribe former Lynn Haven Mayor Anderson or anyone else for that matter. It was then that the prosecutor stated: "James must be guilty of something; he's been in the construction business for decades." That's when I knew that the government was hell-bent on prosecuting these people despite the actual evidence. I told the prosecutor that James would fight this case to the bitter end, and that he would be found not guilty.

Over the next two long years, the government indeed lost over and over and over again. After a series of "fast ball to the head" motions and hearings, Chief Judge Mark Walker dismissed charges, severed counts, severed defendants, and ordered the government to produce favorable evidence being hidden. The Chief Judge suppressed government evidence, threatened sanctions, and eventually ordered the production of the secret Federal Grand Jury transcripts prior to trial. As the thoughtful and experienced Judge stated, his ordering the production of grand jury transcripts prior to trial was a "first" for the District.

Those grand jury transcripts proved to be a bombshell. The evidence showed that James Finch and Mayor Margo Anderson, represented by two of Tallahassee's finest lawyers, Rob Vezina and Tony Bajoczky, were not corrupt as the government repeatedly told the media. Instead, the evidence showed deep rooted corruption by local, state, and federal law enforcement officials in shocking detail. Uncovered evidence from Lynn Haven's Chief of Police described "setting up" people, fixing cases, handing out seized evidence, using the "n" word repeatedly, and other wide-scale police misconduct and corruption.

The evidence showed that the witnesses coached by the prosecutors and agents were themselves lying and scheming, and that their stories changed repeatedly over time. It was wholesale corruption and misconduct on a scale that even as the United States Attorney in Miami I had never seen before. And maybe worst of all, the federal government at every turn tried to suppress and cover it all up. As the avalanche of illegal police corruption and misconduct evidence finally surfaced, the lead federal prosecutor and lead senior FBI Special Agent abruptly resigned immediately before trial rather than face sanction hearings

This legal ground war gripped the entire Panhandle and much of Florida. All the while, Margo Anderson proved to be a graceful, strong and resilient woman who had dedicated herself to her family and to the good people of Lynn Haven. She was an honest, upstanding, admired public official. And her friend of 30 years, James Finch, simultaneously stood by her side, fighting off both cancer and the government with "true grit." In John Wayne fashion, James, sitting tall with the bridle in his teeth, rode directly at the bad guys, repeatedly firing his Colt 45s. Because of this fortitude, James will always be one of my all-time heroes.

It was a hard-fought, lengthy, costly battle. And in the end, Margo and James won. But, as a wise man once asked after being wrongfully vilified in public, "where do I go to get my reputation back?" Maybe what follows in this gripping first-hand account of the investigation and trial will in small measure vindicate these two incredible strong people. They deserve no less.

# CONTENTS

Acknowledgments

Prologue

# ACKNOWLEDGMENTS

This has been a nightmare that no family should ever have to endure, and I offer my prayers of thanksgiving and praise to the Lord who has seen me through so many dark days during this ordeal which as of now has lasted over five years. His grace is truly sufficient. I would like to thank my husband, for his love and support; my brother, who stood by me in the courtroom for every hearing and was a rock of strength; my precious daughter for her love, prayers and belief in me, my three step-daughters, my stepson, sons-in-law and daughter-in-law, fourteen beautiful grandchildren, my aunt, and all of my cousins who believed me and stood by me. I would also like to thank Lynn Haven City Commissioner Judy Tinder, a woman with courage to stand and tell the truth while others remained silent.

To attorneys Ron Johnson, Jimmy Judkins, Rob Vezina, Tony Bajoczky, Jeffrey Forman, and Guy Lewis, both James Finch and I owe our lives, each of these attorneys brought different skills to the defense table: Ron Johnson, saw me through the indictment, arrest, and arraignments with compassion and encouragement, Rob Vezina with his vast knowledge of construction and contract law made fools of the prosecutors and their witnesses during the evidentiary hearings regarding FEMA rebuilding guidelines, and his cross-examination of corrupt Bay County Sheriff's Office Major Jimmy Stanford, was a show-stopper during the evidentiary hearing. Jimmy Judkins, long-time criminal defense attorney helped us with establishing the beginning of our defense preparation, Tony Bajoczky and Jeffrey Forman, the researchers and writers who worked mostly behind the scenes but who as Tony coined them, were the "mules" of the operation; they met all of the filing deadlines with efficiency and semantics which eventually demoralized the Government's case down to one charge. The infamous "666' bribery charge which our attorneys argued correctly, has since been overturned in a Supreme Court decision and would not stand up in court now. Guy Lewis, the former U.S. Attorney for the Southern District of Florida brought us all to the finish line, with all but two of the 64 charges dropped against me, and only a single bribery charge against James Finch in his first trial which ended in a hung jury, and the second trial in which he was acquitted, with a second team of defense attorneys from Indianapolis, Jim Voyles and Jennifer Lukemeyer. Guy Lewis, with his unique perspective, his tenacity and fearlessness in the courtroom, was the modern epitome of the southern lawyer, complete with seersucker suit and tousled white hair, like Spencer Tracy, in *Inherit the Wind*, a courtroom demeanor filled with fire and audacity that literally saved our lives from ruthless and hell-bent prosecutors who cared not about justice or truth, but only a conviction.

*The Burnie Thompson Show* and *The Beacon of Bay County*, two independent news sources who researched the evidence, attended hearings, and looked for the truth, after two years of community scorn and ridicule , would turn the tide of public opinion as they exposed the corruption and lies of the Bay County Florida Sheriff's Department, the FBI agent who was the lone witness to the grand jury, and the Assistant U.S. prosecutor , both who lied to the grand jury to indict us.

Tom Daniel, the former pastor of the First Baptist Church of Lynn Haven, was truly the City of Lynn Haven's pastor in the aftermath of Hurricane Michael. I went to him after the storm for prayer, and then when I was indicted and asked him again for his prayers; throughout the long months and years of struggle, he was a source of strength and courage for me; any time I reached out to him by phone or text message, he responded immediately with prayer and encouragement. I am forever grateful.

Father Michael and Father Rich lifted my heart on so many occasions; may God bless them richly in their continued work for the Lord.

Finally, my precious mom, Geri Deal, whose beautiful soul, filled with grief and pain from watching what her daughter was going through, could no longer endure what was happening, and the Lord took her to be with Him on March 28, 2021, just two weeks after the second indictment against James and me.

The following was written by my fellow City Commissioner, Judy Tinder, from 2017 until the day of my removal, August 19, 2020. I thank her for having the courage to stand for the truth, and most of all, for standing beside me when not one other public official in Bay County was willing to speak up for me when they saw what was happening; their silence was deafening.

*"In 1992, I had the joy of connecting with Margo Anderson, a dedicated drama instructor at Mosley High School in Lynn Haven, Florida, who inspired my daughter and her peers through her passion for the arts. In 2015, Margo's mayoral campaign for Lynn Haven featured a detailed examination of the city's financial structure, yielding multiple proposals to enhance taxpayer savings, employee efficiency, and resident amenities. Her impressive accomplishments motivated me to pursue a commissioner seat in 2017, which I won. As a novice Commissioner, Margo provided guidance on local government intricacies. After my 2021 re-election, I served until 2024. Throughout our collaboration, I witnessed Margo's unwavering honesty, uplifting attitude, and community-focused approach. As Mayor, Margo Anderson demonstrated exemplary leadership, promptly addressing constituent concerns and engaging with residents who brought issues to commission meetings. She took a personal, solution-focused approach, gathering contact information and conducting site visits to drive meaningful outcomes.*

*Her impressive educational background and expertise in revitalization earned her multiple state-level titles and recognition. With deep roots in Lynn Haven, dating back to her grandparents, Margo's commitment to the city remains unwavering, even in the face of legal challenges that have impacted her family's legacy. Her heart and dedication remain firmly rooted in Lynn Haven, Florida. Margo's remarkable leadership has been a testament to the power of hope and determination. By leading our city through a category five hurricane and providing vital support, Anderson has demonstrated that with God and courageous leadership, we can overcome even the most daunting obstacles and emerge stronger."*

**Judy Tinder**
**Lynn Haven, Florida, City Commissioner 2017-2024**

The following statement was written by Jodi Moore and Gerri (GAP) Parker, two citizen journalists who founded the social media news page, *THE BEACON OF BAY COUNTY.* These two women became my friends after they began investigating the Lynn Haven Corruption case, and they attended the evidentiary hearings, court hearings, and the trials of my co-defendant James Finch. They, along with Burnie Thompson, of The Burnie Thompson Show, were instrumental in turning the tide of public opinion in the town where I was born through their tenacious pursuit of the truth through evidence. I am forever grateful to them, and although I did not know them personally at the time I was indicted, I am blessed by their friendship now, and the following was written by The Beacon of Bay County:

*On July 18, 2021, my friend Gap Parker and I created "The Beacon of Bay County Florida" Facebook page as a response to local corruption and unethical politics. We saw a void where local news media not only turned a blind eye to corruption, but in some cases abetted and promoted it. We have seen that our small community of Bay County is a microcosm of what is happening in our country on a larger scale. Despite the risks involved, we realized that the only way to try to make a difference was citizen journalism.*

*Through this process, we came to know Margo Deal Anderson and her story. Like Margo, Gap and I are Hurricane Michael survivors. Before the storm, we knew Margo as the Mayor of Lynn Haven. She was widely beloved, admired and respected in our community before and after the storm. We were shocked to the core when Margo was arrested by the Bay County Sheriff and the FBI on August 19, 2020. Gap and I have extensively followed Margo's case, and that of her friend, James Finch. They are both innocent people railroaded by a system that is supposed to provide justice, but too often does not. I believe in the saying, "Injustice anywhere is a threat to justice everywhere." An injustice has occurred here, and those truly responsible for the corruption should be held accountable. A very few have been, but many of the guilty are walking free as I write this. Civilization eventually breaks down when guilty people are not held accountable but innocent people are prosecuted and jailed. What happened here needs to be exposed. Good people of courage need to stand up and say that enough is enough.*

*It is one of the honors of my life that I have been part of telling the story of Margo and James on the Beacon page. Gap and I were the voice of truth when they were unable to speak for themselves. Now they can speak! It's an incredible, almost unbelievable, story that needs to be told everywhere.*

**Jodi Christine Moore, with Gap Parker**
**The Beacon of Bay County Florida on Facebook**

# PROLOGUE

## Following the Evidence
by Burnie Thompson
Watchdog journalist and talk-show host in Panama City, Florida. His coverage of
my case can be found on Facebook and YouTube at The Burnie Thompson Show.

"There's nothing like looking, if you want to find something."
-JK Rowling

## I thought she did it

Mayor Margo Anderson called me from home the night she was indicted on
64 federal counts of public corruption. All told, she was facing more than a
thousand years in prison.

It took me off guard and I really didn't want to take the call. We knew each
other, and I liked her. She told me that she was innocent, and that I was
the only member of the press she trusted. Her wrists and ankles were
bruised from the shackles that bound her for several hours in a federal
holding cell in Jacksonville.

If shell-shocked had a voice, it was Margo Anderson's on Aug. 19, 2020. I
told her that I'd report the truth, wherever it led me. And I told her that I'd
pray for justice.

At the time, I thought I already knew the truth. The FBI was working
jointly with the Bay County Sheriff's Office, and I was good friends with
Chief Deputy Joel Heape. He's the boss of everybody but the Sheriff
himself. And he assured me that the evidence against Mayor Anderson was
overwhelming.

Earlier that afternoon, I had attended the press conference at which federal
prosecutors announced the charges against her. Along with the FBI and
the Sheriff, U.S. Attorney Larry Keefe promised to root out wide-spread
public corruption in their ongoing investigation.

I had been reporting on public corruption, mostly in Panama City Beach. A week after Mayor Anderson was indicted, the City of PCB was issued a sweeping federal subpoena. I figured they were just starting with Lynn Haven on the way to the bigger crooks masquerading as public servants. The dragnet was wide, I was told.

My friend Joel kept saying that nobody had more integrity than Sheriff Tommy Ford. He said even if the FBI didn't clean up local government, the Sheriff and State Attorney Larry Basford would. I believed him, and I assured my audience that the hounds of justice were on the hunt.

Bay County received more than $300 million in FEMA money after CAT 5 Hurricane Michael ravaged the Florida Panhandle in October 2018. It was the most powerful storm to hit the United States in 50 years. All that FEMA dough kept the cookie jar full. The FBI and Sheriff Ford knew whose hands were in it the most.

About seven months after Mayor Anderson was arrested the feds nabbed her longtime friend and wealthy developer, James Finch. The superseding indictment alleged that Finch and Mayor Anderson had engaged in an elaborate conspiracy to defraud the City of Lynn Haven and the federal government.

I had never met Finch, but I was told Margo would most likely take a plea deal and testify against her friend. Otherwise, she would surely spend the rest of her life in prison. She was 65 at the time.

### It's not so clear

The FBI arrested Finch on March 18, 2021, and I couldn't figure out why Derwin White hadn't been indicted yet. He was the president and co-owner of GAC Contractors along with Allan Bense, former Speaker of the Florida House. Everybody thought that Derwin was the main target in the big crackdown on public corruption.

GAC Contractors had teamed up with national emergency management company AshBritt Inc. after Hurricane Michael. Derwin had allegedly received more than $15 million in kickbacks.

In 2020, the FBI had issued subpoenas to Bay District Schools and the City of Panama City Beach, demanding all communication associated with Derwin White. Local bigwigs who had their hands in the FEMA cookie jar began to avoid him.

Major Jimmy Stanford led the Sheriff's investigation into public corruption, and he was third in command under Joel. Major Stanford had been longtime friends with Derwin until an apparent falling out in late 2017. Not only was Derwin a big contractor, he fancied himself as a local political kingmaker. Since 2019, people all over town had been getting visits from FBI Special Agent Larry Borghini and Maj. Stanford asking about Derwin and GAC Contractors.

But by April 2021, the month after Finch was hit with conspiracy charges, public officials began to suspect that the high-profile investigation was fizzling out. Word on the street was that Derwin had got his mojo back with all the attention on Finch and Margo.

Sources told me that Derwin threatened to support rival candidates against Panama City Beach Councilmen unless they promoted his buddy, the Police Chief, to City Manager. It was a remarkable feat since they had to remove the educational requirements for Drew Whitman to manage City Hall.

By now it appeared that Sheriff Ford and the feds were myopically obsessed with Margo and Finch, who had the money to fight the charges against both of them. His defense attorney, Guy Lewis, had been a federal prosecutor in South Florida until 2002. Then he was appointed to oversee all U.S. Attorneys under Attorney General John Ashcroft. Finch had called in the big guns.

And Finch was fighting mad, saying that Margo blew the damn whistle on FEMA fraud two years prior when she notified Sheriff Ford in his office. Finch himself had stumbled across it by accident in March 2019 when he asked Mayor Anderson who built the new restroom at a City Park. That's how she found the $5 million in fraudulent payments to Erosion Control Specialist (ECS) owned by Mickey White, Derwin's nephew.

Before and after being indicted, Finch gave full access to local news outlets. Rather than dodging questions, Finch even gave a 25-minute interview on WMBB-TV. This time, federal prosecutors had a tiger by the tail.

But Joel and Maj. Stanford said Finch was full of it. They told me the prosecutors had Finch and Margo dead to rights. Just wait until the evidence comes out.

Fast forward to late July 2021. Joel and Maj. Stanford were in my office and we were talking about local corruption. Just before they left, they dropped a bombshell on me: Derwin was in ICU with Covid. He was 55 and in pretty good shape. I was dumbfounded. Why did they wait to tell me until they were about to leave?

Three days later, I received a text from Maj. Stanford: "not sure if you heard, but Derwin just died from covid." It was 2:51 p.m. on Saturday, July 31. It was big news in the community as Derwin was well connected and a big donor to local nonprofits.

Five days after Derwin died, FBI Special Agent Borghini and Maj. Stanford led an all-day search on GAC contractors. I was confident that they had seized a treasure trove of evidence that finally would implicate other local officials. But I couldn't help wondering why they were so quick to act only after Derwin had passed away.

**Margo issues me a challenge**

I began looking more closely into the case in March 2021 after Finch was arrested. Prosecutors tied Margo to Finch in the superseding indictment that alleged the two had been conspiring to defraud the City all along. The drumbeat from local news outlets seemed in lockstep with the federal prosecutors: With the gifts and the bribes and the graft, the Bonnie and Clyde of Lynn Haven had finally been stopped by Sheriff Ford and the FBI.

It had been almost a year since Mayor Anderson was first indicted in August 2020 and removed by Gov. Ron DeSantis. The case had dragged on because of the Covid lockdowns and the superseding indictment that brought Finch into the mix. I was frustrated that more local officials still hadn't been indicted. Be patient, Joel said, the feds move slowly but Sheriff Ford is committed, and you can count on him. Their gooses are cooked one way or another.

I was eager for the other shoe to drop on more local and state officials. Summer 2021 was quickly approaching, and I was hoping for accountability beyond Lynn Haven. Public officials were jumping every time their phones rang, and there were lots of indicators that a reckoning was right around the corner.

That's when I received an earnest Facebook message from Margo bursting with heartfelt sincerity and insistence:

May 12, 2021 at 4:21 PM:
:

Off the record if you are still the person I have always believed you to be and if you are truly searching for the truth; I want you to know that I would continue to loudly proclaim my innocence of ANY wrongdoing more than I do now if I could also present my evidence in the public forum. Evidence which will be surprising to many. But to do that before trial is exactly what this corrupt prosecution hopes that I will do. What surprises me most about you is that you usually are very thorough in your investigative and research processes and connecting the dots.
You didn't dig deep enough on this one…into the local law enforcement leaders and local FBI (LHPD, county and state) to find out why this happened to me; why do you distrust or question the motives and actions of so many elected officials at all levels but you trust elected law enforcement and a police chief who secretly recorded every conversation he had with the sitting Mayor of the City for over six months? Why would he do that? Did he make a deal? (By the way there is nothing incriminating to me in what he recorded) Probably the same reason I have always trusted and respected law enforcement; I love our country and never dreamed the very people we should trust the most can also be corrupt. What was presented to the grand jury, who presented it, and more importantly what was not presented has been

overlooked.
I look forward to my day in court
when I am no longer silenced.
Silence is a terrible thing when you
are innocent and know the truth.
Tom Lewis and Brady Calhoun have
told their story (thanks to Arthur
Cullen, Dan Russell and others who
wanted me gone.
Wait until I can finally tell mine. They
have the public convinced that just
because the government alleged
something it is true.
Best wishes, Burnie. You are
wrong about me and I look forward
to the day when I am vindicated by the truth. I
hope you will cover that story.

I first met Margo in 2008 when she performed her sublime Patsy Cline tribute on the Betsy Ann Riverboat in Panama City. That was seven years before she became the Mayor of Lynn Haven. When she was elected in 2015, I was thrilled. She became the most popular Mayor in Bay County, especially in late 2018 during the aftermath of Hurricane Michael.

Margo's Facebook challenge moved me. Usually, co-conspirators aren't eager to answer questions with federal prosecutors boasting a 98% conviction rate for each count.

"If you are truly searching for the truth"
"You usually are very thorough"
"You didn't dig deep enough on this one"
"You are wrong about me"
"I hope you will cover that story."

The case against them had lots of moving parts in the maze of allegations, and it would take time and focus to understand it all. I'd have to pull my attention away from other stories I was chasing down. Until now, my plan was to cram right before her trial as though it were a college exam. After all, I still mostly trusted what Joel and Maj. Stanford had told me about all that evidence against them.

I couldn't fall asleep, so after midnight I replied to Margo's message:

May 13, 2021 at 12:33 a.m.

Thank you for sending this to me.
I'm always open to the Truth. I
believe that you were targeted for
exactly the reasons you described. I
believe that Arthur Cullen and his
handlers were determined to
destroy you, and they have
very powerful backers who felt
threatened by you. I never go to
sleep upset about what you or
James Finch did or didn't do. There
are so many mean or braggadocios
people who have my attention right
now. All that said, you've always been
so kind to me. I'm happy to talk with
you any time, and I'll always let the
evidence lead me to my conclusions.
If you are ever in a position to join me
on the show, I'll treat you well and would
never ambush you. The questions and
tone would be tough but fair. I'd tell
anyone that we have always been mutual
fans so to speak (the word "fan" seems
so pretentious to me). You have some high
hurdles and I pray that you get a fair
outcome.

But fairness was off the table as I would later discover that prosecutors were hiding exculpatory evidence that would prove the case was negligent at best, or malicious at worst.

### A case full of lies

Prosecutors faced a stunning plot twist in February 2022. After Margo and Finch showed factual errors and legal deficiencies in their earlier indictments, Federal Judge Mark Walker directed prosecutors to hand over the Grand Jury transcripts.

This virtually never happens. It was the first time Judge Walker had ever revealed what the FBI and federal prosecutors had told a Grand Jury in order to secure an indictment. The Judge also ordered prosecutors to include all investigation reports by the FBI and Sheriff's Office.

All of that would remain sealed from the public for about a year. The defendants received investigation notes that were heavily redacted. Prosecutors said they would decide what Finch and Margo were allowed to see.

Judge Walker disagreed, and most of the redactions were lifted. What the defendants saw put the investigators and prosecutors on their heels. Finch's attorney Guy Lewis filed a motion to dismiss all of the conspiracy charges against his client and Margo.

Federal judges are required to lean heavily toward the prosecution, and they don't want to be overturned later by a higher court. Dismissing an indictment requires prosecutorial misconduct that "shocks the conscience." Before issuing a ruling, Judge Walker held an evidentiary hearing with witness testimony a month later on March 31, 2022.

It was a barn burner.

Judge Walker had to decide if the false allegations presented to the Grand Jury constituted a pattern of willful mischief by the government or if they were just sloppy and neglectful.

## What the Grand Jury heard

Assistant U.S. Attorney Stephen Kunz and Special Agent Borghini made the following allegations to the Grand Jury:

1. Mayor Anderson directed the City to clear hurricane debris from her property.
2. She was in Key West floating on Finch's yacht a couple weeks after the CAT 5 storm leveled their hometown.
3. She ripped off the City by using its insurance adjustor for her own home.
4. She gave City contracts worth millions to Finch in exchange for lavish gifts such as a motorhome.
5. Finch bribed Mayor Anderson and another City Commissioner for big contracts.
6. They both made false statements to the FBI.

None of those accusations were true. In fact, they were brazenly false.

1. Other City officials actually did have hurricane debris removed from their property immediately following the storm. A month later the City cleared the public easement next to Margo's home. Her family and friends cleaned her property a few days after the hurricane.

2. Margo couldn't have been on Finch's yacht because he was recovering from a stroke in a Jacksonville hospital at the time. And besides, he had sold his yacht prior to Hurricane Michael.

3. Margo paid the public adjuster for services unlike City Commissioner Dan Russell, who subsequently received $75,000 from his insurance company. The feds named Russell in the indictment but he was never charged. Instead, he became the acting Mayor.

4. The City Commission had voted unanimously for every contract Finch ever won. Mayor Anderson never cast the deciding vote, and state statute required her to cast a vote. The City Manager and staff always recommended Finch as the low bidder with decades of stellar projects under his belt. And sometimes Finch even funded the projects himself. As for the motorhome, it turns out Margo's husband had paid for it after all. The feds gave it back after parking it in a field under the sun for three years.

5. A bribe requires *quid pro quo*, which didn't happen. So prosecutors charged Finch with giving a gratuity, which required no evidence – only "a wink and a nod." Less than a year after the jury returned a not guilty verdict in October 2023, the U.S. Supreme Court issued an opinion prohibiting the catch-all charge they had leveled against Finch.

6. The feds love to use false statements as their final go-to charge when all else fails. They call it their "darling." Margo pled guilty to this charge and served a month in prison after prosecutors threatened to indict her again if she was found not guilty.

There's an old saying that no good deed goes unpunished. That proved true for James Finch.

In 2015, the City didn't have enough money to fix Lynn Haven's most dangerous road that ran alongside a deep ravine. The City Manager and

Commissioners wanted to fix it immediately. Engineers said they could do it for $7.5 million. Finch countered with $5.2 million, and won the bid. The City borrowed the money from Finch at half the going interest rate, and he told the City not to start paying him back until he finished the project in 2016 for only $4.4 million.

City Commissioners publicly thanked Finch, and then asked to borrow another $790,000 to fix stormwater problems. Finch obliged after yet another unanimous vote. He even extended the last payment of the loan until he turns 95.

Think about the absurdity of charging Finch with a crime for fixing the 17th Street Ditch. They accused him of conspiring with Margo to steal his own money after completing the City's most needed road project.

Sixth Amendment concerns

Prior to being indicted in March 2021, Finch suspected the Sheriff and FBI were out to get him because he was paying Margo's defense attorneys. Derwin White was also worried about being indicted. So the two biggest local contractors began putting together a joint legal strategy. By this time, both had legal representation that prohibited investigators from making contact with them directly. That didn't stop Special Agent Borghini who had an informant in Derwin's office.

But on the witness stand, Borghini told Judge Walker that the informant was not an informant at all. He insisted that he never directed the individual to do anything, especially regarding Derwin's hard-drive that was labeled "Attorney-Client Privilege." A few days later, the informant submitted a sworn affidavit with screenshots of text messages from Borghini asking about Derwin's hard-drive.

### I start covering the case

When the evidentiary hearing ended on April 6, 2022, I was convinced that Joel and Maj. Stanford had misled me about Margo and James. I couldn't believe what I had seen, and I was stunned at how deceitful the prosecutors and investigators were right to Judge Walker's face.

I couldn't imagine Sheriff Ford or the FBI wanting it to go to trial at this point. Not after what I seen in the courtroom. Three weeks later, I made the following Facebook post:

## The Burnie Thompson Show
## April 28, 2022

*The charges against Margo Anderson and James Finch appear to be the result of malicious prosecution.*

*Don't be surprised if Chief Judge Mark Walker completely dismisses the charges in late May or early June.*

*And don't be shocked if the Judge holds law enforcement and/or prosecutors accountable before this is all over.*

*I was shocked to see the evidence and hear live testimony when I attended the evidentiary hearings three weeks ago.*

*I don't believe the prosecutors want the case to go in front of a jury trial at this point. I think the FBI, the Sheriff's Office, and the U.S. Attorney's Office would rather the Judge throw it out.*

*The last thing they want is to take the stand to explain their false statements to the Grand Jury or the gifts the BCSO investigator received from the main contractor under investigation.*

*The prosecutors wouldn't even refute the defense in front of Judge Walker to conclude the evidentiary hearing. When asked, they simply said, "No, Your Honor. We'll submit it in writing."*

*Even WMBB-TV, the main propagandist in this case, are softening their accusatory stories. They see the writing on the wall.*

*No doubt that there was major fraud in Lynn Haven. Those who did it have pleaded guilty already. And a couple others remain free.*

*Most notably, City Engineer Chris Forehand. It seems that he has friends in the right places.*

*If this turns out to be malicious prosecution, I'll tell you why and how it happened. I only stumbled across the reason a few weeks ago. Absolutely nobody knew the missing piece to this puzzle and it's a shocker.*

### Sheriff's Office becomes furious with me

In early May 2022, Joel and Maj. Stanford came to my office. They tried to convince me that I was wrong about James and Margo. They were livid that Judge Walker had released the Grand Jury transcripts and investigation notes. Major Stanford told me how Derwin went from being his best friend to his enemy in late 2017. I questioned the integrity of the entire public corruption investigation. After nearly two hours, Joel became angry, and they stormed out.

During the evidentiary hearing a month earlier, Maj. Stanford admitted that Derwin had given him a Harley Davidson when they were friends sometime around 2011. But Maj. Stanford denied receiving a truck, a down payment for his house, a swimming pool, and that Derwin had paid for his sister's funeral. A few days later, he corrected the record: Derwin had paid for some of the funeral expenses.

A few weeks before Maj. Stanford's testimony, the FBI questioned him about it. His answers were entered into a **Form 302** investigation memo:

" STANFORD was aware of some of the allegations going around regarding things that WHITE did for STANFORD. WHITE never paid for STANDORD's pool and never gave STANFORD the down-payment for any house. WHITE did not pay the expenses for STANFORD's sister's funeral, as STANFORD paid for those expenses with his personal credit card. WHITE never gave STANFORD $10,000 and STANFORD "never took a dollar" from WHITE. STANFORD and WHITE had been to the casino together a few times, but STANFORD always used his own money. STANFORD and WHITE were very close for a few years but STANFORD never felt like he crossed any lines. Further, WHITE never asked STANFORD to take any official action to benefit anybody."

The memo read like a preemptive narrative rather than an investigation memo. Clearly, Maj. Stanford made a false statement to the FBI. Whether intentional or not, that's exactly what they prosecuted Margo for after dropping all 64 charges. The night before she was indicted, she told the FBI that first met Derwin's nephew in December 2018 rather than October 2018. For that, Judge Walker sent her to prison for a month and put her on probation for a year.

Maj. Stanford was also questioned about fake invoices Derwin planted at ECS to frame Mayor Anderson. Derwin had his nephew Mickey place them in the office the night before Sheriff Ford's morning raid on April 12, 2019. This was less than two weeks after Margo blew the whistle on Derwin's nephew. Mickey testified that Derwin knew it was coming. Margo's defense attorney Robert Vezina asked Maj. Stanford how he got the fake invoices if he wasn't present during the search.

**Q.** How did that set get in your possession?

**A.** It never got in my possession, but it went from a couple of the people around there and it got back to the sheriff's office. I don't know—hard to—the government anyway. I don't remember exactly how that came about.

## Judge calls prosecution reckless

The prosecution against Finch and Margo took a hit even when her motion to dismiss was denied on July 8, 2022. Judge Walker was fed up with them filing new indictments every time faulty charges were thrown out. Multiple bites at the apple were spoiling the entire case. Here's what Judge Walker wrote in his ruling.

*Though this Court declines to dismiss the second superseding indictment, none should mistake this Order as an endorsement of the Government's conduct. The Government's reckless, haphazard approach is testing this Court's patience. More importantly, it is approaching a threshold, beyond which Defendants are so prejudiced by the Government's conduct that this Court will have no choice but to dismiss the indictment.*

After this scathing rebuke by Judge Walker, my coverage of the case began to reflect my indignation that Margo and Finch were being persecuted.

I made the following Facebook post the same day the ruling was filed.

**The Burnie Thompson Show**
**July 8, 2022**

*BREAKING STORY: Federal Judge rebukes the government as "reckless and haphazard" in its investigation and prosecution of former Lynn Haven Mayor and developer.*

*Judge Mark Walker issued a stern rebuke to the investigators and prosecutors in the Lynn Haven corruption case against Anderson and Finch.*

*The Judge's latest order that denied dismissal of the entire case was just unsealed. It shows that while he threw out Count One (conspiracy) in a separate order, dismissing the entire case would be an extraordinary measure.*

*But it appears to have been a close call.*

*The crux of the decision centers around (1) the government's numerous false statements to the Grand Jury in order to obtain indictments; and (2) Sixth Amendment violations concerning infiltrating attorney-client privilege.*

*Others – including City Attorney Adam Albritton and City Manager Michael White –
have pleaded guilty and await sentencing.*
*More to follow…*

What followed was a second evidentiary hearing in December 2022 that
was even more revealing. On the witness stand were a cast of shady
characters who had orchestrated the entire set up. Police Chief Ricky
Ramie was flippant, and City Manager Vickie Gainer was sanctimonious.
Former City Manager Michael White, awaiting his own prison sentence, was
bizarre.

Their accusations against Margo and Finch were demonstrably false, cringy,
and often differed from their earlier statements to the FBI. But prosecutors
didn't mind false statements as long as they were on script in this saga of
corruption wrapped in corruption.

But something unexpected happened before the second evidentiary hearing
that took place in December 2022.

## More Corrupt than New Jersey and New Orleans

*The Panama City News Herald* broke a major story about the case on August
11, 2022. It confirmed that the FBI and Sheriff Ford had been investigating
public corruption by elected officials and contractors whose names were
not Margo Anderson and James Finch.

A document surfaced that prosecutors didn't want anyone to see. It was the
FBI search warrant affidavit filed by SA Borghini on August 3, 2021 before
they raided GAC Contractors. He accused several elected officials and
contractors of criminal activity in the 45-page document.

The search warrant affidavit implicated Sen. George Gainer and School
Superintendent Bill Husfelt by name. Even so, Sheriff Ford had endorsed
Husfelt in 2020 for his successful reelection on Aug. 18.

The very next day, on August 19, 2020, Mayor Margo Anderson was
indicted. The Sheriff and FBI humiliated her husband in front of local
news cameras as they seized his motorhome. Margo was arrested at their
Jacksonville home and shackled for hours in a federal holding cell until the
afternoon press conference announced the 64 counts against her.

But the newly unsealed document told a different story entirely. The News Herald's lead paragraph shocked the community.

"GAC Contractors, a local company whose top executives include former House Speaker Allan Bense, bilked 'millions of dollars' from local governments in 2018 when it was contracted to clean up debris caused by Hurricane Michael."

Sheriff Ford and the FBI knew that in late 2018 Derwin had conspired with AshBritt Inc. to overcharge the county and its municipalities for debris cleanup after the storm. While they were scheming to defraud taxpayers, Finch was in a Jacksonville hospital recovering from a stroke.

Special Agent Borghini's search warrant affidavit indicated that Bay County was more corrupt than New Jersey and New Orleans.

"Derwin White and GAC made millions of dollars in fees from operations of sites, while Bay County and other municipalities paid an artificial disposal rate that had not been properly bid out," Borghini wrote.

Even though the cat was out of the bag, the search warrant affidavit was sealed again five days later.

### Bad Actor list

Remember the treasure trove of evidence seized from GAC Contractors five days after Derwin died? A year-and-a-half later, at the evidentiary hearing in December 2022, Margo and Finch demanded to examine it for evidence they needed.

Prosecutors didn't want them poking around because they said it could ruin their ongoing investigation. Judge Walker asked why investigators hadn't chased down other illegal deals outside of Lynn Haven yet.

"Is there any doubt that there are a bunch of bad actors robbing the community blind? Is that even— is that even in dispute?"

Federal prosecutor Andrew Grogan replied, "I think there's a lot of corruption there, Your Honor."

The Judge was surprised that the feds put corruption in boxes for so long with no further action. The evidence had been compartmentalized with pieces stored in Pensacola, Panama City, and Tallahassee. Judge Walker said that's not how investigations work, and Grogan agreed.

As the second evidentiary hearing came to a close in mid-December, Finch's attorney again requested that the case be thrown out. The Judge directed him to file a brief outlining the defendants' list of bad actors and bad acts, along with sanctions and remedies based on case law.

Two days before Christmas 2022, the list included the following names:
1. Assistant U.S. Attorney Stephen Kunz
2. FBI Special Agent Lawrence Borghini
3. Bay County Sheriff's Office Maj. Jimmy Stanford
4. Lynn Haven Police Chief Ricky Ramie
5. Former Lynn Haven City Manager Michael White
6. Lynn Haven City Manager Vickie Gainer

Lead prosecutor Stephen Kunz promptly retired before Judge Walker could issue a ruling. Kunz had a history of being sanctioned by higher courts for malicious prosecution. The 5th District Court of Appeals once compared his use of the Grand Jury to "giving a small boy a loaded pistol." Special Agent Larry Borghini had retired mid-case the year before.

Guy Lewis outlined multiple flawed indictments, Sixth Amendment violations, and other reckless misconduct from the bad actors. The entire case had to be thrown out, he argued.

Judge Walker would issue a ruling sometime after the holidays. It was Margo's third Christmas since being indicted on 64 counts of public corruption. Prosecutors had superseded the indictment four times in their relentless onslaught of accusations. Her nerves were shot.

Her face in the courtroom was frozen in fear and disbelief. Now I understand why people describe that look as being petrified. That was the first day I had ever met Finch. I apologized for jumping to conclusions when he was indicted the year before. He wasn't familiar with my show and said it was nice to meet me.

On the first business day of 2023, Judge Walker issued his decision on the bad actor list. He ruled that any misconduct by investigators and prosecutors was "limited" at most. He decided that cross examination during trial was the best remedy for any prosecutorial misconduct in this case.

This surprised me since he had already rebuked them for being haphazard and reckless. In July 2022, Judge Walker warned prosecutors that they were "approaching a threshold beyond which Defendants are so prejudiced by the Government's conduct that this Court will have no choice but to dismiss the indictment."

## Finding the Truth

Until Margo challenged me to look closely at the allegations in March 2021, I thought she and Finch had to be guilty of some of those 79 federal charges against them.

She said I was wrong about her, and that I needed to dig deeper if I really wanted to find the truth. The only way to get there was to follow the evidence with curiosity and humility. Margo had seen me cover several high-profile cases over the years. Nothing compared to hers.

Now I've seen how the deck is stacked against people indicted by a federal Grand Jury. The Constitution provides the Grand Jury to shield against oppressive prosecution. But over time it has devolved into a rubber stamp formality for the government.

No judges or defense attorneys are allowed in a Grand Jury hearing. Only the accusers. And it's done in secret.

There's no accountability for false or malicious allegations. Fewer than one percent of defendants ever know what testimony convinced a Grand Jury to indict them. How can innocent people even begin to mount a defense without that starting point?

Defendants are deprived of basic fairness and due process when evidence is kept secret. The identity of the Grand Jury must remain anonymous, but the transcripts need to be released.

It should be the most pressing legal reform in the federal justice system. Until this happens, there's no deterrent against haphazard, reckless or malicious prosecution.

Margo's book takes you on a journey of legal treachery that will shock the conscience of every American. Through it all, she personifies the faith and strength of Genesis 50:20:

*"You meant evil against me. But God meant it for good in order to bring about a day like this to save many people."*

# 1 PRESUMED GUILTY

*"Keep me, O Lord, from the hands of the wicked; preserve me from violent men who have purposed to trip up my feet.*
*Psalm 140:4*

If one looks at my social media accounts in the aftermath of Hurricane Michael, the Category 5 storm that made landfall in Bay County, Florida, October 10, 2018, leaving behind a path of unimaginable devastation, as Mayor, I quickly gained local, state, and national recognition for my "boots on the ground" work to help the people of Lynn Haven, Florida, a small coastal city of about 20,000 residents, and the people of Lynn Haven and the surrounding area lavished praise such as, "wish you were our Mayor," "Margo for Governor", "where are the other Mayors?", and "Margo for President." The Mayor of Lynn Haven was now a rising political star with some serious talk of my possibly pursuing a state representative or even a Congressional seat because of the leadership and calm so many had observed in the days immediately after the storm.

President Donald Trump walked with me through the streets of the City on October 15th, 2018, and I was pictured with him on the White House website, on the front page of the Wall Street Journal, interviewed by the New York Times, The Weather Channel, and dozens of other national and state level news affiliates. My political capital was growing, and I was not even aware of it because I was unable to watch television or see newspapers until many days later because there was very little outside communication during the first two weeks after the storm. Later, Jeremy Sheftel, a state-level campaign manager, would contact me, and he and his partner discussed with me what they thought the possibilities were, suggesting that we look at a state representative seat first, Jay Trumbull's.

1

I was working sometimes sixteen hours or more each day, meeting with FEMA officials, Governor Rick Scott, Cabinet member Ben Carson, and toured numbers of other officials through my city, on a golf cart, making the case to Representative Kevin McCarthy, Senator Bill Nelson, countless news media personnel, making the case for more assistance for the people of Lynn Haven and Bay County, and leading anyone who would listen through the rubble of the City Annex which was destroyed during the storm, where my husband and I almost lost our lives, along with about 40 first-responders and others, advocating that Hurricane Michael was a Category 5 storm, a fact which would not be announced until months later. I worked to organize a Halloween Festival just 20 days after the storm for the children of Lynn Haven, which was attended by an estimated 7,000 people, a Hometown Thanksgiving Dinner for the entire city, a Christmas tree lighting, Christmas parade and toy drive for the children, and a volunteer street by street cleanup as I worked beside residents, shoveling muck and trash out of the ditches so that they would drain. I raised over $200,000 in Hurricane Relief Funds and these funds were distributed to over 200 Lynn Haven families in $1,000.00 grants to assist in their recovery, grants which did not have to be repaid and could be used for anything they needed, from repairs to food to family bills.

And then, in March of 2019, as everything seemed to be moving forward in the City, the City Manager, Michael White, was arrested for domestic violence, and after he resigned more issues became apparent. The Police Chief shared a screen shot of the City Manager's phone with me, a screen shot which was an invitation from the female Federal FEMA Coordinator who had been working with the city, Amber Guy, stating, "Can we meet in the morning, let's have fun, I love u."

The Police Chief, Ricky Ramie, revealed to me that he had also found $30,000 in a backpack in the City Manager's office. (This amount and the location would change as often as Ramie's story). On March 26th, about a week after Michael White was arrested, I was made aware by my friend, contractor James Finch, that the new building in the park containing a concession stand and restrooms had been erected without a bid by a contractor without a license, Mickey White. James had gone by Sheffield Park to look at the building, because he was contracted to build similar restrooms at the bayside park, Porter Park, and he wanted to find out the cost and why there had been no bid. James told me that he had asked Mickey White, and that Mickey would not tell him, and he had not been able to get a phone call returned from interim City Manager, Vickie Gainer.

I went to Vickie Gainer, who had served as the Deputy City Clerk and was now the interim City Manager. I asked her for a copy of the contractor's information on file. Vickie called the accounting department and provided me with a one- page summary of Erosion Control Specialist

(ECS) which listed work they were doing on the restrooms and concession stand in Sheffield Park. I was surprised to see that the cost was almost $200,000 for the small structure, but even more surprised, that on that same page, at the bottom, there was a list of six very large checks which had been written to ECS by the City of Lynn Haven, totaling almost five million dollars. The checks were listed in an Excel format but in the spaces where there should have been invoice and purchase order numbers, there were none. Only the amounts were listed, and I said nothing to Vickie Gainer to indicate that I was surprised. I was shocked, and went straight to James Finch's office, Phoenix Construction which is only a few blocks from City Hall. I knew something was very wrong, and I knew he could help me find out what was going on. As James looked at the one-page summary of Erosion Control Specialist, the company owned by David "Mickey" White, a dark cloud came over his face, and he began furiously dialing on his flip-phone, since he had declared he would never own an iPhone.

He had dialed Derwin White, the uncle of Mickey White, and asked him if he could come to his office right away. James and I have been close friends for many years, and I wondered why in the world he was calling Derwin about this. Derwin was co-owner of Gulf Asphalt Corporation (GAC) along with Alan Bense, former speaker of the Florida House of Representatives. Within just a few minutes, Derwin's truck pulled up in front of the office, and he came through the door. I will describe this meeting in more detail and its significance later, but suffice to say, this was not a friendly meeting; James told Derwin that someone was stealing from the City of Lynn Haven and that I was going with the information to the Sheriff of what I had discovered. When Derwin left, he was angry with James, did not look at me, and he warned James not to go to law enforcement. As Derwin was driving away, James was looking out the window at the parking lot and asked me if I could see who was in the truck with him, and I answered, "no."

James said, "I can; it's Michael White."

James and I talked a bit longer, and then I went by my house to tell my husband, Lee, who is also James's longtime best friend of almost 40 years. My husband agreed with me, and with James, that the Sheriff would be the person to go to with the information, but I also wanted to take Lynn Haven Police Chief Ricky Ramie with me, as a witness, because of the information he had shown me about Michael White and his apparent sexual relationship with the FEMA coordinator. I went to Police Chief Ramie, told him I had found some financial issues with the City, and I asked him to go with me to Sheriff Tommy Ford as a witness…because I trusted him.

This is where things began to change rapidly after I asked him to go with me to meet with the Sheriff. By now it was mid-morning, and Ricky offered to call and set up the meeting with Sheriff Tommy Ford; he did not ask me for any details, which looking back, I found surprising. Ricky and I had become friends over the months since the storm, and he was very inquisitive and always wanted to be "in the know" if anything was going on. But he asked no questions. I believe now, looking back, and because of the information in his interviews with the FBI that I have been able to read since then, that he asked no questions because he already knew; he and Michael White were the best of friends, and the text messages between them which would later become government "discovery" reveal their relationship.

Ricky Ramie and I met with Sheriff Tommy Ford at the Bay County Sheriff's Office at noon, on April 1, 2019. After the Sheriff saw the one-page summary which I brought to him and discussed at some length what I knew, he asked me to get copies of the checks for him, back and front, and then later that afternoon when I brought him the copies of the checks, he then asked for copies of all the City of Lynn Haven's invoices and purchase orders for the company, Erosion Control Specialist. At this point, Ricky Ramie, to my surprise, volunteered to the Sheriff that he had brought a backpack from Michael's office that Michael had asked him to hold for him, and that the backpack contained $30,000.00 in cash, and he lifted the backpack up which was sitting by his feet on the floor. Later, I would wonder why Ricky chose this meeting as the time to bring the backpack to the Sheriff *after I told him that I wanted him to go with me as a witness regarding some financial discrepancies I had found.*

I had gone to the City's Accounting Department Head, Beverly Waldrup and asked her if she would pull the checks and make copies for me, which she did. I also asked her not to discuss with anyone that I had asked for them. After I took the checks back to the Sheriff, he then asked me if I would get the invoices and purchase orders on file for ECS with the City of Lynn Haven. The next morning, April 2, 2019, I asked Vickie Gainer for these copies, and she had those for me within an hour or so, and there were large stacks of them.

Chief Ramie volunteered that he would meet me in the parking lot of Wal-Mart in Lynn Haven and pick up the materials for the Sheriff so that I did not have to be seen entering the Sheriff's office with the stacks of paperwork. Sheriff Ford had also asked me to get copies of invoices, purchase orders and any other paperwork that the City's accounting consultant, Jay Moody, had for Erosion Control Specialist from his accounting office in Panama City. In retrospect, I wonder how Sheriff Ford knew that Jay Moody was our accounting consultant, and how he knew that Jay would have copies of the ECS invoices and purchase orders; I did not know this at the time. Again, Chief Ramie volunteered to meet me in the parking lot, this time at Moody's office, and take the paperwork to the Sheriff's office for me. I had no reason to think there was anything strange about this at the time, but Ricky Ramie was part of the setup machine which would take me down, and he needed the invoices; so did his buddy, Commissioner Dan Russell.

On April 2, 2019, soon after I delivered all of the stacks of invoices from Erosion Control Specialist I had picked up from Vickie Gainer to Chief Ramie, Sheriff Ford called to let me know that he was going to call in the FBI to begin investigating, and asked me not to discuss what I had told him, or to tell anyone about the checks, invoices and purchase orders. From the conversation, I believed that this was now an FBI investigation, that Sheriff Ford had turned the information over to that agency. But, on April 3, 2019, Tommy Ford had a meeting to begin an investigation which included FBI Agent Lawrence Borghini, the Panama City representative, Major Jimmy Stanford, Lt. Jeremy Mathis, and Crime Analyst Lindsey Miller. This meeting is documented in the Sheriff's investigators reports. Although the FBI Agent, the Sheriff and his investigators all have stated that I was not the whistleblower, they are liars. No investigation of ECS and Lynn Haven started until after James Finch and I discovered what Mickey White had done and made the decision for me to go to the Sheriff. Every single report and warrant (public documents) verify that the investigation began when this Mayor started it. Period. And because of the corruption involving Derwin White, GAC and AshBritt, which I would not find out about until much later, I was targeted by the Bay County Sheriff's office because of their relationship with Derwin White, GAC and others. Derwin White knew of my plans to run for higher office, he ran polls to find out that I had a 92% approval rating, and he knew that I had turned in his nephew Mickey White to law enforcement. I had interrupted Derwin White's sixteen-million-dollar gold mine through his relationship with AshBritt, one of the major haulers.

On April 12, 2019, the Sheriff's investigative team served a search warrant on Erosion Control Specialist properties,(the news media portrayed this as an FBI raid, but this warrant was executed by the Bay County Sheriff's Office, and is when the fake property invoices were planted and photographed in a trashcan, implicating me in a scheme to defraud the City by having my private property cleaned, billed to the City and then to FEMA) but Federal agents and investigators from the Sheriff's department had already begun making appointments and questioning City Department Heads and some officials from the same day I had gone to Tommy Ford. The Sheriff had cautioned me not to not discuss the investigation with anyone, that it would be ongoing; my silence and compliance with what the Sheriff asked would prove detrimental to me in more ways than I could have imagined in the coming days. I was never questioned or interviewed as the investigators made appointment after appointment with city employees and officials. I believed it was because the Sheriff knew I was the one who had discovered fraud and theft and had brought the information forward. I believed he considered me to be *part of the investigation, a trusted source.* I was wrong. Tommy Ford, Ricky Ramie, Derwin White, and Jimmy Stanford started setting me up from the moment Derwin White found out that James Finch and I knew that ECS, owned by Derwin's nephew, Mickey, had billed Lynn Haven for almost five million dollars.

By late April 2019, just after my unopposed re-election as Mayor of Lynn Haven for a second term with a 92% approval rating, the media had gotten word that the FBI and the Sheriff's department were investigating the City of Lynn Haven, the FBI raided the business places of Erosion Control Specialist and Greenleaf Lawncare, both who had done work for the City, and my good name began to take a nosedive as public speculation began on social media. President Donald Trump was scheduling a rally for Panama City Beach in July, and once again I received a call from White House staff inviting me, as the mayor who had walked with Donald Trump four days after the storm, to meet the President, this time at Tyndall AFB, as he arrived. They told me if I met with him at his arrival, I would not be able to attend the big rally at Panama City Beach with all of the other officials because of logistics, but I opted for the personal meeting. Two hours later I received a second phone call from the White House telling me that I would not be allowed to meet with the President because the City of Lynn Haven was under FBI investigation.

All through the summer, the media followed the investigation, casting a shadow over the City of Lynn Haven, and then Northern District U.S. Attorney Larry Keefe announced the indictment of neighboring Holmes County Clerk of Court, Kyle Martin Hudson, on October 4, 2019, then 29 more Holmes and Washington county officials were indicted November 15, 2019, as the U.S. Attorney touted his new Public Corruption Unit and promised that more indictments were coming. And they were. His next press conference would be just four days later after FBI Agent Lawrence Borghini and his partner showed up at night to question me. U.S. Attorney Larry Keefe was sworn in for the Northern District in Tallahassee on January 9, 2019, my 64th birthday.

On the evening of November 18, 2019, Sheriff Tommy Ford telephoned me and told me that I needed to answer my phone, that two FBI agents were sitting in my driveway and wanted to speak with me. I was not living in my home in Lynn Haven at the time, which was being repaired from the hurricane damage, and I gave them directions to the condominium we were renting approximately one mile away. My husband and I had just arrived back in Lynn Haven from spending the weekend in Jacksonville, and we had been driving almost five hours, certainly not expecting this.

The two agents arrived within minutes, and they questioned me for over an hour. This was a huge mistake. I should never have spoken to them without an attorney, but I had nothing to hide, and I was naïve enough to believe that they were probably coming at night to talk with me so that no one would know, trying to protect me from being seen as the "whistleblower," that I was. The more we talked the more uncomfortable I became; Agent Borghini was a bully, and he became more confrontational as he continued to place documents in front of me asking me if I recognized them. When they left, I had a sinking feeling, a feeling of foreboding.

The next day, November 19th, 2019, Michael White, City Manager, David Horton, Community Services Director, David "Mickey" White, ECS owner, Josh Anderson, GreenLeaf lawncare owner, and Shannon Rodriguez, sister of Mickey White, were all arrested. An indictment was read on local news stations in Bay County Florida, with U.S. Attorney Larry Keefe, Assistant Prosecutor Stephen Kunz, Sheriff Tommy Ford, and other members of the FBI. My name, (I was referred to as Mayor Anderson) was read as having allegedly had my personal property cleaned of trees and debris, repaired, and charged to the City of Lynn Haven after Hurricane Michael. From that interview and over the next four years, my photograph was featured countless times in local newspapers, national media, social media, YouTube, and other media, many times placing the photograph beside those pictured in mugshots who had been indicted and pled guilty, and even when I presented documented evidence and property surveys proving that the property cleaned was a stormwater easement adjacent to my property, the media and the Government did not let up.

On August 19th, 2020, the strategically planned one year anniversary of the beginning of U.S. Attorney Lawrence Keefe's Public Corruption Unit, as well as the morning after the election to office and evening of celebration for Sheriff Tommy Ford and State Attorney Larry Basford, the media gathered at about 6 :00 a.m. on the right of way and filmed as FBI agents raided my home in Lynn Haven to arrest me and to seize my husband's motorhome, parked in our yard. I am completely sure that not only had they been celebrating their election for office the evening before but were laughing about the fact that in just a few hours I would be getting the surprise of my life. I was in Jacksonville at the time, where I was arrested later in the morning, but without the media fanfare in my hometown which had been so carefully choreographed, filming instead my 100% disabled husband, a Vietnam veteran, answering the door as agents stormed the home. The story was shared with the Jacksonville media, however, so that my daughter who lives nearby, had to explain to the best of her ability what had just happened to the mayor's 8- and 10-year-old granddaughters…that Mimi the Mayor had been arrested. The beautiful neighborhood in Jacksonville where my husband and I had closed on a home that would be our retirement home when my mayor's term ended, was now no longer a refuge from the ugliness in Lynn Haven. The ugliness had followed me as neighbors watched in horror as FBI agents surrounded my home and arrested me at about 9:00 a.m. in the morning. I remember watching the lawn service workers across the street, most of whom were Hispanic, running in every direction as they saw vests with FBI written on them and the sedans pulled in front of my home.

As Mayor of Lynn Haven, I had brought about many positive changes in the city of Lynn Haven through my active use of social media, encouraging large numbers of people to attend City Commission meetings to have their voices heard. I had exposed a 1.3-million-dollar deficit to the stormwater funds each year that was transferred to general fund to pay the salaries of ten veteran city employees, six of whom were married to each other. Many of the charges made against me in the indictment can be read in accusations made by this same group of people, the "old-guard" city employees, on social media during the months after the indictment against the City Manager and others as my reputation took a slow dive...within forty-eight hours before I was arrested, Jennifer Dutton Williams, daughter of a former city employee, Bobby Dutton, posted on Facebook's Lynn Haven Neighbors, that the Mayor had made an illegal homestead exemption claim in Jacksonville on a $475,000 home she had just purchased; Jennifer's husband is Doug Williams, an employee of the 14th Judicial Circuit, Office of State Attorney Larry Basford in Bay County. Patricia Riemer, wife of the former police chief, and Matt Riemer, both made inflammatory comments on social media about my friendship with local contractor James Finch just hours before my arrest, urging residents to "pay attention." Matt Riemer is also an employee of the 14th Judicial Circuit, Office of State Attorney Larry Basford in Bay County; Reimer is still angry with me because I fought for changes in leadership for the Lynn Haven Police Department; what I could not know then is the new police Chief, Ricky Ramie, would be corrupt. I do not believe Reimer was ever corrupt, just ineffective in his position as the Police Chief, but from his comments on social media one week before my indictment, he and the others who worked for State Attorney Larry Basford knew of my coming arrest.

The United States Attorney for the Northern District, Lawrence "Larry" Keefe, stated in a guest editorial he wrote and had printed on the editorial pages of the *Panama City News Herald*, the *Tallahassee Democrat*, the *Gainesville Sun*, and elsewhere, featured just one month after my arrest, "Today I can report that this specialized unit of dedicated professionals has succeeded beyond expectations, working to restore integrity, responsibility, and trust to public offices across the 23 counties of the Northern District of Florida. Working in close collaboration and unprecedented cooperation with federal, state and local partners, the Public Trust Unit has relentlessly pursued individuals who abused their public positions for personal benefit and those who sought to illegally influence them." He then lists "Mayor Margo Anderson" sandwiched between the names of other public officials who have been tried and found guilty or who have pleaded guilty, one already sentenced and incarcerated, without mentioning my "not guilty" plea, and then ends the article with, "regrettably there is always a small number who see public office as a "golden ticket to undeserved opportunity." This editorial was run in each corner of the Northern District, making sure that any areas of the possible jury pool were covered. The United States Attorney's office had a budget of $455,000 with the Sach's advertising company in Tallahassee, an unheard-of use of taxpayer's funds by a sitting U.S. Attorney to push his name forward. These are editorial, inflammatory remarks, written in such a way as to indicate that I, Mayor Margo Anderson, am one of these who sees public office as a "golden ticket to undeserved opportunity."

The Assistant U.S. Prosecutor, Stephen Kunz, was found guilty by the Florida Bar in 2005 of egregious misconduct, was stripped of his titles within the criminal division and prohibited from trying any criminal case in the Middle District of Florida, costing the Justice Department nearly $2 million dollars—the largest sanction of its kind ever levied against the government for mishandling of a criminal case. And then he simply moved to the Northern District to resume his same tactics from his Tallahassee office.

As Sheriff Tommy Ford and his investigators obviously targeted me for months in this investigation, as he spoke to the public in the press conference after my arrest, no mention was ever made that the Mayor of Lynn Haven came to him with the documents and information which made possible the investigation to go forward. Without me, I believe there likely would never have been an investigation, especially because they currently have an affidavit (which will be discussed at length in later chapters) which refers to corruption throughout Bay County which they have yet to act upon. The Bay County Sheriff's Office continued to assert that they had already started this investigation before I came to Tommy Ford for help, but their own investigative reports and documents prove this is not true, as I stated earlier. The first meeting to begin the investigation was on April 4th, three days after I brought the documentation to Tommy Ford. There was no FBI warrant for Michael White's phone until April 10, 2019, and no raid on ECS until April 12th. They had Michael White's phone after his arrest on March 17, 2019, but the text messages they claim to have read had nothing to do with domestic violence, which is what they were looking for, and without knowing the information that I had, the text messages were largely meaningless.

I believe they started the investigation after I came in with the documents showing that ECS had billed the City of Lynn Haven almost five million dollars, because they had no choice. Everyone involved in the theft was exposed, including some of their cronies and benefactors, and some of their own, notably the lead investigator of the public corruption unit, Major Jimmy Stanford. I had crossed the "blue line" of the police, or the "green line", of the Sheriff's department, the brotherhood of law enforcement, however one wishes to term it, and I would pay. Joel Heap, second in command to Tommy Ford, and at that time, a trusted source for journalist Burnie Thompson, told Thompson that "I was guilty, and that I would either take a plea deal or spend the rest of my life in prison after I was indicted with 64 federal charges."

Every sitting Mayor and other elected officials in Bay County Florida should be thinking now of who they could go to if they discovered something unlawful, if something terrible happened in their respective municipalities? In a position of elected trust such as the Mayor of a City, to have knowledge of or to personally find something illegal and not report it is to be complicit with the wrongdoing, a crime known as, misprision. I did not go looking for financial corruption in the City of Lynn Haven. Finance and the daily operations of the city were not my job. I stumbled upon the misdeeds of Mickey White because one of my friends, and also one of my constituents, James Finch, asked me to find out why a building at Sheffield Park was being constructed without a bid having been solicited. Who could the Mayors of Bay County trust? The Police Chief of the respective City? The Sheriff? The FBI? I was wrong about all three.

I was accused of accepting gifts such as trips, entertainment, and meals from James Finch, the longtime friend of both my husband, Lee, and I, and not reporting these to the Florida Elections Ethics Commission. But what if there were no gifts? What if I paid my way? No one ever asked me. I was never questioned by anyone except the two agents who arrived in the dark of night, the night before the destruction of my life began, when I was already named in an indictment which would be read the next day. The similarities in my case and that of General Michael Flynn are quite striking. General Flynn was questioned with very little notice that the FBI agents were on their way, they did not inform him that any answers he gave them could be used against him to charge him with a felony of making a false statement to a federal agent, and General Flynn, like myself, was not on guard, at least at first, as he answered the questions, because he thought he was helping, that he was not being targeted by them.

The agents and Sheriff's investigators questioned two past City Managers, Michael White and Joel Schubert, the present City Manager, Vickie Gainer, the police chief, the city engineer, the city department heads, employees of ECS and Greenleaf, some of who were incarcerated at the time they were questioned, my neighbors, and they even found trolls on the internet who posted in response to WMBB Channel 13's reporting, and went to them for information, but they never asked me. They never questioned my husband. They were not interested in learning the truth. I have watched many true crime movies and television series, and when someone is suspected of murder, that person is usually one of the first questioned, a person of interest. But there was absolutely no interest from the Bay County Sheriff's Department in asking questions of the Mayor of Lynn Haven. Sheriff Tommy Ford and Lynn Haven Police Chief Ricky Ramie had already decided my fate. On April 1, 2019, when they realized what I knew, that is when they made their decision. They had to get rid of me. I am most probably lucky to still be alive. At one point, I did find a dead fish lying on my doorstep. "Sleep with the fishes." I told Ricky Ramie about it, told him that I was afraid, and asked for protection; he laughed and said that the fish probably just washed up there, or someone threw it out driving by. The fish was perfectly placed on my doorstep where I could not miss it.

My ability to work as a successful entertainer now is gone; if one searches for my name on the internet there is no longer any evidence of my advertised beautiful voice, my nationally known Tribute to Patsy Cline, and the theatres in which I have performed or tickets for those places where I plan to perform. No mention of the fact that I was teacher of the year at three different schools where I taught in Bay County for over 25 years. Instead, videos and news conferences broadcast my name in local, state and national media, as a thief of over five million dollars, taken from the residents of my city in their most vulnerable time, in the weeks after Hurricane Michael.

The purchase of a home in Jacksonville which was posted on social media by Jennifer Dutton Williams, the wife of Doug Williams, an employee of Bay County's 14th Judicial Circuit as something shady or illegal, was bought with a 0% down VA loan with a 3% mortgage for 30 years as a retirement home for me and my husband to live in near our grandchildren when my term of Mayor would have ended in a little more than two years. We had planned to keep our home in Lynn Haven as well, traveling back and forth to visit family and friends there, and should my bid for a Congressional seat be successful, I would still have a home in my Congressional District.

The home we lived in until my indictment and arrest had no mortgage and was a family home built by my father and grandfather in Lynn Haven in the 1940's. The home now belongs to James Finch; I wrote him a quit claim deed in September 2020 after my arrest to begin paying him back for the legal fees he had agreed to pay for me, his longtime friend. I had already paid $25,000 in legal fees to my first attorney, Ron Johnson, and now the proceeds from the home left to me by my parents was the first

$200,000.00 required in an escrow fund for the attorneys in Tallahassee who would defend me, and who would ultimately save my life.

A life well-lived, a life of service to the children I taught, to the community I love, a deep abiding faith in God, a beloved wife, mother, stepmom, daughter, sister, and grandmother.... that life will never again be the same. That life has been taken from me, as surely as if I had been murdered.

Presumed innocent? Or, presumed guilty by those who would use my fall for political gain, to cover their own crimes, and for retaliation because I stumbled upon the corruption in Lynn Haven, and ultimately all of Bay County. This is a mayor's story; it is my story. In many ways, it reads in the same way it happened; it is not smooth reading, nor is it eloquently written; there are long documents which the reader may wish to skip over, or just read in part. Some of the journal entries reveal deep depression, anger, bitterness, and sarcasm. Names are named, not for revenge, but for truth. Before my time on this earth is over, I want my friends and family to know the truth, not to just accept my word, but to see the evidence of why I was indicted; and someday when I am gone, I want my grandchildren to have this book and know this terrible story from my perspective, rather than from the lies given by law enforcement and the prosecutors to the media. I want them to know that I did not bend, nor did I lie, but that I walked through a door of deliverance that God opened for me at the very last moment, that He restored my life and my freedom to me.

Individuals gave interviews to the FBI, some throwing me, as well as my co-defendant James Finch under the proverbial bus, with lies, or omissions, believing that no one would ever know what they said. All of the documents and interviews are not included in my story, only some which have been filed and released as public documents by the Court after our evidentiary hearings, the two trials of my co-defendant James Finch, and many which have been posted in newspapers and online news media during the three years of intense media coverage of the case. The documents filed in this case would fill another book by themselves, but other than the few that remain sealed by the prosecutors, the vast majority of the documents were filed and made public, and hopefully some of our arguments can be helpful to other defendants caught in the hopeless and ruthless clutches of "reckless and haphazard" federal prosecutors, a term given to Assistant U.S. Attorneys Steven Kunz, Andrew Grogan and others of the Northern District of Florida. Judge Mark Walker, praised the legal expertise of defense attorney Guy Lewis when he left the case before the second trial, and even suggested that the motions and strategies of the defense he presented be used in the law school "down the hill." While all of the motions filed and strategies employed by the defense are not contained in this book, they are on file in the Federal Courthouse of

Tallahassee, Florida, and I hope that both law students and practicing attorneys might be able to use what happened in our case to defend someone else who has been wrongfully accused and prosecuted.

No one can understand the walk of a person who has been indicted by the federal government...not even the attorneys, or the Judge. The shoes are too complicated, too hopeless to try and understand without first walking in them. There are many elements in my story; my hope is the reader may find some elements of courage and faith which are redeeming in some way, may see the possibility of the restoration of my soul in the midst of the betrayal, brokenness, depression, and loss which are such a large part of this journey, a journey which I can only describe as feeling as though an anchor were chained to my ankle and I was dropped from a ship in the middle of the sea, knowing that those who did this to me were smug in their belief that I was gone forever, watching me slowly disappear into the depths.

This book is written incorporating the five indictments of the" Lynn Haven Corruption Case," as it has come to be called, as a framework and timeline, and also included are FBI and Bay County Sheriff interviews and investigative reports, interviews which the FBI and BCSO conducted with various city employees, officials, and contractors, and journal entries I made throughout the course of the nightmare which started for me when I was sixty-four years of age...I am sixty-nine as my story is published, and as mentioned before, because of the sheer volume of the documents from the case which has lasted almost five years, all of the motions, exhibits, rebuttals, and filings are not included in this book, but our hope is that the rulings of the Court in our case might prove helpful to other attorneys and their clients who find themselves in the complicated net of a federal indictment. In addition to the motions, supplements to the evidentiary hearings, and rulings, our case also includes the almost unprecedented unsealing of the Grand Jury transcripts by a courageous and lawful jurist, Chief Judge Mark Walker of the Northern District of Florida. Every defendant should be able to see the accusations of the prosecutors which caused him or her to be federally indicted. The transcripts in our case reveal a carefully scripted accounting of the "misstatements" and "unintentional misinformation" given to the grand jury by the sole witness, FBI Special Agent Lawrence Borghini, questioned by Assistant U.S. Attorney Stephen Kunz, as he presented a facially insufficient indictment which took down a duly-elected Mayor of a City...an indictment which was superseded three more times, dropping or dismissing 62 of the original 64 charges against me to a final two charges, and then offering me a sentence of 0- six months if I pled guilty to "making a false statement to the FBI", just two weeks before the scheduled trial of February 27, 2023 to prevent the corrupt government witnesses, law enforcement officers and Special

Agent Borghini, from being called to testify at trial, as well as now retired, previously censured by the Florida Bar, United States Assistant Attorney Stephen Kunz, who should now be permanently disbarred as a result of this case, instead of drawing a government retirement paid for by the taxpayers, living his life without regard for the devastation he has caused in the lives of others.

While editing the book before publication, I noticed how many times I used the word "lies" and "liars" and wondered if perhaps readers would be put off, or offended by my just calling out witnesses by name as liars, but after much contemplation, I feel no remorse at all in stating the truth, taking back my life and my reputation which was taken from me; this entire case was built on lies, almost every sentence of each of the indictments is a narrative of lies from the government which was repeated to the media, to the Judge, to the public, over and over; even Judge Mark Walker never heard my story, because I did not go to trial. I longed to just stand up in the court room and ask for permission to speak, to tell him what really happened. I wanted to take a polygraph to clear my name, and wanted the investigators, prosecutors and all those who had lied in their interviews to have to do the same.

The Bible says, "And ye shall know the truth and the truth shall make you free." The fact that I am not in prison for the rest of my life is a gift from the Lord. He has allowed me to be free, to tell the truth; those who set me up and tried to take away my life to cover their own corruption, failed because of the Grace of my Lord Jesus Christ.

My hope is that our story might be part of a larger movement to prevent this from ever happening again, to expose those who brought this travesty upon both myself and James Finch, to put a stop to the political machine of what I believe to be one of the most corrupt regions of the United States, the Panhandle of Northwest Florida, "the Redneck Riviera", where outspoken and successful women are not welcome, certainly not in public office, and where the corruption reaches from the municipalities to the Capital; where if a corrupt public official they wanted to fit their "public corruption" news story did not exist, they could borrow from the mantra of Joseph Stalin, "show me the individual you want to take down, and we will find a crime to charge her with." And they did. The female Mayor found the fraud perpetrated by David "Mickey" White of ECS and City Manager Michael White of Lynn Haven, which ultimately pointed to GAC (Gulf Asphalt Corporation) owners Derwin White and Allen Bense (former Speaker of the Florida House of Representatives) and national debris hauler AshBritt, leaving the other officials of the Panhandle exposed... the School District Superintendent, the Bay County Commissioners, city and county employees and others...all the way to Tallahassee. She had to go.

# 2 TWENTY DAYS IN THE AFTERMATH OF HURRICANE MICHAEL

*...and who knoweth whether thou art come to the kingdom for such a time as this?*
Esther 4:14

I included the scripture above from the book of *Esther* in the *Old Testament*; a book telling the story of the Jewish woman, chosen to be Queen, who saved her people because she had the courage to confront the King; I believe, in the depths of my soul, that I was elected Mayor, because the Lord knew that someone with a heart for the people of Lynn Haven would need to be in a position of leadership for those first twenty days of hopelessness, chaos, and despair. I believe that I was blessed to be chosen that woman... for "such a time as this".


Monday, October 8, 2018

I was at my daughter's house in Jacksonville for my granddaughter's birthday weekend, and as I woke up that morning, the Tropical Storm in the Gulf of Mexico had increased and was now predicted to become a Category 3 storm. I knew I had to return home, and I had my Mom who was in her eighties with me, as well as my husband's granddaughter who lived in Panama City. I tried to convince my Mom to stay with my daughter, but she insisted she wanted to go home, and my husband's granddaughter wanted to be with her parents. I arrived in Lynn Haven a little before two o'clock in the afternoon, and I went to the City Manager's office to meet with him and to sign the emergency declaration at 3 p.m. Central time. Bay County and the State of Florida had already declared a

16

state of emergency as the storm seemed on track for our area.

We had a scheduled City commission meeting the next afternoon, Tuesday, October 9th, and we waited for a while before deciding to cancel the meeting, to allow not only the City Commissioners, but the city staff who would have been involved in preparing for and attending the meeting, time to make preparations for themselves and their families.

I do not remember much more about that afternoon except that I went and purchased some supplies for my husband and I , as well as for my Mother, who had decided that she and her companion, Bob Gardner, would not evacuate but would stay in his condo at Marina Bay, just across the Bailey Bridge in Lynn Haven, about a mile and a half from both my home and my mother's home on Tennessee Avenue. Bob had an 8th floor unit, and my brother also lives there on the 7th floor. My brother is a doctor at a local psychiatric hospital, and he was on call and would not be able to evacuate or leave the hospital.

Tuesday, October 9, 2018

The air felt much different on this morning, and as the storm continued to strengthen and seem to be on a direct path for Panama City and Lynn Haven, evacuations were begun, officials began moving to the Bay County Emergency Operations center in the northern part of Bay County, in Southport. I made the decision that I would stay in the Police Annex/City Commission Meeting room with the police officers and other first responders, so that I would be available to residents in Lynn Haven after the storm passed. The bridges are usually closed after windspeeds reach 50 mph, and I did not want to be unable to go back to the City afterwards.

The City Manager, Michael white, City Department heads, Police Chief Matt Riemer and Assistant Chief Ricky Ramie, as well as Fire Chief/Emergency Operations Director, John Delonjay were all busy following protocols for getting the city as prepared as possible for what was coming. My husband Lee and I decided to move our cars to the parking lot behind City Hall and to park our motor home in front of the Senior Citizens Center across from the Police Department. I stayed in my home during Hurricane Opal in 1995 and I had lost both vehicles during the tidal surge, and so I wanted to move our vehicles further away from the bay. I had also been without power for over a week after Hurricane Opal, and there was a generator on the motorhome which I was thinking would allow Lee and I to be in close proximity to everyone with the ability to help and to be visible to residents.

As the storm gained in strength, County and City officials from all cities in Bay County Florida began to urge residents in flood zones to evacuate, and the City Manager, Mike White, asked that we have a meeting in the

Police Annex conference/training room at 5 p.m. with the city department heads and first responders. There were television screens on several walls and as we met, we could see updates from various agencies.

After the meeting began, Mike White, City Manager, told everyone that I had declared a state of emergency for the City, and then he let me speak. I told everyone that according to the City Charter, nothing would run any differently than it normally did except that I would be the official head of the city, the spokesperson during the emergency, attending meetings and speaking with the Governor and other officials on behalf of the City. I told them that the City Manager would still be in control of the daily operations of the City and the employees and that the Police Chief, Fire Chief, and other department heads would carry on as usual; I just asked that I be kept informed and up to date on major issues or emergencies as we moved through the storm. The only time of disagreement during the meeting was when the police and fire department were discussing the logistics of deployment before, during, and after the storm. Police chief Matt Riemer wanted to follow the same protocols of placement of his officers as they had during Hurricane Opal and other previous storms, meaning they would be placed all over the city in various locations, many in parking lots, under the car wash, behind Winn dixie, etc. The City Manager and Assistant Police Chief disagreed, and so did I. I made the statement that when I was fourteen, I was in Mississippi to visit my aunt after Category Five Hurricane Camille, and there was nothing left, utter devastation. I expressed my opinion that all of our officers should be called in as soon as the Highway Patrol and other agencies called their people in when winds reached 50 mph. Chief Riemer argued that he did not want everyone in the same building in case we became trapped or even worse, and there was more discussion. The City Manager and I agreed that the officers should be brought in when windspeeds reached 50 mph, and Assistant Chief Ramie spoke strongly for this as well. Chief Riemer finally agreed but was not pleased at all about the decision and said so. In days to follow, more than one police officer spoke to me privately, thanking me for agreeing with a decision that they felt saved their lives. I believe, even now, if they had been deployed outside, many would not have survived.

After the meeting, my husband Lee and I went to the motorhome and got some things together to put at the City Hall Annex because we initially had planned to spend the night in the building. About forty police officers, some of their wives, a few children and pets, as well as Commissioner Dan Russell and his family had brought inflatable mattresses and supplies to stay in the Commission Chambers building and use the offices of the annex. Lee and I placed an inflatable mattress and blankets in the administrative assistant to the Police Chief's office. I stayed at the annex until around midnight when I made a last- minute appeal to residents on Facebook Live urging any residents listening to get in their cars and evacuate; only Officer Willoughby and myself were left in the conference room. He told me it was the best speech I had ever made as Mayor.

The winds were supposed to start picking up at about 8 am the next morning (Wednesday, October 10, 2018), and by this time the predictions included a possible Category 5 at landfall. After my Facebook live post, I went to the motorhome across the street, said goodnight to Lee, said a prayer, and tried to get some sleep.


October 10, 2018, Hurricane Michael makes landfall

Lee and I returned to the annex very early the next morning, around 6 a.m. We were all talking to family members on our phones, and I tried to get my mother to let me come and move her over to the police annex with me because I was worried about her in the condo on the 8th floor, but she would not budge. Later I was thankful she stayed where she was because our building did not survive, and the condominium complex sustained very little damage in comparison to most of Lynn Haven.

Lee's daughter is a radio D.J. in Lexington Kentucky, and she was watching everything about the storm and conveying her complete horror to him of what was about to be on top of us. The last person I spoke with before communicating became sketchy was my daughter. We no longer had television communication, and she was seeing the horror of what was about to hit us dead on from her home on the east coast near Jacksonville. She told me how much she loved me, and then told me as soon as they could get to us that she and my son-in-law were already working with friends to fill up a truck with supplies for the City. We talked about what we would need right away…water, blankets, tarps, batteries, chainsaws, generators, baby formula and diapers, non-perishable foods, and cleaning supplies. I lost connection with her, and then another call came from Fox News. Harris Faulkner's producer had me waiting on the line and then my phone service went dead for good.

Lee and I went down the hallway to the front lobby of the Chambers where the Commission normally meets, and that room holds about 200 people. Most of the first responders' wives, kids and pets were there with their sleeping bags and blankets, and for a while we watched out the front windows as the winds and rains steadily increased, and then the large trees in Sheffield Park across the street started falling over like matchsticks. The pressure began to change, and the windows in the Chambers building were physically bowing out. One or two police officers had come up front, and Lee and I as well as the officers started moving everyone out of the

Chambers building and telling them to go down the connecting hallway to the police annex, which they did. The windows were really rattling now, and as it had once been the Methodist Church, the windows were large, picture windows which did not open. We closed the doors between that building's lobby and the police annex and started moving quickly down the hallway. Water began pouring in through the ceiling now, and even though it was almost noon, the hallways were dark. We heard a large booming sound but did not realize until later that the entire roof of the Chambers building had completely lifted and blown off, and next the large oak rafters from the old church ceiling began to come through the walls at us into the annex hallway.

At one point, my husband pointed up, and we watched a five-ton air-conditioning unit lift off the roof and go straight up. It never came back down. There are so many details of the horror of the next two or three hours as we moved from one hallway to the next, steadily moving everyone to the west side of the building until we were finally in the last hallway near the kitchen, all the children, pets and wives in a small room off the kitchen, and the officers in rain gear by the back door waiting until they could go out. I found myself wondering how many residents had decided to ride out the storm, praying that most had evacuated, praying for those who were in their homes going through this same nightmare, unimaginable terror and worry for their loved ones.

For the most part, everyone remained relatively calm, and encouraged each other that we would get through it, but the police chief's wife, Trisha Riemer, screamed until the assistant police chief, Ricky Ramie told Chief Riemer to move her away from everyone else and to get her under control. The city manager, Michael White, was very upset because he didn't know where his son, Austin was, and he had spoken to him before the storm, trying to get him to come to the annex, which he did not. I think Austin was about 18 or 19. Lee and I had a serious conversation, holding hands in the hallway, soaking wet, when the winds started to finally die down. All of us thought it was the eye of the storm, because the last we had been able to hear, we were the direct hit. What we did not know, was that the eye passed over Tyndall Air Force Base and Mexico Beach, just to the east of us, with us getting a portion of it but not the center of the eye. We were thinking that we had only been through half of the storm, and Lee and I looked at each other, knowing that if we had that much more to go through, that what was left of the building would never make it. It was a difficult moment that I will never forget, but we were together, and we were strangely at peace.

Before long, we all realized that we were seeing the end of the storm, and the decision was made that we would get ready to deploy and start surveying damage, looking for survivors, and trying to restore some communications, because we had none.

The first thing we did was make a big circle, hold hands, and pray before the men and women were deployed outside. Police Chief Matt Reimer was overcome emotionally, and he could not speak. The city manager, Mike White, led the prayer. After that, they all started doing their jobs, meeting at the back entrance and donning their gear. Lee and I made our way through what was left of the hallway into the destroyed lobby of the Chambers building and just stood in the street looking at what was left…it looked as though an atomic bomb had gone off. All the trees were down, and 9th street which led to the Panama Country Club and the residences on the east side of town was completely covered as far as one could see with trees. State Highway 77 was covered in debris and trees, and then suddenly two front-loaders rounded the corner and pulled up in front of the annex. Wesley and Thomas Stone, the grandsons of James finch, had heavy equipment from Phoenix Construction and they yelled at me that they were going to start clearing State Roads 77 and 390 so that emergency vehicles could get in. Lynn Haven is on the North side of Bay County and without those roads being cleared the rest of Bay County was cut off for help. Ronnie Williams, a long-time city employee with the Public Works Department pulled up soon after on another front-loader and said that he would begin clearing Ninth Street to the Panama Country Club and Colorado Avenue, which was a main road running east and west through the City of Lynn Haven. The three of them were heroes that day in every sense of the word. Their efforts made it possible for ambulances and other help to reach all Bay County residents much more quickly than would have been possible otherwise; both hospitals were in Panama City, and ambulances were able to come from the north through Lynn Haven to get to them at the south end of the county.

The next thing we discovered was that Verizon phone service was completely out; the City phones and almost everyone used Verizon service. The only phones that worked to any degree were those with AT&T service and that was sketchy. But, at some point, I was able to borrow an AT&T phone and get a call to my daughter, whose only response was, "oh my God, you are alive." She had already seen the aerial photos of the building which she knew I had been in. We cried, and said a few more words, and then she said, my son-in-law and his friends had a truck loaded and as soon as they get through to us, I would have supplies for Lee and me, and also for the residents of Lynn Haven. They arrived at midnight on Thursday night, the first food and water the residents of Lynn Haven saw from the outside.

I stayed out of the way for the rest of the afternoon, hanging close to our motorhome, parked across the street from the rubble of the City Hall Annex, which had miraculously survived, minus the fiberglass roof torn off right down to the plywood (which we didn't know until later). A few people were out wandering around, and I tried to comfort them, directing those who needed medical attention to the fire station a couple of blocks away where the EMT's were set up, and I passed out bottles of water from city supplies until I ran out. The rest of that evening is a blur, except sometime either that night or the next morning, it was determined that the only building secure enough to set up a perimeter with would be Southerland Funeral Home and Event Center on the corner of Hwy 77 and 12th Street, about three blocks away. Steve Southerland, former Congressman from our District, was more than generous in offering their property, and for the next week or so, that was the Command Center for our emergency operations.

Thursday, October 11, 2018

The day was spent organizing a command center of sorts, with help beginning to arrive from the police, fire, and sheriff's departments from Santa Rosa, Pasco, Escambia, St. Augustine and many other counties and cities. The Forestry Service, power trucks, and ambulances were running non-stop, and the sirens went on hour after hour for days. The EMT's at our fire station were treating injured residents, the firemen had started the door -to- door search and rescue for every house in the city, and the police were patrolling to protect the residents from outsiders and looters. We did not have power for three weeks, and everything was just BLACK DARK at night, with no road signs standing, no traffic lights working, and it was chaotic to try to drive anywhere. All the residential streets were completely blocked with trees and debris, and I remember riding on an all-terrain Polaris vehicle that belonged to Mike White, the City Manager, over trees, fences, through ditches and debris as we searched for people on that first day, hopefully some who had chainsaws. And we found several who were willing to help.

The Assistant Police Chief, Ricky Ramie, entered and took all of the meat and other food from the heavily damaged Grocery Outlet store and began cooking outdoors for the city workers and first responders in the perimeter of the compound set up at the Southerland Event Center, which also had a large kitchen set up for catering which they put into operation within a few days to further take care of the employees and first responders., but it bothered me that people were standing outside the perimeter watching the cooking on the outside grills but were not able to come inside. I assured people that I knew of at least one truck that would be coming within hours loaded with food and supplies for everyone. Even though I had declared the emergency, I had designated the City Manager, the Police Department and Fire Department to continue operating according to their protocols as the charter provided in times of emergency. I found out later that Ramie had no permission to do what he did regarding the Grocery Outlet, which amounted to looting on his part, and that city employees and first responders should not have been eating steaks, chicken and ribs while the residents were wandering the streets looking for food. I asked if the people standing outside the perimeter could come in and eat, and Ramie said, "they were told to have provisions for their families if they decided to stay; my job is to take care of first responders."

My answer to that was, "it wouldn't have mattered if they had a month's supply of food and provisions if their entire home was wiped out."

I had designated the Police Chief and Fire Chief to continue as heads of their operations, and so I didn't argue further, but I was more than annoyed with Ramie. I decided that if the truck of supplies did not get through that evening from my son-in-law, that there would be another conversation between me and Ramie.

Lee and I had Yamaha scooters which we had on a rack on the back of the motorhome, and we used those for transportation because you could not get anywhere by car, and if you did, there were so many nails and debris on the roads that you quickly would destroy the tires. I rode my scooter across the old Bailey Fishing Bridge to Marina Bay condos to find my mom, and when I finally got to the entrance road it was completely covered with piles of pine trees crisscrossing each other. There were about 60 families living there. I crawled over and under the trees for about three hundred yards leaving the scooter beside the road. When I finally got to the front door, there was no power and so I had to climb eight flights of stairs to get to her, rather than using the elevator which of course, was not working. She was shaken, but ok, and after seeing that she had the supplies we had bought still safely stored and intact, I told her that I had to go but would be back the next day. I also told her that she would need to prepare for her and Bob to evacuate to Jacksonville and stay with my daughter for at least a few weeks because there would be no power, and she would have no running water or sewer in the condo. She was not happy about this, and I don't think she took me seriously. I also told the other residents there the same thing, but no one really believed me when I told them it would be a while before they had running water, sewer, or electricity. It would be several days later before the residents there believed me and started preparing to go and stay with family in another town or to find a hotel or condo on the beach. Panama City Beach had sustained very little damage in comparison to the east side of the county where we were.

The City Manager, Mike White, had held a meeting at 6 a.m. that morning, and had given directions to department heads; he had also said that he would have another meeting at 6 p.m. in the evening for a progress report. This would continue for many weeks; I did not learn until later that many of the department heads were extremely unhappy about this because they were living on the beach, and it was about a two hour drive each way to get to and from work because of the unprecedented traffic. Also, many employees did not return to work for days, and some did not return at all, making their jobs very difficult. There was also a shift in duties for employees, because, for example, the library was destroyed, and the librarians were given different work. This was also true for other departments.

I spent the rest of that day riding my scooter around on the streets that were open, offering encouragement to residents, telling them that a truckload of supplies would arrive late tonight or tomorrow from Jacksonville, that my son-in-law and his friends were on the way, just spending time with residents, some crying, some just sitting frozen in disbelief. The devastation was gut-wrenching.

Friday, October 12, 2018

Late Friday night, after another grueling day in the sun, riding around Lynn Haven just talking with people, trying to reassure them that help was coming, the first truck of supplies and help finally arrived for the City of Lynn Haven. My tall, handsome, son-in-law, who is 6'7" tall, and three of his friends pulled into the Southerland Events Center compound in a box truck and a pickup truck with a trailer of cleanup equipment and began unloading the box truck and stacking supplies next to the back wall of Southerland Event Center. The truck contained boxes of baby supplies, bottled water, peanut butter and jelly, hundreds of loaves of bread, non-perishable food items, cleaning supplies, tarps, blankets, pillows, clothing, cases of Gatorade, and I threw both arms around my son-in-law's neck, thanking them for coming and there were tears in his eyes from the shock of the devastation he had seen as they were driving through the darkness to get to us.

After the truck was unloaded they drove the few blocks to my house on the corner of Tennessee Avenue and 6th Street from the 12th Street compound, and began unloading the personal supplies they had brought for our family....a 500 gallon container of potable water to hook to our motorhome, boxes of non -perishables for us, clothing, medicines, cleaning supplies, tarps for our homes, and gift cards for me to pass out to residents and neighbors. Lee had hooked our generator up to our house, and so the guys had a place to sleep, and they could take showers in our motor home which Lee had moved from in front of the Senior Center to our driveway the day before, after they cleared several more streets. The house had electricity from the generator, but we could not use the water or flush the toilets because the water treatment plant was completely down, and all residents were being asked not to flush toilets or run the water in their homes yet.

## Saturday, October 13, 2018

I was so exhausted the next morning, that Saturday was a blur, but my son-in-law and his two friends, began cutting the trees which had fallen from the stormwater easement next to our property onto our pole barn and onto the right of way in front of the pole barn, and also trees which had fallen onto 6th Street to allow traffic to get through. My Mom's house, next door to me had sustained more damage, because a large tree from the property to the north of her had fallen on her roof. The guys cut the portion of the tree that had fallen on her roof away, tarped her roof completely, and began pulling all the wet drywall, carpets and debris out of her house to the street. They also tarped the part of my roof which had been damaged by wind. The other friend that had come with them had family in the Millville area, and he traveled over there to help them. The guys had brought chainsaws and a mini-front loader from one of their businesses in Jacksonville, and by the end of the day all of the trees which had fallen from the right of way and stormwater easement onto our pole barn and in front of it, were cut and pushed back onto the easement behind us, but the power pole on the 6th Street right of way was cracked almost in half and still covered with downed trees and debris from the easement.

I was back at the event center before sunrise, helping to load the supplies back on pickup trucks, including Lee's, to transport over to the parking lot behind the destroyed Police Annex, City Hall and Chambers buildings to set up a distribution center for supplies. We had decided that having hundreds of residents coming to the event center trying to navigate all of the City workers, law enforcement vehicles and very crowded parking lot of the makeshift City Compound would be too confusing, and at this point Michael White told me that if I could take care of the supplies coming in and distribution to the people, that he had the City operations covered. Several of the City workers helped me to get everything moved and some of the police officers came with us to make sure we didn't get overrun by people needing supplies since it had now been three nights since the Hurricane had made landfall. But nothing could have prepared us for the orderliness and kindness that the Lynn Haven residents showed for each other and for us as they began lining up. We placed items by category into large piles and used yellow tape to make a walkway for residents. Many had brought bags or boxes with them, but we also had large plastic garbage bags which we distributed, urging them to take what they needed for two days and assured them another truck was on the way. Over the course of the next few days, my daughter, with the help of her entire neighborhood, organized and sent six more truckloads of supplies to the hometown she loved, and their supplies were the first to meet the needs of the residents, to be followed a few days later by Red Cross and Salvation Army stations, along with Samaritan's Purse, the United Cajun Navy, and many, many other churches and charitable organizations which descended upon our area like angels from heaven. The United Cajun Navy operations were headed by Todd Terrell, of Baton Rouge, Louisiana, who would continue bringing assistance to Lynn Haven and other surrounding areas for months to follow. At one point, General Russell Honore, the General who had overseen the Hurricane Katrina operations visited Lynn Haven, and I was able to meet him and listen to some of his perspective about recovery operations; the conversation with him was helpful to me, because he was optimistic and hopeful in the midst of what seemed hopeless in the first few days after the storm; I was touched by the fact that he was in Lynn Haven on his birthday, and the guys from the United Cajun Navy had a small celebration cook out for him in the area where they had set up their operation in Lynn Haven.

Also on this morning, a Lynn Haven dentist and his wife had set up barbeque grills behind the dentist office which was next door to the destroyed City Hall and Service Center on Ohio Avenue. Over the next few days, churches and other organizations from Santa Rosa, Okaloosa and Walton Counties to the west of Bay County, began sending supplies and cooking hot meals in this same location until it became a distribution center serving hot meals and supplies to thousands of residents each day, not only from Lynn Haven, but all of Bay County. Over the coming days, this POD (point of distribution) became so congested that we created another one on the corner of 17th Street in the parking lot of Tyndall Federal Credit Union. My friend Todd Allen Herendeen, popular entertainer on Panama City Beach, had a large revival tent which he used for outdoor gospel and patriotic shows, which he brought to Lynn Haven, set up himself, and left it there for several weeks, creating a sheltered supply center, which residents from other areas could drive through and get the supplies they needed. The United Cajun Navy, led by Todd Terrell from Baton Rouge, Louisiana also arrived and set up their command post at Tyndall's parking lot, and became instrumental in so many of the projects to help the residents of Lynn Haven and Bay County.

After getting the supplies set up and seeing that there was not a problem with the way residents were coming through getting things they needed, I rode my scooter across the old Bailey Bridge to check on my Mom again. Before climbing the eight flights of stairs at Marina Bay Condos to take bottled water and other items to her, I could see the road to the condos from Hwy 77 was still completely blocked by pine trees which had fallen. I parked the scooter and climbed over and under the trees; I was already hot, scratched up and exhausted by the time I got to the gate of the condos with the small bag of supplies I had brought. I remember telling the residents there, many gathered in the lobby, that I was hearing it would be several weeks before we would have power restored, and I was not sure about water and sewer. I encouraged them again to think about packing some bags and traveling to stay with relatives or friends if they had somewhere to go. Panama City Beach had sustained very little damage in comparison with the rest of Bay County, and many residents had gone out there to stay in hotels, or further west, renting condos or vacation rentals. Many of the residents at Marina Bay were older, retirees, and the thought of packing and leaving did not appeal to them, and at first, they did not believe me about the electricity, water and sewer issues, but within the next twenty-four hours, the reality set in, and most began leaving. I convinced my mom and her companion of many years, Bob Gardner, to begin planning to go to my daughter and son-in-law's home, near Jacksonville. My brother, Roy, who was the medical director at a local in-patient psychiatric hospital where he treated active-duty military patients, was making arrangements to move his patients and staff to the Tampa area to a hospital there, as his entire facility was damaged to the point it would be many months before it was able to be used. Roy had found me the morning after the storm, making his way through streets covered with trees and debris, and each of us had miraculously survived in buildings which were quite literally torn apart. We hugged each other, grateful for our lives, and we talked about whether our Mom should go with him to Tampa where he was evacuating with his medical staff and patients, or if it would be better for her to stay with my daughter, in Jacksonville. We finally decided on Jacksonville, with our next obstacle to be convincing Mom she would need to pack and leave Lynn Haven for a while. After my brother left, he told me he would take care of getting Mom to Jacksonville, and I went back to the distribution center to help with passing out supplies and speaking with residents.

Sunday, October 14, 2018

My Facebook post on this date read:

I'm hoping this post loads on Facebook tonight. We have had a busy day in Lynn Haven, and we are moving forward. We are getting closer to the operation of our water system, we have a station set up behind the City Hall where donations of food, water, baby items, cleaning supplies, tarps, and hot meals cooked by the Reese and Myra Reed Harrison team served almost 7000 people today. I would like to express my appreciation to Governor Rick Scott, FEMA Federal Coordinating Officer Tom McCool and Lt Governor Carlos Lopez-Cantera for listening to my requests for assistance to the people of Lynn Haven and responding so quickly. Today we had a FEMA mobile response unit and team in Lynn Haven taking applications for temporary shelter assistance from residents. They will be here again tomorrow behind City Hall on 9th Street. Please apply as soon as possible to get your number in the system.

After posting on Facebook, delighted that my computer was working using the remote antennae that Verizon had set up at our City Compound at the Southerland Event Center, I received a phone call on the AT&T burner phone my son-in-law had brought me from Jacksonville, because Verizon phones were not working at all, or at best, for moments at a time. The phone call was from a 202-area code, and for a moment I thought it was my daughter, who still had her Washington D.C. phone number since living there for many years. I was wrong. The phone call was from the Secret Service, telling me that President Trump would be visiting Bay County on Monday, October 15, and wanted to know if I could be at the airport with other elected officials to meet him. Of course, I said yes, and the Secret Service agent, Eddie, gave me instructions, and told me to tell no one. I agreed and left to go to my house on my scooter about midnight. I had asked the agent how they were able to reach me on a phone number which was not listed in my name, and he told me that it had been difficult, but he could not tell me, and chuckled when he said it.

When I arrived at our house and went to the motorhome, I told my husband what had happened and that he couldn't tell anyone, which of course he did not. I looked through what few clothes I had, and I found a white shirt that was clean, a reasonably clean pair of jeans, and decided to stay with my "Mayor" ball cap and tennis shoes…. since I had no hair dryer. I also could not find a bra, but hoped the shirt was loose enough no one would notice. I did not sleep very well, and wondered what the next day would bring.

Monday, October 15, 2018

Officer Dutton of the Lynn Haven Police Department drove me to the airport to meet the President, because the traffic was so bad that driving the approximate 15 miles to the airport would take two or more hours without the benefit of a police vehicle with a siren that could go around traffic. He dropped me off at the airport and I went into the waiting lobby area with the other elected officials to await our instructions.

Eddie, the same Secret Service agent who had contacted me the night before was there to speak with us. Initially, after listening to him, I thought it would just be a handshake with the President and maybe a few seconds to speak with him personally to articulate Lynn Haven's most pressing needs.

I had written the number of the generator we needed for our water plant, given to me by Greg Kidwell of the City of Lynn Haven, in the palm of my hand so that I wouldn't forget it. I remember standing on the tarmac and watching with awe as the Osprey aircraft escorting the President arrived first, and then a few minutes later, a helicopter out of which stepped Donald Trump, First Lady Melania, several other officials, and Governor Rick Scott. I remember as he shook my hand, expressing my thanks to him for coming, and then very quickly telling him about the generator we needed. He turned to Rick Scott and said something to him about making sure we had it (which we did receive very shortly thereafter). I remember apologizing to the First Lady for my appearance, and how she took my hand and smiled a beautiful, reassuring smile. She was also in a baseball cap, jeans, and a white shirt, but I am sure that she at least was in clean jeans, and was most probably wearing a bra, which I was not, since I could not find one.

After shaking hands and just being in awe at meeting the President of the United States, we were told to go as a group to a bus which would be part of the President's motorcade. I do not remember everyone who was in our group, but I do remember Congressman Neil Dunn, Bay County Commissioner Bill Dozier, Mexico Beach Mayor Al Cathey, Springfield Mayor Ralph Hammond, and I honestly do not remember the others who were there, but I believe most of the Mayors from Bay County.

As the motorcade pulled out and headed south toward Lynn Haven, I asked the driver if I could video out the front window, because I assumed this would be the first and only time in my life I would ever drive in a Presidential motorcade. The driver allowed me to take the video but asked me not to post it until after the President had left the area later in the day. I promised not to post.

As we approached Lynn Haven the motorcade began slowing down, and then turned onto 5th Street, coming to a stop at the corner of Michigan Avenue. The secret service agent climbed aboard and said the President and First Lady were going to walk down the street in Lynn Haven, and the President had asked the Mayor of Lynn Haven to walk with them. The rest of the party was instructed to stay on the bus. This was a moment which I was to remember later, because there were a few audible comments (not happy ones) as I walked off the bus, leaving the rest of them behind, while the female Mayor became part of the photo ops, many of which ended up in national news and even on the White House website afterwards.

We ended up behind City Hall at the distribution center where the President and First Lady handed out bottled water, shook hands, and took photographs with residents, employees and volunteers. They then left to tour the rest of the area, and I stayed behind to continue working at the distribution center. I had no way of knowing it at the time because I was unable to watch television, but I was on state and national news, my political capital was growing, and the local "boys" were not happy about it, which I will always believe led to most of what was to come later resulting in my removal from office.

My brother posted a YouTube video that night, "President Trump Assesses Damage in Florida following Hurricane", with a post that said, "Proud of my sister Margo Deal Anderson Lynn Haven Mayor with the President and First Lady. Trump 2020. I posted a story I found online that night from NBCNews.COM, "Trump, in hurricane-hit Florida: 'We are doing more than anybody would've done".

Tuesday, October 16, 2018

One of my classmates from Langdon, North Dakota, Class of 1973, Linda Sperling-Mosser posted:
"Margo, this is the video I saw. So heart wrenching. Stay strong and our prayers continue for all."

She had posted an NBCNEWS.COM video, "Hurricane survivors band together after entire Florida towns flattened, "in which I was interviewed.

On this same day, my daughter posted: "The City of Lynn Haven now has a fund set up at Hancock Whitney Bank. The name is the City of Lynn Haven Hurricane Michael relief fund. A Venmo and PayPal account will be posted soon linked to this account. This is a tax-deductible option for donations. (She was working with a friend to set up a 501c3 account to benefit Lynn Haven residents).

An additional Facebook post on this day came to me from Karen Stephens Tayes" shout out to Lynn Haven and Margo Deal Anderson for a hot dinner. So needed and appreciated."

Wednesday, October 17, 2018
Facebook post of Margo Deal Anderson:
"It has been a very long day. I know that everyone is tired, hot, and disgusted with this mess, we will get through it. I will have updates on Facebook tomorrow and with Dr. Shane on 92.5 WPAP. Love and prayers to everyone. I am exhausted and I know you are too. God bless.
There were 221 likes and 60 comments to the post, indicating that many people still did not have connectivity in the area.

*The Lynn Haven Ledger* and Judy Tinder posted on this day, "Amazing teamwork and outpouring of hard work and generosity by hundreds of volunteers in the City of Lynn haven behind the Chambers. The food and supplies were greatly appreciated by so many." The Ledger is Lynn

Haven's newspaper and Judy Tinder is a City Commissioner.

Thursday, October 18, 2018
Facebook post of Jason Taylor
"Wow, Mayor Margo Deal Anderson from the town of Lynn Haven is the most refreshing person to talk to. She has so much love for her town. The people in Lynn haven are lucky to have her advocating for them."

Friday, October 19, 2018
Facebook post of Karen Delaney
"Prayers never stopped. You may or may not have seen Mayor Margo Deal Anderson and the City of Lynn Haven in National News, but they have been. They have done an amazing job securing every possible service known to man to make Lynn Haven whole again. I cried when she escorted GOV Scott, President and Mrs. Trump through Lynn haven. Keep faith and be safe!

Saturday, October 20, 2018
Facebook post of my daughter:
"Mom is on her way to sing the national Anthem at the Mosley football game, but she asked that I share with everyone that there is a mobile medical team at Sheffield Park in Lynn Haven for the next 48 hours. They are available to take care of all medical needs including administer tetanus shots, suture cuts...please share.

Facebook post of Rachal Smoker::
"Day 10 was a long one! I can't even believe what we have accomplished. Made several drop offs to areas in Youngstown, Lynn Haven, and Panama City. Hand delivered ice, charcoal, and food to people in Youngstown. Made drop offs in Lynn Haven. And made a HUGE drop off at a day care in Panama City. They will be opening on Monday and now have everything they need to open and also to give to families in need for their children. This is where your money is going, friends! And we finally got to hug Margo Deal Anderson!

Sunday, October 21, 2018
Facebook post of Mayor Margo Anderson
Thank you to Todd and Angel Herendeen for loaning the City of Lynn Haven your tent to provide shelter for our volunteers distributing food and other items.

U.S. News article today by Natalie Obregon

"Hurricane Michael flattened towns where survivors remain in disbelief"
For a grueling 55 minutes Mayor Margo Anderson didn't know if they were going to survive Hurricane Michael. She rode out the storm in the police headquarters building here with about 40 other people, including police officers, their families and their pets. The group went from room to room, dodging falling debris until the eye came through. Then, silence.
"I looked over at my husband and I took his hand, and I said we're not going to make it," said Anderson. "We are not going to make it."
Fortunately, all 40 people sheltered inside survived. Once the storm passed, they crawled through blown out windows to get out of the demolished building. The first time she went back inside the building, it was almost too much to bear." (The story can be found in its entirety online)

Later that night, I posted the following on social media:
"I can't sleep. Trying to think of how to fix 1000 different things. Please pray for me. God bless each person who feels despair or hopelessness tonight. Give us strength and courage. Jesus take the wheel."
There were 478 likes and 217 comments to that post, which gave me immediate hope that our local connectivity was improving.

Facebook post of Guido Macargel:
"I would like to add, that this storm in a way has been a blessing. It has brought people and strangers together, helping each other, brought love and compassion out in us and slowed down our busy lives. I have always supported First responders, but after 10/10/18 First responders, our military, volunteer organizations, the unrecognized hero's such as the power crews/lineman and Cajun navy, hold a special place in my heart. This also includes those restaurants that opened right after the storm to feed all the help. Special thank you to Sheriff Tommy Ford and Mayor Margo Deal Anderson who really stepped up to the plate and hit grand slams in organizing and taking charge. I know there are numerous people involved and I couldn't start to thank them all. We have lost a lot of lives since that day. My heart goes out to them all, one I knew personally Nick Rivera from FHP who was my instructor for a couple courses. R.I.P. in close Praise God for opening our eyes back up to what is really important. Love and Unity.

Facebook post of Diane Hand McDaniel
"I posted about our Langdon, North Dakota classmate who is the Mayor of Lynn Haven Florida. You've seen her on TV, preparing her citizens for Hurricane Michael and tirelessly working in its aftermath that devastated her city.
She asked us to pray for strength for her with thousands of things that all

have to be done. She said, "Jesus Take the Wheel" Whatever faith you may be, I hope you will send Margo a prayer for strength.

I also realized this morning that I have NO IDEA WHAT POLITICAL PARTY Margo belongs to. And I don't care! I've watched her even before Michael hit put the dignity back in public service.

Sending you prayers for strength, Margo Deal Anderson.

Faccbook post of Pastor John R. Ramsey

"At Harvest Christian Academy we have 5 acres of our 10 acres of property clear and ready for 5 portables so we can open our preschool again in the heart of Lynn Haven. Thank God for City and district and State leaders working so hard to get our community working again Margo Deal Anderson William Husfelt William Harrison Neal Dunn

Facebook post of Margo Deal Anderson

"Tonight, on my way home from our staff meeting there were a few streetlights coming on for the first time. What a beautiful sight they were against the sunset. It was so dark and scary at night without lights. Thank you to the thousands of men and women who came and worked tirelessly to get us to this point. The first prediction was two months. You guys have gotten this almost done in two weeks. You are just one more group of heroes who came to help us, and we love you all. God bless each of you and keep you safe as you complete your mission here in the Panhandle. I keep thinking of the power of God when He said, "Let there be light."

Monday, October 22, 2018

Facebook post of Kelly Anne:

"I missed seeing you when the United Cajun Navy rolled in and we dropped the first trailer…then you got a little busy with a little media and a tiny group from Washington. Glad to see our peeps from Walton County are stationed over there. This is a special group. I'm praying for you, Mayor. Can't wait to hug you soon.

Tuesday, October 23, 2018

Facebook post of Margo Deal Anderson:

"Today the Bay town Trolley will begin making hourly runs from 10-5 from Millville, Parker, Callaway, and Springfield to the Lynn Haven distribution center at 17th street behind Tyndall Federal Credit Union for Supplies. Callaway stop is in front of Grocery Outlet on Tyndall Parkway. I'll post the other locations as well. We want to share our supplies because we have more than we need. God Bless.

*I was encouraged because there were 96 likes, and 89 shares of this post, hoping that many in other cities could benefit from our supplies.

"My Facebook is sketchy again. I can post but I can't respond to anyone. Sorry. I love you all. Be safe. Keep the faith.

Wednesday, October 24, 2018
Facebook post of my daughter
"Two weeks ago, I sat on the phone with Mom holding back tears. I said I love you and promised to send help as soon as I could. We both knew Lynn Haven would never be the same. Thanks to the kindness and generosity of friends and complete strangers we successfully sent 6 box trucks of supplies to my hometown. Others followed and the supply trucks continued to roll in.

Mom has another vision that I am hoping we can make a reality. Please let me know if you would like to volunteer or if you or your company would be interested in making a tax-deductible donation to "hometown thanksgiving". It will be a free event with food, music and fun, celebrating life and the promise that together we can rebuild Lynn Haven.

Thursday, October 25, 2018
Facebook post of Sierra Reece
"One of my favorite high school teachers, Margo Deal Anderson! She has always had a huge and caring heart. In high school I nominated her through a local radio station for teacher appreciation because I sure appreciated everything, she did for us as students. She won!
I can't even begin to tell you how elated I was to hear she became Margo Anderson Mayor!
She has been incredible as mayor! Revamping an old baseball field into one of the greatest dog parks, (that I used weekly) and even put in a splash pad for the littles.
MY HEART BREAKS FOR OUR COMMUNITY. Seeing her walk alongside our president…just brought hope to my heart. #850strong

Facebook post of Margo Deal Anderson
"Today is Day 15. Fifteen days since our town, our lives, our homes were destroyed by a storm like we've never seen. Yet today I am filled with hope for the future. I hope you can be too. There will be rain today, but as it comes, I pray that our tears are washed away and that we continue to lean on each other and the One who saw us safely through the storm. I love you, Lynn Haven.

Comments:

Jeff Zumarraga

We love you, Margo! We hit the jackpot having you as our Mayor of Lynn Haven. God bless you always.

Charlotte Oxley

Thank you and your team for all you have done for our town.

Barbara Wells Steele

Does anyone know when Comcast will be back on? Little thing but big deal to grandkids and old people.

Linda Gunn

Please don't ever stop being our Lynn Haven Mayor

Sherry Poucher Melton

Great job Margo! We love you too!

Kathryn Jones Adams

Lynn Haven Walgreens has a tent set up for a 30-day emergency medicine

Patria Maulden

Incredible job Mayor!! I love you

Nancy Ball Sloan

Margo Deal Anderson if you don't run for Governor, we will write you in. YOU ARE WHAT THE WHOLE STATE NEEDS.

Trudy Lokerson

Thank you, Margo,

Mary Barnes

I am SO glad you are our mayor! God put you there for a time like this. Bless you!

Rhonda Hyler

Margo, do you have anyone who can put a tarp up for us on Redbird St. in Lynn Haven? We've developed two leaks in our bedroom and need to do it before it rains. Thank you in advance.

Rhonda Hyler

Got it done. Thanks. Compliments to you on how you've cared for our town after all this disaster.

Margo Deal Anderson

Sorry for slow response   Was at EOC


Facebook posts of Margo Deal Anderson

"We are having a little taste of normal at Sheffield Park on Wednesday night. Bring your children for a great Halloween. Parking is limited but walking in the areas around the park is safe and law enforcement is present. God bless everyone as we move forward. Lynn Haven Halloween Trunk or Treat, Wednesday, October 31, 2018.

"I love seeing the flag flying all over Lynn Haven. This photo is the tent where our staff meets twice per day to plan and report progress."

"God bless the three linemen who were tragically killed by a driver in Washington County last night. They were here to help us and my heart is broken for their families. Please keep the families in your prayers, and please, please drive carefully near those who are working so hard, many far from home because of their willingness to help our area."


Friday, October 26, 2018

Today I am driving with my husband to Jacksonville to see my daughter and family; this will be my first time to leave Lynn Haven since Hurricane Michael, and it is amazing for the first time in over two weeks to see trees again, landscape that does not look like a nuclear disaster just happened.
A hundred miles away, and no one realizes how bad it is just to the west of them, how could they?
Michael White called an hour after I left Lynn Haven to tell me that he had forgotten to ask me to co-sign a check for a local vendor helping to do push and cleanup in Sheffield Park and asked for permission for Deputy Clerk Vickie Gainer to sign the check as the second signer. I agreed that I would verify that to the bank, and Michael said the bank would be calling me in a few minutes, which they did. The amount of the check was 224 thousand dollars, and under normal circumstances would have given me pause, but we had been told that our total debris removal cost was going to possibly reach 20 to 30 million dollars, and so this did not seem out of the ordinary, and I had no reason not to trust either City Manager Michael White, or the Deputy Clerk, Vickie Gainer at that time. Hancock Bank called me a few minutes later, to verify the check, and as I verified that check, I virtually nailed the first nail in my coffin for the investigation which would begin just a few months later. Michael White had just authorized the first large payment to his buddy, Mickey White, the nephew of Gulf Asphalt President, Derwin White, Adam Albritton had drafted a contract between ECS and the City just days before, signed by Michael and Mickey, and they had fired one of the national haulers, Ceres, to allow the other hauler, Ash Britt to get a larger share of Lynn Haven's debris, in exchange for kicking back money to Derwin. While everyone else was trying to survive, they had just set up a way to defraud the City of Lynn Haven, and over the course of the next five months, ECS would bill Lynn Haven almost five million dollars, and the city employees in the accounting department never came to the Commission to report anything out of the ordinary, even when Michael White would go in and ask for one check to be run, with my facsimile

signature on it, for several hundreds of thousands of dollars.

That same week, on October 23rd, Chris Forehand and Jim Slonina, city-contracted engineers, incorporated a new company, Panhandle Engineering Disaster Services, PEDS, to monitor debris haulers in Lynn Haven, and sub-contracted themselves to Tetra-Tech, the national monitors which Chris Forehand had been instrumental in putting in place according to Michael White's testimony, who stated that Chris persuaded him to bring in Tetra-Tech. City Manager Michael White, his Deputy City Clerk, Vickie Gainer, and the HR Director Kelly Battistini, scored the bid sheet which gave the contract to Tetra Tech, and of course, Panhandle Engineering Disaster Services, who would now be monitoring the debris which would be hauled by Derwin White's nephew Mickey White and his company ECS, and of course, AshBritt, which would now be in position to kick back almost sixteen million dollars to Derwin White and Alan Bense owners of GAC, a company which was named in an Affidavit and raided by the FBI in the summer of 2021. But I get ahead of myself.

Shared on Facebook by Margo Deal Anderson:
Facebook post of City of Lynn Haven

"More progress happening at Sharon Sheffield Park. We are getting Halloween ready so don't forget to come out and enjoy the Trunk or Treat 10/31 from 5:30 p.m. to 7:30 p.m.! We are still looking for community partners interested in helping with this event! Interested? Email **communications@cityoflynnhaven.com** or message us on Facebook!
Facebook post of City of Lynn Haven

"The DEO and the City of Lynn Haven will be hosting a meeting on Monday 10/29/18 at 2:00 pm at the Sheffield Park tent to inform local businesses about financial aid that might be available for their business. This meeting is open to the public. For planning purposes, please contact Ben Janke at the City of Lynn Haven if you would like to attend. Thank you!

Facebook post of City of Lynn Haven
10/25/18 City of Lynn Haven Debris Removal Status Report

| | |
|---|---|
| Total Cubic Yards: | 19,782 |
| Total Trucks Operating | 58 |
| Total loads | 439 |
| Average Cubic Yards per load | 45.06 |
| Disposal sites in operation | 3 |

Facebook post of Margo Deal Anderson
    Lynn Haven Hurricane Michael Pay Pal Information
"This account is a trust fund established for us by an internationally known law firm in Jacksonville, Holland and Knight. Every penny of every donation will go back into the City of Lynn Haven and the donations are fully tax-deductible. My daughter reached out to a friend with this firm, and their services were donated to the city. I will be publishing information on how residents may apply for help from this fund for damages to their property not covered by insurance or FEMA in the very near future. For those who would like to donate, the account is through Hancock Whitney Bank, City of Lynn haven Hurricane Relief Fund!

Saturday, October 27, 2018

Facebook post of Dr. Roy Deal
    "I'm just pausing for a moment to express my gratitude for my hospital family for exceptional sacrifice and courage during Hurricane Michael. Very grateful for no injuries and safe evacuation of our patients. And ever grateful to have been welcomed to the hospital in the Tampa area with my patients and tireless staff working with them to care for our military patients.
Also very fortunate my mother is safe and very proud of my sister Margo Deal Anderson. Margo Anderson Mayor for the incredible job she is doing with our hometown, Lynn Haven, Fl., And my incredible niece, and her husband for showing up with truckloads of relief for Lynn Haven before the Red Cross, FEMA, or any other organization was there. I have an amazing family. At home and at work and I love you all.

Facebook post of Brittany Melissa:
    Proud of my favorite high school teacher, Margo Deal Anderson.

Facebook post of Margo Deal Anderson
    "Today is Day 17. Working on information for the Lynn Haven Trust Fund established at Hancock Whitney Bank to benefit individuals who need immediate assistance. Hoping we have big contributions from corporate America to get us back up again. Assuming all eight thousand homes in Lynn Haven were insured, which I am sure they are not, it will take $40,000,000 to pay the deductibles on each of those policies. It's a big ask, but I am asking. I serve the God of miracles. If our trust collects enough to pay each homeowner back their deductible it would be a huge shot in the

arm for this town. Pray for me as I push this forward with the help of the internationally renowned Holland and Knight law firm in Jacksonville who offered their services to us as a donation. All donations to this trust are 100% tax-deductible and every penny stays in our city for our people. I will keep everyone informed.

Sunday, October 28, 2018

We stopped on our way from Jacksonville back to Lynn Haven at Brooks Rehabilitation Center to see our dear friend, James Finch, who suffered a stroke in early October, and still was not even aware of the damage done by Hurricane Michael in our hometown. James would be coming home on Tuesday, October 30th, and all of their suitcases and things would not fit in their car, and so Lee and I loaded several bags into the trunk of our car before we left and dropped them off at James' home in Lynn Haven. It was so difficult to see him struggling; a music therapist was in the room while we were there, and James' wife Ashley was encouraging him as the therapist sang and asked him to fill in words of familiar songs, nursery rhymes and jingles. He had difficulty remembering words that had just been repeated to him, and his confusion was just heart-breaking; he would later make an astonishing recovery, and within six months' time, he was pretty much back to being our favorite obnoxious friend, insulting and joking with a wit that was known far and wide. But he was not able to make a complete sentence when we left him that day.

Facebook post of Margo Deal Anderson
"Today is Day 18. So, I'm having brunch with my daughter who organized the trucks of supplies from the Jacksonville area. I'm heading back to Lynn Haven now, and they are coming back this week with more stuff....school supplies and clothing."

Facebook post of Judy Tinder
"In just two hours, we gave away and sold 200 pounds of chicken salad, 100 cups of chicken and dumpling soup and chips! Our hearts are filled with joy for this opportunity."

Facebook post of Margo Deal Anderson
"If you need tree removal, tarping, or muck removal at your home and cannot afford to pay, here's help! Call 800-451-1954 and register with Crisis Cleanup. You MUST register to get on the list. Our FEMA rep, my hero, retired General Montague "QUE" Winfield, forwarded this info to me. He

will be compiling a list of local VOADS (Voluntary Organizations Action in Disasters). Call now and register. God bless you all. Hang in there!

Facebook posts of Margo Deal Anderson (with photographs of the remains of the City Hall, Police Annex and Chambers buildings)

"For anyone who has ever had a doubt of God's protective and mighty power, this is the building where my husband and I, the LHPD and several of their wives and children, City Manager Mike White, and Commissioner Dan Russell and his family survived the wrath of Hurricane Michael. "Leaning on the everlasting arms" #lynnhaventogetherandstrong

"This is the Chambers building and Police Dept...None of us doubt the might protective arms of the Lord after 55 minutes in which the building came apart all around us. We are forever bonded in faith and renewed hope for the future."

Monday, October 29, 2018
Day 19

Facebook Post of Margo Deal Anderson
"Small business workshop with Florida Department of Economic Opportunity to discuss recovery strategies, programs, and emergency bridge loans up to 50,000. Thank you, director Cissy Proctor and staff, as well as other guest speakers.
Meeting right now with the Florida Department of Economic Opportunity. A great turnout from business owners!

"Thank you, Walmart, for the generous donations of costumes for Lynn Haven's children. They will all be dressed for Halloween on Wednesday for a great time at Sheffield Park 5:30 til 7:30. Thank you! Bring your children to the area behind City Hall to our new service center. The costumes are absolutely free, and the library staff has them organized by size!

"Photographs of Kaley and Kathryn in their new workspace at the Lynn Haven service center surrounded by donations of candy from Walmart. They have done a great job organizing a Halloween celebration in Sheffield Park for this Wednesday from 5:30 til 7:30. Bring your children out for a safe , fun, two hours of normal.

Facebook post of R. J.

"F—k you FEMA...You act like the money belongs to you...I've been helping a different family ever day since this bullsh%$ happen...It's all the same no help from FEMA at all...My family and I came out ok but I am pissed with insurance and FEMA...A lot of people lost everything with no help at all...Rick Scott f&&k you too. All I've seen you do is walk around and leave it to someone else to figure it out...you lost my vote you prick...trump you better start making shit happen and get in FEMA ass cause I'll dump you ass too...I'm so pissed that I see so many people suffering and are turned down by the very same people who are supposed to help...I still love you Mayor Margo Deal Anderson...You have went way beyond your call of duty and all of Lynn Haven loves you for it.

October 30, 2018
Day Twenty

James Finch is on his way home today, and, his wife, would tell us later that as they neared Blountstown and Marianna, James began to notice the horrendous devastation, the thousands of downed trees, damaged buildings, and a level of destruction which he had not understood until he saw it, and Ashley said he became extremely upset and agitated the closer they came to Lynn Haven.

This day would become extremely important in the grand scheme of things when I was indicted. After the Commission meeting ended on the afternoon of the 30th, I ran into Chris Forehand and Michael White under one of the tents in Sheffield Park and they informed me that they had applied for a permit to open a debris pit for Lynn Haven on some of the property the City owned north of town. Something about the way they said it, the smugness on their faces, it was just a moment that did not feel right, and I became very angry. I told them that if they wanted to permit a pit and go into the debris business, they should have placed that on the Commission agenda, not made such a decision on their own, that the state of emergency was now over, and they were not in charge, they could not make decisions without Commission approval.

Something did not feel right about the City going into the trash business; I had received numerous phone calls from various contractors, some that I knew, some that I didn't know, asking me how they could get approval for their pits to be used by the City of Lynn Haven to accept debris. Each time, I referred them to the City Manager, Michael White. All I could think of was that the city did not need to go into competition with private individuals or large trash companies who were vying for business. We had literally just finished a Commission meeting, and I told them to either rescind the application, or I would reconvene the Commission meeting and they could ask for approval. What should have been the biggest red flag of all, was that they chose to rescind the application rather than go public with it. What James and I learned later as co-defendants, was that their initial plan had been to have a place where Mickey White could say he was hauling debris in much larger amounts than he was without anyone knowing because as mentioned earlier, Chris Forehand had now formed his own company, Panhandle Engineering Disaster Services (PEDS), which was subcontracted to Tetra-Tech, the company doing the debris monitoring for the company. Yet another level of corruption was occurring without anyone knowing. Who could imagine forming a corporation a few days after the storm when everyone else is trying to repair their homes, find water and food, contact insurance companies, and other necessary tasks? Chris Forehand would prove to have his hand in virtually every pot after the storm, making millions of dollars in the aftermath of one of the largest most devasting hurricanes to make U.S. landfall in recorded history. Not only that, but Chris Forehand would receive immunity from the prosecution during the evidentiary hearings, hearings in which one of his most telling text messages to Michael White was made public. Chris commented that Governor DeSantis' appointment for the State Emergency Management Director, Jared Moskowitz, was "an Ash Britt kind of guy," as he and Michael White were texting about FEMA reimbursement. As I was doing research for my own defense preparing for trial, I learned to my surprise, that Moskowitz, before his appointment by DeSantis to a position which determined reimbursement to the cities and counties affected by Hurricane Michael, was the former General Counsel and Vice President of business development for Ash Britt Environmental. Moskowitz would step down from his position in a formal resignation just four weeks before the indictment of James Finch in March of 2021 to "spend more time with his family."

Facebook Post of Margo Anderson
October 30, 2018

Today was a good day. I have rescinded the state of emergency in the City of Lynn Haven, and I have returned normal government operations to the City Manager and to the Commission. The curfew is still in place in Lynn haven until Sheriff Tommy Ford advises that he has lifted the curfew throughout the County. God bless our City as we move forward; I appreciate the support and protection to this Mayor during the time of emergency operations from the LHPD, the LHFD, and the city department heads. God bless each of you and your families as we move a step closer to normal life under very difficult circumstances. I have never been prouder than I have been these last 20 days to stand beside each of you.

Facebook comments to the Mayor October 30, 2018:

Brandy Swett:
I am super impressed with Margo Deal Anderson! You are a true inspiration, go-getter, leader, and just an all-around beautiful, classy lady! Incredibly proud to have you as our mayor!

Leigh Baughn
Just shy of three weeks. She's amazing!!!

Heather Walker
She's amazing. She found her calling! Margo for Governor!
I mean really, how often do you hear praise like this for city officials? I hear it constantly for you. You are a blessing. I thought you were an awesome teacher, but you were made for this.

Brandy Langford
Lynn Haven was truly lucky and blessed to have her as a mayor during this catastrophe, it would have been so much worse without her.

Tambra M Cabrera
Yes, Absolutely Agree…you are amazing leader. We love you Margo Deal Anderson.

Jamie Newell
I just said the same thing today! Great job!

Cheryl Brown
I second that!!

Brett Lanford
Too bad Cain Griffin baseball field had to be trashed for debris collection.

Margo Deal Anderson
It broke my heart as well, but it was a part of a 2013 contract. Sorry. The good news is, once everything is gone the company will restore the park to a beautiful place. I'm already ready.

Willow Rodriguez
Completely agree Brandy Swett. Proud to call Lynn haven home and even more proud of how the Mayor and City Manager have handled things during this unprecedented time in our lives. Bravo to them!!!

Rosemarie O'Bourke
What Brandy said! I'm so proud to be a new Lynn Haven resident. Margo does an incredible job!

Debra Zahara
She has done more for Lynn Haven than any other of the mayors combined east of her, we are still sinking over here with no help and of course most do not have the money Lynn Haven residents have, so I guess that is the dividing line as per usual. But she is amazing.
Margo Deal Anderson you have done an excellent job. I grew up in Lynn Haven spent half my life there. My mother still lives in my childhood home there with damage. My father and his wife live there and they have to rebuild. Believe me I understand. But I can go less than 5-mile diameter from my home alone and count more than 300 completely destroyed homes, lives ended. Depression and suicide are definitely possibilities. I just know we on the east side are not getting the coverage and help from our officials that you are so expertly providing.

Mason Wilkerson
She's been amazing!

John Shepard
Margo Deal Anderson is the most in touch mayor I've ever seen. Other mayors should do what she's doing, and btw, she was like this long before the hurricane.

*I received hundreds of comments similar to these, but wanted to share them in order to show the contrast of how the tide would turn against me, demonstrated by later social media posts, as those who brought this Mayor down set up another "perfect storm."

October 31, 2018

Day 21

I so wish that I had been more observant of the operations of the City under Michael White during the first few weeks after the storm, and that I had more notes of what I was doing each day, which would have proved invaluable to me after I was indicted and charged with 64 federal counts. My social media posts served as a diary of sorts and have been helpful to me in recalling the activities of certain days. The government alleges that I called a meeting at James Finch's house on October 31st, a meeting of contractors led by James Finch to discuss the progress of debris disposal, who was getting debris, the costs and other matters. What is interesting (and faulty) about their timeline, is that they were trying to make it match with an email that Michael White sent to Crowder Gulf directing them to take all chips to James Finch's pit, a direction that Michael White told the Government I forced him to give.

What is faulty about Michael White's testimony, is that James Finch was barely able to walk, his cognitive functions were still poor, and there is no way he could have led a meeting on that day. Three days before, I had witnessed him at the Brooks Rehabilitation Center unable to fill in words for a song with his music therapist. He couldn't remember that Elvis' blue suede shoes were blue. Michael White has been interviewed by the FBI numerous times, and he tells different versions of what happened each time he is interviewed; in short, Michael White has lied from the time he was arrested, saying exactly what the Government wants him to say, to reduce his sentence, and he was sentenced, finally, in June of 2023 to forty-two months in federal prison, below the recommended minimum sentence.

Perhaps his worst lie of all is what he wrote in the email to Crowder Gulf, which the Government presented as truth to the grand jury which indicted me.

Michael White wrote the following in his email of November 1, 2018, to Nick Pratt, the Director of Operations for Crowder Gulf:

"Nick, The Mayor sent me a text from someone stating that you will start utilizing this pit. So, please find attached an FDEP Permit for Yard Trash and Land Clearing Disposal. This is also a site that charges $4.70 per cubic yard. On behalf of the City, please use this email as a directive to haul all mulch from Lynn Haven to this site for disposal. Should you have any questions, please feel free to contact me."
Thanks,
Michael White

*The Mayor sent me a text from someone?* What does that even mean? The prosecutors have never been able to locate the text that they told the grand jury I sent. The reason? There is no such text. Michael White made it up. Another lie used to indict a sitting Mayor. Stephen Kunz had never seen any such text but went forward anyway.

Notice the date on this email. November 1st. The prosecutors had to say the meeting took place at James Finch's house (which it did not) on October 31st to make it fit their narrative. James' pit was used because the people who worked for him had permitted it and it was the closest to Lynn Haven, despite what others have said. Phoenix Construction employees, his company, had worked to get his pit permitted and running while he was ill, with the help of his friend, George Roberts, another contractor. (Roberts' testimony is included in Chapter 6.) The most ironic thing about this is that I did not even know James owned a debris pit until much later, and James certainly did not know he had a pit on November 1, 2018. He could barely speak. Also on this day, just two days after he was home from the rehab center for treatment after his stroke, he had a bad fall, had two black eyes, and was rushed to the emergency room on the day Michael White sent this email. Another interesting point, is that Michael did not "copy" the Mayor on the email; he did not want me to see the lie about "The Mayor sent me a text from someone stating that you will start using this pit"

Facebook Post of Margo Deal Anderson
October 31, 2018

I went this afternoon to a meeting at the EOC (Emergency Operations Center) north of Lynn Haven about six miles. I was honored to meet with Secretary of HUD, Dr. Ben Carson. His staff is committed to our recovery and their innovative ideas for affordable housing will be instrumental to our future and enabling many families to remain in this area. We also discussed options for mortgage payment extensions and small business low interest loans. I was so grateful to Secretary Carson for visiting our area, but the meeting at the EOC was not well organized, and two or three people dominated the conversation, sometimes with questions which were on the rude side for Dr. Carson, who had come with the purpose of trying to help.

I went and sat under the tent at Sheffield Park to watch the final preparations for the Halloween celebration tonight, and to read my emails and text messages. The Verizon antenna at the park seemed to work most of the time and so I would hang out at the tent to read.

Facebook post of Hilary Murphy-Stockwell
"My son is so looking forward to this! Thank you, Margo Deal Anderson!!! I originally told him that Halloween was canceled, and though he is wearing last year's costume, he can't wait!

The Halloween Celebration was wonderful, and thousands of people participated, smiling, laughing with their children for a few hours of normal. Some of the posts I received were:

Facebook post of Mike McLaughlin
"Job well done Mayor Margo Deal Anderson and City of Lynn Haven lifting everyone's spirits by hosting tonight's Trunk or Treat event. Hard to believe how this place looks 3 weeks after the hurricane. A fun time by all including the McLaughlin kids!!

Facebook post of Nancy June Horton
"Fun night of trick or treating and music! City of Lynn Haven and Margo Deal Anderson, Michael White, and of course my husband David Horton along with all the employees out did themselves! It was a much-needed night of fun.

I was so exhausted when I got home, that I just laid down on the bed and fell immediately asleep. I woke up a few hours later and could not go back to sleep. I posted on Facebook:

"My heart is heavy. Hundreds of residents are contacting me asking for help with debris removal, housing, employment, childcare and other needs. Please know that every request lies upon my heart, and nothing is being ignored. I ask for your patience, your prayers and your support. I feel so inadequate and wish I could do more. This is my hometown, and I will do all that I can to bring assistance to all who need it. We are in a dark hour, but I know there is light ahead of us. Pray for me as I do for you. We will get through this. "I know whom I have believeth that He is able."

Reading back over the post of that evening, I realized that even in the midst of so many people having a great time and enjoying being with their children for a few hours of "normal" during the Halloween Trunk or Treat event, that we had so far to go, and I had no idea how our town would get there. I had read that after 9/11, when the baseball game was played in Yankee Stadium, it was the beginning of people feeling hopeful again, that life would go on. That was my motivation in encouraging the Halloween event which had been so much a part of Lynn Haven's history. We had indeed had a few hours of normal, and literally thousands of people, not just from Lynn Haven, but from all over the county, came out that night.

I was overwhelmed by the hugs, by people wanting to shake hands, to talk to me about their problems, their fears, and of course to talk about their personal experience with the devastating storm, Hurricane Michael.

# 3 NOVEMBER'S HOMETOWN THANKSGIVING, CHRISTMAS, AND THE HURRICANE RELIEF FUND

The Halloween Trunk or Treat festival was indeed a turning point for the people of Lynn Haven and the surrounding unincorporated areas. Just as when President George Bush pitched the perfect ball at the Yankees game in the days following the 9/11 attack on our country, lifting the spirits of all Americans and giving hope that life would go on, that we would overcome, this one night of normal in Sheffield Park brought the people of Lynn Haven together for a few hours as neighbors, and reminded us of our resilience, our love for each other and the storm which had forever bonded us in an experience of survival and of faith.

One comment that stayed with me after the Halloween night fun, was from a little girl who posed for a photo with me and then told me that, "I don't like the trees. They are scary and creepy without their branches, and everything is so dark."

She was right. At night we still had no streetlights, and outside of the brightly lit areas of the park where city and law enforcement operations were, no one wanted to go outside at night because it was *really* dark. As the holidays approached, I saw Christmas lights and decorations starting to arrive at Walmart, and I thought about everyone putting up Christmas lights early to brighten up the streets. I posted on Facebook a few days later requesting that anyone who could find their Christmas lights pull them out and put them up on their porches, in the bushes, or trees if they had any. I went into the attic and found our lights, and I didn't have time to be artistic, but covered the bushes around our front porch with them, and I was so pleased with having a little brightness around our house on Tennessee Avenue. We were on the corner, and the lights made it easy to find our house. I had not done a very good job at arranging them in my haste, and the lights looked as though a plane had flown over and dropped them on the bushes.

November 1, 2018
Facebook post of Derek Eubanks:

"Such an incredible mayor. By her actions she's proven that she cares deeply about people and is doing all she can and then some. I've heard so many residents and business owners talk about how good she has been for the city...all before the storm. And now, she's handling the aftermath with such grace and heartfelt kindness. Makes me wish I lived in Lynn Haven again. Mayor Margo Deal Anderson, thank you for what you're doing. We're praying for you too. Last night's event at Sharon Sheffield (park) was a medicine for our family...an oasis in the midst of this. Thank you and the City of Lynn Haven for making it possible.

Facebook post of Anne Pippin:

"Margo Deal Anderson I read your post about how frustrated you feel. Be encouraged. You're doing a great job. (She posted a photo of the sunrise) 6:30 AM in the Sand Hills is beautiful. It reminds me of the song "joy in the morning" "Though the shadows may fall, and life seems so heavy, and sometimes I feel that I'll never see another day dawning. But I remember his word as the night finds me weeping, that he's promised me, and surely there will be Joy in the Morning." Thank you, God, for waking me up to see this beautiful promise."

WJHG television station located on Panama City Beach posted a story about the trust fund my daughter helped me to establish, and the story captured the attention of residents of Lynn Haven as well as the rest of the County:

*"Lynn Haven city leaders held a special meeting Tuesday and talked about Hurricane Michael recovery efforts including opening a trust fund. The trust fund was created to help residents with their recovery expenses. The city is looking to raise $40 million for the fund.*

*"Once that money is in place, we will begin paying grants to our residents to pay the deductible on their insurance policy," said Lynn Haven Mayor Margo Anderson.*

*According to Mayor Anderson, the city is making great progress with recovery efforts. She believes the trust fund will be a way to continue that progress.*

*"It will give immediate relief to residents," said Anderson. "To receive a check to pay the deductible, most owe at least $5,000 on their home insurance, is a very vital thing right now."*

*Anderson says they're seeking corporate donations but would still like for others to pitch in. All contributions are completely tax deductible.*

*The City commission also ended its state of emergency.*

*"It's been a little over two weeks and felt like it was time to end our state of emergency and return power to the city manager and the commission," said Anderson.*

*The city manager says they're still trying to restore phone service and WiFi. The commission decided not to charge residents utility fees until November 15th. Also late fees and disconnect fees will not be charged until 2019.*

November 2, 2018
Facebook Post of Margo Deal Anderson:

"Today is Day 22. On this rainy gray morning I am counting special blessings. My blessings are the people I am privileged to work with at the City of Lynn Haven. Michael White has not taken more than a few hours off at a time since this happened. Vickie Gainer, our Deputy City Clerk, lost her home, everything, but she is still here every day, serving this City. Julie Higby, Kelly Battistini, Kaylee Gardner, Amanda DeLonjay, Greg Kidwell, Bobby Baker, Lori Baker, Chief Delonjay, Chief Riemer, Ricky Ramie, Mark Branstetter, Tracy Johnson, Ramona Bibbs, Beverly Waldrip, Ian Hill, Kelly Tram, Ben Janke, Derek Rizzuto, and Ronnie Williams have given above and beyond to bring Lynn Haven through this. See next post for more heroes of our City.

I also posted a poster for the Disaster Supplemental Nutrition Assistance Program for Bay County (D-SNAP). The poster informed residents of how to apply for this assistance at Bay High School in Panama City, Wednesday, October 31-November 4, 2018. I also posted the following:

"Please share with all who might need this. No time for pride to get in the way. Take care of your family." @lynnhavenstrongtogether, @panhandlestrong

I then posted another superheroes photo, "Thank you to Lynn Haven's facility maintenance guys during this time: Jason Cobbs, John Keen, Dustin May, Brandon Burns, and Kenneth Junger. Another group of superheroes for Lynn Haven.

Followed by:

"Thank you to the Lynn Haven Library staff for categorizing and handing out Halloween costumes for our children! Jill Snipes, Alice Fritz, Julia Cuff, Kris Horst, and Megan Baxley. Amazing Job!!!

Thank you to Gloria Thompson and Amanda Richard who had Lynn Haven's permitting office up and running less than a week after the storm so that we could start rebuilding!!

"Thank you Ivan Rogers, Freya Petit, and Ramona Bibbs for taking care of all of Lynn Haven's furry friends during the storm."

"Thank you Lynn Haven Fire Department for your protection, your service, and your love to this City during and after the storm. We love you, Andrew Miller, John DeLonjay, Darrell Hernandez, Andre Hollendoner, Daniel Kenny, Joseph Bayba, Chase Curti, Benjamin McWaters, Willie Walker, Robert Stephens, Bobby Mayo, Samuel Smith, Jerold Kesinger, Robert Landon, David Rafuse, Austin Holgerson, Robert Jolly, Ryan Fullington, David King, and James McDougall."

"The LHPD has gone above and beyond their call of duty now for 22 days. Most without much sleep, many whose homes were damaged or destroyed, yet they continued to serve. Because that's what they do. Forever bonded with each one after October 10, 2018. Blue has always been my favorite color. Now I know why. Thank you , Brian Blalock, Patrick Hamilton, Kenneth Landingham, Matt Riemer, Sheri Hernandez, Jason Smith, Tom Willoughby, Don Cioeta, William McNeil, Stephen Pointer, Charles Enfinger, Kaitlyn Anglin, Michael Williams, Ryan Shipes, Joshua Thompson, Kerry Dutton, Christopher Meachum, Michael Radcliff,

Joshua Newsome, David Vananda, Matthew Mayfield, Christopher Bieberitz, Kate fugate, Richard Carleton, Khiao Phonchanh, Rickhy Ramie, Chris Parnell, Patrick Grogan, Corey Midyette, Steven Wildes, Gary Schell, John Sumerall, William Mcalinden, Beverly Gilchrist, Janie toth, Dawn Rogers, Lucy Rose, Rhonda Clark, Janet Infiner, Melinda Cullifer, Raymond gates, David O'Connell, Katy Hershey, Barbara Tichey and Alisha Conley."

I had made a special point of posting my gratitude to the city employees, because so many of them had been against me when I was elected Mayor in 2015, many simply because of the many changes I had campaigned for. I was hoping that perhaps our struggles during the storm and working together had helped in building a better relationship with them, that maybe after all we had been through together, they would feel differently about me. I would find out soon that for many of them, nothing had changed. They relished the opportunity to "throw the Mayor under the bus" when the time came.

November 3, 2018
Day 24

I received the following request on my Facebook page on this day from DPB:
"Mayor I live at Arkansas Avenue. Living out of a travel trailer. We have so many trees that fell and no one is picking them up. We need to finish cleaning up but there is no room to put the debris. Also our household trash is sitting by the road they only pick up what's in the can and leaves the rest sitting. Now it's stinking to high heaven. I need another garbage can please! I know you're a great Mayor and working hard for Lynn Haven but I need some help! Thank you.

To which Mary Dell Trent replied:

"We are living in a DISASTER ZONE. Everyone on EVERY STREET has debris and are running out of room. We live on a corner, and we are OUT OF ROOM. Everyone is experiencing the same PROBLEMs with garbage. THANK GOD that they do pick up once a week. I understand what you are saying about the smell. My neighbor, who just returned 4 DAYS AGO CLEANED OUT HIS FREEZER, FULL OF ROTTING FISH. YES!!! IT STINKS. YES THEY ARE IN BAGS. NO, THEY DID NOT PICK THEM UP, BUT THANK GOD, for the regular trash pickup that Lynn Haven has. Some areas are just NOW GETTING THAT. If you need an extra garbage can, I'm SURE that you can walk in a 3 block radius and find one to BORROW. Use it and return it. That's

what I did. We are ALL IN THE SAME....
(As the days continued to pass, the friendly neighborhood spirit of helping began to fade, and my social media page, the main way I had communicated with residents since becoming Mayor, certainly told that story).

On this day I also made a live Facebook post which received 2.7k views, encouraging residents and telling them about the Get out the Vote even which was to be held in the park on November 4, 2018.

I also received a message on my Facebook page from Vonnie Malone: "Margo Deal Anderson, this brought you, and your community to mind...you're all doing an amazing reconstruction up there. What Satan intends for evil; God will turn into a glorious thing of beauty. May He continue to strengthen everyone. Always in my prayers vm.

Gap Parker posted:
"You can get approximately 5-14 channels with this Clear TV Key HDTV antenna. I live in Lynn Haven and get 12 channels. Sure hope Comcast comes back on soon. Also, you can get this at the "As Seen on TV" store in Pier Park for approximately $15 or order from Walmart online.

November 4, 2018
Day 25

The sun was shining, and the wind was blowing on the beautiful Sunday morning we went to mass together at St. Dominics Catholic Church in Springfield. The Church was heavily damaged, and mass was in the open air in the grotto garden behind the Church. My daughter, son-in-law and granddaughters were with me, and it was a beautiful service.

Afterward we went to Lynn Haven Elementary School to the library and toured with Attorney General candidate Ashley Moody, and my daughter enjoyed being back at her childhood school, showing her daughters the library where she had been part of the inhouse television production crew.

Facebook post of Margo Anderson:
"The Lynn Haven Public Works Department has been on the front lines to get our City up and running. They have not only done everything possible in their regular job descriptions but have helped unload trucks of relief supplies and helped to distribute the supplies to those in need.

Facebook post of Dr. Roy Deal: (my brother)
"Great to briefly be home for the first time since evacuating after

Michael with patients to Clearwater and I thank everyone there for your hospitality and friendship and the warm welcome to the patients, staff and me arriving at your hospital. Last night with my mother, Geri Deal, Robert Gardner, Margo Deal Anderson, Lee Anderson, and my niece and her family felt like the first normal night I have had since October 10th. No matter the devastation around us and the distance driven between us temporarily, I am reminded how lucky I am to have my family all alive and here together.

On this same day, my Facebook page reflects a photo of volunteers from the Church of Latter-Day Saints cleaning debris from an elderly couple's home, photos of Governor Rick Scott, Congressman Matt Gaetz, Dr. Neil Dunn, gubernatorial candidate Ron DeSantis, Jimmy Patronis, Pam Bondi, Ashley Moody, and many other political candidates who came to the Get Out the Vote rally.

I had gone to find Mark Anderson many days earlier, making sure we had a place to vote in Lynn Haven, knowing that residents could not travel to Panama City to vote at the Supervisor of Elections office. At that time, traveling five miles could take two or more hours, and usually resulted in a flat tire on a vehicle from nails and debris.

The final post on my Facebook page that night was:

Bret Henderson's who posted the lines of people in front of the stage at Sharon Sheffield Park, where I had closed out the night singing, "Independence Day."
"Wow, check out the lines to get Margo's autograph after tonight's show. Can your Mayor nail "Independence Day" after Hurricaning for 3 weeks? #LynnHaven

There were many, many posts from residents after the Get Out the Vote Rally in Sheffield Park on November 4th, where most of the candidates speaking were Republican, but there were Democrat candidates in attendance who were also given the opportunity to speak. It was a wonderful evening, and the votes from our County would be instrumental in the election of Governor Ron DeSantis, but later, as events would begin to turn, I began to remember who the political players were who were there, those who saw the rising political capital of the female Mayor who had suddenly become a focus in both state and national news, and I would later wonder if any of them, Jay Trumbull, Florida House Representative, George Gainer, Florida Senate, Neil Dunn, Congressional Representative, Matt Gaetz, Congressional Representative, the disgruntled and jealous Bay County Commissioners after President Trump had highlighted his visit to

Bay County with Lynn Haven and walked with me through the town, had played a part in what was about to happen to me. Matt Gaetz was the law partner of soon to be U.S. Attorney Larry Keefe; Gaetz had also lobbied for Keefe's appointment when it wavered in the U.S. Senate. Keefe would be sworn in with his mission of uncovering public corruption on January 9, 2019. He was sworn in on my birthday.

November 5, 2018
Day 26
   This afternoon I drove my scooter out to the Derby Woods subdivision to check on one of my best friends, the Mosley High School principal, Sandi Harrison. She had been picking up all of the boards that were stacked by the road from ruined dwellings, and typical of her "crafty" nature, had been repaneling her garage into a guest bedroom, using the beautifully sanded and repurposed boards she had found.
   I spent time at the City Compound area we had established at Sheffield Park with trailers and tents moved from the Southerland Event Center, and my daughter had brought Lynn Haven shirts and 850 hats as gifts to pass out to our police officers and other employees who were working so hard. Sadly, she, my son-in-law and granddaughters had to go back home today to Jacksonville, and I was sad to see them go.

November 6, 2018
Day 27
   Today the Lord brought a special gift to me that would change my life and become part of my inspiration for each day. A tiny little rescue dog that David Horton, Community Services Director, and Ramona Bibb, Lynn Haven Animal Shelter Director, brought over to the park saying that it was just what I needed. He was a scraggly little thing, a Yorkie mix, black, silver and brown, and so skinny he was mostly hair. He immediately licked me in the face and stole my heart. I told him he was the Vice Mayor.

Today is election day, and I posted the following:
   "Political candidates please consider donating remaining funds in your political accounts after tomorrow to the Lynn Haven Hurricane Relief Trust at the Hancock Whitney Bank. We are a fully sustainable 501C3 which will benefit residents for years to come during our recovery.

The *Panama City News Herald* printed a wonderful article entitled, *Lynn Haven Mayor seeking $40 million for Hurricane Michael relief trust fund.*
I made the following post on Facebook:
   "The first $40 million in donations to this fund will benefit residents

with cash grants to pay insurance deductibles on their homes. This is a sustainable trust fund established by the Mayor of this City with every penny going directly to residents with a simple one-page application and donations to this 501c are 100% tax deductible. Please share this post. Let's get it out nationwide.

Facebook post of Carol D. McAdam:
"Why is Mayor Margo Deal Anderson the only one looking out for her community. She is out there getting stuff and set up a go fund account to help her community to rebuild. What's our Mayor doing for us? Still so many in tents and Thanksgiving is coming. Christmas is around the corner. Do the families eat outside and put their Christmas tree's up outside their tents? That's not normal so many people without and …

November 7, 2018
Day 28
Facebook post of Elisa McDowell

"A great big thank you to our Mayor of Lynn Haven, Margo Deal Anderson for all her hard work and dedication to rebuilding our community and city. Together we stand strong as a community and city that will pull through this devastation.

Facebook post of Margo Deal Anderson

A small scruffy refugee from Hurricane Michael is now snuggled on the couch with us. He is home. His name is Buddy. He lifted my spirits immeasurably today.

November 8, 2018
Day 29
Facebook post of Margo Deal Anderson
Attention Lynn Haven business owners. Beginning tomorrow SBA (United States Small Business Administration) will open a mobile unit in the parking lot behind City Hall in Lynn Haven. They offer low-interest, long-term disaster loans for physical damage and working capital. Reps will provide information and assistance with application process. Open 9-6 Monday-Friday, 10-2 on Saturdays until further notice. Closed this Monday for Veterans Day.

Facebook post of Margo Deal Anderson
Buddy has settled in. He's sleeping a lot which tells me he is starting to relax and feel safe with us. He has lifted me up. I love him already.

November 9, 2018
Day 30
Facebook post of Margo Deal Anderson

According to one of my neighbors on Tennessee Avenue, a man and woman who are working cleaning debris in Lynn Haven are telling people they are related to me because I am the mayor. She said they took her money and then left without completing the work. She is out looking to try and find where they are and working now to turn them in. I have NO relatives who are doing cleanup work in Lynn Haven. If anyone uses my name to try and win your trust, call me. 850-814-6001

November 10, 2018
Day 31
Facebook post of Margo Deal Anderson

It is Day 31 and I cannot sleep. It's cold outside and I know there are many who do not have heat or any comfort. Tired of red tape. Please reach out to your neighbors and offer what you have to help. We must help each other. I'm not saying the government will not help, I'm just saying the system is too slow and this Mayor is not powerful enough to fix it no matter how much I want to. Give generously. Give often. Love more than you ever have and ask nothing in return; and you will be blessed. Jesus take the wheel.
(This post received 1K likes, 183 comments, and 473 shares. Connectivity is definitely increasing on November 10th, my Mom's birthday.)

Today is the FSU Notre Dame game and the television reception is sketchy at best. Buddy is sleeping on the back of the couch and is not impressed.

November 11, 2018
Day 32
Facebook post of Margo Deal Anderson

Happy Veteran's Day to my husband and my hero, Lee Anderson, who is a three- tour combat veteran of the Vietnam Conflict and is still going strong. Thank you to all who have served our great nation. "Freedom is not Free"

I included so many posts from my Facebook page within this book to hopefully remind those who were here of what we were facing each day, and also to help me to produce a journal of sorts to document the challenges we encountered each day on our way back from the absolute devastation of Hurricane Michael.

After the success of the Halloween festival and the "get out the vote" rally we had staged in Sheffield Park, my daughter had been working from Jacksonville helping me to coordinate a "hometown Thanksgiving event." She had met with contacts from Publix, Florida Blue, and Popeyes, and I had met locally with the St. Joe Foundation, contractors, corporate sponsors, and business owners to continue collecting donations for the Hurricane Relief Fund.

Although the Hurricane Relief Fund had not come close to the millions of dollars I had hoped to raise, the donations were coming in, and we decided to start awarding $1,000 grants to families in need as they filled out applications, instead of holding the money until we had a large amount.

The Hometown Thanksgiving was a plan to bring our residents together for a sit-down dinner of traditional turkey, dressing, green beans, mashed potatoes, cranberry sauce and pies, complete with tablecloths, centerpieces, and live music playing in the amphitheater. Hundreds of residents enjoyed this celebration, and many city employees and volunteers helped with the preparation of the event.

Lynn Haven Elementary School is only a few blocks from the park, and we coordinated with the principal, John Cannon, and the cafeteria manager there to use the school cafeteria and walk-in coolers to store the food as we prepared it for warming on Thanksgiving Day. Publix sent over 150 pre-cooked whole butterball turkeys which we sliced, and all the sides were already in containers to be heated in the ovens at the school. The meal was a massive operation, but our efforts were rewarded as Lynn Haven residents as well as those from surrounding areas, joined us for a glorious meal, able to forget for a few hours that most homes in Lynn Haven were not in any condition for preparing a meal.

As I think back on these days of volunteering, attending meetings at the Emergency Operations Center, meetings with school officials, sitting in on City meetings under the tents, I wish that I could have seen what was coming in just a few short months, and I would have taken hundreds more photographs, kept a meticulous calendar and journal of each day documenting where I was and what I was doing, and I would not have been so trusting of the City Manager and those closest to him, city engineer Chris Forehand, Assistant Chief of Police Ricky Ramie, Deputy City Clerk Vickie Gainer, City Commissioner Dan Russell, and HR Director Kelly Battistini.

For those who were not in the area in the first weeks after Hurricane Michael changed our lives in just a few short hours of massive destruction, it is difficult to believe that one could be in the middle of so much financial deceit and corruption and not realize that it was going on. Those who lived through it remember working 14-16 hours daily, just trying to clean and put their homes back together, fighting with insurance companies, dealing with financial issues because businesses were closed, children were not in school, and of all times, in early 2019, there was a federal government shutdown, delaying emergency actions by Congress.

November quickly became December, and my focus was on making sure our City had as much normalcy as possible; one of the most important things I could do as Mayor, as various FEMA representatives and other government officials said over and over, was to advocate for residents not to leave the area, to stay, to rebuild. We knew we had already lost hundreds of residents to other areas by December, and my goal was to push forward a message of hope. I frequently made Facebook live speeches when the internet was working, and visited the local radio and television stations, speaking to residents, urging them to have hope, that we would recover, and we would rebuild.

I remember asking the City Manager and staff if they believed we could have a Christmas tree lighting ceremony as we normally did, the Lynn Haven Christmas Parade, and a toy drive for the children; they all seemed enthusiastic to help. The Hurricane Relief Fund continued to grow, and in early December we were able to present the first seventy-five families with $1,000 checks to use for rebuilding, groceries, gas, clothing, whatever their immediate needs were. With the help of the United Cajun Navy, private donations from individuals, local contractors and businessmen, we were able provide over 14,000 children with Christmas gifts, and once again, the City of Lynn Haven was a beacon of light to the entire area, inviting those from other surrounding areas to bring their children as well. The United Cajun Navy's Todd Terrell, headed a special project which delivered a new winter coat to every child at Lynn Haven Elementary School, just as the cold weather was setting in.

Once the Christmas activities were complete, I told the City Manager that I was going to go to my daughter's home in Jacksonville and spend Christmas with my grandchildren, and also with my Mom and my brother who would be coming there as well. He assured me that nothing much would be going on for the next two weeks, as the debris haulers, city staff, and essentially the entire County took a "breath" from the devastation and celebrated the holidays.

As we spent time in Jacksonville for Christmas, the beauty of the trees, the beaches, the area where my daughter lived, was like an infusion, a breath of fresh air, after the stress, the ugliness, the devastation of Bay County in which I had been living since October 10th, with very little respite. The odd thing about Bay County, was that other than some damage on the east end of the beach at St. Andrews State Park, and some of the businesses and homes, Panama City Beach was virtually unscathed by Hurricane Michael.

The beach was only without power for around twenty-four hours, and many of the employees, first responders and officials were actually living in condos and hotels on the beach, having daily "away" time from the destruction.

This was something I did not realize until later, but City Manager Michael White, Commissioner Dan Russell, Assistant Police Chief Ramie, (and others) and their wives, were eating out, enjoying beachfront views, and living quite normally, while the rest of us were in our homes in Lynn Haven without toilets that flushed. These rooms were provided to the City and reimbursed by FEMA, and my understanding, after the fact, was that they should have been used for first-responders. Some of our police officers were living in their cars. I saw that first-hand; there were heroes in the Lynn Haven Police Department during the storm, selfless, wonderful law enforcement officers who took care of their community. But not all of them were honorable. Assistant Police Chief Ricky Ramie was the "keeper of the keys" and the text messages which were made public later during proceedings in the pretrial evidentiary hearings for James Finch and I, show an ongoing conversation between the Assistant Police Chief Ricky Ramie, Commissioner Dan Russell and Michael White, as they enjoyed the amenities of even a three bedroom condo on the beach while residents and fellow-officers were suffering without basic amenities in Lynn Haven.

I had spoken at Thanksgiving with my daughter about how depressed and exhausted I was, how I was not sure if I wanted to be the Mayor any longer, (the election was coming up in April of 2019), and that I thought what I would really like to do was to move to Jacksonville and be near my grandchildren. My husband, Lee, and I had talked about it, and he told me he would be happy in either place, and we thought that maybe we could look into buying a home there, while keeping my family home in Lynn Haven as a second "vacation" home for when all of us wanted to come to the beaches in Panama City, something we had done all of our lives.

After much soul-searching, I decided it would be cowardly, and almost unethical to leave the City in complete destruction after spending my entire first term with a focus on beautification, restoration of parks, implementation of festivals, and just an overall momentum for Lynn Haven.

I decided to seek a second term as Mayor, but we also decided that we would start looking for a second home in Jacksonville, planning for retirement there at the end of my term should I be re-elected. I even prayed to God to lose the election, hoping that His will was for someone else to step in with a great vision for rebuilding. It was not to be. Commissioner Barnes qualified to run for Mayor, and then after seeing the polls of 92% approval rate for me, he withdrew, and I was re-elected without opposition in February of 2019. How could I have known what was coming next; another storm, almost as destructive as the first was about to tear our City apart…this time irreparably. The storm of corruption was not just beginning; it had been all around us since the day Hurricane Michael made landfall without our knowing it.  Michael White, the City Manager, Adam Albritton, the City Attorney, Assistant Chief Ricky Ramie, Commissioner Dan Russell, and others were not who I believed them to be. Deals were being made, a nefarious contract signed, and the City Engineer, Chris Forehand, even formed his own company within days after the hurricane, PEDS, which he entrenched with the monitors for the City, Tetra-Tech, all without informing the City of this blatant conflict of interest.  Later, the indictments against me would question how all of this could have been going on around me without my knowing.

The Mayor's job, according to the City Charter, has never been to "run the city."  The City Manager is the Chief Financial Officer and is in charge of the day-to-day operations and the employees of the City, not the Mayor, not the Commissioners.  I trusted Michael White and had no reason not to at that time. Even though the Lynn Haven charter states that during times of emergency, the Mayor is the head of the City, or her designee, after declaring the state of emergency and meeting with the Department heads, I designated Michael White to continue his normal duties as the City Manager, and the same for the Police and Fire Departments. This was a logical decision; I was one of five members of the Commission, and I would have had no idea how to run the financial and operational side of the City.  I only asked to be kept informed as we moved through the storm and the aftermath so that I would be able to accurately give reports to the Governor's office, to the County officials, and the news media when I was asked questions concerning our needs and our progress. For the next three months, I rolled up my sleeves and worked fourteen- and sixteen-hour days for my "salary" of $18,000 per year, while City employees were paid at time and a half because of the emergency conditions for many weeks.  I unloaded supply trucks, I led neighborhood ditch and right of way cleanups in rainboots with rakes and shovels clearing the clogged culverts, delivered supplies and checked on elderly and shut-in residents, and made sure our Commission started meeting again six days after the storm, as we would continue meeting weekly for the next 90 days, working and informing residents in the "sunshine",  while also giving a forum for complaints and needs of those residents who attended.  But all around me, something dark and sinister was happening.

While the residents of Lynn Haven were trying to survive, the "boys" of Bay County were lining up to make money from the disaster, forming new corporations, jockeying for position for the hauling and disposal of debris, and taking care of each other as they made millions from one of the strongest Hurricane's to make landfall in United States history.  The "old guard" City employees had been unhappy with me since I was elected Mayor in April of 2015 because my campaign was about change, about fulfilling the promises I made to the residents, and the tenacity with which I worked to bring about the changes I had promised. I thought that after working long hours beside them and getting to know them after the storm I had broken down some of the barriers from the election, that I was accepted, that I had earned their respect, that we were a team, linked forever after going through such a disaster. I would soon find out how wrong I was.

# 4 CORRUPTION AND THE INDICTMENT OF CITY MANAGER MICHAEL WHITE

February 14, 2019

Police Chief Ricky Ramie called me on Valentine's Day, rather late at night, and asked me if I would mind calling Michael White and seeing if he would answer his phone. Without giving me any detail, Ricky told me he was worried about Michael's well-being, that he had been depressed over some "family issues" and that he was concerned that he might even be suicidal. I immediately tried calling Michael, but he did not answer. I then texted him, told him why I wanted to speak with him, that Ricky was worried about him, and would he please call me so that we could talk.

Michael responded by text almost immediately, and told me he was ok, that he just wanted to be alone and think through some things, and that he would talk to Ricky the next day. I relayed this information, and over the course of the next few days, Ricky thanked me for getting an answer from Michael, that everything seemed to be ok, and that he thought it was just a night with too much alcohol, stress from work, and other issues. This did not sound all that unusual to me, and I didn't think any more about it; considering the environment we were all still working in, the daily stress of going to work and then going home to try and deal with repairs, insurance, and all the other family issues was taking its toll on the entire community.

March 17, 2019

While spending the weekend with my family in Jacksonville, I received a call from Police Chief Ricky Ramie, at approximately 2 a.m. in the morning telling me that he was camping with his wife, Kim, in Carrabelle, Florida, and had learned that City Manager Michael White had apparently threatened his wife Amy with a gun, and in the argument that ensued, turned the gun on himself, and threatened to kill her and then himself. He, (Chief Ramie) then went on to tell me that he had asked Commissioner Dan Russell to go to the RV where the Whites were living in the Panama Country Club, in Lynn Haven, and to move Amy White to Russell's residence in his gated community nearby, Osceola Pointe for her safety. (What I did not know, was that this had happened before, Amy seeking shelter with the Russell's). The Chief described to me the fact that because Mike White was the City Manager, and technically his boss, that he would be unable to make the arrest and that the protocol would be to call FDLE; he asked me what my thoughts were, what I thought he should do. This all seemed very odd to me, as the Chief of Police was not sure what to do about arresting someone. Later, much later, it would come to me that Michael White and Ricky Ramie had some type of relationship that Ramie did not want disclosed, and that he was probably afraid to arrest White. I told him that he was the Police Chief and that he should follow his protocols. We talked for a long time by telephone, and one of the things that really stood out to me was the Chief telling me that the cause of the argument was because Amber Guy, the City of Lynn Haven's current Federal FEMA representative, had sent Mike White a text and his wife had seen it. The Chief shared a screenshot of the text to me from Amber Guy's phone (days later) in which she is inviting him to meet with her the next morning to "have some fun", and the obvious is that they are having an affair.

Apparently, Mike White had invited Chief Ramie and his wife Kim to have drinks and dinner a few nights before, and while they were together, Mike "suddenly" noticed that Amber Guy was in the same restaurant and invited her to join them. Chief Ramie told me that it became apparent fairly soon that this was a planned meeting, and he expressed his discomfort with the situation.

I did not know at the time what the extent of the social life was between Commissioner Dan Russell and his wife, Chief Ramie and his wife, and Mike White and his wife, but there was definitely a social media presence with posts of them at different events together, most of which have now been removed as events concerning the Lynn Haven Corruption Case have progressed, but all of the text messages between Michael White and Chief

Ramie have been released after evidentiary hearings of 2022, and they contain shocking revelations about all of them.

I did not realize that there was a domestic violence problem between Mike White and his wife, but I did know there were some types of problems at their home. There had been the previous occasion, only one month earlier, on Valentine's Day, and then I had personally witnessed a temper tantrum in November of 2018 by Michael White's wife, Amy.

On the Sunday evening before the November 2018 election on Tuesday, the city had held an event in Sheffield Park which was attended by Gov Rick Scott, candidates Ron DeSantis, Ashley Moody, and virtually every Panhandle elected official in a get out the vote effort because of the devastation left by the storm. Following this event, I was sitting in the RV in Sheffield Park which was serving as a temporary office for the City Manager, with a few people, but I don't remember exactly who weas there with me, except I do remember my friend Patria, and Ricky and Kim Ramie. The rally was over, and it was probably around 9 p.m., everyone was tired, and we were waiting for the crowds to thin before leaving. The door of the RV opened, and Mike White's wife, Amy, asked if Mike was there. I told her I had not seen him in a while, and started to say something else, when she threw a black trash bag through the door and told us to tell him his clothes were in the bag and not to bother to come home. They were renting a condo on the beach because their home in the Country Club had been destroyed by the storm. Mike White had a camper in Sheffield Park as a convenience when he did not want to drive home to the beach if he was working late, and it had been his primary residence in the first days after the storm. He would later purchase a fifth-wheel RV which he parked on a lot in the Country Club belonging to the City's financial consultant Jay Moody, who lived in the Osceola Pointe neighborhood near Commissioner Dan Russell.

I also remembered a time right after Christmas when Mike White seemed very upset and told me his wife did not like the Christmas gifts he had purchased for her, diamond earrings and a Luis Vuitton purse. He had shown the gifts to me before Christmas, (he had brought them to the office and Vickie Gainer was wrapping them for him) and was very excited about giving them to her. After he gave her the gifts, he told me later that she didn't like the style of the purse and told him to send it back. I found myself wondering how he afforded gifts like those, but didn't think too much more about it.

I don't remember exactly how many times I spoke with Chief Ramie as I was driving home from Jacksonville with my husband the next morning, but it was several times, and we had also spoken over a two- or three-hour period after his initial call to me after the incident happened in the late hours of Saturday night and into the early hours of Sunday. Ricky was also driving back to Lynn Haven from Franklin County where he had been camping, and he sounded alcohol impaired, although I did not mention it to him. In hindsight, even though Ricky and I had become close friends (I thought) after the Hurricane, his talking to me and agonizing over the decision to arrest Michael White should have been a red flag that something else was not right. The relationship between Ricky Ramie and Mike White. What he should have done was let the Mayor and Commissioners know what had happened, and then followed his protocols without asking what to do.

Ramie told me that he decided to have the arrest made by the Sheriff's department after consulting with FDLE (if he even consulted with them; now I am not sure). He would hold off questioning Amy White or Dan and Robyn Russell about what had happened the night before until 7 am Sunday morning, when they would arrive by surprise at Commissioner Russell's home. The Chief told me he did this because Amy was intoxicated the night before and he believed her statement would be thrown out if he did not wait until she was sober. I was uncertain about the time when Mike White was arrested, but later, the police report would reveal that Ricky Ramie did not make sure Michael White was not able to get to Amy White, or to harm himself for many hours. Why?

What I did find out from the Police Chief was that Commissioner Dan Russell was furious that Michael White was arrested and even more furious about the Sheriff's department arriving at his home on Sunday morning, March 18, 2019, without warning to question him, his wife and Amy White.

I made a phone call that Sunday morning, asking Adam Albritton, the City Attorney to draft a statement for me to read regarding the events which had transpired, and I asked the Deputy City Clerk, Vickie Gainer, to call an emergency meeting of the Lynn Haven Commission for 5 pm on Sunday afternoon, notify the media, and to advertise to the public via social media. I did not inform her of the purpose of the meeting at that time, but by the time the meeting took place, many people had already been notified that the City Manager had been arrested for threatening his wife with a firearm and then threatening to turn it on himself.

During the meeting I suggested to the Commission that because I had called an emergency meeting and the City was without a manager, that for the next few days they allow the Mayor to be the head of the City, just as a facilitator to meet with city department heads until a decision was made by the Commission to appoint a temporary City Manager until the situation could be resolved. Commissioner Russell was angry and for some time advocated for Mr. White. Commissioner Antonius Barnes participated by phone and was completely against my proposal. (I had announced my re-election campaign for Mayor with the election coming up in April; Barnes had also qualified to run against me as Mayor, and then later withdrew. He was very angry with me at this time as well, but because he had withdrawn, I had already been re-elected as Mayor on qualifying day in February unopposed.) Barnes suggested that we suspend Mr. White with pay, instead of without pay as had been suggested, and he supported this. Mr. Barnes also suggested that we have the League of Cities place someone as our City Manager until the issue is resolved. I was totally against this, because we were in the middle of recovery from the storm (fifth month) and I could not imagine someone coming from another area who was not familiar with anything we were doing regarding FEMA, cleanup, insurance, etc. This would later be used against me, with investigators saying I was trying to "grab power to continue with the ongoing corruption."

After the emergency commission meeting, I made a phone call to the President of the League of Cities, and friend of mine, Mayor Matt Surrency, who suggested that we move the Deputy City Clerk (Vickie Gainer) into the position temporarily until we could decide about what to do next. The Commission met again two days later, I made this suggestion, and they agreed to this solution. Commissioners Friend and Barnes were both part of the old Commission with Mayor Walter Kelley for many years and have always been against virtually anything I brought before the Commission. Antonius Barnes had planned to run for Mayor in 2015 when I did, and apparently was waiting for Mayor Kelley to serve "one more term". I did not know this when I began my campaign for Mayor in 2015, but after I won, this was the reason for all of the anger from Barnes. The two of them (Friend and Barnes) evacuated to Pensacola before Hurricane Michael hit us, and we saw little of them in the weeks to follow except at weekly Commission meetings initially, and then in the final weeks of his term, February-March 2019, Barnes just stopped coming to the meetings. Chief Ramie, as well as several other city employees who had desks in the attic of the Lynn Haven Service Center at that time, were horrified at my suggestion to the Commission that Deputy City Clerk Vickie Gainer be the interim City Manager. They did not like her, nor did they trust her, were the sentiments they voiced to me. I would certainly find out why as time went on; she had been Michael White's right-hand person and was already aware of the millions of dollars that had been paid to Erosion Control Specialist, ECS.

The next two weeks were very difficult, and I remember asking Chief Ramie to make sure that Mike White's computer was secured (I had no idea what information he had concerning FEMA that could be lost or even erased if Michael became angry during the resolution of his employment with the city. Because Michael White was the one meeting with Amber Guy, he had also basically shut me out of what he was doing as much as possible since the holidays, and even to some degree once I had declared the emergency over at the Commission meeting on October 30, 2018. I was still attending some FEMA and staff meetings and trying to stay on top of what was happening, but it was difficult. I also asked Chief Ramie to make sure the door codes to our administration building were changed because many of the employees had indicated they were uncomfortable or afraid of Mike White after learning of the gun incident. Later, Chief Ramie would tell a completely different story to the FBI about all of this.

Commissioner Russell pushed for Mr. White to have access to City Hall the same as any other citizen, and Russell also threatened both the police chief and the city attorney verbally concerning Mr. White before one of the City Commission meetings. Again, in hindsight, the alliance between Russell, White, and Ramie was probably in play here, and the fact that Russell was threatening Albritton, the City Attorney, as well as his pal Ricky Ramie, would become interesting later as more came to light; they were covering for each other and the corrupt bargains they had made with Michael White.

James Finch, long-time friend of my husband and I, had gone to Las Vegas with his girlfriend of many years, Ashley Hood, to get married on March 9th, and they had asked us to go to Key West with them on March 27th, for a weekend to celebrate with them. That week, James and I were talking about the parks and how they were starting to look beautiful again, and he asked me to find out about the contractor who was building the concession stand and bathrooms at Sheffield Park. He said that he had tried to find out who had bid on the building, the price of the building and the blueprints, because he had the contract to renovate the bathrooms in Porter Park near the Bay. James really liked the building, and he was going to try and emulate the same style at Porter Park, with air-conditioned bathrooms and the same color-scheme so that the parks would look the same with the City colors and building styles. He was not interested in the job at Sheffield, but he said he had not seen any kind of bid process and said the guy building the building, Mickey White of Erosion Control Services would not answer his questions about the bid. James also said that Mickey White did not have a contractor's license. James said something was not right about it and asked me to find out. I went to Vickie Gainer (acting city manager) and asked her for documentation on the bid and the price for the building that was being built…she told me there was no bid packet because there had been no bid, and what she gave me was basically one Excel sheet which had information about the company, ECS. The price of the building was on the sheet, approximately $180,000 plus some other charges listed below that total. Even with my limited knowledge of construction it caught my eye as being a lot of money for that small structure.

But in addition to this information, when I took the sheet over to James to show him the cost, which I could not believe, at the bottom of the sheet was a record of an additional six checks which had been written to Erosion Control Services adding to almost five million dollars. There were no purchase order numbers or invoice numbers on the sheet, just the check numbers and the amounts. One of the checks had cleared the bank on New Year's Eve. I knew something was wrong. James and I continued to look at the amounts of the checks, and James said to me that somebody was stealing from the City and this needed to be taken to the Sheriff. I was just in shock, and he suddenly picked up his phone and called Derwin White, asking him to come to his office that he wanted to ask him about something. I did not know at this time that Derwin White was Mickey White's uncle, and I had only met Mickey White briefly at one of our "One Street at a Time" cleanup events where he was cooking hot dogs and hamburgers in the park for the cleanup volunteers.

When Derwin arrived just a few minutes later at James' office, he seemed surprised to see me sitting there but said hello and asked James what was up. James handed him the sheet of paper and literally all the color left Derwin's face. I also did not know at that time that Derwin was involved as a sub-contractor with one of Lynn Haven's debris haulers, Ash-Britt.

Derwin handed the sheet back to James and began to laugh nervously saying that "that's a lot of money." He continued to look at James and then at me with the nervous laugh going on, when James said something to the effect, of, "somebody's been stealing a lot of money from the City, and the Mayor is going to go to the Sheriff."

Derwin became very upset and told James he thought that was the wrong thing to do, that he was sure this could be handled, whatever was wrong, without going to the Sheriff. James said again that someone had stolen a lot of money and that he and I were turning this over to the Sheriff. Derwin told James that would be a big mistake. James said to Derwin, "No one is going to steal from Lynn Haven, and you can go to Hell!" Derwin turned and stormed angrily out of the office.

James asked me if I could see out the window who was in the truck with Derwin.

I answered him, "no".

James said, "Michael White."

After I left James' office, I went home and told my husband Lee what I was going to do. I was very nervous about the whole thing, but he agreed with me that something was very wrong, and he thought I was doing the right thing. I went to Chief Ricky Ramie, told him that I had found some financial issues with the City, told him I was going to meet with Sheriff Ford, and I asked him if he would go with me as a witness. Ricky did not ask me any questions, but he volunteered to call and set up the meeting.

On the day we went to the Sheriff, Monday, April 1st, I was to meet Ricky there. I went in the front door, and when they led me to the Sheriff's office, Ricky was already sitting there with Tommy Ford; he had come in through the back door instead of meeting me and walking in with me.

Ricky and I were sitting in front of Sheriff Tommy Ford's desk as I shared the excel sheet with Sheriff Ford and told him what had prompted me to ask for the information about ECS, and then to ultimately bring it to him. When I finished telling the Sheriff about the building in the park, and my meeting with James, Ricky Ramie reached for a backpack sitting by his feet which he declared had been in Michael's office and contained $30,000. Later, I would wonder how long Ricky had had the backpack, and even if he was turning it in because he was nervous that I was going to the Sheriff about financial issues in the City. I was so nervous about reporting what I had found that I really did not think about how odd it was at the time that Ricky would suddenly declare in front of me to the Sheriff that he had $30,000 in a backpack from Michael White's office. I still do not know what happened to the $30,000, if it became evidence, or something else.

After I had finished talking, Sheriff Tommy Ford asked me if I could get copies of the six checks, back and front for him, and then later, when I came back with the checks, he asked if I could get copies of all the invoices for Erosion Control Specialist, from both the city and from Jay Moody, the city's accounting consultant., and I told him I would. In hindsight, I also find it odd that the Sheriff knew who our city accounting consultant was and that he would have copies of the invoices and purchase orders for ECS.

I went to Vickie Gainer again and told her that I needed copies of all invoices and purchases orders pertaining to ECS. I told her I could not tell her what they were for, but I would explain when I could. I had gone earlier to Beverly Waldrup, the Finance Department Director and asked for copies of the ECS checks, back and front, before delivering them to Tommy Ford, also asking Ms. Waldrup to please not discuss my request with anyone, and she said that she would not.

There were stacks of paperwork, and Chief Ramie advised me to send the paperwork with him to the Sheriff's office, and even had me meet him at Wal-Mart parking lot with the invoices for him to take to the Sheriff so that no one would see me carrying the stacks of paperwork into the Sheriff's office. He said he thought that "it would be better for no one to see the Mayor carrying large stacks of materials to the Sheriff's office." I would also later regret agreeing to this, which I thought was for my protection, so that no one would know that I was the "whistleblower" on possible wrongdoing in the City. Actually, Ricky would deliver these, not to Sheriff Ford, but to Major Jimmy Stanford, a corrupt investigator who worked hand in hand with Derwin White, his longtime friend, to destroy my life, in retaliation for my reporting the activities of Mickey White and ECS to the Sheriff's office. Much later, I would learn that over the coming months, Mickey White, Michael White, Ricky Ramie, Vickie Gainer, Adam Albritton, Chris Forehand, and others, would assist in covering up and denying that I was the "whistle blower," setting me up in the property cleanup scheme, and implicating me as central to the entire corruption scheme in Lynn Haven.

The Sheriff, when he had asked me to have Jay Moody, our accounting advisor during the storm, to make copies of any invoices he had for Erosion Control Specialist, had also asked me to find out if Jay would be willing to come to the Sheriff's office and talk to him. We did the same thing again, and Ricky met me at Warren Averett CPAs, Moody's office in Panama City, to pick up the invoices to take to Tommy Ford. I had explained to Jay what I needed, and when I asked him, Jay also told me that he was willing to meet with Tommy Ford; I told this to Sheriff Ford. (Ramie and Gainer would later tell the investigators a completely different story about this; their narrative was that Gainer discovered the problems with ECS after becoming interim City Manager when Michael White was suspended, that *she alerted me* of the situation, and that she gave these invoices directly to Ramie, *not to me*.

Ramie's testimony to the FBI mentioned nothing about meeting me in the parking lots to get the invoices; we later found out that he gave these invoices to Major Jimmy Stanford, not to the Sheriff, after holding them for several days. We would also find out later, fake invoices for the cleanup of "my property", actually an easement maintained by the City, were planted at ECS... just in time for the FBI and BCSO raid on April 12th, 2019. Tommy Ford had called me within the next day or so after I had delivered the checks to him and the stacks of invoices and purchase orders to Ricky Ramie and told me that he believed there was definitely a problem, and he was calling in the FBI. He asked me again not to discuss anything about the documents I had brought to him or any of the other information we had discussed. I did not hear anything again until the FBI issued subpoenas to the City of Lynn Haven, and shortly after that, the news media began to report the investigation.

What I know now, in hindsight, is that Sheriff Ford became my judge and jury the day I came forward; he decided that I was guilty and that I was involved, either based on the information he would receive from his corrupt investigator, Major Jimmy Stanford, who was working with Derwin White, or he decided to implicate me because *he was involved himself* with the kickbacks from AshBritt with Derwin White and GAC and wanted me silenced. A later affidavit and raid on GAC would state that Bay District Schools officials and other elected and county officials were also involved in the corruption, although now, over six years after the landfall of Hurricane Michael, none of those named has been charged with a single crime by the FBI or the Bay County Sheriff's Office.

Sheriff Tommy Ford, never, to my knowledge spoke to anyone on my behalf, saying that I was the one who brought the information forward that started the entire investigation, and while the FBI and Sheriff's investigators questioned many City employees in the light of day by appointment, including Chief Ricky Ramie, they never questioned me until the night of November 18, 2019, the night before they made their arrests and read the indictment publicly which implicated me as having received free cleanup and repairs to my property which were charged to the City and submitted to FEMA for reimbursement, implicating me in a federal crime. Sheriff Tommy Ford knew the FBI agents were coming to question me that night; he called me and told me to answer my phone that the FBI had tried to call me. From that point on, my photograph was included both in print and online, over and over, pictured beside the arrested individuals in black and white jail mugshots, and I now believe, based on evidence, that the Sheriff was part of this plan to implicate me, and that he, along with Stanford, was owned by Derwin White and GAC. The week that I went to the Sheriff in April 2019, Ashbritt had made a donation of over $750,000 to the Children's Advocacy Center in Panama City; after that the building contract for the Center was awarded to Derwin White and GAC. Major Jimmy Stanford's daughter is the CEO of the organization, other BCSO investigators are on the board, and Sheriff Tommy Ford was the Treasurer.

The news media began reporting this and from that point on, a small group of past and present City of Lynn Haven employees who were never in favor of me as mayor, as well as those in elected positions who were jealous/envious of all the national media attention and local praise from residents I had received since the storm, began a steady attack on my character, trying to link me with Mike White. I did not learn of Greenleaf's ties with Erosion Control Services until the FBI announcements that they had raided the businesses for computers, and records in April. (Greenleaf was a company under contract with the City of Lynn Haven to maintain the City's sports park and ball fields, the parks, and cemeteries. I was told by the acting City Manager, Vickie Gainer, that both former Commissioners, Rodney Friend and Antonius Barnes were behind the scenes on comments made by their friends and relatives on social media websites, and that Friend had made efforts to have me removed from office by trying to contact the Governor's office.

I do remember during this time being extremely afraid of Micky White, owner of Erosion Control Specialist Inc., Josh Anderson, owner of Greenleaf, and Michael White, because I had taken the information to the Bay County Sheriff's Department and that information had been leaked out by someone either from the City of Lynn Haven or the Sheriff's Department. At the time I did not believe the Lynn Haven Police Chief had told anyone, but Vickie Gainer also knew that I had asked for the invoices and purchases orders, and I didn't know if she made the copies herself, or if she asked someone to do it. There were many days that Chief Ramie had his department park an old patrol car in my driveway at night (unmanned) because I was afraid; this was absolutely a slap in my face, so to speak. I was told later by former members of the LHPD that Ricky joked about this, implying that I was paranoid, or making a "big deal" out of nothing, that I was in no danger from anyone.

I find this laughable now, because Ramie was in on all of it with Jimmy Stanford, Sheriff Tommy Ford, and the other investigators, and he would later wear a wire to record our personal conversations, working with the FBI Agent, Larry Borghini, trying to find something to use against me. I believed this recording was a violation of my 6th Amendment Rights because they both knew I had legal representation at the time they were recording me in April of 2020, but I was told by counsel because Ramie was law enforcement that he could record anyone.

As I mentioned previously, I thought it very strange that the FBI initially questioned Vickie Gainer, Amanda Delonjay (the person who does the check runs for the City), Chief Ramie, David Horton (who was later indicted), Bobby Baker (Public Works Director), Adam Albritton (the City Attorney who was later indicted), and many others, beginning on April 12, 2019, but they never questioned me. I would also find the answer to this later as well. Vickie Gainer would tell me soon after the interviews started that she could no longer discuss the "investigation" with me because she was a *witness* for FBI Borghini and was providing documentation he requested. I could not believe my ears; she was very smug and condescending as she told me this.

They also questioned Commissioner Judy Tinder early on, because I remember her calling me and telling me they had asked to meet with her the next day. She was nervous about it, and I remember encouraging her and telling her not to worry that I was sure it would be fine; Commissioner Tinder had made several public comments about the City being corrupt, and I felt that this was probably what it was about, but I didn't know at the time, and of course, she did not discuss the questions with me. Commissioner Tinder was also aware of the 4.9 million dollars' worth of checks which I discovered and took to the Sheriff; she lives right behind me on Virginia Avenue, and I often would see her in the evenings when I was walking my dog. I had shared with her what I had found, and that I had turned it over to the Sheriff, because I was afraid. I told her this long before the FBI issued subpoenas to the city and the media reported it; I wanted her to know in case anything happened to me. That's how scared I was (and am). I would find out later that the Sheriff's investigators and FBI also questioned former City attorney Rob Jackson and former City Manager Joel Schubert, both who gave false information about me and left out important information in their interviews.

On April 23, 2019, my husband suggested that we take our motor home out to the beach and stay for a few days in one of the RV parks because I was having trouble sleeping in our house. (I live in the old part of Lynn Haven, and my house is very accessible to anyone who wants to find me). I agreed and we went out to the beach for a few days. The second day we were out there, April 24th, I was sitting by the pool reading a book, and Channel 13's Brady Calhoun called me to tell me that he had an invoice stating that the City of Lynn Haven had cleaned my property following the storm amounting to thousands of dollars billed to the City, and wanted to know if I wanted to do an interview before he released the information as a story that evening. I told him that this was not true, and that I was at the beach and not dressed for an interview, but that I would be there as soon as I could get dressed and to the television station which was in downtown Panama City. I also told him I wanted to meet with the station manager and the news director. I realized as we were talking that he was referring to the stormwater easement between Virginia and Tennessee Avenue, and that I had indeed requested that the city remove two or three trees from the easement which had fallen on the electrical pole preventing the power company from doing repair/hookup, on the street on the side of my house, and blocking the pole barn so that we could move our motorhome back underneath it since the fiberglass roof had blown off during the storm and it was down to plywood on top. But what many still do not realize was that my son-in-law and friends came from Jacksonville two days after the storm with a truckload of supplies for the citizens, and then stayed for several days at my house, removing the trees from the pole barn, pushing the debris onto the city easement, and taking care of the cleanup and repairs to my home and my mom's. By the time the City arrived to clear the debris from the easement and right of way on November 9th, my family had taken care of everything on my property and my Mom's who lived next door. But instead of interviewing me, or my Mom, or trying to find out the truth, the investigators asked Mickey White, Michael White, Josh Anderson, and the Lynn Haven Public Works Director Bobby Baker, never questioning me about the fake invoices which had now made their way to the news media, courtesy of one of Derwin White's political hacks, Arthur Cullen, who is also the campaign manager for both Sheriff Tommy Ford and State Attorney Larry Basford.

I called the city attorney, Adam Albritton, who met me at the TV station with a copy of the property description and easement to the east of my property, and then I had the news director pull up the google earth views of my property before and after the hurricane which showed that I had no trees in my yard. After the news director saw the google earth photos and the property description of the stormwater easement, he said to the station manager, "this is a non-story."

After that, I found it odd that the City attorney (Adam Albritton, who later entered a guilty plea) already had a description of my property and the stormwater easement on hand, because he met me at the news station within 45 minutes after I called him. I found out later that the city manager, Vickie Gainer, was already aware that the news media was calling me and had asked Adam Albritton as well as Bobby Baker about the property through emails. The FBI and BCSO had raided ECS and Greenleaf a second time on this date, but I did not know this when Channel 13's Brady Calhoun called me about the invoices that someone had given them.

I didn't hear anything about this matter again until later in the summer of 2019, Commissioner Dan Russell launched a very public attack on me as he made a public records request about the invoices and my property, complained about my having the city golf cart to use, and wanted proof that I had not used city money to pay for baseball caps with my name on them which I gave out as thank you advertising after the Mayor election in April 2019. I read a public statement at the next commission meeting refuting all of his inquiries.

Commissioner Dan Russell had also been questioned about the invoice referring to the cleaning of his gated, private neighborhood at City expense, and he claims they only cleaned a stormwater easement, not private property. He has also been mentioned in both the November 2019 indictment of Michael White and four others, as well as the August 2020 indictment of Adam Albritton and me. I don't know what they cleaned there, because I only became aware of it at about the same time the news media called me about my property. Someone obviously called Channel 13 about the invoice, because my name is not on the invoice, only my address, 513 Tennessee Avenue, and there were so many invoices, that one would have had to know what they were looking for to find it, and then to know that 513 Tennessee Avenue was my address. (And we would find out later that not only did someone know, Derwin White had directed his nephew, Mickey White, owner of Erosion Control Services, to create invoices which would implicate me and then plant them at his office to be found. Major Jimmy Stanford of the Bay County Sheriff's office was part of this, tipping Derwin off as to the date that the FBI would be at ECS. My "invoices" were " found" and photographed there as evidence against me, with crumpled copies conveniently placed on the top of papers in a trash can; the BCSO, the FBI and the prosecutors were all aware of this "setup" before the indictment of Michael White, Mickey White, Josh Anderson,

David Horton, and Shannon Rodriguez in November of 2019, yet I was implicated as a target in their indictment for having received a "property cleanup benefit" from Erosion Control Services and knowingly having it billed to the City and then submitted to FEMA for reimbursement. Chris Forehand's interview with the FBI also reveals that Derwin White gave copies of the fake invoices to Chris and told him to take them to Tetra Tech and make sure that the City of Lynn Haven had paid the invoices and that they had been submitted to FEMA for payment. (This was to make sure that the charges they were going to bring against me would be federal charges involving FEMA).

I believe for many reasons (which I will bring up later) that Dan Russell knew about the fabricated invoices because he was told there were invoices for his neighborhood, probably by Ricky Ramie, to whom I gave the invoices. This would explain why he was in the City Hall attic office combing through piles of invoices right after I went in and received the copies I had requested from Vickie Gainer to turn in to the Sheriff.

At this point in time, we had moved from the Verizon trailer office at Sheffield Park into the Lynn Haven Service Center, the location of the drive-through and walk-in payment center for water and sewage as well as for building permits. The first floor of the building was functioning normally with office space, but the attic of the building was being used as office space for several administrative positions, the City Manager, and the Police Chief. I also had a desk in the corner, in a room of ten or twelve desks, filing cabinets, printers, and stacks of chairs and furniture, and I found it odd to find Commissioner Russell sitting at my desk, which was piled with stacks of pink invoices which he was furiously going through. He set out to prove, unbeknownst to me at the time, that he had done nothing wrong, getting a letter written by his homeowner's association (after the fact) referencing a verbal agreement (that did not exist) with the City to clean the drainage area, and also, his "buddy" Chris Forehand, in his 302 interview with the FBI made elaborate explanation of why the drainage ditch in Dan Russell's neighborhood was a stormwater/flood hazard, and that FEMA would cover those costs. Forehand's interview in which he stated the following, was conducted only three days after I was arrested:
"Forehand was asked if he was aware of the city doing any cleanup work at Osceola Point. Forehand advised that there is a drainpipe that runs from Iowa Avenue to the bay. The pipe runs underground through Osceola Point but there is a drain located just outside of Osceola Point. A lady on Iowa Avenue had complained about her property flooding. At first, the city's position was hurricane cleanup only on public property not private property. The city went to FEMA and was told that if there was a threat to public safety, then the issue could be addressed. Forehand gave the example that if the area was flooded and an ambulance could not access the

area, then that would be justification for the public safety exemption. Forehand understood that the drainage area was cleared so that the area would not flood."

Of course, Forehand made no mention to them that the stormwater easement adjacent to my property which had been cleaned by the City, (and for which I was charged for fraud and charging $45,000 to the City for personal work done in the indictment of August 2020) was a tidewater ditch one block from Maxwell Bayou which also caused extensive flooding during rainstorms to Alabama Avenue, Virginia Avenue, Kentucky Avenue, and parts of Tennessee Avenue. He was aware because he had worked on the City's stormwater study project. The cleaning of the easement by the City was beneficial to all of the homes on Virginia and Tennessee Avenue which backed up to the stormwater ditch and easement.

My asking Michael White to have the City remove three downed trees from the stormwater easement which were on City right of way blocking my property, and also preventing repairs by the power company to the pole, and the trees in the street and covering the ditch and drainage area, was no different than requests made by any other citizen or resident of Lynn Haven. I answered their phone calls personally, visiting them personally to see their complaints and issues, and personally contacting the City Manager and Public Works on their behalf daily after the storm. The fact that the City did not come to even look at the problem on the easement adjacent to my property until a full month after the storm, certainly demonstrated that I was not granted any favor by the City, especially since my son-in-law and his friends from Jacksonville had already moved the trees from my property which fell from the City easement almost a month before the City showed up on November 9th, 2018 to clear the debris from the easement and the right of way.

In the weeks following City Manager Michael White's arrest on March 17, 2019, and his subsequent resignation on March 26, 2019, there was quite a bit of scrambling going on at City Hall by Commissioner Dan Russell, Interim City Manager Vickie Gainer, and others, which would become significant in the months ahead. After discovering Michael White's exclusive payments to Erosion Control Services for debris removal and push, with virtually no payments having been made to the other two haulers, Ash Britt and Crowder Gulf, one of the things that has concerned me most, then and now, is that the City Manager, Vickie Gainer, has stated over and over to the media and to the public that SHE is responsible for making changes in internal accounting procedures after Michael White's departure, without ever mentioning that it was MY IDEA to set up separate accounts for FEMA reimbursements, insurance reimbursements, Bond money, etc., and that I was the one who insisted, going forward, on hand-written checks with blue-ink signatures from she and I to pay the debris haulers, approved by the Commission because the amounts were often in excess of a million dollars each. All of the checks written to ECS (Mickey White) had been run as warrants either in large check runs with my stamped signature, or on singular runs that Michael White had asked Amanda Delonjay to do (which she never reported to anyone on the Commission, nor did her husband, who was technically the Emergency Management Director for the City as the Fire Chief. Why didn't he say something? His interviews reflect that he knew.)

I also insisted after Michael White's departure that the warrant list (checks which had already been written, authorized, and paid for by the City, now be made available to the Mayor and the City Manager *before* the checks were run instead of afterwards, as the system before, during and after the storm, until the resignation of Mr. White had been.

Vickie Gainer could have very easily used the truthful words, "The Mayor and I," concerning these new accounting practices, and a lot of media and public trust might have been averted. I would also like to know if she mentioned to the FBI, with whom she indicated to me that she spoke with frequently and told me she was going to be a witness and could not discuss her conversations with me, that the Mayor is the one who demanded changes to the accounting practices after Michael White's departure, to safeguard the accounts after discovering what had happened. I feel certain after reading all of her interviews with law enforcement and the lies she told them, that she did not tell them. She was the deputy city clerk, the person who oversaw bid packets, saw invoices and purchase orders, and at one point was also the contracts manager under Michael White, the city manager. I saw Vickie Gainer work very hard for the City of Lynn Haven after the storm, for weeks, just as I watched City Manager, Michael White, and many others, seemingly doing everything within their power to bring the City back. I had no reason to distrust any of them, and I was also one of Ms. Gainer's most supportive advocates as she sought the position of city manager, based on the work ethic I had seen from her. I feel much differently in hindsight, just as I do about Michael White. At an earlier point in time the Government had only given our defense attorneys one 302 interview report for Vickie Gainer, yet she told me that they interviewed her numerous times. She would smugly tell me that she was a "witness" and that she would be glad when all of this was over and the City could move forward. Police Chief Ricky Ramie repeatedly told me that this investigation was about "Michael White, Michael White, Michael White," when I expressed my concern that the Sheriff nor the FBI had questioned me like everyone else, and the media appetite increased daily at the same time my public standing diminished. I would find out later that both Vickie Gainer and Ricky Ramie had given more than one interview each, and that they also worked together to provide a type of journal, each time either I or

James Finch met with either of them or spoke to them on the phone. These interviews as well as the notes, or journal of Vickie Gainer were kept from both James Finch and me for almost two years. Had we gone to trial at one of the earlier dates, we would have been without crucial exculpatory information.

In the months following the beginning of the FBI investigation of the City of Lynn Haven in April 2019, our city slowly slipped out of the limelight as the city that had led the way during the storm, offering food, information, clothing, holiday celebrations and a sense of normalcy in the middle of the chaos, and we quickly became the place to make jokes about, to speculate on who was involved and to what degree, a city filled with corruption. Commissioners Brandon Aldridge and Pat Perno, who had each been elected in April 2019 when I was re-elected unopposed for my second term, were somewhat arrogant and condescending to me in meetings at first, but this would grow in the coming months, as they and their "political operative" campaign manager, Derwin White's messenger boy, Arthur Cullen, all worked collaboratively to take down the Mayor; Derwin White had set me up to be indicted because I found the ECS fraud and went to the Sheriff, not knowing that Derwin's "dirty cop" Jimmy Stanford would be there to help, along with LHPD Chief Ricky Ramie, Sheriff Ford, and his "public corruption unit."

The City of Lynn Haven Hurricane Relief Fund for which I had worked so hard, raising over a quarter of a million dollars which was given out in $1,000.00 grants to over two hundred families, now became a subject for jokes, even on the social media sites of WMBB Channel 13, the *Panama City News Herald*, and other news organizations. I was unable to raise more money after the attacks on me began, and I was also too embarrassed to try.

When the President of the United States came during the summer of 2019, I was initially invited to meet him at Tyndall Air Force Base as he arrived, to give him updates of our City's progress since his initial visit just five days after the storm to Lynn Haven; that invitation was rescinded just two hours after I received it because as his Chief of Staff told me, the President could not be photographed or seen with the Mayor of a city under FBI investigation. I tried to explain to him that I was not under investigation, that a contractor doing business with the City (ECS) and the City Manager were. He was not interested in talking further; he obviously knew I was a target of the investigation, even though I did not know.

The President of Florida Blue was scheduled to be a part of our one year Celebration and Commemoration ceremony at Sheffield Park on the anniversary of the storm where he would present us with a $50,000 check for our Hurricane Relief Fund, after I had traveled to the corporate office of Florida Blue to present them with a Key to the City and talk to them about our non-profit relief fund to benefit families in the City. At the last minute his staff notified us that he would not be able to attend but would be sending the check. The staff members from Florida Blue who came brought activities with them and were a large part of the success of the event. I believe that he couldn't be seen with me either because of all of the negative publicity which had now surrounded me as Mayor of Lynn Haven. Also, noticeably absent from the celebration we had planned for thousands, with Publix providing sub sandwiches and desserts for all who attended, was the regional representative for Publix who had worked with me to arrange the generous food donations as they had a year earlier for Thanksgiving. None of the Bay County officials attended the celebration. No other Mayors attended, no other commissioners, no county commissioners; and conspicuously absent was Sheriff Tommy Ford. All those elected officials who had sought the limelight in Lynn Haven in the aftermath of the storm, who I had offered an opportunity to speak at our celebration decided not to attend this one, just one month before the indictment against Michael White, David "Mickey White", David Horton, Josh Anderson and Shannon Rodriguez would be announced. The indictment would also implicate that the Mayor had received fraudulent benefits from the City of Lynn Haven, alleging that her personal property had been cleaned and billed to the City in the amount of $45,000. That same night, I attended the ceremony for Panama City at Tommy Oliver Stadium, and my seat was next to Sheriff Tommy Ford's on the football field as speakers approached the podium, including the Governor of Florida. Tommy spoke to me briefly but did not attempt any conversation. I had been under the impression when I attended that I was to be called on to speak, an honored guest, but I was never called to the podium. How did all these officials know what was coming? Hindsight is truly 20/20. Just before the celebration, in September of 2019, the Panama Country Club held a barbeque dinner at Sonny's because the Country Club was not open because of damages to the building that had not yet been repaired. At this event, our friend, Jim White, a local attorney approached my husband and I and told us that I needed to get an attorney to represent me in this investigation. I was caught completely by surprise and asked him what I needed an attorney for. He was angry, red-faced and became a little belligerent, and this time ignored me, and said the same thing to my husband. What we did not know at the time was that Mickey White had already engaged Mr. White as his attorney. My husband, Lee, and I discussed this on the way home, and I was shaken a bit by what Mr. White had said, and for the next few weeks, I felt more and more distant from the City and my job as Mayor. An ominous foreboding began to descend upon me, and while I had fought off times of depression, probably PTSD, and nightmares since the storm, I found myself giving in more to the depression.

The October 10th Commemoration and Celebration went well, despite the absence of so many officials. I was able to recognize many citizens with plaques and certificates for their work during the storm, and my spirits were lifted again somewhat, especially because my daughter, son-in-law and granddaughters had come to spend a few days and attend the celebration as well. I talked with my daughter again about how unhappy I was and that I thought once again that I was ready to think about possibly buying a home in Jacksonville, and then once the Mayor's term was over move permanently to be close to them, while keeping our home in Lynn Haven for when we wanted to visit our family and friends. I missed them, and while I believed over time that Lynn Haven would flourish, would grow and thrive as a community, I knew that realistically it would be fifty years before there would again be beautiful trees, before the area did not look so desolate.

In November of 2019, I went to spend the weekend of November 15th with my daughter and granddaughters as she and my son-in-law were celebrating their anniversary; Lee and I drove back home on Monday night, November 18th, and at that time we had moved out of our house on 513 Tennessee Avenue to Marina Bay Condominiums (about 1 mile away). At this point, I had not decided what I was going to do, but because of all of the publicity from the investigation, I knew that as soon as the Mayor's term was over (3 more years) that I was ready to move from Lynn Haven. We had moved everything out of our house, done some more repairs, had it painted, and placed it on the market for sale. The condo was gated, and I was able to sleep, something I had not been able to do at our home on Tennessee Avenue since the dead fish had been placed on the doorstep, and all the ugly Facebook and other social media comments continued.

Just after we arrived home from Jacksonville that night, about 8 p.m., Sheriff Tommy Ford called me and told me that FBI agents were at my house and wanted to ask me some questions. I was caught completely off guard, I was tired from driving almost five hours; otherwise, I would not have met with them without an attorney. It felt wrong, it felt sneaky, and not in the light of day. After all these months, after questioning everyone, it seemed in the City of Lynn Haven except me, why now? But I was intimidated, and I told Tommy Ford I was not at my house and gave them directions to where we were living. They arrived in about five minutes, and they stayed asking questions for over an hour. When they left, I felt ok about the interview, and had answered all of their questions to the best of my ability. I had asked them if I could take notes, and they would not allow me to do that, which should have raised many red flags for me. I was very shaken about having them show up at night in a surprise visit; I had no idea what was about to happen the next morning. They arrested the City Manager and others, and at 2:00 pm at the planned press conference in

Panama City, as the indictment was read I, implicating the Mayor as having had her property cleaned and billed to the City of Lynn Haven at a cost of over $48,000, Mayor Anderson's name was called out as much as the names of those who had been arrested in questions by the press. US Attorney Larry Keefe, Assistant US Attorney Stephen Kunz, FBI investigators and Sheriff Tommy Ford stood smugly on the stage for the strategically planned public corruption indictment, following closely on the heels of the previous indictment in a neighboring County in October, and as the media frenzy continued, social media became a modern-day lynching for the Mayor in the twenty-four hour period which followed.

The text of the indictment is included below: (Court records include all of the documents which were unsealed by the Court after the evidentiary hearings and the trials of James Finch. These records were filed on the court document and most are public, revealing who many of the people in our community are who made false or misleading statements to the FBI and BCSO both before and after I was indicted, never thinking what they said would become public, dozens of motions, court orders, grand jury transcripts, and evidentiary hearing exhibits, as well as other information about the case.) The documents reveal in black and white the level of corruption and lies which took place in this "investigation." If reading the indictment and charges against Michael White and the others is something the reader prefers to skip over, the first pages are the part that name me as having received free property cleanup which was billed to the City; but I wanted to include the entire indictment against Michael White, David "Mickey" White and the others for those who were not aware of the charges, and who are curious as to who got the five million dollars. Mickey White was paid the five million dollars by the City of Lynn Haven with portions of it "kicked back" to those who helped him get it. GAC (Gulf Asphalt Corporation) received over sixteen million as sub-contractors to AshBritt; owner Derwin White is deceased, and co-owner Allan Bense was never charged with any crimes. Not one employee of the City of Lynn Haven, ever came to a weekly Commission meeting to ask the city commission or the mayor why Michael White was doing individual "check runs" to ECS, with the stamped signature of the City Manager and the Mayor on them; not Amanda Delonjay, not Beverly Waldrup, and not Vickie Gainer.

Amanda Delonjay, the employee who had been with the City for over 16 years, married to the fire chief, John DeLonjay, the Emergency Operations Manager during the storm, abruptly retired in January 2020 after the indictment against Michael White and the others was brought. Her interview with the FBI will be included later in this book. She told the FBI and the BCSO investigators that the Mayor received a check register every two weeks which listed all of the checks that had been paid, indicating that I was aware of these payments to Mickey White. What she neglected to tell them was that these check registers were not run for many weeks after the storm, and that when they finally were, they were stacked in a corner of the attic on a desk designated as the Mayor's all at once sometime in January of 2019. Until this time, I did not have an office, a desk, or a mailbox. As Mayor, my signature was the third one on the front of the registers which had already been verified by the head of the accounting department and the city manager. The Mayor's signature was not a signature of approval, because the Mayor nor none of the Commissioners had access to the purchase orders, invoices and other accounting documents. The City Manager and Department head for Accounting signed the register indicating that all checks were paid out according to the approved budget, and the Mayor's signature was included as the Treasurer of the City.

Every check written to ECS had my stamped computerized signature on it, run by Amanda Delonjay, except for one. I left town on October 26, 2018, for the first time since the storm, traveling to Jacksonville to meet with the legal firm which had volunteered to set up a 501(c)(3) Hurricane Relief Fund for our City pro bono. I had not been on the road for an hour when Michael White called me telling me that he needed a check authorized to a company for doing the "push" of the trees and debris in Sheffield Park where we had moved all of the City operations and were planning the big community Halloween celebration. He said he had "forgotten" to have me sign the check, and would I give verbal authorization for Vickie Gainer to sign it. The amount was $224K and having been told that our total cleanup of the City was going to be possibly as much as thirty million dollars in total, this did not seem unusual. I gave the authorization. Later the bank called me to verify that I had authorized it which I did. Our area is small, I was well-known in the community, and the bank did not hesitate to authorize the check. When I returned from Jacksonville, Vickie Gainer told me that I needed to write an email to the bank for their records concerning the same check which I did. Later, in the indictment against me in August of 2020, I would be charged in the Erosion Control Specialist conspiracy for authorizing the check for 224,000.

After listening to the press conference and listening to the feeding frenzy of the media calling out my name more than the names of those indicted, I called Sheriff Tommy Ford on the phone and asked him, "What the Hell?" I cannot believe you just stood there and never said a word in my defense. What is this? You knew this last night when you called me. They already had the indictment, naming me before they came to question me."

"The agents said you were not forthcoming with your answers." This is *exactly* what he said to me. I repeated to him again, "they already had this indictment naming me before they ever questioned me, Tommy." At this point, I just lost it and began to cry on the phone and said to him that he knew me, and what did they need to know, that I would be glad to meet with them again if there was something they needed clarification on or more information, that I had told the truth about everything they asked.

He was then sarcastic, as he smugly told me that, "he wasn't going to get in a three-way conversation with me and the FBI, but that he would let them know what I said." There was silence and he then abruptly hung up.

I then went straight to the Lynn Haven Police Chief, and he seemed very surprised, (but he was not, as I would later learn) not only by the indictment, but also by the Sheriff's response to me. He told me to immediately text the Sheriff and refer to our conversation and get the Sheriff to respond to me via text message that he would arrange another meeting for me to speak with them again about the property which was referred to in the indictment. I did this, and I still have the text messages, but there was never another meeting. Police Chief Ricky Ramie, who I trusted, and believed to be loyal to me as his Mayor, as well as my friend, lied to me when he told me he had not known about the indictment that was coming against me in August of 2020; every other law enforcement agent and their wives in Bay County seemed to have known, according to the posts on social media, many of them by former police chief of Lynn Haven, Matt Riemer and his wife Trisha Wright Reimer, (Matt was employed at that time with the State Attorney's Office), and Jennifer Dutton Williams, whose husband Doug Williams was also employed by the State Attorney's Office at the time of my indictment of August 19, 2020.

*The false allegations against me and my mother about having had our property cleaned and billed to the City of Lynn Haven are contained on page 91, in paragraph 12 of the indictment. Although I was not charged, this allegation increased the firestorm of publicity on social media, and local television and newspapers against me, and publicly humiliated my mom.*

THE FIRST INDICTMENT OF THE LYNN HAVEN CORRUPTION CASE


UNITED STATES OF AMERICA
v.
MICHAEL EDWARD WHITE
DAVID MITCHELLE WHITE

84

JOSHUA DANIEL ANDERSON
And
SHANNON DELORES RODRIGUEZ
a/k/a "Shannon Delores Harris"

THE GRAND JURY CHARGES:
COUNT ONE
A.INTRODUCTION

1.    On October 10, 2018, Hurricane Michael caused severe damage to
public and private property, public buildings, public communications
systems, public streets and roads, and public drainage systems within the
City of Lynn Haven, Florida (Lynn Haven).

2.    On October 16, 2018, as a result of Hurricane Michael, Lynn
Haven adopted a local state of emergency for post disaster relief and
planning and approved Hurricane Michael Resolution No. 2018-19-16. In
the resolution, Lynn Haven waived the procedures and formalities
otherwise required under Florida law to take action to ensure the safety,
welfare, and health of the citizens of Lynn Haven, including:  entering into
contracts; incurring obligations; acquisition and distribution of materials,
supplies, and other expenses related to the storm event; appropriation and
expenditure of public funds; and the employment of permanent and
temporary workers.  The resolution delegated emergency powers to the
mayor of Lynn Haven, or her designee, to discharge the duties and exercise
powers for the above described activities until the local emergency declared
had expired and the resolution was rescinded.  The Declaration of
Emergency was to be automatically renewed every seven days until further
action was taken by Lynn Haven.

3.    On October 23, 2018, as a result of Hurricane Michael, Lynn
Haven again declared and reinstated a local state of emergency for post
disaster relief and planning and entered Hurricane Michael Resolution No.
2018-10-23-002.  This Declaration of Emergency contained the same
provisions as the original declaration of emergency and was effective for
seven days.  The Declaration of Emergency was required to be renewed or
it would automatically expire.

4.    On October 30, 2018, Lynn Haven voted to end the local state of
emergency and end the designation of the emergency powers to the mayor
or her designee.

5.    Prior to Hurricane Michael, Lynn Haven had contracted with three
disaster relief companies to provide disaster relief services for Lynn Haven
following a hurricane.  These companies provided debris removal services
for Lynn Haven after Hurricane Michael, submitted invoices with
supporting documentation for their services, and received payment from
Lynn Haven, which was reimbursed by the Federal Emergency

Management Agency (FEMA) for the expenses.

6.     FEMA is an agency of the United States Department of Homeland Security, and is responsible for coordinating the federal government's response to natural and man-made disasters. The primary purpose of FEMA is to coordinate the response to a disaster that has occurred in the United States and that overwhelms the resources of local and state authorities. In addition to on-the-ground support of disaster recovery efforts, FEMA provides state and local governments with experts in specialized fields and the funding for rebuilding efforts for infrastructure. FEMA also provides for the reimbursement of many expenses incurred by local governments in cleaning up and restoration after natural disasters, such as hurricanes.

7.     MICHAEL EDWARD WHITE ("M.WHITE") was hired by Lynn Haven as its City Manager on August 22, 2017. As City Manager, M. WHITE was the administrative head of the municipal government and was responsible for the day-to-day operations and administrative functions of Lynn Haven. The City Manager served at the pleasure of the Lynn Haven City Commission. M.WHITE resigned as city manager of Lynn Haven on March 26, 2019.

8.     Erosion Control Specialists ("ECS") was incorporated in the State of Florida on May 10, 2011. DAVID MITCHELLE WHITE ("D.WHITE") was listed as director of ECS. In a 2018 amended annual report and a 2019 annual report filed with the State of Florida, D. WHITE was listed as a director and Vice President of ECS. ECS was not licensed in Florida to do contracting, electrical, or plumbing activities, and held no business licenses with the State of Florida.

9.     On October 22, 2018 MICHAEL EDWARD WHITE, on behalf of Lynn Haven, and DAVID MITCHELLE WHITE, as owner of ECS, signed an agreement for ECS to provide Lynn Haven with "Emergency And/Or Exigent Services, Ancillary Construction Services, or Construction Due to the Effects of Hurricane Michael." The agreement referenced ECS as a "contractor," with the effective date of October 11, 2018. The term of the agreement was for no more than 90 days to perform services for the project for Lynn Haven. As part of the agreement, ECS agreed to provide detailed invoices requesting payment for services accompanied by such documentation or data, including back-up documentation sufficient for reimbursement of expenses by FEMA for Lynn Haven payments to ECS.

10.     On or about October 28, 2018, MICHAEL EDWARD WHITE, on behalf of Lynn Haven, and DAVID MITCHELLE WHITE, as owner of ECS, signed an amended agreement for ECS to provide Lynn Haven with "Emergency And/Or Exigent Services, Ancillary Construction Services, or Construction Due to The Effects of Hurricane Michael." Notably, the 90-day term in the original agreement was replaced with no

deadline; rather, the agreement provided the duration to be "for such time as necessary to perform the services for the project." Additionally, the amended agreement included new specific language advising D. WHITE and ECS that FEMA financial assistance would be used to fund the contract with Lynn Haven, that ECS would comply with all applicable federal regulations, executive orders, as well as all FEMA policies, procedures, and directives. Under the amended agreement, ECS also agreed to provide FEMA with access to its books and records and was further advised of federal program fraud and false statement prohibitions.

11.   On November 8, 2018, MICHAEL EDWARD WHITE and DAVID MITCHELLE WHITE executed an "Exhibit A-Task order 18-001" that ostensibly was an agreement under the Amended Agreement described in paragraph #9 above, authorizing ECS to assist Lynn Haven in the removal of residential trash. The effective date of this "task order" was listed as three weeks earlier—October 15, 2018, and the "task order" authorized payment to ECS of a rate of $300.00 per hour per crew for removal of trash. The task order stated that it would terminate upon notice by Lynn Haven but was not to exceed 45 days from the effective date (October 15, 2018).

12.   JOSHUA DANIEL ANDERSON operated Greenleaf Lawn Care of Bay County, LLC ("Greenleaf"), which was purchased on or about November 23, 2016, by ANDERSON and his wife. ANDERSON was listed as "CEO" in documents provided to the State of Florida. In an Amended Annual Report for Greenleaf, filed with the State of Florida on December 20, 2016, S.A., the wife of ANDERSON, and T.W., the wife of D. WHITE, were listed as shareholders of Greenleaf. A similar annual report was filed with the State of Florida for Greenleaf on April 4, 2018. Greenleaf equipment was stored and maintained at the business location of ECS, and employees of Greenleaf often reported to work at ECS.

13.   On October 10, 2017, JOSHUA DANIEL ANDERSON, on behalf of Greenleaf, and M. WHITE, on behalf of Lynn Haven, executed a lawn maintenance contract to maintain the cemetery and lawns located at Lynn Haven public parks, cemeteries, and properties. The contract was for a term of four years, and Lynn Haven agreed to pay Greenleaf $10,477.70 monthly for lawn maintenance services. However, the contract allowed for additional services at seven specific Lynn Haven properties on an as needed basis, in accordance with prices stated in the original proposal of Greenleaf. In papers submitted to Lynn Haven in support of the contract, ANDERSON represented himself as the owner of Greenleaf. The contract also provided that in the event of a hurricane, which would prevent performing duties under the contract, the parties would be excused from performance under the contract during the period of disability. Nonetheless, after Hurricane Michael, Greenleaf continued to submit and

receive payment from Lynn Haven for lawn cutting and debris and trash removal.

14.    In the first month of its contract (November 2017), JOSHUA DANIEL ANDERSON and Greenleaf submitted a request for payment to Lynn Haven under the contract for $277,372.80. After Hurricane Michael, ANDERSON and Greenleaf requested a $50,000 payment from Lynn Haven for alleged debris clean-up two days after the hurricane hit Lynn Haven, and $16,398.58 for alleged lawn services for Lynn Haven on October 30, 2018. M. WHITE approved the payments to ANDERSON and Greenleaf and issued a handwritten Lynn Haven check to Greenleaf totaling $66,402.58.

15.    DAVID WAYNE HORTON was employed as the Community Services Director for Lynn Haven and was a department head for Lynn Haven. HORTON, along with M. WHITE, approved invoices submitted by ECS for work allegedly performed by ECS for Lynn Haven relating to post-Hurricane Michael clean-up activities. HORTON also approved ECS timesheets of employees that were submitted in support of ECS invoices to Lynn Haven that were provided to FEMA and falsely verified the attendance of ECS employees at various claimed locations. HORTON accepted payment of some of his travel, lodging, meals, entertainment, and food from D. WHITE on several occasions. After Hurricane Michael, HORTON caused D. WHITE to have ECS provide debris removal and repairs to his personal residence. This service was billed to Lynn Haven by ECS, and Lynn Haven paid ECS. HORTON also requested and obtained from ECS an invoice for the services provided at his residence, which HORTON submitted to his insurance company for payment.

16.    SHANNON DELORES RODRIGUEZ, a/k/a "Shannon Delores Harris" ("RODRIGUEZ") was the sister of D. WHITE and worked with D. WHITE at ECS. RODRIGUEZ supervised a crew of ECS workers allegedly providing services to Lynn Haven for clean-up after Hurricane Michael. RODRIGUEZ prepared and maintained time sheets of ECS workers that were submitted to Lynn Haven in support of ECS invoices requesting payment from Lynn Haven.

## B. THE CHARGE

Between on or about October 10, 2018, and on or about April 30, 2019, in the Northern District of Florida and elsewhere, the defendants,

MICHAEL EDWARD WHITE,
DAVID MITCHELLE WHITE,
DAVID WAYNE HORTON,
JOSHUA DANIEL ANDERSON,

And
## SHANNON DELORES RODRIGUEZ,
a/ka/a "Shannon Delores Harris,"
did knowingly and willfully combine, conspire, confederate, and agree together and with other persons to devise, and intend to devise a scheme to defraud and for obtaining money and property by means of material false and fraudulent pretenses, representations, and promises, and to cause wire communications to be transmitted in interstate and foreign commerce for the purpose of executing such scheme, in violation of Title 18, United States Code, Section 1343.

## C. MANER AND MEANS

The manner and means by which this conspiracy was committed included the following:

1. DAVID MITCHELL WHITE used ECS as a means to fraudulently obtain money from Lynn Haven.
2. JOSHUA DANIEL ANDERSON used Greenleaf as a means to fraudulently obtain money from Lynn Haven.
3. DAVID MITCHELLE WHITE submitted invoices requesting payment for services allegedly provided by ECS to Lynn Haven, but which were false and fraudulent as to a number of material matters.
4. JOSHUA DANIEL ANDERSON submitted invoices requesting payment for services allegedly provided by Greenleaf to Lynn Haven, but which were false and fraudulent as to a number of material matters.
5. MICHAEL EDWARD WHITE, as city manager of Lynn Haven, approved all ECS invoices and directed city employees to immediately pay ECS for those invoices, even though other contracted debris removal companies had to wait for payment of invoices submitted for Hurricane Michael disaster relief and debris removal.
6. **DAVID WAYNE HORTON** approved ECS invoices and recommended payment, often immediately, by Lynn Haven. HORTON also approved timesheets of employees that were submitted in support of ECS invoices to Lynn Haven that were provided to FEMA HORTON falsely verified the attendance of ECS employees at various claimed work locations.
7. After Hurricane Michael, HORTON caused D. WHITE to have ECS provide debris removal and repairs to his personal residence. This service was billed to Lynn Haven by ECS, and Lynn Haven paid ECS. HORTON also requested and obtained from ECS an invoice for the services provided at his residence, which HORTON

in turn submitted to his insurance company for payment.

8.    When DAVID MITCHELLE WHITE and ECS were providing services to Lynn Haven, MICHAEL EDWARD WHITE received things of value from D. WHITE, including repairs to, and debris removal from, M. WHITE'S residence in Lynn Haven and his farm located outside Lynn Haven in Bay County, and money for the purchase of M.WHITE's farm and an automobile.

9.    These repairs to and debris removal from the residence and farm of MICHAEL EDWARD WHITE were billed to Lynn Haven with false invoices submitted by DAVID MITCHELLE WHITE to Lynn Haven with invoices falsely stating that work had been performed at locations in Lynn haven. M. WHITE approved the ECS invoices and directed Lynn Haven employees to pay the invoices.

10.    While DAVID MITCHELLE WHITE and ECs were providing services to Lynn Haven, DAVID WAYNE HORTON received things of value from D. WHITE, including repairs to, and debris removal from, HORTON'S residence in Lynn Haven. Additionally, HORTON , accepted payment of some of his travel, lodging, meals, entertainment, and food from D. WHITE on multiple occasions while D. WHITE and ECS were providing services to Lynn Haven.

11.    When ECS invoices were being assembled for submission to FEMA by Lynn Haven for reimbursement, it was discovered that most of the ECS invoices that had been paid provided no details in support of the requested payments. When directed to provide supporting documentation for the monies requested and already paid, DAVID MITCHELLE WHITE submitted false time sheets prepared by SHANNON DELORES RODRIGUEZ. The time sheets were false and fraudulent in that they included names of individuals who had not worked at the claimed location, were off that day, worked at other projects outside Lynn Haven, or had never worked for ECS at the time of the timesheet. Additionally, in many invoices, the specific Lynn Haven locations of work claimed to have been done by ECS were false. DAVID WAYNE HORTON approved and falsely verified the timesheets claiming attendance of ECS workers at various Lynn Haven locations.

12.    ECS invoices were submitted to Lynn Haven for payment of services that were not authorized under the emergency contract and were for personal residences of some Lynn Haven officials. The performance of ECS post-hurricane debris removal and repairs at the residences of some Lynn Haven officials were concealed and not disclosed in the ECS invoices submitted by DAVID MITCHELLE WHITE. MICHAEL EDWARD WHITE approved the invoices

and caused them to be paid to ECS by Lynn Haven. The unauthorized ECS work for Lynn Haven officials included:

a. The private residence in Lynn Haven and the farm located outside Lynn Haven in Bay County belonging to the Lynn Haven City Manager, M. WHITE.

b. The private residences of the Mayor of Lynn Haven and her mother;

c. The private residence of the Community Services Director of Lynn Haven, DAVID WAYNE HORTON;

d. The private residences of the Lynn Haven City Attorney and others as directed by the City Attorney; and

e. The private gated community of a city commissioner.

13. After the initial declaration of an emergency by Lynn Haven had been revoked and expired, MICHAEL EDWARD WHITE and DAVID WAYNE HORTON sought to locate additional Lynn Haven projects that could provide money to DAVID MITCHELLE WHITE and ECS. One project was the Task Order that M. WHITE issued, ostensibly as part of the Emergency Agreement with ECS, to conduct trash pick-up, using a pick-up truck and a trailer, at a cost of $300 per hour per crew throughout Lynn Haven. This action was implemented despite the ability of Lynn Haven waste trucks to pick-up large amounts of household trash and deposit large amounts of trash at the dump at no increased cost to Lynn Haven.

14. MICHAEL EDWARD WHITE AND DAVID WAYNE HORTON located numerous projects for ECS to handle that were outside the activities described in the Emergency Agreement or Task Order. M. WHITE and HORTON had ECS employees wrap Christmas gifts, prepare locations for a Halloween party, and other miscellaneous acts that were not authorized under any agreement with Lynn Haven. DAVID MITCHELLE WHITE AND ECS submitted invoices that did not describe the actual activities performed, but instead falsely claimed the work was debris removal or cleaning activities. D. WHITE and ECS billed Lynn Haven for a minimum of $35 per hour for ECS employees plus an ECS a supervisor at $90 per hour for these unauthorized activities. M. WHITE and HORTON approved these invoices.

15. On October 22, 2018, DAVID WAYNE HORTON sent a text message to DAVID MITCHELLE WHITE requesting an invoice from ECS for work done at HORTON'S residence after the hurricane, and instructed the invoice be at least $3,500 if not more. D. WHITE subsequently provided to HORTON an ECS invoice in

the amount of $9,600 that was marked, "Paid in Full." Then, HORTON submitted this invoice to an insurance company in support of his insurance claim for $9,600. HORTON had not paid ECS or D.WHITE any money at the time that HORTON submitted the invoice as proof of his claim to an insurance company.

16.  On October 23, 2018, DAVID MITCHELLE WHITE and ECS submitted to Lynn Haven a false invoice for hurricane clean-up in the amount of $180,722.75 that claimed work by ECS was done at a Lynn Haven park and water plant on eight separate days. The ECS supporting documents submitted to Lynn Haven for this fraudulent invoice included individuals who were working at locations outside Lynn Haven for a different contractor. This invoice, and a separate ECS invoice for painting a Lynn Haven building prior to the hurricane, were approved and paid by Lynn Haven as emergency expenditures. MICHAEL EDWARD WHITE issued a handwritten check in the amount of $224,722.75 to ECS within three days after the submission of the invoices.

**17.**  Included in the above-described invoice, ECS billed Lynn Haven for clean-up activities by individuals who were Greenleaf employees, working out of ECS. JOSHUA DANIEL ANDERSON simultaneously submitted a false invoice to Lynn Haven in the amount of $50,004.00 for alleged debris clean-up at the same Lynn Haven locations. MICHAEL EDWARD WHITE approved the payment to ANDERSON and Greenleaf, and on November 7, 2018, issued a handwritten Lynn Haven check to Greenleaf totaling $66,402.58, which included $16,398.58 for alleged lawn services provided by Greenleaf after the hurricane.

18.  Eight days after Hurricane Michael, in October 2018, JOSHUA DANIEL ANDERSON and Greenleaf submitted a false invoice in the amount of $22,658.25, claiming to have provided lawn services to Lynn Haven and claiming "half month service" after the hurricane at various Lynn Haven locations. MICHAEL EDWARD WHITE approved payment of the invoice and issued a handwritten, manual counter check on the account of Lynn Haven in the amount of $22,658.25.

19.  In November 2018, JOSHUA DANIEL ANDERSON and Greenleaf submitted two false invoices, each in the amount of $16,603.62, for "half month service" for lawn care at 37 separate locations in Lynn Haven for the month of November. MICHAEL EDWARD WHITE and DAVID WAYNE HORTON approved and directed the payments from Lynn Haven to ANDERSON and Greenleaf in the total amount in excess of $33,000.

20.	On October 30, 2018, a false invoice for hurricane clean-up in the amount of $202,230.56 was submitted to Lyn Haven by DAVID MITCHELLE WHITE and ECS that claimed work by ECS was done at two Lynn Haven parks during a seven-day period. No supporting documents for the invoice were submitted. ECS merely claimed that various numbers of individuals were utilized by ECS at pay rates consistent with FEMA reimbursement. This invoice was approved by MICHAEL EDWARD WHITE, who directed employees of Lynn Haven to issue a check to ECS in the amount of the invoice. A Lynn Haven check in the amount of $202,230.56 was issued to ECS on November 15, 2018.

21.	On November 6, 2018, a false invoice for hurricane clean-up in the amount of $428,816.13 was submitted to Lynn Haven by DAVID MITCHELLE WHITE, and ECS, that falsely claimed work by ECS was done at two parks and two cemeteries during a seven-day period. No supporting documents for the invoice were provided. Subsequent investigation of the invoice revealed that ECS falsely claimed an excessive number of workers (54), and an overage for equipment such as trucks and dump trailers. This invoice was approved by MICHAEL EDWARD WHITE, who directed employees of Lynn Haven to pay this invoice. This invoice was included in the payment of three invoices to ECS in a Lynn Haven check issued to ECS on November 15, 2018, totaling $1,288,716.54.

22.	On November 12, 2018, a false invoice for hurricane clean-up in the amount of $527,512.65 was submitted to Lynn Haven by DAVID MITCHELLE WHITE and ECS that falsely claimed work by ECS was done at a cemetery and at sports complexes during a seven-day period. Instead of doing the work at the locations described, ECS workers conducted debris removal and clean-up at the residence of MICHAEL EDWARD WHITE located in Lynn Haven, M. WHITE'S farm located outside of Lynn Haven in Bay County, and the residences of the Mayor of Lynn Haven and her mother. The work on these private residences was concealed and not reported in the invoices, and no supporting documents to the invoice were provided. The invoice was approved by MICHAEL EDWARD WHITE, who directed employees of Lynn Haven to pay this invoice. This invoice was included in the payment of three invoices to ECS in a Lynn Haven check issued to ECS on November 15, 2018, totaling $1,288,716.54.

23.	On November 13, 2018, a false invoice for hurricane clean-up in the amount of $332,387.76 was submitted to Lynn Haven by DAVID MITCHELLE WHITE and ECS that falsely claimed trash pick-up was conducted by ECS during a fourteen-day period starting on October 18, 2018. No documentation was submitted in support of this invoice. The claimed trash pick-up did not occur, and there was no record of any trash being dumped at the Bay County refuse location, nor did MICHAEL EDWARD WHITE obtain approval from Bay County for ECS to use the account of Lynn Haven to dump items at the Bay County facility until at least October 31, 2018. This invoice was approved by M. WHITE who directed employees of Lynn Haven to pay this invoice. This invoice was included in the payment of three invoices to ECS in a Lynn Haven check issued to ECS on November 15, 2018, totaling $1, 288,716.54.

24.     For the invoice submitted on November 12, 2018, described in paragraph #22 above, DAVID MITCHELLE WHITE and ECS submitted false Daily Time Sheets purporting to show numerous individuals worked 12 hours per day on November 11, 2018. These time sheets were prepared by SHANNON DELORES RODRIGUEZ, who also prepared time sheets for the same day for ECS to pay its employees. The payroll time sheets prepared by RODRIGUEZ and used to pay ECS employees listed most of the employees as not working when only a few actually worked on that day.

25.     Prior to mid November 2018, MICHAEL EDWARD WHITE allowed DAVID MITCHELLE WHITE and JOSHUA DANIEL ANDERSON to obtain fuel for ECS and Greenleaf vehicles at Lynn Haven fuel facilities for no charge. This activity was in violation of the contracts that ECS and Greenleaf had with Lynn Haven, requiring ECS and Greenleaf to pay for fuel for its vehicles and equipment.

26.     On November 29, 2018, a false invoice for hurricane clean-up in the amount of $297,920.82 was submitted to Lynn Haven by DAVID MITCHELLE WHITE and ECS that falsely claimed work by ECS was done at a sports complex, some Lynn Haven streets, and two water stations during a seven-day period starting after Thanksgiving Day in 2018. Supporting documents provided with the invoice falsely claimed that 61 individuals were at each of the locations for eleven hours daily. This invoice was approved by MICHAEL EDWARD WHITE, who directed employees of Lynn Haven to pay this invoice. This invoice was included in the payment of two invoices to ECS in a Lynn Haven check issued to ECS on November 30, 2018, totaling $433,365.85.

27.     On November 29, 2018, a false invoice for hurricane clean-up in the amount of $135,445.03 was submitted to Lynn Haven by DAVID MITCHELLE WHITE and ECS that falsely claimed trash pick-up was conducted by ECS during a seven-day period starting

on November 23, 2018 (the day after Thanksgiving). There were only 6 dump tickets from the Bay County refuse location for this time period, for which D. White and ECS charged Lynn Haven $19,349 per day. This invoice was approved by MICHAEL EDWARD WHITE who directed employees of Lynn Haven to pay this invoice. This invoice was included in the payment of two invoices to ECS in a Lynn Haven check issued to ECS on November 30, 2018, totaling $433,365.85.

28.    In November and December 2018, a Lynn Haven Commissioner made repeated requests for assistance from MICHAEL EDWARD WHITE to have ECS clean up debris and trash in Osceola Point, a private residential community. M. WHITE directed DAVID MITCHELLE WHITE to have ECS personnel work in Osceola Point, which they did, removing debris. The time spent by ECS workers in clearing debris in the private community was paid to ECS by the submission of subsequent false invoices that claimed ECS worked on projects in Lynn Haven, concealing and not disclosing that ECS was actually being paid for work in a private community for which Lynn Haven had no responsibility.

29.    On December 13, 2018, a false invoice for hurricane clean-up in the amount of $330,228.14 was submitted to Lynn Haven by DAVID MITCHELLE WHITE and ECS that falsely claimed work by ECS done at a sports complex, a park, and a water treatment and sewage plants during a 13 day period. Supporting documents provided with the invoice falsely claimed that 57 individuals were at each of the locations for eleven hours daily Many of the individuals listed by ECS were not at the locations. D. WHITE instead had some of his ECS employees conducting clean-up in Osceola Point, a location for which Lynn Haven was not responsible to conduct cleaning or debris removal. This invoice was approved by MICHAEL EDWARD WHITE, who directed employees of Lynn Haven to pay this invoice. This invoice was included in the payment of two invoices to ECS in a Lynn Haven check issued to ECS on December 14, 2018, totaling $515,731.31.

30.    On December 13, 2018, a false invoice for hurricane clean-up in the amount of $185,503.17 was submitted to Lynn Haven by DAVID MITCHELLE WHITE and ECS that falsely claimed trash pick-up was conducted by ECS during a 13 day period starting on November 30, 2018. The actual dump tickets from the Bay County refuse location for this time period did not support the claims of the invoice. This invoice was approved by MICHAEL EDWARD WHITE, who directed employees of Lynn Haven to pay this invoice. This invoice was included in the payment of two invoices

to ECS in a Lynn Haven check issued to ECS on December 14, 2018, totaling $515,731.31.

31. In late December 2018, while DAVID MITCHELLE WHITE and ECS were providing services to Lynn Haven, D. WHITE paid for a week-long TRIP TO THE Gatlinburg, Tennessee area for DAVID WAYNE HORTON and his family, JOSHUA DANIE ANDERSON and his family, SHANNON DELORES RODRIGUEZ and her family, a Bay County commissioner and his family, and D. WHITE and his family. D. WHITE paid more than $25,000 for the trip that included lodging, meals, entertainment, and rental vehicles for the two public officials.

32. On December 26, 2018, a false invoice for hurricane clean-up in the amount of $244,725.85 was submitted to Lynn Haven by DAVID MITCHELLE WHITE and ECS that falsely claimed work by ECS was done at various Lynn Haven locations during a nine-day period. ECS falsely claimed a number of workers had worked during this period. This invoice was approved by MICHAEL EDWARD WHITE, who directed employees of Lynn Haven to pay this invoice. This invoice was included in the payment of two invoices to ECS in a Lynn Haven check issued to ECS on December 31, 2018, totaling $725,941.09.

33. On December 28, 2018, a false invoice for hurricane clean-up in the amount of $481,215.24 was submitted to Lynn Haven by DAVID MITCHELLE WHITE and ECS that falsely claimed trash pick-up was conducted by ECS during a 17-day period starting on December 13, 2018, and continuing before and after Christmas Day, and through Christmas week. The majority of ECS workers did not work for the two weeks before and after Christmas. The invoice falsely claimed trash pick-up totaling between $21,000 and $32,000 per day during this period. This invoice was approved by MICHAEL EDWARD WHITE, who directed employees of Lynn Haven to pay this invoice. This invoice was included in the payment of two invoices to ECS in a Lynn Haven check issued to ECS on December 31, 2018, totaling $725,941.09.

34. On January 13, 2019, a false invoice for hurricane clean-up in the amount of $416,420.84 was submitted to Lynn Haven by DAVID MITCHELLE WHITE and ECS that falsely claimed work by ECS was done at various Lynn Haven locations during a 12 day period. ECS falsely claimed a number of workers had worked during this period. This invoice was approved by MICHAEL EDWARD WHITE, who directed employees of Lynn Haven to pay this invoice. This invoice was included in the payment of two invoices to ECS in a Lynn Haven check issued to ECS on January 15, 2019,

totaling $895,441.52.

35.    On January 13, 2019, three months after Hurricane Michael, a false invoice for hurricane clean-up in the amount of $479,020.68 was submitted to Lynn Haven by DAVID MITCHELLE WHITE, and ECS that falsely claimed trash pick-up was conducted by ECS during a 13 day period starting the day after New Year's Day. The invoice also falsely claimed that between 11 and 13 crews were used to collect trash daily. The invoice falsely claimed trash pick-up during this period totaling $32,278.68 per day for five days, $38,878.44 per day for seven days, and $45,478.20 for the last day. This invoice was approved by MICHAEL EDWARD WHITE, who directed employees of Lynn Haven to pay this invoice. This invoice was included in the payment of two invoices to ECS in a Lynn Haven check issued to ECS on January 15, 2019, totaling $895,441.52.

36.    On January 20, 2019, a false invoice for hurricane clean-up in the amount of $216,487.92 was submitted to Lynn Haven by DAVID MITCHELLE WHITE and ECS that falsely claimed work by ECS was done at various Lynn Haven locations during a six day period. More than three months after Hurricane Michael, ECS falsely claimed identical and extensive debris removal from various Lynn Haven parks and the clearance of rights of way and access points. This invoice was approved by MICHAEL EDWARD WHITE, who directed employees of Lynn Haven to pay this invoice. This invoice was included in the payment of two invoices to ECS in a Lynn Haven check issued to ECS on January 31, 2019, totaling $433,259.16.

37.    On January 25, 2019, three months after Hurricane Michael, a false invoice for hurricane clean-up in the amount of $216,771.24 was submitted to Lynn Haven by DAVID MITCHELLE WHITE and ECS that falsely claimed trash pick-up was conducted by ECS during a six day period. The invoice also falsely claimed that crews were used to collect trash daily. The invoice falsely claimed trash pick-up during this period totaling $38,878.44 per day for four days, $35,578.56 for one day, and $25,678.92 for the last day. This invoice was approved by MICHAEL EDWARD WHITE, who directed employees of Lynn Haven to pay this invoice. This invoice was included in the payment of two invoices to ECS in a Lynn Haven check issued to ECS on January 31, 2019, totaling $433, 259.16

38.    On February 13, 2019, a false invoice in the amount of $13,800 for filling in three cemetery lots at Mt. Hope Cemetery in Lynn Haven was submitted to Lynn Haven by DAVID MITCHELLE

WHITE and ECS. ECS paid a company $6,000 to fill the three cemetery lots with dirt, but the ECS invoice was in the amount of $13,800. ECS secured a false invoice in the amount of $12,000 from the company that had actually done the work. DANIEL WAYNE HORTON received the invoice from ECS, approved it, and directed employees of Lynn Haven to pay it. A Lynn Haven check in the amount of $13,800 was issued to ECS on February 15, 2019.

39. On February 17, 2019, MICHAEL EDWARD WHITE asked DAVID MITCHELLE WHITE if he wanted to buy his "farm and cows and such" located in Bay County outside Lynn Haven. D. WHITE agreed to pay M. WHITE $300,000 for the farm. On March 8, 2019, D. WHITE provided a cashier's check in the amount of $300,000 to M. WHITE for the farm and a Trans Am motor vehicle. The source of the money paid to M. WHITE was the monies paid by Lynn Haven to ECS for the invoices submitted after the hurricane for alleged debris and trash removal and repair.

40. On February 27, 2019, MICHAEL EDWARD WHITE contacted DAVID MITCHELLE WHITE and asked him if D. WHITE could "be under $20,000" for a metal roof at Sheffield Park, and to provide M. WHITE with a bid and an additional bid. M. WHITE described this matter to Lynn Haven officials as an emergency matter arising from Hurricane Michael, despite having occurred four months after the hurricane.

41. On February 28, 2019, MICHAEL EDWARD WHITE sent a text message to DAVID MITCHELLE WHITE, advising that M. WHITE issued an arrest warrant for an individual who D. WHITE had problems with a day earlier. The individual was a subcontractor used by ECS at one of the Lynn Haven locations and was unhappy with D. WHITE in failing to pay the individual for the services provided to ECS at a Lynn Haven location.

42. On March 5, 2019, MICHAEL EDWARD WHITE sent a text message to DAVID MITCHELLE WHITE relating to Sheffield Park and requested three quotes. D. WHITE did so, and provided M. WHITE with the ECS bid, which was the lowest bid of $85,550 for demolition and replacement of two sidewalks, removal of a couple of trees, and delivery and spreading of fill dirt.

43. On March 11, 2019, JOSHUA DANIEL ANDERSON and Greenleaf submitted an invoice in the amount of $20,798.50 to Lynn Haven for installing flowers at Kinsaul Park. DAVID WAYNE HORTON received the invoice from Greenleaf, approved it, and directed employees of Lynn Haven to pay it. MICHAEL EDWARD WHITE approved the payment. This invoice was included in the payment of two invoices to Greenleaf in a Lynn

Haven check issued to Greenleaf on March 15, 2019, totaling $48,537.25.

44.　　On March 12, 2019, JOSHUA DANIEL ANDERSON and Greenleaf submitted an invoice in the amount of $27,738.75 to Lynn Haven for installing flowers at Sheffield Park. DAVID WAYNE HORTON received the invoice from Greenleaf, approved it, and directed employees of Lynn Haven to pay it. MICHAEL EDWARD WHITE approved the payment. This invoice was included in the payment of two invoices to Greenleaf in a Lynn Haven check issued to Greenleaf on March 15, 2019, totaling $48,537.25.

45.　　On March 13, 2019, an invoice in the amount of $85,550 for Sheffield Park work was submitted to Lynn Haven by DAVID MITCHELLE WHITE and ECS. This invoice related to work performed at Sheffield Park and was approved by DAVID WAYNE HORTON and then MICHAEL EDWARD WHITE, who directed employees of Lynn Haven to pay this invoice as a continuation of emergency work for ECS. This invoice was included in the payment of three invoices to ECS in a Lynn Haven check issued to ECS on March 15, 2019, totaling $118,950.00.

46.　　On March 13, 2019, an invoice in the amount of $22,789.00 for Kinsaul Park work was submitted to Lynn Haven by DAVID MITCHELLE WHITE and ECS. This invoice related to a concrete slab and wall installed at Kinsaul Park and was approved by DAVID WAYNE HORTON and then MICHAEL EDWARD WHITE, who directed employees of Lynn Haven to pay this invoice. Although noted on the Lynn Haven purchase order as not hurricane related, this work was not bid out as required as it was part of a series of work at several Lynn Haven parks at the same time. This invoice was included in the payment of three invoices to ECS in a Lynn Haven check issued to ECS on March 15, 2019, totaling $118,950.00.

47.　　As a result of discussions between MICHAEL EDWARD WHITE, DAVID MITCHELLE WHITE, and DAVID WAYNE HORTON concerning the fraudulent bid submissions for Sheffield Park, Cain griffin, and Kinsaul Park renovations, D. WHITE and ECS performed work at the three parks. On March 27, 2019, ECS submitted three invoices to Lynn Haven seeking payment in the amounts of $163,000 for Sheffield Park, $71,200 for Cain Griffin Park, and $9,000 for Kinsaul Park. DAVID WAYNE HORTON approved the three invoices and directed Lynn Haven employees to issue checks to ECS. However, the acting City Manager, who had replaced MICHAEL EDWARD WHITE on March 19, 2019, blocked payment of the three invoices since a proper bid process had not occurred, there was no contract in place for the work, it had not been approved by the City Commission, and ECS had not pulled any permits for the work. Further, ECS was not licensed to perform the required electrical, plumbing, roofing, and construction work at the parks.

48.    On April 12, 2019, JOSHUA DANIEL ANDERSON and Greenleaf submitted an invoice in the amount of $147,350 to Lynn Haven for landscaping work performed at Sheffield Park that consisted of installing sod, pine straw, and irrigation work. DAVID WAYNE HORTON approved the invoices and directed Lynn Haven employees to issue a check to Greenleaf. However, the acting City Manager, who had replaced MICHAEL EDWARD WHITE on March 19, 2019, blocked the payment of the invoice as fraudulent, since Lynn Haven had purchased the sod for Sheffield Park, and the installation of the sod could not have cost $147,350.

49.    The conspirators performed acts and made statements to hide and conceal, and cause to be hidden and concealed, the purpose of the conspiracy and the acts committed in furtherance thereof.

All in violation of Title 18, United States code, Section 1349.

COUNTS TWO THROUGH TWENTY
A.  INTRODUCTION

The allegations of Count One are hereby realleged and incorporated by reference as if fully set forth herein

B.  THE CHARGE

Between on or about October 10, 2018, and on or about April 30, 2019, in the Northern District of Florida and elsewhere, the defendants,

MICHAEL EDWARD WHITE,
DAVID MITCHELLE WHITE,
DAVID WAYNE HORTON,
JOSHUA DANIEL ANDERSON,
And
SHANNON DELORES RODRIGUEZ,
a/k/a "Shannon Delores Harris,"

did knowingly and willfully devise, and intend to devise, a scheme to defraud and for obtaining money and property by means of material false

100

and fraudulent pretenses, representations, and promises, and for the purpose of executing such scheme did cause wire communications to be transmitted in interstate and foreign commerce.

### C.  SCHEME TO DEFRAUD
It was part of the scheme to defraud that:
The allegations of Count One, Section C, Paragraphs 1-49, are hereby realleged and incorporated by reference as if fully set forth herein.

### D. WIRE COMMUNICATIONS

On or about the following dates, for the purpose of executing the scheme to defraud, the defendants,

MICHAEL EDWARD WHITE
DAVID MITCHELLE WHITE,
DAVID WAYNE HORTON,
JOSHUA DANIEL ANDERSON,
And
SHANNON DELORES RODRIGUEZ,
a/k/a "Shannon Delores Harris,"

knowingly did cause wire communications to be transmitted in interstate and foreign commerce as set forth below:

COUNT
TWO
DATE : October 22, 2018
WIRE COMMUNICATION:  Text messages HORTON/D.WHITE

COUNT
THREE
DATE : October 26, 2018
WIRE COMMUNICATION : Deposit of $224,722.75 check and related wire

COUNT
FOUR
DATE: November 1, 2018
WIRE COMMUICATION:  Deposit of $22,685.25 check and related wire

COUNT
FIVE

DATE: November 7, 2018
WIRE COMMUNICATION: Deposit of $66,402.58

COUNT
SIX
DATE : November 15, 2018
WIRE COMMUNICATION : Deposit of 16,603.62 check and related
wire
COUNT
SEVEN
DATE: November 15, 2018
WIRE COMMUNICATION:  Deposit of $202,230.56 check and related
wire

COUNT
EIGHT
DATE: November 15, 2018
WIRE COMMUNICATION: Deposit of $1,288,716.54 check and related
wire

COUNT
NINE
DATE: November 30, 2018
WIRE COMMUNICATION: Deposit of 16,603.62 check and related wire

COUNT
TEN
DATE: November 30, 2018
WIRE COMMUNICATON: Deposit of $433,365.85 check and related
wire

COUNT
ELEVEN
DATE: December 14, 2018
WIRE COMMUNICATION: Deposit of $515,731.31 check and related
wire

COUNT
TWELVE
DATE: December 31, 2018
WIRE COMMUNICATION: Deposit of $725,941.09 check and related
wire

COUNT
THIRTEEN
DATE: January 15, 2019
WIRE COMMUNICATION: Deposit of $895,441.52 check and related
wire

COUNT
FOURTEEN
DATE: January 28, 2019
WIRE COMMUNICATION: Text message M.WHITE/HORTON

COUNT
FIFTEEN
DATE : January 31, 2019
WIRE COMMUNICATION : Deposit of $433,259.16 check and related
wire

COUNT
SIXTEEN
DATE: February 27, 2019
WIRE COMMUNICATON: Text message M.WHITE/D.WHITE

COUNT
SEVENTEEN
DATE : February 28, 2019
WIRE COMMUNICATION : Text message M.WHITE/D. WHITE

COUNT
EIGHTEEN
DATE: March 5, 2019
WIRE COMMUNICATION: Text message M.WHITE/D.WHITE

COUNT
NINETEEN
DATE : March 11, 2019
WIRE COMMUNICATION : Deposit of $118,950.00 check and related
wire

COUNT
TWENTY
DATE: March 15, 2019
WIRE COMMUNICATION: Deposit of $48,537.25

## COUNT TWENTY-ONE

Between on or about October 10, 2018, and on or about April 30, 2019, in the Northern district of Florida, and elsewhere, the defendants,

## MICHAEL EDWARD WHITE
## AND
## DAVID WAYNE HORTON

being agents of an organization and agency of the local government, that is the City of Lynn haven, Florida, receiving in the one-year period beginning October 10, 2018, benefits in excess of $10,000 under a federal program involving grants, contracts, subsidies, loans, guarantees, and other forms of federal assistance, did knowingly embezzle, steal, obtain by fraud, without authority convert to the use of a person other than the rightful owner, and intentionally misapply property that was valued at $5,000 or more and under the care, custody, and control of such organization, local government, and agency.

In violation of Title 18, United States Code, Sections 666(a)(1)(A) and 2.

## COUNTS TWENTY-TWO THROUGH THIRTY-TWO

### I.      Introduction

1.      Paragraphs 1 through 16 of Count One are realleged and incorporated by reference as if fully set forth herein.

### II.      The Charge

2.      Between on or about October 10, 2018, and on or about April 30, 2019, in the Northern District of Florida and elsewhere, the defendants,

## MICHAEL EDWARD WHITE
## And
## DAVID WAYNE HORTON,

Did knowingly and willfully devise and intend to devise a scheme to defraud and deprive the City of Lynn Haven and its citizens of their right to the honest services of M. WHITE, the City Manager for Lynn Haven, Florida, and HORTON, the Community Services Director for Lynn Haven, Florida, through bribery or kickbacks.

### III. The Fraudulent Scheme

The fraudulent scheme is summarized in paragraphs 1 through 49 of Section C of Count One, which are realleged and incorporated by reference as if fully set forth herein.

### IV. Wire Communications

3. On or about the following dates, in the Northern District of Florida and elsewhere, the defendants,

### MICHAEL EDWARD WHITE
### and
### DAVID WAYNE HORTON,

for the purpose of executing the fraudulent scheme, caused wire communications to be transmitted in interstate commerce as set forth below.

COUNT
TWENTY-TWO
DATE: October 22, 2018
WIRE TRANSMISSION: Text message from HORTON to D. WHITE

COUNT
TWENTY-THREE
DATE: October 24, 2018
WIRE TRANSMISSION: Email from ECS to HORTON

COUNT
TWENTY-FOUR
DATE: November 9, 2018
WIRE TRANSMISSION: Text messages from M. WHITE to D. WHITE and D.WHITE to M. WHITE

COUNT
TWENTY-FIVE
DATE: November 12, 2018
WIRE TRANSMISSION: Text message from M. WHITE to D. WHITE

COUNT
TWENTY-SIX
DATE: November 13, 2018
WIRE TRANSMISSION: Text message from M.WHITE to D.WHITE

COUNT

TWENTY-SEVEN
DATE: December 8, 2018
WIRE TRANSMISSION: Text message from HORTON to M. WHITE

COUNT
TWENTY-EIGHT
DATE: December 26, 2018
WIRE TRANSMISSION: Text messages of M. WHITE and D. WHITE

COUNT
TWENTY-NINE
DATE: January 7, 2019
WIRE TRANSMISSION: Text message of M. White

COUNT
THIRTY
DATE: January 28, 2019
WIRE TRANSMISSION: Text messages of M.WHITE and HORTON

COUNT
THIRTY-ONE
DATE: February 17, 2019
WIRE TRANSMISSION: Text messages of M. WHITE and D. WHITE

COUNT
THIRTY-TWO
DATE: February 27, 2019
WIRE TRANSMISSION: Text messages between M. WHITE and D. WHITE

In violation of Title 18, United States Code, Sections 1343, 1346, and 2.

## COUNT THIRTY-THREE

Between on or about October 10, 2018, and on or about April 30, 2019, in the Northern District of Florida and elsewhere, the defendants,
DAVID MITCHELLE WHITE
and
MICHAEL EDWARD WHITE,

Knowingly made and presented, and caused to be made and presented, to the Federal Emergency Management Agency (FEMA), a department and agency of the United States, a materially false claim against the United

States, knowing such claim to be false, fictitious, and fraudulent, by filing, and causing to be filed, fraudulent invoices to the City of Lynn Haven, Florida, for alleged post-hurricane debris and related work, knowing that the City of Lynn Haven would cause the invoices to be submitted for payment to FEMA for reimbursement to the City of Lynn Haven for payments made to D.WHITE for alleged post-hurricane services.

In violation of Title 18, United States Code, Sections 287 and 2.

## COUNT THIRTY-FOUR

### A.   CHARGE

Between on or about October 10, 2018, and April 23, 2019, in the Northern District of Florida and elsewhere, the defendant,

## DAVID WAYNE HORTON,

Did knowingly and willfully devise, and intend to devise, a scheme to defraud and for obtaining money and property by means of material false and fraudulent pretenses, representations, and promises, and for the purpose of executing such scheme, did cause a wire communication to be transmitted in interstate commerce.

### B.   SCHEME TO DEFRAUD

It was part of the scheme to defraud that:

The defendant, DAVID WAYNE HORTON, made and caused to be made false and fraudulent representations to the American Strategic Insurance Corp. ("ASI") concerning damages to his residence in Lynn Haven, Florida as a result of Hurricane Michael in order to fraudulently obtain money from the ASI insurance company.

1.   DAVID WAYNE HORTON represented in a claim that his residence had been damaged by Hurricane Michael and falsely represented that he had paid for repairs to his residence totaling $9,600.

2.   In fact, repairs to the residence and property of DAVID WAYNE HORTON had been made by Erosion Control Specialist (ECS) at no cost to him as ECS received payment from the City of Lynn Haven for its employees making the repairs and conducting debris removal at his residence.  However, the City of Lynn Haven was not aware that ECS had made repairs to HORTON'S personal residence, as the City of Lynn Haven was falsely billed for alleged work on City properties.

3.   To facilitate the scheme, DAVID WAYNE HORTON solicited ECS to create a false and fictitious invoice attesting to repair work done to his residence after the hurricane by ECS in the amount of

$9,600, which HORTON then submitted to ASI to support his fraudulent insurance claim.

4.    Based upon the false claim, ASI issued a payment in the amount of $5,600 to DAVID WAYNE HORTON. This payment was mailed to HORTON'S address in Lynn Haven. HORTON caused the ASI insurance check to be deposited into the bank account belonging to him and his wife.

5.    By this conduct, DAVID WAYNE HORTON fraudulently obtained approximately $5,600 in insurance funds to which he was not entitled.

## C.    MAILING

On or about November 21, 2018, for the purpose of executing the scheme to defraud the defendant,

### DAVID WAYNE HORTON,

Knowingly did, for the purpose of executing the fraudulent scheme and attempting to do so, caused to be transmitted by United States mail and private and commercial carrier, a $5,600 check through the United States Postal Service.

In violation of Title 18, United States Code, Sections, 1341 and 2.

### COUNT THIRTY-FIVE

Between on or about October 10, 2018, and on or about April 30, 2019, in the Northern District of Florida and elsewhere, the defendants,

### MICHAEL EDWARD WHITE,
### DAVID MITCHELLE WHITE,
### DAVID WAYNE HORTON,
### JOSHUA DAIEL ANDERSON,
and
### SHANNON DELORES RODRIGUEZ,
a/k/a "Shannon Delores Harris,"

did knowingly combine, conspire, confederate, and agree together and with other persons to conduct and attempt to conduct financial transactions affecting interstate and foreign commerce, that is, the interstate transfer of monetary instruments in the form of United States currency within a financial institution, involving funds that were proceeds of a specified unlawful activity, that is, conspiracy to commit wire fraud and wire fraud, in violation of Title 18, United States Code, Sections 1343 and 1349, and that

the defendants knew to be the proceeds of some form of unlawful activity, with the intent to promote the carrying on of the specified unlawful activity, in violation of Title 18, United States Code, Section 1956(a)(1)(A)(i).
All in violation of Title 18, United States Code, Section 1956(h).

## CRIMINAL FORFEITURE

The allegations contained in Counts One through Thirty-Two and Thirty-Four through Thirty-Five of this Indictment are hereby realleged and incorporated by reference for the purpose of alleging forfeiture. From their engagement in the violations alleged in Counts One through Thirty-Two and Thirty-Four through Thirty-Five of this Indictment, the defendants,

MICHAEL EDWARD WHITE,
DAVID MITCHELLE WHITE,
DAVID WAYNE HORTON,
JOSHUA DANIEL ANDERSON,
and
SHANNON DELORES RODRIGUEZ
a/k/a "Shannon Delores Harris"

shall forfeit to the United States, pursuant to Title 18, United States Code, Sections 981(a)(1)(C) and 982(a)(1), and Title 28, United States Code, Section 2461(c), any and all of the defendants' right, title, and interest in any property, real and personal, constituting, and derived from, proceeds traceable to such offenses, including the following:

a.      Real properties located at 9483 and 9711 Highway 20 East, Youngstown, Florida 32466, more particularly described as:
Parcel No. 02796-000-000 (H):
Begin at the Northwest Corner of Northwest ¼ of West ½ of the Southeast ¼ of the Southeast ¼ of Section 31, Township 1 North, 9KN672418 12 West for the POINT OF BEGINNING; thence run East 650.54' thence South 1326.72 feet to the North right-of-way of Highway 20, thence run West along that right-of-way 50 feet thence North 714.70 feet and thence West 603 feet; thence run North 604.07 feet to the POINT OF BEGINNING.

Parcel No. 02796-010-000 (N):
Commence at the Northwest Corner of West ½ of Southeast ¼ of southeast 31, Township 1 North, Range 10 west; thence run South 604.07 feet for the POINT OF BEGINNING; thence run East 603 feet; thence South 714.70 feet to the North right-of-way of Highway 20; thence West along right-of-way 605.96 feet; thence North 714.70 to the

POINT OF BEGINNING.

The total description of which two separate parcels is as follows: The West one half of the Southeast Quarter of the Southeast of Section 31, Township 1 North, Range 12 West.

b.  2016 Dodge Ram Pickup, VIN# 1c6RR7LM1GS304089
c.  2019 Dodge Ram Truc, VIN# 1C6SRFKT9KN672418
d.  1993 International Truck, VIN# 1HTSDPPN0PH533763
e.  2013 Kenworth Dump Truck, VIN# 1NKDX4EX0DJ350365
f.  2013 Kenworth Dump Truck, VIN#1NKDX4EX2DJ350366
g.  2013 Kenworth Dump Truck, VIN#1NKDX4EX7DJ3503693
h.  2013 Kenworth Dump Truck, VIN#1NKDX4EX8DJ350372
i.  2019 Dodge Ram Hell Cat, VIN# 2C3CDZL9XKH502713
j.  1997 International Tractor/Truck, VIN# 2HSFBASR8VC02337
k.  2019 Triton Trailer, VIN# 4TCSM112XKH247309
l.  2018 Bye-Rite Trailer VIN# 7F3B1UG29JR000185
m.  2015 Trailer, VIN# 5VTB1UG24FR002474
n.  2018 Dodge Ram Truck, VIN#3C7WRTCL9JG120614
o.  2018 Dodge Ram Truck, VIN#3C6UR5CL4JG148473
p.  1976 Pontiac Trans Am, VIN#2W87Z6N561781
q.  2005 Oshko Concrete Mixer, VIN# 10TFAAC255S084634
r.  2005 Oshko Concrete Mixer, VIN# 105FAAC255S074150
s.  2002 Oshko Concrete Mixer, VIN# 10TFAAC262S074150
t.  2006 Terex Concrete Mixer, VIN# 5DG8AU4T960011193
u.  2018 Trailstar Trailer, VIN# 4TM19KL22JB001285
v.  2019 Trailstar Trailer, VIN# 71513ZT26KB001256
w.  2019 Suntracker Pontoon Boat, VIN# BUJ11386A919
x.  2018 Tracker Sportsman, VIN# BUJ57530K718
y.  2019 Sea-doo JetSki, VIN YDV21814D919
z.  2019 Sea-doo JetSki, VIN# YDV24929E919
aa.  2001 Ford Truck, VIN# 1FDWW36S71EA76771
bb.  1997 Ford Truck, VIN# 1FTJW35H9VEA61067
cc.  2000 GMC Truck, VIN# 1GDG6H1B6YJ905565
dd.  2000 GMC Truck, VIN# 1GDG61H1B6&J906408
ee.  2019 Empire Cargo Trailer, VIN# 7F81E2021KD006537201
ff.  Big Tex Trailer, VIN # 16VEX2028H3088695
gg.  2018 Ford Truck, VIN# 1FMJU1KTXJEA11481
hh.  2018 Ford Truck, VIN# 1FT7W2BT7jEC35872
ii.  2017 Ford Truck, VIN# 1FTEW1EF3HFC36447
jj.  1993 Jeep, VIN# 1J4FY29S9PP222602
kk.  1998 Eurosport Boat, VIN# ESJ00677F798
ll.  2002 Performance Trailer, VIN# 4DZBA19265P122974

mm. 1989 Pontoon boat, VIN#BUJ45441K889
nn. 2002 Boat, VIN# GDYS1109H102
oo.  Mobile concrete batch plant

If any of the property described above as being subject to forfeiture, as a result of acts or omissions of the defendants:

i.  cannot be located upon the exercise of due diligence;
ii.  Has been transferred, sold to, or deposited with a third party;
iii.  Has been placed beyond the jurisdiction of this Court;
iv.  Has been substantially diminished in value; or
v.  Has been commingled with other property that cannot be subdivided without difficulty,

It is the intent of the United States pursuant to title 21, United States code, Section 853(p), as incorporated by Title 28, United States Code, Section 2461(c), to seek forfeiture of any other property of said defendant up to the value of the forfeitable property.

A TRUE BILL
(Blacked out signature)
FOREPERSON
DATE:  11/06/2019

LAWRENCE KEEFE
United States Attorney

STEPHEN M. Kunz
Assistant United States Attorney

What is interesting about this indictment, is that it was signed on November 6, 2019, but the arrests were not made, nor was the indictment unsealed until November 19, 2019, the morning after the FBI agents had shown up to question me at my house at night, and just four days after interim City Manager Vickie Gainer, was voted to be the new City Manager, on Friday, November 15, 2019.

The indictment was unsealed in a major press conference in Panama City, which began the downslide of my credibility as Mayor, with subpoenas for my financial records issued on December 27, 2019. Josh Anderson, the owner of Greenleaf, who worked with ECS and Mickey White, was referred to in the indictment as Anderson, and as the case progressed, there was no effort made to inform the public that Josh Anderson was no relation to me, and when he was referred to as only "Anderson" the public often confused his name with mine over the next four years of the corruption case.

For all the residents and local news media who have been asking since November of 2019 where the five million dollars went that was stolen from Lynn Haven, for anyone who read the indictment against Michael White et.al., above, it should be clear at this point. David "Mickey" White, the nephew of Derwin White of GAC, deposited the five million dollars in his business account, Erosion Control Specialist, except for the kickbacks he paid to Michael White, Adam Albritton, David Horton, Josh Anderson and others. My co-defendant, James Finch, who would be indicted March 18, 2021, approximately six months after I was indicted, figured out that Derwin White made over 16 million dollars (that we know of) with his "piece of the pie" from national hauler, AshBritt, after Derwin and his attorney, Adam Albritton, worked with Michael White to fire Ceres, the third national hauler who had been hired under blue skies by Lynn Haven.

With Ceres gone, AshBritt was provided with a larger share of Lynn Haven's debris in return for kicking money back to GAC, owned by Derwin White and Allan Bense. I knew nothing of this except that Michael White told me he was firing Ceres because they were not cooperating with him, that having two haulers instead of three would save the city money, and that we only needed two haulers.

At this time, I did not realize that Adam Albritton was also the attorney of record for Gulf Asphalt, (GAC) which was owned by Derwin White and Alan Bense. Of course, all of this is "hindsight 20/20" and a real eye-opener, considering while the rest of us were trying to survive the first 48 hours after Hurricane Michael, Derwin White, Mickey White, Michael White, and attorney Adam Albritton had drafted a contract and were ready to go to work fleecing the City of Lynn Haven, and within a few days after that, Chris Forehand, the City Engineer and his partner, Jim Slonina, had incorporated his Panhandle Engineering Disaster Services (PEDS) company, which would partner with Tetra Tech, the City of Lynn Haven's monitoring service to count the debris. Chris Forehand and his partner, Jim Slonina would make millions as the sub-contractor to Tetra Tech, the company which Michael White testified was "forced down his throat by Chris Forehand." We also learned later that Chris Forehand was listed as senior management with Tetra Tech in their list of employees and consultants. And just a few days after that, Chris Forehand had also introduced Michael White to World Claim, his pick for the city's insurance adjuster, for which Chris would receive a percentage for every client he brought to World Claim along with his friend, attorney DeDe Rowan.

I would later be charged as being part of the conspiracy with ECS, which was a lie; the only signatures on the ECS contract are those of Michael White and D. "Mickey" White, and I was never charged with accepting any money, only for receiving "free" property cleanup, which was proven in the evidentiary hearing of December 2022, never happened. We presented video and photographs of my son-in-law and several of his friends who traveled from Jacksonville on October 12th, tarping the roofs of my home and my Mom's next door, stripping out the carpets and sheetrock from her home, cutting trees from the pole barn on my property which had fallen from the easement behind my property, and doing all of the work that ECS is purported to have done. The property survey clearly shows that what ECS cleaned on November 9, 2018, is a Lynn Haven stormwater easement, an easement which City Manager Vickie Gainer, Public Works Director Bobby Baker, and City Attorney Adam Albritton all knew about, yet Gainer and Baker both gave false statements to the investigators and to the news media, even though there are emails between them containing a copy of the deed to 514 Virginia Avenue, the property directly east of mine, which contains the City stormwater easement.

The invoices which were created by ECS employee, Samantha Lind and used to indict me, were created at the direction of Derwin White, who told his nephew he "better get some" (referring to invoices on my property), placed in the ECS offices the night before the BCSO warrant was executed on ECS on April 12, 2019, and photographed lying on top of a trash can. Major Jimmy Stanford, of the Bay County Sheriff's Department, long-time friend of Derwin White, alerted Derwin when the raid would take place. As both Mickey White and Michael White state in their interviews, Jimmy Stanford had received many things of value from Derwin White...a motorcycle, payment of his sister's funeral, down payment on a home, work on a swimming pool, and not to leave anyone out, another BCSO Deputy, Officer Mickey Vestal, received a free pole barn on his property, which was next door to Derwin's property, and Stanford admitted under oath at the March evidentiary hearing of 2022 that he had indeed accepted a motorcycle, but denied the other gratuities and things of value. After he denied that Derwin had paid for his sister's funeral, he changed that story the next day, again under oath, but was never charged for making a false statement in the Federal courtroom. The Bay County Sheriff's Office spokesperson, Ruth Corley, told the news media that she could not make a comment about Stanford's testimony because they were under a court order, (not true) and Sheriff Tommy Ford reminded everyone of "innocent until proven guilty," certainly a lot more than he afforded me. Major Stanford continues to work for the Bay County Sheriff's Department today.

I was also charged in the original indictment against me in August 2020, with receiving a pro bono contract from World Claim, a public adjustor. It is true that World Claim *sent* me a pro bono contract, but what the FBI did not tell the Grand Jury, *is that I refused it.* I negotiated a contract with them, in February 2019, when they approached me, and I paid it in full. On the other hand, Commissioner Dan Russell, was in on the deal from the beginning, and DID sign a pro bono contract with World Claim insurance adjusters in November 2018, receiving a sizeable claim settlement. Yet, he was never charged, just as he was never charged with his entire gated community being cleaned by ECS and charged to the City of Lynn Haven, ultimately reimbursed by FEMA. Both he and the City's consulting accountant, Jay Moody live in Osceola Point, and Chris Forehand provided a defense for this work being done in his interview with the FBI as stormwater and flooding prevention. But, I get ahead of myself; I have much more to say about that later.

The most interesting part about the first indictment, the one against Michael White, the Lynn Haven City Manager, and Mickey White, the owner of ECS, is that the media had more questions at the press conference about the two sentences in the indictment which allege that the "Mayor and her mother" had their property cleaned and billed to the City of Lynn Haven, than they did about the five people who had stolen five million dollars from the City. And this frenzy would build over the coming weeks. My mother was completely devastated by this horrific lie about her; she had paid a contractor to clean the one and only tree that fell on her house, and my son-in-law and friends had done the other cleanup work, almost a month before the day Michael White and Mickey White claim to have done the work. She was humiliated and never got over the accusations made against her; then when I was indicted a few months later, the accusations against her were more pronounced, and a short seven months later she would die of a sudden heart attack.

Below is the story and some of the social media comments (there were hundreds) from WMBB -Channel 13, the local ABC affiliate of Panama City, the station who would thrive on the fall of Mayor Margo Anderson for many months, and who were complicit in providing the false "evidence" to law enforcement:

LYNN HAVEN, FL. (WMBB)-*Locals are still measuring the fall-out from this week's indictments for corruption and fraud involving FEMA disaster money.*

*A number of Lynn Haven city officials who were named but not charged, are defending themselves against those questioning their integrity.*

*On Tuesday, U.S. Attorney Lawrence Keefe announced that some Lynn Haven City officials participated in a scheme to defraud taxpayers out of $5 million earmarked for Hurricane Michael clean-up projects.*

*The indictment states a company called Erosion Control Specialists performed work at the homes of individuals, then billed the city for it.*

*Prosecutors say the work happened at the homes of Lynn Haven Mayor Margo Anderson, her mother's home, and at gated community where city commissioner Dan Russell lives, among others.*

*On Wednesday, Anderson said workers cleaned-up an easement behind her property, not her home.*

*Russell also told local media that workers only cleaned-up a city owned easement in his neighborhood.*

*We checked these claims with Bay County Property Appraiser Dan Sowell's office.*

*Sowell confirms Lynn haven maintains easements behind Anderson's house, and in Russell's neighborhood.*

*In fact, there are easements all over Lynn Haven that had fallen trees on them after the storm.*

*But not all residents got their easements cleaned up by the city like Mayor Anderson and Commissioner Russell's community.*

*Several Lynn haven residents contacted us to say they asked the city for help cleaning the easements on or near their properties. But the city told them they'd have to do the work themselves or pay someone else to remove debris.*

*News 13 contacted the City of Lynn Haven and requested documents, rules, and policies governing easements.*

Lynn Haven City Manager, Vickie Gainer, responded via email, and to every question News 13 asked her, including whether the property cleaned adjacent to my property was an easement or not, she answered, "No such documents exist."

Vickie Gainer denied that there were any supporting documents for the easements, when, in fact, she, Bobby Baker, and Adam Albritton had just emailed each other and had a copy of the deed which contained the documentation for the easement.

The following are only a few examples from the hundreds of comments from the public on social media and the beginning of the destruction of my character and credibility as Mayor of the City of Lynn Haven, but some residents also stood by me:

*Robbie Williams:*
*Mayor and the Commissioners need to be in jail. CROOKS they screwed the people of Lynn Haven.*

*Debbie Ingram Ward*
*My City's response to your questions is very disappointing.*

*Roger Baldwin*

*No documents exist!! How convenient!*

*Holly Allison Gaddy*
*Sounds like the Mayor and Commissioners days are numbered. Interesting how it will all play out.*

*Todd McGuire*
*Drain that swamp…*

*Fred Bruntel*
*When Margo was elected she was gung ho, going up and down streets, talking to residents, and promising them things will change. She promised to fix storm drainage on Mississippi Ave, blah blah blah. To this day it STILL floods the roadway and my yard. Guess she learned from the best how to BS the City.*

*Judy Tinder*
*My home is located in the same block as the Mayor, but on Virginia Ave. the city easement that runs from 5th Street to 6th Street has always been an issue for storm water and I've experienced rising water right up to my back door in the past. Margo is telling the truth the she nor her mom have trees on their property but after I publicly stated that Commissioner Russell's gated community in Lynn Haven had been cleaned up by Erosion Control on Mr. White's instruction, Russell went fishing to divert the attention away from himself. Mr. Russell made public requests of both Margo and myself asking to see paperwork for my permits for rebuilding my café' and of Margo. I call bs on these allegations!*

*Christie Stray*
*Oh my Lord, this is the definition of being desperate for story and to go so far as to call it corruption? I would hope that our city would offer to help her after all that she's done. We have been displaced here from Mexico Beach and have seen so many improvements and seen her on the streets helping clean up after the storm. These improvements, I believe, have helped raise spirits and encouraged others to move forward. This is a shame and I will keep her and her family in my prayers.*

As the BCSO investigative reports and FBI 302's detail in Chapter 6, the investigators questioned all of my neighbors, many City employees, ECS employees (some even incarcerated as far away as Tennessee for various crimes since the storm), and even City and County officials about the alleged property cleanup, the cleanup which later the Judge would even say was "not my property." But they never questioned me. The story grew larger on social media, and my credibility and popularity as Mayor continued to slide downhill at a rapid pace. The Sheriff's office nor Agent Borghini had any curiosity at all where I was concerned and never questioned me until the night of November 18, 2019, when the indictment against Michael White and Mickey White was ready to be unsealed the next morning. Sheriff Tommy Ford called to tell me that two FBI agents were in my driveway and that I should answer my phone. He was in on it from the beginning and appeared arrogant and smug at the press conference the next afternoon as he stood shoulder to shoulder with the U.S. Attorney Larry Keefe and Assistant U.S. Attorney Stephen Kunz, knowing exactly what was happening to the Mayor of Lynn Haven.

# 5   The Taking Down of Mayor Margo Anderson

My brother and I went out to dinner on the Friday after Thanksgiving, and he encouraged me to get an attorney since I had been named in the indictment; I was reluctant at first, but as the negativity and media attention grew, I decided he was right. He contacted Steve Meadows, former State

Attorney who lives in Panama City, and a friend of my brother. Steve gave us several names, and Ron Johnson in Pensacola was the attorney who answered the phone during Thanksgiving, for which I will ever be grateful.

In December 2019, Lee and I took our motorhome over to a campground in Jacksonville for two weeks to be in close proximity to my daughter and grandchildren during the Christmas holidays; many more family members came, some staying in hotels, others with my daughter and son-in-law and it was wonderful to be away from all of the ugliness in Lynn Haven. When we did return home, December 27th, 2019, I went to the Mayor's office to open mail, and to check and see if they needed my signature on anything or if there was any other business I was needed for since I had been gone two weeks. I had not been in my office even five minutes when Bay County Sheriff's investigators Jimmy Stanford and Jeremy Mathis showed up with a federal subpoena for me. I believe they came to my office in front of staff to embarrass me. Police Chief Ramie told me that he had not been aware that I was going to be subpoenaed, and he seemed angry that he had not been notified. I believe differently now; in fact, I am sure that he is the one who called them and told them I was back, since I found out later that Ramie was working with the FBI to record all of my conversations with him; he was not only the Police Chief that I trusted and respected, but he had become a very close personal friend, and the conversations that we shared were often personal in nature, nothing nefarious but the kind of conversations that people have with close friends that they wouldn't necessarily want to be recorded and shared with the world. He is a snake, with something to hide himself, who worked with the other lying snake, Special Agent with the FBI Lawrence Borghini who retired less than a month after defense attorneys showed that he lied to the grand jury to indict James Finch and me. We also found out from the 302 interviews of Mickey White that ECS did free work on Chief Ramie's personal boat and billed the work to the City, which would also have been reimbursed by FEMA; Ramie should have been charged with a federal crime. (The recordings he made contained nothing harmful to me, because I was not involved in the corruption.) But he tried very hard to steer conversations, and I am trying very hard, even as I write to forgive him; the lying, corrupt Chief of Police of Lynn Haven, who is still there. Something is very wrong when the police chief of any municipality is allowed to record conversations with the sitting, duly elected Mayor with no repercussions. I trusted him; he was there to protect me; Ramie saw me almost every day in the days after the storm, doing everything I could possibly do to bring state and federal attention to the City of Lynn Haven to get help for us. He knew me, he knew I trusted him, and he knew I was not a thief. But he lied about me to protect Commissioner Dan Russell, Michael White, Chris Forehand, Vickie Gainer, the BCSO, and himself. After the storm there was no one, I trusted or thought more of in the City of Lynn Haven than Ricky Ramie; this betrayal of friendship was one of the most devastating of all.

After Jimmy Stanford handed me the federal subpoena, he asked me if I had any questions.

I was thinking, "not for you, you smug, fat, red-neck bastard," but I told him I had plenty of questions just none for him and Mathis. As they were leaving, Mathis, the second investigator laughed. I stepped out of my office and looked him right in the eye and asked him if he thought this was funny. He became angry and said he was not laughing, that he was clearing his throat. I said in a very calm voice, "and you are a liar." He became angry and he was not laughing as they walked out.

The subpoena demanded all of my bank statements from my business account, Anderson Productions LLC, my tax returns, all contracts and correspondence, text messages, and emails concerning performances from 2015 until the present. These documents were to be presented to the grand jury in Tallahassee on January 7, 2020. My attorney, Ron Johnson, made arrangements for me to deliver the documents to the FBI agent in Panama City, (the same one who had interviewed me at night, by surprise, on November 18, 2019, without telling me that I was already named in the Michael White indictment which would be unsealed and read the next afternoon.). I also made a trip to Pensacola with the documents for Ron Johnson to review and to sign the affidavit with the documents as my attorney. I went to the office of S.A Borghini and made sure I did not speak to him at all other than to hand him the documents and say hello. I was shaking as I left the office on the second floor of a local financial institution in Panama City.

Weeks passed after I turned the documents in, and nothing happened. My attorney called the Assistant US Attorney, Stephen Kunz on two or three occasions asking him if we could provide assistance, assuring him that I was not involved, asking if I was a target, asking if there was information we could provide to show him that I was not involved, and we received minimal information. Kunz told Ron Johnson each time he spoke with him that I was not a target of the investigation, but that I was a "subject." He was lying too.

During February and March of 2020 all of those who were indicted except for one, David Horton, the City of Lynn Haven Community Services Director, changed their pleas to guilty, and each time a plea was entered, the media coverage was huge; my name was brought up each time, along with my photograph, sandwiched between photographs of the others in their mugshots and jailhouse striped attire. The comments made on social media on the television and newspaper sites about me became more accusatory and uglier each time. I lost a major concert opportunity on the beach in the Spring and was not hired for a Fall concert because of the negative publicity. I began seeing a therapist for depression, anxiety and sleeplessness after the indictment of November 2019 when I was implicated. The sentencing dates were changed several times and continued to be changed over the next three years; each time a new trial date was scheduled, each time a superseding indictment unsealed, a new wave of media coverage, and speculation began until June of 2023 when all of them were finally sentenced; once my case was resolved they would not need to be on hand to lie for the government any more. Michael and Mickey White would eventually be sentenced to 42 months (below the minimum suggested sentence), David Horton and Josh Anderson received home confinement and probation, Shannon Rodriguez was only given probation, and Adam Albritton, the biggest liar and most deceitful of all, received one year of probation and a fine of $32,000 which was paid in full on the day of his sentencing by Jason Bense, son of GAC owner Allan Bense. The resolution of my case would not come until July of 2023 and is described in a later chapter.

My attorney, Ron Johnson, continued to believe, right up to the day that I was arrested, that I would not be indicted. He felt that it was a local political attack on me out of jealousy, and an effort to make sure that I did not run for higher office; on the day that I was arrested, August 19th, 2020, when I called him, he was completely surprised, and he was also angry that he did not get a call notifying him that I was being arrested from the U.S. Attorney's office in Tallahassee, a four-hour drive for him from Pensacola, and so he had to participate in my initial arraignment in Jacksonville by telephone.

The week before I was arrested, I was in Jacksonville. My mom and my brother had come over to spend the weekend with me and to see our new house we had purchased on June 18, 2020. Lee was in Lynn Haven because he had gone to a race with James Finch to see his son Jake who was in the race that weekend. Thankfully, my Mom drove home with my brother on Monday, and I was planning to drive to Lynn Haven on Wednesday morning. But on Wednesday morning, about 9 a.m. eastern, I received a call from FBI agent Angela Hill asking me my location. She told me that FBI agents were at my home in Lynn Haven and that my husband had told them I was not there, but in Jacksonville. I took a deep breath in absolute horror and asked her if I was being arrested. She said yes. I told her I was packing to leave Jacksonville to come to Lynn Haven, and she told me not to leave the house that agents would be there in just a few minutes. I tried to call Lee, but learned later that he could see me calling him, but they would not allow him to answer the phone. I called my daughter and told her what was happening, I called my attorney, Ron Johnson, and I called James Finch when I could not get Lee and asked him to please find Lee and take care of him. (Lee is a 100% disabled combat veteran of Vietnam; he has diabetes, a triple bypass in 2017, colon cancer in 2012, and prostate cancer in 2010). I was concerned that he would have a heart attack, and James promised to take care of him. He also told me not to worry, that he would help me as I sobbed telling him that I was terrified, that I didn't know what to do. I then called my son-in-law, and asked him to please come and get my dog Buddy, that he would be terrified when they took me out of the house.

When the FBI arrived there were either six or eight of them, I can't remember, and I think there were four vehicles, maybe just three. They wanted to know if anyone else was in the house and I told them no; they wanted to know if I had firearms and I said yes. They wanted to know where they were. They then told me the first lie, wanting to know if I had a passport. They said if I brought a passport to court as my identification that it would help me to secure release or bond. I told them my passport was in the closet in a box with all my important papers, and I would get it, but that my firearms were also in the closet. They knew that my passport would most likely be taken from me, and so they wanted to have it. They gave me permission to go in the closet and one or two of them went with me to get it. I was holding my dog, Buddy, who is a rescue Yorkie mix from Hurricane Michael. They took him away from me and put him in the bathroom, put his food and water bowl with him and closed the door, He began scratching at the door and howling frantically.

We had just moved into our house less than two months before in a gated community in Jacksonville, and for the six weeks we had lived there, I had enjoyed no one knowing who I was, able to sleep and feel safe for the first time in months. They were going to handcuff me as we were leaving the house. I asked them if they would let me walk to the car and put the handcuffs on there so that all of my neighbors would not see, and they agreed. I was not really thinking clearly, because all of the neighbors had already seen all of their vehicles and six or eight of them in their bullet proof vests reading FBI come to my door, and as they put me in the back seat of one of the cars, they left the door open as they handcuffed me and so the neighbors saw plenty.

They did read me my Miranda rights in the car, but I was not told what I was being charged with. I felt like I could not breathe for most of the ride to the Federal Courthouse in Jacksonville, about twenty minutes or so from where I lived

I do not remember much about the ride to the Federal Building because I was so uncomfortable with the handcuffs. I complained they were too tight, but the agent in the backseat with me checked them and said they were not. Once we were at the courthouse, the agents left me with a Federal Marshall who asked questions. I remember one of the agents stayed for a while because she told me she would bring me a turkey sandwich and a drink for lunch because it would be late afternoon before I saw the judge. I told her I did not want any food, but I would appreciate a Coke or something to drink. They took the handcuffs off, but then put leg irons on; I just had sandals on with no socks and the leg irons also hurt. I remember them talking about the fact that I had no prior criminal history, and seemingly were amazed. I would learn why later. I was charged with 63 federal counts. More than John Gotti or Al Capone. They explained that they were asking me so many questions because I had to answer certain questions in order to appear before the judge that day, but I had no lawyer with me, nor was I allowed to call one.     Sometime during this period of time, Kimberly Barrett, an officer of the court, came in and explained about having to answer certain medical and other questions in order to appear before the judge for release, and I agreed to answer and to sign the form. Kimberly Barrett was to become my pre-trial officer as well, and I reported to her for 35 months before my case was completed, although she was not assigned to me until after my appearance in Tallahassee on the 25th of August. What many do not know, (I certainly did not), is that if you are indicted, and given pre-trial release instead of remaining in custody, until your trial, you are under the same conditions as someone on probation. You have no passport, you cannot travel outside of the district in which you live without permission, you are drug-tested each month or even on demand, you are not allowed access to firearms, and if you have any contact with law enforcement, even a speeding ticket, you must call your officer and report it.   I lived like this for three years with the presumption of "innocence" by the court. The presumption of innocence, in my opinion, is guilty until proven innocent. I am so disillusioned with the federal "justice" system.

They asked what prescriptions I was taking, and they also asked if I had ever used marijuana, and if so when was the last time. They wanted to know if I had traveled outside the country and when was the last time, where, etc. They asked for doctors names I was seeing and any medical conditions for which I was being treated. Then Ms. Barrett told me there was a room next door that was private and she would stand beside the door while I obtained a urine sample. I went with her and saw that the "room" next door was a jail cell. While I was in the "private" area of the cell using the cup she provided for the urine sample, the cell door was locked behind me and I found myself handing her the cup back through the bars. While this probably would not seem like a big deal, in hindsight, they were instilling terror and fear within me; she did not tell me I was about to be locked in a cell, they just did it while I was sitting on the toilet behind the partition in the cell.

She left, the FBI agent came back at some point with the sandwich and drink which she left with me, and then I sat for several hours staring at the wall waiting to see the judge. I remember being very cold and shaking. My teeth were chattering. I prayed. I cried, sobbed, dry, aching sobs, and then realized the cell had a camera. I tried not to cry anymore because I did not want them to have that satisfaction. I still did not know why I had been arrested, and most of my thoughts were about my daughter, how humiliated and embarrassed she must be , about my Mom, and the devastation she had to be experiencing , and about my husband Lee and hoping he was alright as I imagined what must be a media "shit show" going on in Bay County as I sat in the stark, brightly lit concrete block jail cell for hours. When the Federal Marshall came and opened the door to tell me I was going to court to see the judge, he had me place the palms of my hands against the wall. He was a tall, African American man, and while he was not unkind, he was just all business and very cold. He then began methodically wrapping chains about my waist which he then attached to handcuffs which he put back on. I began to cry silent tears, shaking uncontrollably. I could barely walk as we went down a long hallway which led to the court room. I was wondering if the media or people were there who would see me chained like this, wearing the jogging clothes I had been wearing after I walked Buddy early that morning, and with my face swollen from crying. I am not sure why I cared at that point, but I was so humiliated, so defeated, I just did not want any more media attention. I think the pre-trial officer was also there and was the one who told me that no one was in the court room except for one man in the back. He turned out to be my son-in-law who lives in Jacksonville who had come there to bring me home if I was released.

As I sat down, I was told that my attorney would be participating by phone from Pensacola and they gave me a headset so that I could hear him. Then someone placed the indictment document in front of me, which was over fifty pages in length. This was the first time I had seen it. I remember wondering why they had let me sit in a jail cell all day without knowing the charges against me, when I could have at least been reading it before I sat before the judge. I would realize later that I saw the indictment at 3:00 p.m. eastern, exactly at the moment in Panama City, where it was 2:00 p.m. eastern when U.S. Larry Attorney, with a speech most likely written by Sachs Media of Tallahassee was presiding over his big press conference, announcing the indictment of the Mayor of Lynn Haven, referring to her as a "virus of corruption" with Sheriff Tommy Ford at his side, both of them wearing Covid masks.

The judge asked me a few minutes later if I understood the nearly 60 pages of charges against me. I remember hearing words like "maximum sentence" "one thousand and twenty-nine years" I think, and $50 million dollars in fines. In the midst of all that, Judge Barksdale was pleasant, she looked me in the eye, and I felt like a human being for the first time that day. She asked me if I understood the charges against me, to which I first answered "no". I had no reading glasses, and I could not read what was in front of me, and once again, silent tears were running down my face. One of the court reporters, very kindly brought me a pair of reading glasses. I answered affirmatively that I understood that many charges were being made against me and that I understood what she was reading to me.

When we got to conditions of release, my attorney told her that I had two homes, one in Jacksonville (The Middle District of Florida), and one in the Northern District of Florida, Lynn Haven. Ron Johnson explained to her that I traveled between them frequently to spend time with my elderly Mom, my grandchildren, my daughter, and my work, and he requested that I be permitted to continue doing so. She stated that she saw no problem and asked the prosecution if they had objection. I remember the prosecutor saying that he saw I had many connections in the state of Florida and saw me as no flight risk. I was released from the Middle District Court in Jacksonville with my passport, with my concealed weapons permit, I was not assigned a pre-trial officer, and I was free to travel freely between the Middle and Northern Judicial Districts of Florida. The only restriction was that I have no contact with City Attorney Adam Albritton (who had also been indicted) without the presence of counsel. I was told that my next court appearance would be in the Northern District, Tallahassee at 2 p.m. on August 25th.

As I left the court room and went back into the hallway, I thought I was released, but the chains were put back on and I was taken back to the cell trying to walk with leg irons. I was told that I would be there until the Federal Marshall completed the paperwork for my release. It seemed like maybe forty-five minutes before he came back and as I stood in the office while he was removing the handcuffs, chains and leg irons I started crying uncontrollably. Not loud, just tears running down my face and I could not breathe. He was wearing a mask because of Covid and so was I, but he told me to, "stop crying," that I should be happy I was not getting in the van going to the prison. He repeated, "I was going home, and I needed to stop crying." I did not answer him, but just stared back, looking straight into his eyes. I do not ever remember feeling that much anger toward another human being, but I said nothing. I was too frightened, too intimidated, too destroyed.

We walked through a hallway, then a door, and I was suddenly in the lobby facing my son-in-law. He hugged me, and then said, "let's get out of here." I asked him to wait for a minute while I went into the Ladies room in the lobby. I had not been to the bathroom all day since giving the urine sample because I was too embarrassed to go in the cell with a camera in the corner.

It was pouring rain, torrential rain, when we got to the front door, and he told me to wait there that he would go to the parking garage and get the car. I said no that I was going with him. We waded through ankle-deep water and walked about a block to the parking garage. Once in the car, he told me that Lee was on his way to the house, that James had flown him to Jacksonville because he was so upset that James didn't want him to drive. My daughter was also waiting at the house for me.

The day after I was charged, Governor Ron DeSantis issued an Executive Order suspending me from public office, *which he did not have to do*, he chose to do so, which prevented me from going to Lynn Haven and calling an emergency Commission meeting to address the Commission and citizens of Lynn Haven. His order stated, "Margo Deal Anderson is prohibited from performing an official act, duty or function of public office; from receiving any pay or allowance; and from being entitled to any of the emoluments or privileges of public office during the period of this suspension, which period shall be from today, until a further Executive Order is issued, or as otherwise provided by law," the statement read.

I was so destroyed by this, that I immediately wrote a letter of resignation. In hindsight, I wish I had not resigned; I did it under duress, and I now regret doing it because I believe it just made me appear to be guilty instead of trying to take a burden off the City in the midst of scandal. I should not have cared. There were those at the City who were involved in doing this to me. I thought at one time that I would have liked to be reinstated just for one day once my name is cleared, but now over four years later, I feel quite differently about politics in Bay County and Northwest Florida; I would never give them the opportunity to hurt me again in the part of Florida in which I was born and had hoped to live out my life.

The next week was strangely like the days right after Hurricane Michael. I couldn't sleep, and when I did sleep I had such nightmares that I would wake up wet with sweat, filled with terror. I was embarrassed and humiliated, even around my family. I felt so violated from being arrested, hand-cuffed, and chained, that I didn't want anyone to touch me, not even Lee. I did not want to see anyone or go outside the house. My daughter told me to turn off my social media and not to look at the news, which was not only in the Panama City area, but statewide and also had made national news, that a Mayor had stolen 5 million dollars in FEMA funds from her City after Hurricane Michael. My daughter had to sit down with my seven and nine-year old granddaughters and explain to them that their Mimi had been arrested, because it also on the Jacksonville news, and she didn't want them to be blindsided at school. I didn't look for days, but when I finally did look, I immediately threw up.

And then, when my arraignment day, the 25th of August arrived, I met my attorney, Ron Johnson and his paralegal, B.J. Greer in Tallahassee and we appeared before Federal Magistrate Judge Fitzpatrick. He read all of the charges again and repeated all of the maximum sentences and fines as I had before, over a thousand years in prison and more than fifty million in fines. Then I listened as they took my passport, and as the prosecutor stated that according to my conditions of release statement that I suffered from anxiety and PTSD and requested that I no longer be permitted to have a gun. My attorney argued for my second amendment right, and the judge finally took a recess and came back with a decision that I could keep my concealed weapon permit. He stated that he did not want me to be alone at a 7/11 store at night unable to protect myself. But then he said that I would not be able to travel freely between my two homes, that facing a maximum sentence of over a thousand years (he said it again) that he wanted to know where I would be. My attorney offered that I was retired, that I was responsible for some of my mom's care, that I had grandchildren...when he was interrupted and they began to talk about 40 hours per week of employment for me. The judge agreed that I was retired but then made a completely inappropriate comment that because of all of this that "maybe my music business would take off now." I was furious. To the contrary, if you Google my name right now, as an agent or venue would for an entertainer, all that you see is that I am the Mayor who allegedly stole five million dollars from the victims in the aftermath of Hurricane Michael. He also assigned a pre-trial officer to my case, which the judge in the Middle District did not do. My attorney, who felt that a small victory had been won with my concealed carry permit, notified me two days later that the prosecution had gone around the Judge's decision and notified the Secretary of Agriculture, Nikki Fried, who rescinded my concealed carry permit, violating my rights. My attorney advised me that I could file a complaint, but I was too terrified of the prosecutors, too destroyed by all of it.

The prosecutor that day was not Stephen Kunz, but another assistant U.S. Attorney, Jason Coody. He was very angry and very aggressive, as though he had personal feelings against me. He insisted that my passport be revoked and that I not be free to travel between my home in Lynn Haven or Jacksonville, that I choose which place I would be staying. I chose Jacksonville, hoping that my mom, who lived in Lynn Haven, would understand. I left the courtroom feeling that we had lost the day, even with the judge deciding in my favor about the concealed carry. I began to wonder what a trial would be like with just Ron Johnson defending me. He is very kind, and I like him very much, but I did not feel confident that he could stand up to this kind of attack if this was a sample of what was to come next. I had another anxiety attack on the way home and cried and prayed most of the night.

The next few days were a blur, and I went to see my therapist to talk with her about the extreme fear and anxiety I was experiencing. I also had lost a great deal of close-up vision (reading) in the last few weeks, even though I had Lasik surgery initially, and then cataract surgery in 2018 with the special lens for reading. I had been able to read the smallest of type fonts without reading glasses, and now suddenly I had to wear 3.0 reading glasses to see my iPhone screen and my computer screen. I had been told it could be because of the stress I was experiencing.

One of the bright spots of the entire arrest and court appearance part of this, is that the carefully choreographed raid on my house in Lynn Haven at 6:00 a.m. with a "no knock" warrant by the FBI to which the media posted across the street had obviously been alerted, was thwarted by the fact that I was in Jacksonville. The utter incompetence of the Bay County Sheriff's Office investigators and the FBI in not even knowing where their "target" was. There was no camera shot of the Mayor handcuffed coming out of her home, no mugshot in the black and white prison jumpsuit as they had done with the others, and no cameras as I was released, because it all happened in Jacksonville, and they did not know. I am a person of faith, and I sincerely believe that God protected me, "hid me" from them on that morning, and they did not get their photoshoot. In Jacksonville, they took a headshot of me when I was arrested, but as far as I know, it was not released to the media. I never saw it until almost three years later when the probation officer of the Northern District prepared a sentencing report for the Judge, and her report contained the photograph which I saw for the first time. *"For in the day of trouble He will conceal me in His tabernacle; In the secret place of His tent He will hide me: He will lift me up on a rock."* Psalm 27:5

The following is the text of the first indictment against me with 64 federal counts, more than John Gotti or Al Capone. Over the next 2 and ½ years, there would be three more indictments against me, with the prosecutors dropping charges or the Judge dismissing charges, until the final one only charged me with two counts. But the saga from this indictment to the last one is a long and unbelievable one; the first indictment is filled with many false statements made by Agent Borghini, which we would find out later when the grand jury transcripts were unsealed. The reader may choose to skip over the 52 pages of the first indictment for now, but I wanted the text in the book to document how the charges changed over time by this "haphazard and reckless" (Judge Mark Walker's words) government team, led by U.S. Attorney Larry Keefe and Assistant U.S. Attorney Stephen Kunz, as well as Bay County Sheriff Tommy Ford and his corrupt "public trust unit."

As I would learn many months later, much of the indictment was written based on the testimony of Michael White, David "Mickey" White, Josh Anderson and others who had months since April of 2019 when I had gone to Sheriff Ford, to talk, to get their stories straight, and to make their deals with the Government as they pled guilty in early 2020 and became government *witnesses* to indict me. The BCSO even questioned people who posted false information on Facebook about what they had "noticed" or "seen" or "had heard rumors about" regarding my alleged property cleanup. Their posts on social media were in response to the news stories on WMBB Channel 13 ABC affiliate in Panama City, as well as the *Panama City News Herald*, concerning my having been named in the indictment against White. The first subpoena for my financial records was made in December of 2019, just about a month after Michael White and the others were arrested, and the grand jury met to begin the process of indicting me in June of 2020, just three months after they all pleaded guilty. Stephen Kunz continued to tell my attorney, Ron Johnson, of Pensacola, that I was not a target of the investigation, that I was a "subject" even after the grand jury had already met in June of 2020. He lied. Just as he would lie at the press conference.

After being held in a jail cell until late afternoon and then being handed the following document to read as I was sitting in front of a Judge, hearing that I was facing over *one thousand years* in federal prison if convicted. I believe I was in some type of shock, not really comprehending the scope of what was happening, and as the Judge in the Middle District of Jacksonville read the indictment to me, I do remember thinking, this is not true, all of this is lies, how can this be possible, and at the same time feeling as though I were going to throw up, as though someone had kicked me in the stomach and I could not breathe. Surely this was a nightmare, and I would wake up at any moment. As the Judge began to read the indictment aloud, I remember screaming in my head, "not true, not true, none of this is true." I needed to stand up and just start refuting what she was saying, and then I remember becoming quite calm.

"I can prove all of this is false," I thought to myself. I will get through this day, and then we will prove that all of this is a lie."

As the Judge continued to read, I was planning an emergency Commission meeting. I would drive to Lynn Haven, call an emergency City Commission meeting and a press conference.

As I would learn later, this would not be possible. Governor Ron DeSantis was already issuing a letter suspending me from office, and the U.S. Attorney's Office of the Northern District was preparing a "no contact" list which would prevent me from not only contacting any City employees of public officials, but I would not even be permitted to attend a City Commission meeting for the next three years. I would be prevented from confronting my accusers, from speaking as the Mayor of the City ever again. My enemies had effectively taken my rights and silenced me, all in one afternoon press conference.

I was also in shock that Adam Albritton, the City Attorney, had been arrested; I considered him a friend and trusted him. At the time I was arrested and until many months later, I believed him to be innocent as well.

The indictment is lengthy, over fifty pages, and I have included all of it, but without refuting each sentence of the narrative spun by the government prosecutors, because virtually every statement is false. I have, in several places, written a comment in bold type, giving explanation of some of the particularly egregious allegations the prosecutors brought.

The first time I saw it, I just stared in disbelief, but it is divided into various conspiracies which the prosecutors charged me with: The conspiracy charge was the overarching charge which tied me to every charge in the indictment; if someone sent a text message or cashed a check, I was charged with wire fraud, because I was charged as a conspirator. The ECS conspiracy charge alleges that I was present and directed Michael White to sign the contract with Mickey White and ECS, and that I had knowledge of all they were doing; therefore, each time they texted each other or the City wrote a check to ECS with my name stamped on it, I was charged with wire fraud. Never mind that I was not charged with receiving kickbacks as the others were, the prosecutors argued that I received a free property cleanup form ECS, and that was my reward. Of course this was a lie as was the rest of it. The World Claim conspiracy charges first alleged that I received pro bono work from the public adjustors working for the city, and that I agreed to this as a part of conditions for signing their contract to be the city's public adjustor. This was disproven in the evidentiary hearing by the 302-interview testimony of the vice president of the company. And finally, the Finch conspiracy charges, alleged that I steered every contract that Finch had with the city, that I signed contracts and checks to him without Commission approval, that he bought my vote by giving me a free motor home and by taking me on trips on his plane. Again, all lies. For each time the city had written Phoenix Construction a check over the six-year period I served as Mayor, I was charged with wire fraud. All of these charges would be dismissed or dropped over the next three years except for a single conspiracy and bribery charge, which was recently overturned by the Supreme Court, the "666" no *quid pro quo* charge; but at the time, the Government had achieved their goal of making national news with charging a small town Mayor with 64 federal counts: more than John Gotti, Al Capone, or even Donald Trump. U.S. Attorney Larry Keefe celebrated his one-year anniversary of "rooting out public corruption" on the day I was indicted, and Sheriff Tommy Ford and State Attorney Larry Basford celebrated their victory in the election which took place the night before, August 18, 2020.

UNITED STATES OF AMERICA

v.

MARGO DEAL ANDERSON
And
JOSEPH ADAM ALBRITTON

THE GRAND JURY CHARGES:

COUNT ONE

    A.  INTRODUCTION

At all times material to this Indictment:

1.    MARGO DEAL ANDERSON was elected as Mayor of Lynn Haven on April 21, 2015. ANDERSON was re-elected as mayor of Lynn Haven on April 16, 2019. As Mayor of Lynn Haven, ANDERSON was the head of the municipal government and supervised the City Manager, who was responsible for the day-t0-day operations and administrative functions of Lynn Haven. ANDERSON, as Mayor, participated in all Lynn Haven Commission meetings, set the agenda for all Commission meetings, and possessed one vote on the City Commission equal to each Commissioner.
**THIS WAS THE FIRST LIE BY THE GOVERNMENT. ACCORDING TO THE CITY CHARTER, I WAS NOT THE HEAD OF THE CITY GOVERNMENT, I WAS NOT RESPONSIBLE FOR DAY-TO-DAY OPERATIONS OF THE CITY, AND I DID NOT SUPERVISE THE CITY MANAGER, OR SET THE AGENDA FOR THE COMMISSION MEETINGS. THE CITY GOVERNMENT WAS A CITY MANAGER RUN GOVERNMENT.**

2.    Between on or about August 22, 2017, and March 26, 2019, Michael Edward White (M. White) was the City Manager of Lynn Haven. As City Manager, M.WHITE was the administrative head of the municipal government and was responsible for the day-to-day operations and administrative functions of Lynn Haven.

3.    JOSEPH ADAM ALBRITTON entered into a contract with Lynn Haven to be the City Attorney for Lynn Haven on or about

October 22, 20189, effective October 15, 2018, for one year. The contract retained ALBRITTON to provide professional legal services and perform other related duties to the Governing Body of the City and its employees as specified in the agreement. ALBRITTON executed an addendum to the professional services contract to be City Attorney on or about October 31, 2019 for an additional period of two years.

4.     As the mayor of Lynn Haven, MARGO DEAL ANDERSON was an agent of the City of Lynn Haven, and had a fiduciary duty to act in the best interests of Lynn Haven and its citizens.

5.     As the City Attorney for Lynn Haven, JOSEPH ADAM ALBRITTON was an agent of the City of Lynn Haven, and had a fiduciary duty to act in the best interests of Lynn Haven and its citizens.

6.     Erosion Control Specialists ("ECS} was incorporated in the State of Florida on May 10, 2011. David Mitchelle White (D. White) was listed as a director of ECS. In a 2018 amended annual report and a 2019 annual report filed with the State of Florida, D. White was listed as a director and Vice President of ECS.

7.     On October 10, 2018, Hurricane Michael caused severe damage to public and private property, public utilities, public buildings, public communications systems, public streets and roads, and public drainage systems within the City of Lynn Haven, Florida (Lynn Haven).

**8.**     On October 16, 2018, as a result of Hurricane Michael, Lynn Haven adopted a local state of emergency for post disaster relief and planning and approved Hurricane Michael Resolution No. 2018-10-16. In the resolution, Lynn Haven waived the procedures and formalities otherwise required under Florida law to take action to ensure the safety, welfare, and health of the citizens of Lynn Haven, including: entering into contracts; incurring obligations; acquisition and distribution of materials, supplies, and other expenses related to the storm event; appropriation and expenditure of public funds; and the employment of permanent and temporary workers. The resolution delegated emergency powers to the mayor of Lynn Haven, MARGO DEAL ANDERSON, or her designee, to discharge the duties and exercise powers for the above described activities until the local emergency declared had expired and the resolution was rescinded. The Declaration of Emergency was to be automatically renewed every seven days until further action was taken by Lynn Haven.

9.     On October 23, 2018, as a result of Hurricane Michael, Lynn Haven again declared and reinstated a local state of emergency for

post disaster relief and planning and entered Hurricane Michael Resolution No. 2018-10-23-002. This Declaration of Emergency contained the same provisions as the original declaration of emergency and was effective for seven days. The Declaration of Emergency was required to be renewed or it would automatically expire.

10.     On October 30, 2018, Lynn Haven voted to end the local state of emergency and end the designation of the emergency powers to the mayor or her designee.

11.     Prior to Hurricane Michael, Lynn Haven contracted with two national disaster relief companies to provide disaster relief services for the city following a hurricane. These companies, referred to as Company C and Company D in this Indictment, provided debris removal services for Lynn Haven after Hurricane Michael, submitted invoices with supporting documentation for their services, and received payment from Lynn Haven, which was reimbursed by the Federal Emergency Management Agency (FEMA) for the expenses.

12.     FEMA is an agency of the United States Department of Homeland Security and is responsible for coordinating the federal government's response to natural and man-made disasters. The primary purpose of FEMA is to coordinate the response to a disaster that has occurred in the United States and that overwhelms the resources of local and state authorities. In addition to on-the-ground support of disaster recovery efforts, FEMA provides state and local governments with experts in specialized fields and the funding for rebuilding efforts for infrastructure. FEMA also provides for the reimbursement of many expenses incurred by local governments in cleaning up and restoration after natural disasters, such as hurricanes.

**13.**     On October 22, 2018, with the knowledge and concurrence of MARGO DEAL ANDERSON, M. White, on behalf of Lynn Haven, and D. White, as owner of ECS, signed an agreement for ECS to provide Lynn Haven with "Emergency And/Or Exigent Services, Ancillary Construction Services, or Construction Due to the Effects of Hurricane Michael." The agreement referenced ECS as a "contractor," with the effective date of October 11, 2018. The term of the agreement was for no more than 90 days to perform services for Lynn Haven. As part of the agreement, ECS agreed to provide detailed invoices requesting payment for services accompanied by such documentation or data, including back-up documentation sufficient for reimbursement of expenses by FEMA for Lynn Haven payments to ECS. JOSEPH ADAM

ALBRITTON drafted this agreement.

**THIS LIE WAS TOLD BY MICHAEL WHITE. I HAD NO KNOWLEDGE OF THE CONTRACT BETWEEN ECS AND THE CITY OF LYNN HAVEN. MICHAEL WHITE AND MICKEY WHITE, OWNER OF ECS SIGNED THE CONTRACT WHICH DID NOT EVEN HAVE A SIGNATURE LINE FOR ME. THEY DID NOT WANT ME TO KNOW ABOUT IT.**

14.     On or about October 28, 2018, with the knowledge and concurrence of MARGO DEAL ANDERSON, M. White , on behalf of Lynn Haven, and D. White, owner of ECS signed an amended agreement for ECS to provide Lynn Haven with "Emergency And/Or Exigent Services, Ancillary Construction Services, or Construction Due to the Effects of Hurricane Michael." Notably, the 90-day term provided for in the original agreement was replaced with no deadline; rather, the agreement provided for in the original agreement was replaced with no deadline; rather, the agreement provided the duration to be "for such time as necessary to perform the services for the project." Additionally, the amended agreement included new specific language advising D. White and ECS that FEMA financial assistance would be used to fund the contract with Lynn Haven, and that ECS would comply with all applicable federal regulations and executive orders, as well as all FEMA policies, procedures, and directives. Under the amended agreement, ECS also agreed to provide FEMA with access to its books and records and was further advised of federal program fraud and false statement prohibitions. JOSEPH ADAM ALBRITTON drafted this amended agreement.

**ANOTHER LIE BASED ON MICHAEL WHITE'S TESTIMONY. FOR EACH CRIME HE COMMITTED, HE SAID WITH THE CONCURRENCE OF MARGO ANDERSON, OR THAT I REQUESTED, OR DEMANDED, OR PRESSURED HIM.**

15.     After Hurricane Michael, MARGO DEAL ANDERSON requested that the City Manager and D. White have ECS provide debris removal and repairs to her personal residence and the private residences of her mother and another neighbor. These services were billed by ECS to, and paid by, Lynn Haven in invoices that falsely claimed services were provided for public areas in Lynn Haven.

**I DID NOT REQUEST ECS TO DO ANY OF THIS; I REQUESTED CITY MANAGER MICHAEL WHITE TO CLEAN THE EASEMENT BEHIND MY PROPERTY. WE PROVED THIS IN THE EVIDENTIARY HEARING.**

16. In late October or early November 2018, JOSEPH ADAM ALBRITTON discussed with D. White expanding the work that ECS was performing for Lynn Haven, to include the pick-up of residential trash in Lynn Haven. ALBRITTON drafted a supplemental agreement between Lynn Haven and ECS authorizing ECS to assist Lynn Haven in the removal of residential trash. The effective date of this "task order" was listed as three weeks earlier—October 15, 2018, and the "task order" authorized payment to ECS at a rate of no more than $300.00 per hour, per crew, for removal of trash. The task order stated that it would terminate upon notice by Lynn Haven but was not to exceed 45 days from the effective date (October 15, 2018).

17. On November 8, 2018, M. White and D. White executed an "Exhibit A-Task order 18-001" that ostensibly was an agreement under the Amended Agreement described in paragraph #12 above, authorizing ECS to charge Lynn Haven for residential trash pick-up, including allowing ECS to bill Lynn Haven for residential trash pick-up that had not been performed by ECS during October 2018.

18. In late October 2018, JOSEPH ADAM ALBRITTON provided to City Manager M. White a list of companies that he claimed had provided prices that would be charged to receive reduced vegetative debris or chips. ALBRITTON advised M. White that a company, referred to as Company A in this indictment provided the lowest price at $4.70 per cubic yard and there was an immediate need to dispose of reduced debris. ALBRITTON told M. White that Lynn Haven had asked that the debris removal companies associated with the City use only locations that charged at a rate that the haulers could bill to Lynn Haven that was higher than several of the individuals and companies who attempted to submit bids for the debris dumping. ALBRITTON also told the City Manager that the dumping location owned by Company A was the most economic solution and should be selected by debris removal companies associated with Lynn Haven to dispose of vegetative debris or chips. At that time, ALBRITTON was also employed by, and provided legal services to, Company A, a fact that was not disclosed by ALBRITTON.

19. After Hurricane Michael, JOSEPH ADAM ALBRITTON directed D. White to have ECS provide debris removal and repairs to his personal residence and the residence of his girlfriend. These services were billed to Lynn Haven by ECS in invoices that falsely claimed services were provided for public areas in Lynn Haven, which paid ECS. ALBRITTON also requested and obtained from

ECS an invoice for the debris removal services provided at his residence, which invoice ALBRITTON submitted to his insurance company falsely claiming he had paid ECS for debris removal and repairs.

## B. THE CHARGE

Between on or about August 1, 2015, and on or about August 11, 2020, in the Northern District of Florida and elsewhere, the defendants,

### MARGO DEAL ANDERSON
And
### JOSEPH ADAM ALBRITTON,

did knowingly and willfully combine, conspire, confederate, and agree together and with other persons to:

1. devise, and intend to devise, a scheme to defraud and for obtaining money and property by means of material false and fraudulent pretenses, representations, and promises, and to cause wire communications to be transmitted in interstate and foreign commerce for the purpose of executing such scheme, in violation of Title 18, United States Code, Section 1343; and

2. did knowingly and willfully devise and intend to devise a scheme to defraud and deprive the City of Lynn Haven and its citizens of their right to the honest services of ANDERSON, the elected Mayor of Lynn Haven, Florida, and ALBRITTON, the City Attorney for Lynn Haven, Florida, through bribery or kickbacks, and to cause wire communications to be transmitted in interstate and foreign commerce for the purpose of executing such scheme, in violation of Title 18, United States Code, Sections 1343 and 1346;

## C. MANNER AND MEANS

The manner and means by which this conspiracy was committed and included the following:

### Public Official Positions

1. The defendants and conspirators used MARGO DEAL ANDERSON'S public official position as the Mayor of Lynn Haven, and JOSEPH ADAM ALBRITTON's public official position as a City Attorney of Lynn Haven, to offer, give, solicit, receive, agree to accept, and accept things of value from companies

and individuals having business interests in Lynn Haven. These things of values were offered to ANDERSON and ALBRITTON with the intent that they would be influenced in the performance of official acts. ANDERSON and ALBRITTON demanded, sought, agreed to accept, and received things of value with the intent that they would be influenced in the performance of official acts.

2.    MARGO DEAL ANDERSON used her position as Mayor of Lynn Haven to take official action favorable to Company A, Company B, and other companies, that included voting on measures pending before the Lynn Haven City Commission, signing resolutions, contracts, agreements, and promissory notes, and pressuring and advising City officials to perform specific official acts.

**NONE OF THIS IS TRUE, AS WE PROVED, HOWEVER, FOR EACH DOCUMENT, CHECK, AGREEMENT, OR VOTE HAVING TO DO WITH ECS, PHOENIX CONSTRUCTION, WORLDCLAIM, OR GAC THAT CONTAINED MY SIGNATURE, EVEN COMPUTER-GENERATED CHECKS, I WOULD BE CHARGED WITH A CRIME. AS MAYOR, MY SIGNATURE WAS VIRTUALLY ON EVERY DOCUMENT IN THE CITY OF LYNN HAVEN.**

3.    JOSEPH ADAM ALBRITTON used his position as City Attorney of Lynn Haven to take official action favorable to Company A, Company B, and other companies, including drafting official documents, signing official documents, conducting alleged bid procedures for contracts, and pressuring and advising City officials to perform specific official acts.

ECS Fraudulent Invoices

4.    D. White used ECS as a means to fraudulently obtain money from Lynn Haven. D. White submitted invoices requesting payment for services allegedly provided by ECS to Lynn Haven, but which were false and fraudulent as to a number of material matters.

5.    M. White, as City Manager of Lynn Haven, approved all ECS invoices and directed city employees to immediately pay ECS for those invoices, even though other contracted debris removal companies had to wait for payment of invoices submitted for Hurricane Michael disaster relief and debris removal.

6.    After Hurricane Michael, MARGO DEAL ANDERSON requested that the City Manager and D. White have ECS provide debris removal and repairs to her personal residence and the

private residences of her mother and a neighbor. These services were valued at approximately $48,000 but were billed by ECS to, and paid by, Lynn Haven in invoices that falsely claimed services were provided for public areas in Lynn Haven.

7.     MARGO DEAL ANDERSON and M. White signed Lynn Haven checks issued to ECS based upon fraudulent invoices that falsely claimed work by ECS was performed at various Lynn Haven public locations when the invoices included work performed by ECS at private residences and premises of public officials, including ANDERSON and the private residences of her mother and a neighbor.

8.     While D. White and ECS were providing services to Lynn Haven, M. White received things of value from D. White, including repairs to, and debris removal from, M. Whites residence in Lynn Haven and his farm located outside Lynn Haven in Bay County, money for the purchase of M. White's farm, an automobile, and cash.

9.     These repairs to, and debris removal from, the residence and farm of M. White were billed to Lynn Haven with false invoices submitted by D. White to Lynn Haven with invoices falsely stating that work had been performed at locations in Lynn Haven. M. White approved the ECS invoices and directed Lynn Haven employees to pay the invoices.

10.     While D. White and ECS were providing services to Lynn Haven, MARGO DEAL ANDERSON received things of value from D. White, including repairs to, and debris removal from, ANDERSON'S private residence in Lynn Haven and the private residences of her mother and a neighbor.

11.     After Hurricane Michael, JOSEPH ADAM ALBRITTON caused D. White to have ECS provide debris removal and repairs to his personal residence and the residence of his girlfriend. These services were valued at approximately $25,000, but were billed by ECS to, and paid by Lynn Haven in invoices that falsely claimed services were provided for public areas in Lynn Haven, ALBRITTON also requested and obtained from ECS an invoice for the services provided at his residence, which invoice falsely stated that ALBRITTON paid the invoice in full, and which ALBRITTON submitted to his insurance company falsely claiming that he paid ECS for debris removal and repairs, and requesting reimbursement from the insurance company.

12.     While D. White and ECS were providing services to Lynn Haven, JOSEPH ADAM ALBRITTON received things of value from D. White, including repairs to, and debris removal from, the

private residences of ALBRITTON and his girlfriend in Lynn Haven, and cash.

13. When ECS invoices were being assembled for submission to FEMA by Lynn Haven for reimbursement, it was apparent that most of the ECS invoices that had been paid provided no details in support of the requested payments. When directed to provide supporting documentation for the monies requested and already paid, D. White submitted false time sheets prepared by another person. The time sheets were false and fraudulent in that they included names of individuals who had not worked at the claimed location, were off that day, worked at other projects outside Lynn Haven, or had never worked for ECS at the time of the timesheet. Additionally, in many invoices, the specific Lynn Haven locations of work claimed to have been done by ECS were false. These time sheets describing the attendance of ECS workers were certified by a Lynn Haven Department Head of Recreation and Parks, as accurate, but they were not, as the public official well knew.

14. ECS invoices were submitted to Lynn Haven for the payment of services that were not authorized under the emergency contract and were for the private residences of some Lynn Haven officials. The performance of ECS post-hurricane debris removal and repairs at the private residences of some Lynn Haven officials and other private individuals were concealed and not disclosed in the ECS invoices submitted by D. White. M. White approved the invoices and caused them to be paid to ECS by Lynn Haven.

15. A check register listing all checks and payments of monies to vendors by Lynn Haven was provided to MARGO DEAL ANDERSON, City Manager M. White, and the Deputy Finance Director on a regular basis. The check register included the amount of the Lynn Haven check, the vendor, and related accounting information. ANDERSON regularly signed off on the check register detailing Lynn Haven payments to vendors, including ECS. ANDERSON signed off on a number of check registers that included the payment of invoices to ECS totaling approximately $5 million between October 26, 2018, and March 2019, and never questioned any of the payments made to ECS until after the resignation of the City manager and the subsequent inquiry concerning the large amount of monies paid by Lynn Haven to ECS.

**AS I WILL DESCRIBE IN DETAIL IN LATER CHAPTERS, IN THE WEEKS AFTER THE STORM, I DID NOT RECEIVE THE LIST OF WARRANTS EVERY TWO WEEKS; I DID NOT RECEIVE THEM UNTIL LATE JANUARY 2019, ALL AT ONE**

**TIME. IN THE BEGINNING WEEKS THERE WERE NO COMPUTERS, PRINTERS, TELEPHONE SERVICE, I HAD NO DESK, NOR EVEN A MAILBOX TO RECEIVE DOCUMENTS.**

16. On October 23, 2018, D. White and ECS submitted to Lynn Haven a false invoice for hurricane clean-up in the amount of $180,722.75 that claimed work by ECS was done at a Lynn Haven Park and water plant on eight separate days. The ECS supporting documents submitted to Lynn Haven for this fraudulent invoice included individuals who were in fact working at locations outside Lynn Haven for a different contractor. This invoice, and a separate ECS $44,000 invoice for painting a Lynn Haven building prior to the hurricane, were approved and paid by Lynn Haven as emergency expenditures. With the approval of MARGO DEAL ANDERSON, M. White issued a handwritten check in the amount of $224,722.75 to ECS within three days after the submission of the invoices, and ANDERSON specifically authorized the cashing of the Lynn Haven check.

17. On November 12, 2018, a false invoice for the hurricane clean-up in the amount of $527,512.265 was submitted to Lynn Haven by D. White and ECS that falsely claimed work by ECS was done at a cemetery and sports complexes during a seven-day period. Instead of doing the work at the locations described, ECS workers conducted debris removal and clean-up at the residence of M. White located in Lynn Haven, his farm located outside of Lynn Haven in Bay County, the residences of MARGO DEAL ANDERSON, her mother, and a neighbor, and the residences of JOSEPH ADAM ALBRITTON and his girlfriend. The work on these private residences was concealed and not reported in the invoices, and no supporting documents to the invoice were provided. The invoice was approved by M. White, who directed employees of Lynn Haven to pay this invoice. This invoice was included in the payment of three invoices to ECS in a Lynn Haven check issued to ECS on November 15, 2018, totaling $1,288,716.54.

18. For the invoice submitted on November 12, 2018, described in paragraph #17 above, D. White and ECS subsequently submitted false Daily Time Sheets purporting to show numerous individuals worked 12 hours per day on November 11, 2018. These time sheets were prepared by a conspirator, who also prepared time sheets for the same day for ECS to pay its employees. The payroll time sheets prepared by the conspirator and used to pay ECS employees listed most of the employees as not working on that day.

ECS Trash Pick-Ups

**19.**     After the initial declaration of an emergency by Lynn Haven had been revoked and expired, JOSEPH ADAM ALBRITTON, MARGO DEAL ANDERSON, and others sought to locate additional Lynn Haven projects that could provide money to D. White and ECS. One project was the Task Order agreement that ALBRITTON drafted and directed the City Manager to execute with D.. White, ostensibly as part of the Emergency Agreement with ECS, to conduct trash pick-up using a pick-up truck and a trailer, at a cost of no more than $300 per hour per crew, throughout Lynn Haven. This action was implemented despite the ability of Lynn Haven waste trucks to pick-up large amounts of household trash and deposit large amounts of trash at the dump at no increased cost to Lynn Haven.

20.     In late October or early November 2018, JOSEPH ADAM ALBRITTON discussed with D. White expanding the work that ECS was performing for Lynn Haven, to include the pick-up of residential trash in Lynn Haven. ALBRITTON drafted a supplemental agreement between Lynn Haven and ECS authorizing ECS to assist Lynn Haven in the removal of residential trash. The effective date of this "task order" was listed as three weeks earlier—October 15, 2018, and the "task order" authorized payment to ECS at a rate of no more than $300.00 per hour per crew for removal of trash. The task order stated that it would terminate upon notice by Lynn Haven but was not to exceed 45 days from the effective date (October 15,2018).

21.     On November 8, 2018, M. White and D. White executed an "Exhibit A-Task order 18-001" that ostensibly was an agreement under the Amended Agreement described in paragraph #14 of Section a above authorizing ECS to charge Lynn Haven for residential trash pick-up, including allowing ECS to bill Lynn Haven for residential trash pick-up that had not been performed by ECS during October 2018.

22.     On November 9, 2018, JOSEPH ADAM ALBRITTON sent an email to City Manager M. White and MARGO DEAL ANDERSON that the trash pickup work order did not require approval by the Commission, as it confirmed the verbal task order approved by ANDERSON and M. White in October. The trash pick-up Task Order was then removed from the agenda for

approval by the Lynn Haven Commission.

23.    On November 13, 2018, a false invoice for hurricane clean-up in the amount of #332,387.76 was submitted to Lynn Haven by D. White and ECS that falsely claimed trash pick-up was conducted by ECS during a fourteen-day period starting on October 18, 2018. No documentation was submitted in support of this invoice. The claimed trash pick-up did not occur, and there was no record of any trash being dumped at the Bay County refuse location, nor did City manager M. White obtain approval from Bay County for ECS to use the account of Lynn Haven to dump items at the Bay County facility until at least October 31, 2018. This invoice was included in the payment of three invoices to ECS in a Lynn Haven check issued to ECS on November 15, 2018, totaling $1,288,716.54.

24.    From the monies fraudulently paid by Lynn Haven for trash pick-up that did not actually occur, JOSEPH ADAM ALBRITTON solicited D. White to pay ALBRITTON money paid to ECS pursuant to the trash pickup agreement. Over the course of the next twelve weeks, ALBRITTON received $10,000 in cash from D. White per week of claimed trash pickup, linking to the payment of twelve weeks of trash pick-up in Lynn Haven.

25.    On November 29, 2018, a false invoice for hurricane clean-up in the amount of $135,445.03 was submitted to Lynn Haven by D. White and ECS that falsely claimed trash pick-up was conducted by ECS during a seven-day period starting on November 23, 2018, (the day after Thanksgiving). However, there were only 6 dump tickets from the Bay County refuse location for this time period, for which D. White and ECS charged Lynn Haven $19, 349 per day. This invoice was included in the payment of two invoices to ECS in a Lynn Haven check issued to ECS on November 30, 2018, totaling $433,365.85. At the direction of ALBRITTON, d. White paid ALBRITTON $10,000 in cash from the proceeds of the Lynn Haven check to ECS.

26.    On December 13, 2018, a false invoice for hurricane clean-up in the amount of $185,503.17 was submitted to Lynn Haven by D. White and ECS that falsely claimed trash pick-up was conducted by ECS during a 13-day period starting on November 30, 2018. The actual dump tickets from the Bay County refuse location for this time period did not support the claims of the invoice. Additionally, the trash-pick-up agreement expired on November 29, 2018, and ECS was not authorized to collect residential trash or receive payment from Lynn Haven for such services. This invoice was included in the payment of two invoices to ECS in a Lynn Haven

check issued to ECS on December 14, 2018, totaling $515,731.31. At the direction of ALBRITTON, D. White paid ALBRITTON $20,000 in cash from the proceeds of the Lynn Haven check to ECS.

27.     On December 28, 2018, a false invoice for hurricane clean-up in the amount of $481,215.24 was submitted to Lynn Haven by D. White and ECS that falsely claimed trash pick-up was conducted by ECS during a 17-day period starting on December 13, 2018, and continuing before and after Christmas Day, and through Christmas week. The majority of ECS workers did not work for the two weeks before and after Christmas. The invoice falsely claimed trash pick-up totaling between $21,000 and $32,000 per day during this period. Additionally, the trash-pick-up agreement had expired on November 29, 2020, and ECS was not authorized to collect residential trash or receive payment from Lynn Haven for such services. This invoice was included in the payment of two invoices to ECS in a Lynn Haven check issued to ECS on December 31, 2018, totaling $725,941.09. At the direction of ALBRITTON, D. White paid ALBRITTON $20,000 in cash from the proceeds of the Lynn Haven check to ECS.

28.     On January 13, 2019, three months after Hurricane Michael, a false invoice for hurricane clean-up in the amount of $479,020.68 was submitted to Lynn Haven by D. White and ECS that falsely claimed trash pick-up was conducted by ECS during a 13-day period starting the day after New Year's Day. The invoice also falsely claimed that between 11 and 13 crews were used to collect trash daily. The invoice falsely claimed trash pick-up during this period totaling $32,278.68 per day for five days, $38,878.44 per day for seven days, and $45,478.20 for the last day. Additionally, the trash-pick-up agreement had expired on November 29, 2018, and ECS was not authorized to collect residential trash or receive payment from Lynn Haven for such services. This invoice was-included in the payment of two invoices to ECS in a Lynn Haven check issued to ECS on January 15, 2019, totaling $895,441.52. At the direction of ALBRITTON, D. White paid ALBRITTON $20,000 in cash from the proceeds of the Lynn Haven check to ECS.

29.     On January 25, 2019, three months after Hurricane Michael, a false invoice for hurricane clean-up in the amount of $216,771.24 was submitted to Lynn Haven by D. White and ECS that falsely claimed trash pick-up was conducted by ECS during a six day period. The invoice also falsely claimed that crews were used to collect trash daily. The invoice falsely claimed trash pick-up during

this period totaling $38,878.44 per day for four days, $35,578.56 for one day, and $25,678.92 for the last day. Additionally, the trash-pick-up agreement had expired on November 29, 2018, and ECS was not authorized to collect residential trash or receive payment from Lynn Haven for such services. This invoice was included in the payment of two invoices to ECS in a Lynn Haven check issued to ECS on January 31, 20199, totaling $433,259.16. At the direction of ALBRITTON, D. White paid ALBRITTON $10,000 from the proceeds of the Lynn Haven check to ECS.

## Disposal of Vegetative Debris or Chips

30. On October 30, 2018, JOSEPH ADAM ALBRITTON provided to City Manager M. White a list of companies that he falsely claimed had provided prices that would be charged to receive reduced vegetative debris or chips and advised M. White that Company A provided the lowest price at $4.70 per cubic yard and there was an immediate need to dispose of reduced debris. ALBRITTON further told M. White that Lynn Haven had asked that the debris removal companies associated with the City use only locations that charged a price of $4.70 per cubic yard or less.

31. At the time that JOSEPH ADAM ALBRITTON advised the City Manager that the dumping location owned by Company A was the most economical solution and should be selected by debris removal companies associated with Lynn Haven to dispose of vegetative debris or chips, ALBRITTON was employed by, and provided legal services to, Company A, and ALBRITTON was the registered agent for 14 companies of the owner of Company A. Additionally, ALBRITTON was a co-owner with the owner of Company A in another company and had been since February 2017. None of these ties, financial interests, and relationships with Company A and its owner were disclosed by ALBRITTON to Lynn Haven.

32. One of the companies that JOSEPH ADAM ALBRITTON falsely claimed had not provided a price for the vegetative debris or chips disposal had actually advised officials in Lynn Haven, including ALBRITTON, in writing that it would accept the vegetative debris or chips for $4.00 per cubic yard, or even lower at $3.50 per cubic yard, and save the taxpayers money both as to the price and the costs of transportation since its disposal sites were closer to Lynn Haven than Company A or the other possible disposal sites.

33. After the selection of Company A became public and an

objection the selection by Lynn Haven of Company A to be used by debris removal companies associated with Lynn Haven to dispose of vegetative debris or chips was made to Lynn Haven officials, one of Company A's owners asked JOSEPH ADAM ALBRITTON to forward ALBRITTON's summary of the obtaining of prices to a representative of Company D, a large debris removal company contracted with Lynn Haven to conduct post-Hurricane Michael debris removal, so Company D could incorporate and justify the use of the Company A site for vegetative debris or chips disposal.

34.    In or about late October, MARGO DEAL ANDERSON convened a meeting with one of the owners of Company A, the owner of Company B, City Manager M. White, and several other persons at the personal residence of the owner of Company B. At the meeting, ANDERSON praised the president of Company B and his previous post-hurricane assistance to Lynn Haven, and the owner of Company B complained about not receiving enough of Lynn Haven post-Hurricane Michael business.

**THIS MEETING DID NOT TAKE PLACE; JAMES FINCH, OWNER OF COMPANY B, WAS STILL IN JACKSONVILLE RECOVERING FROM A STROKE AT THIS TIME.**

35.    On November 1, 2018, at the direction of MARGO DEAL ANDERSON, City Manager M. White issued a directive to Company C, a debris removal company that was contracted with Lynn Haven to conduct post-Hurricane Michael debris removal and clean-up, to utilize a site owned by Company B to dispose of all vegetative debris or chips. Company C, which had been disposing of vegetative debris or chips at another site location, stopped dumping at that site location and commenced disposing of all of its vegetative debris or chips at the site of Company B. Fees totaling more than $1 million for the disposal of items by Company C at Company B's site for the next one-year period were paid by Lynn Haven.

**THIS CHARGE IS BASED ON AN EMAIL THAT MICHAEL WHITE SENT TO COMPANY C, CROWDER GULF, INFORMING THEM THAT THE MAYOR HAD DIRECTED HIM TO HAVE COMPANY C BEGIN BRINGING THEIR DEBRIS TO JAMES FINCH'S PIT. THERE WAS NO SUCH DIRECTIVE IN A TEXT MESSAGE AS MICHAEL WHITE CLAIMED, AND THE GOVERNMENT COULD NOT PRODUCE SUCH A TEXT MESSAGE. IT WAS A LIE.**

36.    On or about November 11, 2018, at the direction of MARGO DEAL ANDERSON, City Manager M. White issued a directive to

Company D, a debris removal company that was contracted with Lynn Haven to conduct post-Hurricane Michael debris removal and clean-up, to utilize a site owned by Company B to dispose of all vegetative debris or chips. Company D, which had been disposing of vegetative debris or chips at another site location, ended dumping at that site location and commenced disposing of all of its vegetative debris or chips at the site of Company B. Fees totaling more than $1 million for the disposal of items by Company D at Company B's site for the next year period were paid by Lynn Haven.

37. On November 19, 2018, at the request of the co-owner of Company A, JOSEPH ADAM ALBRITTON sent to the vice-president of Company D, contracted to remove debris in Lynn Haven after Hurricane Michael, an email with the subject, "Justification Notice," and provided his summary and analysis that the Company A site be used to dispose of vegetative debris or chips by all debris removal companies associated with Lynn Haven.

### Disaster Debris Management Site

38. While Lynn Haven was finalizing its decision concerning the location to be utilized for the disposal of vegetative debris or chips, City Manager M. White consulted with the City Engineer and planned to have real property owned, but not used by Lynn Haven, permitted by the State of Florida to be used by debris removal companies associated with Lynn Haven to dispose of vegetative debris or chips.

39. However, MARGO DEAL ANDERSON instructed City Manager M. White to stop the permitting process for the Lynn Haven property for the disposal of vegetative debris or chips and stated that it would be unnecessary.

40. MARGO DEAL ANDERSON then directed City Manager M. White to seek authorization from the State of Florida for Lynn Haven to obtain a new Disaster Debris Management Site (DDMS) at property owned by Company B in Bay County. Accordingly, on November 7, 2018, City Manager M. White filed a written request with the State of Florida requesting authorization for Lynn Haven to use a new DDMS for temporary storage and processing of disaster debris generated as the result of Hurricane Michael.

41. During the same period of time that the DDMS authorization was arranged for Company B, two disaster debris companies, contracted with Lynn Haven for debris removal, were directed to dispose of the vegetative debris or chips at Company B's site, and

Company B received payment of fees for that dumping from Lynn Haven, MARGO DEAL ANDERSON accepted things of value from the owner of Company B, including travel in a private airplane for ANDERSON and another person to Biloxi, Mississippi, and the Florida Keys, lodging, meals and entertainment, and lodging aboard a private yacht and meals in Key West, Florida.

17th Street Projects and ½ Cent Surtax Design/Build Contract

42.   In August 2015, Lynn Haven approved an agreement for Company B to perform work in the amount of $3.72 miillion for the 17th Street ditch Stormwater Project (17th Street project). Lynn Haven also approved the financing of the project by Company B at an interest rate of 2.55 per cent for a term of 20 years.

43.   On March 20, 2017, MARGO DEAL ANDERSON signed on behalf of Lynn Haven, a promissory note to pay Company B $3.72 million with respect to the 17th Street project. The promissory note was for a period 30 years—10 years greater than what was approved by the Lynn Haven City Commission – and required Lynn Haven to pay interest of 2.55 per cent annually and make monthly payments to Company B. In financing the 17th Street project with Company B, Lynn Haven agreed to pay Company B approximately $1.6 million, as interest, in addition to the $3.72 million the City would pay Company B for its work on the 17th Street project contract.

**THIS WAS THE BIG LIE, THE LIE THAT CAUSED JUDGE MARK WALKER TO UNSEAL THE GRAND JURY TRANSCRIPTS. FBI AGENT BORGHINI TESTIFIED TO THE GRAND JURY THAT I CHANGED THIS PROMISSORY NOTE FROM 20 YEARS TO 30 YEARS WITHOUT COMMISSION APPROVAL, THAT I DID IT ON MY OWN. A VIDEO OF THE COMMISSION MEETING SHOWS THAT THE FULL COMMISSION MADE THIS DECISION BY A UNANIMOUS VOTE, AND OF COURSE, AS MAYOR, I SIGNED THE DOCUMENT.**

44.   On July 29, 2017, MARGO DEAL ANDERSON and the Lynn Haven Commission approved a resolution authorizing the issuance by Lynn Haven of a $3,910,000 municipal revenue bond and a loan agreement to be signed with a financial institution to provide the funding for Lynn Haven to pay for infrastructure work in the City that was to be conducted by Company B. The term of the loan was for 10 years and the interest rate was 2.18 per cent per annum.

ANDERSON signed the resolution and bond loan agreement.

45.     On August 9, 2017, MARGO DEAL ANDERSON signed an agreement between Lynn Haven and Company B designating Company B to be the contractor or vendor for various projects that would be conducted in Lynn Haven under a ½ Cent Surtax Design/Build Contract, utilizing proceeds from the ½ cent Bay County sales tax that was in effect for ten years. This agreement, negotiated by ANDERSON and the owner of Company B, made Company B the contractor for numerous multi-million dollar Lynn Haven infrastructure projects that would not require any bid procedure for any of the projects related to the agreement **WITHOUT BELABORING THE POINT, EVERY SINGLE CONTRACT INVOLVING COMPANY B, PHOENIX CONSTRUCTION, WAS DONE WITH FULL COMMISSION APPROVAL, UNANIMOUS VOTE. ALL OF THESE CHARGES ARE FALSE, AND MISLEADING, BY ASSISTANT U.S. ATTORNEY KUNZ, USING THE WORDS, MARGO ANDERSON SIGNED, OR MARGO ANDERSON APPROVED, INSTEAD OF THE COMMISSION. BOTH KUNZ AND BORGHINI SHOULD HAVE BEEN INDICTED THEMSELVES FOR LYING TO THE GRAND JURY.**

46.     On October 24, 2017, the owner of Company B sent a letter to City Manager M. White advising that he had completed phase one of the project earning the total amount ($3.8 million) authorized to date. The letter further stated that Company B would proceed with the next phase but not invoice Lynn Haven until the City had obtained the new loan. The amount of the referenced additional work was $1.8 million submitted by Company B in an invoice in January 2018.

47.     MARGO DEAL ANDERSON directed M. White to allow Company B to proceed as requested with the work despite no funding being available, a new loan had not been obtained, the City had not approved the specific roads that Company B was paving, and engineering work had not been completed on many of the roads that Company B had finished its work on.

48.     On December 12, 2017, MARGO DEAL ANDERSON and the Lynn Haven Commission approved a resolution authorizing the issuance by Lynn Haven of a $6,090,000 municipal revenue bond and a loan agreement to be signed with a financial institution to provide the funding for Lynn Haven to pay for infrastructure work in the City that was to be conducted by Company B. The term of the loan was for 10 years, and the interest rate was 2.35 per cent per annum. ANDERSON signed the resolution and bond

loan agreement.

49.     On January 4, 2018, Company B submitted an application to Lynn Haven for payment of $1,850,170.66 for work performed on phase two during approximately a two-month period.

50.     In June 2018, the owner of Company B and MARGO DEAL ANDERSON requested City Manager M. White to proceed with an additional phase of the 17th Street project. M. White told ANDERSON and the owner of Company B that he wanted to put the project on hold as it was going to cost the City a large amount of money to continue the project and the City did not have the money to pay for the project at that time. ANDERSON and the owner of Company B told M. White that the owner of Company B wanted to proceed with the project.

51.     ANDERSON pressured M. White to have Lynn Haven proceed with the project and stated that the owner of Company B would finance the additional approximate $1 million cost of the project. Despite protestations by City Manager M. White that Lynn Haven did not need the additional debt, ANDERSON directed M. White to make it happen.

52.     On August 21, 2018, Lynn Haven advertised for sealed bids from businesses to perform additional work on the 17th Street project. Since the Florida Department of Transportation (FDOT) had become a partner with Lynn Haven to provide some of the funding for the project, MARGO DEAL ANDERSON, and Lynn Haven were required to solicit bids for the additional work on the 17th Street project and obtain the concurrence of FDOT.

53.     Three sealed bids for the additional work on the 17th Street Project were submitted: one from Company B, one from a relative of Company B's owner, and one from Company A. In the past, these three companies had bid on contracts with public entities, agreeing among themselves that one company would submit the lowest bid on a specific project and the other two companies would submit higher bids. Then, in another public project, a different company would submit the lowest bid. Company B's $957,000 bid was determined to be the lowest bid and recommended to be awarded to Company B by the Lynn Haven City Engineer.

54.     The sealed bid procedure was intended to make it appear as if the award of the additional work for the project was fair and above board, and would receive the concurrence of the FDOT, which had signed a Joint Participation Agreement with Lynn Haven in the 17th Street project. Seven months before the selection of Company B for the additional work on the 17th Street project, the owner of

Company B arranged to have the Lynn Haven City Engineer sell his 2006 ITAS Motorhome (Motorhome), valued at least at approximately $106,000, to MARGO DEAL ANDERSON without the payment of any money by ANDERSON, by the following means:

a. The owner of Company B issued a personal check to the City Engineer in the amount of $75,000, which allowed the City Engineer to pay off, with additional funds that he possessed, a $105,993.70 loan on the Motorhome.

b. The motor vehicle title for the Motorhome was transferred to the name of ANDERSON'S husband after the City engineer initially listed the purchaser as the owner of Company B;

c. The transfer of title filed with the Florida Division of Motor Vehicles falsely stated that $35,000 was paid by ANDERSON's husband to purchase the Motorhome;

d. The Motorhome was titled in the name of ANDERSON's husband;

e. No money was paid by ANDERSON or her husband to obtain this Motorhome valued at approximately $106,000; and

**ASSISTANT U.S. ATTORNEY STATED THIS AT THE PRESS CONFERENCE, THAT NO MONEY WAS PAID. MY HUSBAND PAID $35,000 IN CASH TO FINCH AS A DOWN PAYMENT AND PAID THE REMAINDER ON DECEMBER 31, 2019. AFTER THREE YEARS, THE GOVERNMENT WOULD FINALLY RETURN OUR PROPERTY TO US. ANOTHER BOGUS CHARGE.**

f. Approximately 22 months after the transfer of the Motorhome to ANDERSON and her husband, ANDERSON's husband issued a $20,000 check to the owner of Company B. This action followed the public reporting of the Federal investigation into public officials in Lynn Haven, including an indictment of two Lynn Haven public officials and three other individuals charged with conspiracy, fraud, and related offenses arising from the defrauding of Lynn Haven. That indictment included allegations that the Lynn Haven Mayor received post-hurricane repairs to her private property and the work was paid for by Lynn Haven based upon fraudulent invoices that concealed and did not disclose that work performed for Lynn Haven was instead performed at a number of public officials' private residences and the private residences of a few other individuals yet billed as work performed at Lynn Haven public properties.

55.     On November 6, 2018, MARGO DEAL ANDERSON voted for and signed a resolution of Lynn Haven amending the Joint Participation Agreement with FDOT relating to the 17th Street project stating that Lynn Haven had agreed to contract for and complete the work as described in the Joint Participation Agreement with Company B.

56.     On November 7, 2018, less than a month after Hurricane Michael and at the time that the owner of Company B complained to MARGO DEAL ANDERSON about not receiving enough hurricane clean-up work, M. White awarded the contract to Company B and executed a contract for Company B to perform an additional amount of work on the 17th Street project in exchange for $957,000. As directed by ANDERSON, this amount was added to the amount of the March 2017 promissory note that Lynn Haven had signed payable to Company B, increasing the amount that Lynn Haven agreed to pay Company B for the project to $5,178,555. In addition, Lynn Haven was required to pay 2.55 per cent interest annually to Company B on the new note amount.

57.     During the same period of time that MARGO DEAL ANDERSON provided approval for Company B to proceed with the 17th Street project, and for which Company B received from Lynn Haven regular monthly payments of approximately $15,000 (including interest) and subsequent work by Company B, and during the same time period that ANDERSON provided approvals for Company B, signed various documents, and caused Lynn Haven to incur significant financial obligations for Company B to proceed with numerous projects in Lynn Haven pursuant to the ½ cent Surtax Design/Build Contract, MARGO DEAL ANDERSON, in addition to receiving a free Motorhome from the owner of Company B, also accepted things of value from the owner of Company B, including travel in a private airplane to Biloxi, Mississippi, and the Florida Keys, and lodging, meals, and entertainment.

World Claim Insurance

58.     Following Hurricane Michael, Lynn Haven received a request from WorldClaim public adjusters to work with Lynn Haven to assist in documentation and adjustment of its claim with insurance companies with respect to losses that Lynn Haven incurred on October 10, 2018, associated with Hurricane Michael. Individual

A, a Lynn Haven public official, strongly recommended to the City Manager that Lynn Haven select WorldClaim.

59. Individual A advised City Manager M. White that a conspirator was to receive a percentage of whatever business the conspirator brought to WorldClaim, and that the conspirator would split with Individual A whatever business was obtained from the City. Individual A told M. White that if Lynn Haven selected WorldClaim, Individual A would give to M. White some of the money that Individual A was receiving from the conspirator, and M. White, MARGO DEAL ANDERSON, and a Lynn Haven Commissioner would not be charged any claims fees by WorldClaim to adjust any private insurance claims for those public officials.

60. On October 24, 2018, and pursuant to the continuing Declaration of Emergency, MARGO DEAL ANDERSON and M. White signed a contract retaining WorldClaim to assist in documentation and adjustment of Lynn Haven's claim under a primary insurance policy with respect to losses that occurred due to Hurricane Michael. The contract obligated Lynn Haven to pay a sliding fee scale from 3 to 10 per cent of the net recovery between $0 and $60 million. This contract was entered into without any request for bids or requests for qualifications, incurring a significant financial obligation for the City, in accordance with a local state of emergency resolution that had been extended by Lynn Haven for seven days the day before the signing of the WorldClaim contract and which emergency resolution was scheduled to, and did expire, six days later.

61. Following Hurricane Michael, City Manager M. White sought a claims adjuster for his personal residence and farm for damages sustained to the properties. White asked Individual A if WorldClaim could help MARGO DEAL ANDERSON, M. White, and a City Commissioner. Individual A advised that WorldClaim would help all three public officials. WorldClaim handled the insurance claims for hurricane damage to the private residences and properties of ANDERSON, M. White and a City Commissioner.

62. WorldClaim sent M. White a bill in the amount of $10,000 for its work in adjusting the insurance claims of M. White relating to his private property. The invoice amount of $10,000 was marked through, there were initials next to the mark, and zero dollars was shown as the amount due. M. White told both MARGO DEAL ANDERSON and a City Commissioner that WorldClaim was going to help them with their insurance claims at no cost to them. WorldClaim agreed to charge both ANDERSON and a City

Commissioner no fee for its work in adjusting the insurance claims of ANDERSON and the City Commissioner relating to their private property.

63. No money was paid by the City Commissioner for WorldClaim to represent him and assisting him in obtaining approximately $75,000 from an insurance company for damages done to his private property. Through the efforts of WorldClaim representing her and assisting her with her insurance claim, MARGO DEAL ANDERSON obtained approximately $81,125 from an insurance company for damages done to her private property. After the federal investigation of ANDERSON and others was made public, ANDERSON issued a check to WorldClaim for a reduced fee of only $3,646.

**WHEN THE GRAND JURY CONVENED IN JUNE 2020, THEY WERE TOLD THAT I RECEIVED A PRO BONO CONTRACT. THEY WERE NOT TOLD THAT I REJECTED THE CONTRACT AND NEGOTIATED A CONTRACT FOR 6% WHICH I PAID IN FULL. COMMISSIONER DAN RUSSELL *DID* SIGN A PRO BONO CONTRACT, RECEIVED 75,000, AND WAS NOT CHARGED WITH A CRIME.**

64. As Mayor of Lynn Haven, MARGO DEAL ANDERSON was a public official who was required under Florida law to file a Form 9, "Quarterly Gift Disclosure" with the Florida Commission on Ethics if she accepted a gift valued at more than $100. This Form 9 was required to be filed during the calendar quarter for which the gift was received, and describe the gift, the name and address of the person making the gift, and the date the gift was received. ANDERSON failed to file a Quarterly Gift Disclosure form as required by Florida law from the date of her election as Lynn Haven Mayor in 2015 through June of 2020, despite receiving numerous things of value in excess of $100 from various individuals. ANDERSON concealed the receipt of these items.

65. As the City Attorney for Lynn Haven, JOSEPH ADAM ALBRITTON was a public official who was required under Florida law to file a Form 9, "Quarterly Gift Disclosure" with the Florida Commission on Ethics if he accepted a gift valued at more than $100. This Form 9 was required to be filed during the calendar quarter for which the gift was received, and describe the gift, the name and address of the person making the gift, and the date the gift was received. ALBRITTON failed to file a Quarterly Gift Disclosure form as required by Florida law from the date of his appointment as City Attorney in October 2018 through June of 2020, despite receiving numerous things of value in excess of $100

from various individuals. ALBRITTON concealed the receipt of these items.

66.     MARGO DEAL ANDERSON directed Lynn Haven employees to assemble, print, and provide various city records to her that she in turn provided Company B relating to ongoing and planned Lynn Haven projects.

67.     On or about July 13, 2020, the owner of Company B made false statements to a Special Agents of the Federal Bureau of Investigation concerning the transfer of the 200 ITAS motorhome to MARGO DEAL ANDERSON and her husband, and provided to the Special Agents a claimed bill of sale relating to the motor home that falsely stated the motor home was sold by the owner of Company B to Anderson's husband on July 6, 2018, for $70,000 that was paid "half down and half due with 6 percent interest."

68.     The conspirators performed acts and made statements to hide and conceal, and cause to be hidden and concealed, the purpose of the conspiracy and the acts committed in furtherance thereof.

All in violation of Title 18, United States Code, Section 1349.

### COUNTS TWO THROUGH TWENTY-EIGHT
#### A.   INTRODUCTION

The allegations of Count One, Section A, are herby realleged and incorporated by reference as if fully set forth herein.

#### B.   THE CHARGE

Between on or about August 1, 2015, and on or about August 11, 2020, in the Northern District of Florida and elsewhere, the defendants,

### MARGO DEAL ANDERSON
### And
### JOSEPH ADAM ALBRITTON

did knowingly and willfully devise and intend to devise a scheme to defraud and for obtaining money and property by means of material false and fraudulent pretenses, representations, and promises, and for the purpose of executing such scheme, did cause wire communications to be transmitted in interstate and foreign commerce.

#### C.   SCHEME TO DEFRAUD

It was part of the scheme to defraud that:

The allegations of Count One, Section C, Paragraphs 1-68, are hereby realleged and incorporated by reference as if fully set forth herein.

### D. WIRE COMMUNICATIONS

On or about the following dates, for the purpose of executing the scheme to defraud, the defendants,

**BECAUSE I WAS CHARGED WITH 'CONSPIRACY' I WAS CHARGED WITH EVERY ONE OF THESE WIRE COMMUNICATIONS, WHICH WERE BETWEEN MICHAEL WHITE, ADAM ALBRITTON, AND MICKEY WHITE, AS WELL AS EVERY CHECK WRITTEN BY THE CITY TO ECS, WORLDCLAIM, AND OTHERS.**

MARGO DEAL ANDERSON
And
JOSEPH ADAM ALBRITTON,

Knowingly did cause wire communications to be transmitted in interstate and foreign commerce as set forth below:

COUNT          DATE                         WIRE COMMUNICATION

TWO            October 24, 2017             Email with letter from M. White
to engineering firm

THREE          October 23, 2018             Text messages between
                                            ALBRITTON and D. White re
Work @306 N. Palo Alto

FOUR           October 23, 2018             Text message ALBRITTON to
D.White requesting ECS invoice

FIVE           October 24, 2018             Text messages between
ALBRITTON and D. White requesting electrician at girlfriend's residence

SIX            October 26, 2018             Deposit of $224,722.75 check
and related wire

SEVEN October 30, 2018          Email from ALBRITTON to City
Manager re use of Company A pit

EIGHT October 30, 2018          Text message from M. White to City
Engineer to cancel permit application

NINE          November 1, 2018          Email from M. White to
Company C directing it to use Company B pit

TEN          November 8, 2018          Email including letter of M.
White to State of Florida requesting approval for DDMS site for Company
B

ELEVEN          November 8, 2018          Text messages between
ALBRITTON and D. White requesting D White to come sign task **order**

TWELVE          November 9, 2018          Text messages between
ALBRITTON and D. White to go to 2114 CC Dr., tarp and patch broken
windows

THIRTEEN          November 9, 2018          Text messages between M. White
and D. White re ANDERSON'S property clean-up

FOURTEEN          November 15, 2018          Text messages between
ALBRITTON and D. White re needing invoice

FIFTEEN          November 15, 2018          Deposit of $1,288,716.54 check
and related wire

SIXTEEN          November 19, 2018          Email from ALBRITTON to
Company A Executive re justification for Company A pit

SEVENTEEN  November 28, 2018          Text message from D. White to
ALBRITTON ("$$$")

EIGHTEEN          November 30, 2018          Deposit of $433,365.85 check
and related wire

NINETEEN          December 14, 2018          Deposit of $515,731.31 check
and related wire

TWENTY          December 26, 2018          Text messages of M. White and
D. White re ANDERSON has a "good job" for D. White

TWENTY-
ONE          December 31, 2018          Deposit of $725,941.09 check
and related wire

TWENTY-

| TWO | January 7, 2019 | Text messages of ALBRITTON |

and M. White

TWENTY-
THREE  January 14, 2019  Text messages between
ALBRITTON and D. White requesting D. White to sign addendum to
Lynn Haven contract

TWENTY-
FOUR  January 15, 2019  Deposit of $895,441.52 check
and related wire

TWENTY-
FIVE  January 16, 2019  Text messages between
ALBRITTON and D. White re trailer invoice

TWENTY-
SIX  January 31, 2019  Deposit of $433,259.16 check
and related wire

TWENTY-
SEVEN February 18, 2019  Text message from ALBRITTON to d.
White re need for enclosed trailer

TWENTY-
EIGHT March 9, 2019  Text message from ALBRITTON to D.
White re need for invoice for both storage units

In violation of Title 18, United States Code, Sections 1343 and 2.

## COUNT TWENTY-NINE

Between on or about October 10, 2018, and on or about April 30, 2019, in the Northern District of Florida, and elsewhere, the defendants,

### MARGO DEAL ANDERSON
And
### JOSEPH ADAM ALBRITTON,

being agents of an organization and agency of the local government, that is, the City of Lynn Haven, Florida, receiving in the one-year period beginning October 10, 2018, benefits in excess of $10,000 under a federal program involving grants, contracts, subsidies, loans, guarantees, and other forms of federal assistance, did knowingly embezzle, steal, obtain by fraud, without authority convert to the use of a person other than the rightful owner, and intentionally misapply property that was valued at $5,000 or more and under the care, custody, and control of such organization, local government, and agency.

In violation of Title 18, United States Code, Sections 666(a)(1)(A) and 2.

## COUNTS THIRTY THROUGH SIXTY-TWO

### I.        Introduction

The allegations of Count One, Section A, are hereby realleged and incorporated by reference as if fully set forth herein.

### II.        The Charge

Between on or about August 1, 2015, and on or about August 11, 2020, in the Northern District of Florida and elsewhere, the defendants,

### MARGO DEAL ANDERSON
### And
### JOSEPH ADAM ALBRITTON,

did knowingly and willfully devise and intend to devise a scheme to defraud and deprive the City of Lynn Haven and its citizens of their right to the honest services of ANDERSON, the elected Mayor of Lynn Haven, Florida, and ALBRITTON, the City Attorney for Lynn Haven, Florida, through bribery or kickbacks.

### III.        The Fraudulent Scheme

The fraudulent scheme is summarized in paragraphs 1 through 68 of Section C of Count One, which are realleged and incorporated by reference as if fully set forth herein.

### IV.        Wire Communications

On or about the following dates, in the Northern District of Florida and elsewhere, the defendants,

### MARGO DEAL ANDERSON
### AND
### JOSEPH ADAM ALBRITTON,

for the purpose of executing the fraudulent scheme, caused wire communications to be transmitted in interstate commerce as set forth below.

| COUNT | DATE | WIRE TRANSMISSION |
|---|---|---|
| THIRTY and related wire | October 6, 2017 | Deposit of $2,272,669.87 check |

THIRTY-
ONE            October 13, 2017            Deposit of $72,000 check and
related wire

THIRTY-
TWO                        October 25, 2017            Email of letter from M.
White to engineering firm

THIRTY-
THREE            November 6, 2017    Deposit of $1,455,330.13
check and related wire

THIRTY-
FOUR            January 8, 2018            Deposit of
$1,850,170.66 check and related wire

THIRTY-
FIVE            February 16, 2018    Deposit of $75,000
check from owner of Company B into the account of Individual A for
Motorhome and related wire

THIRTY-
SIX            October 23, 2018            Text message
ALBRITTON to D. White requesting ECS invoice

THIRTY-
SEVEN            October 24, 2018        Text messages
between ALBRITTON and D. White requesting electrician at girlfriend's
residence

THIRTY-
EIGHT            October 26, 2018    Deposit of $224,722.75
check and related wire

THIRTY-
NINE            October 30, 2018    Email from
ALBRITTON to City Manager re use of Company A pit

FORTY            October 30, 2018    Text message from M.
White to City Engineer to cancel permit application

FORTY-
ONE            November 1, 2018        Email from M. White

to Company C directing it to use Company B pit

FORTY-
TWO                November 8, 2018        Email including letter
of M. White to State of Florida requesting approval for DDMS site for
Company B.

FORTY-
THREE        November 8, 2018     Text messages between
ALBRITTON and D. White requesting D. White to come sign task order.

FORTY-
FOUR             November 9, 2018     Text messages between M.
White and D. White re ANDERSON property cleanup

FORTY-
FIVE             November 9, 2018     Text messages between
ALBRITTON and D. White to go to 2114 CC Dr., tarp & patch broken
windows

FORTY-
SIX             November 15, 2018     Text messages between
ALBRITTON AND d. White re needing invoice

FORTY-
SEVEN          November 15, 2018    Deposit of $1,288,716.54
check and related wire

FORTY-
EIGHT            November 28, 2018        Text message from D.
White to ALBRITTON ("$$$")

FORTY-
NINE             November 30, 2018       Deposit of $433,365.85
check and related wire

FIFTY             December 14, 2018       Deposit of $515,731.31
check and related wire

FIFTY-
ONE             December 26, 2018          Text messages
of M. White and D. White re ANDERSON has a "good job" for D. White

FIFTY-
TWO                    December 31, 2018        Deposit of
$725,941.09 check and related wire

FIFTY-
THREE                  January 7, 2019          Text message of M.
White and ALBRITTON

FIFTY-
FOUR                   January 14, 2019         Text messages between
ALBRITTON and D. White requesting D. White to sign addendum to
Lynn haven contract

FIFTY-
FIVE                   January 15, 2019         Deposit of
$895,441.52 check and related wire

FIFTY-
SIX                    January 16, 2019         Text messages
between ALBRITTON AND d. White re trailer invoice

FIFTY-
SEVEN                  January 31, 2019         Deposit of
$433,259.16 check and related wire

FIFTY-
EIGHT                  February 8, 2019         Email from
WorldClaim to Anderson including attachment of contract and no fee
addendum for WorldClaim to be private insurance adjuster
FIFTY-
NINE                   February 12, 2019        Email from
ANDERSON to WorldClaim including signed contract for WorldClaim to
be private insurance adjuster

SIXTY                  February 18, 2019        Text message from
ALBRITTON to D. White re need for invoice for enclosed trailer

SIXTY-
ONE                    March 9, 2019            Text message from
ALBRITTON to D. White re need for invoice for both storage units

SIXTY-
TWO                    January 16, 2020         Deposit of $20,000

check on ANDERSON account payable to Company B owner and related wire

In violation of Title 18, United States Code, Sections 1343, 1346, and 2

## COUNT SIXTY-THREE

On or about November 18, 2019, in the Northern District of Florida and elsewhere, the defendant,

## MARGO DEAL ANDERSON

did knowingly and willfully make materially false, fictitious, and fraudulent statements and representations in a matter within the executive branch of the Government of the United States, that is, the defendant falsely stated that:

    a.    ANDERSON was unaware of the role of Erosion Control Specialists (ECS) in the post-Hurricane Michael clean-up of Lynn Haven; and

    b.    ANDERSON was first introduced to David "Mickey" white in December 2018 or January 2019, when volunteers were used to clean up various streets designated by Lynn Haven as needing some attention and clean-up.

These statements and representations were false because, as ANDERSON then well knew:

    a.    ANDERSON was aware that ECS had been contracted by Lynn Haven to conduct debris removal and repairs in the City of Lynn Haven after Hurricane Michael;

    b.    ANDERSON was introduced to David "Mickey" white through City Manager Michael White shortly after Hurricane Michael and requested David "Mickey" White to have ECS clean up her private residence.

In violation of title 18, United States Code Section 1001(a)(2)

## COUNT SIXTY-FOUR

## A. CHARGE

Between on or about October 10, 2018, and April 1, 2019, in the Northern District of Florida and elsewhere, the defendant,

## JOSEPH ADAM ALBRITTON,

Did knowingly and willfully devise, and intend to devise, a scheme to defraud and for obtaining money and property by means of materially false and fraudulent pretenses, representations, and promises, and for the purpose of executing such scheme, did cause a matter to be delivered by the United States Postal Service and commercial interstate carrier.

## B.   SCHEME TO DEFRAUD

It was part of the scheme to defraud that:
1.      The defendant, JOSEPH ADAM ALBRITTON, made and caused to be made, false and fraudulent representations to the St. John's Insurance Company concerning damages to his residence in Lynn haven, Florida, as a result of Hurricane Michael in order to fraudulently obtain money from the St. John's Insurance Company.
2.      JOSEPH ADAM ALBRITTON represented in a claim that his residence had been damaged by Hurricane Michael and falsely represented that he had paid for tree removal, debris removal, and installation of a tarp to his residence totaling $9,600.
3.      In fact, the tree removal, debris removal, and installation of a tarp to the residence and property of JOSEPH ADAM ALBRITTON had been made by Erosion Control Specialist (ECS) at no cost to him, as ECs received payment from the City of Lynn haven for its employees making the repairs and conducting debris removal at ALBRITTON'S residence.  However, the City of Lynn Haven was not aware that ECS had made repairs to ALBRITTON'S personal residence, as the City of Lynn Haven was falsely billed for alleged work on city properties.
4.      To facilitate the scheme, JOSEPH ADAM ALBRITTON solicited ECS to create a false and fictitious invoice attesting to repair work done to his residence after the hurricane by ECS in the amount of $9,600, and that the amount of the invoice was paid in full on October 24, 2018, which invoice ALBRITTON then submitted to St. John's Insurance Company in support of his fraudulent insurance claim.
5.      Based upon the false claim, St. John's Insurance Company issued payment in the amount of $6,100 to JOSEPH ADAM ALBRITTON that was based upon the false ECS invoice for the tree removal, debris removal, and installation of a tarp to ALBRITTON's residence and represented payment of the $9,600 less a deductible under the insurance property.  This payment was mailed to ALBRITTON'S address in Lynn Haven.  ALBRITTON

caused the St. John's Insurance Company insurance check to be deposited into a bank account belonging to him.

## C.   MAILING

On or about November 29, 2018, the defendant,

### JOSEPH ADAM ALBRITTON,

knowingly did, for the purpose of executing the fraudulent scheme and attempting to do so, cause to be transmitted by United States mail and private and commercial carrier, a $6,100 check issued from the St. Johns Insurance Company.

In violation of Title 18, United States Code, Sections 1341 and 2.

### CRIMINAL FORFEITURE

The allegations contained in Counts One through Sixty-Two, and Sixty-Four of this indictment are hereby realleged and incorporated by reference for purpose of alleging forfeiture. From their engagement in the violations alleged in Counts One through Sixty-Two, and Sixty-Four of this Indictment, the defendants,

### MARGO DEAL ANDERSON
And
### JOSEPH ADAM ALBRITTON,

Shall forfeit to the United States, pursuant to Title 18, United States Code, Section 981(a)(1)(C), and Title 28, United States Code, Section 2461(c), any and all of the defendants' right, title, and interest in any property, real and personal, constituting, and derived from, proceeds traceable to such offenses, including the following:

a.   2006 ITAS Motorhome, VIN#4UZACKDC26CW30357

If any of the property described above as being subject to forfeiture, as a result of acts or omissions of the defendants:

i.      Cannot be located upon the exercise of due diligence;
ii.     Has been transferred, sold to, or deposited with a third party;
iii.    Has been placed beyond the jurisdiction of this Court;
iv.    Has been substantially diminished in value; or
v.     Has been commingled with other property that cannot be subdivided without difficulty,

It is the intent of the United States, pursuant to Title 21, United States Code, Section 853(p), as incorporated by Title 28, United States Code, Section 2461(c) , to seek forfeiture of any other property of said defendant up to the value of the forfeitable property.

A TRUE BILL:
(SIGNATURE BLACKED OUT)
FOREPERSON

08/18/2020

LAWRENCE KEEFE
United States Attorney

STEPHEN M. KUNZ
Assistant United States Attorney

 

This initial indictment was a travesty; a document which was legally insufficient but was also based on the lies of Michael White and others who had pled guilty, who knew that I was the person who had gone to Sheriff Tommy Ford with the information which led to their arrests. Just a few months after I was arrested, the government would drop 38 of the 64 charges against me, in a second, or superseding indictment, which would include my friend, owner of Phoenix Construction, James Finch.

My therapist, Denise Folsom, suggested to me that when I became overwhelmed, to write down whatever I was feeling, and to keep a type of journal. I started seeing her in November of 2019, after I was first named in the indictment of Michael White and the others; I was still devastated from all that we went through with Hurricane Michael, and processing the public outlash and the media covering the "corruption of Lynn Haven" just became overwhelming. Throughout this book there will be journal entries of what I would sometimes write on a single sheet of notebook paper, or sometimes sit at the computer and pour out my heart, sitting at the desk in my bedroom, usually late at night when I could not sleep. Writing became a mode of survival for me during the nearly three years of living as an indicted defendant, under conditions of release, always mindful of the phrase, The United States of America vs. Margo Deal Anderson.

AUGUST 28, 2020

"Woke up many times feeling like I can't breathe, wondering how this can be happening to us. Lee keeps holding his breath in his sleep, and waking up, sitting up in bed. Yesterday, my concealed carry permit was suspended by the Department of Agriculture Secretary Nikki Fried, after the prosecution was angered by Magistrate Judge's ruling to allow me to keep one firearm for my person protection. My 2nd amendment rights have been taken and I have not gone to trial yet. Guilty until proven innocent."

"Who was the private investigator following me about and who hired him or her? How did they know when I was traveling and why? We have made no secret of our friendship. (I am speaking of James Finch and the videos on the news media of our traveling together on his plane.)

"It is only 7:45 a.m. and I am supposed to call my pre-trial officer to discuss directions for travel. I am so shaken and nervous that I feel afraid. I don't know why. The last time I met Kimberly Barrett (the pre-trial officer) I was chained by ankles and handcuffs and answered her questions to be able to see the judge. She was business-like, but kind. Why am I afraid?"

"I read at all times of the night last night about federal indictments and the statistics for acquittal are horrible—how will I prove I am innocent?"

"I am so worried about Lee—he is so sick. I am afraid he will have a heart attack. Lord, help us!"

"What does my daughter think of me, how humiliated and embarrassed she must be right now. Will my granddaughters ever be able to feel the same about me? Will they be distrustful or fearful of Mimi, who loves them so much?"

"My Mom, by brother, they must be just sick with worry; I cannot imagine how I would feel if I were helpless, watching one of them go through this. It has to almost be worse than the one it is happening to."

SEPTEMBER 20, 2020

"I listened to Joel Osteen's sermon before I went to bed last night entitled, "The Rewards of Integrity" and I realized how much I have lost. The Bible speaks of how a good name is worth more than riches."

"Why has this prosecutor and this Sheriff targeted me? They have taken everything from me. The pastor of the church in Lynn Haven, my friend, Tom Daniel, sounded different on the phone when I spoke to him, cordial, but cold, distant. My daughter has supported me, and I know she loves me, but I also know how embarrassed she is because I know how embarrassed and ashamed I feel, and I know I am innocent."

"My devotional today is to find peace by bringing my needs, my hopes and my fears to the Lord, to stop trying to plan and control what will happen to me in the future."

"I have been afraid because the meeting Lee has planned with the lawyers has been cancelled twice, first because of a death in the lawyer's family and now because of the hurricane in Pensacola, Hurricane Sally. I am so anxious and need to know this decision about my defense has been made and a plan for how we can sell the house to pay the attorney's fees, but I will "be still and have peace", I will wait on the Lord and praise His name."

Lee and James went to meet with my attorney, Ron Johnson, after the arraignment in Tallahassee, to speak with him and talk with him about my defense. I was not allowed to have contact with James after the arraignment, of August 25, 2020, but James had told me that he was going to help me to find attorneys who could represent me against such an overwhelming indictment. Lee and I had paid Ron Johnson $25,000 at this point, and while I really liked Mr. Johnson, I was terrified after the arraignment hearing in Tallahassee and the demeanor of the Assistant U.S. Attorney, Jason Coody, who had been in the courtroom that day.

James gave Lee the name of an attorney he knew in Tallahassee, and Lee set up the appointment with Rob Vezina. I met with Rob, who had also brought in criminal attorneys Jimmy Judkins and Tony Bajoczky for the meeting. The three of them talked with me for a long time, and the question they asked me that I liked the most was, "you are not planning to plead guilty?" I assured them that I was innocent, and I was ready to fight. I signed a contract with them, and James sent them the $200,000.00 for the escrow account which meant they would begin my defense. (I had given James a quit claim deed to my house in Lynn Haven).

I wrote Ron Johnson a letter, thanking him for his help through the indictment and arraignment, and let him know that I was terminating our relationship.

The prosecutors, within the next months, tried to disqualify my attorneys because James was paying for them; they failed.

December 21, 2020

An Unmailed Letter to James Finch
(James and I were not allowed to have contact as a condition of my release when indicted as he had been named as Company B in the indictment. Later our attorneys would petition the Court for us to work together as co-defendants, but in the interim, the Government even came after our attorneys and tried to disqualify them.)

Dear James:
I cannot believe that Christmas will be here in just four more days. I am excited about the Christmas star tonight, they say it is a once in a lifetime to see the star so close to earth; I am doing all that I can to be optimistic and full of hope, because this is my favorite time of year.

I have lived under such stress and humiliation since April of 2019 that I no longer feel like the same person I was. I have watched my photograph in the local news as a criminal for almost two years, and I learned what it felt like to be chained by the ankles in the basement of a federal courthouse for eight hours not knowing what I had been charged with.

I know that I am blessed beyond measure to have your friendship and the support that you have already given me is something I will never understand but will forever be thankful for no matter how this turns out. If you ever have doubt that you are loved in this world, lease do not ever doubt mine, because I love you as much as if you were my own brother, and there is nothing I would not do for you.

I cannot sleep because I have nightmares of spending the rest of my life in a prison; I have read the jury instructions for 64 counts, entangled with Adam and the charges against him, and knowing the average intelligence and beliefs of the people in the area that this jury pool will come from, I am not optimistic at them being able to understand the instructions, or that they will be able to even understand what I am charged with, because I still do not understand how I am charged with being a conspirator to steal 5 million dollars when I am not connected with any money in the indictment.

I have always been a strong person, but this is not just about me, it is about the lives of Lee, you, my Mom, my brother, my daughter, my granddaughters, and it is breaking my heart. They have worried that I would have a heart attack or a stroke, or even do something to myself because the stress has gone on for so long, but I want you to know that I will be there to fight for myself and everyone I love, including you.

I am hoping for a miracle from the meeting with the attorneys and the prosecutors on January 5th, but if it does not happen I will continue to work to do everything I can to help the attorneys with evidence, and I continue to have faith that we will win and the Lord is on our side. I have not had a lot in my life, but I have never stolen from anyone, and I have never done anything intentionally to hurt anyone. I don't have that gene.

I hope that you can forget about all of this for a few days and enjoy a blessed Christmas with Ashley and your family, and I pray for a better New Year for all of us. I continue to pray for your complete healing and recovery.

Merry Christmas, James, maybe next year this will all be over for us; 2021 has to be a better year.


Sometimes it is better not to be able to see the future; we would spend two more Christmas seasons after this one fighting for our lives. Just three months after writing this unsent letter, James would be indicted, and my precious Mom would pass away from a massive heart attack two weeks after that.

Throughout that terrible first Christmas season after my indictment, the media in Bay County continued to report about our case, and on January 21, 2021, *The Panama City News Herald,* story, "Federal court denies indicted former Lynn Haven mayor's motion to withhold some charges," was on the front page. My attorney, Rob, Vezina, wrote a searing response to them because the article was so biased and inaccurate. The editor never printed an apology but instead, corrected the story, to some degree, and added the following: *Editor's note:: This story has been corrected from its original version. The previous version misstated the federal government's response to the defendant's motion.*

All three of the media outlets in Bay County, Florida were used to push the narrative of the prosecutors throughout our case, and the following is the letter my attorney wrote to the Executive Editor of the *News Herald:*

Panama City News Herald

c/o Lisa Nellessen Savage, Executive Editor
501 W. 11th Street
Panama City, Florida 32401

Re: Inaccurate Article about former Lynn Haven Mayor

"Dear Ms. Savage:

We represent Margo Deal Anderson. On January 21, 2021, the News Herald published an article about Ms. Anderson titled, "Federal court denies indicted former Lynn Haven mayor's motion to withhold some charges." The article is demonstrably inaccurate. The article makes repeated references to decision made or actions taken by the Court when, in fact, the Court has made no such decision and takes no such action. The attached copy of the docket report as of the writing of this letter demonstrates that the Court order(s) referenced in the article does not exist. Instead, the author recklessly conflates the government's opposition to the motions as an order of the Court, and the News Herald published it. We demand that the article be retracted with the same prominence with which it was inaccurately published.

As a secondary matter, the motions discussed in the article are procedural in nature, and the Court's ultimate ruling on the motions bears no relationship to the merits of the allegations or the outcome of the case. A federal judge (unrelated to this case) once commented that the government, if it so chooses, can indict anyone, anytime, for any reason. The statement is not far from the truth. The government solely controls the scope and diligence of the investigation; it solely controls the facts alleged in an indictment; and it solely controls the facts presented and the manner and means of the presentation of facts to a grand jury that decides whether to indict an accused person. The accused person has no recourse in the federal justice system to rebut inaccurate and incomplete allegations until his or her day in court. This is critical and should not be overlooked.

With this in mind, we would ask that you respect a fundamental tenet of the American justice system that presumes the innocence of an accused until proven guilty. Ms. Anderson has never wavered on her innocence and intends to prove as much at trial. In the interim, however, it is astounding how quickly a community prejudges facts, jumps to conclusions, and turns on those who care for them the most. The degree to which members of the community accept a stranger's word and character over that of their neighbor is likewise astounding. As a protector of the First Amendment, you know as well as anyone that we must question the veracity of allegations and their sources, regardless of the source (whether a federal prosecutor, investigator, or otherwise), before accepting them as the gospel.

Therefore, we demand that you retract the inaccurate article and verify any facts included in future articles. These statements are defamatory and paint Ms. Anderson in a false light. We further ask that you remember the presumption of innocence and the old parable that says: the hunter is always the hero until someone tells the lion's story. The government is not always the hero, and Ms. Anderson has not told her story. She must wait until trial. For better or worse, that's how the American justice system works.

Please govern yourself accordingly.

Sincerely,
W. Robert Vezina, III "

 The letter from Rob was copied to Tim Thompson, the publisher, and helped my feelings at the time tremendously. As a defendant, when the media blatantly publishes lies or distorted facts, one feels even more downtrodden, and Rob's letter buoyed my spirits and helped me to stand back up again to fight. The original version of the story is not available any longer, but the corrected version is available in digital form.

# 6   James Finch and Commissioner Antonius Barnes are Indicted, the Superseding Indictment of March 2021, Thirty-Eight Charges Dropped, The Mayor's Mom Passes Away, The Blue House, and FBI and BCSO Interviews/*Brady* Material

After my indictment and arrest of August 19, 2020, James had hired Guy Lewis, an attorney he had known for some time; James described him as a big shot former prosecutor who had worked directly with Ashcroft in the Bush administration. On September 5, 2020, about three weeks after my indictment, the *Panama City News Herald* featured a story in which the author repeated the allegations from the indictment against me as though they were fact, naming Finch's company again, as well as Derwin White and GAC, stating that "the indictment was a road map of sorts to where the investigators might be planning to go next in their effort to root out corruption."

In reply to questions posed by the *News Herald,* James said, "I've never been accused of bid-rigging, but it reads in there (the indictment) like we've been doing it a whole long time," Finch said. "If it were true, it would be a bad big deal. If it's a lie, it's pretty slanderous."

"Finch said he and his company have never made deals strictly with Anderson but have always worked through the Lynn Haven City Commission. Finch said he had been very sick and was hospitalized just four days ahead of Hurricane Michael striking Bay County a devastating blow. He said that by the time he was able to work again all of the contracts for things like debris removal had been signed and work was underway."

"While James was in the hospital in Tallahassee and then in rehab following the stroke he suffered, he said all of his contractor "friends" from Bay County came to visit him. He laughed, and said they came to make sure he was "asleep" since they were busy securing all of the work. James and his attorneys brought up his alibi many times to the government: he was not involved in the corruption because he was in a coma."

The Assistant U.S. Attorney had the audacity to say that James had been "out of pocket" instead of saying that he had suffered a stroke in the days before Hurricane Michael, and then went through a month of rehabilitation in Jacksonville. James was not even aware there had been a hurricane in Lynn Haven and Panama City.

He told the reporter that, "he did open his debris disposal facility so that Crowder Gulf and Ashbritt would have a location to drop debris, but he denied Anderson applied pressure on anyone to get him a contract. He said he has cooperated with the FBI all along as it has conducted its investigation into Bay County corruption and will remain available if they want to talk to him."

"If they want to see me or arrest me they can call me up and I'll be there," he said. "I'll even bring the doughnuts."

James told me later, that he said that because they were "fat sonofabitches."

James had answered the subpoena of the government with hundreds of thousands of pages of tax returns, business records, and Lewis and his partner Jeffrey Foreman had met with the government to present evidence of James' innocence, but the presentation was to no avail, even when the attorneys told the government that James would take a polygraph. He had nothing to hide.

At that point, Lewis believed James' indictment to be imminent, and James asked to self-surrender, to which the government's reply was, "they would let him know when it was appropriate."

"I decided then to pack my bags and go to Tallahassee rather than wait for helicopters to appear over my house or to see a SWAT team crawling on their bellies with knives in their teeth," said James.

James and my husband, Lee, had been good friends for over thirty years. Since my arraignment on August 25, 2020, the court had put James on my "no contact" list and so I was not able to speak with him at all, or risk losing my pre-trial release status. When James called Lee to let him know what was happening, Lee went with him to Tallahassee.

They had been in Tallahassee for two days staying at the Hotel Duval, waiting for the Grand Jury to indict him, and nothing had happened. In their usual cavalier style, on Tuesday morning, they had gone as far as to "tour" the Federal Courthouse lobby, looking at paintings, to see if they could get a glimpse of the devil himself, AUSA Stephen Kunz, but it was not to be.

On the morning of March 16, 2021, just as they had done with me, the US Attorney's office and the FBI raided the home of James Finch on 2nd Street in Lynn Haven. His wife, Ashley, answered the door, having been up each morning by 5 a.m. for several days, like James, after the attorneys were sure an indictment against James was imminent.

SA Lawrence Borghini was furious when she told him that James was not home, and when asked where he was, she calmly told him, "Tallahassee."

"You are welcome to come in and look if you like, but he is not here," she told him.

With a fit akin to Rumpelstiltskin in the fairy tale, he called James and screamed at him over the phone, "Where the fuck are you?"

To which James calmly answered, "At my attorney's office in Tallahassee waiting on you."

James said that Borghini continued to shout at him, wanting to know a physical address where he was, to which James replied, "You should calm down, you are too fat to be upset and screaming like this."

Borghini continued to shout, repeating, "I want a physical address of where you are!"

James was at Rob Vezina's office, my attorney. Guy Lewis, James' attorney was in Miami and could not get to Tallahassee in time for the arraignment because the government had not contacted him to tell him that James was being arrested, even though James had come to Tallahassee to turn himself in after being frustrated just waiting at home for them to surround his house after learning that a grand jury was being convened.

When Borghini asked James again for the physical address of where he was, James answered as only he would have the nerve to do in a situation like this. "I am at an attorney's office and he's in the bathroom taking a shit; when he comes out, I will get the address for you."

Borghini, as he was driving to Tallahassee, continued to shout, wanting a physical address where James was located, and James asked Borghini where he should turn himself in.

Borghini yelled, "663 E. Jefferson Street! 663 E. Jefferson Street!"

Then to add insult to injury, after the FBI agent arrived in Tallahassee two hours later, it was pouring rain and he called James demanding that he come to the courthouse to turn himself in. James told him he would be there as soon as it stopped raining.

James was delaying going to turn himself in as long as possible to avoid sitting in the "cage" as he called it for so long. If there was any bright spot in this horrible situation, the Bay County Sheriff's Office and the FBI missed their big media moment of James walking out of his house in handcuffs, with the local mugshot for WMBB Channel 13-Panama City; while James was sitting in Tallahassee attempting to self-surrender, the Assistant U.S. Attorney and entourage were driving one hundred miles *west* to Panama City for their big afternoon press conference at the same time SA Borghini was driving at a high rate of speed one hundred miles *east* to Tallahassee, cursing James on the phone. Karma sometimes works out.

Once James arrived at "663 E. Jefferson Street," in Tallahassee, he said they fingerprinted him and did a DNA swab, took his photograph, and then he waited in a cell, "the cage," until he could see the magistrate judge. While sitting in the cell, James said a very large black man was also in the cell, and after a while, James asked him, "Are you Gen Barnes?" "Gen" was Commissioner Antonius Barnes' nickname, and most people who knew him called him "Gen." Antonius affirmed that it was him; James said he felt bad, but he had not seen him in so long that he did not recognize him, and he was much heavier than he used to be.

James did not engage in any conversation with him because he said at that point he didn't know if they were being recorded or maybe Barnes was wearing a wire for the government to see what James would say.

Once he was before Magistrate Judge Fitzpatrick, the prosecutors told the Judge that James had two airplanes, was wealthy, and they believed him to be a flight risk; they asked the Judge to restrict him from using his airplanes.

James asked the Judge if he could speak, and the Judge affirmed that he could, saying, "you are the star of the show."

"Your honor, I am 69 years old, and I have lived in Lynn Haven all my life. My construction business office is two blocks from where I was born, and if you put me in jail or I go free, Lynn Haven is the only place I have to go; all of my children and my family are there, and that is where I will be."

The Judge ruled that James could be released without bond, that he should meet with his pre-trial officer to work out the details of his travel, but that his airplanes would not be restricted from his use. The Judge did order his passport surrendered, and then James was free to go home and begin the two-year battle for his acquittal. The prosecutors had lost their first battle with James Finch.

The sarcasm and arrogance James had displayed to the agent came from months of the continued investigation following my indictment of August 19, 2020, in which I had been literally destroyed, and then they had started the same media storm and leaks of information about James or "Company B" as he was referred to in the indictment of myself and City Attorney Adam Albritton. But the real surprise of the indictment was that instead of just adding James, former Commissioner Antonius Barnes was indicted on charges of bribery, checks he had received from James as a loan for his insurance business. Our attorneys had expected that Derwin White, Commissioner Dan Russell, or city engineer Chris Forehand would have been added in the superseding indictment, but Antonius Barnes was a surprise. My first trial had been scheduled for March 3, 2021, and when I look back now at how that trial would have ended for me, I shudder. Sixty-four counts against me, and what I did not know at that time was that the discovery we had been given thus far was largely useless to us. The 302's which would prove us innocent had been withheld. We would not be given this discovery until several months later, and even then, it would not be complete, the "*Brady*" information was heavily redacted, (Brady information is any information possessed by the government which could be helpful or exculpatory for the defendants) sometimes paragraphs, sometimes entire pages. After months of filing motions and battling the Government, we finally received the un-redacted 302's and the puzzle-pieces came together, implicating Major Jimmy Stanford of the Bay County Sheriff's Department as corrupt, and revealing that Derwin White had directed his nephew, Mickey White, to fabricate the invoices indicating that my personal property had been cleaned and billed to the City of Lynn Haven.

The Government, after meeting with my attorneys in January of 2021 and corresponding with James' attorneys, had taken some hits in our motions of deficiencies in the indictment of 64 charges against City Attorney Adam Albritton and I, who were scheduled for trial March 3, 2021. I was so exhausted by the months since the indictment, and I fought to go to trial, but co-defendant Adam Albritton asked for an extension, and the Government indicated that they would be seeking a superseding indictment within 30 days of our hearing in February. The prosecutors had dropped 38 charges against me in their "superseding" indictment, reducing the charges against me from 63 to 26, but still more than any high-profile drug or mafia cases I had ever heard of, which I just found incredible. The indictment is printed just as it was written, and I do not try to refute any of it as I did earlier with the indictment of August 19, 2020, because the entire document is a Government narrative of lies; lies which we would prove over the next two years, until all of the charges were dropped or reduced except for the conspiracy and bribery charge, "666" which has now been struck down by the Supreme Court as a viable charge. Our lawyers argued this in court over a year before the Supreme Court decision, but to no avail. The superseding indictment reads as follows:

| | |
|---|---|
| THE UNITED STATES VS. | SEALED |
| MARGO DEAL ANDERSON | SUPERSEDING |
| ADAM ALBRITTON | INDICTMENT |
| ANTONIUS BARNES | Case No.: 5:20cr28-MW |
| And | |
| JAMES D FINCH | |

THE GRAND JURY CHARGES:
### COUNT ONE

#### A.  INTRODUCTION
At all times material to this indictment:

1.      The City of Lynn Haven was a municipality incorporated under the laws of the State of Florida. The City of Lynn Haven's Charter provided for a City Commission, consisting of a "Mayor-Commissioner," described throughout as the "Mayor," and four Commissioners. The Charter required, among other things, that the Mayor Preside at all meetings of the Commission, that the Mayor was the official head of the City I certain circumstances, and the Mayor may take command of the police and fire departments and govern the city by proclamation during the times of grave public danger or emergency and shall be the judge of what constitutes such danger or emergency. The administrative head of the city government was a City Manager, appointed by the Commission, and subject to its direction and supervision.

2.      MARGO DEAL ANDERSON was elected as Mayor of Lynn Haven on April 21, 2015. ANDERSON was re-elected as Mayor of Lynn Haven on Aril 16, 2019. As Mayor of Lynn Haven, ANDERSON acted as the de facto head of the municipal government and sometimes directed the activities of the City Manager, who was responsible for the day-to-day operations and administrative functions of Lynn Haven. ANDERSON, as Mayor, presided over and participated in Lynn Haven Commission meetings, contributed to the agenda for all Commission meetings,

and possessed one vote on the City Commission equal to each Commissioner. As the Mayor of Lynn Haven, MARGO DEAL ANDERSON was an agent of the City of Lynn Haven and had a fiduciary duty to act in the best interests of Lynn Haven and its citizens.

3.    JOSEPH ADAM ALBRITTON entered into a contract with Lynn Haven to be the City Attorney for Lynn Haven on or about October 22, 2018, effective October 15, 2018, for one year. The contract retained ALBRITTON to provide professional legal services and perform other related duties to the Governing Body of the City and its employees as specified in the agreement. ALBRITTON executed an addendum to the professional services contract to be City Attorney on or about October 31, 2019 for an additional period of two years. As the City Attorney for Lynn Haven, JOSEPH ADAM ALBRITTON was an agent of the City of Lynn Haven and had a fiduciary duty to act in the best interests of Lynn Haven and its citizens.

4.    JAMES DAVID FINCH was the owner of Phoenix Construction Services, Inc. ("Phoenix") and JDF Properties, LLC ("JDF Properties"), businesses incorporated in the State of Florida, which sought contracts with the City of Lynn Haven.

5.    ANTONIUS GENZARRA BARNES was a City Commissioner for the City of Lynn Haven between 1996 and April 2019. BARNES was an agent of the City of Lynn Haven and had a fiduciary duty to act in the best interests of Lynn Haven and its citizens.

6.    Between on or about August 22, 2017 and March 26, 2019, Michael Edward White ("M. White") was the City Manager of Lynn Haven. As City Manager, M. White was responsible for the day-to-day operations and administrative functions of Lynn Haven.

7.    Erosion Control Specialists ("ECS) was incorporated in the State of Florida on May 10, 2011. "D. White was listed as a director of ECS. In a 2018 amended annual report and a 2019 annual report filed with the State of Florida, D. White was listed as a director and Vice-President of ECS.

8.    On October 10, 2018, Hurricane Michael caused severe damage to public and private property, public utilities, public buildings, public communications systems, public streets and roads, and public drainage systems within the City of Lynn Haven, Florida ("Lynn Haven").

9.    On October 16, 2018, as a result of Hurricane Michael, Lynn Haven adopted a local state of emergency for post disaster relief and planning and approved Hurricane Michael Resolution No.

2018-10-16. In the resolution, Lynn Haven waived the procedures and formalities otherwise required under Florida law to take action to ensure the safety, welfare, and health of the citizens of Lynn Haven, including: entering into contracts; incurring obligations, acquisition and distribution of materials, supplies, and other expenses related to the storm event; appropriation and expenditure of public funds; and the employment of permanent and temporary workers. The resolution delegated emergency powers to the mayor of Lynn Haven, MARGO DEAL ANDERSON, or her designee, to discharge the duties and exercise powers for the above-described activities until the local emergency declared had expired and the resolution was rescinded. The Declaration of Emergency was to be automatically renewed every seven days until further action was taken by Lynn Haven.

10.     On October 23, 2018, as a result of hurricane Michael, Lynn Haven again declared and reinstated a local state of emergency for post disaster relief and planning and entered Hurricane Michael Resolution No. 2018-10-23-002. This Declaration of Emergency contained the same provisions as the original declaration of emergency and was effective for seven days. The Declaration of Emergency was required to be renewed, or it would automatically expire.

11.     On October 30, 2018, Lynn Haven voted to end the local state of emergency and end the designation of the emergency powers to the mayor or her designee.

12.     Prior to Hurricane Michael, Lynn Haven contracted with two national disaster relief companies to provide disaster relief services for the city following a hurricane. These companies, referred to as Company C and Company D in this Indictment, provided debris removal services for Lynn Haven after Hurricane Michael, submitted invoices with supporting documentation for their services, and received payment from Lynn Haven, which was reimbursed by the Federal Emergency Management Agency (FEMA) for the expenses.

13.     FEMA is an agency of the United States Department of Homeland Security and is responsible for coordinating the federal government's response to natural and man-made disasters. The primary purpose of FEMA is to coordinate the response to a disaster that has occurred in the United States and that overwhelms the resources of local and state authorities. In addition to on-the-ground support of disaster recovery efforts, FEMA provides state and local governments with experts in specialized fields and the funding for rebuilding efforts for infrastructure. FEMA also

provides for the reimbursement of many expenses incurred by local governments in cleaning up and restoration after natural disasters, such as hurricanes.

14.     On October 22, 2018, with the knowledge and concurrence of MARGO DEAL ANDERSON, M. White, on behalf of Lynn Haven, and D. White, as owner of ECS, signed an agreement for ECS to provide Lynn Haven with "Emergency and/or Exigent Services, Ancillary Construction Services, or Construction Due to the Effects of Hurricane Michael." The agreement referenced ECS as a "contractor," with the effective date of October 11, 2018. The term of the agreement was for no more than 90 days to perform services for Lynn Haven. As part of the agreement, ECS agreed to provide detailed invoices requesting payment for services accompanied by such documentation or data, including back-up documentation sufficient for reimbursement of expenses by FEMA for Lynn Haven payments to ECS. JOSEPH ADAM ALBRITTON drafted this agreement.

15.     On or about October 28, 2018, with the knowledge and concurrence of MARGO DEAL ANDERSON, M. White on behalf of Lynn Haven, and D. White, owner of ECS, signed an amended agreement for ECS to provide Lynn Haven with "Emergency And/Or Exigent Services, Ancillary Construction Services, or Construction Due to the Effects of Hurricane Michael." Notably, the 90-day term provided for in the original agreement was replaced with no deadline; rather, the agreement provided the duration to be "for such time as necessary to perform the services for the project." Additionally, the amended agreement included new specific language advising D. White and ECS that FEMA financial assistance would be used to fund the contract with Lynn Haven, and that ECS would comply with all applicable federal regulations and executive orders, as well as all FEMA policies, procedures, and directives. Under the amended agreement, ECS also agreed to provide FEMA with access to its books and records and was further advised of federal program fraud and false statement prohibitions. JOSEPH ADAM ALBRITTON drafted this amended agreement.

16.     After Hurricane Michael, MARGO DEAL ANDERSON requested that the City Manager and D. White have ECS provide debris removal and repairs to her personal residence and the private residences of her mother and another neighbor. These services were billed by ECS to, and paid by, Lynn Haven in invoices that falsely claimed services were provided for public areas in Lynn Haven.

17.    In late October or early November 2018, JOSEPH ADAM ALBRITTON discussed with D. White expanding the work that ECS was performing for Lynn Haven, to include the pick-up of residential trash in Lynn Haven.    ALBRITTON drafted a supplemental agreement between Lynn Haven and ECS authorizing ECS to assist Lynn haven in the removal of residential trash.  The effective date of this "task order" was listed as three weeks earlier—October 15, 2018, and the "task order" authorized payment to ECS at a rate of no more than $300.00 per hour, per crew, for removal of trash.  The task order stated that it would terminate upon notice by Lynn Haven but was not to exceed 45 days from the effective date (October 15, 2018).

18.    On November 8, 2018, M. White and D. White executed an "Exhibit A—Task order 18-001" that ostensibly was an agreement under the Amended Agreement described in #12 above, authorizing ECS to charge Lynn Haven for residential trash pick-up, including allowing ECS to bill Lynn Haven for residential trash pick-up, including allowing ECS to bill Lynn Haven for residential trash pick-up that had not been performed by ECS during October 2018.

19.    In late October 2018, JOSEPH ADAM ALBRITTON provided to City Manager M. White a list of companies that he claimed had provided prices that would be charged to receive reduced vegetative debris or chips.  ALBRITTON advised M. White that a company, referred to as Company A in this Indictment, provided the lowest price at $4.70 per cubic yard and there was an immediate need to dispose of reduced debris. ALBRITTON told M. White that Lynn Haven had asked that the debris removal companies associated with the City use only locations that charged at a rate that the haulers could bill to Lynn Haven that was higher than several of the individuals and companies who attempted to submit bids for the debris dumping. ALBRITTON also told the City Manager that the dumping location owned by Company A was the most economical solution and should be selected by debris removal companies associated with Lynn Haven to dispose of vegetative debris or chips.  At that time, ALBRITTON was also employed by, and provided legal services to, Company A, a fact that was not disclosed by ALBRITTON.

20.    After Hurricane Michael, JOSEPH ADAM ALBRITTON directed D. White to have ECS provide debris removal and repairs to his personal residence and the residence of his girlfriend.  These services were billed to Lynn Haven by ECS in invoices that falsely

claimed services were provided for public areas in Lynn Haven, which paid ECS. ALBRITTON also requested and obtained from ECS an invoice for the debris removal services provided at his residence, which invoice ALBRITTON SUBMITTED TO HIS INSURANCE COMPANY FALSELY CLAIMING HE HAD PAID ECS FOR DEBRIS REMOVAL AND REPAIRS.

21. At the request of JAMES DAVID FINCH, MARGO DEAL ANDERSON caused City Manager M. White to issue a directive to Company C and Company D, debris removal companies that were contracted with Lynn Haven to conduct post-Hurricane Michael debris removal and clean-up to utilize a site owned by FINCH TO DISPOSE OF ALL VEGETATIVE DEBRIS OR CHIPS. As directed, Company C and Company D commenced disposing all of its vegetative debris or chips at a FINCH'S site. Fees totaling more than $1 million for the disposal of items by Company C and Company D at FINCH'S site for the next one-year period were paid by Lynn Haven.

22. JAMES DAVID FINCH and MARGO DEAL ANDERSON attempted to have the City of Lynn Haven switch from its approved preliminary plan for the rebuild of municipal facilities to allow FINCH to conduct construction of a new municipal building/police station in accordance with his plan.

THE CHARGE

23. Between on or about August 1, 215, and on or about February 2, 2021, in the Northern District of Florida and elsewhere, the defendants, MARGO DEAL ANDERSON, JOSEPH ADAM ALBRITTON, ANTONIUS GENZARRA BARNES and JAMES DAVID FINCH,
did knowingly and willfully combine, conspire, confederate, and agree together and with other persons to:

(a) Devise and intend to devise, a scheme to defraud and for obtaining money and property by means of material false and fraudulent pretenses, representations and promises, and to cause wire communications to be transmitted in interstate and foreign commerce for the purpose of executing such scheme, in violation of Title 18, United States Code, Section 1343; and

(b) To devise a scheme to defraud and deprive the City of Lynn Haven and its citizens of their right to the honest services of ANDERSON, the elected Mayor of Lynn Haven,

ALBRITTON, the City Attorney for Lynn Haven, and BARNES as Commissioner, through bribery or kickbacks, and to cause wire communications to be transmitted in interstate and foreign commerce for the purpose of executing such scheme, in violation of Title 18, United States Code, Sections 1343 and 1346;

### MANNER AN MEANS

The manner and means by which this conspiracy was committed included the following:

### Public Official Positions

24.    The defendants and conspirators used MARGO DEAL ANDERSON'S public official position as the Mayor of Lynn Haven, JOSEPH ADAM ALBRITTON's public official position as a City Attorney of Lynn Haven, and ANTONIUS GENZARRA BARNES' position as City Commissioner, to offer, give, solicit, receive, agree to accept, and accept things of value from companies and individuals having business interests in Lynn Haven. These things of values were offered to ANDERSON, ALBRITTON, and BARNES with the intent that they would be influenced in the performance of official acts. ANDERSON, ALBRITTON, and BARNES demanded, sought, agreed to accept, and received things of value with the intent that they would be influenced in the performance of official acts.

25.    MARGO DEAL ANDERSON used her position as Mayor of Lynn Haven to take official action favorable to Company A, JAMES DAVID FINCH and FINCH'S business interests, and other companies, that included voting on measures pending before the Lynn Haven City Commission, signing resolutions, contracts, agreements, and promissory notes, and pressuring and advising City officials to perform specific official acts. Among other things, ANDERSON directed City officials to take official action favorable to JAMES DAVID FINCH and FINCH's business interests in exchange for financial benefits from FINCH.

26.    JOSEPH ADAM ALBRITTON used his position as City Attorney of Lynn Haven to take official action favorable to Company A, Phoenix, and other companies, including drafting official documents, signing official documents, conducting alleged bid procedures for contracts, and pressuring and advising City officials to perform specific official acts.

27.    ANTONIUS GENZARRA BARNES used his position as City Commissioner to take official action favorable to JAMES DAVID FINCH and his business interests, including moving, seconding,

and voting on items on the Commission agenda.

28.    JAMES DAVID FINCH, through his businesses, and otherwise, provided money and other benefits to ANDERSON and ANTONIUS GENZARRA BARNES in exchange for official acts favorable to his business interests.

ECS Fraudulent Invoices

29.    D. White used ECS as a means to fraudulently obtain money from Lynn Haven. D. White submitted invoices requesting payment for services allegedly provided by ECS to Lynn Haven, but which were false and fraudulent as to a number of material matters.

30.    M. White, as City Manager of Lynn Haven, approved all ECS invoices and directed city employees to immediately pay ECS for those invoices, even though other contracted debris removal companies had to wait for payment of invoices submitted for Hurricane Michael disaster relief and debris removal.

31.    After Hurricane Michael, MARGO DEAL ANDERSON requested that the City Manager and D. White have ECS provide debris removal and repairs to her personal residence and the private residences of her mother and a neighbor. These services were valued at approximately $48,000 but were billed by ECS to, and paid by, Lynn Haven in invoices that falsely claimed services were provided for public areas in Lynn Haven.

32.    MARGO DEAL ANDERSON and M. White signed Lynn Haven checks issued to ECS based upon fraudulent invoices that falsely claimed work by ECS was performed at various Lynn Haven public locations when the invoices included work performed by ECS at private residences and premises of public officials, including ANDERSON and the private residences of her mother and a neighbor.

33.    While D. White and ECS were providing services to Lynn Haven, M. White received things of value from D. White, including repairs to, and debris removal from, M. White's residence in Lynn Haven and his farm located outside Lynn Haven in Bay County, money for the purchase of M. White's farm, an automobile, and cash.

34.    These repairs to, and debris removal from, the residence and farm of M. White were billed to Lynn Haven with false invoices submitted by D. White to Lynn Haven with invoices falsely stating that work had been performed at locations in Lynn Haven. M. White approved the ECS invoices and directed Lynn Haven employees to pay the invoices.

35.     While D. White and ECS were providing services to Lynn Haven, MARGO DEAL ANDERSON received things of value from D. White, including repairs to, and debris removal from, ANDERSON'S private residence in Lynn Haven and the private residences of her mother and a neighbor.

36.     After Hurricane Michael, JOSEPH ADAM ALBRITTON caused D. White to have ECS provide debris removal and repairs to his personal residence and the residence of his girlfriend. These services were valued at approximately $25,000, but were billed by ECS to, and paid by Lynn Haven in invoices that falsely claimed services were provided for public areas in Lynn Haven. ALBRITTON also requested and obtained from ECS an invoice for the services provided at his residence, which falsely stated that ALBRITTON paid the invoice in full, and which ALBRITTON submitted to his insurance company falsely claiming that he paid ECS for debris removal and repairs and requesting reimbursement from the insurance company.

37.     While D. White and ECS were providing services to Lynn Haven, JOSEPH ADAM ALBRITTON received things of value from D. White, including repairs to, and debris removal from, the private residences of ALBRITTON and his girlfriend in Lynn Haven, and cash.

38.     When ECS invoices were being assembled for submission to FEMA by Lynn Haven for reimbursement, it was apparent that most of the ECS invoices that had been paid provided no details in support of the requested payments. When directed to provide supporting documentation for the monies requested and already paid, D. White submitted false time sheets prepared by another person. The time sheets were false and fraudulent in that they included names of individuals who had not worked at the claimed location, were off that day, worked at other projects outside Lynn Haven, or had never worked for ECS at the time of the timesheet. Additionally, in many invoices, the specific Lynn Haven locations of work claimed to have been done by ECS were false. These time sheets describing the attendance of ECS workers were certified by a Lynn Haven Department Head of Recreation and Parks, as accurate, but they were not, as the public official well knew.

39.     ECS invoices were submitted to Lynn Haven for payment of services that were not authorized under the emergency contract and were for the private residences of some Lynn Haven officials. The performance of ECS post-hurricane debris removal and repairs at the private residences of some Lynn Haven officials and other private individuals were concealed and not disclosed in the

ECS invoices submitted by D. White. M. White approved the invoices and caused them to be paid to ECS by Lynn Haven.

40.    A check register listing all checks and payments of monies to vendors by Lynn Haven was provided to MARGO DEAL ANDERSON, City Manager M. White, and the Deputy Finance Director on a regular basis. The check register included the amount of the Lynn Haven check the vendor, and related accounting information. ANDERSON regularly signed off on the check register detailing Lynn Haven payments to vendors, including ECS. ANDERSON signed off on a number of check registers that included the payment of invoices to ECS totaling approximately $5 million between October 26, 2018, and March 2019, and never questioned any of the payments made to ECS util after the resignation of the City manager and the subsequent inquiry concerning the large amount of monies paid by Lynn Haven to ECS.

41.    On October 23, 2018, D. White and ECS submitted to Lynn Haven a false invoice for hurricane clean-up in the amount of $180,722.75 that claimed work by ECS was done at a Lynn Haven Park and water plant on eight separate days. The ECS supporting documents submitted to Lynn Haven for this fraudulent invoice included individuals who were in fact working at locations outside Lynn Haven for a different contractor. This invoice, and a separate ECS $44,000 invoice for painting a Lynn Haven building prior to the hurricane, were approved and paid by Lynn Haven as emergency expenditures. With the approval of MARGO DEAL ANDERSON, M. White issued a handwritten check in the amount of $224,722.75 to ECS within three days after the submission of the invoices, and ANDERSON specifically authorized the cashing of the Lynn Haven check.

42.    On November 12, 2018, a false invoice for hurricane cleanup in th4e amount of $527,512.65 was submitted to Lynn Haven by D. White and ECS that false claimed work by ECS was done at a cemetery and sports complexes during a seven-day period. Instead of doing the work at the locations described, ECS workers conducted debris removal and clean-up at the residence of M. White located in Lynn Haven, his farm located outside of Lynn Haven in Bay County, the residences of MARGO DEAL ANDERSON, her mother, and a neighbor, and the residences of JOSEPH ADAM ALBRITTON and his girlfriend. The work on these private residences was concealed and not reported in the invoices, and no supporting documents to the invoice were provided. The invoice was approved by M. White, who directed

employees of Lynn Haven to pay this invoice. This invoice was included in the payment of three invoices to ECS in a Lynn Haven check issued to ECS on November 15, 2018, totaling $1,288,716.54.

43. For the invoice submitted on November 12, 2018, described in paragraph #17 above, D. White and ECS subsequently submitted false Daily Time Sheets purporting to show numerous individuals worked 12 hours per day on November 11, 2018. These time sheets were prepared by a conspirator, who also prepared time sheets for the same day for ECS to pay its employees. The payroll time sheets prepared by the conspirator and used to pay ECS employees listed most of the employees as not working on that day.

### ECS Trash Pick-Ups

44. After the initial declaration of an emergency by Lynn Haven had been revoked and expired, JOSEPH ADAM ALBRITTON, MARGO DEAL ANDERSON, and others sought to locate additional Lynn Haven projects that could provide money to D. White and ECS. One project was the Task Order agreement that ALBRITTON drafted and directed the City Manager to execute with D. White, ostensibly as part of the Emergency Agreement with ECS, to conduct trash pick-up using a pick-up truck and a trailer, at a cost of no more than $300 per hour per crew, throughout Lynn Haven. This action was implemented despite the ability of Lynn Haven waste trucks to pick-up large amounts of household trash and deposit large amounts of trash at the dump at no increased cost to Lynn Haven.

45. In late October or early November 2018, JOSEPH ADAM ALBRITTON discussed with D. Whit expanding the work that ECS was performing for Lynn Haven, to include the pick-up of residential trash in Lynn Haven ALBRITTON drafted a supplemental agreement between Lynn Haven and ECS authorizing ECS to assist Lynn Haven in the removal of residential trash. The effective date of this "task order" was listed as three weeks earlier—October 15, 2018, and the "task order" authorized payment to ECS at a rate of no more than $300.00 per hour per crew for removal of trash. The task order stated that it would terminate upon notice by Lynn Haven but was not to exceed 45 days from the effective date (October 15, 2018).

46. On November 8, 2018, M. White and D. White executed an "Exhibit A –Task order 18-001" that ostensibly was an agreement

under the Amended Agreement described in paragraph #14 of Section a above, authorizing ECS to charge Lynn Haven for residential trash pick-up, including allowing ECS to bill Lynn Haven for residential trash pick-up that had not been performed by ECS during October 2018.

47.    On November 9, 2018, JOSEPH ADAM ALBRITTON sent an email to City Manager M. White and MARGO DEAL ANDERSON that the trash pick-up work order did not require approval by the Commission, as it confirmed the verbal task order approved by ANDERSON and M. White in October. The trash pick-up Task Order was then removed from the agenda for approval by the Lynn Haven Commission.

48.    On November 13, 2018, a false invoice for hurricane clean-up in the amount of $332,387.76 was submitted to Lynn Haven by D. White and ECS that falsely claimed trash pick-up was conducted by ECS during a fourteen-day period starting on October 18, 2018. No documentation was submitted in support of this invoice. The claimed trash pick-up did not occur, and there was no record of any trash being dumped at the Bay Count refuse location, nor did City manager M. White obtain approval from Bay County for ECS to use the account of Lynn Haven to dump items at the Bay County facility until at least October 31, 2018. This invoice was included in the payment of three invoices to ECS in a Lynn Haven check issued to ECS on November 15, 2018, totaling $1,288,716.54.

49.    From the monies fraudulently paid by Lynn Haven for trash pick-up that did not actually occur, JOSEPH ADAM ALBRITTON solicited D. White to pay ALBRITTON money paid to ECS pursuant to the trash pickup agreement. Over the course of the next twelve weeks, ALBRITTON received $10,000 in cash from D. White per week of claimed trash pickup, linking to the payment of twelve weeks of trash pick-up in Lynn Haven.

50.    On November 29, 2018, a false invoice for hurricane clean-up in the amount of $135,445.03 was submitted to Lynn Haven by D. White and ECS that falsely claimed trash pick-up was conducted by ECS that falsely claimed trash pick-up was conducted by ECS during a seven-day period starting on November 23, 2018 (the day after Thanksgiving). However, there were only 6 dump tickets from the Bay County refuse location for this time period for which D. White and ECS charged Lynn Haven $19,349 per day. This invoice was included in the payment of two invoices to ECS in a Lynn Haven check issued to ECS on November 30, 2018, totaling $433,365.85. At the direction of ALBRITTON, D. White paid

ALBRITTON $20,000 IN CASH FROM THE PROCEEDS OF THE
Lynn Haven check to ECS.

51.  On December 13, 2018, a false invoice for hurricane clean-up in
the amount of $185,503.17 was submitted to Lynn Haven by D.
White and ECS that falsely claimed trash pickup was conducted by
ECS during a 13-day period starting on November 30, 2018. The
actual dump tickets from the Bay County refuse location for this
time period did not support the claims of the invoice. Additionally,
the trash-pick-up agreement had expired on November 20, 2018,
and ECS was not authorized to collect residential trash or receive
payment from Lynn Haven for such services. This invoice was
included in the payment of two invoices to ECS in a Lynn Haven
check issued to ECS on December 14, 2018, totaling $515,731.31.
At the direction of ALBRITTON, D. White paid ALBRITTON
$20,000 in cash from the proceeds of the Lynn Haven check to
ECS.

52.  On December 28, 2018, a false invoice for hurricane clean-up in
the amount of $481,215.24 was submitted to Lynn Haven by D.
White and ECS that falsely claimed trash pick-up was conducted by
ECS during a 17-day period starting on December 13, 2018, and
continuing before and after Christmas Day, and through Christmas
week. The majority of ECS workers did not work for the two
weeks before and after Christmas. The invoice falsely claimed
trash pick-up totaling between $21,000 and $32,000 per day during
this period. Additionally, the trash-pick-up agreement had expired
on November 20, 2020, and ECS was not authorized to collect
residential trash or receive payment from Lynn Haven for such
services. This invoice was included in the payment of two invoices
to ECS in a Lynn Haven check issued to ECS on December 31,
2018, totaling $725,941.09. At the direction of ALBRITTON, D.
White paid ALBRITTON $20,000 in cash from the proceeds of
the Lynn Haven check to ECS.

53.  On January 13, 2019, three months after Hurricane Michael, a false
invoice for hurricane clean-up in the amount of $479,020.68 was
submitted to Lynn Haven by D. White and ECS that falsely
claimed trash pick-up was conducted by ECS during a 13-day
period starting the day after New Year's Day. The invoice also
falsely claimed that between 11 and 13 crews were used to collect
trash daily. The invoice falsely claimed trash pick-up during this
period totaling $32,272.68 per day for five days, $38,878.44 per day
for seven days, and $45,478.20 for the last day. Additionally, the
trash-pick-up agreement had expired on November 29, 2018, and
ECS was not authorized to collect residential trash or receive

payment from Lynn Haven for such services. This invoice was included in the payment of two invoices to ECS in a Lynn Haven check issued to ECS on January 15, 2019, totaling $895,441.52. At the direction of ALBRITTON, D. White paid ALBRITTON $20,000 in cash from the proceeds of the Lynn Haven check to ECS.

54.     On January 25, 2019, three months after Hurricane Michael, a false invoice for hurricane clean-up in the amount of $216,771.24 was submitted to Lynn Haven by D. White and ECS that falsely claimed trash pick-up was conducted by ECS during a six-day period. The invoice falsely claimed trash pick-up during this period totaling $38,878.44 per day for four days, $35,578.56 for one day, and $25,678.92 for the last day. Additionally, the trash-pick-up agreement had expired on November 29, 2018, and ECS was not authorized to collect residential trash or receive payment from Lynn Haven for such services. This invoice was included in the payment of two invoices to ECS in a Lynn Haven check issued to ECS on January 31, 2019, totaling $433,259.16. At the direction of ALBRITTON, D. White paid ALBRITTON $10,000 from the proceeds of the Lynn Haven check to ECS.

## Disposal of Vegetative Debris or Chips

55.     On October 30, 2018, JOSEPH ADAM ALBRITTON provided to City Manager M. White a list of companies that he falsely claimed had provided prices that would be charged to receive reduced vegetative debris or chips and advised M. White that Company A provided the lowest price at $4.70 per cubic yard and there was an immediate need to dispose of reduced debris. ALBRITTON further told M. White that Lynn Haven had asked that the debris removal companies associated with the City use only locations that charged a price of $4.70 per cubic yard or less.

56.     At that time that JOSSEPH ADAM ALBRITTON advised the City Manager that the dumping location owned by Company A was the most economic solution and should be selected by debris removal companies associated with Lynn Haven to dispose of vegetative debris or chips, ALBRITTON was employed by, and provided legal services to, Company A, and ALBRITTON WAS THE registered agent for 14 companies of the owner of Company A. Additionally, ALBRITTON was a co-owner with the owner of Company A in another company and had been since February of 2017. None of these ties, financial interests, and relationships with Company A and its owner were disclosed by ALBRITTON to

Lynn Haven.

57.     One of the companies that JOSEPH ADAM ALBRITTON
falsely claimed had not provided a price for the vegetative debris or
chips disposal had actually advised officials in Lynn Haven,
including ALBRITTON, in writing that it would accept the
vegetative debris or chips for $4.00 per cubic yard, or even lower at
$3.50 per cubic yard, and save the taxpayers money both as to the
price and the costs of transportation since its disposal sites were
closer to Lynn Haven than Company A or the other possible
disposal sites.

58.     After the selection of Company A became public and an
objection to the selection by Lynn Haven of Company A to be
used by debris removal companies associated with Lynn Haven to
dispose of vegetative debris or chips was made to Lynn Haven
officials, one of Company A's owners asked JOSEPH ADAM
ALBRITTON to forward ALBRITTON's summary of the
obtaining of prices to a representative of Company D, a large
debris removal company contracted with Lynn Haven to conduct
post-Hurricane Michael debris removal, so Company D could
incorporate and justify the use of the Company A site for
vegetative debris or chips disposal..

59.     In or about late October, MARGO DEAL ANDERSON
convened a meeting with JAMES DAVID FINCH, one of the
owners of Company A, City Manager M. White, and several other
persons at FINCH'S personal residence.  At the meeting,
ANDERSON praised FINCH and his previous post-hurricane
assistance to Lynn Haven, and FINCH complained about not
receiving enough of Lynn Haven post-Hurricane Michael business.

60.     On November 1, 2018, at the direction of MARGO DEAL
ANDERSON, City Manager M. White issued a directive to
Company C, a debris removal company that was contracted with
Lynn Haven to conduct post-Hurricane Michael debris removal
and clean-up , to utilize a site owned by JAMES DAVID FINCH
to dispose of all vegetative debris or chips at another site location,
stopped dumping at that site location and commenced disposing all
of its vegetative debris or chips at FINCH's site.  Fees totaling
more than $1 million for the disposal of items by Company C at
FINCH'S site for the next one-year period were paid by Lynn
Haven.

61.     On or about November 11, 2018, at the direction of MARGO
DEAL ANDERSON, City Manager M. White issued a directive to
Company D, a debris removal company that was contracted with
Lynn Haven to conduct post-Hurricane Michael debris removal

and clean-up, to utilize a site owned by JAMES DAVID FINCH Phoenix to dispose of all vegetative debris or chips. Company D, which had been disposing of vegetative debris or chips at another site location, ended dumping at that site location and commenced disposing of all of its vegetative debris or chips at FINCH'S site. Fees totaling more than $1 million for the disposal of items by Company D at FINCH'S site for the next year period were paid by Lynn Haven.

62. On November 19, 2018, at the request of the co-owner of Company A., JOSEPH ADAM ALBRITTON sent to the vice-president of Company D, contracted to remove debris in Lynn Haven after Hurricane Michael, an email with the subject, "Justification Notice," and provided his summary and analysis that the Company A site be used to dispose of vegetative debris or chips by all debris removal companies associated with Lynn Haven.

Disaster Debris Management Site

63. While Lynn Haven was finalizing its decision concerning the location to be utilized for the disposal of vegetative debris or chips, City Manager M. White consulted with the City Engineer and planned to have real property owned, but not used by, Lynn Haven, permitted by the State of Florida to be used by debris removal companies associated with Lynn Haven to dispose of vegetative debris or chips.

64. However, MARGO DEAL ANDERSON instructed City Manager M. White to stop the permitting process for the Lynn Haven property for the disposal of vegetative debris or chips and stated that it would be unnecessary.

65. MARGO DEAL ANDERSON then directed City Manager M. White to seek authorization from the State of Florida for Lynn Haven to obtain a new Disaster Debris Management Site (DDMS) at the property owned by JAMES DAVID FINCH IN Bay County. Accordingly, on November 7, 2018, City Manager M. White filed a written request with the State of Florida requesting authorization for Lynn Haven to use a new DDMS for temporary storage and processing of disaster debris generated as the result of Hurricane Michael.

66. During the same period of time that the DDMS authorization was arranged for the company of JAMES DAVID FINCH, two disaster debris companies, previously contracted with Lynn Haven for debris removal, were directed to dispose of the vegetative debris or chips at FINCH'S site, and FINCH'S company received

payment of fees for that dumping from Lynn Haven, MARGO DEAL ANDERSON accepted things of value from the FINCH, including travel in a private airplane for ANDERSON and another person to Biloxi, Mississippi, and the Florida keys, lodging, meals and entertainment, and lodging aboard a private yacht and meals in Key West, Florida.

17th Street Projects and ½ Cent Surtax Design/Build Contract

67.  In August 2015, Lynn Haven approved an agreement for JAMES DAVID FINCH'S company to perform work in the amount of $3.72 million for the 17th Street Ditch Stormwater Project ("17th Street project"). Lynn Haven also approved the financing of the project by Phoenix at an interest rate of 2.55 per cent for a term of 20 years. ANTONIUS GENZARRA BARNES was not present for the vote.

68.  On or about February 28, 2017, the City commission considered a modification to the 17th Street project. The City Manager recommended adding $668,000 to a promissory note to JAMES DAVID FINCH'S company for piping on the west side of the street, and to increase the promissory note term to 30 years. ANTONIUS GENZARRA BARNES moved to approve these recommendations. BARNES and MARGO DEAL ANDERSON voted in favor.

69.  On March 20, 2017, MARGO DEAL ANDERSON signed, on behalf of Lynn Haven, a promissory note to pay Phoenix, JAMES DAVID FINCH'S company, $3.72 million with respect to the 17th Street project. The promissory note was for a period of 30 years and required Lynn Haven to pay interest of 2.55 per cent annually and make monthly payments to Phoenix. In financing the 17th Street project with Phoenix, Lynn Haven agreed to pay Phoenix approximately $1.6 million, as interest, in addition to the $3.72 million the City would pay Phoenix for its work on the 17th Street project contract.

70.  On July 29, 2017, MARGO DEAL ANDERSON and the Lynn Haven Commission approved a resolution authorizing the issuance by Lynn Haven of a $3,910,000 municipal revenue bond and a loan agreement to be signed with a financial institution to provide the funding for Lynn Haven to pay for infrastructure work in the City that was to be conducted by JAMES DAVID FINCH'S company, Phoenix. The term of the loan was for 10 years and the interest rate was 2.18 per cent per annum. ANDERSON signed the resolution and bond loan agreement.

71.     On August 9, 2017, MARGO DEAL ANDERSON signed an agreement between Lynn Haven and JAMES DAVID FINCH designating Phoenix to be the contractor or vendor for various projects that would be conducted in Lynn Haven under a ½ Cent Surtax Design/Build Contract, utilizing proceeds from the ½ cent Bay County sales tax that was in effect for ten years. This agreement, negotiated by ANDERSON and the owner of Phoenix, made Phoenix the contractor for numerous multi-million dollar Lynn Haven infrastructure projects that would not require any bid procedure for any of the projects related to the agreement.

72.     On October 24, 2017, JAMES DAVID FINCH sent a letter to City Manager M. White advising that he had completed phase one of the project earning the total amount ($3.8 million) authorized to date. The letter further stated that FINCH'S company would proceed with the next phase but not invoice Lynn Haven until the City had obtained the new loan. The amount of the referenced additional work in the amount of $1.8 million was submitted to Lynn Haven by FINCH in an invoice in January 2018.

73.     MARGO DEAL ANDERSON directed M. White to allow JAMES DAVID FINCH'S company to proceed as requested with the work despite no funding being available, a new loan had not been obtained, the City had not approved the specific roads that Phoenix was paving, and engineering work had not been completed on many of the roads that Phoenix had finished its work on.

74.     On December 12, 2017, MARGO DEAL ANDERSON and the Lynn Haven Commission, including ANTONIUS GENZARRA BARNES, approved a resolution authorizing the issuance by Lynn Haven of a $6,090,000 municipal revenue bond and a loan agreement to be signed with a financial institution to provide the funding for Lynn Haven to pay for infrastructure work in the City that was to be conducted by JAMES DAVID FINCH'S COMPANY. The term of the loan was for 10 years and the interest rate was 2.35 per cent per annum. ANDERSON signed the resolution and bond loan agreement.

75.     On January 4, 2018, JAMES DAVID FINCH submitted an application to Lynn Haven for payment of $1,850,170.66 for work performed on phase two during approximately a two month period.

76.     In June 2018, JAMES DAVID FINCH and MARGO DEAL ANDERSON requested City Manager M. White to proceed with an additional phase of the 17th Street project. M. White told ANDERSON and FINCH that he wanted to put the project on

hold as it was going to cost the City a large amount of money to continue the project and the City did not have the money to pay for the project at that time. ANDERSON and FINCH told M. White that FINCH wanted to proceed with the project.

77. ANDERSON pressured M. White to have Lynn Haven proceed with the project and stated that the JAMES DAVID FINCH would finance the additional $1 million cost of the project. Despite protestations by City Manager M. White that Lynn Haven did not need the additional debt, ANDERSON directed M. White to make it happen.

78. On August 21, 2018, Lynn Haven advertised for sealed bids from businesses to perform additional work on the 17th Street project. Since the Florida Department of Transportation (FDOT) had become a partner with Lynn Haven to provide some of the funding for the project, Lynn Haven was required to solicit bids for the additional work on the 17th Street project and obtain the concurrence of FDOT.

79. Three sealed bids for the additional work on the 17th Street project were submitted: one from JAMES DAVID FINCH's company, one from FINCH's relative, and one from Company A. In the past, these three companies had bid on contracts with public entities, agreeing among themselves that one company would submit the lowest bid on a specific project and the other two companies would submit higher bids. Then, in another public project, a different company would submit the lowest bid. Phoenix's $957,000 bid was determined to be the lowest bid and recommended to be awarded to Phoenix by the Lynn Haven City Engineer.

80. The sealed bid procedure was intended to make it appear as if the award of the additional work for the project was fair and above board, and would receive the concurrence of the FDOT, which had signed a Joint Participation Agreement with Lynn Haven in the 17th Street project.

81. Seven months before the selection of JAMES DAVID FINCH's company for the additional work on the 17th Street project, FINCH arranged to have the Lynn Haven City Engineer sell his 2006 ITAS Motorhome (Motorhome), valued at approximately $106,000, to MARGO DEAL ANDERSON without the payment of any money by ANDERSON, by the following means:

    a. FINCH issued a personal check to the City Engineer in the amount of $75,000, which allowed the City Engineer to pay off, with additional funds that he possessed, a

$105,993.70 loan on the Motorhome;

b. The motor vehicle title for the Motorhome was transferred to the name of ANDERSON's husband after the City Engineer initially listed the purchaser as Finch;

c. The transfer of title filed with the Florida Division of Motor Vehicles falsely stated that $35,000 was paid by ANDERSON'S husband to purchase the Motorhome;

d. The Motorhome was titled in the name of ANDERSON's husband;

e. No money was paid by ANDERSON or her husband to obtain this Motorhome valued at approximately $106,000; and

f. Approximately 22 months after the transfer of the Motorhome to ANDERSON and her husband, ANDERSON'S husband issued a $20,000 check to JAMES DAVID FINCH. This action followed the public reporting of the Federal investigation into public officials in Lynn Haven, including an indictment of two Lynn Haven public officials and three other individuals charged with conspiracy, fraud, and related offenses arising from the defrauding of Lynn Haven. That indictment included allegations that the Lynn Haven Mayor received post-hurricane repairs to her private property and the work was paid for by Lynn Haven based upon fraudulent invoices that concealed and did not disclose that work performed for Lynn Haven was instead performed at a number of public officials' private residences and the private residences of a few other individuals, yet billed as work performed at Lynn Haven public properties.

82. On November 6, 2018, MARGO DEAL ANDERSON and the Lynn Haven Commission, including ANTONIUS GENZARRA BARNES, voted for and ANDERSON signed a resolution of Lynn Haven amending the Joint Participation Agreement with FDOT relating to the 17th Street project stating that Lynn Haven had agreed to contract for and complete the work as described in the Joint Participation Agreement with JAMES DAVID FINCH's company.

83. On November 7, 2018, less than a month after Hurricane Michael and at the time that JAMES DAVID FINCH complained to MARGO DEAL ANDERSON about not receiving enough hurricane clean-up work, M. White awarded the contract to FINCH's company and executed a contract for Phoenix to perform an additional amount of work on the 17th Street project in

exchange for $957,000. As directed by ANDERSON, this amount was added to the amount of the March 2017 promissory note that Lynn Haven had signed payable to FINCH, increasing the amount that Lynn Haven agreed to pay FINCH for the project to $5,178,555. In addition, Lynn Haven was required to pay 2.55 per cent interest annually to FINCH on the new note amount.

**84.** During the same period of time that MARGO DEAL ANDERSON provided approval for JAMES DAVID FINCH'S company to proceed with the 17th Street project, and for which FINCH received from Lynn Haven regular monthly payments of approximately $15,000 (including interest) and subsequent work by FINCH's company, and during the same time period that ANDERSON provided approvals for FINCH, SIGNED VARIOUS DOCUMENTS, AND CAUSED Lynn Haven to incur significant financial obligations for FINCH to proceed with numerous projects in Lynn Haven pursuant to the ½ Cent Surtax Design/Build Contract, MARGO DEAL ANDERSON, in addition to receiving a free Motorhome from FINCH, also accepted things of value from FINCH, including travel in a private airplane to Biloxi, Mississippi, and the Florida Keys, and lodging, meals and entertainment.

85. Between August 2015 and December 2017, ANTONIUS GENZARRA BARNES moved, seconded, and voted on matters before the Lynn Haven City Commission favorable to JAMES DAVID FINCH's business interests, including the 17th Street project. Meanwhile:

    a.   On or about September 8, 2015, FINCH provided BARNES' business, Barnes Insurance Services, Inc. with a check in the amount of $8,000. Marked in the memo section of the check was the word "Loan." The check was deposited by BARNES into his Barnes Insurance Services, Inc. account.

    b.   On or about September 28, 2015, FINCH provided a check in the amount of $12,000 to BARNES' business, Barnes Insurance Services, Inc. Marked in the memo section of the check was the word "Loan." The check was deposited by BARNES into his Barnes Insurance Services, Inc. account.

    c.   On or about October 28, 2015, FINCH provided a check in the amount of $5,000 to BARNES' business, the Antonius G. Barnes Insurance Agency, Inc. Marked in the memo section of the check was the word "Loan." The check was deposited by BARNES into his Antonius G. Barnes Insurance Agency, Inc. account.

d. On or about January 26, 2016, FINCH provided a check in the amount of $10,000 to BARNES BUSINESS, THE Antonius G. Barnes Insurance Agency, Inc. Marked in the memo section of the check was the word "loan." The check was deposited by BARNES into his Antonius G. Barnes Insurance Agency, Inc. account.

e. On or about November 14, 2016, FINCH provided a check in the amount of $2,500 to BARNES' business, the Antonius G. Barnes Insurance Agency, Inc. The check was deposited by BARNES INTO HIS Antonius G. Barnes Insurance Agency, Inc. account.

f. On or about March 15, 2017, FINCH provided a heck in the amount of $2,500 to BARNES' business, the Antonius G. Barnes Insurance Agency, Inc. The check was deposited by BARNES into his Antonius G. Barnes Insurance Agency, Inc. account.

g. On or about December 4, 2017, FINCH provided a check in the amount of $5,000 to BARNES, which was cashed by BARNES.

WorldClaim Insurance

86. Following Hurricane Michael, Lynn Haven received a request from WorldClaim public adjusters to work with Lynn Haven to assist in documentation and adjustment of its claim with insurance companies with respect to losses that Lynn Haven incurred on October 10, 2018, associated with Hurricane Michael. One of Lynn Haven's engineers recommended to the City Manager that Lynn Haven select WorldClaim.

87. Individual A advised City Manager M. White that Individual A was to receive a percentage of whatever money was brought in by WorldClaim from Lynn Haven, and agreed to share some of the money with M. White, and that M. White, MARGO DEAL ANDERSON, and a Lynn Haven Commissioner would not be charged any claims fees by WorldClaim to adjust any private insurance claims for those public officials.

88. On October 24, 2018, and pursuant to the continuing Declaration of Emergency, MARGO DEAL ANDERSON and M. White signed a contract retaining WorldClaim to assist in documentation and adjustment of Lynn Haven's claim under a primary insurance policy with respect to losses that occurred due to Hurricane Michael. The contract obligated Lynn Haven to pay a sliding fee scale from 3 to 10 per cent of the net recovery between

$0 and $60 million. This contract was entered into without any request for bids or requests for qualifications, incurring a significant financial obligation for the City, in accordance with a local state of emergency resolution that had been extended by Lynn Haven for seven days the day before the signing of the World Claim contract and which emergency resolution was scheduled to, and did, expire six days later.

89.    Following Hurricane Michael, City Manager M. White sought a claims adjuster for his personal residence and farm for damages sustained to the properties. White asked Individual A if WorldClaim could help MARGO DEAL ANDERSON, M. White, and a City Commissioner. Individual A advised that WorldClaim would help all three public officials. WorldClaim handled the insurance claims for hurricane damage to the private residences and properties of ANDERSON, M. White, and a City Commissioner.

90.    WorldClaim sent M. white a bill in the amount of $10,000 for its work in adjusting the insurance claims of M. White relating to his private property. The invoice amount of $10,000 was marked through, there were initials next to the mark, and zero dollars was shown as the amount due. M. White told both MARGO DEAL ANDERSON and a City Commissioner that WorldClaim was going to help them with their insurance claims at no cost to them. WorldClaim agreed to charge both ANDERSON and a City Commissioner no fee for its work in adjusting the insurance claims of ANDERSON and the City Commissioner relating to their private property.

91.    No money was paid by the City Commissioner for WorldClaim to represent him and assist him in obtaining approximately $75,000 from an insurance company for damages done to his private property. Through the efforts of World Claim representing her and assisting her with her insurance claim, MARGO DEAL ANDERSON obtained approximately $81,125 from an insurance company for damages done to her private property. After the federal investigation of ANDERSON and others was made public, ANDERSON issued a check to World Claim for a reduced fee of only $3,646.

## City of Lynn Haven Design & Rebuild

92.    On September 24, 2019, the Lynn Haven City Manager reported to the City Commission that staff was working with legal counsel and FEMA on issuing the first round of Request for Qualifications (RFQ) for architectural design and engineering services for Lynn

Haven's rebuild of municipal facilities. She further explained that contractors to rebuild the municipal facilities would be in the second round.

93.    On January 14, 2020, the Lynn Haven City Commission voted to approve the City Manager to proceed with negotiations and contracts to the top three Architect/Design teams for the Lynn Haven rebuild.

94.    In the days after, the City Manager began negotiations of contracts with three architect firms for the Lynn Haven rebuild of municipal facilities. The contracts included designs for the old City Hall, new City Hallk Police Department, Commission Chambers building and the sports complex.

95.    On April 3, 2020, Defendant JAMES DAVID FINCH, through JDF Properties, purchased land at 201 14th Street West, Lynn Haven, for $750,000, which property was represented by FINCH and ANDERSON sought to be the property for the rebuild of municipal facilities to be built by FINCH.

96.    On April 15, 2020, MARGO DEAL ANDERSON requested that the City Manager and Police Chief meet with JAMES DAVID FINCH at his place of business to discuss an alternative plan for the City rebuild to be done by FINCH.

97.    On April 20, 2020, the City Manager and Police Chief met with JAMES DAVID FINCH and MARGO DEAL ANDERSON at FINCH's office. FINCH advised that he had purchased property that would be good for the Police Department and Fire Department, that he would build a fortified concrete building, and that the architects will cost too much. FINCH claimed that his property was the best place in Lynn Haven, and that the City Commission would be interested in hearing his price for a design, build, and finance plan of $13 million for 37,000 square feet. MARGO DEAL ANDERSON supported FINCH's plan and told the City Manager and Police Chief that FINCH was willing to finance the costs of building the facilities like he did for the 17th Street ditch.

98.    On April 22, 2020, MARGO DEAL ANDERSON discussed with the Police Chief the Architects meeting from the previous day and the price. ANDERSON stated that JAMES DAVID FINCH has advised her since becoming Mayor, and that she didn't trust the City employees and their knowledge. ANDERSON stated that FINCH would stay out of the rebuild until the architects make their presentations and the City has workshops. Then, FINCH would come in and show the Commission what he can do. ANDERSON further stated that FINCH will finance the rebuild at

2% like the 17th Street Ditch, and FINCH makes more money than putting his money in a bank.

99.     On April 23, 2020, JAMES DAVID FINCH discussed with the Police Chief renderings that FINCH had already provided to MARGO DEAL ANDERSON for the new police building.

100.    On April 30, 2020, JAMES DAVID FINCH met with the Police Chief and discussed the rebuild of the Police Department building. FINCH also stated that he wanted to rebuild all city buildings. After discussing rebuilding with the architects' plans and having FEMA involved, FINCH stated that he could receive the insurance money that the City is going to obtain and financing the rest of the building costs at 2.5% interest. At the meeting, FINCH had in in his possession documents that had handwriting and notes on them by MARGO DEAL ANDERSON as Mayor relating to the presentations of three different architects regarding their proposed projects and pricing for City Hall, the Police Department, and renovation of the old City Hall. FINCH told the Police Chief that he would get a least 4 votes from the City Commission on rejecting the architects' plan. When the Police chief tried to explain that the Emergency Operations Center (EOC) should not be separated from the Police Department, FINCH threatened the Police Chief that if he did not agree with FINCH's plan, the easiest thing to do is for the Sheriff's Office to come in and take over the Police Department at a cost of half the Police Department's budget.

101.    On May 12, 2020, at the City Commission workshop, the Architects made a presentation of renderings of the new City Hall, City Buildings, and Police Department, and Sports Complex and ball fields. JAMES DAVID FINCH attended the workshop. At the City Commission meeting later that day, the City Manager reported to the City Commission that the City had eight projects planned in the City with FEMA funding.

102.    On May 19, 2020, MARGO DEAL ANDERSON called the City Manager and asked her to call JAMES DAVID FINCH to get him on the agenda for the upcoming City Commission meeting. The City Manager was concerned that ANDERSON wanted FINCH placed on the agenda by the City Manager instead of ANDERSON who was making the request. Later that day, FINCH met with the City Manager and complained about the architect fees and the drawings that had been submitted. FINCH claimed that he could build his building much cheaper and he would do a workshop with the commission for the Police Department building, and he wanted to add the Community

Building to the project, but the City Manager refused. FINCH asked the City Manager how much money she had for the rebuild, which the City Manager refused to provide a dollar amount.

103.  On May 26, 2020, JAMES DAVID FINCH made a presentation at a City Commission workshop regarding problems he claimed existed with the projects proposed by the Architects. FINCH presented his proposal for rebuild of the City at a cost of $15 million, 2% financing, which included the property that FINCH recently purchased at 201 14th Street West in the City. MARGO DEAL ANDERSON stated at the workshop that FINCH'S proposal was a wonderful idea.

104.  On May 28, 2020, JAMES DAVID FINCH called the City Manager multiple times complaining that the City Commission had already made a decision to deny his proposal for the Police Department. The City Manager advised FINCH that the City Attorney had advised that any project over a specific amount had to be bid out or it would be in violation of state law. FINCH continually stated that the architect was going to the charge the City $40 million to build the Police Department and City Hall, which the City Manager told FINCH was not true. The responses appeared to anger FINCH.

105.  On May 29, 2020, the City Manager spoke to MARGO DEAL ANDERSON, who told the City Manager that JAMES DAVID FINCH had spoken to City Attorney ALBRITTON who determined it was legal to bid out the project that FINCH wanted and it could be placed on the Commission agenda. The City Manager told ANDERSON all she wanted was to make sure things were done legally and if the Commission wanted to do this, it would be up to them. The City Manager further advised ANDERSON that ALBRITTON had contacted the Commissioners about the project and that anything over $300,000 would have to be bid out. The City Manager stated that she had spoken with one of the architects who was very disappointed that the City is going in a different direction and he stated that it was being done illegally.

106.  On June 8, 2020, MARGO DEAL ANDERSON called the Police Chief and mentioned giving him a raise. She stated she wanted to fulfill her promise of making him a highly paid Police Chief. She said she did not want him to ever leave the City and go somewhere else. ANDERSON also told the City Manager that she wanted to do the same thing with the City Manager and her salary. Salary increases for City employees are determined by the City Manager and not the Mayor.

107. On June 9, 2020, MARGO DEAL ANDERSON placed on the City Commission meeting agenda Item #19 concerning the planning and construction of Municipal facilities and at the meeting urged re-consideration of JAMES DAVID FINCH's plan. FINCH spoke at the meeting and complained about the architects' proposal as too expensive and stated that the Police Chief wanted a "Suite" as his office and a $400,000 kitchen. The Commission voted to hold a workshop on the matter. The Police Chief later met with ANDERSON and told her he was angry that FINCH referenced his office as a "Suite" and had inflated the price of the kitchen and told her that FINCH did not need to threaten the Police Chief with the Sheriff taking over the Police Department in the future for not supporting ANDERSON'S and FINCH's proposed plan.

108. On June 23, 2020, MARGO DEAL ANDERSON placed on the City Commission meeting agenda Item #17 concerning the City rebuild process. At the City Commission meeting, ANDERSON discussed JAMES DAVID FINCH's proposal and the architect's proposal, highlighting benefits of a guaranteed maximum price that FINCH offered. ANDERSON stated priority should be to get started on the Police Department. J.T advocated for moving forward with design build with guaranteed price of FINCH and moved that the Commission do so. However, no Commissioner seconded the motion. ANDERSON then passed the gavel to the Mayor pro tempore and seconded the motion. The City Manager explained such a path may result in loss of FEMA funds. ANDERSON replied that she wanted to use insurance funds because they were not subject to FEMA guidelines and complained about not always receiving good advice from the FEMA consultants. ANDERSON stated she wanted to get off this $40 million dollar ship and go a different course. The motion to have Staff work on a plan and proposal to bid out a portion of the City work through design build process and bring back before the Commission passed on a 3-2 vote.

109. On July 2, 2020, MARGO DEAL ANDERSON called the City Manager and discussed the design/build proposal of JAMES DAVID FINCH. The City Manager explained to ANDERSON that she was concerned about losing FEMA funds. ANDERSON responded there was no guarantee the City would receive the FEMA money. However, the City Manager advised ANDERSON that in the May Commission meeting it was clearly explained to the Commission that the project was designated a "428" project and the money had already been set aside as a fixed cost and bridge funds of $1 million dollars had already been obligated and any of

the bridge money not used could be used for the Police Department. As she had expressed to the City Commission and ANDERSON, the City Manager reiterated that the City stood to lose in excess of $5 million by doing a design/build project as proposed by FINCH.

110. On July 14, 2020, MARGO DEAL ANDERSON placed on the City Commission meeting agenda Item #21 concerning the creation of an Assistant City Manager position.

111. On July 22, 2020, JAMES DAVID FINCH met with the City Manager and stated the City was dragging its feet on the rebuild. FINCH ACCUSED THE City Manager of being against him on this project. The City Manager stated she was against leaving $5 million dollars on the table and not following the law. FINCH then claimed the City was going to spend $40 million dollars rebuilding to which the City Manager told FINCH that he kept repeating false information as to the cost. In his conversation with the City Manager, FINCH spoke as if he had already been awarded the Police Department contract. FINCH stated that no one could do his architect fees of $150,000 for the building. He then accused the City Manager of holding up the process. The City Manager replied that she had no reason to work against anything, that she had been given a task by the Commission and she was following it, and she was not going to break the law for anyone. FINCH stated that he had supported the City Manager for her position, but they were now going in two different directions.

112. On July 27, 2020, MARGO DEAL ANDERSON contacted the City Manager and requested copies of the contracts with the architects for the rebuild projects and the amount of money spent on renting the temporary Police Department and City Hall. The City Manager suspected that this information was, in reality, for JAMES DAVID FINCH. She emailed the requested documents to ANDERSON.

113. On July 28, 2020, JAMES DAVID FINCH appeared for the City Commission meeting approximately 40 minutes prior to the beginning of the meeting and had in his possession all of the City documents that the City Manager had provided by email to MARGO DEAL ANDERSON. During the Commission meeting, FINCH commented on architect's design issues on the agenda, and objected to concession stand costs and the City paying rent for temporary buildings. FINCH quoted some numbers that the architects had in their designed build of the City Buildings and Ball Fields, and quoted the amount of money the city was spending on renting the two temporary buildings. The City Manager explained

that the projects were "428" FEMA projects and that the City is only responsible for any project costs in excess of the FEMA and insurance proceeds for the projects.

114.    On July 30, 2020, MARGO DEAL ANDERSON contacted the City Manager and asked the City Manager who authorized her to pay the architects. The City Manager told ANDERSON that the Commission authorized it and that the architects had been working since February and not received any payments. ANDERSON stated the architects did not have a contract. Prior to this discussion, ANDERSON had already been advised by the City Attorney that the City Manager was well within her authority to pay the architects.

115.    On August 11, 2020, the City Manager advised the City Commission at the Commission meeting of the tentative re-building of City and budget, FEMA reimbursement amounts, and the City's share of rebuild projects. The City Manager noted that the City had $19 million in its' restoration account and anticipated FEMA to reimburse the City $20 million dollars to cover the cost to rebuild the City.

116.    On August 12, 2020, MARGO DEAL ANDERSON met with the City Manager and stated that she had wanted someone from Tetra Tech and FEMA at the next workshop. ANDERSON stated that she was upset with a statement that the City Manager made during the workshop about saving the City $19.3 million dollars. The City Manager advised ANDERSON that the Commission meetings were getting out of control and that people from the audience should not be allowed to attack people on the dais. The City Manager provided ANDERSON with two examples where JAMES DAVID FINCH personally attacked the City Manager. ANDERSON told the City Manager that FINCH used to like the City Manager but no longer. The City Manager asked ANDERSON about information that FINCH was talking with City employees and vendors telling them that he and ANDERSON had spoken and FINCH recommended that the Mayor hire an Assistant City Manager and fire the City Manager, so that ANDERSON could do what she wanted or go around the City manager. ANDERSON denied that she was trying to get rid of the City Manager and stated that FINCH was just being mean.

117.    On August 14, 2020, JAMES DAVID FINCH sent a letter to the City Manager withdrawing his offer to build the new Police Department and offering to sell the land located at 2011 14th Street West to the City.

Concealment of Benefits

118. As Mayor of Lynn Haven, MARGO DEAL ANDERSON was a public official who was required under Florida law to file a Form 9, "Quarterly Gift Disclosure" with the Florida Commission on Ethics if she accepted a gift valued at more than $100. This Form 9 was required to be filed during the calendar quarter for which the gift was received, and describe the gift, the name and address of the person making the gift, and the date the gift was received. ANDERSON failed to file a Quarterly Gift Disclosure form as required by Florida law from the date of her election as Lynn Haven Mayor in 2015 through June of 2020, despite receiving numerous things of value in excess of $100 from various individuals. ANDERSON concealed the receipt of these items.

119. As the City Attorney for Lynn Haven, JOSEPH ADAM ALBRITTON was a public official who was required under Florida law to file a Form 9, "Quarterly Gift Disclosure" with the Florida Commission on Ethics if he accepted a gift valued at more than $100. This Form 9 was required to be filed during the calendar quarter for which the gift was received, and describe the gift, the name and address of the person making the gift, and the date the gift was received. ALBRITTON failed to file a Quarterly Gift Disclosure form as required by Florida law from the date of his appointment at City Attorney in October 2018 through June of 2020, despite receiving numerous things of value in excess of $100 from various individuals. ALBRITTON concealed the receipt of these items.

120. As City Commissioner of Lynn Haven, ANTONIUS GENZARRA BARNES WAS A PUBLIC OFFICIAL WHO WAS REQUIRED UNDER Florida law to file a Form 9, "Quarterly Gift Disclosure" with the Florida Commission on Ethics if he accepted a gift valued at more than $100. This Form 9 was required to be filed during the calendar quarter for which the gift was received, and describe the gift, the name and address of the person making the gift, and the date the gift was received. BARNES failed to file a Quarterly Gift Disclosure form as required by Florida law from the date of his election as City Commissioner of Lynn Haven in 1996 through April 2019, despite receiving numerous things of value in excess of $100 from various individuals BARNES concealed the receipt of these items.

121. MARGO DEAL ANDERSON directed Lynn Haven employees to assemble, print, and provide various city records to assemble, print, and provide various city records to her that she in turn provided to JAMES DAVID FINCH relating to ongoing and

planned Lynn Haven projects.

122.    On or about July 13, 2020, JAMES DAVID FINCH made false statements to Special Agents of the Federal Bureau of Investigation concerning the transfer of the 2006 ITAS motorhome to MARGO DEAL ANDERSON and her husband, and provided to the Special Agents a claimed bill of sale relating to the motor home that falsely stated the motor home was sold by FINCH to ANDERSON's husband on July 6, 2018, for $70,000 that was paid "half down and half due with 6 percent interest."

123.    On or about October 1, 2020, JAMES DAVID FINCH caused a wire transfer of $200,000 from FINCH's revocable trust to attorneys representing MARGO DEAL ANDERSON in this matter.

124.    On or about May 10, 2016, ANTONIO GENZARRA BARNES, on behalf of Antonius G. Barnes Insurance Company, executed a line of credit agreement with Whitney Bank, a Mississippi state-chartered bank, d/b/a Hancock Bank ("Hancock Bank"). On the application for the line of credit, BARNES did not disclose any loan obligations to JAMES DAVID FINCH or any businesses owned and-or controlled by FINCH. BARNES personally guaranteed the loan. On or about October 25, 2017, Hancock Bank filed a lawsuit against Antonius G. Barnes Insurance Company and BARNES, alleging that the loan was in default due to lack of payment and $20,675 was owed to Hancock Bank.

**125.**    On or about December 13, 2019, ANTONIO GENZARRA BARNES, on behalf of The Barnes Insurance Agency, LLC, executed loan documents for a $23,681 loan from Innovations Federal Credit Union. On the loan application, BARNES did not disclose any loan obligations to JAMES DAVID FINCH or any businesses owned and-or controlled by FINCH.

The conspirators performed acts and made statements to hide and conceal, and cause to be hidden and concealed, the purpose of the conspiracy and the acts committed in furtherance thereof.

All in violation of Title 18, United States Code, Section 1349.

## COUNTS TWO THROUGH FORTY
### A.   INTRODUCTION

1.    The allegations of Count One, Section A, are hereby realleged and incorporated by reference as if fully set forth herein.

## B.   THE CHARGE

2.    Between on or about August 1, 2015, and on or about August 11, 2020, in the Northern District of Florida and elsewhere, the defendants,

MARGO DEAL ANDERSON

JOSEPH ADAM ALBRITTON

ANTONIUS GENZARRA BARNES,

AND

JAMES DAVID FINCH

Did knowingly and willfully:

(a) devise, and intend to devise, a scheme to defraud and for obtaining money and property by means of material false and fraudulent pretenses, representations, and promises, and to cause wire communications to be transmitted in interstate and foreign commerce for the purpose of executing such scheme, and

(b) devise and intend to devise a scheme to defraud and deprive the City of Lynn Haven and its citizens of their right to the honest services of ANDERSON, the elected Mayor of Lynn Haven, ALBRITTON, the City Attorney for Lynn Haven, and BARNES, the elected City Commissioner, through bribery or kickbacks, and to cause wire communications to be transmitted in interstate and foreign commerce for the purpose of executing such scheme.

## C.  SCHEME TO DEFRAUD

3.    The allegations of Count One, Section C, Paragraphs 24-125, are hereby realleged and incorporated by reference as if fully set forth herein.

## C.   WIRE COMMUNICATIONS

4.    On or about the following dates for the purpose of executing the scheme to defraud, the defendants,

MARGO DEAL ANDERSON,

JOSEPH ADAM ALBRITTON,

ANTONIUS GENZARRA BARNES,

And

JAMES DAVID FINCH

Knowingly did cause wire communications to be transmitted in interstate and foreign commerce as set forth below:

COUNT   TWO

DATE 1/26/2016
WIRE COMMUNICATION Deposit of $10,000 check and related wire
NATURE OF DEPRIVATION    Honest Services
DEFENDANTS CHARGED      BARNES AND FINCH

COUNT THREE
DATE 11/14/2016
WIRE COMMUNICATION Deposit of $2,500 check and related wire
COUNT FOUR
DATE 3/15/2017
WIRE COMMUNICATION Deposit of $2,500 check and related wire
NATURE OF DEPRIVATION  Honest Services
DEFENDANTS CHARGED   BARNES AND FINCH

COUNT FIVE
DATE 12/4/2017
WIRE COMMUNICATION Deposit of $5,000 check and related wire
NATURE OF DEPRIVATION Honest Services
DEFENDANTS CHARGED    BARNES AND FINCH

COUNT SIX
DATE 10/6/2017
WIRE COMMUNICATION Deposit of $2,272,669.87 check and related
wire
NATURE OF DEPRIVATION Honest Services & Money and Property
DEFENDANTS CHARGED  ANDERSON, BARNES AND FINCH

COUNT SEVEN
DATE 10/13/2017
WIRE COMMUNICATION Deposit of $72,000 check and related wire
NATURE OF DEPRIVATION Honest Services & Money and Property
DEFENDANTS CHARGED  ANDERSON, BARNES AND FINCH

COUNT EIGHT
DATE 10/25/2017
WIRE COMMUNICATION  Email with letter from M. White to
engineering firm
NATURE OF COMMUNICATION  Money and Property
DEFENDANTS CHARGED  ANDERSON AND FINCH

COUNT NINE
DATE 11/6/2017
WIRE COMMUNICATION  Deposit of $1,455,330.13 check and related

wire
NATURE OF DEPRIVATION  Honest Services & Money and Property
DEFENDANTS CHARGED  ANDERSON AND FINCH

COUNT TEN
DATE 1/8/2018
WIRE COMMUNICATION  Deposit of $1,850,170.66 check and related wire
NATURE OF DEPRIVATION  Honest Services and Money and Property
DEFENDANTS CHARGED  ANDERSON AND FINCH

COUNT ELEVEN
DATE  2/16/2018
WIRE COMMUNICATION  Deposit of $75,000 check from FINCH into the account of Individual A for Motorhome and related wire
NATURE OF DEPRIVATION  Honest Services
DEFENDANTS CHARGED  ANDERSON AND FINCH

COUNT TWELVE
DATE 10/23/2018
WIRE COMMUNICATION  text messages between ALBRITTON and D.. White re work @ 306 N. Palo Alto
NATURE OF DEPRIVATION  Honest Services and Money and Property
DEFENDANTS CHARGED  ALBRITTON

COUNT THIRTEEN
DATE 10/23/2018
WIRE COMMUNICATION  Text message ALBRITTON to D. White requesting ECS invoice
NATURE OF DEPRIVATION  Honest Services and Money and Property
DEFENDANTS CHARGED  ALBRITTON

COUNT FOURTEEN
DATE 10/24/2018
WIRE COMMUNICATION  Text messages between ALBRITTON and D. White requesting electrician at girlfriend's residence
NATURE OF DEPRIVATION  Honest Services & Money and Property
DEFENDANTS CHARGED  ALBRITTON

COUNT FIFTEEN
DATE  10/30/2018
WIRE COMMUNICATION  Deposit of $224,722.75 check and related wire

NATURE OF DEPRIVATION  Honest Services & Money and Property
DEFENDANTS CHARGED  ANDERSON AND ALBRITTON

COUNT SIXTEEN
DATE 10/30/2018
WIRE COMMUNICATION  Email from ALBRITTON to City Manager
re use of Company A pit
NATURE OF DEPRIVATION  Honest Services and Money and Property
DEFENDANTS CHARGED  ALBRITTON

COUNT SEVENTEEN
DATE  10/20/2018
WIRE COMMUNICATION  Text message from M. White to City
Engineer to cancel permit application
NATURE OF DEPRIVATION  Honest Services and Money and Property
DEFENDANTS CHARGED  ANDERSON AND FINCH

COUNT EIGHTEEN
DATE 11/1/2018
WIRE COMMUNICATION Email from M. White to Company C
directing it to use FINCH's pit
NATURE OF DEPRIVATION  Honest Services & Money and Property
DEFENDANTS CHARGED  ANDERSON AND FINCH

COUNT NINETEEN
DATE 11/8/2018
WIRE COMMUNICATION  Email including letter of M. White to State
of Florida requesting approval for DDMS site for FINCH company
NATURE OF DEPRIVATION  Honest Services & Money and Property
DEFENDANTS CHARGED  ANDERSON AND FINCH

COUNT TWENTY
DATE 11/8/2018
WIRE COMMUNICATION  Text messages between ALBRITTON and
D. White requesting D. White to come sign task order
NATURE OF DEPRIVATION  Honest Services & Money and Property
DEFENDANTS CHARGED  ALBRITTON

COUNT TWENTY-ONE
DATE 11/9/2018
WIRE COMMUNICATION Text messages between ALBRITTON and
D. White to go to 2114 CC Dr., tarp and patch broken windows
NATURE OF DEPRIVATION  Honest Services & Money and Property

DEFENDANTS CHARGED  ALBRITTON
COUNT TWENTY-TWO
DATE 11/9/2018
WIRE COMMUNICATION  Text messages between M. White and D. White re ANDERSON'S property clean-up
NATURE OF DEPRIVATION  Honest Services & Money and Property
DEFENDANTS CHARGED  ANDERSON

COUNT TWENTY-THREE
DATE 11/15/2018
WIRE COMMUNICATION  Text messages between ALBRITTON and D. White re needing invoice
NATURE OF DEPRIVATION  Honest Services & Money and Property
DEFENDANTS CHARGED    ALBRITTON

COUNT TWENTY-FOUR
DATE 11/15/2018
WIRE COMMUNICATION  Deposit of $1,288,716.54 check and related wire
NATURE OF DEPRIVATION  Honest services & Money and Property
DEFENDANTS CHARGED  ANDERSON AND ALBRITTON

COUNT TWENTY-FIVE
DATE 11/19/2018
WIRE COMMUNICATION  Email from ALBRITTON to Company A Executive re justification for Company A pit
NATURE OF DEPRIVATION  Money and Property
DEFENDANTS CHARGED  ALBRITTON

COUNT TWENTY-SIX
DATE 11/28/2018
WIRE COMMUNICATION  Text message from D. White to ALBRITTON ("$$$")
NATURE OF DEPRIVATION  Honest Services & Money and Property
DEFENDANTS CHARGED  ALBRITTON

COUNT TWENTY-SEVEN
DATE 11/30/2018
WIRE COMMUNICATION  Deposit of $433,365.85 check and related wire
NATURE OF DEPRIVATION  Honest Services Money and Property
DEFENDANTS CHARGED  ANDERSON AND ALBRITTON

COUNT TWENTY-EIGHT
DATE 12/14/2018
WIRE COMMUNICATION  Deposit of $515,731.31 check and related wire
NATURE OF DEPRIVATION  Honest Services & Money and Property
DEFENDANTS CHARGED  ANDERSON AND ALBRITTON

COUNT TWENTY-NINE
DATE 12/26/2018
WIRE COMMUNICATION  Text messages of M. White and D. White re ANDERSON has a "good job" for D. White
NATURE OF DEPRIVATION  Honest Services & Money and Property
DEFENDANTS CHARGED  ANDERSON

COUNT THIRTY
DATE 12/31/2018
WIRE COMMUNICATION  Deposit of $725,941.09 check and related wire
NATURE OF DEPRIVATION  Honest Services & Money and Property
DEFENDANTS CHARGED  ANDERSON AND ALBRITTON

COUNT THIRTY-ONE
DATE  1/7/2019
WIRE COMMUNICATION  Text messages of ALBRITTON and M. White
NATURE OF DEPRIVATION  Honest Services & Money and Property
DEFENDANTS CHARGED  ANDERSON AND ALBRITTON

COUNT THIRTY-TWO
DATE  1/14/2019
WIRE COMMUNICATION  Text messages between ALBRITTON and D. White requesting D. White to sign addendum to Lynn haven contract
NATURE OF DEPRIVATION  Honest Services & Money and Property
DEFENDANTS CHARGED  ANDERSON AND ALBRITTON

COUNT THIRTY-THREE
DATE  1/15/2019
WIRE COMMUNICATION  Deposit of $895,441.52 check and related wire
NATURE OF DEPRIVATION  Honest Services & Money and Property
DEFENDANTS CHARGED ANDERSON AND ALBRITTON

COUNT THIRTY-FOUR
DATE 1/16/2019
WIRE COMMUNICATION  Text messages between ALBRITTON and D. White re trailer invoice
NATURE OF DEPRIVATION  Honest Services & Money and Property
DEFENDANTS CHARGED   ALBRITTON

COUNT THIRTY-FIVE
DATE 1/31/2019
WIRE COMMUNICATION  Deposit of $433,259.16 check and related wire
NATURE OF DEPRIVATION  Honest Services & Money and Property
DEFENDANTS CHARGED  ANDERSON AND ALBRITTON

COUNT THIRTY-SIX
DATE 2/8/2019
WIRE COMMUNICATION  Email from WorldClaim to ANDERSON including attachment of contract and no fee addendum for WorldClaim to be private insurance adjuster
NATURE OF DEPRIVATION  Honest Services & Money and Property
DEFENDANTS CHARGED  ANDERSON

COUNT THIRTY-SEVEN
DATE 2/12/2019
WIRE COMMUNICATION Email from ANDERSON to WorldClaim including signed contract for WorldClaim to be private insurance adjuster
NATURE OF DEPRIVATION  Honest Services & Money and Property
DEFENDANTS CHARGED   ANDERSON

COUNT THIRTY-EIGHT
DATE 2/18/2019
WIRE COMMUNICATION  Text message from ALBRITTON to D. White re need for enclosed trailer
NATURE OF DEPRIVATION  Honest Services & Money and Property
DEFENDANTS CHARGED  ALBRITTON

COUNT THIRTY-NINE
DATE 3/9/2019
WIRE COMMUNICATION  Text message from ALBRITTON to D. White re need for invoice for both storage units
NATURE OF DEPRIVATION  Honest Services & Money and Property

DEFENDANTS CHARGED   ALBRITTON

COUNT FORTY
DATE 1/16/2020
WIRE COMMUNICATION  Deposit of $20,000 check on ANDERSON account payable to FINCH and related wire
NATURE OF DEPRIVATION  Honest Services
DEFENDANTS CHARGED  ANDERSON

In violation of Title 18, United States Code, Sections 1343, 1346, and 2.

## COUNT FORTY-ONE

1.   The allegations of Count One, Sections A and C, are hereby realleged and incorporated by reference as if fully set forth herein.
2.   Between on or about October 10, 2018, and on or about April 30, 2019, in the Northern District of Florida, and elsewhere, the defendants,

### MARGO DEAL ANDERSON
And
### JOSEPH ADAM ALBRITTON,

Being agents of an organization and agency of the local government, that is, the City of Lynn Haven, Florida, receiving in the one-year period beginning October 10, 2018, benefits in excess of $10,000 under a federal program involving grants, contracts, subsidies, loans, guarantees, and other forms of federal assistance, did knowingly embezzle, steal, obtain by fraud, without authority convert to the use of a person other than the rightful owner, and intentionally misapply property that was valued at $5,000 or more and under the care , custody, and control of such organization, local government , and agency.

In violation of title 18, United States Code, Sections 666(a)(1)(A) and 2.

## COUNT FORTY-TWO

1.    On or about November 18, 2019, in the Northern District of Florida and elsewhere, the defendant,

### MARGO DEAL ANDERSON,

did knowingly and willfully make materially false, fictitious, and fraudulent statements and representations in a matter within the executive branch of the Government of the United States, that is during a criminal investigation of public corruption involving the City of Lynn Haven conducted by the Federal Bureau of Investigation, the defendant falsely stated that:

214

a. ANDERSON was unaware of the role of Erosion Control Specialists (ECS) in the post-Hurricane Michael clean-up of Lynn Haven; and

b. ANDERSON was first introduced to David "Mickey" White in December 2018 or January 2019, when volunteers were used to clean up various streets designated by Lynn haven as needing some attention and clean-up.

These statements and representations were false because, as ANDERSON then well knew:

a. ANDERSON was aware that ECS had been contracted by Lynn Haven to conduct debris removal and repairs in the City of Lynn Haven after Hurricane Michael;

b. ANDERSON was introduced to David "Mickey" White through City Manager Michael White shortly after Hurricane Michael and requested David "Mickey" White to have ECS clean up her private residence.

In violation of Title 18, United States Code Section 1001(a(2).

## COUNT FORTY-THREE

1. On or about July 13, 2020, in the Northern District of Florida, the defendant,

### JAMES DAVID FINCH

Did knowingly and willfully make materially false, fictitious, and fraudulent statements, representations, and writings in a manner within the executive branch of the Government of the United States, that is, during a criminal investigation of public corruption involving the City of Lynn Haven conducted by the Federal Bureau of Investigation, the defendant falsely stated that

a. FINCH had sold a 2006 ITAS motorhome to ANDERSON and her husband for $70,000 that he had purchased from Individual A for $75,000; FINCH presented a false bill of sale dated July 6, 2018 that stated the sale of the motorhome was $70,000 of which half was paid down and half due to FINCH with 6% interest; and

b. FINCH stated that he sold the motorhome to ANDERSON and her husband for $70,000 and they had paid him with a check and the difference in cash;

c. FINCH stated that he purchased the motorhome to flip.

These statements and representations were false, and the claimed bill of sale dated July 6, 2018, contained false statements, because as FINCH then well knew:

a.  FINCH was aware that ANDERSON's husband had registered the purchase of the motorhome from Individual A, as the seller, and ANDERSON'S husband as the buyer in early March 2018;

b.  The transfer of title to the motor home was signed by Individual A as the seller and ANDERSON's husband as the purchaser with a sale price of $35,000 with a sale date of February 13, 2018;

c.  The motor home was titled in the name of ANDERSON'S husband'

d.  FINCH issued a check to Individual A in the amount of $75,000 on February 14, 2018;

e.  Approximately 22 months after the transfer of the motorhome to ANDERSON and her husband, ANDERSON'S husband issued a $20,000 check to FINCH allegedly in relation to the motorhome.

In violation of Title 18, United States Code Sections 1001(a)(2)&(3).

## COUNT FORTY-FOUR

### A.  CHARGE

Between on or about October 10, 2018, and April 1, 2019, in the Northern District of Florida and elsewhere, the defendant,

## JOSEPH ADAM ALBRITTON,

Did knowingly and willfully devise, and intend to devise, and intend to devise, a scheme to defraud and for obtaining money and property by means of materially false and fraudulent pretenses, representations, and promises, and for the purpose of executing such scheme, did cause a matter to be delivered by the United States Postal Service and commercial interstate carrier.

### B.  SCHEME TO DEFRAUD

It was part of the scheme to defraud that:

1.  The defendant, JOSEPH ADAM ALBRITTON, made, and caused to be made, false and fraudulent representations to the St. John's Insurance Company concerning damages to his residence in

Lynn Haven, Florida, as a result of Hurricane Michael in order to fraudulently obtain money from the St. John's Insurance Company.

2. JOSEPH ADAM ALBRITTON represented in a claim that his residence had been damaged by Hurricane Michael and falsely represented that he had paid for tree removal, debris removal, and installation of a tarp to his residence totaling $9,600.

3. In fact, the tree removal, debris removal, and installation of a tarp to the residence and property of JOSEPH ADAM ALBRITTON had been made by Erosion Control Specialist (ECS) at no cost to him, as ECS received payment from the City of Lynn haven for its employees making the repairs and conducting debris removal at ALBRITTON's residence. However, the City of Lynn Haven was not aware that ECS had made repairs to ALBRITTON'S personal residence, as the City of Lynn Haven was falsely billed for alleged work on city properties.

4. To facilitate the scheme, JOSEPH ADAM ALBRITTON solicited ECS to create a false and fictitious invoice attesting to repair work done to his residence after the hurricane by ECS in the amount of $9,600, and that the amount of the invoice was paid in full on October 24, 2018, which invoice ALBRITTON then submitted to St. John's Insurance Company in support of his fraudulent insurance claim.

5. Based upon the false claim, St. John's Insurance Company issued payment in the amount of $6,100 to JOSEPH ADAM ALBRITTON that was based upon the false ECS invoice for the tree removal, debris removal, and installation of a tarp to ALBRITTON'S residence and represented payment of the $9,600 less a deductible under the insurance property. This payment was mailed to ALBRITTON'S address in Lynn Haven. ALBRITTON caused the St. John's Insurance Company insurance check to be deposited into a bank account belonging to him.

## C. MAILING

On or about November 29, 2018, the defendant,

### JOSEPH ADAM ALBRITTON,

Knowingly did, for the purpose of executing the fraudulent scheme and attempting to do so, cause to be transmitted by United States mail and private and commercial carrier, a $6,100 check issued from the St. Johns Insurance Company.

In violation of Title 18, United States Code, Sections 1341 and 2.

## CRIMINAL FORFEITURE

The allegations contained in Counts One through Forty-One, and Forty-Four of this Indictment are hereby realleged and incorporated by reference for the purpose of alleging forfeiture. From their engagement in the violations alleged in Counts One through Forty-One, and Forty-Four of this Indictment, the defendants,

MARGO DEAL ANDERSON
JOSEPH ADAM ALBRITTON,
ANTONIUS GENZARRA BARNES,
And
JAMES DAVID FINCH

Shall forfeit to the United States, pursuant to Title 18, United States Code, Section 981(a)(1)(C), and Title 28, United States Code, Section 2461(c), any and all of the defendants' right, title, and interest in any property, real and personal, constituting, and derived from, proceeds traceable to such offenses, including the following:

A.     2006 ITAS Motorhome, VIN#4UZACKDC26CW30357

If any of the property described above as being subject to forfeiture, as a result of acts or omissions of the defendants:

    i. cannot be located upon the exercise of due diligence;
    ii. has been transferred, sold to, or deposited with a third party;
    iii. has been placed beyond the jurisdiction of this Court;
    iv. has been substantially diminished in value; or
    v. has been commingled with other property that cannot be subdivided without difficulty,

it is the intent of the United States, pursuant to Title 21, United States Code, Section 853 (p), as incorporated by Title 28, United States Code, Section 2461 (c), to seek forfeiture of any other property of said defendant up to the value of the forfeitable property.

A TRUE BILL

Redacted Signature
FOREPERSON

3/16/2021

JASON R. COODY
Acting United States Attorney

STEPHEN M. KUNZ
Assistant United States Attorney

ANDREW J. GROGAN
Assistant United States Attorney

Lynn Haven and Bay County once again reeled under the news of yet another indictment in the "corruption" case in which Sheriff Tommy Ford and U.S. Attorney Larry Keefe continued to promise to "root out" the virus of corruption of public officials. With the election of President Joe Biden, U.S. Attorney Larry Keefe was forced to resign his position, and U.S. Attorney Jason Coody was now serving as the "interim" U.S. Attorney for the Northern District of Florida. The website of the United States Attorney's Office for the Northern District of Florida's press release stated:

**Former Lynn Haven City Commissioner and Developer
Charged in Superseding
Indictment Against Former Lynn Haven Mayor and
City Attorney**

**TALLAHASSEE, FLORIDA:** In an ongoing case arising from alleged public corruption by Lynn Haven City's former Mayor and Attorney, James David Finch, 70, and Antonius Genzarra Barnes, 55, were indicted Tuesday by a federal grand jury on charges of conspiracy to commit wire fraud and honest services fraud, and substantive counts of wire fraud and honest services fraud. Finch is also charged with making false statements to the FBI. The 44-count superseding indictment alleges that Finch, a Lynn Haven developer, and Barnes, a former Lynn Haven City Commissioner, conspired with Lynn Haven's then-Mayor, Margo Deal Anderson, and then-City Attorney, Joseph Adam Albritton, to ensure that contracts for numerous multimillion-dollar infrastructure and construction projects and post-Hurricane Michael debris clean-up activities were awarded to Finch. In return, Finch allegedly provided money and gifts to Anderson and Barnes, and Albritton received money from a company doing debris clean-up.

Acting United States Attorney Jason R. Coody of the Northern District of Florida, Special Agent in Charge Rachel Rojas of the FBI's Jacksonville

Field Office, and Bay County Sheriff Tommy Ford announced the superseding indictment at a press conference this afternoon.

The original indictment, returned by a federal grand jury in Panama City in August 2020, charged Anderson and Albritton with conspiring to commit wire fraud and honest services fraud, substantive counts of wire fraud, honest services fraud, and theft concerning Federal programs. Anderson was also charged with making false statements to FBI agents, while Albritton was charged with submitting a false invoice to an insurance company for hurricane debris removal from his residence. These charges were directly related to activity that took place in the aftermath of Hurricane Michael in October 2018.

The August 2020 indictment also charged Anderson and Albritton with devising a scheme to defraud Lynn Haven and its citizens of their right to honest services of Anderson, as Mayor, and Albritton, as City Attorney. These allegations, that both Anderson and Albritton solicited and received bribes or kickbacks from City projects that they approved, are related to yesterday's charges against Finch and Barnes. The indictment charged that Albritton drafted and implemented an agreement for trash pick-up with co-conspirator David White, owner of Erosion Control Specialists (ECS). In exchange for orchestrating the agreement, Albritton allegedly demanded kickbacks from White. Specifically, the indictment alleges that Albritton received money from ECS for each trash invoice paid by Lynn Haven.

The superseding indictment alleges that Anderson halted progress on plans to permit a city-owned site for disposal of vegetative debris, even though using the city-owned site would have saved Lynn Haven millions of dollars in disposal fees. Instead, the indictment alleges Anderson directed the City Manager to use Finch's company for vegetative debris disposal. According to the indictment, the city of Lynn Haven paid disposal fees in excess of $2 million to Finch.

The superseding indictment also alleges that between 2015 and the present date, Anderson helped Finch win multiple multimillion-dollar contracts with the city of Lynn Haven. In August 2017, Anderson , as Mayor of Lynn Haven, signed an agreement known as "1/2 Cent Infrastructure Surtax Design/Build Contract" with Finch's construction company—Phoenix Construction Services, Inc. The agreement made Phoenix the contractor or vendor for numerous multi-million-dollar Lynn Haven infrastructure projects that would not require any bid procedure. As alleged in the indictment, Phoenix was paid a total of $5.6 million for work related to this contract.

Additionally, during the same time period, Finch was awarded a contract for the 17th Street Ditch Stormwater project. For this project, Anderson signed a 30-year promissory note on behalf of Lynn Haven to Finch that eventually totaled more than $5 million, obligating the city of Lynn Haven to pay Finch the principal amount of the note along with millions of dollars in interest. Both Anderson and Barnes voted for this arrangement and received benefits from Finch as a result.

Between April and August 2020, the superseding indictment alleges that Anderson and Finch sought to have Finch construct the rebuild of municipal buildings, despite a City Commission approved plan in place to have architects prepare designs for the rebuilding and have FEMA and insurance proceeds pay for most of a $19 million dollar project. Anderson, as Mayor, attempted to thwart that plan and have Finch instead handle the rebuild for $15 million, most of which the City would have to finance since FEMA would not approve the Finch design/build proposal. Anderson and Finch allegedly pressured the City Manager and Police Chief to support their plan to the detriment of City residents.

In return, the superseding indictment charges Anderson with accepting things of value from Finch, including travel in a private airplane, lodging aboard a private yacht, meals and entertainment. According to the indictment, Anderson and her husband also received a $106,000 motorhome from Finch in February 2018.

In the superseding indictment, Finch is alleged to have provided Barnes with $45,000 in loans, which were never repaid. As Commissioner, Barnes voted consistently to approve Finch and his projects before, during, and after receipt of the monies that he received from Finch during a two-year period. Between August 2015 and December 2017, Barnes moved, seconded, and voted on matters before the Lynn Haven City Commission favorable to Finch's business interests, including the "1/2 Cent Infrastructure Surtax Design Build Contract" and the 17th Street project.

During the time periods when the alleged crimes were being committed, neither Anderson, Albritton nor Barnes filed required quarterly gift reports documenting that they received gifts in excess of $100 according to the indictment.

The superseding indictment also charges Finch with making false statements to FBI agents when he was interviewed relating to the criminal investigation. Finch is charged with making false statements and submitting a false document to the FBI in July 2020 concerning the transfer of a motorhome to Anderson and her husband. Finch provided the FBI with a bill of sale for the motor home, falsely stating he sold the motorhome to Anderson's husband on July 6, 2018, for 70,000. Although the bill of sale indicates that $35,000 was already paid and that another $35,000 was owed "with 6 percent interest," the indictment alleges that there is no record any money was ever paid to finch by Anderson's husband for the motorhome other than a $20,000 check issued to Finch by Anderson's husband 22 months after the motorhome transfer when the federal investigation of public officials had been publicized.

This investigation was conducted by the Federal Bureau of Investigation and the Bay County Sheriff's Office. The case is being prosecuted by Assistant United States Attorneys Stephen M. Kunz and Andrew J. Grogan.

If convicted, Anderson, Albritton, Finch, and Barnes each face prison terms of up to 20 years for conspiracy to commit wire fraud and honest services fraud, substantive wire fraud and honest services fraud, and mail fraud. Anderson and Albritton also face up to 10 years for theft concerning programs receiving federal funds. Both Anderson and Finch face an additional 5 years if convicted for making false statements to federal agents. Albritton faces a maximum of 20 years for submitting a false invoice to an insurance company.

Finch and Barnes made their initial appearance in court at 1:30 EST this afternoon before U.S. Magistrate Judge Martin Fitzpatrick, at the U.S. Courthouse in Tallahassee. Anderson and Albritton will be scheduled by the Court for an arraignment on the superseding indictment.

This indictment is a follow-up to the indictment returned in November 2019 of five defendants, including former Lynn Haven City Manager Michael White, former Lynn Haven Community Services Director David Horton, and Erosion Control Specialist owner David White, for conspiring to commit wire fraud, substantive counts of wire fraud and honest services fraud, relating to post-Hurricane Michael clean-up activities in Lynn Haven. All five of the defendants indicted in November 2019 have pled guilty to charges from the first indictment and are awaiting sentencing.

An indictment is merely an allegation by a grand jury that a defendant has committed a violation of federal criminal law and is not evidence of guilt. All defendants are presumed innocent and entitled to a fair trial, during which it will be the government's burden to prove guilt beyond a reasonable doubt.

I cannot describe what it is like to see one's name on a document like the indictment, United States Government vs. Margo Deal Anderson and James David Finch, then to read a press release that is completely false, and not be able to respond until trial. After reading such a narrative, to then read the last single sentence which states "all defendants are presumed innocent and entitled to a fair trial," is just "insult to injury." The damage has been done to the defendant in his community, in his workplace, his church, his family, to anyone who has ever known him, this is now the defining moment of his life, and for someone who is completely innocent, it is gut-wrenching.

March 28, 2021

Just seven months after I was indicted, and two weeks after James was indicted by the superseding indictment of March 16, 2021, my beautiful Mom, Geri Deal, died suddenly of a heart attack on Palm Sunday, March 28th, 2021. She had lived with the constant stress of the local news media accusing her of receiving free property cleanup after Hurricane Michael, and the devastation of watching her daughter going through the absolute Hell of a federal indictment and being harassed and humiliated daily by the media and the community which had once hailed her as the best Mayor ever in Bay County. The pain of losing my mom, knowing how all of this had just devastated her, just broke my heart into a thousand pieces, and in the months to follow, my grief was overwhelming, and so was that of my brother and my daughter.

She had just spent the last week in Jacksonville with my daughter and granddaughters, who were the joy of her heart, before returning home to Lynn Haven; I hugged her on Saturday morning as we all watched my granddaughter in her gymnastics class, and I told her I would see her the next weekend for Easter; the next day, Palm Sunday, my brother called me after midnight , wracked with grief , telling me that we had lost her. I just sat on the edge of my bed and sobbed, calling out to God, "Oh, please no, please God, no." My husband drove me to my daughter's house to tell her instead of calling her.

The following Wednesday, before the weekend of Good Friday and Easter began, Father Michael officiated at her funeral mass at St. Dominic's Church in Panama City; Todd Allen Herendeen, our dear friend, sang for her service, and my daughter read a beautiful tribute to her grandmother.

James had known my mother since childhood, and he was not allowed to be at her funeral because he and I could not have contact due to the orders of the prosecutors. His wife attended and sat with our family.

On the way from Kent-Forest Lawn Funeral Home to the church, the Bay County Sheriff's Office provided an escort to the church, speeding past us with lights flashing, and seeing them was extremely upsetting to me. When we arrived at the church, I spoke to the funeral home director and told him to let them know we did not want them to escort us back to the cemetery; my mother would not have wanted them around her, and neither did we.

The following is what I wrote and read at her funeral mass:

*Heaven has opened its gates to welcome Geri Deal, our beautiful, sweet Mother,*

223

*Grandmother, and "GG" to be with the Lord.*

*Geraldine (Geri) Davidson Deal was born November 10, 1937, in Geneva, Alabama.*

*Her early years were spent in Westville, Florida, and she attended Ponce de Leon School, where she was known for her abilities playing basketball, and where she spent a great deal of time with her grandparents, Cora and William Stafford, before later moving to Panama City.*

*She married Louie W. Deal, on November 22, 1952, and after living several years in Lynn Haven, Florida, they began a journey of over 30 years with the Corps of Army Engineers in many areas of the United States and abroad. Geri particularly enjoyed the three years spent in Hokkaido, Japan, where she immersed herself in the culture, and was a wonderful ambassador there, forming friendships of a lifetime because of her compassion, her love of learning, and her ability to communicate quickly as she studied Japanese in night classes.*

*Because she married very young, Geri did not go to college, but was a stay-at-home Mom, making her children and educational opportunity for them one of the most important priorities of her life. She made herself a part of each school her children attended as a room mother, member of the PTA, and began pushing them at an early age, and then never neglecting to tell anyone that her daughter has a master's degree, her son is a doctor, and her only granddaughter, an attorney. She also began working as a substitute teacher later in life, and was at Mosley High School almost every day, again, forging friendships and relationships with teachers and students there because of her warmth, her love of young people, and because she discovered another talent, she had not realized she possessed, the gift of teaching.*

*Throughout her life, Geri Deal enjoyed sewing, music of all kinds, reading, dancing, aerobics classes and travel, and she was also known for her wonderful cooking and baking, especially during holidays. Geri was particularly delighted with the boat named after her by her son Roy Deal and companion, Bob Gardner, the GERI D, expeditions to Shell Island, and watching the sunsets with Bob at Marina Bay. She loved going to church, and her personal relationship with the Lord began as a young girl, remaining at the core of her beliefs throughout life, and in later life converted to Catholicism, spending many hours discussing her opinions, objections, beliefs, and questions with Father Michael, who she adored, as she attended classes with her longtime companion and significant other, Bob Gardner.*

*Her children and grandchildren were her purpose for living, and she held a special place in her heart for each of them.*

*I was born at Lisenby Hospital in Panama City when my Mom was just seventeen years old; she had a dream for me, that my life would be filled with all of the things she never had. She started working on that dream by having me take piano lessons before I was five years old and planning how I would someday go to college. She could not afford to buy me the clothes like many of the little girls had, and so she learned to sew. She would sit for hours, sewing beautiful clothes for me and for my dolls. When I was a junior in high school she became very sick, and was in the hospital for over a month for a serious spinal surgery, and one week before she was to check in for the surgery, she stayed up all night for three days in a row to make sure she had finished my prom dress, sewing in agonizing pain, but she never told me about it until later. While she was in the hospital, I wrecked both of the family cars, wash and dried my father's tailor-made silk suits he had had made while stationed in Japan, which shrunk to the size of a charm bracelet, and while trying to cook for us in Mom's absence, burned many dinners, and actually set the entire stove on fire once while trying to fry chicken. I was so relieved when she was finally released from the hospital and came home to us. We were very close during my high school years, and I would come home from school each day, sit on the kitchen counter and tell her everything about school while she was preparing dinner; she was my best friend, the person I could always depend on, the one who taught me about the love of Jesus, who took me to church, who pushed me to succeed in school, and later when I would try for a successful career as an entertainer, she was my biggest cheerlead, attending as many shows as she possibly could, telling everyone in the audience within earshot, "that's my daughter."*

*To my brother, I will tell you that Mom never spoke of you without her face lighting up; you were sunshine in her life. She loved you so much, and I remember when you were a little boy, so ill with severe allergies, often causing bronchitis and pneumonia, she would be sitting up, rocking you all night, holding you up so that you could breathe easier. Your first year in college, Dad was working in Saudi Arabia, and Mom moved to Ole Miss, renting a house there and became a support for not only you, but all of your friends, as once again, her kitchen and her home were a gathering place where everyone felt welcome. You were her hero, her tall handsome son always standing by her side; becoming the medical doctor she was so proud of, the one who was with her at the end, doing everything in your power to save her.*

*My daughter, as you so eloquently said just a few moments ago, the two of you were inseparable from the beginning. As a working Mom, I was blessed to have her to be there for moments in your life when I could not be there. She was your Geri, and you came along in her life at a time when she needed you most and you brought joy to every day of her life from the moment you were born. To quote Forrest Gump, "you were two peas in a pod" and her love for you was immeasurable.*

*My granddaughters, I cannot even begin to tell you how many dreams your GG had for you, and she often said that she hoped to be in your lives for a long, long time. She worried that a time might come when you would not remember her. She saw a little piece of herself in each of you and knew in her heart that the legacy of strong women from which she came will continue on in all of us. She saw herself watching you play sports, and she said many times that your dance moves were inherited from her. She will always be a part of you; your successes, your joys, and when you have disappointments or heartaches, you will have a special angel watching over you, your GG.*

*"Her children arise up and call her blessed," a scripture from Proverbs, epitomizing the Mother and Grandmother who was Geri Deal; indeed her children and grandchildren were the ones who were truly blessed. The scriptures tell us that we each have a day to be born, and a day on which we are called home. To my beautiful mother who now no longer sees through a glass darkly but is face to face with her Lord and Saviour, for he is*

*indeed the resurrection and the life, the conqueror of death. I love you so much, and I will miss you every single day until we meet again.*


April 28, 2021

Tonight is the last night I will spend in the little blue house in Lynn Haven, built by my grandfather, and lovingly remodeled many years later by my Dad for my daughter and I. It is a very special house and has sheltered many members of my family for several generations. My baby bed was in the front bedroom with my parents, right across the hallway from my grandparents in 1955.

One of my favorite dogs is buried in the little grassy area between the driveway and the house, a little Shitzu I named Dumpling. Further toward the tree line are more of my childhood pets, two brown and white pointers, Rusty and Dusty, a beautiful cocker spaniel, Blondie, and a small black terrier, Sputnik.

The house has provided a home for various cousins, aunts and uncles through the years; there was a garden of giant watermelons planted by my grandfather, and a tide stream ran behind it when I was little that we played in when all of the streets in Lynn Haven were white sand. The places to be at that time included the little league ball games at Kinsaul Park, hanging out at the tennis courts behind the McMullen library on Pennsylvania Avenue, or the Big R root beer stand.

I wrote a quit claim deed to the house a month after I was indicted and my husband delivered it to James Finch because I was no longer allowed to speak to James after my arraignment of August 25, 2020. James did not record the deed until after he was indicted when I insisted that he file it. He had deposited $200,000 to the attorney's trust account who were going to represent me, and the quit claim deed was collateral for that money. I had no idea what legal representation was going to cost for the case, but quickly found out when the entire $200,000 was gone by the time James was indicted on March 16, 2021. By April, Judge Mark Walker changed the conditions of release and allowed James and I to communicate again because we were co-defendants in order to prepare for trial, and I insisted that he sell the house to pay him back the $200,000. He finally agreed.

I will always visit Lynn Haven because my brother, my cousins, and many close friends are here. One of my dearest friends, and co-defendants, James Finch is like a homing pigeon to the town which betrayed us both; you couldn't jackhammer him out of this place, and both of my parents were laid to rest in Mt. Hope Cemetery.

But Lynn Haven will never be my home again; this is my last night in my house. The last night to sleep here where generations of my family lived. This is the last morning I will wake up in my house on the corner of Tennessee Avenue and Sixth Street. I feel sick, I feel betrayed, and I feel abandoned by the place I have loved my entire life.

I have been a teacher in this community for over twenty-five years, I was a musician, and for six years, I was the Mayor. I was born here, I went to church here; I loved and gave so much of myself to this special little city…in the best of times and in the worst of times.

I have been accused of unbelievable wrongs, and I have had everything taken from me—for no reason other than lies, envy, and the political ambition of those in power who feared the success of a Mayor who was loved and trusted by the people of Lynn Haven.

Yet, when all is said and done, I still have what is important. I have my daughter, my husband, my brother, my family, my friends who know and believe that I am still the same person I have always been, and I have my faith in the Lord, who continues to hold me in the palm of His hand…through it all.

There will be a day when truth will prevail and when exoneration will come. But at what price?

July 2021

After the indictment and arrest of James Finch, his lawyers Guy Lewis and Jeffrey Forman, continued the requests that my attorneys had been making since August 2020 for *Brady* material pertaining to the investigation. (*Brady* material is information which is potentially exonerating or beneficial to defendants and prosecutors are required to provide this material in a timely manner.) If not for the efforts of the four high-powered attorneys working to exonerate James and me, and the absolute "bulldog" way they went after the documents we needed to defend ourselves, I do not believe we would have ever seen the documents.

Before James was indicted, I had been scheduled to go to trial March 3, 2021, on an indictment of 64 charges which was flawed and insufficient; the prosecutors informed my attorneys in February 2021 that they planned to supersede the indictment (rewrite it, possibly indicting others). This came about after all three of my attorneys, Jimmy Judkins, Rob Vezina, and Tony Bajoczky, met with the prosecutors, including U.S. Attorney Larry Keefe, presenting them with evidence which was clearly sufficient to prove the property cleaned was not mine, along with a multitude of other evidence proving that the investigation was faulty. As one of my attorneys put it, "there was no hiding of the ball." What the prosecutors did at this point, instead of looking at the evidence for truth, took everything we gave them, and rewrote the indictment. The charges went from 64 to 27; and two defendants were added, James Finch and former commissioner, Antonius Barnes.

When the FBI interviews a witness or target, their notes are formalized in a memo known as a "302", and as James and I quickly learned, 302's are written to benefit the government's "narrative", and witnesses often lie to protect themselves. A large number of 302's were publicly filed as exhibits, and so many of the interviews and reports were made public after the evidentiary hearings of March 2022 and December 2022, and after the two trials of my co-defendant James Finch. Here, I have included many of these interviews and reports with my comments and annotations. If I had gone to trial in March or May of 2021 as had been planned, this information would not have been in my possession. As you look at the dates on these various interviews, keep in mind that I was the whistleblower in this case, even though the FBI and the Bay County Sheriff's office deny this. They admit that I came to them on April 1· 2019, with the information, and there is not one report from either the FBI or the Bay County Sheriff's Office written before that date, nor is there a warrant for phone records or property search until after that date. Some of the Sheriff's investigators refer to my bringing in the information, but Sheriff Tommy Ford has never publicly acknowledged this, and he stood beside the FBI and prosecutors at the press conferences and never opened his mouth to defend me. Instead, he referred to me as an official who "took advantage of residents at their most vulnerable time."

## FBI Interview of Amanda Delonjay
## Accounting Specialist for the City of Lynn Haven

**April 12, 2019 (*The same day the Sheriff's department raided ECS warehouse and found the planted invoices placed on top of the trash implicating me as having had my property cleaned*)**

## By: Special Agent Lawrence P Borghini

After being advised of the nature of the interview, Delongay provided the following information:

Amanda Delongay, date of birth (redacted), was interviewed at the City of Lynn Haven City Hall in Lynn Haven, Florida, by Special Agent (SA) Lawrence P. Borghini and Bay County Sheriff's Office Major Jimmy Stanford.

After being advised of the identity of the interviewing Agent and the

Delongay is employed by the City of Lynn Haven as an Accounting Specialist. She has worked for the City of Lynn Haven for sixteen (16) years. During that time, she has been responsible for various accounting functions such as payroll, fixed assets and paying all bills. Her direct supervisor is Beverly Waldrup. Waldrup is the Director of Finance for the City of Lynn Haven and as such is a department head. All department heads report to the city manager.

Delongay believes the first time that the City of Lynn Haven paid Erosion Control Specialists, Inc. (ECS) was in January of 2018. She was not aware of a contract, bid or request for proposal (RFP) for the work that ECS performed. The City of Lynn Haven's purchasing department would have that information.

The process normally requires that a purchase order (PO) be prepared and submitted. The purchase order contains the approval to purchase goods or services. When an invoice for the item comes in, Delongay stamps the invoice with the date received and forwards it to the department which purchased the item for verification and approval to pay the invoice. The invoice and the PO are then returned to the finance department and a check is prepared and mailed. The finance department keeps all the documentation for all expenditures.

After Hurricane Michael, the invoices for ECS were brought to DeLongay by either Michael White or David Horton. There were no purchase orders with the invoices. Sometimes the invoice(s) would be signed off on or she was given verbal authorization to pay the invoice(s). The checks for ECS and Greenleaf were held out and put in David Horton's box. David Horton is the Director of Community Services and a department head.

The checks that were being printed and issued to ECS and Greenleaf were in excess of $35,000. ($35,000 was the city manager's daily spending limit without commission approval). A lot of money was being paid to ECS and Greenleaf. Delongay never saw a contract nor a purchase order regarding the payments. Delongay understood that some of the money that was being paid was for emergency circumstances, so she questioned the city manager, Michael White. White told her that "they were working on a project for me" and/or "get Ashley to prepare a purchase order for me". White would tell Delongay to pay the invoice. Delongay reported the activity to her supervisor, Beverly Waldrup, but nothing seemed to happen. After each check run, a check register of the warrants would be printed off and sent to the City Manager, Mayor and Deputy Finance Director. The City Manager, Mayor and Deputy Finance Director were to review and signoff on the check register so that they would be aware of how much money was being spent by the City of Lynn Haven.

**What Amanda Delonjay neglects to tell the FBI agent here, is that after the storm the warrant list was not printed every two weeks as it was in the past under normal circumstances, and if it was printed in some form, I did not receive copies. Computers were down, printers**

not available, and the warrant lists were not available to me for many weeks. I had no office, no desk, no mailbox. When I finally received them, I found them in a big stack on a desk which had been designated to me in the attic of the City Service Center next door to the old City Hall. This was in January of 2019. The mayor's signature is the last signature on the warrant list (checks that have already been sent out), and the City Manager and Accounting Department Head have already signed their approval. The mayor is the Treasurer of the City, and the signature is symbolic in nature; however, I had aways been diligent at looking over the warrant lists as Mayor, just to be informed as to what the city expenditures were each month. All of the Commissioners had access to these documents, not just the Mayor.

Delongay was also responsible for payment of the City of Lynn Haven's credit cards. She would receive a master copy of the credit card statement. DeLongay would stamp the statement as received and then separate the pages according to the individual issued a card and responsible for the charge. She would forward the pages to each department head so that they could put the purchase order number next to the charge on the statement. The individual statements and purchase orders approving and authorizing the charge paid were returned the finance department. Delongay would then pay the whole credit card bill.

Ben Jenke purchased $400 worth of alcohol for Hurricane Michael with this credit card. The City of Lynn Haven purchased a drone, and it is on the fixed assets list. The drone costs approximately $1,200. Any item over $1,000 is placed on the city's fixed assets list.

Prior to city manager Michael White leaving, DeLongay was told to hold off payment of $140,000 worth of invoices to various vendors while ECS and Greenleaf invoices were being paid in full. As far as Delongay could tell, there had been no bids, quotes, contracts or approval by the city council authorizing the payment of the ECS and Greenleaf invoices. This is a violation of city policy and state statute. Delongay had also heard that ECS employees were stealing stuff from the City.

David Horton had been hired by Michael White. Michael White had terminated the former director/department head of Community Services and hired Horton.

**End of interview with Amanda Delonjay; the agent misspelled her name in his interview. My question is why an employee of fifteen years with the City did not go to the Commission, or even one Commissioner or the Mayor with this information? Her husband was the Fire Chief of Lynn Haven, (he retired in 2023) and also the Emergency Management Director. Surely, she was telling him about this. Why did he say nothing? Amanda Delonjay, like so many**

others in this case, suddenly retired in January of 2020, just after
Michael White, David Mickey White, Josh Anderson, David Horton,
and Shannon Rodriguez were indicted in November of 2019 and then
pleaded guilty in early 2020. The timing of her retirement, like so
many others in Lynn Haven and Bay County, is noteworthy.


FBI Interview of Robert Jackson
Former City Attorney of City of Lynn Haven

April 15, 2019 (two weeks after I went to Sheriff Ford)

By Special Agent Lawrence P Borghini

Former City attorney who was let go in September 2018 one month
before Hurricane Michael. I had been advocating that the City hire
an inhouse attorney and an in-house engineer from the time I
became Mayor. Jackson's billing to the City for the previous 5-year
period was almost 900K, for the firm Harrison, Sale McCloy. He was
very angry with me.


ROBERT JACKSON (Protect Identity) was interviewed in Panama City,
Florida. After being advised of the identity of the interviewing Agent and
the nature of the interview, Jackson provided the following information:

Jackson was the City of Lynn Haven's attorney from 2002 until 2018.
Jackson was let go by the city commission in September 2018 at the last city
commission meeting before the start of the new fiscal year beginning on
October 1, 2018. Jackson described the way the commission handled the
matter as unprofessional. Jackson noticed in the last commission meeting
there was a change in the city's budget for the new fiscal year and the
budget did not contain money for a city attorney. Jackson first learned of
his dismissal in that public meeting. Jackson had just had dinner with the
mayor, Margo Anderson, two days prior to the commission meeting and
she never mentioned it to Jackson.
He makes this sound like we had a private dinner together. We were
at the Bay County League of Cities meeting at Captain Anderson's
and we happened to be seated at the same table. The Commission
could not have discussed his possible dismissal outside of a public
meeting; that would have been a Sunshine violation, as he knew.
Jackson advised that the city attorney position was a charter position
that has never been approved by the commission. The hiring of a city

231

attorney was a procedural matter with no Request for Qualifications (RFA) advertised by the city before hiring.

Jackson learned that the city wanted to save money and planned to use a city employee (Kelly Tram) who was working as a police dispatcher as their in-house city attorney. The city planned on paying for Tram to take the Florida Bar exam in February 2019. Jackson advised that the city was spending approximately $100,000 to $120,000 a year on legal fees with his firm. The city justified the change from outside council to in-house council because the city was going to pay Tram a salary of $50,000 to $60,000 a year plus employee costs. The city commission voted 3-2 to make the change with Margo Anderson and Commissioners Judy Tinder and Dan Russell voting for the change while Commissioners Rodney Friend and Antonius Barnes voted against. Jackson was concerned about Tram's lack of experience and legal knowledge. During the transition, Jackson provided the city with a list of the files he was working on and offered to help the city with its transition to in-house council.

Jackson explained the mayor had run on the platform that the city had too many senior employees costing the city a lot of money and these employees needed to go because of their high pay. Jackson was concerned because by getting rid of these employees, the city would greatly reduce its knowledge and experience.

**This statement is not true. My platform pointed out that the City of Lynn Haven had 10 employees, 6 of whom were married to each other, who were making 1.2 million dollars annually in salary and benefits, while a large number of employees were barely making minimum wage, or a livable wage. The City was transferring over a million dollars a year from the stormwater enterprise funds to cover these salaries, and I promised if elected I would bring this before the Commission, which I did. I never stated that we needed to "fire or get rid of anyone." My campaign brochures are still in existence to verify this.**

Jackson advised that after the hurricane, the city entered a FEMA contract to clean up the city's parks. The contract was not bid out and nobody knew about it. The contract was for at least six figures. Commissioner Friend advised him that it appeared the contract was being covered up. Jackson explained that the city manager only has spending authority up to $35,000. Any expenditure by the city greater than $35,000 needed to be approved by the city commission. By Florida Statute, any construction contract by the city greater than $250,000 had to be advertised. With regard to emergency situations, any sole source contract needed to involve the public's health and safety and get the best value for the city.

**When I first read this, all I could think was, if Commissioner Rodney Friend had this information, why did he not bring it up to the**

rest of the Commission?  He was in office until April 2019, and he was in attendance at public commission meetings beginning the week after Hurricane Michael in October 2018.  Why didn't he speak up?  Another interesting point, is that the FBI agent never interviewed Commissioner Rodney Friend, even though he was a sitting Commissioner during the time of Hurricane Michael and the aftermath?  Why?  Or was he interviewed, and it was just another document the government did not give us?  Michael White and Mickey White, in their text messages to each other, discuss a driveway that Mickey White is to pour for Rodney Friend.

Jackson advised that goods and services were being transferred between Lynn Haven's city manager Michael White and Erosion Control Specialist (ECS) owner Mickey White.  ECS had the city parks cleanup contract.  The property being transferred between the two were land and vehicles.  So, if Robert Jackson, a member of the Florida Bar and officer of the court knew that there were illegal activities going on in Lynn Haven, why did he not report it to someone?  And how did he know?  Did Commissioner Friend tell him this information as well?

After Hurricane Michael, Lynn Haven hired Adam Albritton as their city attorney.  Albritton did not disclose to the city that he represents GAC Contractors.  Albritton also represents the Bay County Contractors Association (BCCA).  BCCA lobbies local governments.  In addition, Albritton represents Derwin White on property sales.  Michael White recommended Adam Albritton to the Commission after Kelly Tram was unable to fulfill the position of city attorney because her husband was deployed to another area.

Bobby Baker is the public works director for the City of Lynn Haven.  Baker's staff was fired and the city's vehicles are now being maintained by James Finch.  Finch and the Mayor have a long-time relationship.  The mayor's husband worked for Finch at one time.  Jackson is aware that the mayor has taken trips with Finch to Key West, Florida.  Jackson advised that such trips are a violation of Florida law unless they are paid for by the mayor.  Chris Forehand sold Finch a motor home.  The motor home was expensive and is now with Mayor Anderson.  The city built a splash park at Cain Griffin Park (616 E 17th St; Lynn Haven, FL 32444).  The original budget for the project was $200,000.  The city ended up spending $1,000,000 on the project.  Finch owns the property across the street from the park and is building a new subdivision on it.  Finch was the best man at Anderson's wedding.  I do not even know where to begin here.  Rob Jackson was just full of information about me, the Mayor.  First of all, my husband never worked for James Finch.  He was a member of the Phoenix Race Team as a volunteer, and he traveled every weekend racing with James and the team for years.  Never for a salary.  It was a hobby for him. James was the best man at our wedding in 2001, over 20 years before this investigation. As I read the information Jackson volunteered about trips to Key West, the motorhome transaction, and speculation concerning whether I paid for trips or broke Florida law I am just amazed at what a fountain of information he was, and also that the FBI agent never asked me or my husband any of these questions. SA Larry Borghini, the sole witness to the grand jury which indicted me, had absolutely no curiosity or inclination to verify what the angry former city attorney had to say about me. My husband did pay for the motorhome, it was not a gift, when we traveled there are records of our payments for meals and lodging, and my travel on Mr. Finch's airplane, by Florida statute was only equal to the cost of a ticket on any commercial flight to the same destination for which Mr. Finch and I had a payment agreement, if anyone from the FBI or the BCSO had bothered to ask, but they had no curiosity. They did not want the truth. They wanted me to go to prison for exposing the GAC/ AshBritt conspiracy and theft in Bay County.

FBI 302 Interview

Ricky Ramie, Lynn Haven Police Chief

7/17/2019

This interview was conducted by SA Lawrence Borghini on 7/17/2019 but was not entered formally into his records until 06/02/2021, almost two years later. Attorney Guy Lewis brought this to the Court's attention, that for an agent not to type or enter his notes into a formal report until months or even years after the fact, is a credibility issue, as the agent would be looking at hand-written notes and trying to remember the entire context of an interview. And there were many 302 reports which were not entered until months after the actual interviews were conducted by SA Borghini.

Ramie was interviewed at the Federal Bureau of Investigation in Panama City, Florida by Special Agent Lawrence P. Borghini. After being advised of the identity of the interviewing Agent and the nature of the interview, Ramie provided the following information:
On February 1, 2018, Ramie was hired by Lynn Haven City Manager Michael White as Assistant Police Chief for the City of Lynn Haven. Ramie had gone through Lynn Haven's hiring process and been selected. Ramie

had 25 years of experience in law enforcement starting with the Bay County Sheriff's office (BCSO) in November 1992 and retiring in November 2017. During his time at the BCSO, Ramie started in patrol and worked his way up holding various ranks and positions before retiring as a Major.

Ramie had known Michael White from coaching t-ball. In January 2018, Ramie was approached about the Lynn Haven police chief position because the current police chief Matt Riemer was retiring. Michael White and Ramie discussed the Lynn Haven police department and Ramie ended up applying for the position. Ramie was formally interviewed for the position and ranked number 1 of the 4 or 5 candidates that had made the cut. Ramie was hired as the deputy chief with the understanding that Matt Riemer would be retiring in two years.

After Hurricane Michael, Lynn Haven began offering buyouts. It was announced that Riemer would be retiring on May 10, 2019, and he was going on 90 days terminal leave starting February 7, 2019.

Ramie was introduced to Mickey White by Michael White one day when Ramie was pointing out the screw ups in a curb that ECS was pouring at the police department.

Ramie was at the police department during Hurricane Michael. A number of people, to include Michael White, Mayor Anderson and Dan Russell, had come to the police department to monitor the hurricane and shelter. A decision was made to bring everyone that was out working in and wait for the hurricane to pass before sending them back out. Once the conditions became safe, the officers were sent out to conduct welfare checks, etc.

After the hurricane, because the city hall and police station were damaged, the city set up at Southerland's. **Southerland's was a funeral home and event center owned by former U.S. Congressman Steve Southerland.**

There were briefings at 6 am and 6 pm. Michael White was meeting with city department heads and contractors assessing the damage and assigning the priorities. After approximately 3-4 days, there began to be secondary meetings with Gulf Power, Crowder Gulf and Chris Forehand. Michael White fired CERES. Michael White was trying to run the city like he did the Co-op and went with two debris companies.

**Michael White had told me that he was letting Ceres go, one of the three national debris hauling companies hired during "blue skies" by the City in case of a disaster, in order to save money for the City. What I did not know, was that Michael, in agreement with Derwin White and Adam Albritton, GAC's attorney, let Ceres go, and drafted a contract with ECS, Derwin White's nephew David Mickey White's company, the company that working with Michael White would bilk**

the City of Lynn Haven for almost five million dollars, the conspiracy that I would be charged as having been a part. **Derwin White made a deal with AshBritt, that Derwin would get rid of Ceres, which would give AshBritt and Crowder Gulf more work, and in exchange, Ash Britt would "kick back" money to GAC.**

Eventually the city's operations were moved to behind the city library. Ramie noticed ECS, dressed in their orange t-shirts, began to appear at the meals the city was providing after the hurricane. Mickey White had ECS employees working and doing various things that included cooking. Ramie asked what the ECS employees were doing and was told they were helping out. Ramie had asked the question because the city had its' own people.

The mayor was pushing to clean the park (Sheffield Park) for Halloween. **This statement is not entirely true; the park was being cleaned in order to move the City temporary operating trailer, tents, and various police and Sheriff's office trailers from other counties, out of Southerland's property to the City park. I was pushing for the City to have its normal Halloween in the park celebration for the children since trick or treating would be impossible because of no streetlights and the condition of the City, and to try and push the message of recovery to encourage people not to move away, but to stay and rebuild.**

Lyon Smith from Gulf Power was out at the ball fields and ran their operations from there.

Michael White wore 5.11s and a badge around his neck. He appeared to be law enforcement. The city manager, mayor and city commissioners were all given badges (for credentials) for presentation at roadblocks and entrance into the EOC. **Ricky makes this sound to the FBI agent as though the badges were just given to us by him. The Mayor and members of the Commission all had badges which were given to us when we were sworn in after being elected to office.** Michael White wanted a gun, so he was issued a .40 caliber S & W for a desk gun. When the city went to AR-15's, Michael White wanted one, but Ramie never issued one to him. Michael White purchased a .380 handgun. Ramie went to Money Miser with White when he purchased the firearm. **Ricky is trying to distance himself from Michael White in this interview with SA Borghini. The text messages between Ricky and Michael, which were also made public during the evidentiary hearings tell a completely different story about their relationship and the guns.**

Michael White was assigned to take care of the city employees and operations while the mayor oversaw the citizens coordinating with her daughter in Jacksonville and the Cajun Navy.

**This is crucial exculpatory evidence provided by Ricky Ramie**

about the fact that Michael was in charge of the city employees and operations. What Ricky does not say was that when I declared the emergency that I delegated all of Michael's normal responsibilities to him and did not take over any of the operations, as I could have by the Charter. SA Borghini testified to the grand jury, that I was the head of the City and that I supervised Michael White; this one statement alone made everything else that was said about me to the grand jury believable. In later indictments, this would be corrected, but it is too late once one has been indicted.

Ramie recalls Mickey White telling Michael White that he needed money to pay ECS employees. Robert Brannon (Robert was the City facilities manager) and Michael White got into an argument. They were arguing about ECS, the pay he (Brannon) was seeing and the work they had done at the police department. Michael White was wanting to sub-contract stuff out, including the police dispatch, to cut costs. Ramie believes this occurred while they were operating from the Verizon trailer.

Michael White told Ramie he needed a police escort. Ramie had to assign an officer to Michael White for approximately 2-3 months. The officer was tasked with taking Michael White everywhere White needed to be. Michael White also wanted to be issued radio so he could talk to the officers on Lynn Haven's primary channel.

On one occasion, Mayor Anderson approached Ramie before a commission meeting. She asked Ramie about getting to the beach to get her hair done. The Mayor was concerned about getting back in time for an event that was being held in the lunchroom. Mayor Anderson was given a ride back from her hairdresser on the beach by the Lynn Haven police department. Ramie doesn't recall giving the mayor any rides to her residence and explained the mayor used the city golf cart to get around after the hurricane.

**This is not a true statement. I had driven myself to the beach after over two weeks of not having a way to wash my hair except the limited water in our motorhome to have my hair washed and dried by my stylist who had moved out there because her salon in town was destroyed. After she finished my hair, when I returned to my truck it had a flat tire and I was trying to get back to an important meeting. I called the LHPD and one of the officers brought my husband out to the beach to get the truck tire repaired and drove me back to town. Several others who were interviewed by the FBI told versions of my having gone to the beach to get my hair done.**

The day the FBI showed up **(the interviews began in the City just a few days after I had gone to Sheriff Ford as the whistleblower. Not one document, interview, affidavit or warrant in the corruption case**

**was issued until AFTER I went to the Sheriff, despite their denials that I was the whistleblower in the case)** Vickie Gainer had a meeting with staff and advised they (staff) were probably going to be approached by FBI to speak with them. After David Horton's first meeting with the FBI, Horton treated Ramie differently. Michael White and Horton had a long-standing relationship. **(David Horton was the Community Services Director who was indicted and arrested with Michael White in November of 2019).**

ECS employees were used to clean out the police station, city hall and sports complex. A number of items were removed from the police department and put into a Conex box. Corporal Enfinger noticed that ECS employees were posting stuff online for sale that had a City of Lynn Haven sticker on it. Cpl. Enfinger identified an individual selling the city's property and located him in Fountain, Florida. Cpl. Enfinger found city property in the subject's vehicle. More city property recovered in Alabama and a truckload of it was brought back from that location.

On the days that ECS was working at Michael White's farm or other properties, Michael White would hold Austin White, Josh Horton and a third individual back from working with ECS on those projects. On New Year's Eve, Michael White complained about not having a jacket because Mickey White's guys had packed up Michael White's belongings. Michael White also got on to Austin White (Michael White's son) about all the money Austin was making for ECS. Michael White wanted Austin to use some of that money to pay for the repairs on Austin's truck instead of Michael White having to pay for the repairs for him.

**Why did Ricky, as a member of law enforcement, not report any of this work being done on Michael White's property by a contractor who was apparently working for the City? Again, the text messages between Ricky and Michael show a very close relationship up until the time Michael resigns as City Manager on March 26, 2019, after having been arrested for domestic violence. Ricky continues to distance himself from Michael White in his interview with the FBI.**

The mayor approached Ramie and told him that Mickey White had made an invoice with her address on it. The mayor explained that there was an easement behind her property and a tree had fallen on her pole barn. The mayor had Google pictures before the hurricane and after. The mayor went to Tom Lewis and the news director at News 13. She claimed News 13 was not going to run a story because of what she had presented them. Ramie advised that Amanda had told him that the mayor was just down there and that there was no easement. The mayor claims to have the original survey for the property which shows the easement.

**This is regarding the property cleanup accusations which were the center of the Government's case against me, and of course, were**

completely false. Amanda Richard, the City Planner, knew there was an easement and so did Bobby Baker, Vickie Gainer, the city attorney and others. Their emails prove this. Channel 13 called me and demanded a statement from me, and I went to the station. Notice that Ricky says the mayor "claims" as though I were not being honest.

The city purchased a golf cart approximately a month before the hurricane. The golf cart was to be used by the city for various events. The golf cart was given to the mayor to use when they were at Southerland's. **The city manager assigned the golf cart to me because there were so many nails on the roads and debris, that you could not drive a car without getting a flat tire, and I was using my own Yamaha scooter to drive around Lynn Haven. Once I started delivering blankets, water, food, and other supplies to residents who were unable to get to the distribution center, Michael assigned the golf cart to me to use for deliveries. As various dignitaries and news media came to Lynn Haven, I also used the golf cart to drive them around the city, showing them damage and telling the story of the day of the storm. Some of the visitors included Senator Bill Nelson, Attorney General Ashley Moody, Congressman Kevin McCarthy, reporters from the Wall Street Journal, the New York Times, and many others. My having the golf cart, as I would find out later, really pissed off Commissioner Russell and Chief Ramie; in September of 2019, they were so vocal about my having it that I returned it to the City and stopped using it altogether. To this day it now remains parked in Chief Ramie's front yard in Lynn Haven for his personal use.**

Ramie has no idea where the city's drone is at. It was purchased to photograph various city events such as concerts, etc. Ramie never saw the drone. Ben Jenke (Ben was the City's CRA director and Economic Director) was told by Michael White if he found a liquor store open to let him know. Twenty (20) bottles of whiskey were purchased from Publix and placed in the city's motorhome. **Ricky is very sanctimonious here and does not mention that he often had a red solo cup of Crown and coke which he referred to as "brown water."**

Ricky went to RV Connections looking for something the police department could use for a command post. Ramie met the owner outside the business. Ramie brought back a motorhome, and the owner agreed to settle up with the city later. Michael White took the motorhome for the city's use. Michael White eventually purchased a 5$^{th}$ wheel for dispatch to use.

Michael White had two vehicles which he let the city use after the hurricane. Both buggies were jacked up with one being larger than the other. Right after the hurricane, Michael White had $10,000 in cash. After they moved the motorhome to behind the city library, they needed a place to hide the money. The money was hide {sic} under one of the seats in the motorhome.

**Ricky Ramie, Michael White, Chris Forehand, and Mickey White, all have different and varying stories of bags of cash that were floating around in the aftermath of the hurricane. No one ever accused me, through all the 64 charges of taking cash or having bags of cash. Even at my sentencing hearing, I was given no fines or ordered to pay any restitution because I was never charged with stealing anything, despite the fact that the *Washington Post, AP*, and other major news outlets reported that the Mayor of Lynn Haven had been indicted for helping to steal five million dollars in FEMA funds.**

Ramie believes that Ben Lee, the president of Hancock Bank, was able to get the city the money. Some of the money was loaned to Antonius Barnes, LH police officer Chris Meachem and Robert. Meachem's money was paid back through payroll deductions. After the city moved to the Verizon trailer, Julie Higby was tasked with tracking down how the money was used.

Michael White was buying a piece of property from Jim Slonina (one of the owners of Panhandle Engineering with Chris Forehand). Slonina was donating a boat to the city. Ramie drove with Michael White to look at the boat. They drove by the property that White was going to purchase. A couple days later, Michael White threw a bag of cash to Ramie to hold for White. Ramie believes the bag contained the cash ($35,000) that White was going to use to purchase the property from Slonina.

Ramie heard from Michael White that he was selling his farm to Mickey White. Ramie rode with Michael White one time to feed the cows on Michael White's property. The cows looked like they were starving. Michael White advised that he was selling the farm to Mickey White for $300,000, cows and everything. White intended on paying off the mortgage on the property and putting $100,000 in his pocket.

Mickey White invited Ramie to go with him to Destin for dinner. Mickey White had a limo rented. Ramie declined. David Horton went on the trip with Mickey White. Mickey White also invited Ramie on a hunting trip. Mickey White was complaining that people were bailing on him regarding the trip.

**The FBI agent seems to have no curiosity about the fact that while those of us living in the City were trying to survive, Ramie, Michael White, Commissioner Russell, and others were enjoying the amenities of restaurants, condos, and bars on the beach, which only 14 miles away was virtually untouched with hurricane damage, and their good times are documented in text messages which are public records from the court hearings.**

Michael White and David Horton came back from someplace. Michael White then asked Ramie to be on a committee. Ramie, Horton, and Joe Footen were on the committee that scored the bids that came in on an RFQ for a new building. Horton was the one who scored the bids.

ECS employees cleaned the ditch in Dan Russell's subdivision. (Osceola Point). A call for service came in for a medical emergency at Osceola Point. Prior to the hurricane, Dan Russell and Michael White would get into arguments about the ditch in Russell's neighborhood. Michael White's position was when the subdivision purchased the property they assumed responsibility for the ditch. Dan Russell claimed that the ditch was an easement and therefore the city's responsibility. When the call came in, Michael White went down there. Ramie did not. **Commissioner Dan Russell was named in the first indictment as an unindicted conspirator for property cleanup, just as I was. Bobby Baker and others testified that ECS cleaned truckloads of debris from the privately owned neighborhood, stacked it by the road, charged it to the City and ultimately submitted the costs to FEMA. Russell was never indicted for private property cleanup, and he actually *had private property cleanup* as a sitting Commissioner, as did many other Bay County officials. I am the only elected official who was indicted and arrested, and we proved in court that what was cleaned was a city easement, and that the easement was on the neighbor's property to the east of me. The city easement was not even on my property but the property to the east of mine, 514 Virginia Avenue.**

Dan Russell called Ramie about an incident involving Michael White while Ramie was camping at an RV park in Franklin County. Ramie then called Mayor Anderson about the matter. The next morning, Ramie called Bay County Sheriff Tommy Ford to discuss the incident. Sheriff Ford planned on taking statements and doing an investigation. Ramie packed up his camper and drove back to Bay County.

**This paragraph is not even close to what happened; Michael White got into an argument with his wife because she found a text message on his phone which alluded to an affair between Michael White and the FEMA coordinator, Amber Guy. Michael turned a gun on his wife and then threatened to kill himself before running out of the RV they were staying in. Ricky was driving home from camping in Franklin County celebrating his birthday or some other occasion, and his voice on the phone to me, sounded alcohol impaired. Commissioner Dan Russell as well as Ramie were aware of domestic violence issues with the Whites, and at this point in time, Ramie was involved in the corruption and did not want to arrest Michael White. He kept asking me what he should do, which I thought was so very odd; I told him he was police chief, to follow his protocols. The**

entire arrest process by the BCSO, and the coverup by Commissioner Russell and Chief Ramie are suspect in hindsight; based on the interviews and information we now have, Russell and Ramie, as well as the BCSO were covering for Michael White. Also, another fact that has never been discussed by the media, is that Michael White was on probation for domestic violence with a firearm when he was indicted and arrested by the FBI. Even Ricky Ramie had stated to me that Michael would probably be arrested for violation of probation charges, but he never was. Apparently, his state probation for domestic violence charges went away as part of his deal with the Government, although this has never been made public if it is true.

James Finch noticed construction was going on at Sheffield Park and made inquiries with Margo Anderson. There were questions about the bids. Finch advised that ECS was putting up a building and they didn't even have a contractor's license.

Again, Barghini is the special agent who at this point is now part of the Sheriff's task force, and he is questioning Ramie about the building in Sheffield Park which is the reason I found out about the ECS fraud and went to the Sheriff. SA Borghini has no curiosity to question me and ask me what I know about any of this. Instead, he relies on Ramie and others, because he obviously either believes what the Sheriff and Ramie have told him about me, (that I am guilty), or he is part of the corruption scheme to take down the mayor because she has exposed the GAC corruption which is far-reaching. I was willing to take a lie detector test to prove my innocence, but I was told that a lie detector test is inadmissible.


FBI INTERVIEW
RICKY RAMIE (2ND Interview of Ramie)
Police Chief for the City of Lynn Haven

05/08/2020

This interview with Ramie is nearly a year after the first interview, and at this time, Ramie is wearing a wire and recording every conversation he has by phone or in person with me and with my co-defendant James Finch. All of the tape recordings are court record, and they were released to us on the evening of my Mom's funeral in March of 2021. Ramie is now working with the FBI to indict me because he is involved in the corruption himself, and he is also trying to push forward the plans for the new City Hall and Police Department with Florida Architects; plans which were, in the beginning plans, over 40 million dollars. After this amount was exposed in public commission meetings, City Manager Vickie Gainer, Ramie, and staff began to work with the architect to bring the cost more in line. His tone in this interview, just three months before I was arrested, is completely different than the first one. Also, it is interesting that only one FBI agent interviews Ramie; their protocol is for two agents. Ramie is law enforcement; he is one of their own.

Ricky Ramie was interviewed at the Federal Bureau of Investigation. Ramie was aware of the identity of the interviewing Agent and the nature of the interview. Ramie thereafter provided the following information:

On January 12, 2020, the City of Lynn Haven through an RFQ began the process of rebuilding the city as a result of the damage from Hurricane Michael. Vickie Gainer, Ben Jenke, Chief Ramie and others were involved in the process. The group had had eight (8) meetings with Florida Architects and was working on the plans for the rebuilding of the City Hall and Police Station. The process had reached the point where the city staff was fine tuning the designs and getting ready to present them {sic} the City Commission.

On Saturday, Ramie was contacted by James Finch. Finch had just purchased a piece of property behind the Walgreens in Lynn Haven and wanted to build the city a Police Station and Fire Station on the property. Finch stated that he was going to get Chris Forehand to draw up plans for a 4,000 square foot building. Finch wanted to do the project as a design-build and the city could either pay for the project or he would finance it. Ramie let Vickie Gainer know on Monday about his conversation with Finch.

On Wednesday, April 15, 2020, Ramie received a call from Vickie Gainer. Gainer was crying. Gainer advised that she had received a call from Mayor Margo Anderson. Mayor Anderson told Gainer that she wanted Gainer to meet with Finch on Monday, April 20, 2020, at 2:00 p.m. to "hear James out." Gainer stated that she did not think that was a good idea since Jimmy Stanford had come to the city and asked for copies of the City's contracts with Phoenix Construction and GAC. Mayor Anderson blew up. The Mayor was mad that a public records request had been made and she knew nothing about it. Gainer was aware that Finch had built and financed the 17th Street ditch project and now he was trying to do the same thing with the police department. At the Monday meeting, Finch was going to make a proposal and present plans drawn up by Forehand.

Ramie explained that FEMA, Tetra Tech, and the City had been working on hardening the current Fire Department, building a new Police

Department and new City Hall. The city was going to pay for the projects with insurance money and FEMA funds. Ramie had heard that after the hurricane, Kelli Battistini was working on the City's insurance claim and the city was to receive the policy limits before Chris Forehand talked Michael White into using World Claim. Forehand claimed that World Claim had helped other communities in similar situations in the past.

Ramie advised that he had been contacted by Forehand and asked "what do you think about the Beach's Police Department building." Forehand sent Ramie a set of plans for the PCBPD's building.

**This interview with Ramie was conducted in the middle of Covid-19 when the City was working administratively from home, and also, after months of the negative publicity of the FBI investigation, and after having been named as an unindicted co-conspirator in the November 2019 indictment of Michael White and all the rest, my reputation had plummeted, City Commission meetings were filled with people who did not usually attend, including political operatives such as Arthur Cullen.**

**I had attended one of the final meetings with Florida Architects by Zoom, and when I heard the 40-million-dollar price tag I was completely taken aback, knowing that the City could not afford this. I spoke with James Finch about it, and he wanted to present an alternative idea to the City Manager, the Police Chief and others of how the rebuild could be accomplished much more cost-efficiently, and there was absolutely nothing nefarious or underhanded about the meeting which he requested and which I requested to talk about possible alternatives to present to the Commission.**

**This interview with the FBI was done with Ramie in May of 2020, and the FBI agent did not memorialize it by filing it until June of 2021 when our attorneys were hammering the Government for Discovery containing *Brady* material that we had not received.**

**The meeting which I arranged with Vickie Gainer and Ricky Ramie with James Finch to hear his ideas was recorded by Ricky who was wearing a wire, and later on the recording the voice of Borghini could be heard as Ricky was asking him, "can you hear me," before he entered James' office. None of the numerous tape recordings which Ricky made for the Government were damaging for Finch or for me. We were not corrupt; the law enforcement of Bay County, Florida was then and is now.**

**FBI INTERVIEW**
**RICKY RAMIE (3ᴿᴰ INTERVIEW)**

## Police Chief for the City of Lynn Haven

**12/01/2022**

This interview with **Ricky Ramie** was with a different FBI agent, SA Daniel Crecelius. The interview was conducted after the evidentiary hearings of 2022 which exposed the lies of both Ricky Ramie and Vickie Gainer in the federal courtroom. This interview is what I call "the big lie." My attorneys exclaimed, "Ricky Ramie has gone rogue," because this interview is so completely different than the first one, he gave, volunteering outlandish information that he could have given in the beginning if it were true. Below is the entire interview Ramie gave, and after each paragraph, my annotations. This interview is much more important to the Government than the previous ones with Ramie, and so Assistant U.S. Attorney Grogan is listening in to the telephone interview. The previous interviews of Ramie only had a single FBI agent instead of two agents as they had with me when they showed up at my home, unannounced, at night to intimidate and terrorize me.

Ricky Ramie was interviewed via telephone. Also present for the interview was Assistant United States Attorney Andrew Grogan. After being advised of the identity of the interviewing Agent and the nature of the interview, Ramie provided the following information:

Michael White was arrested around March 17, 2019, for domestic violence after White's wife called Ramie. White's wife was incoherent and drunk, so Ramie asked Dan Russell to take care of her since Ramie was out of town on a camping trip. Ramie also called Bay County Sheriff Tommy Ford and told Ford about the situation. White was Ramie's boss so Ramie recused himself from any future investigation. Ramie also called former Lynn Haven Mayor Margo Anderson and let her know what was going on with White. Ramie told Anderson that White may be arrested. The Bay County Sheriff's Office (BCSO) eventually arrested White and White gave investigators consent to search his phone.

**Ricky does not tell the story of the nearly two-hour phone call he had with me as he was driving back from his camping trip in Franklin County to Bay County. Ricky sounded alcohol impaired when he called me, and he kept asking me what I thought he should do regarding Michael White. In hindsight, Ricky did not want to arrest Michael White because of the corruption he was part of; he and Michael were buddies, and Ricky was now afraid of all that would be exposed about him. I told Ricky that I had no idea who should make the arrest, the FDLE or the Sheriff's Department (as Ricky was**

suggesting to me), but I finally told him that he was the police chief, that Michael had a gun and was apparently threatening his life and his wife's and to follow his protocols. We would also find out later, through the text messages and other information that Commissioner Dan Russell was aware of Michael and Amy White's domestic violence and alcohol issues, and like Ramie, had covered it up. Ramie also does not disclose to the new FBI agent who is interviewing him that he (Ramie) is aware of the affair going on between Michael and FEMA coordinator Amber Guy, which Ricky suddenly told me about after Michael's arrest and even texted me a screen shot of the message between Michael White and Amber Guy that had started the argument between Michael White and his wife. The comment that Ricky makes about Michael White giving consent for the investigators to search his phone, is added here, two years after my arrest in his new and improved interview, to fit with the BCSO story that they already knew about the corruption in Lynn Haven from Michael's phone and had started their Lynn Haven corruption investigation *before* I went to Sheriff Ford, which is proven false by the dates on all of their investigative reports, search warrants and affidavits.

Around the time of White's arrest, Erosion Control Specialist (ECS) had a contract to build a concession stand at Sheffield Park. ECS was owned by David "Mickey" White (Mickey). By this time, James Finch (Finch) had been released from the hospital and was back in Lynn Haven. Finch had another contract for work being done at Porter Park and saw ECS working at Sheffield Park. Finch called Anderson and complained that his company didn't get the opportunity to get the job at Sheffield Park. **Ricky is such a poor liar that he has his timeline confused. He says "by this time James Finch had been released from the hospital and was back in Lynn Haven). James Finch had been back in Lynn Haven since November of 2018, four and a half months before Michael White's arrest for domestic violence on March 17, 2019. He and Vickie Gainer also made up the story that Finch had complained about not getting the opportunity to build the concession stand at Sheffield Park. Finch already had the contract at Porter Park, and he was actually trying to find out who was building the concession stand at Sheffield Park to either sub-contract them to build the concession stand at Porter Park, or at the very least, try to make the design of the building at Porter Park look similar to the one being built at Sheffield. When he contacted Vickie Gainer to ask her who had bid the job at Sheffield, she would not give him information; then James went to the park to find out who was building the building and saw that it was Mickey White, Derwin's nephew, who James knew did not** possess a contractor's license. James then asked me to go to Vickie Gainer and find out who had the contract or who had been awarded the bid on the building in the park, the inquiry which precipitated my going to Sheriff Ford with the information about ECS which Vickie Gainer gave to me when I asked her for it after she told me there had been no bids on the building at Sheffield Park. The information she gave me on a single Excel sheet contained not only the cost of the concession stand, which was close to $200,000.00, but the Excel sheet contained a listing of six checks written by the City of Lynn Haven to ECS in the amount of 4.6 million dollars, without listing invoice or purchase order numbers. This is when I knew something was wrong and went to James' office as detailed in an earlier chapter.

Around the same timeframe, Ramie and Anderson spoke about the fact that the City had paid a lot of money to ECS. Anderson told Ramie that she was going to do some research, but she told Ramie that ECS had received a lot of money after the storm. Anderson told Ramie that she was concerned about White's relationship with ECS. At that time, Anderson did not disclose that ECS had done any work on her property.

**This paragraph is another complete fabrication by Ramie, and as my attorneys and I went through this interview together, the depth of Ramie's involvement in the corruption became more and more apparent to us, because his entire interview with Crecelius is a lie; a lie he told after he perjured himself during the federal court evidentiary hearing, along with City Manager Vickie Gainer. I had never spoken to Ricky Ramie about the City paying a lot of money to ECS, because I did not know. I never told Ramie I was going to do more research, and I never told Ramie that ECS had received a lot of money after the storm, or about any concern of Michael White's relationship with ECS. I did not know anything about Michael White's relationship with Mickey White or about ECS. I did not disclose that "ECS had done any work on my property" because they did not do any work on my property; I had asked Michael White to have the City of Lynn Haven clean the easement behind my property, and was completely unaware that he had ECS to do the work, until much later; however, as the interviews of others disclose, Ricky Ramie was actually present in some of the financial meetings with accountant Jay Moody, Michael White, Mickey White and others as they were going over discrepancies and concerns with one of Mickey's employees.**

Anderson started acting paranoid after White's arrest. After the initial conversation, Ramie and Anderson had nearly daily calls. Anderson told Ramie that she believed Derwin White (Derwin) White, and Mickey were "dirty." Ramie consistently encouraged Anderson to file an official complaint with Ford or with federal law enforcement. Anderson told Ramie that she felt like her life would be in danger if she reported anything to Ford. Anderson told Ramie that she heard that Mickey was Derwin's nephew and that Derwin was "not a good guy." Anderson asked for a police radio and for Ramie to put a marked patrol unit at her house.

**Ricky Ramie and I had spoken almost every day as we worked together after the storm in October, by phone and in person; this was not something that started after Michael White's arrest. He never encouraged me to file any kind of report with the Sheriff, and I never said to him that I believed Derwin, Michael White and Mickey were "dirty" until long after the investigation started (which I initiated) by going to the Sheriff. When I asked Ramie to go with me as a witness to Sheriff Tommy Ford on April 1, 2019, all that I told him was that I had found some financial issues with the City that I needed to report, and I wanted him to go with me to the Sheriff as a witness. In hindsight, I can imagine the frantic phone call that Ramie must have made to Sheriff Ford as he set up the meeting for he and I to go, as he offered to do. It was probably an "oh my God, the Mayor knows," call. I never asked Ricky for a police radio or a marked car at my house until after I had gone to the Sheriff and the Sheriff told me that he had indeed found problems with what I had given him and that he was starting an investigation and calling the FBI. He also asked me to be quiet about the investigation and not to discuss it with anyone, which was a huge mistake on my part. But after I had turned in the information about Michael White, Derwin White and Mickey White that James and I had figured out, I was afraid. I would find out later that Ricky made fun of me because I was afraid, and the patrol car that he parked at my house was not manned, an old Crown Victoria that looked as though it would not even start. I did ask for a radio so that I could call for help if I needed to. I never used the radio or spoke on it.**

Ramie thought Anderson's paranoia was strange because he remembered how Anderson bragged about an interaction that she had with Derwin about a week after Hurricane Michael passed. Anderson told Ramie that Derwin went to Anderson's house to apologize after he tried to cut Finch out of "the whole pit ordeal." Anderson bragged that she just kept making Derwin stronger drinks and how Derwin kept talking about how he tried to cut Finch out of business while Finch was "down."

**This is another paragraph which is completely fabricated to try and implicate me further to the FBI by Ricky. The interaction I had with Derwin White was not about a week after the hurricane, but actually on October 30, 2018, the same day that I had told Michael White and Chris Forehand, who had just told me they were permitting a pit for**

the City of Lynn Haven, that they had no authority to do that without Commission approval. We had just had a Commission meeting that day, and I had just lifted the state of emergency in Lynn Haven. I told them to cancel the permit unless they wanted me to reconvene the Commission meeting and present their permit for approval. The fact that they did not want to do this and immediately withdrew their permit is something that I would not understand until much later, but the indictment charged me with having them to cancel their permit accusing me of being in a conspiracy with James Finch for him to have a pit, which was proven false. They had hoped to have a pit where Mickey White and ECS could claim to dump vast quantities of trash and debris as they were overcharging the City of Lynn Haven, and the invoices were submitted to FEMA for reimbursement.

I did tell Ricky about Derwin White coming to my house, but it was because it was so strange. Although I knew Derwin White, he was not a social friend, just an acquaintance, (he had come up on stage and sung with me from time to time when I was performing at local events or at James Finch's Blue Moon Bar and Grille, but he had never been to my home. He appeared on my front porch that night (October 30th), there were still no streetlights in Lynn Haven, everyone was on edge because of looters, but when he knocked on the door and I saw who it was I invited him in. He asked me if Lee and I had anything to drink, and I made us drinks and invited him to sit at my kitchen counter on one of the bar stools. The conversation was about everything *except* what had happened that afternoon. He wanted to talk about how we were doing, he asked about James and his health, (James had just been released from the hospital that day and was on the way home), and then we talked about two hours about his family from Vernon, about his religious upbringing, about gospel music, and about my long family history in Lynn Haven. At some point in the conversation, he said something about his being James' friend and how he would never do anything to hurt James, and then he left. Again, in hindsight, my attorneys and I would realize that the entire purpose of Derwin's visit that night was to find out how much I knew: if I knew about the ECS contract, about the kickbacks from AshBritt the national hauler; when I had stopped Chris Forehand and Michael White from going forward with the permitting of the City of Lynn Haven property as a pit, it had set off alarms for all of them that maybe I knew what they were doing. He was trying to find out if I knew of their corrupt scheme, of firing Ceres, the third hauler in exchange for giving AshBritt a larger portion of the debris with AshBritt kicking back the money to GAC, and Michael White, Chris Forehand and others receiving kickbacks from ECS and Mickey White, with his contract with Lynn Haven that he and Michael White had signed, without my knowledge just after the storm.   Ricky, in this paragraph about Derwin, makes it appear that I am knowledgeable about Derwin White's corruption and that my cancelling the permit for the City of Lynn Haven pit was to benefit James as the indictment charged.

Anderson never gave Ramie any specific details about her concerns with Derwin, White, and Mickey.  Anderson only spoke generally about the fact that she was concerned by how much money the City was paying ECS.

**Again, Ricky lies; I did not know about the 4.6 million the City had paid to ECS until the last week in March of 2019 when I went to Vickie and asked her for the information on the concession stand in the park, which started my actions as a whistleblower.**

On the night of March 22, 2019, Ramie called Ford because the City was concerned about White's computer potentially being accessed by White or Russell.  Ford met Ramie in an alley later that night and Ford took possession of White's computer. Ramie informed Anderson that he was going to ask Ford to take the computer.

**This entire alley story is quite amazing.  If Ramie had planned to take Michael White's computer to Sheriff Ford, why would he need to meet in an alley?  I asked Ricky Ramie two things immediately after the emergency Commission meeting on Sunday, March 17th after Michael had been arrested.  I asked him to change the entry codes on all of the City office doors because the employees were nervous after hearing of Michael pointing a gun at his wife and then at himself, and I asked him to secure Michael White's laptop computer which Michael had worked on every day , outside under the tents, in the Verizon trailer, anytime you saw Michael he usually had the computer with him.  I was concerned that as any corporation or entity would be, that a disgruntled employee might take records with him or even destroy records.  I knew that all of the city business, including our FEMA records would be on Michael's laptop.  That was my reason for asking Ricky to secure the laptop, not because I thought Michael was involved in any corruption, at that point.  Ramie never told me that he was going to ask Ford to take the computer or anything about meeting in an alley.**

Ford and Ramie had a brief conversation in the alley.  Ford didn't go into specifics, but Ford told Ramie that White's phone revealed "some shady shit going on Ramie told Ford that he felt uneasy about Anderson after looking back on some of the interactions that Ramie had witnessed. Ramie told Ford that he witnessed Anderson "jump all over White" about one of the City's haulers and a pit that Chris Forehand and White wanted the City to start using. Ramie recounted that Anderson told Ramie how she was getting fed up with White and that she was close to firing him and having Greg Tidwell take over. Anderson told Ramie that she had already spoke with Tidwell about replacing White as the City Manager. At the time, Ramie thought Anderson's concerns were odd because the City had just gone through a catastrophic event and Ramie didn't understand why Anderson was so upset with White.

**Again, Ramie has lied in this paragraph to the new FBI agent who is questioning him during the time of the second evidentiary hearing in the federal court in Tallahassee. The original FBI agent, Borghini, as well as the assistant US Attorney, Stephen Kunz, both retired after the evidentiary hearing and were no longer involved in the case as far as we knew. The Government insisted that Borghini retired because he 'aged out', and that Kunz' retirement had been long-planned. We found the timing to be suspect after the grand jury transcript was opened for all to see the "misstatements" made to the grand jury by both Kunz and Borghini. The BCSO reports demonstrate that Major Stanford (the corrupt one who accepted gifts from Derwin White of GAC) was on vacation the week after Michael White was arrested for domestic violence and that Capt. Jason Daffin had looked through Michael's phone. When downloaded, there were thirty thousand pages of text messages on Michael White's phone which we as defendants had access to and which were made public during the evidentiary hearing; however, while the phone showed lots of "shady shit" as Ricky says the Sheriff said, without knowing about the six checks written by the City to ECS for 4.6 million dollars, the phone by itself, in that short period of time which Daffin was looking at it, would not have shown the corruption that I exposed when I went to the Sheriff, unless of course, the BCSO was already involved in the Derwin White corruption, which we believe based on the evidence we have, some of which was presented in the evidentiary hearing in Tallahassee. Ramie feeling uneasy about Anderson, is probably because I asked Ramie to secure the computer. Ramie says the "City" was concerned about the computer; I am the one who asked him to secure it, not the "City." Ramie was involved and was worried about what might be on Michael White's computer and phone for very different reasons than mine. I just wanted to protect the City FEMA records and other crucial information that we would need as we began the rebuild, and Michael had certainly demonstrated that he was unstable. Ramie never told me that he was going to give the computer to Ford. I have already discussed the matter about permitting the pit, except that here, Ramie says that he was present when this happened. He was not. I am sure that Chris Forehand**

and Michael White, his buddies, told him about the conversation and how heated it was, or possibly one of his LHPD officers, Tom Willoughby, who was sitting there when the conversation took place, because he told me later that he thought I had "big balls." Ramie also has his timeline messed up again in his lies here, because the conversation I had with Greg Kidwell, (not Tidwell) as the FBI report says, was very early in the first days after the storm, not in relation to what had just happened with Michael White's arrest. Michael had an altercation with the Gulf Power Company manager out at the Sports Complex and I was on the dune buggy vehicle with him after someone called and told him Gulf Power was setting up their sleeping and living quarters in the same area where he wanted the debris trucks to be able to get in an out of. Michael was so angry and driving so fast on the way out there that I was afraid we were going to be injured, and I asked him to slow down. He did not, and then when we finally stopped, he was in the face of the manager cursing and screaming at him about blocking the trucks. I got out of the vehicle and stepped into the argument telling Michael to calm down and I apologized to the manager. They finally worked something out and we drove back to the park where employees were milling around and getting ready for the 12:00 noon meeting. I was still very upset about the altercation that had taken place and the temper that Michael White had displayed, which later I would just attribute to lack of sleep and the stress that everyone was living with, but we had not yet undeclared the emergency and I still felt responsibility for the City. I saw Greg Kidwell, longtime public utilities director and city employee and went over to talk to him. I told him about what happened, asked him to keep it confidential, but I also asked him that if for any reason that Michael White became unable to continue serving as the City Manager could I count on him to serve until the Commission could find someone else. He agreed on confidentiality and that he would do whatever I needed him to do to keep the City working. That was the end of the matter, and we never discussed it again. I did not tell Ramie about this and so the only way he would have known is if Kidwell told him about what I had said. Many of the city employees did not like me as the Mayor from the beginning of my term in 2015 because of my campaign for change, and Kidwell may have been one of those without my knowing it. In the weeks after the storm, I witnessed Michael White working long hours, and still had no reason to suspect him of anything corrupt or illegal.

Anderson eventually accepted Ramie's offer to set up a meeting with Ford. The meeting happened around April 1, 2019. Anderson arrived at the BCSO before Ramie did. Anderson was already seated and engaged in small talk with Ford when Ramie arrived. Ford shut both doors to his office and Anderson started talking about ECS's invoices and ECS's work at the concession stand. Anderson was extremely nervous and jittery during the meeting. Ramie felt like Anderson's physical demeanor was "odd."

**This paragraph is false. After meeting with James Finch and deciding to go to the Sheriff, I approached Ricky Ramie and asked him to go the Sheriff with me, as I have stated before. Ricky offered to call and set up the meeting *after* I asked him to go with me as a witness for something I wanted to discuss with the Sheriff about financial issues in the City. Ricky was already at the Sheriff's office when I arrived, not just the opposite as he states. I was not talking about ECS's invoices because I did not have them, nor had I seen them at this point. I had one Excel sheet of ECS information which I had requested from Vickie Gainer and one sheet was all that she provided to me. I was quite nervous and jittery in the meeting because I had come to the Sheriff to report what I believed was probably going to be a financial crime. Anyone would have been nervous. Ramie is using his "cop" vocabulary telling the FBI agent that my "demeanor was odd". The fact that Ricky would lie to the FBI agent, telling him that he, Ricky, had tried to persuade *me* to go the Sheriff, was just shocking when I read this interview. This interview, after the evidentiary hearing, was described by my attorneys as "the police chief has gone rogue," and it is when I knew without doubt, that Ricky Ramie was involved with the Lynn Haven corruption and was covering his tracks.**

Anderson told Ford that she had already looked through some of the city's documents related to ECS and she was going to continue her review. Ford asked Anderson to compile whatever documentation she deemed relevant and provide it to Ford. During the meeting with Ford, Anderson gave Ford a little bit of documentation, but Ramie didn't know what it was.

**I did not tell Ford that I had already looked through some of the city's documents related to ECS and that I was going to continue my review because I had not. This is totally false, and Ramie is setting me up to the FBI agent as already knowing about ECS and the large amount of money paid by the City to them, which I had denied. Ford did not ask me to compile whatever documentation I deemed relevant and provide it to Ford. He specifically asked me if I could get copies, back and front, of the six checks listed on the one sheet of information I had provided to him. When I brought the checks back to him later, he then asked me if I would get copies of the purchase orders and invoices for ECS which would provide documentation for the checks. I agreed to go back to the City and ask for the copies; the Sheriff did not ask me to compile whatever documentation I deemed**

relevant as Ramie says.

After the meeting with Ford, Ramie told Ford that he should meet with Jay Moody (Moody) because he would have a lot of knowledge related to the City's spending. Ford eventually called Moody and obtained documentation from him.

**Another completely false statement by Chief Ramie. Ford asked me in our meeting if I would get copies of Jay Moody's invoices and purchase orders for him at the same time he asked me to get the City's invoices and purchases orders relating to ECS. What did *not* occur to me at the time, was how would Sheriff Ford have been aware that Moody was our financial consultant. I believe in hindsight, that Ramie told him and that they were making sure to have copies of everything from anyone who had invoices and purchase orders from ECS in order to start covering their own involvement. Ricky Ramie and I went to Jay Moody's office and got the copies of the invoices and purchase orders on the same day that I met Ricky Ramie at the Wal-Mart parking lot with the invoices and purchase orders from the City as previously stated. Ramie was going to take the stacks of paperwork to the Sheriff's office so that I would not be seen taking stacks of information to the Sheriff. Ramie was doing this for my protection as the "whistleblower" is what he told me at the time. They were really making sure that no one saw me and making damn sure that I could not prove that I was the one who brought the documentation into the BCSO. We had tried to retrieve the parking lot surveillance tapes from the Wal-Mart parking lot once we realized from the 302's that Ricky was lying, but it was over a year later, and the manager and store security told us they did not have the tapes any longer, that the store did not retain them for that long.**

Anderson requested documentation from Vicky Gainer (Gainer). Anderson told Gainer "When you get it ready, give it to Ramie and he will get it to Ford." Anderson never gave anything to Ramie directly. Gainer gave it to Ramie and Ramie called Ford immediately upon receiving the documentation. Ford told Ramie that he was not in the office and asked Ramie to give the documentation to BCSO Major Jimmy Stanford (Stanford). Ramie left his office and went to the BCSO. Stanford and Ramie didn't have any conversation because Stanford was busy doing something else at the time. Stanford accepted the documents and just "fist bumped Ramie.

**These lies, along with those in Vickie Gainer's interviews let us know that Ricky and Vickie were involved in the corruption. They would have had no other reason to say the exact opposite of what happened. I asked for and picked up the copies from Vickie Gainer**

of the ECS invoices and purchase orders from the City, took them to the Wal-Mart parking lot and met Ricky Ramie there, where I handed them over to him. We then went to Jay Moody's office where I told Jay Moody what I needed, and why, and he seemed very surprised and nervous, but he made the copies while Ricky Ramie and I waited, and then Ricky put the copies in the front seat of his truck in Jay Moody's parking lot. I offered to take a polygraph about this, even though it is not admissible in court, and I am still willing to do so, maybe at some point for the media if the opportunity arises.

Ramie heard the allegations that Stanford leaked information related to the investigation, but Ramie didn't have any evidence of any kind of wrongdoing by Stanford. Ramie knew that Derwin and Stanford did not get along after a falling out they had over Greg Wilson. Derwin came to Ford's office and asked Ford to drop the case against Greg Wilson and Ford kicked Derwin out of his office. Ever since then Derwin hated Ford and Stanford.

There are many versions from all of the conspirators, indicted and un-indicted of the relationship between the Sheriff, Derwin White, Jimmy Stanford and Greg Wilson. What Ramie does not mention about evidence of wrongdoing against Stanford, is actually a lie in his interview to the FBI. Stanford had recently admitted in federal court that he accepted a motorcycle and the payment for his sister's funeral from Derwin White. Mickey White made allegations against Stanford that he received a lot more, although Stanford denied this. It also came out in the federal court that Stanford had tipped off Derwin White the night before the April 12, 2019 raid on ECS to enable Mickey White to place the false invoices on top of the trash for the FBI and BCSO to "find" which would implicate the Mayor (me) of having had her "property" cleaned by ECS, billed to the City, and then submitted to FEMA. James and I both believe that Derwin White was an informant and probably was holding dirt over the heads of the local law enforcement is why he remained an unindicted conspirator who was named in the indictment against me. Derwin White died on July 31, 2021, and just a few days later an FBI and BCSO raid took place on the GAC property where boxes and boxes of evidence were taken, and no arrests were ever made. Our belief is that after Derwin passed away from COVID, law enforcement was retrieving any evidence in his and Allan Bense's (co-owner and former Speaker of the Florida House) offices to protect themselves and others who had been named in the Affidavit which was accidentally unsealed by *The Panama City News Herald* and published. The affidavit names wrongdoers ranging from the Superintendent of Schools in Bay County to the State Senator, none of whom were ever indicted.  The Government immediately had the affidavit resealed, and then it was unsealed again by the Court, who stated "that skunk was already loose in the room," after learning that the document was in the newspapers and on the television websites in Bay County.

During the investigation, Ramie told Ford and the Federal Bureau of Investigation that he wanted to make sure his cooperation was confidential. Ramie specifically brought up Stanford because Stanford was very good friends with Jerry Wilson (Wilson).  Wilson was also very close to Finch, so Ramie wanted to make sure Finch didn't find anything out about Ramie. Ford assured Ramie that his actions would remain confidential.

Ramie did believe there was a leak coming from somewhere because Judy Tinder seemed to have accurate information about the investigation before it happened.

**Jerry Wilson is a local roofing company contractor and Ramie is insinuating that maybe Wilson is leaking information from Stanford to Finch.  Ramie does not like Judy Tinder, and in the text messages which were revealed in the evidentiary hearings, Ramie texts Michael White that Judy is "a butch p-ssy-licking c--t," and Michael White responds that she is a "bitch."  Ramie's credibility and ethics have been in question since that time, as the text messages also revealed that he had fixed tickets for friends and officials, had Michael White's friend's ex-girlfriend set up and arrested, given a gun out of the evidence locker to Michael White, knowing of his mental issues, and a multitude of other infractions.  The text messages sent between City Manager Michael White and Chief Ramie also contained memes of African Americans, including one of a little girl, holding a popsicle shaped like a penis with disgusting captions, yet the City Manager, Vickie Gainer, refused to take any action against Ramie other than a letter in his file even after Commissioner Judy Tinder questioned him about the texts in a public meeting, and he denied making the comment.  The letter written by Gainer for his file did not even describe the infractions; the texts are racist, prejudicial against Commissioner Tinder's sexuality, and against the code of ethics for police officers.  Ramie's most recent infraction has been the "hit and run" accident on December 30, 2023, when he left Newby's bar on Panama City Beach at 3:30 a.m. in the morning and video shows him crashing into another vehicle in the parking lot, causing $3500.00 in damage and then leaving the scene.  BCSO's Officer Heape, son of Major Joel Heape, second in command at BCSO, was called to the scene after a citizen chased Ramie down who saw what happened. Ramie drove himself to another location and was never given an alcohol test or arrested that evening, and Officer Heape turned off his**

camera when he saw whose drivers' license he was dealing with. The entire Ramie case lasted from December 2023 until August of 2024, with his Zoom court hearing occurring just two days *after* the re-election of Sheriff Tommy Ford and State Attorney Larry Basford. Ramie pleaded *nolo contendere,* he was given a four hundred dollar fine and told to write a letter of apology to the victim. There is still great community outcry in the City of Lynn Haven at the time of this book's publication, with every City Commission meeting attended by residents continuing to call for Ramie's dismissal. Vickie Gainer, "FBI witness" who lied to the FBI on record, unrefuted, refuses to fire Ramie, and it has been stated by many that it is because she is afraid of what he will tell about her. This situation remains ongoing in the City of Lynn Haven where Ramie was placed on suspension without pay for twenty-five days following the court hearing of August 22, 2024, was not allowed on City property and had to take a safe driving course. He has been re-instated and is back in his office as the Police Chief of Lynn Haven. Chief Ramie, proven to have violated the moral and ethical standards of a police officer, should never have power over other people's lives and liberty. He continues to be protected by the Bay County Sheriff's Office and the State Attorney of the 14th Judicial Circuit, who recused himself from the case and appointed his ex-girlfriend who is the State Attorney from a neighboring district to prosecute the case. The assistant prosecutor who attended the hearing on August 22, 2024, showed very little interest and was totally uninspiring in his preparation.

## FBI INTERVIEW

Agent Larry Borghini

Lynn Haven City Manager Vickie Gainer

April 12, 2019

The first interview with Vickie Gainer was conducted on April 12th, 2019, the same day the BCSO warrant was served on ECS and the FBI and BCSO raided the business; the report was drafted on April 19, 2019 by SA Borghini and was entered into files on May 16, 2019, almost a month after the day the interview took place, which seems to be a pattern for Borghini. This was brought up during the evidentiary hearings, that in many of the interviews conducted by SA Borghini during the investigation, Borghini let time lapse in between the time the interview took place and the date in which the interviews were formalized and entered using notes. Guy Lewis, defense attorney for James Finch, pointed out during the hearing that waiting weeks, and sometimes many months to formalize the interview notes was not protocol for the FBI. Mr. Lewis had served as the U.S. Attorney for the Southern District of Florida before becoming a defense attorney.

On April 12, 2019, Vickie Lynn Gainer, was interviewed at the City of Lynn Haven Town Hall by Special Agent (SA) Lawrence P. Borghini and Bay County Sheriff's Office Major Jimmy Stanford in Lynn Haven, Florida. She was advised as to the identity of the interviewing agent and the nature of the interview. Gainer thereafter provided the following information:

On March 19, 2019, Gainer was appointed the acting city manager for the City of Lynn Haven (CLH). Prior to becoming acting city manager, Gainer was the Deputy City Clerk. Gainer was first hired by the CLH in April 2017, as a grant and contracts manager. During that time, she worked on both federal and state grants for the CLH. She eventually became the Director of Administrative Support Services and held that position for approximately one year.

Prior to Hurricane Michael, Gainer was living in Calloway. After her property was damaged from the hurricane, she moved into her son's residence in Lynn Haven. Gainer came back to work at the CLH on Saturday following the hurricane.

Gainer advised the CLH received invoices from Erosion Control Specialist (ECS) for Hurricane Michael cleanup. Gainer recalls the invoices did not have very much detail on them. Gainer expressed the need for the invoices to have more detail. An emergency contract was put in place for the work ECS was performing. Greenleaf Lawn Care already had a contract in place and the CLH used that contract to support the work Greenleaf was asked to perform. Gainer stated all the ECS invoices for hurricane cleanup were paid and ECS was paid the most out of all the vendors submitting invoices.

**Gainer's testimony here indicates that she knew of the ECS contract signed by Michael White and Mickey White, that she knew the invoices did not have the correct detail and information, yet she makes no mention of telling this information to anyone. Of note, after we received discovery materials from the Government, there is a letter which Vickie Gainer wrote on April 4th, (the day the Sheriff's investigation in the City of Lynn Haven began after I went to see him with information I had requested of Gainer) to FEMA in which she is documenting and trying to justify the work that ECS has been paid to do thus far. The timing of this letter is suspect, and when a public**

records request was sent to find out if the letter was an email or a formal letter as well as who the letter was sent to, the City did not provide the information. The letter may not even have been sent, as it is written to FEMA without a name or address in the heading.

CLH had pre-negotiated contracts in place for disasters such as Hurricane Michael. The contracts were for three (3) years with a three (3) year renewal. All the contracts had been reviewed in 2016. The contracts had been put out for bid and three (3) haulers were awarded contracts. AshBritt Environmental, Crowder-Gulf Joint Venture, and Ceres Environmental Services were each awarded contracts under this process. The contracts were at unit prices and standard rates for such work. All the vendors were in contact with CLH prior to the hurricane and standing by. CLH also had a pre-negotiated contract with Tetra Tech for monitoring and verifying the work of the vendors hired by the CLH.

The haulers under contract were responsible for pushing debris off the city roads, pickup and transporting of debris, stabilization and cleanout, and other services as directed. After the hurricane all of the vendors came and performed the services they were contracted for. The contracts called for the submission of invoices within 30 days of the completion of the work. The contractors were to submit a list of crews and equipment used, the start and stop times of work performed, and the dump tickets. The invoices were also to include the Tetra Tech reports that verified the work as invoiced had been completed. City manager, Michael White was receiving weekly emails with the stats regarding the hurricane cleanup.

**This paragraph demonstrates that Vickie Gainer was aware of what was happening with debris contracts and payment. She was the deputy city clerk. She is giving this information to the FBI agent in April of 2019. While I would learn of all these processes and how they worked as the investigation continued, these contracts and processes were not part of my job, and I was not familiar with them. Vickie Gainer was Michael White's right arm, and she obviously understood the process and the contracts.**

Gainer believes there was a problem with Ceres and the job they were doing. Gainer was not part of any discussion on the hiring of ECS or Greenleaf. Gainer believes in the beginning, nobody was monitoring or verifying ECS' work. She is not sure about Greenleaf. Gainer has seen some dump tickets in ECS' file.

**Gainer makes sure to distance herself from the discussion/hiring of ECS although she said earlier in the interview that she was aware of their contract. Greenleaf, owned by Josh Anderson, already had a contract with the City of Lynn Haven for lawn services for parks and sports complex long before Hurricane Michael, yet Gainer, who was the contracts manager, says she is not sure about Greenleaf.**

For the first two weeks after returning to work, Gainer worked at the Emergency Operations Center (EOC). Mayor Anderson was in charge and was having weekly meeting. ECS and Greenleaf turned in invoices for work being performed. The invoices did not have much detail on them. When questions were raised, the response was Michael White was there.

**Gainer states that I was in charge and having weekly meetings. This is false. Michael White was designated to run the City and he conducted daily meetings at 6 am, 12 noon, and 6 p.m. at first and then tapered off to two meetings per day, finally one, and then back to weekly staff meetings after the holidays. The only part I had in these meetings was to give a report on emergency supplies that had been received and distributed by the City, Christmas gifts for children, the Thanksgiving Day Dinner celebration, and reports on meetings I attended at the EOC or interviews I had with officials and news media who visited the City. For her to say that I was in charge and having weekly meetings was her first lie about me, that I know of.**

The city's process calls for the preparing of a purchase order for the invoices being submitted. Gainer questioned Josh Anderson regarding the Greenleaf invoices that had been submitted. Gainer asked why Greenleaf was submitting invoices for lawn care maintenance when virtually all of the city property had been damaged by the hurricane. Josh Anderson submitted the invoices as for being for unbilled work before the hurricane. Most of the time the invoices were sent down having been signed off on.

Gainer questioned the invoices that had been dropped off. Gainer brought the invoices to Michael White and brought them to his attention. Michael White stated that the work being performed at the cemetery was labor intensive. Gainer questioned the Greenleaf invoices a second time. She is not sure if they were paid. The city manager, Michael White made the call on paying the ECS invoices. Gainer believed ECS was overcharging the CLH. ECS was being paid before the other vendors.

**Gainer mentions questioning the invoices that she believed ECS was overcharging CLH, and that ECS was being paid before the other vendors. If she knew something was wrong, why did she not approach the Commission or the Mayor? She has no problem telling the FBI about it after she knows the Mayor has taken documentation to the Sheriff.**

Jay Moody was aware of the situation. Kelly Tram resigned for personal reasons. She initially stayed on with the CLH even after her husband's orders changed.

**Kelly Tram, the newly hired attorney from the last Commission meeting before Hurricane Michael (September 2018) told me that she was resigning because of stress and that she was trying to get**

pregnant again. The conditions of her employment as the City Attorney had also changed because of her husband's deployment after the storm; his deployment changed the provision for her out of state license from Texas. She was very unhappy after the Commission selected Vickie Gainer as the interim City Manager when Michael White was arrested in March of 2019. Ricky Ramie, Kelly Battistini, and Julie Higby, the City Manager's assistant, all expressed dismay to me that Vickie would now be in charge of the City. I had suggested to the Commission, based on the recommendation of the League of Cities President, Matt Surrency, that the Commission put the Deputy City Clerk in place as the interim City Manager until a new manager could be hired.

Gainer advised that it is against city policy to clean up private residences or private property.

This random statement appears to be an answer about the property cleanup, which is just rich, considering that April 12th is the day of the raid on ECS when the fake property cleanup invoices were placed at ECS, and Jimmy Stanford is the investigator asking Gainer the questions. According to testimony by Mickey White, Derwin White directed him to make the invoices and Jimmy Stanford tipped Derwin off as to the date of the raid on ECS.

Gainer was also aware of the easement abutting my property on the east because there are emails from, she, Bobby Baker and Adam Albritton to each other concerning the easement, and the government had a copy of it, as do I. The email between Gainer and Albritton is on April 24th, the day the news media called me asking for a statement about purported invoices in which my property had been cleaned and charged to the City. Gainer also answered questions to Channel 13 which were made public on the air in which she stated that "no such document exists." Her statement created a firestorm of social media comments accusing me of wrongdoing.

Michael White purchased a drone with city funds for use by the CLH. Gainer is not sure where the drone is at or who has it.

Each of the city's department heads have a city credit card. A purchase order is needed for all purchases made with the credit card.

City contracts for goods and services are secured depending on the size and scope of the project. CLH puts out an RFQ (Request for Qualifications) or RFP (Request for Proposal) or forms a selection committee. Bids are selected based on low bid, high bid, or quality of the vendor. Projects under $35,000 can be awarded via quotes. Projects $35,000 or over are awarded through the bid process.

One day, Gainer saw some men working on one of the concession stands at one of the city's parks. She learned the concession stand project had not been bid out. She understood the project was being worked under ECS' previous contract. They had supposedly turned in bids for the project.

This paragraph starts out like a fairy tale, "one day,". My question is which day? Gainer knew this project was being done without a bid and had said nothing until the day I walked in her office and asked her about it. She had scored the bid sheets with Michael White and Kelly Battistini when Tetra Tech was selected. Gainer was part of the operations of the City. She then said immediately, "there is no bid," and when I asked her who was doing the work she answered ECS. At that point is when I asked her for the information on ECS and the concession stand that led to my finding out about the 4.6 million dollars in checks.

When ECS turned in an invoice for the project, Gainer advised she could not pay it since ECS did not have a contract. According to Gainer, the only way the CLH could have paid ECS' invoice was if the City Commission had approved the project and there was a contract in place.

When Gainer took over on March 19th, she learned there were no permits for the project. When she asked for ECS' contract, David Horton brought her the quotes for the project. There was no contract (s) in place for the project. Gainer called Michael White (White had resigned as city manager) and he told her the work was being performed under the emergency contract. Gainer told Mickey White that she was not going to pay the $234,000 ECS invoice. Gainer asked Amanda to pull all of ECS' invoices and then alerted the mayor.

When the Government finally provided me with this *Brady* information a year after I was arrested, it was easy to see that Gainer was involved as well. The paragraph above is not true; it is the complete opposite of what happened. She did not contact Mickey White by letter/email until the day I went to her asking about the concession stand, (documented by the date of the email) and she gave me one sheet of information containing the costs and the list of additional checks written to ECS. She then tells the big lie to the FBI agent, that *SHE ASKED* Amanda to pull all of ECS' invoices and then alerted the Mayor. Instead of the exact opposite, I went to HER and asked for copies of all of ECS' invoices and purchase orders after taking the Sheriff copies of the six checks. If Borghini believed Gainer, or if the Sheriff had already told Borghini that I was guilty, who knows? But Borghini either chose to ignore that I was the whistleblower or went with the theory that I went to the Sheriff because I was guilty and was trying to cover up. Gainer's lie in this interview was a huge part of the Government's case against me, and like I said before, I know that lie detector tests have been used by law enforcement in murder cases to try and eliminate suspects, why are they not willing to administer them in cases like this? Even if the test is not admissible in court, law enforcement would at least know who was lying to them before they turned evidence over to the prosecutors, and I would never have been indicted. But BCSO did not need a lie detector test; they already knew the truth, and they needed to cover it up.

Michael White had expressed that he wanted ECS to do a lot of work for the CLH. The projects included the concession stands, restrooms, concrete work and various other projects. The emergency contract with ECS ended in the first part of February 2019.

Yet, Vickie was trying to justify another emergency contract for ECS on April 4th in her letter/email to "FEMA".

ECS always seemed to have the lower quote. 850 Construction had submitted the other quote on the project.

Greenleaf had submitted an invoice in the amount of $143,000 for work completed at Sheffield Park. Gainer sent the invoice back to Josh Anderson and requested an itemization of the amount being invoiced with documentation. The CLH had purchased the grass for the project ($13,000) because Greenleaf would have marked it up 30% if they had ordered it and included it in their invoice.

The city purchased gas after Hurricane Michael and had it available for city vehicles. Vendors of the city should not have been using the city's gas.

**FBI Interview**
**Vickie Gainer**
**(9/30/2022)**

This interview took place over two years after my initial indictment and arrest and after the first evidentiary hearings in the Spring of 2022. We were preparing to go to trial in the fall of 2022, and the Government was preparing to supersede the indictment for the third time against me. This interview was conducted by SA Daniel Crecelius since SA Borghini had now "retired", along with Assistant U.S. Attorney Stephen Kunz.

Vickie Gainer, was interviewed at Lynn Haven, Florida. Also present for the interview was Federal Bureau of Investigation (FBI) Staff Operations Specialist Saisha Freeland. After being advised of the identity of the interviewing Agent and the nature of the interview, Gainer provided the following information:

Christy McElroy, (McElroy), Jody Moore (Moore), and Jerry Parker

(parker, had been coming to every City of Lynn Haven commission meeting and attempting to ruin the reputation of Gainer and Lynn Haven Police Chief Ricky Ramie (Ramie). McElroy, Moore and Parker were very good friends with former Lynn Haven Mayor Margo Anderson (Anderson) and current City Commissioner Judy Tinder (Tinder). After Anderson was charged by federal authorities, McElroy, Moore, Parker, and Tinder have been "doing her bidding" by trying everything they could to discredit Gainer and Ramie, who are potential federal witnesses in Anderson's case. Recently, the current Mayor of Lynn Haven, Jesse Nelson, had to tell the public to stop talking about the criminal case of Anderson during City meetings because it had become so disruptive.

**Vickie Gainer perjured herself again with this lie. All three of the women named here will be testifying in the upcoming civil depositions, under oath, that we were not friends at this time; they have already stated this publicly in City Commission meetings after the evidentiary hearings in our case. Gainer is angry because both she and Ramie made false statements at the federal court evidentiary hearing and Moore and Parker reported on this using their citizens journalist page, The Beacon of Bay County.**

McElroy recently filed a criminal referral with the State Attorney's Office claiming that City employees knowingly used former Building Inspector Mike Gordon's stamp after he had been arrested by local authorities and fired as the City's Building Inspector. Gainer knew the allegations were untrue, as Gordon's stamp had been locked up in the Human Resources Director's Office since Gordon was fired. Tinder questioned the City of Lynn Haven's Director of Customer Services, Stephanie Nichols (Nichols), about the allegations regarding Gordon's stamp. Nichols was so upset by Tinder that she sent an email complaining about the interaction to Gainer and the City's Human Resources Department.

Anderson Tinder, Moore and Parker all spend a lot of time on "The Beacon" Facebook page talking bad about Gainer, the City, the Department of Justice, and the FBI. Anderson was very good with social media and controlled a lot of what happened on The Beacon. Tinder, Moore, and Parker were very good friends and were always with Tinder at Tinder's restaurant.

**Mike Gordon, the building inspector referred to by Gainer, was arrested because of her and others in the City of Lynn Haven. All charges against him have since been dropped and he has filed civil litigation in the matter.**

**Again, Vickie lies about me by stating that I controlled a "lot of what happened on The Beacon". I had no part in what was being said at that time on The Beacon, and the administrators of that page**

will be stating as much under oath.  The owners of the social media page attended both evidentiary hearings, the trials of James Finch, my plea hearing and sentencing hearing, and since that time, we HAVE become friends.  But we were not friends at the time as Gainer stated, under oath, once again trying to do harm to me in her testimony to protect herself.

Tinder filed a lot of public records with the City of Lynn Haven.  This information always made its way to the Beacon and to McElroy.  Before Anderson and James Finch were arrested, Tinder would always vote no, when it came to Finch.  After Finch's arrest, Tinder was a big supporter of everything that Finch said.

**Another lie by Vickie Gainer.  Tinder's voting record was in favor of Finch both before and after he was arrested.  Gainer was the Deputy City Clerk who prepared the agenda and counted the votes of the Commission on each agenda item.  She knew this was not true, yet when she was caught in her lie, she simply said she was mistaken, that she "misspoke."  I have become a convicted felon and served one month in federal prison because I pled guilty to a false statement.  (I did not make a false statement.  I pled guilty to making a false statement because I was unwilling to go through another indictment and another trial as the Government promised to do, even if I was acquitted.  There is a more detailed explanation of this in a later chapter).**

Gainer heard rumors and believes that Burnie Thompson (Thompson) is being financially supported by Finch.  Thompson uses his media presence to support Finch and Anderson and to attack Gainer and Ramie.

**Another lie in the same interview.  Burnie Thompson believed both James Finch and I to be guilty in the beginning.  He also attended the evidentiary hearings, both of Finch's trials, my plea hearing, as well as my sentencing hearing, and he was also present on many of the telephone hearings with Federal Judge Mark Walker listening in.  Burnie Thompson will also swear under oath that James Finch had made no financial contributions to him at the time that Vickie Gainer swore in her interview with the FBI that he had.  She was malicious in her lies, not caring who she harmed with them.  When we read these interviews for the first time, I was so angry and wanted to confront her, as well as other City employees who had made false statements or omitted information to hurt both me and James Finch.  But we were denied even confronting our accusers.  We had a list of people on a "no contact" list from the Government prosecutors.    To speak to them or contact them in any way would have brought us before the Judge and possibly ended our pre-trial release agreement, sending us to prison until trial.**

The testimony of Vickie Gainer in the evidentiary hearing, as well as her testimony to the FBI was particularly hurtful, because, like Police Chief Ricky Ramie, I trusted her, considered her to be my friend, and when I read in her interview that she told the FBI agent that *she* alerted *me* to the financial fraud rather than the way it really happened, I knew that she had lied , either to cover her own involvement, or at the direction of those who were setting me up, or both.

FBI Interview

Chris Forehand, Lynn Haven City Engineer

8/26/2019

This interview with Chris Forehand occurred on 8/26/2019, about four months after I went to Sheriff Tommy Ford with the financial information I had discovered concerning ECS (Erosion Control Specialist owned by Mickey White).  Special Agent Lawrence Borghini and Bay County Sheriff's Office Major Jimmy Stanford conducted the interview, and the interview was formalized by the agent almost a month later and entered into record on 9/18/2019.

Forehand provided the following information:
Forehand is an owner of Panhandle Engineering, and they do work for the City of Lynn Haven.  Prior to Hurricane Michael, the City of Lynn Haven had an established hurricane preparedness plan.  Forehand was not involved in the preparing of the plan.  Forehand also advised the City of Lynn Haven had pre-negotiated contracts with three (3) haulers and one (1) monitoring service for storm and disaster related services.  Forehand was not involved in the negotiation or signing of those contracts.  After Hurricane Michael, Forehand did assist the city with securing a contract with Tetra Tech for financial services regarding FEMA and recovery services.
Chris Forehand made no mention to me as Mayor, and as far as I know nor the Commission, that he and his partner, Jim Slonina, on October 23, 2018, just two weeks after Hurricane Michael made landfall, incorporated their own company, PEDS (Panhandle

---

Engineering Disaster Services).  According to the later testimony of Adam Albritton, the City contracted attorney, Chris Forehand pushed Michael White to choose Tetra Tech, and Michael White, Vickie Gainer and HR Director Kelly Battistini were the employees who scored the bid sheet designating Tetra Tech.  Chris Forehand, who was also a board member of Tetra Tech, would then sub-contract his own new company, PEDS, to Tetra Tech, and all of them moved into Forehand's office space.  Lynn Haven now had Mickey White, Derwin White's nephew hauling debris in Lynn Haven, and Chris Forehand had his hand on the monitoring service, where in the end, his company made millions.  He was also granted immunity by the Government in this case.

After Hurricane Michael, Forehand was asked by Lynn Haven's City Manager, Michael White, to assist in helping with various storm related activities and projects.  After the hurricane, the city was without phone service, electricity and water.  At first, the city had meetings three (3) times a day (morning, noon, and night).  All of the city's department heads would attend those meetings as well as the haulers and entities involved in the cleanup and restoration of services.

Forehand's house was damaged by the hurricane.  He and his family were living in Watercolors.

**Watercolor is an exclusive beach resort at the far west end of Panama City Beach, completely unaffected by Hurricane Michael's devastation.**

His days were long as he had to get up early to travel into Lynn Haven and would get home late as a result of the travel conditions.  Forehand has known Michael White for more than twenty (20) years.  Forehand was working for Preble Rish Engineering when Michael White was working for Gulf Coast Electric.

The first thing Forehand recalls working on after the hurricane was logistics.  That involved getting things such as generators, etc. in place so that services and facilities could begin to be brought back online.  Forehand also worked on debris monitoring.  Forehand is a subcontractor to Tetra Tech and employed all the monitors being used by Tetra Tech who were monitoring the haulers and debris sites in the cities of Lynn Haven, Springfield, Parker, and Callaway.  Forehand also worked on a Request for Proposal (RFP) for the City of Lynn Haven advertising for financial services regarding FEMA and recovery services.  Forehand lastly worked on demolition documents for the various city buildings which were destroyed by Hurricane Michael and the setup of temporary facilities by the city.

**Chris Forehand, the city-contracted engineer, had his hands in virtually every aspect of cleanup and recovery of the City of Lynn Haven as well as other cities in Bay County.  He either did not**

disclose his position with Tetra Tech to the FBI agent here, or the agent did not include it in the report.

Forehand was not involved with anything to do with Erosion Control Specialists (ECS). The first time Forehand heard of any discussion about ECS was after a meeting between Michael White, Tetra Tech and Jay Moody. The discussion was about the amount and size of the ECS invoices. Forehand was not involved in the discussion, he only heard about it. Forehand did, however, help with emergency services involving Kenny Strange Electric (KSE) and Gulf Coast Utilities Contractors (GCUC). Since there was no power, KSE and another electrician were putting out generators at various locations such as lift stations, etc. GCUC had equipment which vacuumed the city's sewer lines. Forehand also believes GAC and Marshall Brothers Construction did some emergency push work after the hurricane. Push work is the process of pushing debris to the side of the road making them passable.

**An interesting point in this paragraph of the interview is that Michael White's text messages with Chris Forehand reveal a close relationship and comments about AshBritt, the hauler which subcontracted Derwin White and GAC after Derwin struck the "deal" with AshBritt to give them more business by Michael White's firing of the third hauler in Lynn Haven, Ceres. Chris Forehand also refers to Governor DeSantis' Emergency Management Director, Jared Moskowitz, as an "AshBritt kind of guy" in his texts to Michael White. Moskowitz served as general counsel to AshBritt until 2017; he was appointed by DeSantis in December of 2018 just after the November election in the aftermath of Hurricane Michael.**

**Forehand, in this first interview also makes no mention of me, Mayor Anderson, being in the meeting about ECS; only Michael White, Tetra Tech and Jay Moody, the accounting consultant. This recurring theme, my absence from the financial meetings is reflected in other 302's yet the Government relied almost solely on Michael White, the city manager's testimony that I "directed" or "pressured" him, when in truth, he was the city manager who controlled the day-to-day operations of the City both before and after Hurricane Michael.**

Forehand was asked to assist with the permitting of the various debris management sites (DMS) and Disposal Sites by the City of Lynn Haven with the State of Florida. Lynn Haven had DMS sites at the Sports Complex, Cain-Griffin Park, Kinsaul Park and a site off of Highway 77. Forehand was unaware of Lynn Haven having a site on Allen Spikes' property. Forehand understood that site was an Ash Britt and GAC DMS site.

Forehand and Jim Slonina started Panhandle Engineering Disaster

Services, LLC (PEDS). PEDS hired a group of monitors and Tetra Tech oversaw the work they were performing. Tetra Tech had a process of advertising, hiring and training the monitors. The training was about a three-hour block and covered the basics.

The monitors would go along with the trucks and were in the towers at the DMS sites. The monitors would make the call on the amount of debris in the trucks. The trucks would then dump their loads at the DMS sites where the debris was chipped. The trucks were then loaded with the chips and transported to a final resting place. The monitors would then make a call on the amount of chips each truck was loaded with.

A copy of the dump ticket was given to the driver at each location. Tetra Tech would retain a copy of the ticket which was turned in. When the billing came
in from the haulers, a copy of the dump tickets would be attached to the invoice to make sure they matched and verify the loads.

The Mayor of Lynn Haven, Margo Anderson, had emergency powers and was involved in the daily meetings. Once things got going, she was there about half the time.

**Chris Forehand's description of me as having emergency powers is not quite honest here. The Charter of the City gives the Mayor the power to declare an emergency and also gives the Mayor the power to either assume authority or designate authority during the period of emergency. When I declared the state of emergency as Hurricane Michael was approaching the City, I designated Michael White, the City Manager to continue his control as CFO and manager of the city operations, and also designated the Police and Fire Chiefs as well as other city department heads to continue their roles as they normally did. The only thing I asked of them (all of this in a meeting with department heads, City Manager, Fire Chief and Police Chief) was that I be kept informed of the City's needs and any information that needed to be relayed to the government officials at the EOC. I did attend almost every meeting which the City Manager had in the beginning because I wanted to have accurate information to relay at the Emergency Operations Center for the County as well as to the residents of the City. I took responsibility for working with city employees as the trucks of supplies came in to unload them and to make sure the residents had food, water and other emergency supplies because of the devastation. My responsibilities, as many would testify, "were taking care of the people." When Forehand says that I was there about "half the time", this was hardly the case. I worked shoulder to shoulder with employees and volunteers from the outside fourteen and sixteen hours daily in the weeks after the storm.**

The City of Lynn Haven was initially going to permit property that it owned as a final resting place for chipped debris. Michael White asked Forehand to permit LH Debris Disposal Site (DDS) 62-701 which he did. Forehand was shown and reviewed copies of emails as well as Panhandle Engineering check number 12885, dated 10/23/2018 payable to F.D.E.P in the amount of $100.00. Forehand was then shown a copy of a text message that was sent to him on 10/30/2018 at 13:08:12 by Michael White. Forehand explained that the Mayor told both Michael White and Forehand that "We are not permitting that site. She was in charge and responsible for the city. No one asked her about permitting this site." Forehand was thereafter asked to discontinue and withdraw the permitting of that site.

**The permitting of this site and Forehand's as well as Michael White's same testimony resulted in my being charged with conspiring with James Finch, my co-defendant, for the City to use Finch's pit for debris. The dates of Forehand's testimony above are very telling. On the date that he wrote a check to the Florida Department of Environmental Protection for $100.00 to permit a site for Lynn Haven, we had a City Commission meeting. Neither Michael White nor Chris Forehand mentioned that they were applying for a permit for a city-owned debris pit on city property. On October 30th, the day that the text message from White told Forehand to cancel the permit, was the day that both of them told me what they had done. The commission met on October 30th, the meeting in which I rescinded the state of emergency for Lynn Haven. Michael White and Chris Forehand had every opportunity to bring this matter before the Commission, including me as the Mayor, but they chose not to. They were hoping to permit this property which would allow Mickey White and ECS to claim to be dumping large amounts of debris there, as Chris Forehand's monitoring company provided the documentation. Of course I did not know this at the time, I just knew they were proposing to permit a debris pit in competition with all of the private companies which were asking for business for the debris, and I believed they should have placed this on the agenda for discussion and a vote of the Commission. They withdrew the permit and never brought it before the Commission because they did not wish for us to know of the fraud and conspiracy in which they were involved. I did not know that James Finch had a pit at this time, and neither did he. He was in a coma in Tallahassee after having had a stroke the week before the hurricane. His company President and operations manager had applied for a pit permit for his company on his behalf at that time, but I was unaware and so was James. We proved this at the evidentiary hearing. To make the "façade" of what Forehand and Michael White, the City Manager, were trying to do even more telling, the property they were trying to permit was only**

about **10 acres, had no passable roads which would handle the debris trucks, and would not have worked, according to the testimony of several contractors who spoke in defense of Finch.**

Forehand, was asked if there was an advantage to the City of Lynn Haven permitting and using its' own property versus sending the debris to a vendor. Forehand stated that there was an advantage to using its' own site versus sending the debris to a vendor's site because the City of Lynn Haven would save from having to pay tipping fees.

**The advantage was for him and his monitoring company as well as to ECS and Michael White if they had a city site where no one would have been monitoring them as they falsified invoices.**

Forehand was then shown a string of emails dated 11/06/2018 through 11/12/2018 in which Panhandle Engineering was in contact with the Florida Department of Environmental Protection (FDEP) regarding the permitting of a new Disaster Debris Management Site (DDMS) at the JDF Properties Disposal Facility on behalf of the City of Lynn Haven. Forehand stated Panhandle Engineering was hired to permit the JDF Properties site. The JDF site was to serve two purposes. The JDF site was to be used as a final resting place for the chipped debris and a C & D (construction and debris) site. The plan was to take Lynn Haven C & D debris to the site, crush it and then take it across the street to the Waste Pro site for disposal. The FDEP requires that a contract be in place with a public entity before a permit for a DMS can be issued.

**Forehand neglects to tell the FBI that Panhandle Engineering has partnered with Phoenix Construction on numerous projects for many years. At this point in time, Forehand will begin to "throw James Finch under the bus" because Forehand is "in" with Derwin White, GAC and Michael White, they know that I, Mayor Margo Anderson and James Finch discovered the fraud, and that I went to the Sheriff as the whistleblower. The protection racket is in full force, and all of those involved who know that I went to the Sheriff are working together to protect themselves against "guaranteed mutual destruction".**

Forehand advised that Panhandle Engineering met with FEMA about once a week. Panhandle Engineering had been tasked to go out and document all the damage to the city properties and produce engineering reports. Forehand stated that took approximately a couple of months. Panhandle used a drone to fly a number of the city locations. Forehand believes the drone shots were taken somewhere around 2-3 weeks after the hurricane and then a month later. Panhandle has been using the photos in the engineering reports that they have been producing and further believes they may have given copies of the photos to Tetra Tech.

**I believe at this point the FBI is hoping for photos of the easement**

property which was cleaned behind my property; we produced our own photos in the evidentiary hearing which proved my property was not cleaned by the City nor was it cleaned by ECS, the charges which brought about my suspension as Mayor of the City.

Amber Guy was Lynn Haven's FEMA representative. At one point, Michael White and Guy started having one-on-one meetings. Tetra Tech noticed this and stated that the meetings were not normal. In February 2019, there was an issue between Michael White and his wife regarding some text messages between Michael White and Guy. After that, Guy was not there anymore. Forehand was shown some text messages between Michael White and Forehand regarding Michael White's alleged involvement with Guy. Forehand's only comment was to reiterate his last comment to Michael White which was I told him "to keep his guard up." Michael White did not go on a hunting trip with Forehand in February because of the incident with his wife.

**Forehand was aware of what was happening between Michael White and the Federal FEMA coordinator; the text messages between White and Forehand, known as "Foreskin" by Michael White, had exchanges describing Michael White's "great white snake" and Forehand calling him, "you dog," as they talked of how Amber agreed to work with Lynn Haven. Ricky Ramie shared screen shots from his phone with me in March 2019 when Michael White was arrested which demonstrated that the police chief also knew about the affair. I went to interim city manager Vickie Gainer in the days following and asked her if she had known about what was going on, and she described to me walking in on Amber Guy and Michael White having sex in the upstairs attic room where administrative city officials were located at that time. She would later deny this in the evidentiary hearing and say that they were only "slumped over together." When I learned of the affair after Michael was arrested, I contacted one of the former FEMA coordinators the city had been assigned (there had been several). Tom McCool, the first FEMA coordinator with who I had contact, after the storm, apparently had her removed because the next I heard she had gone to work with the consulting company hired by the city of Panama City in Bay County. There was no discovery ever given to my co-defendant and I of any interviews by the BCSO or the government with Amber Guy. They either had no curiosity about the federal FEMA coordinator's involvement with the manager of the City who was involved with almost five million dollars of FEMA fraud, or if they interviewed her, this would be one more piece of *Brady* evidence we were not given.**

After the hurricane, Michael White was going to rent Forehand's RV from him. When Michael White found out how much insurance money he was going to get for living expenses, Michael White decided he could buy one instead which he did.

Forehand was shown three (3) ECS invoices:

1.  Invoice #1697 dated 11/26/2018 for 513 Tennessee Avenue in the amount of $18,466.00
2.  Invoice # 1698 dated 11/26/2018 for 511 Tennessee Avenue in the amount of $12,482.10
3.  Invoice #1699 dated 11/23/2018 for 514 Virginia Avenue in the amount of $17,177.60.

**These are the false invoices which Derwin White told his nephew Mickey White to create implicating me in the cleanup of my private property and charging the costs to the City and then to FEMA for reimbursement.**

Forehand was at Porter Park the first time he saw the invoices. James Finch had a contract for the work at the park and GAC had been sub-contracted to do the asphalt. Derwin White handed Forehand the invoices. Derwin White states, "you need to see if the City of Lynn Haven paid these invoices." Forehand contacted Andy Burns and provided him the invoices. Forehand had looked up the addresses on the invoices and learned they belonged to the mayor, her mother and the mayor's neighbor. After speaking with Burns it was also noticed that the invoice numbers were consistent with invoice numbers issued by ECS in March 2019 while the invoices were dated late November 2018.

**Andy Burns worked with Tetra Tech, and Chris was making sure the false invoices had been paid and submitted because that would make sure that I would be charged with federal FEMA fraud.(We tried to contact Andy Burns as a defense witness, and we were told that _he had left the country_ and was working in Europe). The invoices were manufactured by ECS as soon as Derwin knew that I was going to the Sheriff. The invoices would be left on top of a trash can in the ECS office just in time for the BCSO/FBI raid on ECS on April 12, 2019. Major Jimmy Stanford, who was actually helping to conduct this interview with Chris Forehand, tipped Derwin White off to the date of the search warrant execution by the Bay County Sheriff's Office and the FBI on the ECS property and Derwin had told his nephew, owner of ECS, Mickey, "they were coming."**

Forehand was asked if he was aware of the city doing any cleanup work at Osceola Point. Forehand advised that there is a drain pipe from Iowa Avenue to the bay. The pipe runs underground through Osceola Point but there is a drain located just outside of Osceola Point. A lady on Iowa Avenue had complained about her property flooding. At first, the city's position was hurricane cleanup was only on public property not private property. The city went to FEMA and was told that if there was a threat to public safety, then the issue could be addressed. Forehand gave the example that if the area was flooded and an ambulance could not access the area, then that would be justification for the public safety exemption. Forehand understood that the drainage area was cleared so that the area would not flood.

**Forehand is now covering for their other unindicted co-conspirator, Commissioner Dan Russell. After Russell heard about the invoices for "my property" he panicked in early April 2019 and was in the upstairs office at my desk going through stacks of invoices one afternoon as I walked through. I did not think much about it at the time, except that I was annoyed that he was at my desk. The news media contacted me on April 24th, asking me for a statement about my having had my property cleaned and billed to the city. I was of course blindsided, and immediately went to meet with the news director, which is described earlier. On April 26th, Dan Russell wrote a letter to the City of Lynn Haven referring to a "verbal" agreement between his privately owned neighborhood and the City, an agreement which did not exist. Russell's letter was signed by this HOA board, who later said in interviews they just "took Russell's word" about the verbal agreement, that they had no personal knowledge of such an agreement. Forehand could have said the same thing about the drainage easement which was located on the 415 Virginia Avenue property directly to the east of my former home in Lynn Haven, because that drainage empties into Maxwell Bayou and controls flooding for Tennessee Avenue, Virginia Avenue, Kentucky Avenue, and Alabama Avenue, all public city streets, not part of a gated community as Russell's, and others' homes were. But Forehand did not mention this to the FBI; instead, he covered for Russell. Bobby Baker, the public works director, in his interview, stated that debris was cleaned up in the Osceola Pointe neighborhood and stacked on the road outside its gates, with the City trucks picking up the debris, hauling it away, and submitting the charges to FEMA. Baker stated that Osceola Point was not the responsibility of the City of Lynn Haven.**

Forehand was asked about an RV that he had sold in February of 2018. Forehand had purchased a motor home in 2008 and financed it with US Bank. In early 2018, Forehand had another motorhome that he was wanting to purchase from Derwin White. Before Forehand could purchase the motor home from Derwin White, he needed to sell his motor home. Forehand listed his motor home for sale on RV Trader and Facebook. Forehand could not recall the initial listing price but does recall lowering the asking price to $99,000 at some point.

Forehand had asked Derwin White if he knew of anyone looking to purchase a motor home. Derwin White said he would ask around. James Finch came forward and offered to purchase Forehand's motor home for $75,000. After some back and forth, Forehand accepted Finch's offer and Finch gave Forehand a check for $75,000. Forehand used the $75,000 he received from Finch plus $25,000 he had of his own money to pay off the loan at US Bank.

Forehand later learned that Lee Anderson was actually going to buy Forehand's motor home and Finch was going to finance it. Lee Anderson came to Forehand's office on a Friday afternoon to complete the paperwork. Lee Anderson told Forehand that he was purchasing the motor home and Finch was financing it. Lee Anderson had paperwork with him which included a Bill of Sale. Before signing the paperwork, Forehand confirmed with Finch that Lee Anderson was purchasing the motor home and Finch was financing the purchase.

Forehand noticed that on the Bill of Sale the selling price was listed at $35,000. When asked if Forehand questioned Lee Anderson about the selling price on the Bill of Sale, Forehand stated that he guessed Lee Anderson wanted to show a lesser value for the motor home. Forehand was shown a copy of the Bill of Sale, the motor home title and an Affidavit which had been filed with State of Florida Department of Motor Vehicles regarding the sale of the motor home. Forehand confirmed that he signed the Bill of Sale but that the signature on the Affidavit was not his. Forehand stated that he does not recall signing an Affidavit. SA Borghini then showed Forehand the signatures on the Bill of Sale and the Affidavit and pointed out that they looked the same. Forehand stated that he had not signed the Affidavit and that was not his signature.

After selling his motor home, Forehand purchased the motor home from Derwin White. Forehand stated that he gave Derwin White some cash and financed the balance of the selling price with Panhandle Federal Credit Union. SA Borghini asked Forehand who filled out the paperwork regarding the sale. Forehand stated that he did not recall. SA Borghini then pointed out that the Bill of Sale listed the selling price of the motor home as $25,750 which happened to be the same amount of the check Forehand had given to Derwin White.

**The last sentence which says Forehand paid Derwin White $25,750 for an American Eagle motorcoach valued at much more than the motorhome Forehand had just sold, says it all about this lie. The Government had no curiosity about why Chris was able to procure an American Eagle motorcoach for $25,000. Chris Forehand secured a lawyer soon after this interview, David McGee of Pensacola, a former assistant prosecutor with the Northern District of Florida.**

**There are so many questions about this part of the interview. Who had brought to the attention of the Bay County Sheriff's Office and**

the FBI public corruption team that the mayor's husband had purchased a motorhome from James Finch, his friend of over thirty years? Derwin White? A jealous city employee who saw the beautiful motorhome we already owned with a for sale sign in its window sitting next to the motorhome my husband had just purchased from his friend, James Finch in our front yard? Everyone in Lynn Haven knew where I lived, and the two motorhomes sat side by side for weeks in our yard after my husband, Lee, purchased it from James in February of 2018.

This interview happened in August of 2019 after I went to the Sheriff in April of 2019. If there were questions about the propriety of the purchase of the motorhome, again, why was the BCSO investigator Jimmy Stanford not at all interested in questioning me, or questioning my husband? Was there no curiosity? They did not want to know the truth. We already owned a motorhome which we were selling; our motorhome was in beautiful condition but was more situated for family camping; the motorhome my husband purchased from James Finch was only two feet longer, the same year model (2006) but had larger storage bins below which Lee felt would better suit our needs because of all of the music equipment we hauled with our band for shows, festivals and concerts I performed in. I did not like the motorhome when I saw it because it was dirty, had been used for hunting, the interior ceiling was falling down, the carpet and flooring needed replacing, and many other cosmetic issues, but my husband made the deal, and after he explained to me how he planned to fix the cosmetic and other issues I was fine with it. My husband paid James Finch for the motorhome; over their thirty-year friendship they traded, sold, and bought vehicles from each other, one of the most recent before the motorhome, a Big Dog motorcycle. The investigators were all too happy to listen to community gossip. Derwin White who had provided gifts and services to the corrupt investigator in this case, Major Jimmy Stanford, and apparently, according to testimony of everyone from the former City attorney Rob Jackson to the corrupt City Manager Michael White, many conspirators and officials were pleased to add their opinions about the motorhome. No one with law enforcement asked a single question to my husband or to me, but in the last months in which I was Mayor, WMBB Channel 13 ABC affiliate in Panama City's reporters were certainly interested; and Derwin White approached me after a social event I attended and said, "how do you like that motorhome that James gave you?" I responded to him angrily that he knew that was not true, but all he did was just stare back at me with the most evil grin that one can imagine. I will never forget it.

Derwin White truly despised me because I had gone to Sheriff Tommy Ford about his nephew's theft of almost five million dollars from the City of Lynn Haven. The five million that his nephew had stolen was nothing compared to what Derwin White, Allan Bense and their company GAC were alleged to have done in the affidavit of August 2021, and Derwin knew that he would now be targeted because of me. He made me pay...with a little help from his corrupt law enforcement friends. Derwin passed away on July 31, 2021, from Covid complications approximately one year after I was indicted and arrested. The motor home was returned to us after three years of sitting in a government lot in Montgomery, Alabama. My husband paid for it just as he said he did. Chris Forehand, continued to lie to the government as he changed his testimony, added to his testimony, was granted immunity and is still an unindicted conspirator who made millions of dollars from the FEMA fraud in Bay County, and is living his best life now that the statute of limitations on his crimes has run out; however, at the time of the publication of this book, my friend and co-defendant, James Finch has entered civil litigation against Forehand. Forehand's motion to dismiss the civil suit was denied on October 10, 2024, and the case is continuing.


FBI Interview
Chris Forehand, City Engineer for City of Lynn Haven

09/25/2020


This interview was conducted by SA Lawrence Borghini with no other agent listed, but Chris Forehand now has his lawyer, David McGee present. The interview took place exactly one month after I was arraigned in the Tallahassee Federal Court on August 25, 2020, charged with 64 federal counts, and facing over 1,000 years in federal prison and fifty million dollars in fines according to the Federal Magistrate Judge Fitzpatrick who read the fifty-seven page indictment to me. While this interview was conducted on September 25, 2020, according to the date of entry for which it was typed and filed by the FBI agent, the entry date is March 10, 2021, just six days before my friend, James Finch would be indicted himself. I will have no further comment on this interview except to present it as Chris Forehand testified to the agent. Chris had been named in my indictment as an un-indicted co-conspirator and he had "lawyered up". Chris begins to implicate James Finch as being unethical in his practices, and nothing could be further from the truth. Finch does less than 1% of his work for the City of Lynn Haven where he lives and where his business is located, and he is one of the most respected pavers and contractors by the FDOT as is exhibited by numerous awards. Finch had a long-standing relationship with Panhandle Engineering's longtime owner, Jim Slonina, with Chris Forehand being the newer partner in the company. This interview clearly portrays how Chris begins to weave the narrative to protect his corruption and the millions of dollars he made in Bay County through fraudulent means. He was rewarded for this testimony by the Government and by the Bay County Sheriff's Office "public corruption task force" by his never facing any charges and by his receiving immunity.

CHRISTOPHER BRIAN FOREHAND, was interviewed at Panhandle Engineering in Lynn Haven, Florida. Forehand's attorney, David McGee was present for the interview. After being advised of the identity of the interviewing Agent and the nature of the interview, Forehand provided the following information:

Panhandle Engineering was asked to assist the City of Lynn Haven with a paving plan. All the roads in the city were ranked. The roads were to be paved under a continuing contract after one was awarded and approved by the city commission. The project was discussed with Lynn Haven's Director of Public Works Bobby Baker and City Manager Joel Schubert. Lynn Haven Mayor Margo Anderson and Phoenix Construction's owner James Finch talked Schubert into making it a design build project.

Schubert, in his interview, would truthfully state that all projects of Phoenix were done in the Sunshine with Commission vote of approval. Forehand begins to build the story that James and I are in a conspiracy that we are the criminals in Bay County. He and his lawyer, David McGee beginning with this interview, and in the subsequent interviews Forehand gives, will achieve immunity for Forehand in the World Claim charges and he also was never indicted for any other charges in the Hurricane Michael corruption case.

Lynn Haven put out a Request for Qualifications (RFQ) for the project. Margo Anderson's car would be at Finch's office a lot. Forehand saw the writing on the wall and teamed up with Finch on the project. Finch told Lynn Haven that a six percent engineering fee was too much. Finch's invoices to Lynn Haven would show a 3 ½ % engineering fee, however Finch agreed to pay Panhandle Engineering a 6% fee. Finch only did this to make it appear as if the city was receiving the lower fee. Forehand advised that Panhandle Engineering's contract with and invoices to Phoenix Construction show the 6% fee. Forehand's partner in Panhandle

Engineering, Jim Slonina worked on Phase I of the project and Forehand worked on Phase II of the project.

Forehand recalls almost immediately after the project was approved getting a call from Bobby Baker. **(Baker was the Public Works Director for the City of Lynn Haven).** Bobby stated that "James has already started and he is paving roads not on the list." Forehand advised that this was a problem because the engineering had not been completed. According to Forehand, Baker requested Phoenix Construction not do any paving until Panhandle Engineering had provided the plans. All through the process, changes were being made and the plans would need to be adjusted. Roberts and Roberts did all the paving on the projects.

Lynn Haven asked Forehand to assist with the city's water and sewer systems. Both systems were old and had issues. Panhandle Engineering scoped the work and determined that the city's water system needed approximately $3 million dollars' worth of work and the sewer system needed approximately $6 million dollars' worth of work. Lynn Haven went to the State of Florida Department of Environmental Protection (FDEP) to access State Revolving Funds (SRF) to finance the project.

Lynn Haven sent the project to the SRF people and asked if the city could do a design build for the project. After the project was reviewed by the SRF, Lynn Haven was told that they could not do a design build because of "local preference". Lynn Haven went to Mott MacDonald who prepared a new RFQ for Lynn Haven's water and sewer projects. Forehand again saw the writing on the wall and decided to have Lynn Haven use one of its other engineering firms to prepare the city's RFQ and Panhandle Engineering partnered with Phoenix Construction to bid on the project. On the sewer and water projects, Finch billed Lynn Haven the amount Panhandle Engineering charged Phoenix Construction.

Once the paving project was completed, Lynn Haven had Panhandle Engineering prepare a storm water master plan for the city. The plan encompassed the whole city. A portion of the plan addressed structural flooding. In particular, there were five (5) homes on Colorado Avenue that the city wanted to provide relief from the flooding. A couple of other areas that needed addressing were Minnesota and Mississippi. In all, four storm water projects were identified and incorporated into a task order and added to the 17th Street ditch project. The amount of the work was to be $795,000 and financed with the Highway 390 tie in work being done by Finch. Panhandle Engineering's file number for the project was PX 17th Street 14243-J.

Lynn Haven was doing the 17th Street ditch in small sections. After bidding on it, Phoenix Construction was awarded Phase 5. As part of the city's storm water and capital improvement plans, Finch asked Panhandle Engineering to prepare an assessment of the costs to address the 17th Street ditch. Finch thereafter went to Lynn Haven and proposed doing the project as a design build project which he would finance. Panhandle Engineering was advised that they needed to do a package for the project. Lynn Haven consulted their City Attorney Rob Jackson. Jackson advised the city could the project as a change order and Panhandle Engineering could do the engineering on the project under Panhandle's continuing contract with the city.

Highway 390 in Lynn Haven was being widened. It was a Florida Department of Transportation (FDOT) project. FDOT was needing a piece of property owned by Lynn Haven for the widening. Schubert went to the FDOT and proposed trading the property for FDOT piping the rest of the 17th Street ditch. FDOT accepted the proposal. FDOT was going to use their own engineers and contractor to do the project. Finch called State Representative Jay Trumbull, Jr. and Jay Trumbull, Sr. and requested they contact the FDOT and ask them to do a joint participation agreement (JPA) on 17th Street ditch project. A JPA would allow state funds to be passed down to the local municipality to pay for the project. A JPA has a number of requirements such as the project being bid out and there needed to be an engineer on the project. The project was estimated to cost approximately $950,000. The FDOT agreed to fund $750,000 on the project under the JPA. The low bid for the project was $957,000 by Phoenix Construction.

For the last part of the project, Finch went to Lynn Haven and requested Panhandle Engineering do the engineering on the project. The last part of the project included all four of the projects the city wanted done. City Manager Michael White and Finch negotiated that part of the project.

After Hurricane Michael, Lynn Haven applied for and received $1,000,000.00 in state funds on a legislative line-item appropriation for paving. The money went through FDOT. The funding could be used for the engineering and design on the paving project. There were two bidders for the project, Phoenix Construction and GAC Contractors. Dewberry Engineering was hired as the construction engineer inspector for the paving project. Lynn Haven paid $30,000 to $40,000, plus another $60,000 on the project because it came in over budget.

In the beginning, there was two weeks needed to get ready. Within a couple of days, Forehand received a call from Bobby Baker. Baker said that "James is milling 5th Street." Forehand went down to the location. Finch stated that he wanted to lower the road to stop the flooding of residences' driveways. The project called for the asphalt to be mixed in place. Dewberry was not prepared to start the project two weeks early.

Forehand pointed out that the Lynn Haven paving work bids and the Callaway paving work bids were both to be opened on the same day two (2) hours apart. The work was exactly the same in each location. The clerk was responsible for opening the bids in Callaway. Phoenix Construction was awarded the work in Lynn Haven with a bid just over budget and GAC second. GAC was low bidder on the Callaway paving project with a bid just over budget and Phoenix Construction was second. GAC did the paving on Iowa Avenue in Lynn Haven for Phoenix Construction on the Lynn Haven paving project. On the Callaway paving project, Phoenix Construction showed up to do part of that paving project for GAC.

Forehand does not consider himself or Panhandle Engineering Lynn Haven's city engineer. Panhandle Engineering does approximately 70% of the work it does for Lynn Haven in house while subcontracting out such work as surveying, etc.

**Forehand was referred to as the City Engineer by himself and by the City officials; only recently did the City of Lynn Haven place other engineering firms on their list of three consulting engineering firms. When I became Mayor in 2015, Panhandle Engineering's Jim Slonina, now Forehand's partner, was referred to as the City Engineer and even had his own key to City Hall. Forehand is now distancing himself from the corruption to the FBI agent as he tells him that "he does not consider himself the city engineer."**

After the hurricane, Forehand teamed up with Tetra Tech. Jim Slonina had worked with Tetra Tech in the past. Forehand and Slonina assisted with the monitoring. Forehand advised that approximately 30% of the monitors were working for Forehand while the remaining 70% were working directly for Tetra Tech.

**Forehand is giving up more information now than in his previous interview about "his workers" but it is interesting that his new company which is aligned with Tetra Tech, PEDS, is not mentioned here. He also does not mention that he, Forehand, is listed as a board member of Tetra Tech. James Finch, my co-defendant and I, would learn this as we continued to get discovery materials from the Government as we prepared for trial over almost three years' time. Forehand, and his company, Panhandle Engineering, was "knee-deep" in the debris counting business, and Lynn Haven financial documents show the millions he made, after directing his buddy, City Manager Michael White, to hire Tetra Tech. Both Adam Albritton and Michael White's testimony speak of this, as well as cash which Forehand gave to Michael White.**

Forehand stated that the Debris Management Sites (DMS) were getting full. WastePro had provided a bid of $4.70 at one of the meetings. All the attendees agreed that $4.70 was the amount that was going to be the price charged to dispose of the vegetative debris. Michael White asked Ralph Natale, Director of Operations for Teta Tech to check the price. Natale advised that he thought the price was reasonable. Michael White told

Forehand that he wanted to get a site and start filling it up with chips. Forehand started the permitting process on land owned by Lynn Haven.

Shortly thereafter, Forehand received a text instructing him to withdraw the permit. Forehand went to a meeting in which the mayor was in attendance. The mayor, Margo Anderson, asked Michael White, "what are you doing?" The mayor went on to tell Michael White, "I didn't tell you to do that. Look, I'm in charge of this city. You don't do anything I don't tell you to do." Margo Anderson thereafter instructed Michael White not to do anything unless he runs it by her first.

**Chris Forehand and Michael White embellish this story each time they tell it. As I said before, I angrily asked them why they were trying to permit city land to compete against vendors for chips without bringing it before the Commission. I told them that I would call another Commission meeting to get approval or they could withdraw the permit. They obviously did not want the Commission to know what they were doing because they withdrew their permit rather than bring it as an agenda item for a vote. This would be used against me later in the indictment in which I was accused of refusing to allow them to permit a city property for a pit in order for James Finch's pit to get the business. Another lie in which they cooperated. I had no authority to stop them from permitting the property; they knew that if they did it, the Commission was now going to know. Again, neither the FBI agent nor BCSO ever asked me about the pit until I was already named in an indictment. City Manager Michael White, City Engineer Chris Forehand, ECS owner Mickey White, Police Chief Ricky Ramie, Interim City Manager Vickie Gainer, and many others had from April 1, 2019, when they knew that I had gone to the Sheriff with the information I had found until November 19, 2019, when the first indictment was unsealed to talk to each other and "get their stories straight". Unfortunately for them, their interviews and testimonies change from interview to interview, as well as when they testified in the hearings and the trials, or in Forehand's case, when he was given immunity and in the first hearing his attorney told our attorneys that if he testified in the hearing, he would take the 5th amendment so there was no need to call him.**

Forehand advised that there was an agreement about where the chips were to go. The meeting was at James Finch's house. Ralph Natale was there. Finch was complaining that the cleanup was not going fast enough and that all the work was going to outside contractors and the local guys were not getting any of the work. Finch wanted Lynn Haven to put out a new RFQ for Lynn Haven's work. Natale stated that FEMA would not reimburse the city for the costs if Lynn Haven did that. That is when Finch said "what about the wood chips." Forehand advised there were two meetings which occurred at Finch's. The mayor was in attendance during the meetings.

Forehand lies again about the meetings at Finch's house, and the dates for this meeting changed, even in the indictment, as the witnesses found out their first stories did not work because James was still in rehabilitation in Jacksonville at the time of the "meeting" which they said occurred.

FBI Interview
Chris Forehand (Interview #3)
03/30/2021

This interview, the third for Forehand, that we know of, occurred either on 3/12/2021, six days before James Finch, my co-defendant, and Commissioner Antonius Barnes were indicted by the Northern District of Florida, or two weeks after. The FBI agent has two different draft dates on his interview which makes it difficult to determine if the interview happened six days before or two weeks after James was arrested. Guy Lewis, James' defense attorney brought this up several times in the evidentiary hearing, that it was not FBI protocol to interview someone and then wait days, weeks, and in this agent's case, sometimes months before actually memorializing and filing the reports. This report, if the date is accurate, was actually entered into official record on June 2, 2021, about two months after the interview took place. James and I would finally receive our first discovery which included the actual interviews of the witnesses against us, *Brady* material, during the summer of 2021, a full year after I had been indicted. I would have gone to trial facing initially 64 counts without this information in March of 2021, and again in May of 2021 had the indictment not been superseded when James Finch was arrested and indicted himself.
Because I have included the first two rather long interviews of Chris Forehand, instead of including the next three interviews of Forehand I just summarize for the reader to avoid repetition.

In this interview, Forehand goes back through the details of the sale of the motorhome, and while he had stated previously that he did not sign the Affidavit stating that the motorhome was sold to Virgil Anderson for $35,000, Forehand now states in this interview to the FBI that the signature on the Affidavit appears to be his (Forehand's). This should have been a charge against Forehand for lying to the FBI, but that never happened.

The following paragraph from the third interview in which Forehand was interviewed by SA Borghini and with his lawyer present, is a blatant lie:

"Finch wanted Michael White to put out an RFQ for all the stuff that the haulers were already doing. Finch already knew the haulers prices so he knew he could out bid them and claimed he could do the cleanup faster than it was being done. Margo Anderson had a meeting at Mosley High School's fine Arts building which all the city's haulers were there. During the meeting, Margo Anderson publicly stated that the city was not getting cleaned up fast enough and she wanted Finch involved in the cleanup. Forehand stated that when he was helping the city permit their land to use for the disposal of debris, Margo Anderson has told him that she runs the city. Margo Anderson instructed Forehand not to do anything without running it by her or unless she tells him to do it. Forehand claims that Michael White would call him and tell him about stuff the mayor was wanting him to do like fire someone or something that wasn't right."

I did not have a meeting at Mosley High School. On one occasion after Hurricane Michael the City Commission meeting was held at Mosley High School's Fine Arts Auditorium because we had no meeting space large enough, and Lynn Haven Elementary School was not available on that date. There are commission minutes and a video of the meeting. After the city commission meeting was completed, Michael White was standing over to one side speaking with the contracted haulers and others about being off for the holidays, and I sat down to listen. When he finished his meeting, he asked if I wanted to say anything, and I had plenty to say which made them all angry. I complained about the fact that they were still not doing street by street debris pickup, and that they were still selectively picking up the lightest debris from all over the City to fill their trucks and make their "loads" of cubic yards, leaving behind all of the heavier debris. I made a comparison of Phoenix Construction's cleanup of the City of Lynn Haven after Hurricane Opal in 1995 which was done in a street-by-street manner and gave my opinion of what a much more efficient and better job he had done, cleaning up the city so quickly. Hurricane Opal was a Category 3 hurricane which devastated the city with flooding and debris. Forehand also tells his tired lie about the pit again as he did in his previous interviews.

The second part of this interview is about the rebuild of the City of Lynn Haven after Hurricane Michael, and Chris Forehand repeats the same lie that Commissioner Brandon Aldridge and City Manager Vickie Gainer would push at the final Commission meetings in which I was Mayor in the summer of 2020, that FEMA would not allow the design build process if the city wanted the project to be reimbursed by FEMA. Forehand talks extensively to the FBI about Finch and the rebuild of the City here, and both James and I would ultimately be charged with conspiring together to make sure that James would be the contractor who rebuilt the City, another lie which was disproven in the evidentiary hearings. James Finch, a lifetime resident and philanthropist to the City of Lynn Haven did meet with City officials and offer them an alternative plan to present to the City Commission which ultimately was presented and approved; his plan would have saved the City millions of dollars, and included an offer of the best possible location in the City for a police department and Emergency Operations Center in a separate location from City Hall. Even though this plan was voted and approved by a majority of the Commission to be sent out for proposals, once I was indicted and removed from office, the plan never happened. The City went back to the plan that had been pushed by the present City Manager Vickie Gainer, as well as Chris Forehand, who would benefit handsomely from engineering fees, spending millions more than should have been spent and leaving the City library out of the rebuild as well as other park facilities because they overspent on the City Hall and Police Department.

The final part of this third interview of Forehand's targets both James and me and Forehand continues his fabrications to the agent:

"Finch wanted the city to do everything design build. Finch wanted to use the city's insurance money and get things started. Forehand advised Pat Perno, Dan Russell, and Brandon Aldridge to be careful with Finch. If the city did not follow FEMA's rules and the city lost the FEMA money, it would be unfair to the taxpayers. Finch and Mayor Anderson were upset with City Manager Vickie Gainer. The mayor wanted to put in an assistant city manager and get rid of Vickie Gainer. Forehand believes he hears this from Finch when Forehand was at a SRF (State Revolving fund) meeting. He also heard stuff when he was around Finch at various other project meetings."

"On January 8th, 2021, Forehand had a meeting with Phoenix Construction regarding the Steelfield Landfill project. Ron Golinowsky and Ted Schoppe from Phoenix and Cliff Wilson from DewBerry were there. Panhandle Engineering had teamed up with DewBerry on the project. Finch came into the meeting last. Finch asked Forehand to step into his office. Finch asked Forehand if he had heard about the documents Finch sent to the Sheriff's Office. Finch stated that the Sheriff's Office had been provided an article and minutes of a commission meeting where the commission voted to finance the 17th Street ditch project for 30 years. Finch advised that his attorney was going to meet with Kunz next week."

After I was indicted, James sent Sheriff Tommy Ford the minutes of the Commission meeting which refuted what the indictment had said about my signing without commission approval an extension of an agreement from 20 to 30 years. Instead of trying to help James in pushing forward the truth, the Sheriff, instead, just sent the information to Assistant U.S. Attorney Stephen Kunz, along with the negative information James had provided him about Kunz. We proved in the evidentiary hearing that what Assistant US Attorney Kunz and FBI Agent Borghini told the grand jury about this was a lie, which eventually resulted in the Court ruling to unseal the entire grand jury transcript. In the final paragraph of this third interview, Chris tells the FBI agent several more bits of information to do all that he could to hurt James Finch:

"Finch stated that he had a meeting with Glen Osborn and asked Forehand to come to his office for the meeting. When Forehand arrived, Lee Anderson was in the kitchen. Finch did not talk about anything relating to Steelfield Landfill. Finch brought up issues about documents. Finch's attorney had told him that the government was going to be indicting Finch and several others soon. Finch mentioned the motor home and stated that he had financed the motor home and it was being paid for over time. Finch next handed Forehand a letter that Guy Lewis had written to Kunz. Forehand read a couple of lines of the letter and handed it back to Finch. Forehand told Finch that the letter had nothing to do with Forehand. Finch stated that the United States Attorney Larry Keefe was going to resign soon. Finch further stated that if Kunz moved forward with the case against Finch, Kunz was going to be embarrassed about a case in south Florida. **(More about this in Chapter Eight).** Finch told Forehand that the city commission always voted 5-0 and that the charges against Margo were bogus. Finch claimed that he has never been involved in any bid rigging in his entire career. Finch then asked Forehand about the 17th Street Ditch project and what did he tell the FBI. They talked vaguely about the process and contract before Forehand ended the meeting and left. On March 8th, 2021, Finch asked Forehand about Bobby Baker. Finch asked about 10 acres on a piece of property the city owned and disputed the ownership. Finch further asked if Forehand had applied for a permit on the property. Finch advised that something had come up regarding that property. **(Finch was asking about the property that Michael White and Forehand had tried to permit for debris disposal that belonged to the City that I was charged with)**

**FBI Interview**
**3/15/2022**

## Chris Forehand (4th Interview)

This is a much shorter interview and conducted approximately a year after the last interview with Chris Forehand by the FBI; this one takes place just before the first evidentiary hearing which provided so much evidence to the public and to the Court about an investigation which the Court termed "haphazard and reckless" by the prosecutors, and for which he considered dismissing the entire case approximately two years after I was indicted, but ultimately, allowed the case to go forward. One interesting point about this interview, is there is now a different FBI agent, and the interview is entered into the file the next day after the interview, rather than weeks or months later as had been done by SA Borghini. Also, in addition to the new Agent, Daniel Crecelius, Assistant US Attorneys Kunz and Grogan are also present, this interview does not take place at Forehand's office as the three previous ones had, but instead was at the United States Attorney's Office in Tallahasssee. Forehand's attorney, David McGee was also present.

Christopher Forehand was interviewed at the United States Attorney's Office in Tallahassee, Florida. Also present for the interview was Forehand's attorney, David McGee, and Assistant United States Attorneys Stephen Kunz and Andrew Grogan. After being advised of the identity of the interviewing Agent and the nature of the interview, Forehand provided the following information:

Forehand saw Derwin White on and off before White died. White wanted to speak to Forehand about the Federal Bureau of Investigation's FBI investigation, but Forehand didn't want to talk to White about it. Around May 2021, White called Forehand and told him that White was in possession of Forehand's bank records and surveillance pictures of Forehand's house. White was in possession of various documents that the Government turned over during the discovery process. White asked Forehand if Forehand had spoken to the Government. Forehand told White that he might be a witness in the investigation.

Forehand and his company, Panhandle Engineering, had a lot of work with James Finch and Finch's company, Phoenix Construction over the years. After the FBI's investigation broke, the City of Lynn Haven, through Vicky Gainer, made an agreement with Forehand that Forehand shouldn't do anymore work with Finch.

Forehand remembered former Lynn Haven Mayor Margo Anderson being upset because of a permit for a property that Michael White asked Forehand to submit. Anderson wanted to know who authorized the permit. When Forehand told Anderson that Michael White authorized the permit, Anderson told Forehand that Michael White didn't run the city.

Anderson also told Forehand not to do anything without her permission. *This interaction with Anderson was not normal, as a decision like this would usually go through the City Council.*

When I read this last sentence for the first time I could not believe my eyes. Of course, the interaction should have gone through the City Commission, which is precisely why I told them if they did not withdraw their permit I was going to reconvene the Commission. Forehand was helping the Government with the lie they had told in the first indictment... that I was the head of the City and that I supervised the City Manager. The City Charter would have told them otherwise if they had bothered to read it or ask about it. Instead, the lies of Michael White and Chris Forehand were preferable. Through the course of the nearly thirty-six months of pre-trial Hell that James and I went through, I cannot describe how reading blatant lies in the government discovery told by Chris Forehand and the others, affects one, especially when the defendant is not allowed to contact or confront any of these "witnesses" without threat of arrest and imprisonment until trial.

Finch wanted all of the work in Lynn Haven after Hurricane Michael. Forehand remembered meeting at Finch's house on at least two occasions. Finch wanted the City of Lynn Haven to issue a Request for Qualifications in order to remove the haulers that were moving debris from Hurricane Michael. Forehand remembered sitting around Finch's dining table. Anderson, Michael White and some guys from Tetra Tech were also present for these two meetings. Finch had a stroke or some kind of medical emergency before these meetings. Finch seemed fine at the meetings and sat at the dining table like everybody else.

**Forehand repeats the same lie, just to a different FBI agent.**

Forehand would meet at Finch's office on a weekly or bimonthly basis. Anderson was often at the meetings at Finch's office which was why Forehand felt like the meetings at Finch's house were so unusual. It was clear that Anderson wanted all of the work to go to Finch, to include the vegetative chips. Anderson was always praising Finch and his work publicly.

During the time of the first stage of the ½ cent surtax paving project in which 25 miles of roads were paved in Lynn Haven in 2017 and 2018 before the Hurricane, there were weekly meetings at the contractor's office, Phoenix Construction, and as Mayor, I often attended these meetings. I rarely asked questions; I was simply there to inform myself of progress. Paving of streets had been a campaign promise of mine in 2015 when I ran for Mayor, and I was pleased with the fact that Lynn Haven was receiving surtax money from the state/county after the referendum had passed in 2016 which projected

that Lynn Haven would receive approximately 17-22 million dollars in infrastructure funding. Finch was simply not capable of holding a meeting on the dates the government accused him of doing so due to his health. There was a meeting held at his house at some time in late November, but nothing as Chris Forehand described, and I was invited to attend by City Manager Michael White because I was the Mayor. The declared emergency had long passed. The City had no suitable conference rooms, and Finch's dining table seats 16-20 if I recall; he has a large, beautiful home just a few blocks from the City Hall in Lynn Haven, and I really do not recall too much about that meeting except several contractors and engineers, as well as city personnel were there discussing the progress of the cleanup and next steps. In the months just after the storm, I knew very little about the process for cleanup, the debris pits, who owned or managed them; I was just concerned that the eight-to-ten-foot piles of debris on every street in the City of Lynn Haven did not seem to be going away at a very fast pace. While I compared to Michael White in conversation, more than once, what James Finch had done in the earlier 1995 Hurricane aftermath to clean up the City with what was being done now, after Hurricane Michael, I never pressured anyone to fire the national haulers because I did understand what a blue skies contract agreement was as a member of the Commission because I had voted on its renewal long before Hurricane Michael
was thought of. Chris Forehand and others lied about this over and over, to please the prosecutors, and to reduce their sentences.

Forehand used to own a motor home that Finch financed for Lee Anderson to buy. The motor home was in great condition and had new tires. The motor home was not dated. The motor home did not need any interior repairs. The motor home did not need any engine repairs.

Chris lies again. The motorhome did have new tires, but it was twelve years old, and it was dated. We redid the interior including dashboards, headliner (which was falling down) new furniture, and bedroom mattress. While Forehand was "under water" and owed 106,000 dollars on the twelve-year old motorhome, even the Government in their own value of it later, valued it at only $57,400, after our initial improvements, and after having it repainted and a new roof and windshield installed after Hurricane Michael. Assistant U.S. Attorney Stephen Kunz lied in the Panama City Press Conference when he stated that the Andersons paid no money for the motorhome that was given to them valued at $106,000.

Forehand wanted to buy another motor home from White because it was bigger than the one Forehand was selling. Forehand originally listed his motor home for sale for $100k on RV Trader and Facebook. Forehand tried to sell the motor home for about a month.

Finch inquired about Forehand's motor home while Forehand was at Finch's office. Forehand questioned why Finch would be interested in the motor home because Finch was the type of guy to have the "half a million dollar motor home" Finch told Forehand that he wanted the motor home because Finch planned on putting the motor home at his track. Finch offered Forehand $75K for the motor home. Forehand declined Finch's request and tried to negotiate with Finch but Finch would not budge. White knew that Finch and Forehand were negotiating on the price of forehand's motor home. White ended up lowering the price of the motor home that he was selling to Forehand by $5k. After White lowered his asking price, Forehand agreed to sell Finch his motor home for $75K.

Forehand went to Finch's office to drop off the keys to the motor home and the title to the motor home, but Finch was not at his office. Forehand left the keys and title on Finch's chair in Finch's office and called Finch to let him know where he left everything. Forehand wrote Finch's name on the title since the motor home was being transferred to Finch's name. During the phone call, Finch never mentioned anything about Lee Anderson.

About a week after dropping off the title and keys at Finch's office Finch told Forehand that Lee Anderson was actually going to buy Forehand's motor home and that Finch was financing the purchase for Lee Anderson. Finch told Forehand that he was going to send Lee Anderson to Forehand's office so Forehand can fill out the bill of sale.

Forehand felt uneasy about Lee Anderson buying the motor home because Lee Anderson was married to Mayor Anderson. Forehand did not think it was "good optics doing business with the Mayor's husband." Forehand specifically remembered three or four conversations that he had with Finch after Finch told him that Lee Anderson was going to buy the motor home. Forehand specifically asked Finch if Finch was going to make Lee Anderson pay for the motor home. Finch told Forehand "Yes, I 'm going to finance it for them." After Michael White was arrested, Forehand asked Finch about making sure Lee Anderson was going to pay for the motor home and Finch again told Forehand that he was financing the purchase.

When Lee Anderson arrived at Forehand's office, Lee Anderson had the title to the motor home with him. Finch's name had been crossed out and Lee Anderson's name was now on the title. Lee Anderson also had a bill of sale for the motor home.

Forehand did not remember writing any affidavit, but Forehand believed that he signed it. The title also listed that the motor home was being sold for $35K. Forehand was not the one that wrote $35K and assumed Lee Anderson listed that amount on the title in order to avoid paying higher taxes.

In this interview after the first evidentiary hearing, by a new FBI agent, Chris is now speaking with the confidence of his immunity for the World Claim conspiracy, and he is an un-indicted conspirator named in my indictment. His statements about asking James over and over if my husband Lee is *actually paying him* for the motorhome are just ludicrous. My husband agreed to pay James half down and the other half after the motorhome we owned at the time was sold. The Government made a huge deal out of the fact that James Finch had crossed his name off the title and my husband's name was written on the title. When James and my husband decided on their deal for the motorhome, James had not gone to pick up the motorhome as far as I know, they had made many handshake and handwritten bill of sale deals over thirty years of friendship, and this one was no different; after three years of lies by the government witnesses and the corrupt investigators, my husband drove to Montgomery, Alabama in March of 2023 and got his motorhome back after it sat in a field for three years. Chris Forehand purchased an over-the-top American Eagle motorcoach from Derwin White, apparently for just a *little over 25,000* according to the affidavit that Chris Forehand signed at the tax office when he paid the taxes on his purchase, affirming that he bought a luxury American Eagle motorcoach for $25,000. What a bargain price that was.

FBI Interview
Chris Forehand (04/01/2022)
Fourth Interview of Chris Forehand

This last interview of Chris Forehand pertains to the World Claim public adjusters used by the City of Lynn Haven and the interview was conducted during the time of the first evidentiary hearing by telephone, again, with Assistant US Attorneys Kunz and Grogan listening, Forehand's attorney on the phone, and again, the new FBI agent, Crecelius conducted the interview, and entered it into record on the same day, April 1, 2022, exactly three years to the day that I walked into Sheriff Tommy Ford's office as the whistleblower which began the entire investigation and ultimately made me their target The World Claim charges against me were dropped by the prosecutors in their fourth indictment against me in October 2022, but they would later tell me when they offered a plea of 0-6 months two weeks before my trial of February 27, 2023, that if I did not accept the plea, that even if I was acquitted of the two charges left against me in the February trial, that they would indict me again and bring back the World Claim charges.

**We proved in the evidentiary hearing, that I did not accept a pro bono contract, nor did I pay a reduced fee to World Claim, but that I had a legal contract with them which I paid in full. We also proved that Commissioner Dan Russell, an unindicted conspirator, actually *signed* a pro bono contract with World Claim, the city public insurance adjuster, and gained over $70,000 through the contract. He was never charged with a any crimes.**

"Forehand understood the terms of the immunity letter and had a chance to review it with his counsel. As way of background, after Hurricane Michael, a lot of people moved out of their homes and lived at the Watercolor subdivision in Walton County. Several of Forehand's friends rented houses near each other. After work, Forehand and his friends would gather up and socialize with each other.

Denise "Dede" Rowan and her husband were staying at Watercolor. Rowan is a local attorney. Rowan told Forehand that WorldClaim contacted her and said they would hire her to assist with hurricane-related insurance claims. Rowan asked if Forehand knew anybody that might want to use WC. Forehand was having problems with his current insurance, so he ended up hiring WC for his personal home, business, and another property that he owned.

Forehand told Rowan that the City of Lynn Haven might be interested in hiring WC because Lynn Haven was also having problems with insurance claims. Rowan told Forehand that she would split the fees that WC paid her if Forehand brought in additional clients. Forehand and Rowan agreed to split the fees in half. Rowan sent a contract to forehand to document their agreement. Rowan introduced Forehand to Michael Fusco and Lauren Brubaker from World Claim.

WC had a lot of experience with disasters. Forehand set up a meeting with Michael White and asked if the city needed to hire an adjuster. White said he had a personal need for an adjuster at his farm home. Forehand recommended WC and told White that he hired them personally. Forehand also recommended WC for the City of Lynn Haven. Forehand explained the deal that he had with Rowan to White. Forehand explained that he would financially benefit from any contract that WC had with the City of Lynn Haven. Forehand showed White his contract that he had with Rowan.

It was not uncommon for Forehand to ask White for work from the city. Forehand periodically sat down with all of his clients to discuss further opportunities. After the meeting with White, Forehand didn't get involved with anything related to the City of Lynn Haven and World Claim.

Based on Forehand's reading of the indictment, Forehand thinks that White misunderstood what Forehand said during their meeting about WC.

White asked Forehand if he could be part of the fee that Forehand and Rowan earned from WC Forehand told White that he could not take part in the fee-sharing agreement between Forehand and Rowan. White asked Forehand if WC would do work at White's personal residence for free. Forehand told white that White would have to work out any specific details like that with WC personally.

Forehand introduced White to Fusco.

Forehand also mentioned WC to Dan Russell. Forehand told Russell that he might want to consider hiring WC. Forehand believed that Russell hired WC and later fired them, but Forehand didn't have anything to do with Russell and WC's relationship.

Forehand was unaware that Margo Anderson hired WC. Forehand found out that Anderson hired WC after reading the indictment.

Forehand did not coordinate everything with WC and believes the indictment made it seem that way. After the introduction of White and Fusco, Forehand didn't have anything to do with White and WC's relationship.

Forehand was aware of an email from Rowan claiming that White didn't pay because Forehand was on the email and because he was owed part of the fee. Forehand should have received a portion of any fees from White, the City of Lynn Haven and Russell. Forehand never followed up with any of these fees because he was so busy with other work. Forehand may have had a conversation with Rowan about pending fees, which may have prompted the aforementioned email.

Forehand had no knowledge of any personal agreements between Fusco or his VP, and White, Russell, or Anderson. Forehand was not present in any meeting setting up the City of Lynn Haven's contract with WC. Forehand knew the City of Lynn Haven signed a contract with WC but did not have anything to do with any meetings related to the contract other than making the introductions.

**Forehand says he did not know about my contract with World Claim; Forehand had a conversation with my husband about how our insurance claim on our home was going and told my husband that he had used World Claim and what a good job they had done for him. My husband expressed interest, and we received an email from Lauren Brubaker in February of 2019. This was long after Michael White, Chris Forehand, and Dan Russell had already received their pro bono work from World Claim. I have already gone into detail about the World Claim and the lies in the federal indictment, but I did want to clarify once more that, Michael White signed the contract with World Claim, brought the contract with him to a commission meeting with a place for my signature, and I signed it after the meeting. Michael White also told the entire commission, including**

me, that he had entered into a contract with World Claim as the city's public adjuster, and this is on record, a public City Commission meeting. I did not sign a contract in a dark room with Michael White so that I could get free adjustment services. I did not sign a pro bono contract. But unindicted co-conspirator Commissioner Dan Russell did, and Chris Forehand received immunity about World Claim benefits he received. His immunity letter is a filed public document and was an exhibit in the first hearing. The letter is dated March 29, 2022.

Lauren Brubaker, the Vice President of World Claim's interview follows, in which she states that I refused a pro bono contract.

FBI Interview
Lauren Brubaker (7/30/2020)

This interview was conducted by SA Lawrence Borghini at the FBI office in Columbus, Georgia with Lauren Brubaker and her attorney on July 30, 2020, about three weeks before I was arrested and indicted. The interview clearly states that I rejected a pro bono contract and the Government clearly had this evidence before I was indicted in August of 2020, although the first grand jury had already met in June of 2020 , targeting me, while U.S. Attorney Stephen Kunz continued to tell my attorney that I was not a target, but a subject of the investigation.

"Dr. Williams referred Deedee Rowan to Worldclaim. Michael fusco met with Rowan in person at her house to setup a homeowners claim and referral agreement. The referral agreement was to compensate Rowan for people in the area she referred to Worldclaim. Chris Forehand is an engineer who works with the City of Lynn Haven. Worldclaim assisted Forehand with the handling of his claim (s). Rowan and Forehand were working together to share their network with Worldclaim however Worldclaim's referral agreement was with Rowan.

Forehand introduced Worldclaim to Michael White. White was Lynn Haven's city manager. The first meeting Worldclaim had with Lynn Haven was with Michael White and the Mayor. They discussed Worldclaim's services and what they could provide to the city. The city had already been briefed on Worldclaim's resume and fee structure. After Lynn Haven signed a contract, Worldclaim came onsite and started working.

I do not remember meeting with anyone from Worldclaim with Michael White to discuss their services, but I do not deny it, because in the days after the hurricane, I literally met with hundreds of people. Most meetings were outside under tents, in the emergency portable buildings in the park, or the Verizon office trailer on loan to the City. The World Claim contract was signed on October 24th, 2018, just two weeks after the landfall of the Cat 5 storm, and so if there was a meeting it would have been impromptu and sometime before then. I signed the World Claim contract after Michael White brought the contract to the Commission meeting and told the Commission he had entered into contract with Worldclaim, which he had the authority to do at that time because the emergency did not end until October 30th, 2018. Adam Albritton's interview with the FBI speaks of the initial meeting with Worldclaim and he does not mention my being present.

Worldclaim met inside Lynn Haven's trailer to discuss the city's claim and properties. Present for those meetings were Jay Moody (city's accountant), Kelli Battistini (risk management) and Adam Albritton (city attorney). The process included going over insurance contracts, joint inspections, assigning priorities and the normal process of handling such a claim and the people involved such as field people, adjusters and estimators.

Michael White had four (4) properties that Worldclaim handled for him. His residence in the Country Club, his farm and his rental property. Michael White approached Brubaker about handling his work "pro bono". Michael White phrased it as it would be "helpful if they handle" his claims. At first, Michael White asked for himself but soon after asked if Worldclaim could do the same for the mayor and Dan Russell. Brubaker claims she did not know there was anything wrong with handling their claims pro bono until February 2019 when she approached Mayor Margo Anderson about handling Anderson's claim. Anderson told Brubaker, "I can't do that, I could lose my job."

**Although I do not think those are the exact words I used, the point is, I did refuse the pro bono contract, and the Government knew it. *Before* they indicted me.**

Brubaker was specifically asked about a fee not taken document for Michael White and his properties. Brubaker stated that she thought she had prepared a "not taking a fee" document for Michael White. Brubaker tried to locate the document in Worldclaim's records but could not find it. Brubaker was also asked about documents having information redacted from them. Brubaker stated that some documents submitted to insurance companies have some information redacted from them.

Brubaker had initially sent Margo Anderson a contract stating that Worldclaim's fee was 10%. The contract also included an agreement that Worldclaim would not be taking a fee for the work. Brubaker had a conversation with Margo Anderson about Michael White arranging for

Worldclaim to do the mayor's claim pro bono. After discussing it with the mayor, Brubaker agreed to handle the claim for a 5% fee and sent Anderson a revised contract reflecting such which Anderson signed and returned.

Brubaker stated that she was told to help Michael White with his claim because he was an important guy. Dan Russell was also discussed. Brubaker was told to get with Adam Albritton which she did but it never went anywhere.

**It is interesting that Brubaker does not state who told her to help Michael White, Dan Russell and Adam Albritton, or either the agent doing the interview left it out. I believe this would be Chris Forehand since he, by his own words, arranged everything, and then received government immunity, but of course, I do not know that for sure.**

In November 2019, Brubaker learned of the indictment regarding Lynn Haven. Worldclaim continued to work for the City of Lynn Haven attempting to reach settlements on the open parts of the claim. Worldclaim worked with Adam Albritton and Vickie Gainer regarding the matter.

**In the indictment of November 2019, when Michael White, David "Mickey" White, Josh Anderson, David Horton and Rodriguez were indicted and Commissioner Dan Russell and me were named as un-indicted co-conspirators, there was no mention of World Claim or the World Claim charges. The investigators came after me on the false Worldclaim charges because of the testimony of City Manager Michael White, Chris Forehand, and possibly others.**

## The FBI Interviews of David "Mickey" White

**The five interviews of Mickey White, the owner of ECS (Erosion Control Specialist) are filled with information of the level of corruption occurring in Lynn Haven and all of Bay County Florida in the aftermath of Hurricane Michael. Because they are so lengthy I chose to use paragraphs from the interviews which were specifically related to charges against me. James Finch was never charged with any of the conspiracy known as the "ECS conspiracy" and in October of 2022, both the World Claim and the ECS charges were dropped against me as well as Federal Judge Mark Walker ruled against the Government in their wanting to try us together in the same trial in two conspiracies in which James was not charged. In the third superseding indictment, the fourth indictment against me, the Government dropped both the ECS charges, and the World Claim charges against me, leaving me facing only two charges for the**

**February 27, 2023, trial, conspiracy and a "666" bribery charge.**

**David "Mickey White"**
**Interview of 4/19/19**
**This interview was just seven days after the Bay County Sheriff's**
**Office and the FBI raided ECS, Mickey White's place of business.**

After learning that law enforcement was executing a search warrant at the business, upon arrival, White wanted to know what was going on. It was explained to White that a search warrant was being executed for certain business records of the company. White was advised that he was not under arrest and was free to leave if he wished. After being advised of the identity of the interviewing agents. White agreed to speak with the agents and answer questions. White was interviewed by FBI Special Agent Lawrence P. Borghini, SA Heather C. Johnson and Bay County Sheriff Office Major Jimmy Stanford. White thereafter provided the following information:

"After Hurricane Michael, ECS began helping the City of Lynn Haven with the initial clean up response. The "big guys" (referring to the large contracting companies) were there doing work. Everyone was trying to get a contract. The Mayor and City Manager, Michael White, called ECS and hired them to perform cleanup work. Jay Moody, the CLH's attorney and Tetra Tech prepared the contracts for the work which included a fee schedule for various types of work that could be performed. The contract was reviewed by the Mayor and City Manager. White knows the City of Lynn Haven city manager, Michael White. White used to work for Michael White at the power company many years ago."

**Michael White and Mickey White, as well as others involved, had now had seven days to talk and think about what was probably coming since they knew that I had been to Sheriff Tommy Ford on April 1st. Mickey says that the Mayor and City Manager "called ECS" And hired them to provide cleanup work. How did we make this call? Mickey also states that he knew Michael White, but he does not say the same about me. The contract that Adam Albritton drew up for ECS was signed by Mickey White and Michael White. There was not even a signature line for the Mayor. I did not know about the contract, nor did I sign it. This was a real problem for the Government, and this is why they charged me with lying to the FBI because my testimony was that I met Mickey White sometime in December of January, which is true, but they needed me to say that I knew him in October when this contract was signed.**

"White participated in meetings twice a day which occurred at 6 am and

6 pm with the City of Lynn Haven. Attending the meetings were City of Lynn Haven department heads, Gulf Power, the gas company and contractors. Attending for ECS were White, Wilson and Shannon, (White's sister.)

**The City was actually having meetings three times each day, and I was at all of them in the first days of the storm, but not so many after the first week or ten days because I was busy at the distribution centers handing out supplies to residents and also meeting at the Emergency Operations Center with other Mayors and officials. Mickey signed the contract with Michael White on October 22nd, 2018, and so by the time he started attending meetings I was probably hardly ever there, and he does not mention me in his interview as being at the meetings. But Mickey and Michael were government witnesses who were eventually sentenced to 42 months in federal prison; below the recommended sentence guidelines, thanks to their testimonies against me. Michael White, whose false testimony against me and against James was the testimony which the prosecutors relied on most heavily in the narrative of their indictment, in the opinion of our attorneys, and according to the Bureau of Prisons website, he is scheduled for an even earlier release date which will mean that his prison time is less than two years.**

After the hurricane, ECS went to a few police officers' residences to work because City Manager, Michael White, said the City of Lynn Haven was responsible for the police officers. The police officers were having to work long hours and CLH wanted to make sure the police officers were not having to worry about their residence. ECS did not charge the police officers for the work performed; however, ECS was paid by the City of Lynn Haven for the work performed.

**Robert Brannon, the Facilities Manager, in his interview stated that many city employees, not just police officers had work done at their residences and charged to the City. This was illegal, yet no one else was questioned about property cleanup, nor were they charged, even though these charges were ultimately reimbursed by FEMA making the charges federal.**

City of Lynn Haven Mayor Margo Anderson asked White to perform work at her house and her mother's house. White's crew worked four (4) days at the residences per the Mayor's request.

**This is blatantly false. The entire cleaning of the easement request details are outlined earlier in this book, but the request I made was to City Manager Michael White for the City of Lynn Haven to clean the easement adjacent to the east side of my property. I never spoke to Mickey White about any type of cleanup, my property nor the easement.**

## Mickey White's Second Interview (12/02/2019)

**Mickey White's second interview was on 12/02/2019 at the Federal Bureau of Investigation in Panama City by Special Agent Laurence Borghini. Also present for the interview was Mickey's attorney, Jim White (no relation), and U.S. Assistant Attorney Stephen Kunz.**

**I am including more of Mickey White's second interview because there is so much information about the web of corruption happening in Lynn Haven and beyond in the weeks immediately after the storm. Mickey White is the owner of ECS, and he is the nephew of Derwin White, the owner of GAC along with his partner, former Florida House Speaker Allan Bense.**

The interview was conducted pursuant to a proffer agreement which was executed by White and his attorney Jim White.

Prior to Hurricane Michael, Mickey White and his family were living on Veal Road in Panama City. After the hurricane damaged their residence, they stayed with his mother-in-law in Lynn Haven, Florida. After Hurricane Michael, White went to Michael White, Lynn Haven's city manager and talked to him about the cleanup of city properties. Michael White advised White that he (Mickey) needed to speak with Crowder Gulf about cleanup work.

Not long after the hurricane, White went to GAC offices in Panama City to get ice. GAC had a contract with Bay County District Schools. GAC hired White's company, Erosion Control Specialist (ECS), as a sub-contractor for cleanup work at Bay High School and Springfield Elementary School.

White first started doing work for the City of Lynn Haven at the water plant, the water towers, and Southerland's Funeral Home. White hooked up generators at each of these locations which cost $38,000. White had used Tony Wishnett of Tony's Electrical Services to do the work. In addition to the generators, White tarped Michael White's house in Country Club and Lynn Haven police officers' houses. Michael White requested that White bill the City of Lynn Haven for the work but show the invoice in man hours. Michael White wanted to make sure the city would get reimbursed for everything it was doing.

White was asked to cleanup hurricane debris at Mayor Margo Anderson's house. That was the first time he had met the mayor's husband, Lee Anderson. White's crews spent the day cleaning along the

street and behind three (3) houses on Tennessee Avenue with Mayor
Anderson's being one of them. White was asked not to bill the mayor for
the work that was performed, but instead was requested to bill the city like
he had done for everything else to that point. White billed the work to
Sheffield Park along with the work ECS had performed at the police
officers' houses.

Notice that Mickey White has contradicted his first testimony
about "my property cleanup" when he told the agent that he was
there for *four days* doing cleanup for my property and that of my
mom who lived next door to me. In this interview he states that his
crews spent "*the day*" cleaning along the street and behind three
houses on Tennessee Avenue with Mayor Anderson's being one of
them. The ECS crew that Michael White sent did work on the
easement for only one afternoon as Mickey now states in this second
interview. Michael White sent Mickey White to the easement behind
my house which is a drainage ditch that runs behind the houses on
Tennessee Avenue on the west and Virginia Avenue on the east, on
November 9th, a full month AFTER the hurricane. I described in an
earlier chapter of the cleanup and repair to my home and that of my
mom which was done the weekend after the storm by my family
members and friends who traveled from Jacksonville. All of this is
documented with photographs as well as the testimony of others who
saw them there; even the testimony of those interviewed by the Bay
County Sheriff's investigators trying to implicate me, actually became
evidence which helped me, because they testified seeing workers
tarping my home and my Mom's home on the weekend after the
Hurricane rather than a full month later when Mickey White and
Michael White's text messages prove they were on the easement
behind my property on November 9th, a full month after Hurricane
Michael, not the weekend after. The entire property cleanup
conspiracy and the charges against me were false, but my point here
is that Mickey has contradicted himself from the first interview.

ECS crews did work at David Horton's house. They tarped his house
and cleaned up hurricane debris. Josh Anderson removed a tree from the
property. Horton requested a bill for the work that he paid after the fact.

David Horton was the community services director for the City of
Lynn Haven who was indicted in November 2019 and Josh Anderson
was the owner of Greenleaf, the lawn service company which had a
contract with the City of Lynn Haven. Josh Anderson was also
indicted along with Horton, Michael White and Mickey White. Josh
Anderson also gave false testimony against me regarding the
"property cleanup". He was ultimately sentenced to house arrest and
probation as was David Horton, even though both received cash

**kickbacks from ECS and were part of the fraud. They were
government witnesses rewarded for their testimony against me.**

White's crew gutted Michael White's house in the Country Club. He
also sent crews and equipment to Michael White's farm in Youngstown on
at least three (3) separate occasions. The crews cleaned out the houses on
the property and cleaned up hurricane debris on the properties. All the
hours for the work performed at Michael White's properties were billed to
Lynn Haven and shown as having been worked at Mount Hope Cemetery.
White estimates he had approximately thirty (30) employees as well as
equipment working on Michael White's properties. Michael White's son,
Austin White, was on ECS' weekly payroll and received a paycheck each
week. According to White, Austin never showed up to work.

White was asked by Adam Albritton to gut Albritton's house in Lynn
Haven. White sent Dustin Turner and some Mexicans over to Albritton's
house to start the work. White believes he had approximately 10 people on
the Albritton job for a couple of days. White had approximately $6,000 in
the job plus any cost for the haul off of materials. Additional work White
did for Albritton included tarping ($3,000), demo of a fence (2,500), and
debris cleanup and removal of 5-6 stumps ($6,000). Albritton needed a
trailer to store his household goods in until Albritton's house could be
repaired. White rented a storage container at $600-$800 a month for 3-5
months. White never billed Albritton for the work or the expenses
incurred. White charged the time to the City of Lynn Haven as hours being
worked at Mount Hope Cemetery.

**Albritton was the City Attorney hired by Michael White, who was
also the attorney for Derwin White and GAC. Albritton drafted the
contract for Derwin's nephew Mickey after Michael White fired one
of the national haulers, Ceres, so that Derwin White and AshBritt
would benefit. Albritton was indicted when I was in August of 2020,
and at the time I believed him to be innocent of the charges, just as I
was. I considered him a friend; he volunteered and helped me with
supplies for the residents after the storm. He pled guilty, and he was
taking $10,000 per week kickbacks from Mickey White. He would
also be a government witness against me, and he ultimately received
no prison sentence, only a year of probation, because Judge Mark
Walker said he had suffered enough collateral damage by losing his
license to practice law. I was sickened by both his behavior and by
the way he was rewarded for his lying about me to protect his own
interests and those of his co-conspirators in the fraud. On the day he
was sentenced, he was ordered to pay $32,000 in restitution, a fine
which was paid in full immediately by Jason Bense, the son of Allan
Bense, former co-owner of GAC, Derwin White's partner.**

White was taken to Osceola Point by Michael White. Michael White told White to have his guys clean out the area around the lift station and drainage ditch to the bay. White told his guys to hold up because they needed certain equipment to do the work. White left Osceola Point to get the equipment. After leaving White learned that one of his guys was hurt and had broken his back in three places.

**There is no mention here about the fact that this small, gated area is where Commissioner Dan Russell lives concerning the large amounts of debris that Public Works director Bobby Baker told the Bay Count Sheriff's office investigators was hauled from the neighborhood, charged to the city and then submitted to FEMA. Russell was an un-indicted conspirator named in the indictment for having had his property cleaned by the City (ECS) and reimbursed ultimately by FEMA, but Michael White, Chris Forehand and others protected their buddy, the Commissioner who also accepted pro bono work from World Claim.**

White did some work for Lynn Haven Police Chief Ricky Ramie. White repaired Ramie's personal vehicle at ECS' shop as well as changed out an axle on Ramie's boat trailer. Ramie paid for the axle and White's shop did the work. White estimates the axle change took approximately 4-5 hours.

**These hours were billed to the City and then to FEMA. Ramie is the corrupt police chief who at the time of the publication of this book has been on suspension without pay by the City of Lynn Haven, this time for a hit and run arrest at 3:30 in the morning at a local bar. Residents continue to call for his firing because of continued infractions, yet unindicted co-conspirator and witness Vickie Gainer, the City Manager, refuses to fire him. The protection continues even now, six years after the landfall of Hurricane Michael. Mutual assured destruction is my description of why they protect each other.**

White discussed the trash pickup work with Michael White. White had spoken to Jason Tunnell and received a price of $300 an hour for trash pickup around the city. Michael White asked White if he could do it for less than $300 an hour. White agreed to provide a truck, trailer and men. White already had a contract with the city with a price list for trucks, trailer and man hours attached. Michael White and Adam Albritton prepared the paperwork. White advised that Jay Moody was present when the topic was discussed and agreed upon. White stated that no trash pickup was done prior to the task order being executed. Albritton back dated the task order. White claims that he paid Albritton $10,000 a week after the task order was signed.

White would purchase certified checks payable to Greenleaf and have Josh Anderson cash them. After Josh Anderson cashed them, he would give the money right back to White. White used this cash to pay Albritton. White believes he had Josh Anderson cash 4-5 checks for him. White would make the payoffs to Albritton at places like the Blue Moon. White and Albritton would meet and White would give Albritton the money. White made some payoffs outside Lynn Haven's office at Sheffield Park.

**There were text messages between Mickey White and Adam Albritton which verified that Adam was meeting him for cash. Another interesting part of Mickey's statement is that in these meetings drawing up the contract, there is no mention of my being present even though the Government continued to push that I was part of the ECS conspiracy. Michael White was the chief government witness against me, but Mickey agreed with whatever Michael told him to say against me to get his sentence reduced, and Mickey was also taking direction from Derwin White, one of the owners of GAC who was so angry with me for going to Sheriff Ford. Because as I would learn later, GAC's corruption scheme extended beyond Lynn Haven to all of Bay County, and I had interrupted a massive fraud operation.**

Nobody ever asked any question regarding invoices that White submitted to the City of Lynn Haven for payment. Everything got paid. At first, White did not have any documentation or records regarding the work that ECS had been doing . They had to go back and create the documents supporting the invoices.

**Vickie Gainer, the Deputy City Clerk, Amanda Delonjay, who actually printed the checks, and other city employees who knew Michael White was writing these checks did not bring any of this to the City Commission's attention. The Commissioners, including the Mayor, were not responsible for running the financial operations of the City. The Commission does not see invoices, purchase orders or other daily financial matters unless they have a specific question about something, or staff presents budget reports or other financial matters at a commission meeting.**

Keith Baker was calling around and trying to get some work. White advised that the Lynn Haven trash pickup contract did not limit on the number of trucks that could be used so White told Keith Baker to get a truck and come on. Keith Baker borrowed a trailer from GAC and started doing trash pickup under the Lynn Haven contract. Keith Baker eventually added a second truck and trailer. White furnished the guys throwing the trash and they split the income the truck produced.

When the trash business died out, White and Keith Baker decided to get fence jobs. Keith Baker knows a lot of people and was going to call around. The idea was to use Keith Baker's position as county commissioner and contacts to get jobs. The plan was to get big jobs like $100,000 jobs. The first job they got was at Oakland Terrace Park. The job had some issues and White ended up having to do all the work but split the money with Keith Baker.

Josh Anderson and Ryan Regan paid for their own accommodations, meals and entertainment in Gatlinburg, Tennessee over the Christmas holiday. White had rented a cabin and invited Keith Baker. Keith Baker invited David Horton. White rented a passenger van which Keith Baker drove to Gatlinburg. While in Gatlinburg, White paid for meals at steakhouses, entertainment at Dollywood and purchased gifts such as airsoft guns for the children. White paid the expenses of Keith Baker and David Horton during the trip. In the past White has paid for meals for David Horton such as the time they went to a fight night and dinner at the Grand Marlin. White has also purchased meals for Michael White and his wife, Ricky Ramie and his wife, Dan Russell and his wife.

**This portion of Mickey White's testimony was regarding County Commissioner Keith Baker, who made approximately 150K hauling trash with fraudulent invoices submitted to FEMA by the City of Lynn Haven, while he was a sitting Commissioner for Bay County. Baker was ultimately arrested for text messages that implicated him for bid rigging on White's phone. Baker was never federally charged; he was arrested by the Bay County Sheriff's Office, he was charged by the state, and was allowed adjudication, a nolo *contendere plea*, and probation. Bay County justice with Larry Basford as the State Attorney for the 14th Judicial Circuit and Sheriff Tommy Ford takes care of the good old boys. I have no anger against Baker, I do not even know him; I am simply pointing out the selective and malicious prosecution of the BCSO in my case as opposed to Baker, who, according to his own testimony, *did* receive expensive travel gifts from Mickey White, yet was not charged, and for more serious crimes, he was given probation. He is now living his best life and is not a convicted felon.**

White prepared invoices for Michael White to submit to his insurance company. One invoice in the amount of $13,600 was prepared representing the demo work on the inside of the house and another in the amount of $3,000 was prepared representing tarping of the house. Michael White asked for the amounts on the invoices. After the invoices were prepared, they were given to Michael White.

Derwin White called White and asked if he had any invoices or documentation for the work done at the mayor's property. White told Derwin White "no"; Derwin White told him "You better get some and bring them to me." White prepared (3) invoices purporting to capture the work done on the Andersons' properties. White brought the invoices to Derwin White at the Blue Moon. White is not sure what happened to the invoices after he gave them to Derwin White or what Derwin White did with the three invoices. The one invoice that had 514 Virginia Avenue on it was incorrect. The correct address for the invoice should have displayed the address for the residence that belonged to Margo Anderson's cousin (at 507 Tennessee Avenue)

**The invoices would mysteriously show up at ECS on the day that the BCSO and FBI raid took place at ECS on April 12, 2019, just eleven days after I had gone to the Sheriff. The original invoice contained the reference to 514 Virginia Avenue, because that property is the property to the east of my former home which contained the city easement. My cousins *did* own the rental property at 507 Tennessee Avenue which abutted the north side of my mom's property, and when they found this out, they changed the invoices yet again to reflect my cousin's property.**

Mickey was aware that Derwin White bought Michael White a car. Mickey was needing a place to live. White called Michael White and asked if he (Mickey) did the work on the little house on Michael White's farm in Youngstown, could he stay in it. White had just received $400,000 from his insurance company for his house on Veal Road. Michael White offered to sell White his farm for what he (Michael White) owed on it. White took $300,000 from his insurance proceeds and paid Michael White with a cashier's check. The cows on the farm and cars Michael White sold White were part of the deal. Michael White got Adam Albritton to do the paperwork. White has started building a house and pond on the property.

In addition to Adam Albritton, White made payments to Michael White and David Horton. White paid Michael White various amounts approximately four times. He made the payments to Michael White at the Blue Moon or would just pick him up (Michael White) and drive him around the block. White hand delivered the invoices to David Horton for the work ECS was doing for Lynn Haven. White paid David Horton $5,000 in cash one time.

**No one, not even Mickey White or Michael White, ever accuses me, the Mayor of knowing about these exchanges of cash, and they never accuse me of accepting cash. I was not part of their conspiracy. They had ONE text message between Michael White and Mickey White which said, "are you at the Mayor's yet", on November 9th, the day the easement was cleaned. That was the Government's "evidence" against me other than testimony of government witnesses, including some of Mickey White's employees who were incarcerated for other crimes at the time they were interviewed, one in another state.**

**Mickey White's Third Interview with the FBI**
**January 8, 2020**

This interview is more about the GAC and Bay County Sheriff's office corruption, but I wanted to include the information to demonstrate the corruption of GAC, the company owned by Derwin White and Allan Bense, and also because as was shown in the evidentiary hearings, Major Jimmy Stanford, who is employed by the Bay County Sheriff's Office and was the lead investigator in this case which destroyed my life and that of my co-defendant James Finch, was corrupt. The hypocrisy of Bay County and Northwest Florida "justice" is palpable. This interview was conducted by SA Borghini, and White's attorney Jim White was present because Mickey had already pled guilty and was now cooperating with the Government in his second interview since his guilty plea.

ECS worked on GAC's Panama City city hall project. Brett Hitchcock was the project manager. ECS worked on the project for approximately 5-6 months. ECS did all the demo work, dry wall, concrete work and grading work on the project. ECS billed GAC for the work performed. White claims he was told what amounts to bill GAC. White further claims he was required to pay J.D. White and Scott Joiner $10,000 in cash. If White did not make the payments, he would not get any more work as a subcontractor for GAC. White made the payments out of the money he received from GAC.

**Derwin White, Mickey's uncle, was still alive at the time of this interview Mickey is giving; Derwin passed away from Covid on July 31, 2021, five days before the FBI raided GAC properties.**

White was paid $150,000 to demo three (3) floors on the city hall project. The job was estimated to take three weeks. White completed the work in 3-4 days. White received $300,000 for the exterior demo work which took approximately two months. ECS spent approximately another month cutting in new windows and doing other work on the exterior of the building.

White was paid approximately $500,000 to $600,000 for the interior build out of city hall project. ECS spent approximately 3-4 months on the build out. White claims he had to pay J.D. White and Joiner $7,500 each for a total of $15,000 on that part of the project.

White advised that he had to pay certain individuals in GAC's building department. They helped White get the jobs and therefore wanted a pinch off. White claims that he did not have a choice. If White stopped making the payments, he would not get any more GAC jobs.

White advised that Derwin White has been trying to find out what White has told law enforcement. White has done work at both of Jimmy Stanford's residences. At Stanford's previous residence, White did some grading work and laid sod around Stanford's pool. White never charged Stanford for the work or was not reimbursed by GAC or Derwin White for the work. White advised that Derwin White claimed to have paid for Stanford's pool. White did the work in 2007 and 2008.

At Stanford's current address, White painted the inside of the house, did some tractor work, stamped the patio concrete and built an in-ground fire pit. White did not bill Stanford for the work. White was not reimbursed for the work. White estimates the work to have been valued at approximately $30,000-$40,000. White claims that Stanford called him and asked for the work to be done. Derwin White has told White that "if anyone calls and asks you for something, you take care of them."

White has heard that Stanford has gotten White's cousins (Derwin White's daughters) out of trouble before so they would not go to jail. White has only known Greg Wilson since Wilson ran for the State Attorney's Office during the last election. White has heard that Stanford has a poker game at his house above his garage every Tuesday or Thursday night. White believes Derwin White gave Stanford the money for the down payment on his house. Derwin White has also supposedly purchased Stanford a motorcycle, paid for Stanford's sister's funeral and given Stanford $10,000 to go to Biloxi, Mississippi to gamble a couple of times. White heard from his cousin, Christy white that Derwin White and Stanford set up Wilson in the current matter that Wilson has been convicted of.

**During the evidentiary hearings of 2022 in Tallahassee federal court, Major Stanford admitted to accepting a motorcycle as a gift from Derwin White and at first denied that Derwin White had paid for his sister's funeral. He came back the next day and corrected himself under oath again, that he had been "mistaken," that Derwin had paid for the funeral. There are numerous public record police reports of DUI and other crimes committed by Derwin White's daughters which demonstrate they did not receive the same type of sentences normally given; also, Greg Wilson, an attorney who was campaigning for State Attorney was arrested, lost his attorney's license, and was working for Mickey White and ECS during the hurricane cleanup. A second attorney, Billy Joe "Hoot" Crawford, who pursued the State Attorney position in the 14th District was recently arrested by the Bay County Sheriff's office and prosecuted by State Attorney Larry Basford. He was convicted and lost his license as well. The case is currently being appealed, and the Judge, Kelvin C. Wells has since resigned. The fact that SA Borghini was aware that**

the lead investigator of the BCSO Jimmy Stanford was possibly corrupt and yet continued the investigation, targeting James Finch and me, was part of the motion by attorneys Guy Lewis and the others defending us to dismiss the case. The motion failed for dismissal, but the Court did rule for the grand jury transcripts to be unsealed in our case, which was a huge victory for us in demonstrating the lies and misrepresentations which were heard by the grand jury of the FBI agent and the assistant U.S. Attorney, Stephen Kunz.

Derwin White put up a pole barn on Bay County Sheriff's Deputy Mickey Vestal's property. Vestal lives next to Derwin White. Derwin White stores stuff in the pole barn on Vestal's property.

Michael White told White that he would often meet in James Finch's office to discuss City of Lynn Haven business. Finch bought Lynn Haven mayor Margo Anderson a motor home. The motorhome was purchased from Chris Forehand. Finch purchased some property across from one of Lynn Haven's parks. Finch developed the land and sold it to D.R. Horton to build townhouses on it. White believes Finch purchased and donated the playground equipment to the city at Cain Griffin Park. According to White, Finch gets everything in Lynn Haven. White was doing work at Porter Park for Finch. White and Finch were going back and forth on stuff regarding the project. While White was working on the project, Finch got another crew to come in to take over and finish the project.

White was going to bid the Porter Park project when Lynn Haven put it out for bid. Before submitting a bid on the project, White received a phone call from Derwin White. Derwin White stated, "that looks like a job for James Finch." That was White's signal not to bid the job. Finch won the bid and White received some of the subcontract work.

**Mickey makes a random statement here that Finch bought the Mayor a motorhome (which was not true and the government gave the motorhome back), and Mickey could not have bid on the job he refers to above because Mickey did not have a contractor's license.**

After Michael White got in trouble, the mayor (Margo Anderson) brought ECS' invoices to Finch to look over. Finch told Anderson that she needed to bring the invoices to the sheriff. Derwin White told them (the mayor and Finch) that was not a good idea. Finch was mad about the build-out of Lynn Haven's parks.

**Mickey is repeating what Derwin White has told him about the meeting that occurred between Derwin White, James and me at his office when we told Derwin we had discovered the fraud, and I was going to the Sheriff. I did not have the *invoices* as Mickey states here. I had a single excel sheet, given to me by Vickie Gainer when I requested information about the concession stand, with a list of the**

checks that had been paid to ECS by the City of Lynn Haven and the price of the concession stand that Mickey was building in Sheffield Park. I did not see the invoices or purchase orders until after I went to Sheriff Ford and he requested me to get copies of the checks, and then the invoices and purchase orders for him. Also as pointed out by attorney Guy Lewis in the evidentiary hearing, SA Borghini conducts interviews and then waits months to actually enter them into record. This interview was not entered until five months afterward.

## The Fourth Interview of Mickey White of ECS
## February 7, 2020

This interview was conducted one month after the third interview and was not entered into record by SA Borghini until five months later, May 6, 2021. Mickey White's attorney, Jim White, is present for this interview as well as Assistant U.S. Attorney Stephen Kunz. I am including the information from this interview because it is all about the cash payments exchanging hands, and again I am not mentioned as having asked for or received any payments. I was not part of their conspiracy as the government told the grand jury.

White admitted to making cash payments to Lynn Haven City Manager Michael White. White started making the cash payments to Michael White after receiving the first check from the City of Lynn Haven for hurricane debris cleanup. White would have the cash either in a paper sack or bank bag. White would normally pick up Michael White and drive around or meet him at the Blue Moon Bar & Grill.

On the first payment, White picked up Michael White at Sheffield Park and the pair drove around. White handed Michael White the cash. Michael White asked White, "what's this." White responded that he appreciated Michael White helping him out. White told Michael White that he needed to take the money and use it to help his family. Michael White stated he appreciated it and accepted the cash. The cash White used was from the money White had received from the City of Lynn Haven.

White also made cash payment to Lynn Haven City Attorney Adam Albritton. White stated the payment was approximately $30,000 to $40,000 dollars. White owed Albritton for 3-4 weeks of trash pickup billings. White paid Albritton at the Blue Moon Bar and Grill. White went inside and had drinks before making the payment to Albritton.

White explained that he had an agreement with Albritton. The agreement was made outside the Lynn Haven command post. Albritton stated that there was already a contract in place. The trash pickup was to be for under $300.00 per hour. White was paying Albritton to make sure everything was done right. As long as everything was good, White paid Albritton in cash from the billings to the City of Lynn Haven.

White advised that he made cash payments to both Michael White and Albritton at the Blue Moon Bar & Grill. When White texted Albritton the $$$$ symbols, that was one of the occasions he paid Albritton money at the Blue Moon. The payments White made to Michael White and Albritton were always in cash and after he had received a check from the City of Lynn Haven for debris cleanup and/or trash pickup.

White made a total of 5 or 6 cash payments to Albritton. The agreement was that White would pay Albritton 10,000 for each week the trash pickup contract was in place and White received payment from the City of Lynn Haven.
White also made 5 or 6 payments to Michael White. There was no set amount for the payments White made to Michael White. The cash payments varied based on what White wanted to give Michael White at the time.

White further stated that he had made a cash payment to David Horton in the amount of $1200-$1400. White gave Horton the cash for signing off on the invoices White had submitted to the City of Lynn Haven and making sure his guys (White's crews) had somewhere to go. Horton was surprised to have received the money from White.

White was getting the cash to make the payments by having Josh Anderson cash checks for him. White told Anderson that he needed the cash to pay sub-contractors and buy equipment such as trailers.

**Mickey has different testimony in this interview about the amounts paid; in a previous interview he stated that he paid David Horton $5,000.00, and that he made three or four payments to Adam Albritton. Liars have a hard time keeping their "facts" straight, but maybe there was just so much cash changing hands that Mickey cannot remember the exact amounts.**

**The Fifth Interview of Mickey White**
**March 3, 2022**

**This interview again included Mickey White's attorney, Jim White, Assistant US Attorney Stephen Kunz, but this time Assistant U.S. Attorney Andrew Grogan is added and there is a new FBI agent**

conducting the interview, SA Danie Crecelius.
This interview was conducted after the first evidentiary hearing for
James Finch and I at the Federal Court in Tallahassee. Mickey
describes his version of the "planted evidence" of the property
cleanup invoices for which I was charged and prosecuted.

White had no advanced knowledge of the search warrant that was
executed on his business, Erosion Control Specialists Inc. in April of 2019.

Derwin White was White's Uncle. A few weeks before the search of
ECS, Derwin asked White if he had invoices for the work that he did at
former Lynn Haven Mayor Margo Anderson's property. White told
Derwin that he thought he had invoices. Derwin told White to "make
sure." Derwin asked if White had invoices for "everybody" not just
Anderson. White told Derwin that he did not have invoices for everybody
and that he "just billed it to the city."

White already had documents that showed how many people were
working at Anderson's property and the equipment that was used. Based
on Derwin's instructions, White had Samantha Lind use these documents
to create invoices and back-date them. White told Lind which dates to use
on the invoices. White had three invoices created for the work that was
done on Anderson's property. White delivered the invoices that he had
Lind create to Derwin during a meeting that White had with Derwin at the
Blue Moon Bar and Grill. This meeting happened the night before ECS
was searched.

White did not do anything to try and frame Anderson. White had
documents that proved he worked on Anderson's property, but they didn't
reflect Anderson's name. White told Lind to create invoices so they would
accurately reflect Anderson's information and the work that was completed
on her property. During the course of creating the new invoices, White
even called people to verify the work that was done. White remembered
calling Josh Anderson.

**Mickey states that he did not try to frame me, but he states that he
delivered these invoices to his uncle, Derwin White, the night before
ECS was raided by the BCSO and the FBI, and of course the invoices
were photographed lying on top of the trash in plain sight. I will not
belabor the point about the property that was cleaned being an
easement and city right of way, but it was proven in the evidentiary
hearing. While I do not include the testimony of Samantha Lind,
Mickey's employee, she does state that she "created" the invoices at
Mickey's instruction in her testimony, and as far as White calling
Josh Anderson for information to create the "new invoices", Josh
Anderson and Mickey were business associates, both testifying for
the government in hopes of lesser sentences.**

During White's meeting with Derwin at the Blue Moon Bar and Grill, Derwin insinuated that the Federal Bureau of Investigation (FBI) was "coming," meaning that the FBI was investigating White and the others. This conversation between Derwin and White occurred the night before the FBI's search warrant on ECS in April 2019

Derwin never mentioned how he knew that the FBI was "coming." Derwin and White were having alcoholic drinks, and anybody who knew Derwin knew that he was "halfway full of shit." Derwin liked to play mind games and pretend that he knew everything. White had grown up around Derwin, so he knew how Derwin liked to gossip. For this reason, White "didn't pay it no attention." Derwin never mentioned a search warrant specifically, only that the FBI would be "coming".

**Even though the FBI was involved in the raid, the search warrant for ECS came from the Bay County Sheriff's Office and Major Jimmy Stanford was part of the raid.**

Despite Derwin's comments, White was still shocked when he received a phone call from his employee informing him that ECS was being searched by law enforcement. White even thought his employee was kidding. White's employee passed his phone to an FBI Agent who confirmed the execution of the search warrant at ECS. White also received a telephone call from Jimmy Stanford. Stanford told White about the search and told White "it wasn't a big deal" and asked White to come to ECS so he could speak to investigators.

White may have called Derwin after finding out about the search warrant at ECS. White didn't remember the conversation he had with Derwin, but White believed he did speak to Derwin. White may have told Derwin that he was correct when he said the FBI was coming. White did not remember calling James Finch after learning about the search warrant at ECS. White could not think of any reason why he would call Finch because they weren't very close. White remembered calling Greg Wilson because Wilson was a friend of White.

**Wilson is the attorney who was dating Derwin White's daughter who was arrested by the BCSO and ultimately lost his license to practice law. He worked for ECS after the hurricane and was also a confidential human source for the FBI whose testimony was helpful to the case of James Finch and I during the evidentiary hearings as he contradicted the FBI agent's testimony and proved it by text messages he had preserved on his cell phone.**

After White was placed under arrest, he was transported to Tallahassee for his initial appearance by Stanford and Jeremy Mathis. White did not believe that he spoke about anything during the car ride to Tallahassee. White did not remember saying anything negative about Anderson.

**Jimmy Stanford had stated in his report that Mickey had called me**

a "cock-sucking lying bitch."

White stated, "the only cocksucker I talked about was telling Stanford that he was a cocksucker." White could have been upset with Anderson at the time, but White did not remember talking about the case during his transport to Tallahassee. White "wouldn't talk to those mother fuckers,' meaning anybody from the Bay County Sheriff's Office.

After White's arrest, Derwin always wanted to know what White was telling law enforcement. The FBI interviewed White during the search of ECS, along with Stanford and a "young lady." Immediately after the search, Derwin knew everything that White told law enforcement. After that, White told the FBI that he was willing to talk to the FBI but was not willing to talk to anybody from BCSO.

**Mickey's implication here is that Derwin is hearing everything that is happening from Jimmy Stanford, the lead investigator against James and me, who is "owned" by Derwin White. Derwin passed away just a year after I was indicted, and we were never given any interviews that law enforcement or the Government conducted with Derwin, if there were any. James and I believe that Derwin was a government informant who was given immunity. As the affidavit for the search of GAC five days after Derwin's death will demonstrate, had Derwin lived, he would have most likely been the witness for the Government about not only local Bay County and state officials, but against AshBritt the national debris hauler, possibly his own partner, Allan Bense, former Speaker of the Florida House, and beyond. All of that evidence remains in boxes according to what the FBI told the Court during our evidentiary hearing.**

A few weeks before the search of ECS, Derwin called White. Derwin told White that he had picked up Michael from jail and then received a call from Finch. Finch asked Derwin to come to Finch's office. When Derwin and Michael arrived, Finch had all of ECS' bills with Lynn Haven on his desk. Finch told Derwin and Michael that he was going to make Anderson go to BCSO with the bills and file a complaint. Derwin told Finch not to go through with his plan, and said "don't give it to them, make them come get it." Michael was present for the phone call between Derwin and White and confirmed everything that Derwin told White on this phone call.

**Again, Mickey states this incorrectly. Finch did not have any of the bills from Lynn Haven on his desk. I had come to James' office with the one-page Excel sheet that Vickie Gainer had given me when I went to the City at James' request to find out about the building at Sheffield Park. As I said earlier, James had seen Mickey White working on the building and knew he did not have a contractor's license. The excel sheet had the amount that the City had paid to Mickey (almost 200K) for the small concession stand, and then had a**

list of the 6 checks which had been paid to ECS totaling almost five million dollars. Also, Michael White, the former City manager who Derwin had just picked up from jail for the domestic violence arrest in March of 2019, did not come inside. He was waiting outside in Derwin's truck. I did not know that Michael was with Derwin until James, looking out the window of his office, asked me if I could see who was in the truck with Derwin. James said, "it is Michael White."

Finch's greed "fucked" White, his sister, David Horton, and Hosh's lives up.

Here, Mickey is referring to Michael White, Shannon Rodriguez, David Horton and Josh Anderson, all of whom were indicted and arrested in the first indictment of November 2019, in which I was named as well as Commissioner Dan Russell. Michael White, the city manager whose testimony the entire government case is based, their chief witness, would push the narrative that James Finch was controlling Lynn Haven through me, and that he, Michael, was forced to do all of the things that he did because of pressure from the mayor, me. Less than 2% of James Finch's multi-million-dollar business has come from the City of Lynn Haven over the decades he has been in business, and because of the quality of his work, in the years before, during and after my tenure as Mayor, every contract his company has received has been in the light of day with a unanimous vote of the Commission, without exception.

Derwin and Stanford used to be really close friends. White did not know the details of Derwin and Stanford's friendship, but he knew they were very close. White remembered going to Stanford's previous residence before Stanford's current marriage and "doing all kinds of work." White believed the work was done around 2007 or 2008. White remembered laying sod, grading, and possibly doing some concrete work at Stanford's residence. White was not paid for any of the work that he did at Stanford's residence. White went to Stanford's because Derwin asked him to. White would do a lot of work "pro-bono" and didn't ask questions when Derwin told him to do something. Derwin told White "You got to keep people like that close to you."

Derwin might have mentioned that he paid for Stanford's pool. Derwin also mentioned that he gave Stanford the down-payment for Stanford's house, gave Stanford cash for gambling trips to Biloxi, bought Stanford a motorcycle, bought Stanford a pole barn, and might have bought Stanford a truck.

White also did a lot of work on Stanford's current residence. White remembered doing some "interior stuff," building a patio and a fire pit. Stanford also called White and asked him to send over some painters which White did.

Derwin would ask White what work White was doing at Stanford's residence. Derwin told White that he would make it up to White if he took care of Stanford. White could not remember the specific dates of the work that was done at Stanford's new residence, but White believed he had pictures of the work on his phone.

Christy White told White that Stanford and Derwin set up Wilson one night while she was at White's house. Christy told white that Derwin was a "piece of shit" and that if people knew who he really was, they wouldn't be around him. Christy told White about Wilson's case and how Wilson passed a note between Christy and her sister, Clista Robbins while both were in jail. Christy made it seem like law enforcement knew exactly what Wilson would do so they set up cameras in the room.

White told Wilson that Christy told him about being set up by Stanford and Derwin because he was friends with Wilson and believed Wilson deserved the right to confront Derwin if he wanted to. White didn't believe Christy's story, but he wanted to tell Wilson anyway. White didn't think that Wilson believed that Derwin and Stanford set him up.

Christy and Robbins were Derwin's daughters. Derwin tried his best with them, but both had experienced problems with drugs and had run-ins with the law. Wilson had an intimate relationship with Robbins at one time.

Derwin and Wilson told White that Stanford was upset with Wilson because Wilson didn't intervene after Stanford's wife was arrested in downtown Panama City. Wilson was the Assistant State Attorney at the time that Stanford's wife was arrested and Stanford wanted Wilson to get the case dropped.

**Again, Greg Wilson, whether set up or not, was running for the office of State Attorney, was accused of passing notes between the sister of his girlfriend while meeting with her in his capacity as attorney at the jail, was caught on camera in the client/attorney meeting room and arrested by the BCSO. And in the next campaign for State Attorney of 2024, Billy Joe "Hoot" Crawford, another Bay County attorney who had announced his intention to run for office was arrested by the BCSO, lost his license to practice law, and his case is being appealed.**

**Mickey's testimony is filled with contradictions and like the other government witnesses was giving the government all kinds of information.**

**While I do believe that he intentionally had the invoices made to implicate me in being involved in wrongdoing (which I was not), I believe he did this task the way he seemed to do everything else by his testimony. Whatever his uncle, Derwin White, told him to do, he did. Derwin was his key to contracts and work. Derwin was angry with James Finch and I because I went to the Sheriff as the**

whistleblower, and he told Mickey to make the invoices which would implicate me in federal fraud.

On November 9th when ECS cleaned the easement east of my property, the ditch and easement stretched the length of the block, emptying into Maxwell Bayou dividing the properties of the homes on Virigina Avenue to the east of the easement and Tennessee Avenue to the West of the easement. The easements are on the Virginia Avenue side of the ditch, not the Tennessee Avenue side where my property, and my moms were located. My cousin's property to the north of my mom's property was added in later after the investigators found out that relatives of mine owned the property at 507 Tennessee Avenue. They did not clean the easement behind 507 and they did not clean the property. A contractor was living in that house in the aftermath of the storm, and he cleaned that property in exchange for his rent while he was in the area working, another fact that we presented at the evidentiary hearing. Mickey White may have truly believed he was cleaning my property because he had been asked to clean the property of so many other officials and employees by Michael White. But the facts proved that he did not, in federal court. Additionally, the prices, hours worked, and equipment listed on ALL of the ECS invoices presented to the City of Lynn Haven were enormously inflated and false, many containing no documentation at all, and the cleaning of the easement would not have cost anywhere near the $48,000.00 stated on the three false invoices.


Interviews of Michael Edward White
City Manager of the City of Lynn Haven


Although the FBI and the BCSO interviewed dozens of my neighbors, many city employees, ECS employees, contractors, county and at least one state official during, I have included only those interviews which were filed publicly and of those, the interviews most crucial to my story.

Michael White was the "witness in chief" for the government's case against me, and his interviews and testimony are filled with lies and contradictions, supporting the Government's narrative and ultimately getting him what he was working for, a lesser sentence. Michael White was sentenced to 42 months, as Mickey White was, in a minimum security federal prison camp, his sentence well below the minimum recommendation. As of the publication of this book,

Michael White is scheduled to be released in May of 2025, just 23 months after beginning his sentence of 42 months. (BOP website) Michael White's lies for the government paid off.


**First Interview of Michael White**
**City Manager for the City of Lynn Haven**

**July 25, 2019**

This interview was conducted by SA Lawrence Borghini about four months after I went to Bay County Sheriff Tommy Ford. Borghini states that he had BCSO members with him when he approached Michael White, but Michael White refused to talk to the BCSO, agreeing only to talk to the FBI agent.

White had just exited his residence and was in a red Dodge Hell Cat bearing Florida license plate when he was approached by SA Borghini and members of the Bay County Sheriff's Office (BCSO). SA Borghini identified himself and then asked White if he was willing to speak with law enforcement. White stated that he was willing to speak with the FBI but not the BCSO. White invited SA Borghini into his residence.

SA Borghini explained to White that he wished to speak with White about the City of Lynn Haven and White's time as city manager of Lynn Haven. White advised that he was willing to speak with SA Borghini but he wanted to contact his attorney Waylon Graham first. White attempted to call Graham and left a message. White then text messaged Graham.

White stated that he was from Gadsden, Alabama and had recently accepted a job in Alabama as the general manager of wholesalecars.com in Alabama. White was back in Florida for a few days and had spent the day prior with David White aka Mickey White riding around looking at various jobs Mickey White's company was working on. Mickey White had picked White up at the apartment. Mickey White needed to go to a location in Chipley and did not want to drive White back to the apartment, so Mickey White let White drive the Dodge Hell Cat back to Panama City Beach. White was to return the Hell Cat to Mickey White on his way back to Alabama. White has known Mickey White since Mickey White was 19 years of age and had worked for White.

**I did not know that Michael White and Mickey had known each other for so long until we read this information; in the months after April 1, 2019 when I went to the Sheriff, Michael and Mickey had months to talk together before they would be indicted in November, and all those months I had expressed my anxiety and fears to Police**

**Chief Ramie, who at the time, I believed was a trusted friend, that I was afraid of them because I knew they were angry with me because I was the whistleblower.**

At this point, White received a return call from Graham. SA Borghini could hear Graham advise White not to speak with the agent. SA Borghini requested White place the cell phone on speaker phone. SA Borghini advised Attorney Graham that he understood that White was invoking his right to counsel and the agent would not ask White any questions and would leave the residence. After terminating the cell phone call with Graham, White expressed a desire to speak with the agent, however based on the advice of counsel, he needed to consult with his attorney first.

**Apparently, Michael White's attorney advised him to not speak with the agent again, because the next time Michael was interviewed by the government in his second interview, was after he was indicted in November of 2019, and he has entered a guilty plea.**

White is from Gadsden Alabama and attended Auburn University. White studied agribusiness and pre-vet. White obtained a master's degree from Florida State University in Business Administration. He is currently a full-time doctoral student at Walden University. White started his professional career working for Coosa Valley Electric Co-op for three years. White next worked for Gulf Coast Electric Cooperative for twenty years starting as the marketing manager and leaving as the CEO. After leaving the co-op, White did consulting work for Pragmatic Solutions, LLC. At Pragmatic Solutions, White prepared business plans, and employee and procedure manuals. In 2017, White was hired as the city manager for the City of Lynn Haven. The city commission voted 4-1 to hire White with Commissioner Judy Tinder voting against him. White was most recently employed at wholesalecars.com in Alabama as the general manager until he was arrested. He was fired from the position after being arrested.

White applied for the city manager position and was interviewed by the Lynn Haven City Commissioners. Three applicants were presented to the city for possible hire. Each of the applicants took questions from the public after which White was offered the position. White was paid a salary of $140,000 a year plus allowances. White had been approached by Chris Forehand regarding the city manager position. White has known Forehand for a long time and Forehand was trying to help White get a job. Forehand advised that there were two jobs but they had not come out yet. White talked to Derwin White quite a bit and Derwin knew White needed a job. Forehand, Derwin White and Matt Marshall vetted White for the city manager position. White met with each one of them.

Joel Schubert was Lynn Haven's city manager. The Bay County assistant county manager position was coming open. Schubert was going to decide which position he wanted, and White was going to be placed in the remaining position. Schubert decided he wanted the Assistant County Manager position. Schubert did not want to remain in the Lynn Haven City Manager position because of Mayor Margo Anderson. The group was going to help both Schubert and White obtain the positions.

**Schubert told me that he was applying for the Assistant County Manager position because it was a better salary, and it offered a retirement package. But I also knew that Schubert was not particularly fond of me because I was a very popular Mayor, not afraid of expressing my opinions to him or anyone else, and the city commission meetings had become quite full after I was elected because people knew they would be heard, and they were excited about the new ideas of my campaign of 2015.**

Matt Marshall called White to his office at Marshall Brothers Construction and Engineering to speak with him. The two discussed the city manager position and White's philosophy on things. White had to meet with Derwin White and James Finch at lunch to discuss the position. After the meetings, White was advised that they were going to bat for him. Derwin White had influence with Lynn Haven City Commissioner Antonius Barnes and Rodney Friend. James Finch (Matt Marshall's father-in-law) had influence with Mayor Margo Anderson and Antonius Barnes. Forehand had access to Lynn Haven City Commissioner Dan Russell and Rodney Friend. White was advised that Jimmy Maulden's wife was friends with the mayor as well. In addition, White called Rodney Friend himself. White knew Rodney Friend from when White was at the Co-op. White also knew Dan Russell from when Russell owned a liquor store.

White had to meet with Lee Anderson (Mayor Margo Anderson's husband) because they did not want anyone to see White meeting directly with the mayor. White had to answer questions the mayor wanted to ask him. White knew he had the job prior to going into the city commission meeting.

**I believe this paragraph to be typical of Michael White, half-truths and lies, but I do know that my husband attended lunch with some of those named above because he told me he had met Mike White, some guy that Derwin White was pushing for the city manager position. I interviewed Michael White in a one-on-one interview just as all the Commissioners did and no one, including my husband was involved with my decision. Of the three people we interviewed he seemed to be the most qualified. Another candidate, Brian Davis, was my second choice, and I wish that I had chosen him instead. He was soft-spoken and small in stature, and he spoke of "servant leadership" styles. The "swamp" of embedded city employees who were unhappy with the new mayor, me, already, would have run him into the ground, in my opinion. After interviewing Michael White, I**

thought he would be able to manage the employees more effectively. I was wrong about this, as I would be wrong about many of my initial impressions of Michael White.

White advised that the mayor believed in "you have my back and I've got yours." When White would not do a good job on something, the mayor would text him drunk in the middle of the night. The first thing the mayor had White do after he started the city manager position was to fire Laurie Baker. Laurie Baker had talked back to the mayor on something. The mayor told White that he needed to find a way to get rid of Laurie Baker which he did. After Laurie Baker, the mayor next wanted Ronnie Williams gone. The Mayor also hated Robert Baker. The mayor wanted Lynn Haven Police Chief Matt Riemer gone. White was told to fire Reimer or he (White) was going to be fired. The mayor did not like these employees because they were making too much money, dead weight and/or set in the old way of doing things. The mayor wanted Ricky Ramie to be Lynn Haven's police chief. After White was fired from the City of Lynn Haven, White was not allowed back on city property. They cleaned out his office and gave him back his stuff.

**Laurie Baker resigned her position, Ronnie Williams retired. I did not hate Robert (Bobby) Baker. I was critical of Bobby Baker's management of the Public Works department then and now, nine years after I was first elected, he is still with the City and I still believe he does a terrible job. Lynn Haven's drainage system is a system of ditches and culverts, and they remain overgrown with grass and the culverts full of trash and overgrowth on any day one drives through the city to look; any time there is a heavy rainstorm, parts of the city floods. I was not in favor of Joel Schubert, the former city manager hiring Matt Riemer as the police chief, because when the chief before him, David Messer retired, Matt would just be more of the same, and I believed that Lynn Haven needed someone from outside as the new police chief. But Joel Schubert told me that he had three members of the Commission who supported his choice and he hired Riemer. The Mayor had no power of hiring and firing employees other than the City Manager, who is hired by the entire Commission. As far as Ricky Ramie, I did not know Ricky Ramie until Michael White brought him to the City. And Ricky, another friend of Michael White's, at the time of the writing of this book was on suspension without pay for twenty-five days as the Police Chief for an arrest for hit and run, as previously mentioned.**

White has heard that Derwin White purchased Jimmy Stanford a motorcycle, a pickup truck and done some work at Stanford's house. Mickey white has done a lot of work at Stanford's house. White is not sure if Stanford paid for the items or services. Stanford use to host gambling at his house. Former Bay County Sheriff Frank McKeithen use to have BCSO Deputy Derrick Groves prepare deer hunting plots while on duty.

**Michael White is apparently angry with either Stanford or Derwin at this point in his government interviews.**

Prior to becoming city manager, White was arrested for a DUI in Lynn Haven. White refused to blow. White claimed he was actually texting his girlfriend (now wife) at the time. After being arrested, White talked to attorney Waylon Graham but did not retain him. White also spoke with Derwin White and Chris Forehand about the DUI. Derwin White told White not to worry about it because "we are going to get it taken care of". Derwin White was working with Greg Wilson in the State Attorney's office. Derwin White told White that he had everything taken care of. White was told to come to Derwin White's office to sign the papers. White gave Derwin White $2,000-$3,000 which he understood was to be paid to an attorney. White never went to court in the matter. White did the things required in the case such as taking classes and within a month he was off probation. White did not know Greg Wilson before the DUI case. White has been told by Derwin's daughter that Derwin White and Jimmy Stanford set Greg Wilson up regarding Wilson's recent conviction. The first time White met Greg Wilson was at a Christmas party that Derwin White and James Finch were hosting at the Blue Moon. White briefly talked to Wilson a couple of times about the DUI. Wilson told White that it takes a while to get things worked out.

The City of Lynn Haven worked out a deal with James Finch regarding the ½ cent sales tax which was to be in place for ten (10) years. The deal was negotiated by Margo Anderson and Finch. White only recalls one time that Finch attended a meeting at the City of Lynn Haven regarding city business. The rest of the time, meetings were held in Finch's office at Phoenix Construction. Margo Anderson would always be at Finch's office when White arrived. White advised the ½ cent sales tax money would come in from the State of Florida and he would put it into a city account. White would then make the city's $100,000 bond payment from the fund and let the rest of the money accumulate in the account. The account balance reached $2.5 million dollars and looked good on the city's balance sheet.

**As stated before, if the FBI agent and other investigators had bothered to look at the City Charter or the city commission meeting videos and minutes, they would have known that Michael was lying. Every contract with Phoenix Construction was a unanimous vote by the City Commission. Michael does admit here that he was not doing what had been the direction of the Commission, which was that all of the surtax money was to be swept from the account each time the City received a payment from the state and applied to the**

ten million dollar paving bond. He was not doing that as we found out.

Finch was wanting White to release the 5th Street project. The 5th Street project was one mile of paving. White stated the 5th Street project was not ready to be done. The engineering was not complete, the city did no have the money to pay for the project and the street did not need to be re-paved. Finch went ahead and did the project anyways. It was a pattern with Finch. Finch would do the work, finance the project and the city would make payments to Finch. In addition to the 5th Street project, there were other projects this occurred on.

**Michael White paints a picture of a very corrupt James Finch, when James had loaned money to the City for projects at a much lower rate than prime, with again, a unanimous vote of the Commission. James is a lifelong resident of Lynn Haven and loves the City; he has been voted Citizen of the Year two different times because of his philanthropy to Lynn Haven.**

Finch has taken the mayor (Margo Anderson) on several trips on his airplane. Margo Anderson has been to the Florida Keys and gambling in Mississippi with Finch. Margo Anderson also has a recreational vehicle (RV) that was purchased by Finch from Chris Forehand. Forehand told White that Finch was going to purchase Forehand's RV and park it at the go kart track that Finch owned. Two weeks later, the RV that Finch had purchased from Forehand was parked at the mayor's residence and the mayor got rid of her old RV.

**The entire indictment against me is filled with the narrative of Michael White to the investigators. James Finch and I have been friends since childhood, and my husband and James have been friends for almost 40 years. James was the best man at our wedding in Key West over twenty years ago, 2001. We have traveled together for decades, vacationed together, and are very close friends. During the time that I was Mayor, I was on James Finch's airplane six times in a period of six years. In the years prior to that, my husband flew with him every weekend as part of his NASCAR team, and I flew with them often. Florida Statutes state that the cost of flying on a private plane as an elected or other official is the same as the cost of a commercial airline ticket, which put another way, from Panama City to Key West at that time would have been anywhere from 300.00 to 500.00 at most. I sang at James' restaurant and bar, almost every Wednesday night from 2014 until 2018 for no charge, as well as many private events he hosted, when as an entertainer my fee as a solo artist for my shows was $1200.00, which is also documented. James paid his other bands and musicians $600.00 per night, and so even at that rate, I more than paid for the six times I flew on his plane while I**

was Mayor, something I have done for decades. What we found out later was that Derwin White had hired a private investigator to follow us and video me on the plane in Key West in September of 2018, and also a trip to Biloxi with James and his wife. These were delivered to WMBB Channel 13 ABC affiliate in Panama City by Arthur Cullen, the political operative and campaign manager for both the State Attorney and the Bay County Sheriff. The videos were actually provided by the television station to law enforcement according to our sources. One of the photographs Channel 13 broadcast as me, was instead, James' adult daughter who is tall and has long blonde hair. The FBI agent presented to the grand jury that my flights on the airplane were equal to around $40,000 in gifts from James, because he presented the costs as though I had chartered a plane which was completely false. According to Florida Statutes, the cost for a public official flying on a private plane is documented at the same cost as that of flying on a commercial flight to the same destination. The FBI agent presented to the grand jury that I had been on nine trips on the plane during my time as Mayor which was also proven false. I had credit card charges in other cities during those times. The most egregious lie to the grand jury was that during the time just after the hurricane when all of the residents of my city were suffering, I was reported to have been floating around on James' yacht in Key West. The problem with this story was that James had sold the yacht. As far as the motorhome, Mike White says the "mayor got rid of her old RV" as though it was a piece of junk; it was the same year model and in much better condition than the one my husband purchased from James Finch that James had purchased from Chris Forehand; the motorhome he purchased from Finch was two feet longer and had larger storage bins which would suit our travel with our band and all of the equipment better than the one we had. These trips and the motorhome were what my attorneys referred to as "the shiny objects" that the Government would use at trial to inflame the jury against me as a "corrupt" politician, when nothing could have been further from the truth. Channel 13 has probably shown the video loop of the motorhome (which was later returned) being seized from my property hundreds of times. They continue to show it to this day any time a story comes up in the news about the Lynn Haven corruption scandal, even though they know it was returned to us.

Derwin White gave White tickets to an Alabama football game being played in Atlanta, Georgia. When White and his wife arrived, Derwin White and Chris Forehand had their RV's parked next to each other's tailgating. Derwin White wanted a bar that he owned delivered to the location they were tailgating at, so he had a GAC employee (Nathan

Westry) deliver it to him in Atlanta.

**Chris Forehand's relationship with Derwin is pointed out by Michael White.**

White advised that as city manager, he had complete spending authority up to $35,000. Any expenditure over $35,000 needed to be done with a sealed bid. White did not need to get quotes for expenditures under $35,000. However, White would get quotes if he thought the price he was given was off or to make sure he was getting the best value for the city. White believed at first, the spending limit of the city manager was either $5,000 or $10,000, but it was increased to $35,000 by the city commission. White advised that city department heads had $1,000 spending authority which he got raised to $2,000. Department heads needed to get three quotes on expenditure. White also got department heads city credit cards so they did not have to wait for accounting to issue a check before an approved expenditure could be made.

**White appeared, in the beginning, to be a hard worker, who was trying to modernize some of the past policies of the City. When the Commission approved the $35,000 daily spending limit for the City Manager, I was the "nay" vote. I thought this was too much, because a city manager could spend a lot of money with commission authority in the two weeks between meetings.**

White does not like City Commissioner Judy Tinder. According to White Tinder pays herself under the table from her business, so she does not affect her social security benefits. Lee Anderson told White that Tinder comes to their house all the time and talks city business with Margo Anderson. This is a violation of Florida's Sunshine law. Margo Anderson hated former city attorney Rob Jackson and his firm. Margo Anderson wanted to get rid of both the city's law firm and accounting firm. White spoke to Adam Albritton about the city attorney position at Lynn Haven. Former City Commissioner Antonius Barnes always advocated for the city to retain the both of them. Barnes had concrete work done at his house that Derwin White paid for. Finch once told White that "Antonius Barnes would dance for me if I wanted him to. He probably wants more money."

**Judy Tinder is the most honest person I have ever known and a well-respected member of the Commission for years. She and I never discussed city business outside of meetings and she has never been inside my home. Ever. There are text messages between Michael White and Ricky Ramie which were in evidence in which they were disparaging Tinder, with the police chief referring to a sitting commissioner as a "p-ssy-licking c--t," and lied about this to the entire City Commission when Tinder confronted him. He was not fired by his protector, City Manager Vickie Gainer, who was the deputy city clerk for Michael White. I did not hate Rob Jackson, the**

former attorney, I hated what the city was paying his firm, almost one million dollars for five years of legal consulting for a city as small as Lynn Haven.  I had proposed that we consider an in-house attorney, which the city eventually did in September of 2018 by Commission vote.  I had also advocated for a new accounting firm when I became Mayor, because the city had the same firm for over twenty years. Best practices says that a municipality should consider a different firm every five years according to my research.  Michael White would embellish his story about Commissioner Barnes in a later testimony to try and inflame the jury against James Finch by saying that James used the "n" word in the dance quote above.  A blatant lie, again. Antonius Barnes, in the first trial of James Finch said that he was not bribed by James Finch.  After a hung jury, when James was tried a second time, the prosecutors did not even call Antonius Barnes, and the entire case was a bribery charge involving Barnes.  Finch was acquitted.

After the hurricane, the mayor gave White spending authority up to $500,000.  Just prior to the hurricane, White pre-positioned his two ATVs' at the city.  The four-seater ATV White had purchased from James Finch for $20,000. White paid Finch with two personal checks.  One drawn on his Regions Bank account and one from his Co-op Credit Union account. White's two-seater ATV came from his farm in Guntersville, Alabama. After the hurricane, the ATVs were used to get around the city.  White let the police department use the smaller ATV which they bent the frame on it.

**I never gave Michael White spending authority of half million dollars.  I didn't even want him to have $35,000 spending authority and voted against that.  Why would I have given him $500,000?**

Prior to the hurricane, White had purchased a golf cart for the City. White found the golf cart online.  White sent two Lynn Haven employees to Jacksonville to pick it up.  White paid $5,000 for the golf cart which he got from the city's accounting department.  According to White, the city had a need for the golf cart and was to be used for a number of purposes. After the hurricane, the Mayor wanted to use the golf cart to get around the city.  Lee Anderson would drive the golf cart.  Mayor Anderson went to Assistant Chief Ramie and told him that Lee Anderson needed a city badge. Mayor Anderson stated that Lee Anderson was very critical to her.  The city had issued badges to the Mayor, city manager and city commissioners.

**The Mayor and Commissioners had city issued badges long before the storm; I did ask Ramie for a temporary badge for my husband or some type of City identification, because it was dangerous for weeks in our area after the storm, especially at night with no street lights, and my husband went with me a lot as I was delivering supplies and going to visit residents who had asked to see me.  I did not ask to use**

the golf cart; Michael White asked the police department to let me use it as long as I needed it because of what I was doing with supplies, and I continued to use it for months until Commissioner Russell complained about it, as I described earlier.

The city had pre-negotiated contracts with CERES, Crowder Gulf and Ashbritt. CERES was the first one to arrive. The local contractors were coming to White complaining about not getting the cleanup work. Mayor Anderson was pressuring White to give the city's cleanup work to the local contractors. White told the contractors that they had to sub-contract with the major haulers who had the contracts. The contractors did not want to do that because they did not like the major haulers' sub-contractor rates and complained the haulers did not pay anything.

**Another lie from Michael White. I did not pressure him about this because I did not know anything about the local contractors trying to get work.**

After the hurricane passed, White went to Southerland Funeral Home's parking lot. Ricky Ramie was in the parking lot cooking a steak and drinking a beer that had come from the Grocer Outlet. White thereafter contracted with Southerland's to use the parking lot as a place for city operations and in order to provide meals. White employed the services of Kenny Strange Electric, an old guy who was an electrician and electrician that Mickey White recommended. They assisted with hooking up generators, etc. or whatever else the city needed to get back up and running. White could not find any of James Finch's guys. White went to GCUC and got them to do the work that the city needed done. The next thing White knew, the city started getting bills from Phoenix Construction. White paid GCUC directly for the work that was done.

After the hurricane, the City of Lynn Haven needed help cleaning things that needed to be cleaned. As a result of the hurricane, Lynn Haven lost approximately 10-15 city employees. In addition, the city was in the process of transitioning from city employees/staff to contractors (outsourcing) to provide certain services to the city. Another disadvantage the city faced after the hurricane was a lack of equipment.

White advised, that despite the condition of Lynn Haven, the mayor still wanted the events the city had scheduled to continue and take place when they were scheduled. The mayor put a lot of pressure on White to make this happen. White recalls being in the Verizon trailer with the mayor, Adam Albritton and Mickey White when it was decided to use ECS for cleanup. Albritton prepared a 90-day contract between the city and ECS for cleanup. Mickey White was able to provide the city with what was needed most, bodies. The people that Mickey White (ECS) provided were used for everything. ECS was contracted to cleanup and rake the city parks and cemeteries as well as supplement the city staff.

This was Mike White's most crucial lie; he says that I was present with he, Mickey White and Adam Albritton as they prepared the contract for the cleanup of the city. This lie is why I was charged with the "ECS conspiracy". Later, SA Borghini would say that I lied to him when I stated that I met Mickey White for the first time in either December or January at a city volunteer cleanup event. They needed to place me at the signing of the contract with ECS in October. The contract did not even have a signature line for me. Michael White did not intend for me to ever know about it. The irony of SA Borghini charging me of "lying" to him, is that this same agent lied to the Grand Jury in order to get the indictment against me, and faced no consequences, because the prosecutors maintained his false statements were mistakes, not intentional lies.

White claimed he had no knowledge of the work the ECS submitted on its' first invoice had not been performed. White further claimed that he had not seen the invoice because it was submitted to the city through Robert Brannon. White reviewed a copy of check number 353 in the amount of $224,722.75 that paid the invoice and verified that he and the mayor had signed the check. White did not trust Beverly Waldrup and cautioned against believing everything that Vickie Gainer says. After the hurricane, Jay Moody was put in charge of assisting the city with accounting and financial matters.

I discussed the $224,722.75 check in an earlier chapter; the only check of the nearly five million dollars paid to ECS that had my signature on it was signed by Vickie Gainer. On October 26th, I was driving from Lynn Haven to Jacksonville and Michael White called me to say that he had forgotten to have me sign a check to a vendor who was doing the push and cleanup of trees and debris in Sheffield Park so that he could move the rest of the city operations there and also to prepare for the big Halloween festival we were planning for residents. In normal times, a check this size would have seemed extraordinary, but because we had been told that our total debris invoices were probably going to be in the range of $30 million dollars, this did not seem strange. I verified the check over the phone, and Vickie Gainer signed it as Michael White's co-signer. The bank called me to verify the transaction which I did. I would later be federally charged for "conspiracy" and "wire fraud" with ECS because of this check and the fake invoices concerning my property cleanup. The other checks that were written to ECS which had my signature were those that had a computer-generated signature run by the payroll clerk, Amanda Delonjay. I knew nothing about them until later. Michael White says nothing about any of this to the FBI agent, and I was never questioned by the FBI until November 18, 2019, the night before Michael White and the others were indicted and arrested. When the FBI agents were questioning me, I had already been named in the indictment that was to be unsealed the next morning as an unindicted co-conspirator, which they of course knew, and so did Sheriff Tommy Ford, who had called me that evening to tell me that the FBI was in my driveway and that I needed to answer my phone call from them.

White stated that he was getting complaints about the garbage that was accumulating in the city as a result of everyone removing stuff from their residences and dumping it by the side of the road. At the time, the city had only one one-arm bandit in service picking up trash. White claims he was instructed to get the trash out of the city. The city had one additional old trash truck but did not have the people to operate it. White spoke to Jason Tunnell about getting a price for trash pickup in the city by BCC. Tunnell quoted White a price of $300 an hour for a truck and two slingers. After speaking with Tunnell, White was advised that Mickey White could put more people on the pickup of city's trash than BCC and for less than $300 per hour. White decided to go with Mickey White.

**Each time that Michael White said he "was instructed" or "pressured" as he states above, he was telling the investigators that I was directing him to take the illegal actions in which he was involved. I had no power to do this even if I had wanted to. The Commission was meeting weekly, Michael was the CFO of the City, and the investigators chose to believe what Michael said rather than question me, read the City Charter, or more importantly, review the videos of City Commission meeting meetings, which they never did until after I was indicted. Then, they began dropping charges and correcting their "mistakes" with each of the three superseding indictments against me.**

White spoke with Adam Albritton about having Mickey White pick up trash and requested Albritton prepare a contract. According to White, Albritton was very interested in the contract and got it done quickly. White told Albritton the price that he (White) had been quoted by Tunnell of $300 an hour for a truck and two slingers. Albritton was advised that Mickey White could provide more trucks and more slingers than BCC. White worked it out with the Bay County Landfill to let ECS trucks working for the city dump their trash at the landfill and the city would be billed directly for the disposal of the trash. When the contract ended, ECS was no longer allowed to dump trash at the landfill on the city's dime.

White stated again that Albritton was very interested in the trash contract and there was a rush to get the contract done. For some reason, this contract seemed to be a bigger deal than the other contracts. The contract was pushed through quickly. FEMA, through the city's FEMA representative, Amber Guy, approved of the city getting the trash removed. It was only after everything started to come out about ECS that Mickey White told White that Albritton was getting kickbacks off of the trash pickup contract and that ECS had performed work at Albritton's residence that had been paid for by the city. It was also at that time Mickey White told White that work had been done at the mayor's house and the city paid for it. Lee Anderson was at the house when the work was done.

**Michael White was getting kickbacks from Mickey as Mickey described in his interviews, but here Michael throws Adam Albritton under the bus telling the FBI of the kickbacks Adam is also receiving. Michael also uses the term "when everything started to come out about ECS" instead of telling them that he knew I was the whistleblower. Michael is making sure that his story as well as Mickey's story portrays me as being part of their conspiracy.**

One day, White was in the event tent at the park when the mayor came up to White and told him the city had a drainage ditch behind her house that floods the area when it rains. The mayor also stated that she needed someone to clean her property. White told the mayor that she could hire Mickey White to clean her property. White texted Mickey White about the mayor's residence. White had been told by the mayor and Bobby Baker about the easement. White traveled to the mayor's residence.

When White got to the mayor's residence, he saw what she had been talking about. There was pipe in the ground and in White's mind, because no one could build there, the easement was the responsibility of the city. White also observed trees on the mayor's pole barn. Mickey White, Josh Anderson and Lee Anderson were there with White. White showed Mickey White the area he wanted cleaned and instructed him to clean the easement. White later learned that in addition to the easement, Lee Anderson had Mickey White and Josh Anderson clean all the yards of the Andersons' residences. White did not review the invoices that ECS submitted for work that day and claims he did not know that the city had been billed for the work performed by ECS at the mayor's residence.

**Michael White's testimony about the property cleanup begins as many of the interviews conducted by SA Larry Borghini, no date is given by the witness, but rather, "one day," as though beginning a fairy tale. This property cleanup lie by Michael White was the basis for the honest services fraud charges against me for which I was suspended from office by Governor DeSantis. I have described the property cleanup in detail previously; the day that the City, and/or ECS came to clean the easement abutting my property and that of my mom's on the east side was a full month after the storm, and our homes and property had already been cleaned by my family. Photos and video proved this in the evidentiary hearing. The Bay County**

Sheriff's office investigators Stanford, Mathis, Chance, and others would question all of my neighbors, ECS employees, city employees, and of course Michael White, Mickey White, and Josh Anderson, who were all under investigation and angry at me because they knew I was the whistleblower. But the investigators never once questioned me. They had no curiosity about the truth.

White stated that Tetra Tech was shoved down his throat by Chris Forehand. White had known Forehand for a long time and trusted Forehand. The monitoring services were already in place, but the city needed help with FEMA reimbursement. White was getting packets from a lot of different companies wanting to be hired. Forehand helped White vet the companies and pick one to hire.

**Chris Forehand subcontracted his own company, Panhandle Engineering Disaster Services LLC to Tetra Tech; he and Michael White would now be able to "monitor" Mickey White's debris.**

White recalls there being an issue at Osceola Point. Mickey White's crew had been tasked to clean an area around the lift station. Bobby Baker told White that if the ditch that ran to the bay was not cleaned out, the street would flood. White went to Osceola Point to look at the situation. White instructed ECS to clean the ditch. White then went and talked to the homeowners at Osceola Point. White told the homeowners that by the city doing this, they were going to benefit from it. White told the homeowners that they needed to fence around the lift station and put nice shrubbery around it as well. White stated that he had instructed Mickey White to bill the work to the city. White claims that FEMA representative Sid Melton approved the city to do the cleanup work. White was shown an agreement executed by the residents of Osceola Point and forwarded to the City of Lynn Haven. The agreement was dated April 2019, which is after White's departure as Lynn Haven's city manager. The terms contained within the agreement were consistent with the terms White had outlined to the residences of Osceola Point. White pointed out that the information provided by Sid Melton regarding Osceola Point was used by Bay County to cleanup Bay Point and another sub-division which were both private gated communities.

**This elaborate explanation by Michael White refers to a letter written by Commissioner Dan Russell, his buddy, who lives in Osceola Point, a very small, gated neighborhood, along with Jay Moody the city's financial consultant who was hired by Michael White after Hurricane Michael. Dan Russell wrote a letter, dated April 26, 2019, to interim City Manager Vickie Gainer, referring to a "verbal agreement" between Osceola Point and the city to clean the ditch easement. Chris Forehand, in his testimony, also covered for Commissioner Russell, with his stormwater report as I described**

earlier. The agreement was hastily put together in April of 2019, *after*, Commissioner Russell learned that I had found the fraud taking place in Lynn Haven and had gone to the Sheriff on April 1, 2019. Forehand, White, Gainer and Russell all worked together to justify the cleanup of the private community which was ultimately billed to FEMA. Russell was an unindicted co-conspirator who was named for having had his property cleaned by the City and billed to FEMA, but he was never charged.

White believes ECS performed work on Rickey Ramie's personal boat (wheel bearings on the trailer and work on the boat's motor) that was billed to the City of Lynn Haven.

**Mickey White's testimony about Ricky Ramie's boat repair is similar to this account by Michael White.**

White asked Chris Forehand to permit some city property that had been used in the past by the city to dispose of Hurricane Opal's debris. The city owned 200 acres of land which was unable to be and could not be used for any other purpose. White planned to redo the permit for the property and use it as a final resting place for Hurricane Michael debris. By doing such, the city would only have to pay for the monitoring fees.

After getting the process started, White recalls coming out of the Verizon trailer and observing the mayor with Chris Forehand. The mayor asked White who gave him permission to permit the site and use it to dispose of debris. White responded that the site already had trash on it and was not worth much. The mayor wanted the permit withdrawn and told White that he could not use the site. The mayor then stated, "Michael White does not run the city. I run the city."

**Chris Forehand and Michael White had carefully rehearsed this testimony which would be used against me, as I have stated before, as well as the reasons they wanted this property permitted so badly, yet did not want to bring it before the commission as I told them they would have to do. Instead, they withdrew the permit.**

White was next called to a meeting. The meeting was called not long after James Finch got home from rehab. Chris Forehand picked White up and they went to James Finch's residence on the bay in Lynn Haven. In attendance was the mayor (Margo Anderson), James Finch, Jim Slonina (Panhandle Engineering and Forehand's partner), Matt Marshall (Marshall Brothers Construction and Finch's son-in-law), Troy Syfrett, George Roberts and Derwin White. The meeting was about how everyone had teamed up (Derwin White teaming up with Ashbritt was specially mentioned) and how all kinds of side deals had been cut. There were lots of complaints during the meeting. The mayor wanted to get rid of all the haulers because they were out of towners. The mayor further stated that after Hurricane Opal, James Finch took care of everything and things went well. After a while of listening to all the complaining, Derwin White said to James Finch, "what do you want. You want some chips? I'll send you some damn chips."

**I have addressed this "meeting" and when it occurred previously but wanted to include Michael White's version. The testimony at the evidentiary hearing of those contractors named by Michael White refuted their having attended such a meeting. The Government would change the dates of when this meeting was supposed to have been held when they learned that James Finch could not possibly have been there because of his physical condition after rehab from a stroke, and then shortly after returning home, a serious fall.**

White was asked about the use of Spikes' debris management site (DMS) by the city especially in light of the fact that the city already had permitted and were operating several DMS sites on city properties. White advised that Albritton negotiated the use of the site and Chris Forehand handled the permitting. White was further questioned why the city paid a number of GAC invoices for work to prepare a road to the site. White claims that he was told that the site prep and road work was the city's responsibility. The Spikes DMS site was used by Derwin White. White had heard that Allen Spikes had been paid by Derwin White for use of the property.

White was in the Verizon trailer looking at cars one day when Derwin White came in. White's daughter's car had been totaled by the hurricane. Derwin White took White to Bay Chrysler Dodge to look at cars. White told Derwin White that he could not afford any of the cars. Derwin White told White to pick out a car and Derwin White would work out a good deal with Jeffery Gainer. White picked out a white Hyundai Tucson. White took the vehicle and paid no money that day. The price of the vehicle was more than $18,000. White anticipated receiving $5,000 of insurance proceeds from his daughter's totaled car. White also had just sold some cows before the hurricane and had a new crop of calves that would be ready for sale soon. At $1,500 a head, White planned on selling 5-6 calves. White also anticipated that his wife's ex-husband would pitch in and pay for half of the vehicle.

Before White could get the vehicle, they had to call Albritton and ask if the vehicle could be sold to White because Albritton had been looking at the vehicle. White did not sign any paperwork for the vehicle. White stated to Jeffrey Gainer that I thought you had worked that out with Derwin. After getting the vehicle, White kept asking for the title to the vehicle. White was instructed to go to the DMV and talk to the lady to get a copy of the title. On the trip to the dealership, Derwin White had mentioned that he (Derwin White) had purchased a truck for Bill Dozier. Dozier is a Bay County Commissioner and Derwin White insinuated Dozier could not afford a truck like the one Dozier was driving. White stated that he had planned on paying Derwin White at least $5,000 and some cows. After everything broke about ECS, White paid Derwin White for the vehicle. White went to Derwin White's office to pay him with a check. When White arrived, Derwin White asked White if he was wearing a wire.

**After this information came out, County Commissioner Bill Dozier made a statement on the local news denying that Derwin White had purchased him a truck, and there was no further mention of it by the news media. Derwin White had passed away by the time of the evidentiary hearings and release of the information. White repeats the phrase again, "after everything broke about ECS" rather than saying, "after the Mayor went to the Sheriff." Michael White knew that I was the whistleblower; either he never said that in his interview, or the agent chose to leave it out. One of the interesting points again, about this interview of Michael White of December 11, 2019, is that according to Agent Borghini's date of entry, the agent did not write it up and enter it formally until May of 2021, which was over a year later. Defense Atttorney Guy Lewis excoriated the agent about this in the evidentiary hearing, pointing out FBI protocol and asking how he could remember information accurately even with notes after waiting so long.**

After the hurricane, White sent Robert Brannon to all the city employees' houses to have the employees' roofs tarped and assist with whatever else they could assist with. White wanted to make sure the employees could focus on things at work and not be worried about their residences.

**Robert Brannon was the Facilities department head and all of the work these employees did tarping city employees' homes and assisting with "whatever else they could assist with" was billed to the city and reimbursed by FEMA; Brannon never came to my home to ask if I needed any assistance, and I certainly did not expect it. I also was unaware that all of the city employees had received this service from the city, which was illegal. My family tarped my home and my mom's home and cleaned our property, yet I was federally charged with the "city cleaning my property," a charge that was proven false in the evidentiary hearings; none of the city employees whose homes were repaired, tarped, and cleaned and billed to the city were charged with crimes, and we were given no interview reports in which law enforcement questioned the employees about the repairs and cleanup of their homes by the City of Lynn Haven.**

White used Mickey White to work on his house in the Country Club and on his farm. White gave Mickey White a $10,000 check which Mickey White cashed and gave the money back to White. White claims that regarding the work ECS did on his house in Lynn Haven, White traded

Mickey White a policy manual for ECS that White drafted. White sent Mickey White the manual. Mickey White did not return the manual to White requesting any revisions and therefore assumed the manual met ECS' needs. White advised the value of the policy manual was $4,000. White knows the value of the manual was not equal to the value of the amount of work that White received. White also acknowledged that the time ECS employees spent working on White's properties and farm was billed to and paid for by the City of Lynn Haven.

White claims that Mickey White gave him cash on at least three (3) separate occasions. Mickey White would tell White to come outside and meet him. White recalls Mickey White giving him $10,000, $15,000 and $10,000 in cash on the occasions that he can recall. White has since talked to Mickey White about the payments. Mickey White claims that he paid White $172,000 which White disputes.

White was asked about the hiring of Greenleaf by the City of Lynn Haven. White advised that Greenleaf was awarded the contract because they were low bidder. Mickey White had told White that he needed to look at Greenleaf that Josh was a good guy. Greenleaf was awarded a contract that included a base amount for lawn care maintenance service plus add-ons. After the contract was in place, White started adding properties to Greenleaf's contract. The city could not hire an employee to do the work that Greenleaf was performing at the price Greenleaf was charging. At the time the contract was awarded, White was unaware that Mickey White was associated with Greenleaf. After the contract was awarded, White learned that Mickey White's wife was listed as one of the owners of Greenleaf.

**The Greenleaf contract was awarded by the City of Lynn Haven before the storm by a vote of the commission, and they were recommended by Michael White. Here, Michael White is trying to avoid charges of awarding a bid to a friend by saying he didn't know of Mickey White's association with Greenleaf when it was Michael White who recommended the Greenleaf contract to the Commission.**

White advised that Greenleaf's contract was for billable hours. After the hurricane, White did not want to lose the local guys that the city had contracts with. White instructed Greenleaf to take the parks off and to maintain the city properties that could be serviced. Greenleaf was then told to take those hours that were associated with the parks and use them for hurricane cleanup. After all of Greenleaf's billable hours to the city under the contract were worked, Greenleaf was free to work for Mickey White. White instructed Josh Anderson to continue to bill the city that way that he had been billing the city.

**Josh Anderson's interview revealed that he had been cashing checks for Mickey White during the time of the fraud that had been taking place. After almost three years of waiting to testify against me**

at trial as a government witness, he was sentenced only to home confinement and probation, just as David Horton, the community services director was. Josh Anderson also lied in his interview about being at my home, cleaning flower beds, and other yardwork on the day the city was there to clean the easement. Even though they had months to talk about their stories, they still could not get their stories straight on how many hours or how many "days" they spent cleaning the property of the Mayor, her mom, and her relative.

Michael White would be interviewed four more times by Special Agent Borghini between January 10, 2020, and October 19, 2021, with the last interview occurring just before my co-defendant, James Finch, was indicted for the second time and I was indicted for the third time. The interviews contain a lot of repetitive information, but I am including some of the new "information" which Michael White provided to the FBI agent, and Assistant U.S. Attorneys Kunz and Grogan as a cooperating government witness.

Vickie Gainer told Kelli Tram who told Kelly Battistini that White was inappropriately texting with FEMA representative Amber Guy. White was supposedly sending pictures to Amber Guy. Gainer further claimed that White had a meeting with Amber Guy in his office one evening. When Gainer was leaving, she observed Amber Guy straddling White with her breasts exposed and they were having sex. White stated that Gainer's accusations are completely fabricated and that he never touched Amber Guy.

**Police Chief Ricky Ramie, after Michael White was arrested, sent me a screen shot of Michael's texts with Amber Guy which had caused the argument and domestic violence between Michael White and his wife, and he also shown me a photograph that Michael and Amber Guy had exchanged. The texts, which are in evidence refer to their meeting the next morning, "to have fun," and "love you." I reported this to FEMA coordinator Tom McCool, and shortly thereafter Amber Guy was no longer in Lynn Haven but was working in Panama City with their consulting firm. Vickie Gainer testified in federal court that she did not see them having sex as she had said before, but that they were "slumped over" when she walked in.**

White took Gainer over to Sheffield Park and went through the plan with her. Other city department heads and managers were aware of the project and had even taken pictures that had been sent to the mayor. The footprint of the concession stand was changed, the playground was resurfaced, and new equipment was put into the park. James Finch had the Porter Park contract. Finch even asked Mickey White to give him a price on the bathrooms for Porter Park. The Sheffield Park rebuild was widely known by the city and staff.

**Michael White reveals that he had gone over the concession stand information with Gainer as well as the rest of the park, so Gainer knew that Mickey White was doing the work. After James saw Mickey White building the concession stand, he asked me about who had the contract/bid on the concession stand at Sheffield Park, this precipitated my going to Vickie Gainer and ultimately to the Sheriff.**

White gave ECS, Greenleaf, city employees, Dan Russell, the mayor and Ricky Ramie permission to use the city's gas after the hurricane. White also used to fill up his Polaris ATVs as well because they were being used for city business.

**Michael White told me that I could use gas from the city in the days after the storm, and I did. I also signed for the gas that I put in the golf cart I was using to deliver supplies, as well as other gas I used from the city. I do not know who else Michael allowed to do this or if they signed for the gas they used from the city supply.**

After the hurricane, the mayor and Ricky Ramie got closer. Ramie use to brag that he had the mayor so wrapped up, that he could tell her that Michael was fucking a goat and she would believe him.

**Chief Ramie was definitely not the person I thought him to be, as I stated earlier.**

White arranged for Ramie to come work for Lynn Haven. White approached Ramie one night at the Blue Moon. White told Ramie that he needed a number two man at the police department until Chief Matt Reimer retires. After Reimer retires, Ramie would move into the chief's position. The chief's position pays $90,000-110,000. White never discussed money with Ramie but planned on moving him up to the pay Reimer was receiving.

**Michael White hired former Bay County Sheriff's deputy Ricky Ramie in a meeting at the Blue Moon Bar and Grill; I had nothing to do with Ramie's hiring and did not know him until Michael White introduced him to me after he made the decision to hire him before the hurricane.**

**In the next two paragraphs of the interview, Michael White lies about the 17th Street Ditch project which James Finch had financed for the city, a project that was voted on by the City Commission while Joel Schubert was the City Manager. Michael's testimony looks a lot like the indictment against me of August 19, 2020, with 63 charges, all of which were dropped through the more than three years of pre-trial battle except for two for which I was to face trial. Michael White was the principal witness for the government against both James Finch and me. The jury did not believe Michael White in Finch's trial, and**

Finch was acquitted in October of 2023 as detailed in later chapters. Michael White tells the FBI agent that I put pressure on him, told him to make it happen, and that Finch is putting the money from the project into his son's trust account. As said earlier, Finch did finance the project for the city at a rate four points below the best rates at the time; he was given the project on a unanimous vote by the Commission. At one of the evidentiary hearings, as Michael White exited the courtroom, he winked and smiled at my husband when he walked past us, after his testimony of lies.

The city had a project to fix a ditch that ran along 17th street. The State of Florida owned some of the property and the state was going to give Lynn Haven approximately $450,000 towards the project for piping. It was going to be a lot of money to do the project. White told the mayor that he wanted to put the project on hold. Finch wanted to pick up the project again because he was not getting all the city's hurricane cleanup work. The mayor put pressure on White to do the project and that Finch would finance the project. White argued that the ditch needed to be fixed but the city did not need the debt. The mayor finally told White to make it happen. Chris Forehand was also backing the project. Forehand wanted to see the project go through because he would get all the engineering and inspection work associated with the project. The city did the project and Finch financed the cost of the project which was $5,178.555. The money that the city is paying back to Finch for the project is being put into trust for Finch's 13-14 year old son.

**Again, watching the video of the city commission meeting completely negates Michael White's testimony.**

White advised that after the hurricane, the City of Panama City purchased comfort centers. William Harrison, Representative Jay Trumbull and Randell McElheney purchased several of the comfort centers and sole them to Panama City. William Harrison helped the city make the decision to buy the comfort centers. White understood the comfort centers cost approximately $1 million dollars apiece. White knows that Panama City had the comfort centers and people used them. White is not sure what happened to them after Panama City got done using them or where they are now.

**Here, Michael is apparently answering questions about the "no bid" comfort stations that appeared in Panama City after the hurricane. There are no interview reports which were made available to James and me regarding the comfort stations for William Harrison, Jay Trumbull, or others if such reports exist.**

Bay County Commissioner Keith Baker is lying about not knowing the ethics rules on accepting gifts. White received a call from Derwin White asking him if he (White) had anything that Baker could do. Derwin White

said that Baker needed a job.  Shortly thereafter, Mickey White pulls up and
Keith Baker was in Mickey White's passenger's seat.  White asked them
what they were doing.  Mickey White said that Keith Baker was working for
him now.  Mickey White told White that Derwin White made him (Mickey)
hire Keith Baker.  White asked Mickey White what do you have him doing.
Mickey White responded, he is supposed to be driving a garbage truck.
Keith Baker didn't drive the garbage truck, Baker's son ended up driving
the garbage truck.  Mickey White told White that Keith Baker cost him
$200,000.

**I referred to former County Commissioner Keith Baker earlier, and
how he was charged by the state, not the federal government, was
allowed to plead no lo contendere, was adjudicated with probation,
and did not lose his rights.  Larry Basford is the 14th Judicial Circuit
State Attorney, as I mentioned before, and the former State Attorney,
Glenn Hess, remained employed by the office.  Hess's sister, Nancy
Hess, was appointed the Criminal Chief of the Northern District's
management team by U.S. Attorney Larry Keefe on February 4, 2019.
She was in this position at the time I was indicted.**

White advised that he had authorized the cleanup of the easements
behind the mayor's house and at Osceola Point.  White stated his decision
was based on Bobby Baker claiming the areas flooded and after consulting
with FEMA.  White stated that he thought that he had made the right
decision but that the crews cleaned up a lot more than he had directed them
too.

**Michael tells a little different version of the "property cleanup"
here.**

Mickey White gave White a couple pair of boots.  One pair was used,
and White estimates they were worth $300.  The second pair of boots were
from a trip Mickey White had gone on.  White estimates that pair of boots
were worth approximately $200.

At the time of the first Christmas after White became the city manager
for Lynn Haven, Chris Forehand asked White to get into Forehand's truck.
Forehand handed White an envelope with cash in it.  The envelope
contained $3,000 - $5,000 in it.  Forehand told White that he (White) was
under appreciated.  White had not asked for the money.  White asked
Forehand "what is this for?"  Forehand told him it was "a Christmas
present."

While at Lynn Haven, White would get traffic tickets that had been
issued fixed when it was requested.  There are a number of text messages
on his phone regarding the subject.

The City of Lynn Haven had a concert which featured the country
group Shenandoah.  The mayor, Margo Anderson, opened for them.  James
Finch and Derwin White paid for Shenandoah while Chris Forehand paid

for Margo's appearance.

This concert took place in April of 2018, and I did not accept any money for my performance with my band to open the concert *because* I was the Mayor. There are text messages between Michael White and I (documented on my phone) when he asked me about opening, and I told him that my performance would be pro bono, but if they wanted my band of six musicians, the band would need to be paid. Panhandle Engineering's sponsor check was written to the band lead guitarist and cashed by him. Because of this testimony, all of my business and tax records as a musician were subpoenaed by the Government just after the indictment of Michael White and presented to a grand jury in January of 2020. The government also questioned the staff and manager at James Finch's bar and restaurant to verify that all of my performances there had been without charge by me.

On one occasion, White asked Lynn Haven Assistant Police Chief Ricky Ramie to hold some money for him. The amount was approximately $20,000 to $30,000. White needed Chief Ramie to hold the money because White did not want to leave the money unattended while he took care of some business and before White could properly secure the money.

On the day that Ricky Ramie met me at the BCSO, April 1, 2019, he had a backpack with him that he told the Sheriff had come from Michael White's office and that it contained $30,000.00. I do not know what happened to that backpack; it has been the subject of much public speculation.

White advised that David "Mickey" White called him and asked him to go for a ride with Mickey White. During the ride, Mickey White gave White $10,000 in cash. White used the cash to pay the rent at the condo he and his family were staying at and a number of other things.

White explained that he withdrew cash from Lynn Haven's bank account for use by the city. The money was kept at the city.

The day before the hurricane made landfall in Lynn Haven, at a meeting of the city department heads, Commissioner Dan Russell, the police chief and the fire chief, Michael White said that he thought he should withdraw some cash for the city before all of the power went down in case the banks became inaccessible for needs we might have. We agreed, and according to what Michael said, he withdrew $25,000 for emergency use by the City, and I believe the city accounting department did keep track of that money.

White met Mickey White in the parking lot of the Blue Moon Bar & Grill. On that occasion, Mickey White gave White $15,000. After receiving the money from Mickey White, White did not go inside and left.

Another time, White went to Mickey White's truck in the parking lot at Lynn Haven's offices. White received cash from Mickey White. In all,

White believes he received at least $35,000 from Mickey White. Mickey White set up the meetings with White by contacting him on his cell phone.

After Hurricane Michael, the Mayor delegated some emergency powers to White. However, White had to run everything by Mayor Anderson first. Anderson had the last say on what was happening on hurricane matters.

**This is the lie that Michael White continued to repeat and because it fit the narrative of U.S. Attorney Stephen Kunz and FBI SA Lawrence Borghini, it was repeated to the grand jury as fact.**

**The Lynn Haven Commission meeting minutes and videos proved all of this to be a lie, after three years of pretrial motions and over five million dollars in attorney fees for James Finch and me. Lynn Haven is a city manager run government, and Michael White was completely in charge both before and after the Hurricane, as I said earlier, yet he continued to lie at the trials of James Finch, and had I gone to trial , Michael White, Mickey White, Adam Albritton, Chris Forehand, and others would have testified against me, stating that I was involved in the ECS and World Claim corruption as they had been doing in their interviews, in exchange for the lesser sentences and in Forehand's case, the immunity he received. James Finch and I believe that Vickie Gainer and Ricky Ramie most likely received immunity from the government as well; Vickie Gainer was tasked with keeping a journal of her interactions with both me and with James, and Ricky Ramie recorded our telephone conversations as well as in person interactions for the FBI.**

White stated that he told Mayor Anderson and Dan Russell that Worldclaim would do their stuff for free and that Forehand negotiated getting it done. Anderson and Russell were ok with it.

**Michael White continues to repeat the World Claim lie, which even the Vice President of the company refuted concerning my contract. Michael White and Dan Russell received pro bono contracts; I turned the pro bono contract down and paid a negotiated contract in full.**

White stated that Chris Forehand said that the City of Lynn Haven needed to use Worldclaim. Forehand claimed that Lynn Haven needed an expert when it came to handling its' insurance claim. Attorney Denise Rowen was referring business to Worldclaim and was to get paid a fee from Worldclaim for the referral. According to Forehand, Rowen had agreed to pay Forehand a portion of her fee for any business he was able to refer. Forehand told White that he was going to give White some of the money he received for the referral of Lynn Haven. White stated there was no further discussion about White receiving Worldclaim money from Forehand.

Forehand arranged for White, Margo Anderson and Dan Russell to get their personal residence done for free from Worldclaim. Forehand told them that since Worldclaim would be doing the city, Worldclaim was going to take care of them. Both Margo Anderson and Dan Russell understood that their property would be done for free. Both said alright. The no fee arrangement was made and discussed with Anderson and Russell prior to the signing of the Lynn Haven contract.

**I have refuted this with evidence earlier, but wanted to include Michael White's repeated lies against me as he worked for the government to try and save himself . I know that Dan Russell signed a pro bono contract because we have a copy of it in our evidence, as well as the emails verifying that Michael White and Chris Forehand benefitted from Lynn Haven using Worldclaim as the city public adjuster. Again, Chris Forehand received immunity and Dan Russell was not charged by the government nor the state.**

## Michael White's Final Interviews
## March 13, 2022 and October 17, 2022

**These interviews with Michael White were conducted by a different FBI Agent; SA Borghini and Assistant U.S. Attorney Kunz both would "retire" soon after the evidentiary hearings. The Government stated that both retirements were planned and not due to our case as our defense questioned.**

**This interview of March 13, 2022, was conducted by SA Daniel Crecelius and White's attorney Barry Beroset as well as Assistant US Attorneys Kunz and Grogan were present.**

Former Lynn Haven Mayor Margo Anderson would tell White when she wanted James Finch to be involved with city projects. Anderson brought up Finch's previous work experience on multiple occasions, to include a meeting at Finch's house. White could not remember whether or not adding Finch as an additional hauler came up in the meeting at Finch's house.

After Hurricane Michael, Anderson would always bring up the work that Finch did after Hurricane Opal. Anderson would say that Finch was "better and faster" than other companies. The work that Lynn Haven needed after Hurricane Michael was similar to what Finch did after Hurricane Opal.

**Michael continues his narrative that I was responsible for James Finch getting contracts from the City of Lynn Haven, when we proved with Commission minutes and videos that all of Finch's work**

was done by a unanimous vote of the City Commission.

It was "common knowledge" that Jimmy Stanford was corrupt. White didn't know anything personally, but Derwin White mentioned that Stanford was corrupt. Greg Wilson knew first-hand that Stanford was corrupt. David "Mickey" White told White that Derwin knew about the Federal Bureau of Investigation's search warrant at ECS ahead of time because Stanford told Derwin.

**Major Jimmy Stanford was called as a witness and admitted to accepting gifts from Derwin White during the evidentiary hearings.**

## Michael White's Second Interview with Agent Crecelius
## October 18, 2022

**This interview was conducted the week that Finch and I were indicted again, the third time for him and the fourth time for me. All charges had been dropped against me in this indictment except a conspiracy charge with Finch and a "666 bribery charge" of accepting a motorhome. Finch was charged with these same two charges as well as bribing Antonius Barnes and lying to the FBI. After we had filed the motion to sever the ECS and Worldclaim charges we were successful, and instead of charging me in a separate indictment for these two conspiracies, the government dropped the charges against me completely.**

**Most of the interview is repetitious of previous information but White becomes more descriptive and so here I include some of his final interview:**

Finch often called White "stupid and dumb" at meetings with Margo. White felt pressured by Margo and Finch to agree with whatever Finch and Margo wanted to do out of the fear of being fired. Margo was very narcissistic and if White didn't do what she wanted, Margo would call and text White threatening to fire him by "getting the votes from the city council." Margo only needed to convince one other city council member fire White because Margo already had Judy Tinder's vote. Tinder was always at the Anderson's house and would do whatever Margo wanted. Margo would call and text White while she was drunk and tell White that she would get the City Council to fire White and that she would go onto Facebook and "blast him." Margo threatened to fire White all the time.

**I have addressed my relationship with Commissioner Judy Tinder previously, but again she had never been to my house in all of the time that I knew her. Michael White had alcohol and anger issues and was arrested for pointing a gun at himself and his wife during the**

domestic violence incident. The text messages between him, his wife, the police chief, Forehand and Dan Russell, point to a lifestyle in which he and his wife were often drinking, driving while intoxicated, fighting, threatening to leave each other, suicide, and worse. For him to say I was texting or calling him while I was drunk is ludicrous. The Government never produced any of these "texts" from me as evidence. In fact, I was never charged for any text messages on my phone because I was not engaged in the fraud; many of the charges against me were made from what was contained in the text messages of Mickey White and Michael White *to each other*.

Derwin received a phone call from Finch one day while White was with Derwin. Derwin told White that he had to go meet with Margo and Finch and told White to stay in the truck. When Derwin returned, he told White that Finch and Margo wanted to "turn White in." White told Derwin that Finch and Margo shouldn't "throw stones" because White believed that Margo and Finch did a lot of business illegally. White was arrested a few weeks after Derwin had the meeting with Margo and Finch. Finch decided to turn White in because Finch was upset after Erosion Control Specialists received a contract with the City of Lynn Haven.

**Actually, Michael White was arrested seven months later, not a few weeks later. While the FBI refers in their reports to "one day" quite frequently, this date was prior to April 1, 2019 when I did indeed go to Sheriff Tommy Ford. Also, Derwin had no idea I was in Finch's office that day until he walked through the door. He was quite surprised to see me sitting there.**

White didn't speak to Derwin too much but Derwin would call and check on White occasionally. Derwin sold White a vehicle but Derwin would not let White pay for it. Eventually, "after everybody had been arrested," Derwin told White, "yeah, you need to pay me." Derwin also asked White if he was "wearing a wire" when White paid Derwin for the vehicle.

**Michael's lying memory fails him again; in his previous testimony he said that he paid Derwin after "everything broke about ECS", which would have been in April 2019, when there was a virtual flurry of activity apparently of officials paying for goods and services they had received from GAC, when they found out the Mayor of Lynn Haven had gone to the Sheriff. Above he says he paid for the car after everyone was arrested, which was November 2019, not April 2019 which was the correct date of the payment.**

**FBI Interview of Joseph Adam Albritton**

## Lynn Haven City Attorney

## April 17, 2019

This interview with Adam Albritton was just five days after the raid on the ECS owned by David "Mickey" White. Adam was indicted and arrested on the same day I was August 19, 2020, and when I was charged as a co-defendant with him, charged as being part of the conspiracy. Of all those who lied to me and lied about me to the FBI, Adam is the biggest disappointment to me. His lawyers initially told my lawyers that Adam was a "friendly" witness, that his testimony did not implicate me. When we received copies of his FBI interview "302's" in September of 2021 we would learn differently. He is the biggest liar of all; according to the news report from his plea hearing Judge Walker stated, "If he cooperates and testifies against the remaining defendants, Albritton could earn a substantial assistance agreement but was not entitled to one," Walker said. The remaining defendants at this point were James Finch, Antonius Barnes (who would plead guilty three weeks after Adam Albritton) and me.

Joseph Adam Albritton was interviewed at the Federal Bureau of Investigation by Special Agent Lawrence Borghini. Albritton provided the following information:

Albritton explained that the City of Lynn Haven had terminated their previous city attorney, Robert Jackson. When Hurricane Michael hit, the City of Lynn Haven did not have an attorney. The mayor of Lynn Haven (Margo Anderson) and city manager (Michael White) contacted Albritton and asked if he was interested in helping the City of Lynn Haven's attorney. Albritton was familiar with the mayor and Michael White because he had seen them at various social functions.

I was not aware that Michael White had contracted with Adam Albritton as the City of Lynn Haven's attorney until after Hurricane Michael when Michael White announced that he had done so at one of the first City Commission meetings held after the storm. Adam had "shown up" at the city compound set up at Southerland's Event Center in the aftermath of the storm, and he was volunteering helping with distributing supplies with me to residents. The Commission had just hired Kelly Tram as the in-house city attorney at the September 28, 2018, Commission meeting and ended the contract with Rob Jackson, the former City Attorney.

Albritton is a sole practitioner with an assistant. He is also part owner of a title company which is at the same location of his law office. Prior to going into private practice, Albritton was a prosecutor in the 1st Judicial

Circuit (Walton County) and an Assistant Public Defender (part time) in the 14th Judicial Circuit (Gulf County). Albritton's private practice consists of clients in the construction industry. Albritton is also the city attorney for the City of Port St. Joe.

Albritton advised the City of Lynn Haven did not advertise nor put out a Request for Qualifications (RFQ) regarding the city attorney position. The City of Lynn Haven had an employee who had passed the bar in Texas and was planning on taking the bar in Florida in February 2019. Albritton advised that Florida Bar has a mentorship program in place that was being considered regarding Kelly Tram.

**Again, Adam is not accurate. Kelly Tram was a military wife, and under provisions of such, she was eligible to practice law in another state under the mentorship of a bar member in that state until she passed the bar. The City Commission was not "considering" Kelly Tram; she was hired as the new in-house City Attorney by a vote of 3-2 of the Commission with that understanding. After Michael White announced that he had hired Adam Albritton as the City Attorney at a Commission meeting, I was told that Kelly was no longer eligible under the mentorship program because her husband had been deployed after the storm. Kelly Tram continued to assist the city with her legal expertise in the months after the storm, and seeing her often, I got to know her better and considered her a friend.**

Albritton has a one (1) year contract with the City of Lynn Haven. Michael White signed the contract on behalf of the city. The contract was negotiated and signed while the city was under a declaration of emergency. In that situation, the mayor or her designee has the ability to enter into a contract on behalf of the city. Albritton is paid a rate of $160 an hour for the work he performs for the City of Lynn Haven and $180 an hour for any kind of special circumstance and/or work.

**Michael White was the person who signed the contract with Adam Albritton, and I was not aware of it until the Commission meeting.**

Albritton put together the contract between the City of Lynn Haven and Erosion Control Specialist, Inc. (ECS). It was an emergency contract. Albritton received copies of standard forms from the City of Marianna and put together the ECS contract. ECS was to be a troubleshooter. In total, Albritton believes there were 3 or 4 emergency contracts the City of Lynn Haven needed. GCUC was to do construction (below groundwork), and he believes the City of Lynn Haven needed one for electrical work. They were all done in the month of October. The scope of the work and rates to be charged were either in the contracts or attached to the contracts. Albritton advised that at the time they were under tough conditions. While working on the contracts, Albritton learned the definition of push and pull work as used by the industry. Albritton's basic understanding of the contract with

ECS was that ECS was to provide manpower where the City of Lynn Haven lacked it.

**This interview is only a little over two weeks after I had gone to Sheriff Ford as the "whistleblower" concerning what James Finch and I had found about Mickey White and ECS. Adam does not mention here that he is Derwin White and GAC's attorney, that Mickey White/ECS is Derwin White's nephew, and that as he put together this contract for Michael White and his employer Derwin White, that one of the major haulers, Ceres, has been fired by Michael White to enable Derwin to make his deal with AshBritt, and ECS has been put in place in Lynn Haven by Derwin and Michael White as well.**

Albritton was unaware that ECS workers had performed work at the Mayor's residence. Albritton learned that ECS workers had performed work at Michael White's farm after the news story. Albritton was unaware of any other irregularities except for the City of Lynn Haven police car at Michael White's farm.

**Here, Special Agent Borghini is questioning Adam Albritton about the property cleanup at my address. The fraudulent invoices prepared by Mickey White have just been "found" by law enforcement in the raid on ECS five days before this interview. So, just two weeks after I went to the Sheriff for help with what I had found, the FBI agent is questioning Adam about the "property cleanup" at my address, but again, he, nor anyone else bothered to question me. Also, Adam does not mention any work done at his property or his girlfriend's by ECS as he is later charged in the indictment.**

Albritton was aware that Michael White purchased some land from Jim Slonina of Panhandle Engineering around the end of February 2019. There should be emails with Michael White which has details regarding the sale of the land. Albritton was asked to prepare a purchase agreement and deed for the sale. They did not want a survey or any title work, so the sale was not handled by his title company.

**Vickie Gainer, the deputy city clerk at the time of this sale, notarized the transaction between Michael White and Slonina. The purchase price is interesting as well, $30,000. The same amount of money which keeps coming up about the backpack recovered by Police Chief Ricky Ramie from Michael White's office according to Ramie. Ramie only chose to disclose about the backpack after I asked him to go with me to the Sheriff's office about financial issues I had discovered with the city; he brought it with him to the Sheriff's office and during my discussion with Sheriff Ford, Ramie said, "oh, by the way, I have a backpack here with $30,000 in it from Michael**

**White's office."**

The following discussion with Albritton pertains to text messages recovered from Michael White's cellular telephone:

Albritton was asked to do it and draw up the paperwork. The sales price was $30,000. Albritton had just received the deed back on the Friday before Michael White was arrested. Albritton felt obligated to record the deed. The recording fee was approximately $223. Albritton's office called Michael White and got a new address from him. Michael White was told that the deed would be mailed to him after it had been recorded.

Another text message was regarding a land sale. As far as Albritton knows, that sale never closed. Once again, all the details should be in Michael White's city email account. Albritton was asked to draft a purchase agreement and property deed selling Michael White's farm to Mickey White. Michael White advised the agreement did not require a survey or title insurance. Albritton prepared the agreement in blank since he was not provided with a sales price. He prepared a deed using the legal description for the farm. The deed was drafted to transfer the property to David M. White. All the draft documents were sent to Michael White's city email account.

**This interview contained photocopies of the text messages between Adam and Michael White, another interesting point. There was no warrant for Michael White's phone until April 10, 2019, ten days after I went to the Sheriff with the information I had found. Again, all of the investigation into the Lynn Haven "corruption" began after I went to the Sheriff on April 1, 2019, not after Michael White was arrested on March 17, 2019. Every BCSO report in this investigation is dated after April 1, 2019, as well as the FBI reports and warrants. I was the whistleblower in this case, no matter how many times they deny it or construe it.**

Text Message:
Michael White: I need make sure James project goes through
Adam Albritton: Understand
Adam Albritton: Town homes deal is a go

The text message was regarding a Jame Finch project. The project was before the planning board and Michael White was wanting to make sure all the legalese matched. The project was passed by the planning board.

**Again, every single project done by James Finch and Phoenix Construction was passed by the Lynn Haven City Commission and I was never the deciding vote.**

Text Message:
Michael White: See if you can determine how many days we cut Mickey short around Christmas/new year as well we will look at adding those days to the days tetra tech had them cease...do not count Christmas Eve,

Christmas Day, or New Years. I want to leave those holidays off.
Delivered: 01/07/2019
Adam Albritton: Will do. I was going to get a total number and then we
can add days back in as you decide.

The text message had to do with the "where as" clause in the emergency
contract. The emergency contract with ECS had to be amended several
times. The original contract was for professional services. Then the
amended contract fixed that issue but the 90 days was left off that contract.
A pdf document adding the 90 days was then prepared, initialed by Michael
White and Mickey White, and added to the contract. They eventually got to
the point where the emergency contract was for a maximum 90 days from
the effective date of the contract, at the maximum FEMA reimbursement
rate and the City of Lynn Haven could terminate it at any time.

The emergency contract with ECS was a sole source procurement. The
evaluation points for continuing work should have been 30 day, 60 days and
90 days. The City of Lynn Haven understood that regarding FEMA
reimbursement, the City of Lynn Haven should have been alright regarding
the first 30 days, at 60 days they would probably be alright and at 90 days
they were pushing it. In November 2018, Tetra Tech stopped ECS from
working because their invoices lacked details.

**In November of 2018, Adam Albritton sent an email to Michael
White and Vickie Gainer, and I was included in the chain which said
that he was preparing a task order and that it would not need to be on
the agenda to go before the City Commission. I answered, "ok" on
my iPhone. I would later be charged for wire fraud by answering
"ok" because the Government included me in the ECS conspiracy.
November was still just weeks after the storm, with total devastation
everywhere. I was probably out doing something, saw the message,
and said "ok" without even thinking twice about it. Vickie Gainer,
on April 4, 2019, after I went to the Sheriff, and the day the Bay
County Sheriff's Office and the FBI began their investigation, wrote
her own "CYA" letter to FEMA, justifying the work of ECS with a list
of exigent circumstances, requesting an emergency contract. The
April 2019 timing, like that of other officials, smells.**

In late November or early December, Albritton was part of a meeting
that included Michael White, Jay Moody, John Buri (Tetra Tech) and
Albritton believes Mickey White. The meeting was about the lack of details
in the ECS invoices. The meeting also included discussion about paying the
full amount of the ECS invoices. It was recommended that the ECS
invoices not be paid in full. The City of Lynn Haven was advised not to
pay the invoice or hold a portion of the invoice until the proper
documentation had been provided. The City of Lynn Haven was warned
that if the invoices were paid, it was on the City of Lynn Haven. Michael

White defended the paying of the invoices by stating, "ECS is going to be here, they are not going anywhere.".

**The Mayor (me) was not invited to this meeting, just as I was not invited to the other meetings about ECS invoice payments. They did not want me to know, yet I was charged as being part of a conspiracy with Michael White, Mickey White, and the others. This interview with Adam Albritton is over a year before he is indicted, but at this time, he is receiving $10,000 per week in kickbacks from Mickey White and ECS, which is documented in his own text messages.**

Albritton recalls another meeting with Michael White. Michael White stated that there was some work needing to be done and that the mayor was on him about it. Michael White wanted to extend ECS' emergency contract. Michael White was justifying the extension by saying that ECS had not worked the full 90 days the contract allowed for. Therefore, Michael White wanted to extend the emergency contract in place extending it for the additional days equal to 90 days less the number of days that ECS did work under the contract. Albritton did not believe the emergency contract could be extended. Albritton therefore prepared an additional contract for the City of Lynn Haven which recaptured the number of days equivalent to the number of days that ECS did not work under the emergency contract.

On Sunday around noon, Albritton was going to lunch when he received a call from the mayor. Anderson advised him that Michael White was arrested or was to be arrested on domestic violence charges. The mayor wanted to call a special meeting. Proper notice was given and a number of questions were discussed at the meeting. Michael White was put on administrative leave. Anderson wanted to assume the position of both the mayor and the city manager. Albritton did not think that was a good idea and advised against it. The City of Lynn Haven negotiated a severance agreement with Michael White and Michael White resigned as city manager. After Michael White resigned, the mayor, Vicki Gainer, Jay Moody, and Albritton met at the water plant. They discussed sole source contracts, FEMA and the need to start bidding contracts.

**The FBI agents' interviews leave out dates many times, but this would have been Sunday, March 17, 2019. Several of the government witnesses have said that I wanted to be both Mayor and City Manager, but what I was really asking at the emergency meeting was the authority to meet with the city department heads as a facilitator and make sure that the city was operating smoothly until a decision was made. I pointed out that I had declared an emergency after the storm, and that this was an emergency as well. The Commission was not in favor of this, I contacted the League of Cities for advice, and they advised to appoint the Deputy City Clerk as interim manager**

until a new city manager was selected. Vickie Gainer became the interim city manager by agreement of the City Commission.

In late February or early March 2019, it was brought to Albritton's attention that ECS was doing work on some of the city's parks. There were no contracts in place and ECS was doing the work on an internal purchase order with no definition as to the scope of the work. ECS had submitted on invoice in the amount of $118,000 that had been paid and there was an invoice in the amount of $243,000 that had been submitted and was outstanding. It was determined that ECS did not have a general contractors (GC) license and therefore working unlicensed. That made any agreement ECS may have had for the work with the city null and void. Dan Russell spoke to Mickey White about donating the labor and materials. Albritton drafted an agreement and release. Albritton advised that he is not aware of it being signed and does not know where the matter stands.

**Michael White did not resign until March 26, 2019; therefore, the late February early March dates that Adam cites above would have been before Michael White was arrested and was still the City Manager. Adam is already starting to fabricate here because he knows that I have been to the Sheriff on April 1st, and this will go along with Vickie Gainer's narrative that she is the one who alerted me to the problem with the building in the park rather than the opposite. Vickie was questioned by the FBI a few days before Adam, and became a "witness" for them. The fact that Commissioner Dan Russell is involved at this point trying to solve Mickey and the others' problems by getting him to donate his labor and materials was a revelation to us as we read the 302. Dan Russell was involved in the World Claim conspiracy with his "pro bono" contract, and with Mickey White with the cleanup of his gated private community which was charged to the City and to FEMA; he is an unindicted conspirator.**

ECS did some work at Albritton's residence. Albritton had talked directly to Mickey White about doing the work. ECS tarped his roof and cleared his property of debris. ECS invoiced Albritton $9,600 for the work. Albritton submitted the invoice to his insurance company.

**Adam did not tell the agent that ECS also did work at his girlfriend's home putting up a new fence; the ECS invoice he sent to his insurance company would also become a problem—insurance fraud.**

Albritton prepared the paperwork for the Bay County Contractors & Associates, LLC (BCCA). The BCCA is a 501c3 organization. Jay Moody does the accounting work for BCCA. The mission of the BCCA is to support contractor issues.

**Derwin White was the President of BCCA.**

Albritton has done work for GAC Contractors, Inc. since 2015. Albritton assists GAC employees with legal issues. Over the years, Albritton estimates he has helped approximately (8) GAC employees with filing paperwork forming LLCs. After Hurricane Michael, Albritton helped Brandon Mayhan form 850 Construction Services, LLC. Mayhan formed the LLC to do sheetrock work.

## FBI Interview of Joseph Adam Albritton
## September 12, 2021

**This interview was conducted by Special Agents Lawrence Borghini and Daniel A. Crecelius. His attorneys were with him and the interview was conducted pursuant to a proffer agreement executed between Albritton and the government. United States Attorney Jason Coody and Assistant United States Attorneys Stephen Kunz and Andrew Grogan were present.**

Albritton advised that after Hurricane Michael, Chris Forehand was working for Tetra Tech and the City of Lynn Haven (hereafter "Lynn Haven"). Lynn Haven had a contract in place with Tetra Tech for debris monitoring. Lynn Haven did not have a contract in place for FEMA consulting and was looking to negotiate a consulting contract for assistance with FEMA reimbursement and projects.

Lynn Haven City Manager Michael White, Forehand and Ralph Natale (from Tetra Tech) initially wanted to piggyback off of Walton County's contract with Tetra Tech. Albritton reached out to Walton County to get more information. Albritton determined that although a state rule allowed Lynn Haven to do that, the Feds did not. Albritton informed Michael White and Natale of what he had learned. Albritton researched the matter with FEMA and Lynn Haven moved to the bid process. Forehand provided Albritton with a generic bid form that Forehand had obtained from Tetra Tech.

In October 2018, Albritton and Kelli Tram worked on putting together a bid. The bid was to close three days after being put out. Lynn Haven went through their normal means of advertising for the bid. Albritton and Tram Googled and called companies in the consulting business for this type of work, as well as 5-7 companies that Natale provided, to ensure that they were aware of Lynn Haven's bid package.

Jay Moody contacted a firm in his network and invited them to bid. Moddy and Michael White talked to an individual in that firm about the bid package. The individual was going to fly to Lynn Haven to discuss his company's qualifications with Lynn Haven. The bid only being open for three days became a concern. Albritton spoke with Panama City's city attorney Neven Zimmerman. Panama City had determined that it was not an emergency and extended their bid closing date. Vickie Gainer extended Lynn Haven's bid from three days to ten days to make sure it complied with the procurement process.

Albritton and Moody talked about how awkward it was that everyone was assuming that Tetra Tech was going to be awarded the bid. Michael White liked the company that Moddy was recommending. Moody was skeptical because if Lynn Haven selected that company, they would be going against Forehand.

Albritton recalls being in the trailer with Michael White, Moody and Forehand when Michael White told Forehand that he (Michael White) was going with the consulting firm Moody was recommending. Forehand asked Michael White to step outside the trailer. After about five minutes, Albritton left the trailer and went to the tent outside the trailer where drinks and snacks were available. Albritton witnessed Michael White and Forehand engaged in a discussion. As Albritton passed the two, Forehand was asking Michael White to reconsider his discussion. Albritton heard Forehand say, "I've helped you get here, and I am going to help you get a raise." While getting items from the tent, Albritton tried to pay attention to what else was being said. The two eventually returned to the trailer and Michael White advised that Lynn Haven would be going with Tetra Tech. Kelly Battistini, Vickie Gainer and Michael White reviewed and ranked the bids submitted. Tetra Tech was ranked the highest and awarded the bid.

**Besides the implied rigging of the bid for Tetra Tech that is stated here, the most important thing about this testimony, is that as in other testimonies, these meetings by city officials do not include my name. This is another contract that was decided by Michael White and others. I knew nothing of this, just as I knew nothing about the ECS contract that did not even contain my signature.**

Albritton was talking with FEMA about the contract to be used with the consultant and the FEMA regulations. Two conditions that FEMA regulations specified were that 1.) the bid needed to solicit minority owned businesses, and 2.) that the company awarded the bid would attempt to use minority owned businesses as sub-contractors. The bid was awarded in October 2018, but the contract was not signed until January 2019. Albritton could not say with certainty that Lynn Haven had reached out to minority owned businesses regarding the bid.

In December 2018, Albritton spoke with Michael White about his concern. The issue was later discussed with Tetra Tech's John Buri at Panhandle Engineering's office. It was brought up that a lot of times, the Chamber of Commerce picks up and puts out the requests for bids to its members. Forehand volunteered to call the Chamber of Commerce to see if they picked up and ran Lynn Haven's bid package. Forehand claimed he contacted a member of the Chamber of Commerce and they said they saw the bid. Albritton recommended that Lynn Haven award a 90-day contract for consulting services and then re-bid the contract for FEMA consulting services. Albritton asked John Buri what he thought, and he was fine with Albritton's recommendation. Albritton wanted the matter presented to the City Commission.

Albritton never saw anything from the Chamber of Commerce on whether Lynn Haven's bid had been picked up and put out by the Chamber. In December 2018, Albritton reiterated his concerns about the Chamber of Commerce in emails and advised he never received any proof or follow up about whether the FEMA regulations had been met. Albritton again advised the safest way for Lynn Haven to proceed was to execute a 90-day temporary contract and re-bid the contract. Michael White denied Albritton's request.

In December 2018, Forehand sent a text to Albritton regarding the contract. The text stated, "kids need shoes for Christmas." Albritton advised that there is going to be a memo that stated he spoke with someone at the Chamber of Commerce but advised that what really happened Forehand called someone at the Chamber of Commerce to affirm that FEMA regulations regarding the minority owned business requirements were met for the bid. The contract with Tetra Tech was eventually approved by Lynn Haven's City Commission. John Buri was asked if the Chamber of Commerce disseminating the bid met the FEMA requirement. Buri stated if the Chamber did that, then Lynn Haven was good to go as far as meeting the FEMA requirement.

**Again, Chris Forehand, who received immunity is at the center of more corruption. Their text messages often contained "kids need shoes" as a code for "I need this money," in the messages we had in our discovery evidence. As I read this testimony, I asked myself why Adam didn't come to me or one of the commissioners if he was having an issue with Michael White and Chris Forehand, but the answer is simple; Adam was deep into the corruption himself and could not risk making them angry since he was the attorney for Derwin White as well. He had made a 10,000 a week kickback "deal with the devil."**

Lynn Haven's FEMA representative at the time was Annie Ford and the person Albritton had contacted regarding the matter. Forehand rented space to Tetra Tech. Albritton believes Tetra Tech used Forehand and Panhandle Engineering for assessing and documenting the damage to Lynn Haven's city properties and engineering projects.

Tetra Tech also received Callaway and Springfield's business. Forehand implied that he got Tetra Tech Callaway's business and bragged about getting Tetra Tech Springfield's business. Eddie Cook is Callaway's City Manager. The City of Callaway used Ashbritt to clean up debris after Hurricane Michael. Derwin White provided Cook with a camper.

**This paragraph reveals that Derwin White "provided the city manager of Callaway with a camper." Really? After the Government accused me of receiving a "free" motorhome from James Finch that my husband paid for, why was Callaway City Manager Eddie Cook not questioned by the FBI about this "camper?" We received no BCSO or FBI interview with Eddie Cook in our discovery from the prosecutors. There was no curiosity about the "camper." Was it a fifth wheel, or a motorhome or something else? Adam either did not know that Chris Forehand had a company, PEDS, subcontracted to Tetra Tech, and that Chris Forehand was also listed as senior management with Tetra Tech, or he just does not mention it in the interview. James and I found this information out about Chris after we received the 302's in the summer of 2021.**

Albritton stated that approximately eight to ten months before he became Lynn Haven's city attorney, he was asked to lunch at Smitty's by Michael White and Forehand. Albritton was told that Rob Jackson was getting fired and they wanted to know if Albritton was interested in the position. The first time Albritton believes he me Michael White and Chris Forehand was at a men's social function.

A few months later, Albritton met and had lunch with Lynn Haven's Mayor Margo Anderson at the Olive Garden. Anderson stated that she was not happy with Rob Jackson. Anderson was upset about Commissioner Rodney Friend. Albritton recalls the conversation at lunch involved general discussion and Anderson's daughter.

**Albritton's statement about our lunch is a truthful one. We talked about my thoughts of running for higher office, either Jay Trumbull's Florida House seat, or Neil Dunn's Congressional seat, and I did talk with him about wanting an inhouse attorney for Lynn Haven that I was not happy with what we were paying to Harrison Sale McCloy law firm for Rob Jackson. He immediately said that he would not be interested in an "inhouse" attorney position because of his own private practice and because he was also the city attorney for Port St. Joe. He did not tell me that he was Derwin White and GAC's attorney. I was also unhappy with a recent opinion that Jackson had delivered to the Commission regarding Commissioner Rodney Friend not living in the city limits of Lynn Haven, which is required by charter. Citizens were upset about it and had voiced this to me when I campaigned for Mayor, and I was confronted about it at city commission meetings. Albritton encouraged me about a run for**

Congress, expressed that he had thought about running for State Attorney, and I told him if I were elected that I would love to have him as Chief of Staff. He expressed sincere interest in this and thought I had a good chance in a challenge to Neil Dunn. Adam's brother had been a student of mine when I taught high school, and I also knew his family and liked them. His betrayal of me with false statements to the Government was literally a stab in the heart; I considered him a friend. I did not know about Michael White and Chris Forehand's meeting with Adam about a position as the City's attorney.

Albritton was eventually contacted by Michael White and told that Lynn Haven had or will be firing Rob Jackson as Lynn Haven's city attorney. Michael White wanted to use Kelli Tram as Lynn Haven's attorney. Tram was a licensed attorney in Texas who was living in Panama City as a result of her husband being in the United States Air Force. Florida has a mentorship program and Lynn Haven wanted to use Albritton to mentor Tram. Albritton declined the offer.

After Hurricane Michael, Albritton went up to Southerland's where Lynn Haven had staged at. Albritton went up there to use a phone. Michael White asked Albritton to help and wanted Albritton to come up to the Emergency Operations Center (EOC). Albritton was asked to assist by providing legal services. Lynn Haven had meetings at 6:00 AM each day. Crowder Gulf, CERES, and Ashbritt attended the meetings. Crowder Gulf and CERES started cleaning up Lynn Haven. CERES was fired by Lynn Haven. Derwin White started coming to Lynn Haven and meeting with Michael White.

On October 30, 2018, Michael White and Derwin White were in a conference room in Lynn Haven's trailer. Albritton was called in and handed a list of sites that chips could be disposed at. The list was supposed to have been provided by Bay County. Albritton was instructed to call the places on the list and see what they charged to dump chips at their location. Albritton called the sites and provided the results in an email. Albritton claims the prices he reported in his email were the prices he received and had not falsely reported any price. The only thing not accurately represented in his email was that fact that he had not called GAC because Derwin White was in the room and gave hi a price of $4.70 in person.

Albritton advised that Michael White had people calling him about the chips. Mike Swearington had called about getting chips and came to Lynn Haven on the morning of October 30, 2018. Albritton believes he sent a text message to Allan Byrd and thanked him for reaching out to Lynn Haven and Byrd may have quoted a price around d$3.60 or so. Derwin White had Michael White in his pocket and the price of $4.70 had been floated around. Albritton wanted to stay out of having to decide on picking a site to dispose of the chips because it became very political. Albritton thereafter drafted a notice to the haulers that a site charging $4.70 or less be used and recommended the lowest price be selected. Michael White wanted the memo/email sent to the haulers.

**Again, this meeting is held without my presence. Adam does not mention me at all as Michael White and Derwin White are meeting in the Lynn Haven conference room of the temporary trailer. The date is the day the Commission met, and I asked that we end the state of emergency in the City of Lynn Haven which was approved by the Commission by unanimous vote.**

Prior to Hurricane Michael, Albritton had been to Bay Dodge to look at purchasing a vehicle for his title business. After the hurricane, Albritton received a call from Jeffery Gainer asking if he was still interested in one of the vehicles Albritton had looked at. Albritton advised he was no longer interested in purchasing the vehicle.

**This paragraph refers to the vehicle that Derwin White was purchasing for Michael White from Gainer, mentioned in another interview; they were making sure that Albritton no longer wanted it since he had been looking at it.**

Albritton claims the email he drafted regarding the chips was accurate and drafted in order to cover himself because of a conflict that existed because of his representation of GAC. The email was drafted in response to a letter from a local attorney representing Allen Byrd and Troy Syfrett. Albritton advised that he not seen the letter until after Michael White had been terminated and Vickie Gainer gave it to Albritton. Lynn Haven responded to the attorney with a letter.

Albritton was aware that Lynn Haven was trying to permit some land to use for the disposal of chips. Forehand had said they had a meeting with James Finch and not to worry about the site because Finch was going to get the chips. Albritton was not at any of the meetings with Finch, but Michael White wanted Albritton to see how Lynn Haven could give the debris pickup to Finch and asked him to look at the contracts with the haulers.

Albritton contacted FEMA regarding the matter. Albritton prepared a memorandum at his office detailing what he had learned and found during his research of the matter. Albritton stated they were trying to slide Lynn Haven's debris cleanup contract to James Finch. Forehand contacted Albritton and told him that Finch was going to be calling Albritton. Albritton stated to Forehand that he did not have good news for them. Albritton met with Margo Anderson, Michael White and Forehand about what he had found out. Albritton explained to them that they could fire the haulers that the City had under contract but they would have to go through the procurement process in hiring a new hauler.

**And with this paragraph Adam begins the narrative the**

Government will eventually reward him for. Adam received a
sentence of probation from federal Judge Mark Walker. I never met
with Michael White, Forehand and Adam Albritton about giving a
cleanup contract to James.

Finch called Albritton and wanted him to come to Finch's house.
Albritton took the memorandum that he had prepared and took it to Margo
Anderson's house and gave her a copy Finch called Albritton again.
Albritton went from Anderson's house to Finch's house After Albritton
arrived at Finch's house, he met with Finch and another Phoenix
Construction employee who Albritton did not know. Albritton handed
Finch a copy of the memo that he had prepared and just given to
Anderson. Albritton told Finch that he did not think it was a good idea for
Lynn Haven to fire their haulers and hire Finch. Finch responded that
Lynn Haven had the "wrong guy". Finch was implying that Albritton
should be going along with what they wanted done. Finch claimed that the
current haulers were not picking up the debris properly and wanted to burn
the vegetative debris chips. Finch was not happy with Albritton and spoke
to him very harshly. Albritton advised that Finch's comments to him that
day were the worst that anyone has ever spoken to him.

**Adam Albritton did not come to my home, nor has he ever been to
my home. When James and I received this 302 in discovery he said
that Adam had not been to his house either. I never advocated for
James to haul debris, and James was just out of the hospital from
having a stroke. As I said previously in the book, I *did compare* the
way James and Phoenix Construction cleaned the City of debris after
Hurricane Opal in 1995, using a street by street method, which was
far superior than what was happening in Lynn Haven at this time.
The haulers were being paid by the cubic yard instead of weight, and
so they would just drive around the city picking up the lightest
branches off the mountains of debris to fill their trucks, leaving tons
of debris behind. What I could not have known was that they were
defrauding the city, and they didn't care how long it took to clean it
up; they were making millions.**

In November 2018, Derwin White asked Albritton to forward the
October 30th email that Albritton had prepared regarding the chip disposal
prices to Joel Schubert at Bay County. Derwin White then told Albritton
that he needed Albritton to attend the County Commission meeting to talk
to them about the prices that were in the email. Albritton learned from
Schubert that Allan Byrd was upset about not getting any chips. Albritton
understood that Bay County was relying on their haulers and consultants to
dispose of the chips at the best location with the best price. Albritton was
next contacted by Ashbritt's Matt Gierden. Albritton and Gierden
discussed Albritton's October 30th email. Albritton prepared a proposed

response to Bay County and sent it to Derwin White. Albritton later learned that his proposed response was used by Landfall Strategies to send an email/letter to Don Murray at Bay County.

Albritton was not wanting to go to the County Commission meeting to talk about the chips. Schubert told Albritton not to worry about it because they had it figured out. Albritton however did attend the County Commission meeting because Keith Baker was being sworn in.

**Joel Schubert has it figured out for Albritton.**

Albritton stated that Michael White asked him to prepare a task order for ECS for Lynn Haven's trash pickup at a price not to exceed $300.00 an hour. The task order was dated to track the date on the existing ECS debris cleanup contract and to be eligible for reimbursement from FEMA.

Shortly after the task order was executed, Albritton received a text message from Mickey White. The text message was all dollar signs. ($$$$). Within a couple of days, Mickey White came to Albritton's house and gave Albritton $10,000 in one hundred-dollar bills. The money was a kickback from the task order that Albritton had just prepared between Lynn Haven and ECS. Later in 2018, Albritton received a second payment of $10,000 from Mickey white. This time the money was strapped. Once again, the money was a kickback on the task order that ECS had received. Albritton stated that taking the money was wrong and he should not have done it.

**Mickey White claims that he gave Albritton money on more than two occasions as Adam states here. Also, when Adam prepared the task order he sent an email to Vickie Gainer telling her that she didn't need to put the task order on the commission meeting agenda because it did not need Commission approval. He copied me on the email, and I answered on my iPhone "ok" as I did anytime someone emailed me as the Mayor, just to acknowledge that I had read their emails. There was nothing suspect about a task order for trash pickup, and my quick answer of "ok" on my phone became a federal charge of conspiracy with ECS in the indictment.**

Albritton explained that the first contract prepared between Lynn Haven and ECS was an emergency contract that was later edited. The emergency contract and task order were back dated in order to fit within the emergency period and avoid FEMA scrutiny. Albritton was later asked to prepare a contract to add back days that ECS was allowed to work under the contract. That should have gone to the city Commission for approval.

**I was not part of the contract with ECS, there was not even a signature line for me as I have stated before. Albritton does not mention me here, but Michael White, in his interview, as well as Mickey White, said that I was present when the contract was signed and negotiated and that I was part of the deal. They would have sworn this at trial, and I assume so would have Albritton, as part of**

his deal with the Government.

Albritton explained that ECS performed work at his residence at his request. ECS removed hurricane debris (approximately 7-10 trees) from his yard as well as worked on cleaning the debris from the interior of his house (living room, two bedrooms and hallway). Mickey White helped Albritton with a storage shed and supplied him with a Conex box which was used to store Albritton's household items while his house was being repaired from storm damage. Albritton also requested Mickey White help at his girlfriend's residence with a fence and tarping her roof. Albritton did not pay Mickey White for the work and claimed he did not know that Mickey White was charging Lynn Haven for the work. Albritton heard from Greg Wilson that Mickey White was paying money to Michael White and David Horton. Albritton advised that Mickey White appeared to be doing well as he was riding around in a new truck.

**Adam's girlfriend at the time, Caitlin Lawrence, was the Public Information Officer for the City of Panama City and accepted work from ECS on her fence and property. She was not charged with any crime.**

## FBI Interview of Joseph Adam Albritton
## September 30, 2021

This interview with Adam Albritton was conducted by Special Agent Lawrence Borghini, a few days after Albritton pled guilty to two charges, wire fraud, and honest services fraud, with all other charges dropped.

After reading the interview that Adam gave to the Government, I am convinced that he would have been one of their main witnesses against me had I gone to trial. Adam was not sentenced until after the trial of James Finch in October 2023, and he received no prison sentence, a year of probation, and his restitution was $31,000. The $31,000 was paid in full by Jason Bense, the son of Allan Bense, former co-owner of GAC with the late Derwin White. Neither Derwin White nor Allan Bense were charged with a crime despite the allegations in the affidavit included earlier which prompted the raid on GAC.

Albritton's attorney stated that "Albritton didn't get jail time because he suffered immense collateral consequences."

Parkman, Albritton's attorney also said in an interview with local news, "The fact that if you're an attorney and you lose your license, everybody knows that. That's devastating, and all the work, time, effort that you put into, that's gone."

Parkman also says Albritton's conduct throughout the entire case sets him apart from the other defendants.

"He came forward very quickly and said, look, I did this, and that's hard for people to do."

Adam was a government witness against me and James Finch to protect himself; everything I had worked for in my life was taken from me, but apparently the court did not see that as "collateral damage." Government prosecutors are fine with lies…as long as you are lying for them.

Joseph Adam Albritton was interviewed at the Federal Bureau of Investigation in Panama City, Florida. Albritton was aware of the identity of the interviewing agent and the nature of the interview.

Albritton stated that Chris Forehand brought Michael Fusco of WorldClaim to Lynn Haven and introduced him to Michael White and Jay Moody while the City of Lynn Haven was using the Verizon trailer. Albritton recommended to Lynn Haven that they not hire WorldClaim because it was too soon after the hurricane. Albritton advised Lynn Haven that they needed to give their insurance company a chance and to work through the process with them. Michael White and Moody agreed.

**Once again, there is no mention of my being present at this meeting. The same players are always there, but not me, the mayor.**

The very next day, World Claim was hired. They had just discussed how Lynn Haven would keep more money if the City did not hire WorldClaim at this time and they could hire WorldClaim in the future if needed. Albritton was never part of any discussions regarding people getting their property done for free if WorldClaim was hired by Lynn Haven. Albritton had no idea that people got work done for free by World Claim.

**The people who got work done for free, that we know of, are Chris Forehand, the City Engineer, Michael White, the City Manager, and Commissioner Dan Russell. Neither Forehand nor Russell were charged. Forehand received immunity.**

At one point, Albritton did contact Michael Fusco by phone to get a quote regarding his personal residence. Albritton was quoted a fee of ten percent. Albritton thought the fee was too high. Albritton was already getting a pay out from his insurance company and decided not to use WorldClaim.

In November 2018, Michael Fusco asked Albritton who the city manager for the City of Port St. Joe was. Albritton referred Fusco to Jim Anderson. Fusco continued to ask Albritton about getting the City of Port

St. Joe and Gulf District Schools as clients for WorldClaim. In December 2018, Forehand was really pushing Albritton hard to help Fusco in Port St. Joe. Forehand stated to Albritton, "it would be worth your time getting Fusco work in Gulf County." Forehand implied that there would be a financial benefit to Albritton. Forehand had a deal with WorldClaim and implied he could probably get Albritton the same deal. Fusco continued to contact Albritton about the matter until January 2019.

Albritton explained that a few days prior to the emails regarding the vegetative debris chip emails, he received a call from Mike Swearington. Swearington told Albritton that Michael White told him that Albritton was in charge of the chips. Albritton had no clue what Swearington was talking about. Michael White and Albritton had a conversation about the chips. Albritton interpreted that conversation as don't worry about it, the chips are already spoken for. Derwin White was at Lynn Haven's trailer every day and was trying to get Ashbritt in at Lynn Haven. Swearington continued to check on the chips with Albritton. Albritton told Swearington that Derwin White had been coming up to Lynn Haven each day and spending a good portion of the day there.

**Adam Albritton was Derwin White/GAC's attorney. At the time of this interview, Derwin had passed away just two months earlier, James and I were preparing for trial in October, and the Government was preparing to indict us again.**

On the Day Albritton wrote the email regarding the chips, Michael White and Dewin White were in the conference room of Lynn Haven's trailer. Albritton was handed a list of disposal sites. Albritton was asked to call some of the places on the list and get some prices. Albritton was told that Bay County was at $4.70 and they wanted to justify $4.70 to FEMA. Albritton stated that all the prices recorded in his email were the prices he had received that day and the only thing not accurate about his email was that he had not called GAC. Derwin White was in the trailer with Albritton and Derwin White gave Albritton the price of $4.70 in person. After calling around and getting prices, Albritton gave the results to Michael White. Michael White told Albritton to tell the haulers that they were to dispose of the chips at a price of $4.70 or less and for them to pick the disposal site.

Forehand told Albritton that James Finch was upset. Finch was wanting the cleanup and is either getting or going to get the chips.

**The following part of the interview is about the rebuild process in Lynn Haven. Adam's narrative is false and fits in quite nicely with the Government's version of the rebuild process in Lynn Haven.**

Lynn Haven was wanting to start the rebuilding process. Albritton assisted Lynn Haven with working on the bids by looking at the State procurement process. Albritton believed Lynn Haven also needed to incorporate FEMA in the process. Lynn Haven was going back and forth with Tetra Tech. Vickie Gainer wanted to use (3) architects and divide up the work that needed to be done. Eventually, Lynn Haven picked three (3) architectural firms and the architects began presenting ideas.

**Adam gives Vickie Gainer credit for wanting to use three architects; however, the City Commission was in favor of this idea, and the City Commission picked the architects recommended by staff.**

Joe Sorci from Florida Architects presented Lynn Haven with all the options regarding their part of the rebuild. The plan was for Lynn Haven to pare down the project to what Lynn Haven wanted and what their budget allowed.

**Sorci had been meeting with Vickie Gainer, Police Chief Ricky Ramie, and city staff, and this was also during the onset of Covid in 2020. I was invited in early 2020 to attend a meeting of their progress via a Zoom tele meeting. I listened without comment in horror as Sorci and the staff presented a rebuild plan in excess of 40 million dollars, with office suites as large as a small house, with the police department located on the second floor of city hall with a gym, a $400,000 kitchen, and a monstrosity of a building located in a small area with limited parking space for a meeting hall that would hold over 200 people. There was also no re-build of the library included in the plan. Vickie would later deny over and over that the original cost was to be over $40 million. The only reason they began to bring the cost down was because James Finch began to attend Commission meetings pointing out to the public what the City Manager was about to do. Even though he was indicted for it, James was looking out for the best interest of the City, and his ill-fated intervention saved the residents millions of dollars…again.**

**I got a copy of the plans from Vickie Gainer and shared them with several people, including my friend James Finch, who was just as horrified over the cost as I was.**

**James had recently purchased the property behind Walgreens on the corner of State Road 77 and State Road 390 in the center of Lynn Haven; probably the most valuable piece of business/government real estate in the City. The property had been a mobile home park which had been devastated during Hurricane Michael and was several acres. James had a drawing of a one-story police department, and an emergency operations center drawn up on the property and showed his ideas to me. There could be entrances in and out from both major highways, plenty of parking, and room on the back side of the acreage to expand the public works department buildings and equipment storage. He said that he (or another contractor) could build it using a design build concept much more economically and**

efficiently than what had been proposed, and he wanted to share the idea with the Commission when the architects shared their ideas. (Even though the City had selected three architects to submit proposals, there were no contracts at this time.)

Margo Anderson contacted Albritton about using James Finch because "James had a plan." Finch wanted to do the project as a design build. Albritton was concerned about Lynn Haven losing funds and prepared a memo documenting such. In May 2020, Albritton advised Anderson that proceeding the way they were trying to do the project with Finch was a bad idea and the project needed to be bid out.

**This is a false statement by Albritton. I had taken James Finch's ideas to Vickie Gainer and told her that James would like to show his idea to both her and Police Chief Ramie, and then he would like to be on the agenda to show his plan to the Commission as an alternative to the 40-million-dollar plan presented by Florida Architects. Ricky Ramie and Vickie Gainer met with me at James' office where he shared his plan with them, but what we did not know was that Ricky Ramie wore a wire and was recording for the FBI and BCSO as we talked. There is nothing out of the ordinary for a Mayor or a Commissioner to meet with a business person and listen to a proposal, and then if the Commissioner has interest to place the proposal on the agenda. If the Commission doesn't like the agenda item, they don't vote for it. There was never a suggestion by me nor by James that that he be given the project without it being bid, and he also said in that meeting as well as to the Commission, that if he were not the contractor selected that he would be willing to sell his property to the City for the project if they wanted it, and that he would also finance it as he had done other projects, at below bank lending rates. The Government, with the help of Vickie Gainer, Adam Albritton, Commissioner Aldridge, and others, made a sensible and legal proposal seem corrupt and illegal. While all of this was going on, I had no idea that a grand jury was convening in June of 2020 for the purpose of indicting me. Joe Sorci, the architect, was fuming mad about James's proposal, and that he was allowed to present it to the Commission; his administrative assistant Sue Hudson, was on social media the week before I was indicted with inflammatory comments:**

**August 17, 2020: Sue Hudson, Facebook**

**"Ryan you obviously haven't done your research into James Finch. The city is and has been in enough trouble with federal authorities, they need to be very careful who they accept any kind of "offer" from**

at this point."
Ryan Scray replied to her, "I can only read what's on public record. Which I have."
"Dig deeper. Everything doesn't make it to public record. With your background you should know there are ways to try and hide information."
"Seems there's lots of hanky-panky going on in this city."

James Finch was upset about the deal and called city manager Vickie Gainer. Gainer gave Albritton a heads-up regarding Finch. Albritton received a call from attorney William Harrison. During the call, the two discussed the City Commission's ability to fire someone, however, they agreed Lynn Haven could not sole source the project. Albritton advised the project needed to be bid out and that Lynn Haven could lose FEMA funding by going this route.

**William Harrison is a Panama City attorney and is known as one of the kingmakers for Bay County politics; the fact that Adam was consulting with William Harrison about Lynn Haven is interesting, when Adam, according to his interviews, knew the FBI scrutiny and investigation was centered on what was happening at the Lynn Haven Commission meetings with the rebuild. Again, neither James nor I ever advocated for sole sourcing his idea as a project, and as far as losing FEMA funding, this lie was being perpetrated by Commissioner Brandon Aldridge and his wife who worked for an agency in Panama City and served as Brandon's "advisor." Our attorneys proved in the evidentiary hearing that losing FEMA funding because of a design build method was false.**

During this period of time, Anderson would call Albritton to discuss the project. Anderson kept saying "James' is better" meaning plan. Albritton believed Anderson was trying to fire Florida Architects and hire James Finch. Albritton advised, that if that was done, the project would need to be put back out to bid. Albritton specifically recalls receiving phone calls from Anderson around June 7, 2020. Albritton was in the hospital in Gainesville, Florida with his father at the time. It was a long conversation specifically about firing Florida Architects and hiring James Finch. Albritton cautioned Anderson again about the federal investigation.

**Albritton was correct that I wanted to get rid of Florida Architects because of the unbelievable prices they had put forth with their plans; but he states this as if I had the power to do this. This is months after the storm, there is no emergency, and any firing or hiring of an agency voted on by the Commission could only be done by Commission vote. Adam knew this, yet made it sound to the FBI agent as though I had the power to fire Florida Architects and hire**

James Finch. An utter lie. He is telling the truth about our phone conversation, because when I realized he was with his father, who was dying, I apologized for calling and we did not talk for very long as I recall. The phone call was primarily about the fact that I had discovered that Vickie Gainer had already paid the architects over 100k without Commission approval and the architects had no contract. I was concerned that Gainer was writing checks of this size without Commission approval and without a contract in place; the behavior was exactly what former city manager Michael White had just been indicted for. One of the checks she had written was paid from a letter using it as an invoice. I do not recall Adam mentioning a federal investigation at this point, cautioning me about what? I am the one who started the investigation. He was the one taking $10,000 weekly kickbacks, as we learned from Government discovery months after my indictment.

Albritton stated that he didn't even know how to prepare a bid package for a project that included the bidder to provide the land for the project and was included in the project.

Albritton could see that Commissioner Judy Tinder was helping Anderson and Finch. Tinder would show up to meetings with document sand pictures of Finch's plans. The documents and pictures had Finch's writing on them. It was clear to Albritton that Anderson and Tinder were working to direct the project to Finch.

James had most probably shared his ideas, with every member of the Commission. From the way Dan Russell and Brandon Aldridge reacted to the plans, Judy was probably the only one besides me who thought the design build might be a better way to go. Judy Tinder and I were not working together to direct anything; we did not speak outside the Commission meeting about this.

In June 2020, the matter of pursuing the project as design build was brought before the City Commission. The Commission voted 3-2 with Commissioner Pat Perno voting with Anderson and Tinder for design build. Albritton was surprised by the way Perno voted. After the meeting, Albritton asked Perno why he voted the way he did. Perno stated that he got confused as to what they were voting on during the vote. Albritton also asked Anderson why it was so important that Finch gets this project. Albritton cautioned Anderson again about the federal investigation and the possibility of this conduct leading to an indictment.

Albritton leaves out a great deal of information here. The Commission voted to have Albritton prepare an RFQ for a design build project for the police department only for contractors to submit their bids and qualifications and to advertise. Florida Architects was furious, of course. If Commissioner Perno didn't understand what he was voting for he should not have voted. We did not vote for Finch to get the project; we were voting to advertise the project. Joe Sorci, of Florida Architects made an angry statement accusing me as the Mayor and the Commission of doing something illegal. Albritton says exactly what the Government wants him to say here: that somehow, as Mayor, that I am steering a contract to James Finch, instead of what I really did, bringing his proposal in front of the Commission to consider a more cost effective alternative than what Florida Architects had presented.

Albritton advised Anderson that Lynn Haven should not fire someone in order to give James Finch a project and that Finch should not be preselected to get the project. It was at this point that Anderson took a step back and Judy Tinder started to bring things up and doing things to assist in Finch getting the project like showing up with documents on Finch's plans. The plans Tinder had appeared to have come directly from Finch as they had Finch's handwriting and notes on them. Albritton again cautioned Anderson against cherry picking the project to get the outcome they wanted. Albritton told them they needed a reason why they were doing what they were doing. Albritton explained to Anderson that firing Florida Architects was possible, but it was their intent is what mattered. If Lynn Haven fired Florida Architects, they needed to provide the general public with a fair chance to provide the services.

Adam just repeats the same things again. I am not sure how he knew the writing on Tinder's information was Finch's handwriting, but I am sure it probably was if Tinder had met with Finch to get more information about his proposal. There would be nothing wrong with her asking him questions. The intent for firing Florida Architects, if the Commission voted to do so, was because of the exorbitant costs and the overbuild of the building on such a small piece of property. Also, when the rebuild process started, one of the tenets we agreed upon was that putting city hall, the police department and the EOC all in the same building was probably not a good idea in case another catastrophe occurred. It was better not to have "all eggs in one basket." We were left with no building to meet as a City after Hurricane Michael because everything was in the one complex that was destroyed. Also, had the proposal gone forward, we would not have been firing Florida Architects at that point, because they did not have a contract yet, even though Vickie Gainer had paid them almost 100k without Commission approval.

Anderson thereafter consulted Albritton about Vickie Gainer paying Florida Architect's invoice. Albritton believed Anderson was going to use that issue as a reason to fire Gainer. Albritton followed up the conversation with Anderson in an email documenting their discussion.

This last paragraph is mostly true. I not only consulted Albritton about Vickie Gainer paying Florida Architect's and Dewberry's invoices without Commission approval, I brought it up at a Commission meeting which is on record. He is absolutely correct that I was prepared to pass the gavel and make a motion that we fire Vickie Gainer. Michael White had paid vendors without Commission approval, and now Vickie was doing the same thing. She needed to be fired. She still does, yet she is remains in place as the City Manager for Lynn Haven at the time of this book's publication. Adam was protecting her because she was part of everything that he was. She had been a "witness" for the Government from the day after I went to the Sheriff; and after Adam pled guilty, he was their boy, too.

One of the most disturbing aspects of Adam's testimony against me is that in the weeks and months following Hurricane Michael, as my political capital grew and I was approached about running for a higher office, I had lunch with Adam one day and told him I was considering running for Congressman Neil Dunn's seat. I was very disappointed in Dunn's lack of action in getting a disaster bill passed for our area over six months after the storm. Adam expressed interest and told me that he had been thinking of maybe running for State Attorney for the 14th Judicial District, but that he would also be interested in working as Chief of Staff for me if I should go through with running for that office. He seemed excited about it, and he also encouraged me and thought that I had a real shot at winning if I went forward. What never occurred to me until much later was that Derwin White would not have wanted me to have that seat; he knew I could not be controlled or owned, and the other "good ol' boys knew it too." And Adam was Derwin White's attorney.

I do not hate Adam Albritton; I try to forgive what he did to me to save himself, but I am not there yet. I have not seen him since August 19, 2020, the day that I was indicted, but I hope someday to have an opportunity to speak with him. I would just like to ask him, "why?' and see if he has the male anatomy to look me in the eye. I doubt it.


FBI Interview
SA Lawrence Boghini

Commissioner Dan Russell
September 1, 2020

**This interview took place about two weeks after I was indicted, on August 19, 2020:**

Daniel Clyne Russell, was interviewed in Panama City, Florida, by FBI Special Agent Lawrence P. Borghini and Bay County Sheriff Tommy Ford and BCSO Major Jimmy Stanford. Russell was accompanied by his attorney William "Bill" Henry of the law firm Burke and Blue. Russell provided the following information:

Russell is a first term Lynn Haven City Commissioner. His term ends in April 2021. He ran for Lynn Haven Seat 3 that was held by Roger Schad. Russell was friends with LH City Manager, Joel Schubert. Russell had met Schubert at a baseball game and the two had been friends ever since. Margo Anderson wanted Schubert gone.

**Why Commissioner Russell would make such a random statement to the FBI agent that "I wanted Schubert gone" is beyond me. Joel Schubert was not fond of me because I was a "people's" Mayor, dozens of residents came to each meeting after I became Mayor of Lynn Haven, and I allowed them to speak freely during public commentary, something which had not been happening in the years before. Russell was elected two years after I became Mayor, and in that first election cycle of 2017, the citizens fired two of the old Commissioners because of their negativity toward me and the new ideas I had brought. Judy Tinder was also elected in 2017, replacing another longtime, commissioner, Joe Ashbrook. Joel Schubert did not like it when I disagreed with him or spoke against something he proposed in meetings that I was not in favor of, but I did not want him "gone" as Russell stated above. But I would find out after reading Shubert's statement to the FBI, a year after I was indicted, that he spoke against me as well.**

When Russell was running for City Commissioner, Chris Forehand recommended that Russell use Arthur Cullen for his campaign. James Finch asked Russell to come to his office and pick up a $1,000 campaign contribution. Russell claimed that all Finch wanted him to do was make decisions that were best for the City. Russell has known Forehand for a long time. The two would occasionally socialize. Forehand would lobby on behalf of the City for projects and grant money. Russell interviewed Michael White for the LH City Manager position. Russell did not know Michael White prior. Forehand told Russell that he knew Michael White. After Michael White became City Manager, Russell would socialize with White. Russell was surprised by the indictment of White and what White had been involved in.

**Russell accepted the pro bono contract in November 2018, just after Hurricane Michael, with a City vendor, WorldClaim, that**

Michael White told him about. He received free adjustment services from WorldClaim as Michael promised him. Russell was named in the first indictment as an unindicted co-conspirator, just as I was, for receiving property cleanup and billing it to the City, but he was never charged. Russell was also asking Michael White to fix speeding tickets, which Michael White arranged with Police Chief Ricky Ramie, documented in their text messages shown in the evidentiary hearings.

Russell stated that Erosion Control Specialist (ECS) was hired after the fact. Russell claimed to have not known about ECS. Russell saw ECS in Country Club. Russell had heard that ECS was cleaning Mayor Anderson's house. David Horton told Russell that ECS was at Mayor Anderson's house and that Lee Anderson was there directing them on what to do.

**Dan Russell was present at every commission meeting after the storm, just as I was, and he claims, just as I did, not to have known about ECS; he was on holiday Facebook posts and other social event posts with Michael White and Ricky Ramie in the weeks after the storm. The FBI takes Russell's word that he didn't know about ECS yet claims that I lied when I said I didn't know. Russell also repeats the same sentence found in Mickey White, Josh Anderson, and other 302's, "Lee Anderson was there directing them on what to do." They all use the word "directing" as though the testimony is collaborative.**

Russell explained that there is a ditch that runs through his subdivision. The lady across the street from the ditch was having problems with storm water because trees had fallen into the ditch. Russell went to City Manager at the time, Joel Shubert and asked that the ditch be cleaned. Russell claims that because it is private property but there is an easement.

After Hurricane Michael, Russell stated there was a verbal agreement to clean the ditch. FEMA has a program for cleaning waterways. They were looking for more work so the ditch at the subdivision was cleaned. Russell checked with and secured the approval of the subdivisions' board members regarding the work to be performed. The subdivision agreed to fence a city lift station within the subdivision as part of the agreement. Russell emailed City Manager Vickie Gainer with a copy of the agreement. Russell stated that they had only put up the fence a couple of months ago. Before putting up the fence around the lift station, Russell checked with Lynn Haven's Director of Public Utilities Greg Kidwell. Kidwell advised that he did not care about what type of fence was put up as long as it met the setback requirements.

**These two paragraphs are an elaborate lie which Chris Forehand assisted Commissioner Russell in putting forth. The email that Russell refers to that he sent to Vickie Gainer, the city manager, was written on April 26, 2019, two days after the BCSO and the FBI raided**

ECS for the second time, on April 24th. The local news media had been given the fake property cleanup invoices for my property on April 24, 2019, and this is when I found Dan Russell, sitting at my desk in the crowded, temporary office in the attic of the water department where administrative personnel, the police chief, and City Manager had moved in late December. Vickie had stated to Channel 13 that there was no documentation of an easement for my property on this date. He was going through a huge stack of pink invoices which had been provided to him by Vickie Gainer, looking for invoices for his gated subdivision, Osceola Pointe, and then two days later he wrote her the email.

The email refers to a verbal agreement that did not exist, and Bobby Baker, the Public Works Director gave an interview in which he stated that "truckloads" of debris were hauled out of the private neighborhood, stacked on the road, and Lynn Haven hauled it away picking up the bill and submitting it to FEMA.

The entire "lift station fence agreement" and FEMA waterways program, was all done *after the fact*, aided by Chris Forehand, to cover his buddy Commissioner Russell's ass. Russell did have his HOA board members to sign, acknowledging the "verbal agreement" they were not part of, just signing to acknowledge that Commissioner Russell told them there was a verbal agreement as one of the board members, Jay Moody clarifies in his 302 interview. We have a copy of Russell's email to Vickie Gainer of April 26th, 2019.

Russell was named in the indictment as having had his property cleaned and charged to the City. He also signed a pro bono agreement with WorldClaim in November of 201. His buddy, Chris Forehand, the city contracted engineer, who received immunity, took care of Russell with his elaborate explanation of flooding and stormwater concerns, as I mentioned previously in reference to the stormwater ditch adjacent to my property which is a city-maintained easement and is not in a privately owned gated community like Russell's.

Russell stated that the City was in the process of rebuilding. The projects were proceeding using the design, bid, build method. Committees were in the process of developing budgets for the projects. Forehand told Russell that James was wanting on of the projects. Finch had come to Russell before and wanted the Cain Griffin project stopped.

Finch was against the exorbitant prices in excess of 40 million dollars, initially, that Vickie Gainer, Chief Ricky Ramie and other staff were negotiating with the architects, and he was speaking out about it. Russell, Forehand, and others were pushing a six-million-dollar baseball field project on the City before the City Hall and other necessary infrastructure had even started. Many people were speaking out about this.

Forehand asked Russell to lunch. Russell initially refused but Forehand eventually talked him into it. Russell and Forehand were sitting in Sonny's BBQ when Finch called Forehand. Finch ended up joining them for lunch. Russell believes the discussion was about LH's City Hall.

Derwin White came to one of the recent commission meetings. Derwin White talked about how design build was the way to go with the City's rebuild projects.

Russell advised that when the Cain Griffin project was advertised regionally and bid out, the project cost came out lower than the City had estimated and expected.

Russell stated there was a rumor that Commissioner Judy Tinder had accepted money from Finch. Chris Forehand and Arthur Cullen have each talked about it.

**Arthur Cullen is a local political operative who was not only Commissioner Russell's campaign manager, but also for Sheriff Tommy Ford, State Attorney Larry Basford, and State Representative Griff Griffitts. Cullen has several social media aliases, notably, Alex Cantone, in which he disparaged me and pushed the narrative of my dishonesty and urged residents to watch carefully. He also began attending Lynn Haven Commission meetings in the weeks just before I was indicted, something he had never done in the six years I had been mayor. Commissioner Judy Tinder is known for her honesty, and for not accepting campaign donations over $50.00. I find it amazing that there is a sentence in an official FBI interview which even entertains, "there was a rumor that", but it happens over and over in this investigation.**

Facebook posts of Alex Cantone/aka/Arthur Cullen

Campaign manager for Sheriff Tommy Ford, SA Larry Basford, State Representative Griff Griffitts, and many other Bay County elected officials These posts were nine days before I was indicted.

**August 10, 2020**

"I promise you there are bigger eyes than just "the public" watching this. Watch the video again, listen to how many times she says "staff" and "City Manager," the meeting tonight is designed to beat up on the City Manager make this look like poor decisions by her team, the LH staff, architects, and all the while pushing business for her buddy. This is a well-choreographed opus designed to benefit a few. Don't be sheep. You've already followed her "strong Mayor" agenda after the storm. What did that get ya? Over $5 million documented gone from the city. The FBI is on this city like a bee on honey. If you're a council member, know we the citizens are watching.

September 10, 2020

"Yall go ahead and start a go fund me, the FEDS have the best canteens. Finch won't be able to send her money from prison."

Mayor Anderson would often threaten Michael White when he was City Manager. Russell could overhear Michael White's conversations with the Mayor through Michael White's cell phone.

**If Commissioner Russell was listening to my phone calls with Michael White concerning City business without my knowledge, he was violating Florida Statutes and the Florida Sunshine law; also, Michael White is a very large, loud, man who was fired from his position as CEO at the Electric Coop and sued by several women there for his behavior toward them; he was arrested for domestic violence with a gun in March 2019, yet Michael's buddies were of one accord in their testimony that "I threatened him." A lie.**

Michael White introduced Russell to Worldclaim. Michael White told Russell that he was getting the work done on his properties done for free by Worldclaim as well as the Mayor's property. Worldclaim had offered to do his public adjusting work for free as well. Russell met with Lauren Brubaker and her estimator. Brubaker confirmed that the work on Russell's claim would be free. Russell's insurance company did an estimate on his property. Worldclaim then did an estimate regarding Russell's claim. The insurance company then came back out and did another estimate which came out higher than the first. Russell ended up getting a check from the insurance company for approximately $75,000 which was based on the second estimate the insurance company had done. Russell cashed the check.

Russell contacted his attorney Bill Henry because he felt that the insurance company still had not paid him enough on his claim. After speaking with Henry about the matter, Russell terminated his relationship with Worldclaim and paid Henry $34,000 to handle the matter.

Russell did not know that Lynn Haven had received a settlement offer from its' insurance company prior to WorldClaim doing work for Lynn Haven. The contract between Lynn Haven and WorldClaim was never brought before the City Commission.

Dan Russell signed a pro bono contract in early November with WorldClaim , and according to the indictment received 75,000 because of his relationship with them. Keep in mind that as he is interviewing with the FBI agent, he has read the indictment against me charging me with conspiracy in the WorldClaim matter, and so he has his story ready and his attorney sitting beside him.

He knew about WorldClaim because Michael White announced at the October 30' 2018, commission meeting that he had contracted with World Claim as the city's insurance public adjuster. Michael had signed the contract, and he brought the contract to the meeting with my name and date he had signed (October 24' 2018) preprinted in his handwriting; I signed the contract after the meeting. None of the Commissioners questioned Michael's actions, including Russell, in the same way none of the Commissioners, including me, questioned his actions in hiring Jay Moody as the Financial consultant and Adam Albritton as the attorney. Michael had emergency powers from October 10th-October 30, 2018, which I had delegated to him as the City Manager when I declared the emergency.

Russell was the mayor pro-tem after Governor Ron DeSantis suspended me from office on August 20, 2020, and like many other public officials in Bay County in the aftermath of the storm, he did not seek re-election, and quietly slithered away from the public eye.


## Statement of Denise "Dede" Rowen (attorney and friend of Chris Forehand)

### Defendant's Exhibit 87
### Evidentiary Hearing

Rowen learned of WorldClaim from a client of hers from Atlanta, Howard Williams. Williams had used WorldClaim before regarding a claim he had in North Carolina. Williams suggested that WorldClaim could assist Rowen with her claim in Florida as a result of Hurricane Michael. Shortly thereafter, Rowen was introduced to and met with Michael Fusco at her house in Panama City. Rowen's personal residence had sustained substantial damage as a result of Hurricane Michael. After the initial meeting with Fusco, Rowen had a follow up meeting with him at the residence they were renting in Watercolors (a community in Walton County that was not affected by Hurricane Michael).

Rowen continued to have contact with Fusco and Lauren Brubaker. In addition to signing Rowen, WorldClaim was also interested in developing additional clients in the area. Chris Forehand was introduced to Fusco. Before Rowen agreed to sign on with WorldClaim, she requested some additional information from them such as prior experience and references. WorldClaim had offered Rowen a rate of 10% to handle her personal claim. Attorneys handling such work normally charge a fee of 30%. Rowen talked to Clayton Syfrett about using WorldClaim. Rowen was hesitant but signed on with WorldClaim towards the end of October 2018 after she was offered a discounted rate.

Rowen also became involved in referring clients/people to WorldClaim. It was discussed that if Rowen played a substantial role in getting someone to sign with WorldClaim, that she would be paid a fee. For residential work, Rowen was to be paid 10% of the fee WorldClaim received. For non-residential clients, it was a tiered fee structure, 15%, 12.5%, and 10%.

Rowen advised she had a part in referring to WorldClaim to Royal American, Richard Maddox, Toucans, the City of Lynn Haven, Bay District Schools, the City of Mexico Beach, the City of Port St. Joe, and the shops at Edgewater. Rowen also introduced Chris Forehand to WorldClaim. Rowen discussed with Forehand that if he brought in someone that signed with WorldClaim, she would split the fee she received from WorldClaim with him. Forehand presented a written agreement to Rowen but she never signed it. They way it worked, after Rowen received a payment from WorldClaim, Forehand would invoice Rowen for consulting fees for his share of the fee. Some of the referrals that Rowen was tracking were: Joe Littleton, **Michael White, Dan Russell**, Boys & Girls Club, Dr. Campbell, **City of Lynn Haven,** the Kings.

In December 2018, Rowen emailed Michael Fusco wanting to compare notes and began a list of referrals she had made to WorldClaim. In a January 9, 2019, email response Rowen received from Michael Fusco regarding Lynn Haven, Fusco stated that **Mike White and Dan Russell** were not paying WorldClaim a fee because it was part of the City of Lynn Haven deal.

After receiving a breakdown from WorldClaim showing an amount of $39,209.55 she was to receive, Rowen responded with her email dated 10/6/2019. The email contained a number of questions and comments regarding the calculation of the fees to be paid by WorldClaim to Rowen.

On October 11, 2019, Rowen received an email from Lauren Brubaker. The email advised Rowen that **Dan Russell and Mike White** were pro bono clients.

Rowen continued to follow-up with WorldClaim over the next five months to determine which referrals had signed up with WorldClaim and what the status of their claims were. Nick Brubaker sent out an email with a calculation of the fee Rowen was to receive as a result of her referrals. Rowen then received a second email in which the referral fees had been reduced. Rowen saw Michael Fusco and Laren Brubaker in the airport one day and questioned them about the amount of payment she was to receive. After that, Rowen sent an email to WorldClaim advising that she was troubled by WorldClaim *not charging Lynn Haven city officials a fee.*

**Michael Fusco and Lauren Brubaker are President and Vice-President of WorldClaim, respectively.**

Chris Forehand would tell Rowen the names of people that he had mentioned WorldClaim to that she needed to keep them on her list. Rowen did not speak to Adam Albritton regarding WorldClaim, nor was there mention of Margo Anderson being referred to WorldClaim. Rowen was aware that **Dan Russell received $75,000** from working with WorldClaim. Chris Forehand was keeping track of who was getting settlements as a result of WorldClaim. Forehand had requested that Rowen check on it meaning the payment they were to receive for referring the work to WorldClaim.

Chris Forehand told her that he never did that. Forehand denied it when asked.

As of April 2020, WorldClaim was still getting payments from clients Rowen had referred.

**I contracted with WorldClaim in January of 2019, months after Michael White, Dan Russell and Chris Forehand made their "deals." WorldClaim offered me a pro bono contract, I refused it, negotiated a 6% contract and paid it in full when we received our check from the insurance company. Yet I was charged with committing a crime and Dan Russell was not; and Chris Forehand received immunity from the Government. Why?**

**FBI Interview with George Roberts, Contractor**

**SA Lawrence Borghini and Sheriff Tommy Ford**

**This interview was actually conducted on March 6, 2020, several months I was indicted, and a year before James Finch was indicted. Once again, Borghini does not memorialize or file the report until much later. This report was filed June 6, 2021, over a year after the interview. Guy Lewis, the lead defense attorney for James Finch, excoriated the FBI agent in the evidentiary hearing, asking him if**

this was proper procedure for drafting and filing 302 reports.

I include this report without any comment, just to demonstrate that the FBI and the Bay County Sheriff's office was aware that James nor I were involved with his having a "pit" selected for chips as we were charged in the indictment. This testimony from Geroge Roberts, a fellow contractor, is quite plainly stated. The Sheriff was present for this interview.

Geroge Roberts provided the following information:
Roberts owns and operates Roberts and Roberts, Inc. located at 1741 N. Sherman Aven., Panama City, Florida. After Hurricane Michael, Roberts did not have any local contracts but did have State contracts. Roberts ran four-man crews in five locations: Franklin County, Gulf County, Panama City, Panama City Beach, and Highway 231. Roberts was a subcontractor for Roads, Inc. of NWF (a Pensacola Company) and did cut and toss on State roads. Roberts dealt with Cody Rawson at Roads, Inc.

Roberts advised that during the first week he had sixteen crews that worked on the first pass of State roads 65, 71, 98, Business 98, 231, 77, and 15th Street. This was first pass cut and toss operations. On the second pass, they worked on clearing hurricane debris 3' outside the white line on the roads. Roberts crews did this for a couple of weeks. Roberts also had crews that worked at Tyndall for approximately two months. The pace of operations were such that they were working 7 days a week. Roberts eventually bid on and awarded road repair work.

Roberts had met Randy Perkins of Ashbritt during the oil spill. Perkins had called Roberts prior to Hurricane Michael. Perkins wanted Roberts to call Florida Governor Rick Scott and recommend to the Governor that the Army Corps of Engineers come in and run the hurricane cleanup operation. If the Corps ran the operations, the reimbursement rates would pay double the rates than if the operations were run by the local governments. In addition, if the Army Corps of Engineers were put in charge of the Bay County cleanup operations, Ashbritt would receive 100% of the work in Bay County. Perkins was also connected to the Governor's people.

At the time of Hurricane Michael, Rick Scott was still the Governor of Florida; three weeks after the storm Ron DeSantis was elected Governor and Rick Scott was elected Senator. Roberts mention that Perkins was also connected to the Governor's people may be referring to the fact that AshBritt's former legal counsel, Jared Maskowitz was appointed as Florida's Emergency Management director in December of 2018 after DeSantis' was elected governor. Chris Forehand, in his text message to Michael White, states, in reference to him, "he is an AshBritt kind of guy." Or there may be

**other "people" Roberts is referring to.**

Roberts had inquired about work after the hurricane and was told by Ashbritt that they had signed a contract with GAC and that he needed to go through them to get work. Roberts was trying to make sure that he had work for his guys and they were able to collect a paycheck after the hurricane. While at the EOC, Roberts was told to call Ashley Ramsey at Crowder Gulf. Roberts called Ramsey and told her that he had 100 pieces of equipment. Robert met Ramsey at the Hombre Golf Course in Panama City Beach to discuss what work was available.

Roberts explained that Bay County cleanup operations were split with Crowder Gulf being assigned everything East of Highway 77 and Ashbritt assigned everything West of Highway 77. The City of Lynn Haven was divided the same way. The City of Panama City used Crowder Gulf and the City of Calloway used Ashbritt. The City of Springfield was split between Ashbritt and Crowder Gulf.

Roberts advised that he owned two pits that could be used as the final rest place for hurricane debris. Roberts sent Crowder Gulf the information on his sites. Troy Syfrett also had a pit that was used by Crowder Gulf. Derwin White wanted all of the hurricane debris to go to his pits. Because James Finch had had a stroke, Roberts was going to assist Finch with Lynn Haven. Roberts claimed to have contacted Chris Forehand about the approval of Finch's site as well as Finch's wife and daughter. Ron Golinowsky was handling things at Phoenix Construction in Finch's absence. Nick Pratt was the head of operations for Crowder Gulf. Roberts claims that he was told the price for disposal of the vegetative debris was $4.70 per cubic yard.

Roberts was asked by SA Borghini if he had attended any meetings at Finch's residence where hurricane debris and/or a final resting place for reduced vegetative debris chips was discussed with Finch, Derwin White and/or others. Roberts denied attending any such meeting or having any knowledge of Derwin White making a statement in any kind of a meeting. Roberts advised that he did have some emails regarding the permitting of his pit and Finch's pit that he would provide to SA Borghini.

**George Roberts was interviewed again on November 7, 2022, by the new FBI Agent on the case, Daniel Crecelius, after Agent Borghini and Assistant U.S. Attorney Stephen Kunz abruptly retired after the evidentiary hearings. This interview was by telephone with Assistant US Attorneys Andrew Grogan and Justin Keen participating:**

After Hurricane Michael struck Bay County, Florida, Robert's company,

Roberts and Roberts, Inc. received debris from the City of Lynn Haven, Florida and from Bay County, Florida. Roberts considered himself the "local voice" of Crowder Gulf while Derwin White was the "local voice" for Ashbritt. Roberts owned a debris management site and had to submit a letter to Crowder Gulf that detailed how Roberts' authorized site would receive debris at a rate of $4.70 per cubic yard. Roberts could not remember who set the rate at $4.70, but Roberts knew that $4.70 was the established rate that everybody was charging. Roberts heard that Allen Byrd offered to charge less for debris disposal, but Roberts didn't know all of the details.

**As detailed earlier, Adam Albritton and Derwin White set the price of $4.70. Also, Derwin White may have been the local voice for Ashbritt, but his co-owner, Allan Bense signed the teaming agreement of GAC and AshBritt, but the local law enforcement and FBI continue to refer to Derwin White and GAC, rarely mentioning Allan Bense.**

Roberts also submitted a similar letter to Crowder Gulf on behalf of Phoenix Construction (Phoenix). Roberts submitted the letter to Crowder Gulf because James Finch, who was the owner of Phoenix, was a close friend of Roberts and had been in the hospital at the time of the Hurricane. Roberts had partnered with Finch on several jobs over the years, to include the concrete and asphalt at the airport. Roberts believed that Finch would have received a lot of work from Hurricane Michael if he hadn't been in the hospital. Roberts wanted to make sure that Finch received some work. At some point, White told Roberts that Finch would not be able to get any work because Finch was in the hospital. Roberts confronted White and told White that Roberts was going to make sure that Finch received some work from the Hurricane. Roberts also "steered" debris from Troy Syfrett's site in favor of Finch. Roberts only wanted to help Finch because they were close friends.

Roberts did not coordinate with Finch at all regarding the letter that Roberts sent to Crowder Gulf on behalf of Phoenix. Roberts sent the letter on October 26th, but Finch did not get home from the hospital until October 30th. Roberts coordinated everything through Ron Golinowsky who was running Phoenix's operations while Finch was in the hospital, along with Mike Swearington. Roberts called Golinowsky and told Golinowsky to create the letter that Roberts eventually sent to Crowder Gulf.

While Finch was in the hospital, Roberts never went to visit Finch, but Roberts did speak to Finch on several occasions over the phone. Roberts and Finch never spoke about business when Finch was in the hospital.

Roberts was also the Chairman of the Northwest Florida Water Management District. In this capacity, Roberts had the ability to see various permit applications. Roberts received a telephone call from Michael White, regarding the permitting process of Finch's debris site. MW wanted to know when Finch's site was going to be ready. Roberts later sent a text message to MW that read "Michael this is George you need to call me ASAP per James Finch." Roberts sent the message to tell MW that Finch's site was almost ready. Even though the text read "per James Finch" Finch didn't have anything to do with the text because Finch was in the hospital.

Crowder Gulf discovered Finch's site while they were flying overhead. Nick Pratt called Roberts and asked who owned the site, and Roberts told Pratt that Finch owned the site. Crowder Gulf was always looking for sites and Roberts would help Crowder Gulf identify the owners. After identifying the sites, Chris Forehand or Ron Rogers would help getting the proper permits from the state.

**City Manager Michael White repeatedly lied, telling the FBI that I directed him to tell Crowder Gulf to use James Finch's site, which was not true as shown in the paragraph above.**

Roberts had gone to Finch's office on a few occasions, but the meetings were always one on one. Roberts was never present in any meeting with Finch and other people where the hurricane debris was discussed. A few weeks prior to the captioned interview, Finch and his attorney visited Roberts at Roberts' office. Finch's attorney wanted to discuss the letter that Roberts sent to Crowder Gulf on behalf of Phoenix. Roberts never really discussed Finch's criminal case with Finch. Once, Finch told Roberts that White paid to have somebody take photos of Margo Anderson on Finch's plane.

**We learned later that Derwin White had paid a local private investigator, to get photos of my husband and I traveling with James on his plane, something we had done for over thirty years, and after I became Mayor, the few times I flew on James' plane with my husband were paid for as I had outlined earlier.**

**The photos and video were given to Channel 13 WMBB by local political operative Arthur Cullen, aka, Alex Cantone on social media.**

**There are many, many more interviews of many individuals in the course of this investigation, and the majority of them are filed and available on PACER in the federal court, along with over three years of motions, rebuttals, and other documents pertaining to this case. I am concluding this section of the book with excerpts from interview reports of the Bay County Sheriff's Office, which exemplify the fact that they interviewed employees of the City of Lynn Haven, officials, and even my neighbors, but they never once questioned me. Their reports all verify one glaring fact, that none of this investigation**

would have likely happened had I not stumbled upon the fraud perpetrated by Mickey White, Michael White, Derwin White, Adam Albritton, Chris Forehand, Ricky Ramie, Vickie Gainer, and others, all because James Finch noticed that Mickey White was the contractor building a concession stand in Sheffield Park…without a contractor's license. The dates on every single report by both the Sheriff and the FBI are AFTER the date that I went to Sheriff Ford.

The following is a report by Lt. Jeremy Mathis, an investigator with the Bay County Sheriff's office. The report is dated November 25, 2019, six days after Michael White and the others were indicted, and I was implicated in having had my "property cleaned for free." Social media had hundreds of nasty comments about me on the Channel 13-WMBB website after they broke the story of the indictment which named me as having had my property cleaned and billed to the city, and this report outlines Investigators Mathis and Chance questioning my neighbors:

On November 25, 2019, myself and Inv. Chance traveled to the 500 blk of Virginia Avenue to speak with neighbors about the drainage ditch behind their house. Virginia is one road East of Tennessee, and the properties are bordered on their West side by the same ditch Margo Anderson's property is bordered by.

We initially made contact with Lynn Haven City Commissioner Judy Tinder, who said when she moved into the area, she was under the impression that the ditch behind her house is indeed a city easement. Tinder said after the storm, she had multiple trees and limbs in her back yard from the ditch, and the city never came to clean those items up. Tinder said in fact, those trees are still laying in her yard as she is, "old," and couldn't clean them up by herself. Tinder went on to say that she regretted the fact that she told local media outlets that there was an easement, as she talked to employees of Lynn Haven Public Works who sent her documentation showing there was no city maintained easement behind her property. Tinder did say she recalled some years ago having a crew of 12-15 inmates from the jail in her backyard clearing brush and trimming limbs back. Tinder could not be specific on when this occurred or exactly how long ago it occurred. I provided Tinder my email address and she agreed to forward the documents provided to her by public works.

Public Works Department head Bobby Baker and others were not truthful about the easement. They caused Judy Tinder to believe that she was mistaken, something she would figure out as time went on. If the Sheriff's investigators had bothered to come to my house and question me, I could have shown them photos of 2016 with the city trailers loaded with equipment labeled Bay County Sheriff's Office and City of Lynn Haven which cleaned the easements using community service workers from the Bay County Jail. I also had photos of the easement after it was cleaned, as well as other areas in the city. They never asked. We showed the photos in the evidentiary hearing when we proved the property cleaned was not mine, but is a city easement and ditch which drains into Maxwell Bayou. The Sheriff and Agent Borghini would question Judy Tinder again, in an official 302, and she stated that she had investigated and knew that it was an easement. She would tell me months later when my case was complete, that the Sheriff was so angry after the interview that he left red-faced, in quite a huff after questioning her repeatedly and trying to make her say that the ditch area was not an easement.

Investigator Mathis goes on to say that at about 1600 hrs I received the e-mail from Judy Tinder which she received from "Roy," at the Lynn Haven Public Works Department. This e-mail was saved as a PDF document and added to my folder in the network drive being used for this case. That e-mail reads, *"the right to use the property of another for a specific purpose. The easement is itself a real property interest, but legal title to the underlying land is retained by the original owner for all other purposes. Typical easements are for access to another property, redundantly often stated access and egress, since entry and exit are over the same path, for utility or sewer lines both under and above ground, entry to make repairs on a fence or slide area, and other uses. Easements can be created by a deed to be recorded just like any real property interest."*

This email from Roy at Public Works to Commissioner Tinder is just insulting, as he sent her the definition of an easement. Tinder figured it out in time for the next interview. The entire public works department was all too eager to join in throwing me, the mayor, under the bus, because a large part of my campaign to be mayor in 2015 was regarding the overgrown drainage ditch system in Lynn Haven, and the culverts full of trash and foliage, all of which contributed to horrible flooding every time it rained in any significant amount. I had also used the appearance of the City, with trash, old furniture, and debris which sometimes remained on the right of ways in neighborhoods for weeks before being picked up. When I was elected, I was extremely popular with the people of Lynn Haven, but not so much with the old Commissioners and the city employees. After my arrest, one of the public works employees who had recently retired, Jerry LuCante, posted a large jail cell on social media with my photograph inserted. The Public Works Department was pleased to see me gone. Especially the director, Bobby Baker.

We next spoke with Rodney Plante. Plante said he paid $3,000.00 to have trees removed from his yard, but said these trees were within his yard and not from the ditch. Plante invited us to the rear of his property and showed us several trees still down in the ditch that were never cleared. Plante said if the city was indeed responsible for the maintenance of the ditch, then he thought they would clean these trees out as they were blocking the movement of the water through the drainage ditch. (Photographs were taken behind Plante's residence which have been added to the photographs taken as part of this case.)

**The City (using ECS) only cleaned the southern end of the ditch to the east of my property to clean the trees and debris off the busted power pole; typical of the City they did not clean the ditch the entire length of the block between 5th and 6th street from south to north. The last time they had cleaned the entire thing was in 2016-2017 when the City had the community service workers from BCSO as described before.**

We made contact with the resident of (redacted) who said they were not there post hurricane, and didn't move in until March, so they had no information about the debris from the easement or how it was cleaned.

We left messages at (redacted) and (redacted) as those homeowners were not home.

Upon arrival back at the sheriff's office, I received a phone call from the owner of (redacted) Lonnie Mings. Mings said about two weeks after the hurricane, he left a note on Margo Anderson's door, inquiring about whose responsibility it was to cut the trees from the ditch which were on his property. He said a couple of days later, he returned and found where an unknown person cut a tree in his driveway with a chainsaw, however the tree was still there. He said a couple of days after that, he returned to his house to find two trees cut up and removed along with a utility trailer that got "smashed" in the storm. He said again, he had no idea of who cut those trees. Mings said the remainder of the trees, including several on his house were removed by a company he paid $15,000.00 to. At the time of my call with him, Mings could not recall the company name he used for this work.

**The Mings were neighbors who lived on the opposite corner of my block from me, facing Tennessee Avenue. I do not recall getting a note from them, and I have no idea who cleaned the trees from their ditch, but there were also many volunteers going through Lynn Haven at this time with chainsaws from various organizations that came to Lynn Haven to help residents.**

A short time later I got a call from Justin Davis, the owner of (redacted). Davis said he was under contract to purchase his house when Hurricane Michael hit and closed approximately two weeks post storm. He said he didn't like purchasing the property with an easement but said he did anyway. According to Davis, he spent about 30 days cleaning his backyard of the debris from the easement and using his own dump trailer to haul the debris to the landfill. Davis said he was aware of the media coverage talking about Anderson's house being cleaned, but said he was never offered, nor sought, help from the city cleaning his property.

**Again, the presence of the easement is verified.**

At about 1600 hrs., I was made aware that Lori Castillo, was in the lobby. Castillo lives at (redacted) and has been vocal on social media about the city easement behind her property not being cleaned post hurricane. Castillo said after the hurricane hit, she was left with a large tree leaning in the easement. Castillo said the ground in that area is very soft, and she was concerned the tree would fall and either strike her house, or her neighbor's house. She said she called Michael White and was told someone would come out to see if the tree was a hazard, however nobody ever showed up. She said she contacted White several times, to the point that he became rude and eventually refused to speak to her. Castillo said she finally paid $2,000 for the removal of the upper half of the tree so if the remainder fell, it would not strike a house. Castillo went on to say she has attempted to get reimbursed from the city's fund being used to assist citizens, however she has been told that fund is for people on hard times, and not reimbursement for removing trees. Castillo also said the easement is still clogged behind her house, causing flooding when it rains, and still the city will not come clean it out. Castillo provided, via e-mail, pictures of the tree she believed to be hazardous, as well as her back yard while flooded. Those pictures have been introduced into evidence in this case, as well as added to the network drive being used for this investigation, stored in a folder titled, 'ditch pics'.

**Again, none of this exculpatory material was given to us until almost a year after I was indicted, and even then, I was not permitted to speak to any of my neighbors because the prosecutors had placed them on a "no contact" list for me. If Mathis and Chance, the "investigators" had bothered to come to my house and question me, I could have walked my property line with them, showed them the survey stakes, showed them what was cleaned around the broken power pole, showed that the city right of way is only feet away from my front porch on the south and west sides of the lot, showed them photographs of my family tarping, repairing and cleaning my property, the weekend after the storm, but they had no curiosity to hear from the Mayor of the City of Lynn Haven. They were on a mission. Major Jimmy Stanford, the corrupt lead investigator, was doing the bidding of Derwin White and GAC.**

## Report of Major Jimmy Stanford
## Lead Investigator for the Bay County Sheriff's Office

**April 4, 2019**
**(This report is written three days after I went to Sheriff Ford for help after I asked Vickie Gainer for information on Mickey White and ECS, taking Police Chief Ricky Ramie with me as a witness.)**

On March 17, 2019, Captain Jason Daffin with the Bay County Sheriff's Office led an investigation into domestic violence between Lynn Haven City Manager Michael White and his wife, Amy White. During this investigation, Captain Daffin interviewed Michael White, post-Miranda, and during that interview, Michael White stated that he had phone conversations and text messages with a FEMA worker, Amber Guy, and that his wife, Amy White, had seen these messages and that was the cause of the arguments between he and his wife. Michael White said that some of those text messages were on his phone. He showed Captain Daffin some of these messages but not all of them.

Believing that there were more messages and more evidence of the ongoing domestic violence between Michael White and Amy White, Captain Daffin wrote a search warrant for the contents of Michael White's phone.

The following week, I was away from work. Upon my return to work, I met with Captain Daffin, who updated me on this investigation and stated that he had found several things while looking through Michael White's phone, looking for evidence supporting this case. Captain Daffin said a lot of data was contained on the phone and asked my assistance to help locate the text messages between Michael White and Amber Guy, which he had not found, as well as other evidence.

I then began looking at the contents of the phone dump, which was copied to an external hard drive. While looking at this, I found several text messages and photographs that disturbed me, including a conversation between Michael White and Mickey White, wherein Michael White was telling Mickey White to give him a bid under $20,000 for a roof and to obtain several other bids for them. There were several instances where Michael White had taken care of tickets for people and either obtained property from them later or stated to the officer that he was going to use this as a bargaining chip. There was also a conversation between Mike White and Chris Forehand where Forehand calls him a "dog" because Fema female had passed on all Bay County municipalities except Lynn Haven. Mike White's reply was "Alabama white snake." There is also a conversation between Dan Russell and Mike White where White admits to texting the female but denies any sexual contact.

I reported my findings to Sheriff Ford. On April 1, 2019, Lynn Haven Mayor Margo Anderson met with Sheriff Ford and asked the Sheriff's Office conduct an investigation into improper actions by ex-City manager Mike White and his dealings with ECS. Sheriff Ford and I met afterward and chose a small group to work on this complaint. The group included Lt. Jeremy Mathis, Inv. Aubrey Chance, and Analyst Lindsey Miller. On April 3, 2019, Sheriff Ford and I met with this group and briefed them on this investigation which would start on April 4th. On April 4th, this group, Sheriff Ford, and FBI agent Larry Borghini all met and discussed this case.

**Although again, we did not see this report until much later, I believe this to be a carefully crafted report meant to implicate that Stanford and Capt. Daffin had already figured out that there was corruption and had reported it to Sheriff Ford before I came in. The first sentence, "I reported my findings to Sheriff Ford" does not give a date, and Stanford also says that he was out the previous week. I went to Ricky Ramie to ask him to go with me to see the Sheriff about some financial issues that I had found, and Ricky, as I said previously, offered to set up the meeting, which he did, for April 1, at 12 noon, a Monday. I had gone to Vickie Gainer the week before as I said earlier about the building in Sheffield Park, and she gave me the excel sheet on ECS which contained not only the information about the building, but the six checks totaling almost 5 million that had been written to ECS by the city. Based on evidence we received, the blatant lies we know that Ricky Ramie and Vickie Gainer told in their later FBI interviews, the BCSO presented to the FBI agent that when I came to the Sheriff, they already knew. Vickie Gainer told the FBI agent that *she* alerted me about the ECS fraud instead of that when I came in asking questions, requesting information about ECS, she went into a panic. They made it seem as though I only came in to the Sheriff with the information because Michael White had been arrested and I was afraid that the "conspiracy" was going to come out, and so to get ahead of it, that I was the whistleblower. This is how the prosecutors presented my going to the Sheriff in the hearings, that somehow, I felt the "jig" was up and so I went running to law enforcement to try and make myself appear innocent.**

**Jimmy Stanford, the lead investigator was corrupt and at Derwin White's bidding; he alerted Derwin White when the raid would be at ECS, Derwin White directed Mickey White to have the invoices prepared which implicated me in the illegal property cleanup, and the invoices were planted in plain sight on top of the trash to be "found" in the raid. Mickey, in his interview, stated that he delivered the invoices to Derwin White the night before Jimmy Stanford led the raid on Erosion Control Specialist, Inc.**

The following is a report conducted by Lt. Jeremy Mathis, an investigator with the Bay County Sheriff's Office. I do not include his entire report here, because it is 63 pages long; however, I do include large portions of the report with my comments:

Again, notice that the investigation begins after April 1st, 2019, the day I went to the Sheriff's office, and then afterward, went back to the city to gather copies of the invoices and purchase orders relating to ECS that he requested. Their investigation into Lynn Haven corruption began with information that I provided.

I also believe that the Sheriff's office was and is involved in widespread corruption stemming from their relationship with Derwin White and GAC; a source who is a former deputy, reports that Derwin was in and out of the Sheriff's office on a regular basis, as though he had his own key.

Throughout the report, Mathis uses the pronoun, "myself and Major Stanford" which are his words; I refrained from correcting the grammar.

On April 3, 2019, I was made aware of a complaint of possible fraud involving the former city manager of Lynn Haven, Michael White, and a company called Erosion Control Specialist, Incorporated. I was informed that along with Major Jimmy Stanford, Investigator Aubrey Chance, and Crime Analyst Lindsey Miller, I would be assigned to conduct this investigation.

Mathis does not mention my name as the whistleblower in his "I was made aware of a complaint." Almost every report filed by the BCSO refers to information obtained from the "city," or other phrases, rather than stating that the Mayor of Lynn Haven brought the complaint, although some of the reports do mention that I "met with the Sheriff" or "the Sheriff met with the Mayor". They are deliberately careful with how the reports refer to me to make sure I am not seen as the "whistleblower," since I was a target of their investigation as soon as I walked out of the meeting with Sheriff Ford and Lynn Haven Police Chief Ricky Ramey on April 1st.

On April 4, 2019, myself and Major Jimmy Stanford met with Amanda DeLonjay, an accounting clerk for the city of Lynn Haven. Mrs. DeLonjay said she has been employed with the city for approximately 15 years. She said she is in charge of paying invoices, employees, taxes, and other expenditures. Mrs. DeLonjay said she became suspicious of the payments being made to ECS when the amount of the payments exceeded the amount, $35,000, which requires a request for bids according to city rules. Mrs. DeLonjay said she took this information to her supervisor, but would be instructed to make the payments to ECS by City Manager Michael White. She said she has made payments in excess of $4,000,000.00 to ECS since the hurricane, while being told not to pay other outstanding bills owed by the city. Mrs. DeLonjay also talked about a company called Greenleaf, which would also be paid while other accounts were left in arrears. In speaking with Mrs. DeLonjay, she said some of the work was suspicious including $85,000 for the removal and replacement of sidewalks in Sheffield Park, paying $450.00 a load for fill dirt, and the fact that ECS was paid to build a building at the park. Mrs. DeLonjay also talked about a painting job at the fire department where ECS was paid $8,000.00 to prime half of the building, when the paint was already purchased by the city. According to her husband, Fire Chief DeLonjay, a bid was already out to paint the entire building with a total price of $11,000.00. Chief DeLonjay said he was instructed to sign the purchase order for payment to ECS for this paint job by Michael White.

**Amanda Delonjay's interview is included earlier, but my question still remains, if she and her husband, the fire chief and the emergency management director for the city, knew something was wrong with ECS, why did they not speak up to the Commission? They had both been with the city many years; even if they did not like me, there were two longtime commissioners, Antonius Barnes and Rodney Friend who they did like and had known for many years and who they could have alerted. Why did they remain silent? Rodney Friend apparently knew something was wrong and said nothing, according to former attorney Rob Jackson. Yet, there is not one interview with Rodney Friend from either the Bay County Sheriff's Office or the FBI. If they interviewed him, James and I did not get a copy of the interview. Rodney Friend is another elected official who did not seek re-election and slithered away in the midst of the corruption investigation; text messages between Mickey White and Michael White speak of Mickey White being asked to pour a driveway for Commissioner Friend, but there is no record in the discovery we were given of the Sheriff's Office or the FBI questioning Commissioner Friend.**

Also on April 4, Major Stanford and myself met with Bobby Baker, the public works director for the city of Lynn Haven. Mr. Baker said ECS came to be involved with city clean-up when the amount of work became overwhelming for the city employees to handle. According to Mr. Baker, Michael White called ECS in to help, and Mr. Baker considered ECS and its employees to be working directly for Michael White. In speaking with Mr. Baker, he said he considered it suspicious that the ECS crews were used to clean up Osceola Point, a totally private gated subdivision. Mr. Baker said the city had a very strict policy against working on private property, and said he would not have sent his workers into that subdivision based on that policy. According to Mr. Baker, ECS employees were removing debris from Osceola Point, then placing it on the right of way on Iowa Avenue for city employees or other contract debris haulers to pick up. Mr. Baker said he also believed ECS was working on Michael White's private property possibly at the time they were being paid by the city of Lynn Haven. He further referenced both ECS and Greenleaf getting fuel from the city yard with the permission of Michael White and believed as part of the reimbursement to them they would be being paid for fuel costs. Mr. Baker said logs were available for those who obtained fuel from the city yard, which could be obtained by him and turned over to the Sheriff's office investigators.

**Osceola Point is the private, gated community in which Commissioner Dan Russell lives, and he denies it was cleaned by the City. Russell was an un-indicted co-conspirator who was never charged with either the property cleanup or the pro bono contract he signed with WorldClaim, the City contracted public adjuster.**

On April 8, 2019, I spoke with Donnie Jacobs, an investigator with the Florida Department of Business and Professional Regulation. Mr. Jacobs confirmed that the structure built in Sheffield Park would require a licensed contractor as long as city employees were not completing the work. As of this date, I have been unable to locate any indication of Mickey White or any of his employees possessing a Florida Contractor's License, which would permit them to complete structural, plumbing, roofing, or electrical work.

**This is the building which James Finch asked me to check into to see who was building it and who had bid the contract. When I went to Vickie Gainer, I discovered a lot more than the building being built without a contract; I discovered the five million paid to ECS by the City.**

Also on April 8, 2019, myself and Inv. Chance traveled to the Osceola Point neighborhood. We knew from his text messages that Michael White was asked about cleaning a drainage ditch in this property as it ran directly off of Iowa Ave. During the investigation, we learned that this neighborhood is private property for which the city of Lynn Haven has no responsibility. We were able to locate a connector ditch between Iowa Avenue and the Osceola Point neighborhood, but it was overgrown and didn't appear to have been maintained or cut back in several months. Photographs were taken which were added to this case file.

**According to Baker, large amounts of debris were stacked on the**

**road that came from Osceola Point; apparently the debris didn't come from the easement drainage ditch.**

On April 10, 2019, we went to the Osceola Point neighborhood, where ECS employees had done clean up work post hurricane. A report from the Lynn Haven Police Department identified an ECS employee, Gary Temple, being hurt in the neighborhood, specifically at 700 Rue Esplanade. Myself and Lindsey Warren traveled to that address and could see a drainage ditch behind the residence, however, could not determine where it would run off water from Iowa Avenue, given the distance apart from each other and there being no obvious drainage connection between Iowa Avenue and 700 Rue Esplanade. The ditch behind the 700 address appeared to dump into the bay. I also noted that the area of the ditch appeared to contain a lot of debris, such as tree limbs, and did not appear to have been cleaned up. The area noted on April 8, was found to have a for sale sign on it, and appeared to be a low-lying lot, not a drainage ditch.

**The BCSO investigators continue to shoot holes in Commissioner Russell's story, and he was named in the November indictment, but then, he was never charged, as I have said several times.**

On April 11, 2019, I met with Judge Chris Patterson and presented him a search warrant application for ECS business office located at 3620 Frankford Avenue. Judge Patterson did find probable cause and did issue the warrant for the business.

On April 12, 2019, myself and other investigators from the sheriff's office served the search warrant on ECS. We arrived at about 0800 hr., and made contact with three employees in the office, Danny Henley, Jamie Schulte, and Brandon Mayhann. Schulte was provided with a copy of the search warrant for the business, at which time overall photographs were taken by Inv. Matt Cutcher (BCSO Crime Scene Investigator,) and the search was begun.

**The photographs taken at ECS included the planted invoices with my address on them implicating me in a property cleanup billed to the city.**

While on-scene, I learned an employee Johnny Vickers had been taken into custody in reference to outstanding warrants. Vickers was transported to the office, where I conducted an interview with him. Vickers said he had been working for ECS for about 2 years. He said he went to work the day after the storm and the company began working in Lynn Haven. According to Vickers, one of the first jobs he was assigned was working on Michael White's house in Lynn Haven, doing work including tarping the roof, replacing windows, and doing demolition inside the house. Vickers said he also worked on Mayor Anderson's house as well as an attorney's house. Although he could not identify the attorney he said the house was in the area of Louisiana Avenue and the clothing in the yard had his name on them.

**Mr. Vickers makes a reference to working on the Mayor's house, but he doesn't say where the house is, or how he knew whose house it was.**

On April 15, 2019, I began to review the contents of the Apple iPhone collected from Mickey White's truck. In one text chain, I saw messages between Mickey White and Keith Baker, (then the city of Panama City's Parks & Recreation Head) where they were talking about bidding a job. White begins the conversation with, "I've got the three quotes." Baker responds, "Need that text." White sends a text to Baker, which says "Greenleaf 22,500 ECS 15,000 and Precision Concrete 25,000, with a follow up text that says "ECS 15,000" Baker responds to these messages that says, "How about $19,500, $14,750 and $18,000." These messages are sent on April 25, 2018 between 1637 and 1939 hours. On April 26, 2018, at 1841 hrs, Baker sends a message to White which reads, "Need you to drop off those quotes," to which White responds," Can you text me your email address"

**The investigation would lead to County Commissioner Keith Baker's arrest; however, he was not federally indicted. He was charged by the State Attorney, pleaded *nolo contendere*, adjudication withheld, two years' probation, and so is not a convicted felon. He made over $150,000 driving a trash truck for Mickey White in the City of Lynn Haven according to testimony while he was a sitting Bay County Commissioner.**

Samantha said on January 15, 2019, she was called by Mickey and told to meet him at the city hall in Lynn Haven. She said when she and Mickey walked in, Jay Moody, Michael White, and another official was there she believed to be named Ramie. She said the meeting was in reference to the manner in which she completed their invoice documentation and the fact that it needed to be done a different way. She said she was instructed on a different manner to complete the documentation and said on her computer which was seized during the search warrant, would be a spreadsheet where she had begun completing the paperwork in the manner she was told to do it.

**Samantha Lind was a clerk for Mickey White and ECS. What I pointed out in my defense about this meeting is that City Manager Michael White and the city's financial consultant, Jay Moody, are present, and the police chief, Ricky Ramie is there. My question has been, why was the police chief included in the financial meetings raising questions with ECS but not the Mayor?**

Mrs. Lind was asked about private residences she completed invoices for, and said she was asked to do 3 or 4 invoices for residences on the

Wednesday or Thursday before we did the search warrant on ECS. She believed these addresses to be on Tennessee Avenue and Virginia Avenue, but didn't remember the names attached. According to her, Mickey White told her what equipment and labor to bill for, as well as the date to put on the invoice. She said she printed four copies of the invoices for Mickey, and initially they had the date she made the invoice, but he told her to back date them to a date he identified using his cell phone.

**These are the fabricated invoices which Derwin White directed Mickey to bring to him the night before the raid on ECS.**

On May 20, 2019, myself and Major Stanford spoke with Kelly Tram, a former employee of the city of Lynn Haven. Mrs. Tram said she was initially hired as an administrative assistant in the police department, however, was asked to apply for the city attorney position, as she is licensed to practice law in the state of Texas. (Mrs. Tram said she was awaiting passage of a law which would have allowed her to practice law in Florida, based on her husband's military career.) Ms. Tram said she was given a position as the assistant to the city manager, specifically dealing in FEMA related issues. Ms. Tram said she went back to work on the Monday after the hurricane (October 15, 2018) and was working as a liaison between the city and FEMA. She said almost immediately, she saw a bill from Greenleaf which was concerning to her, based on the fact that the bill encompassed October 1 through October 18 for $16,000 and another from October 15 through October 31, which was for $55,000.00 She said she, along with Vicki Gainer, confronted Josh Anderson about the bills, and said the first included their normal contracted work, which she believed to be suspicious given the work was entirely after the hurricane, and due to the debris down, he would not have been able to cut grass. Ms. Tram said she recommended to Vicki Gainer that neither of these bills be paid. Mrs. Tram also said she believed the bills for the concession stand at Sheffield Park to be suspicious, as it was for approximately $200,000, which she could build a house for. She said she recommended a work stop order on this project, based on the amount of money being charged. Mrs. Tram said as the FEMA person for the city, she believed it to be suspicious that meetings would be held specifically about FEMA or payments being made, and she would not be invited. She said she believed others involved in those meetings, such as Chris Forehand from Panhandle Engineering, were not needed while she was excluded. Ms. Tram said during one meeting, she and Mayor Anderson walked in, and even Mayor Anderson was questioning certain parties involvement. Mrs. Tram said in the initial billing from ECS, the math didn't add up, which was caught by Andy, an employee of Tetra Tech. She said at that time, Julie Higbee, a city employee, was tasked with completing the oversight of the invoice, to ensure the figures matched what was being billed. She also said Michael White made clear after the storm that all bills over $2,000 had to go through him and could not be paid unless approved by him. In speaking with Mrs. Tram, she said the considered the friendships between contractors and the city manager to be suspect, and considered Josh Anderson, Mickey White, and Panhandle Engineers to be who she was specifically talking about. She said the business of the city was ran by Michael White, while the mayor acted as a liaison to the residents and business owners of the city. We asked Mrs. Tram if she could think of anything else she believed to be out of the ordinary, and she said she believed GAC billing the city of Lynn Haven, when they were sub-contracted to Ashbritt was certainly not normal practice, and when she saw that bill she also recommended it not be paid, as she believed it may lead to a double billing situation. Mrs. Tram said due to stress being caused by her employment, she decided to leave her position, and said this became effective on about April 10, 2019.

**What stands out to me about Kelly Tram's interview is that Vickie Gainer did not stop payments to ECS and Greenleaf until after I went to her and asked for a copy of the ECS file. Kelly also verifies that financial meetings were taking place with interesting attendees and *without* the Mayor; she also verifies that Michael White was in charge of running the city, while I served as a liaison to the people and to the business owners. The FBI agent told the grand jury, in the initial indictment, that I was the head of the city and that I supervised Michael White. Completely untrue. All he had to do was read the City Charter to see that Lynn Haven was a city-manager form of government, but he did not bother to do so until after the first indictment. The Government's description to the grand jury of the Mayor's authority and job description changed with each new and improved indictment.**

On May 22, 2019, while leaving Regan's house, we drove by 511 Tennessee Avenue, the home of Margo and Lee Anderson. We noticed a black golf cart, with an aftermarket lift and tires, sitting in their driveway which resembled the one described by Mr. Brannon, that was purchased by the city of Lynn Haven and had since gone missing. Pictures were taken of the golf cart and sent to Mr. Brannon. He said it appeared to be the same golf cart to him. Those pictures have been transferred to the sheriff's office drive for use in this investigation. A video found on the Lynn Haven Facebook page shows Anderson and her husband in what appears to be the same golf cart in the Lynn Haven Christmas Parade.

**Robert Brannon, the Lynn Haven Facilities Maintenance manager had apparently told the investigators that I had stolen the golf cart that City Manager Michael White had assigned to me after the hurricane; it was not missing; everyone knew I had it. Why would I**

have used it in the Christmas Parade for the whole town to see if I was doing something I wasn't supposed to be doing? Commissioner Russell, and Police Chief Ramie were irritated that I had the golf cart and made a huge issue of it as I described earlier. Why in the world if the two BCSO investigators were driving by staring at the golf cart in my yard, did they not just pull in and ask me about it? I was the Mayor of the City; they knew me. They just did not want to hear anything I had to say. They were on a mission for the Sheriff and Derwin White. They also have the incorrect address for my former home; it should be 513 not 511. The golf cart saga continues in paragraph 132 of Investigator Mathis' report as he speaks again to Bobby Baker, Public Works Director:

While speaking with Baker, I asked him about the golf cart which was purchased by the city. He said he felt that transaction was out of the normal course of city business, as he had to send a mechanic to Jacksonville with $5,000 in cash to get this golf cart, at the direction of Michael White. He said cash transactions are not a part of city business and also said three bids should have been obtained for a transaction over $3,000.00 He further said the golf cart, which is on the fixed asset list for the city, was supposed to have been purchased for the use of the special events employees, however was almost immediately given to the mayor for her use, further saying the special events employees didn't even know a golf cart was purchased for them.

Bobby does not mention here that the golf cart was assigned to me the day after Hurricane Michael to use for delivering supplies to the residents who were older or could not walk to the area behind the old city hall where supplies were being distributed. I had no idea how the golf cart was purchased, but Bobby was a longtime city employee, and if he knew the city manager made a cash purchase which should not have been made, he should have come to a member of the commission. Many of the Lynn Haven City employees were complicit in their silence in the weeks and months after the storm, in their omissions of information, and in giving false information.

We also talked about the use of city paid crews to clean up employees' houses, specifically Michael White's house on Hwy 20, Margo Anderson's house and the drainage ditch in Dan Russell's subdivision. Baker said this work was completely outside of what the city should have paid for saying it was a matter of city officials taking advantage of the situation. He said although there is a 20' easement behind Anderson's house, this easement is on her neighbor's property, and not hers. He also said the fact that trees fell on her property are not the responsibility of the city, and instead were her responsibility, just as all the other property owners in the city had to take care of. He said he knew that building maintenance and leisure service employees were used on White's property on Hwy 20 as he had to send a mechanic up there to get a city truck running. He again verified that no work should have been completed in Osceola Point, as this is a completely private subdivision and not in the scope of the city's responsibilities for clean-up, although he knew the city sent crews in there to clean up.

**Baker is the first one, although accidentally, to point out, that even the easement that was cleaned behind my house by the City was not on my property but abutted my property and was owned by the neighbors. Bobby Baker was not part of the cleanup and as far as I know he never visited my home to look or even to say hello to me in the first days after the storm, but if he had done so, he would have seen that my family had already cut the trees off the pole barn and even off the city right of way that he was responsible for a full month before the day that Mickey White and ECS showed up to clean the easement. My family had also cut the trees that were lying across 6ᵗʰ street, the street that runs beside my former home to allow traffic to pass through. He was all too anxious to throw me under the bus because I had been very critical of his job performance both before and after I was elected Mayor.**

On August 30, 2019, myself and Inv. Chance made contact with Jacqueline Vickers who was also an employee for ECS post hurricane. Vickers said she was mainly cleaning city owned properties, specifically the parks, city hall, and the sports complex, however she said she did work on other projects like the mayor's house, a house in the country club, and a drainage ditch in a gated community on the East side of Hwy 77. Vickers said at the mayor's house, she and about 9 other workers cleared trees from the yard, moving them to the side of the road for later pickup. She said she did not recall any trees leaning on the pole barn or power lines with the exception of one on the side of the road, right at the corner of the property. Vickers estimated she was at the mayor's house for "several hours," but only on one day, and said when she left, Virgil Anderson gave her a deep freezer which was sitting on the side of the road.

**This testimony, as well as others, was exculpatory for me in the hearings because Mickey White and others had several different testimonies ranging from one day to several days they were "at my property". I believe that the ECS workers in some cases, may have thought they were cleaning my property, because there was certainly not a line drawn showing them where my small yard of 150 x 50 ended and the easement began; there were no trees on my lot at all, and when she referred to one tree right at the corner of the property, the city right of way takes most of my front yard; the only tree right at the corner of my property would have been where the easement**

meets the city right of way near the broken power pole. The city right of way on the south and west sides of my lot was thirty feet from the middle of the street. One can literally jump from my former front porch and be on city right of way.

On November 14, 2019, SA Borghini asked that we conduct interviews with the members of the board of directors for the Osceola Point Homeowners Association in reference to the cleanup of the drainage ditch in that subdivision. He also provided written correspondence to Mrs. Vicki Gainer, dated April 26, 2019, pertaining to this cleanup which was signed by all members of the HOA board. The main question to be addressed was any agreement, in writing, from an employee of the city of Lynn Haven which originally accompanied this correspondence from the HOA.

On November 15, 2019, we made contact with Chris Donlan the secretary of the Osceola Point HOA, and one of the signers of the letter to Gainer. Donlan said he was told about the agreement by Dan Russell, further saying he was never told which city employee agreed to the clean up of the ditch. When asked about the letter written to Gainer, Donlan said he believed this correspondence was written to cover the HOA's agreement, even though the entirety of the letter was written by Dan Russell, (Osceola Point HOA President, and Lynn Haven City Commissioner) and he was not present for the talks between Russell and the city of Lynn Haven, and also said he never saw anything in writing from any city employee agreeing to the clean-up of the ditch.

At about 1020 hrs, we made contact with James (Jay) Moody, the Treasurer of the Osceola Point HOA, and a signer on the letter to Gainer. Moody, like Donlan, said he was told by Russell, prior to the first of 2019, (unknown exact date) that the city agreed to clean the ditch. He said he recalled an e-mail received from Russell which talked about the city agreeing to clean the ditch, but didn't think it covered who the employee was who agreed for the city to undertake this work. Moody said he would try to locate the emails concerning these matters and send them. Also like Donlan, Moody said he was not a part of these communications with the city, and was relying on what Russell told him for his knowledge of the agreement. Moody said he agreed to sign the letter provided to the city, as it only recapped the conversation he had with Russell, and did not encapsulate other details he was not told. In speaking with Moody he said this drainage issue had been an ongoing issue with the city for several years, and at one point he talked to a friend who recommended telling the city they were going to block the ditch and not allow the water to flow through the HOA property.

**Chris Donlan, the HOA secretary referred to above, is also the resident of the property referred to earlier in this report, 700 Rue Esplanade, where the "ditch" that Russell claimed was cleaned was**

not cleaned, according to the investigators, indicating that all of the debris hauled out of Osceola Pointe did not come from cleaning the ditch, or the "easement." Donlan denies knowing anything about an agreement with the city other than what Dan Russell has told him; Jay Moody, like Donlan, tells the investigators that he relied on Russell for the information about the "verbal agreement." Russell's "verbal agreement" does not exist except in the fantasy letter he wrote to Vickie Gainer.

At about 1499 hrs., we made contact with Daniel Russell at his home in Osceola Point. Russell said he spoke with Michael White about getting the ditch cleaned as he was concerned for possible flooding in the area of Iowa Avenue, (immediately West of the subdivision.) Russell said he could not recall exactly when this agreement was made, and confirmed nothing was put in writing between the two. He said prior to becoming a commissioner, he was trying for years to get the ditch cleaned out and could not as the city employee in charge of storm water, (believed to be Robert Brannon), would not agree to maintain the ditch. Russell said this has been an on-going issue which basically started when he moved into Osceola Point. Russell said at one point, he told the city he would block the ditch so the water could not flow through and was told that a state statute prohibits the stopping of flowing water, therefore legally he could not block the ditch. Russell also expressed concern for the neighbors outside of the HOA, saying one lady came to his former business complaining about flooding from the HOA. (We talked to this neighbor, Brenda Caldwell, on August 30, and she confirmed there was no flooding post hurricane on Iowa. Avenue.) I asked Russell about other interviews we conducted where Michael White was overheard telling him the city could not clean the ditch in the private subdivision, and Russell said he, "did not recall," any such conversation. I asked Russell if he could send me the emails between himself and HOA board concerning the city cleaning the ditch, and he agreed saying he never deleted any correspondence and would find them and forward to me. During the conversation about maintaining e-mails, I made a comment about the ease in, "doctoring," the contents of e-mails. Russell replied, "yeah, like those invoices?" He then began talking about being shown the invoices for clean up at the mayor's house and the dates and amounts not being correct. We did not talk about this with Russell, however the fact that he immediately connected my comments to those invoices was interesting.

This interview with Russell is one day before the FBI came to my house at night to interview me, November 18, 2019. The fact that Russell knew about the fake invoices which had been used to build a case against me is indeed interesting; his neighbor, Brenda Caldwell, who says there was no flooding on Iowa Avenue after Hurricane

Michael, blows a hole in both Dan Russell's and Chris Forehand's testimony of flooding on Iowa could cause an emergency situation if the "easement" in Osceola Pointe was not cleaned.

On November 17, 2019, I received a second and third e-mail from Russell. One was an e-mail sent to the Osceola Point HOA asking permission to send the previously mentioned correspondence to Mrs. Gainer at Lynn Haven and included an unsigned copy of the letter. Third e-mail is from Moody to the remainder of the board speaking specifically about the fence around the lift station as far as type of fence to be installed and who they would use for the installation. (It is important to note that the fence has still not been installed around the lift station in Osceola Point).

The next two paragraphs, #184 and #185 from Mathis' report refer to subpoenas which were issued after the arrest of Michael White, Mickey White, Shannon Rodrigez, Josh Anderson (owner of Greenleaf, no relation to me), and David Horton.

On December 19, 2019, I received two subpoenas from SA Borghini who asked me to serve them. One of the subpoenas was for Blue Moon Bar & Grill, via James Finch. Also on December 19, 2019, we made contact with Mr. Finch as his office on Hwy 390 and served the subpoena to him there.

The investigators wanted the records at the Blue Moon Bar and Grill, which James Finch owned, because I sang there on a weekly basis, and they were checking to see if he paid me to sing there. As I have said previously, I never charged James for my singing because we were friends, and the records showed that. As I would tell my lawyers later, the few times that I had traveled on James' plane since I had been Mayor, was paid for through my singing, an unspoken exchange between us; The state statute only requires reimbursement by an elected official the cost of a commercial plane ticket to fly on a private plane, and my singing more than adequately did this. Before I was Mayor, we traveled with Finch more frequently because of my husband's volunteer position on the race team Finch owned, and family vacations. After I became Mayor, I did not have time to travel like we had done in the past. We presented evidence to the prosecutors of all of this after I was indicted, but they were hell-bent that James Finch and the Mayor of Lynn Haven were corrupt. If the investigators had asked me about this instead of assuming the worst, and portraying my friendship with James Finch in the worst possible light, there would have been no indictment; but an indictment was what they were after, and as I said before, none of the BCSO investigators or the FBI SA Borghini ever questioned me until the night before the first indictment was unsealed, and I was already named in it as an un-indicted co-conspirator. "The dye had been cast."

The second subpoena was for Anderson Productions, via Margo Anderson. On December 27, 2019, myself and Major Stanford made contact with Margo Anderson at Lynn Haven City Hall, and she was served her subpoena there.

**Mathis and Stanford arrived at my office with the subpoena in front of the employees there to embarrass me. They knew where I lived, since they had apparently been driving by my house taking photos of the "stolen" golf cart. After I was named in the indictment of November 19, 2019, my brother had convinced me to hire an attorney, which I did, on Friday, the day after Thanksgiving. My brother had a list of names given to him by a dear friend who is also an attorney, and after calling several on a holiday weekend, Ron Johnson, a criminal attorney from Pensacola answered his phone and agreed to meet with me on the first Saturday in December. I paid my first $10,000 to secure an attorney, and on December 27th, I called him to tell him I had received a subpoena for business and tax records to be delivered to a grand jury in January.**

On February 12, 2020, myself and Major Stanford conducted interviews of four city of Lynn Haven employees in reference to a bid review package submitted. The bid was for fencing on two city properties, and several mistakes were found in the bid review. All of these mistakes seemed to point the outcome to GAC, and away from the other two bidding companies.

We first interviewed Joe Footen, director of facility maintenance for the city, and one of the group of three employees who reviewed the bid packages and graded those packages. Footen said he was hired by Mike White approximately 1 ½ years prior to our contact with him. He said he was a part of four bid review teams for the city, and pointed out one in which White's Wrecker was awarded a contract for the city's towing. He said when he reviews the bids, he considers other work he knows the company to have done in the past, specifically saying he has had issues in the past with McFatter Fence Company's work. He said even though the bid packages covered two jobs, he would have completed one review form for the entire bid. Major Stanford pointed out to Footen that his math was incorrect, and he said it was an honest mistake, and nothing intentionally done by him to try to get GAC the contract. Footen denied he had been in contact with the owners or employees of any of the bidding companies about the bid, although it would not be uncommon for them to call him inquiring about specifics of the job, or materials required if that information was not listed in the RFQ.

**City staff was used routinely to score bid sheets, or qualifications**

sheets. Interesting that Stanford takes Footen's word that he made a "math mistake" referring to GAC getting the job, and Vickie Gainer took the item off the city commission agenda because of a "math mistake."

Next, we spoke with Julie Higby, who would receive paperwork from the review committee. Ms. Higby said the fencing bid was taken off of the city commission agenda due to issues with the scoring. She said when she receives the paperwork, she only looked at the bottom-line total score, and didn't add the scores herself to ensure accuracy. She did say that Vickie Gainer came to her and told her to take the job off of the agenda as it was, "pointed out," that the scoring was not correct.

After Ms. Higby, we spoke with Bobby Baker, another city employee who reviewed the bids and made a recommendation on who should be awarded the job. Baker scores were also noted to be lower than the other two grading employees. Baker said he didn't grade for items not included in the bid, like warranty of work, therefore giving these grades a 0. He said he thought the bid process for this particular job was, "a little weird," as it did ask him to grade for items not specifically requested in the bid packages. Baker also confirmed that he had no contact with any of the bidding company's owners or employees prior to his review of the bid, although he did know some of them from other jobs performed for the city.

We also asked Baker about the easement on the mayor's property as we heard he was changing his view on the clean up work paid for by the city. Baker said he never changes his position on that, saying the debris on Anderson's property was her responsibility to clean up. He confirmed there is an easement on the property behind hers, but said that does not encompass her property, nor is it the responsibility of the city to clean up what fell on her property from the easement. Baker again explained that the easement gives the city access to the property to maintain the piped ditch that is there, however the property itself is still privately owned and not a city property.

**Baker, again, omits crucial information that he knew to be true. The entire ditch is not piped, and the city has done much more than just "access" the easement in the past. Baker does not mention the community service workers from the Sheriff's Department and the partnership that had occurred cleaning this easement and others; the photos we presented in federal court showed that the trees which had fallen on my property had already been cut and pushed back onto the easement before the city came to clean the easement a month later. Also, a large portion of my former property is city right of way on both the south and the west side of the lot; if the Sheriff's investigators or the FBI agent had bothered to come to my house and ask me about the property cleanup, I could have walked the lot with**

them and shown them the property lines and the photos of the cleanup done a month before the City/ECS came out.

Finally, we spoke with Greg Kidwell, who said on his grading form he made an error in grading a line that had a maximum score of 10 with a 20. He said some instead of all items being a 1-10 score, some are 20 and even 40, and he believed he looked at the wrong line when tabulating his score. I asked Kidwell about his scoring for warranty where there was no mention of warranty in the deed and he said he graded that based on his knowledge of past jobs the company had with the city, and what they would do to fix issues down the road, calling his warranty score, "subjective." He said he has had dealings with Bay Fence and GAC in other jobs, however, like the other grading employees, did not have contact with them prior to submitting his grade on this particular bid.

**Three city department heads made "mistakes" on scoring the same bid sheet, but nothing more was said about this. Adam Albritton in his interview of September 10, 2021, also refers to another bid sheet, the scoring of Tetra Tech, which was scored by Vickie Gainer, Michael White, and Kelly Battistini, in which Tetra Tech was given the contract. Albritton stated that he had stepped outside from the meeting to get a soft drink from under the tent, when he overheard Chris Forehand telling Michael White to "reconsider his discussion" that "I've helped you get here, and I am going to help you get a raise" as he strong-armed Michael to select Tetra Tech because Michael was considering another company that Jay Moody had suggested. According to Albritton, Michael went back inside and advised they would be going with Tetra Tech. HR Director Kelly Battistini, Vickie Gainer and Michael White reviewed and ranked the bid submitted. Tetra Tech was ranked the highest and awarded the bid. Chris Forehand was senior management with Tetra Tech, and he also subcontracted his brand-new company formed October 23, 2018, just thirteen days after the hurricane, PEDS, to Tetra Tech for debris monitoring. He also shared his office space, Panhandle Engineering with them. Forehand was paid millions by the city of Lynn Haven through his new company PEDS, in the aftermath of the storm.**

On March 12, 2020, at about 1400 hours, SA Borghini and I made contact with **Joel Schubert,** the Assistant County Manager for Bay County, at the Bay County Administrative Building on W. 11th Street. Schubert has been in this position since July 2017 and worked as the city manager for Lynn Haven prior that. We wanted to speak with him about his time at Lynn Haven as well as his knowledge of the hauling contracts post hurricane.

Schubert said he was mainly covering FEMA reimbursement after the hurricane as well as was placed in charge of temporary housing. He said he was aware that several independent haulers showed up in Bay County after the hurricane wanting to haul debris. He specifically named GAC as one of these companies, and said all of the independent haulers were pointed to Ashbritt or Crowder Gulf as the county was relying on them to handle the debris pickup and transportation. He said like Murray, they were also counting on Landfall Strategies and Tetra Tech to look out for the best interest of the county, however felt like Landfall had let them down in that aspect. He said the county was using three levels of, "eyes" to oversee the incoming invoices, including the haulers, the monitors, and clerk of courts, who acts as the county's comptroller. He said he did recall receiving phone calls from Derwin White wanting money from the county from retainage, and also said he was aware that Bob Majka and Bill Kinsaul were receiving similar calls from Derwin White.

**Joel Schubert does not mention his property cleanup by GAC which came out in the FBI Affidavit of August 2021 here.**

Schubert said he went to work for the city of Lynn Haven when Walter Kelly was mayor and said when Margo Anderson got elected, she wanted him to fire three long term employees. He said one of her platforms when running for election was getting rid of city employees who were costing the city too much money. He said he didn't initially fire these employees and said once Anderson was elected it became, "dirty politics." Schubert said Jim Slonina, owner of Panhandle Engineering was a, "quasi," city manager, even billing the city for attending meetings when his attendance was not required. Schubert said one point, he gave Slonina his invoice back and told him he would not be paying for him to attend meetings on his personal time. Schubert said with some persuasion of the city commission, he had two other engineering companies awarded contracts, even though initially they continued to use Panhandle.

**Schubert is so disingenuous here in his answers. I was elected Mayor by a 64% vote in 2015, and then re-elected six months after Hurricane Michael unopposed with a 92% approval rating. I had campaigned not on firing anyone, but in changing the salary scale of the City, because there were many, many employees doing manual labor type jobs not making a living wage. There were 10 employees making over 1.2 million per year, and six of them were married to each other. The 1.2 million was being transferred from the stormwater enterprise fund to general fund to pay these people, most of whom had not more than a high school diploma, including the police chief and his wife, (David and Charlene Messer) the fire chief and his wife, (John and Amanda Delonjay, and the public works director and his wife, Bobby and Laurie Baker.) The police chief and his wife together were making over $250,000 including benefits, and the average income of a Lynn Haven resident at that time was less**

than $30,000.  People were incredulous when they saw the salaries, as well as the nepotism within the ranks of the city employees.

Stormwater was a huge issue in the City of Lynn Haven, and mitigating flooding is still an issue today.  After I brought attention to this, Schubert stopped the transfers from the enterprise funds to the general fund.  The old guard city employees were furious with me for pointing out the salary disparity in the city.  The old mayor, Walter Kelley, had been in office for 17 years, was a pleasant old gentleman who cut ribbons and attended events, and Schubert and the other four commissioners were livid that I had won the election.  Every meeting was contentious as I brought up new ideas, and the commission room filled with residents anxious to speak and for the most part, supporting changes and new ideas I proposed, especially having evening meetings to allow more people to attend. As far as Jim Slonina, he would become partners with Chris Forehand, who is at the center of the entire Lynn Haven corruption case.  When I became Mayor, Panhandle Engineering had done 11 million dollars of engineering for which no projects had been constructed.  I brought attention to this fact, and I asked for an in-house engineer and an in-house attorney.  I also asked that we consider changing our accounting audit firm, since the City had the same one for over twenty years.  Joel did not like having an outspoken woman for the mayor, and apparently this interview was his opportunity to help throw me under the proverbial bus, accusing me of "dirty politics."

Schubert said initially upon election, Anderson "loved him." He said this came to a stop as soon as he told her no the first time, and she spent a couple of weeks not talking to him. He said Anderson didn't like the fact that Schubert wouldn't conform to how she, "did business." He said he also had issues with the city doing a request for qualifications for everything, to include pretty simple jobs like fencing or landscaping. Schubert said he changed this policy, and did change this type of work to a bid submission, with a qualification identification along with the bid.

I never "loved" Schubert as he states.  Even when I was campaigning for Mayor we clashed when I would meet with him for information that I requested for my campaign.  I have no idea what he is referring to when he says, "the first time I told her no," as though I were a child.  He had no power to do anything to me other than make a complaint to the commission, or to the state ethics board; I was an elected official, not his employee.  Schubert also proposed that the city manager have a $35,000 spending allowance without Commission approval, which passed with 4-1 vote; I was the dissenting vote.

Schubert talked about the ½ cent sales tax, which was passed in the county, and which the city got some of. He said there was a sum of money which was pulled from that income stream to do work on the city's roads, and Phoenix won the RFQ for those projects. He said he wasn't there when Phoenix was awarded the RFQ from the city, but said he believed Bobby Baker would have knowledge of that particular contract. Schubert said he did believe Finch and Anderson were "tight," but said he was never directed to award jobs to him, even saying when the commission was questioning a bid or proposal submitted by Phoenix, Anderson would, "remain quiet." He said he has heard of videos where Anderson and Finch are traveling together but hasn't personally seen them.

**Schubert has to tell the truth about how jobs were awarded to Phoenix because the commission minutes and videos are evidence that everything was done in the sunshine and by unanimous vote. It is interesting that he already knows that there are "videos" of my travel with Finch, when these did not appear publicly until several months later when I was indicted and WMBB TV had the videos. Joel knew that my husband was part of the race team at Phoenix, and he knew that we traveled occasionally, because if I was out of town for the weekend, I told him where I was going. At this point in time, the Lynn Haven investigation is headlines, my reputation has taken a nosedive because of it, and to be fair, Schubert is probably scared, because as the affidavit would show, there was plenty of stuff going on all over the county, with Schubert along with others implicated, but Sheriff Ford and his "corruption unit" were focused on me and James Finch.**

In paragraph 258 Mathis continues:

On August 19, 2020, I was assigned to the arrest team tasked with arresting Margo Anderson. We arrived at her Lynn Haven residence, and made contact with Virgil Lee Anderson, her husband. Anderson said she was in Jacksonville at their residence there, and had been for about a week. Anderson allowed consent to search the residence for her, and it was cleared without locating her. While other team members were clearing the house, Anderson asked me what she was charged with and I told him, "various fraud counts," from the federal grand jury. Anderson asked, "for what, she didn't do anything." I told Anderson that one of the counts involved the clean up of the yard by ECS employees and he then said their property bordered a city easement and so the city was responsible for any clean up of debris from the easement. I explained to Anderson that an easement only grants another party access to a piece of property, it doesn't mean they own the property. At that time, Anderson immediately pivoted in his statement to say the only trees cleaned up were in the roadway, that they had no trees down in their yard. When I told Anderson we had aerial photographs from right after the storm that showed that to be false, he discontinued his conversation with me. Margo Anderson was later located in Jacksonville and arrested there. A seizure warrant was served on the Anderson's RV, and after personal property was removed, it was driven to the sheriff's office by Inv. Aubrey Chance.

**The aerial photographs Mathis referred to do not show trees in my yard and we proved this in Federal court at the evidentiary hearing. Mathis does not mention that the media had been tipped off and were standing on the right of way filming the arrest team that it took to subdue a 64-year-old woman. They were so incompetent they had not even checked to see if their "target" was in town, and the RV was later returned to us after the humiliation they put my family through for over three years.**

In the afternoon of August 19, we watched the Lynn Haven Commission meeting, and overheard Commissioner Dan Russell say he was cleared of wrong doing in the first indictment, as his gated community had a city drainage ditch on the property. According to Russell, he verified that with the property appraiser. Knowing city employees had not acknowledged responsibility for that drainage ditch, we decided to make contact with the property appraiser and see what was in their records about the matter.

**This commission meeting is on video, and it is difficult for me to watch, even four years later. Commissioner Russell and City Manager Vickie Gainer are just smug in their demeanor.**

On August 20, 2020, myself and Major Stanford met with Dan Sowell, Bay County Property Appraiser at his office on W. 11$^{th}$ Street. Mr. Sowell said he could look and see what records they have in an effort to determine the responsible party for the drainage ditch, where ECS employees performed work. Mr. Sowell was able to provide a part of the deed, when the land was sold to the Osceola Point Land Owners, which is dated February 9, 1998. The dedication of the land specifically reads, "know all by these presents, that Sylvia Ann Calo, as trustee of the Calo Trust U/A last will & testament of Emogene Chapman Atwater, owner of the lands described and platted hereon, hereby dedicates to and for the private use of Osceola Point Land Owners Inc. all streets and drainage easements as designated on this plat "Osceola Point." A copy of this paperwork was provided to SA Borghini, as well a scanned and made an attachment to this case file.

**The BCSO investigators proved that Russell's claims were false, yet they chose never to indict him, on the property or the World Claim pro bono contract, or the text messages requesting tickets to be fixed by Chief Ramie. Why? Who protected him?**

On September 22, 2020, myself and SA Borghini met with Bill Gainey and his daughter Paula Jones at the FBI office. The meeting was in response to some photographs provided to the FBI by Gainey showing school board members working at a private residence after the hurricane.

Jones was asked about the photographs provided by Gainey, and said she lives close to Sandra Davis, the Assistant School Superintendent. She said she noticed Bay District School trucks at Davis' home, and between she and her husband they took photographs of the workers present. She said she can see Davis' backyard from her house, and said there were district maintenance personnel at Davis' house for several days. According to Jones there were several crews working there, and she talked to at least one of the crew members who acknowledged they shouldn't be there, but they had to, "do what they're told." Jones said as a teacher, she was never asked if she needed help cleaning up around her house, or had any major issues that could be fixed, specifically saying she was told, "they weren't for teachers." Jones said after the storm, she received an e-mail from her principal to make sure she survived the storm, but nobody inquired about her needing help with anything around her house. Notes Jones took around the time, identified the worker being at Davis' residence around the 23rd of October, 2018. SA Borghini is in possession of those notes written by Jones.

On October 5, 2020 I made contact with Collier "Wayne" Beach, in reference to this investigation. Beach is a former employee of Bay District Schools in their maintenance department and is believed to have information pertaining to this case.

Beach said after the hurricane, he did recall seeing trucks owned by Bay District Schools as well as a crew consisting of Lee Walters and other school board employees working on a house on Highpoint Rd. Beach said he didn't know who's house it was, and doubted he could find the house again, bus said he recalled them working on the roof of the house. Beach further said he was confident no work was done on private property that Bill Husfelt was not aware of saying Husfelt was aware of all of this type of work. He further said Husfelt may not be trutyful about his knowledge of it., but again assured me he was aware of it.

**Borghini presents evidence in the Affidavit of 2021 that work was done on a school board employee's home on Highpoint Rd referenced by Mr. Beach above.**

**I do not include any further interviews although there were many more, and both James and I believe there were interviews that we never saw, withheld by the Government as they did so much of the information for months, even years. My hope is that I have included enough that the reader may see how the investigation was conducted.**

**The Bay County Sheriff, Tommy Ford, was interviewed only once, as far as we know, and his interview was by telephone. He agreed to**

"cooperate in any way that he could" with the FBI in the investigation.

The goal of the Bay County Sheriff and his "public corruption unit," was to silence me, to punish me for exposing the corruption of Mickey White, the nephew of Derwin White, who along with City Manager Michael White, Adam Albritton, and others, defrauded the City of Lynn Haven of almost five million dollars. They also punished James Finch for coming to my defense and paying over a million dollars for me to have great defense attorneys; otherwise, my story would have ended differently. My bringing evidence to Sheriff Tommy Ford, forced the investigation of the county-wide corruption, and I believe had I not gone to Sheriff Ford, the investigation of Lynn Haven, Bay County, and of GAC and AshBritt would have never happened.

There are many civil lawsuits pending at this time against the City of Lynn Haven and the Bay County Sheriff's office, including mine, and my hope is that the civil courts will expose what the criminal investigators had no interest in doing, and while criminal statutes of limitations ran out in 2023, the trials in civil courts may finally bring some measure of justice to those who destroyed innocent lives with such calculated cruelty in order to protect themselves and their criminal enterprises.

"So do not fear, for I am with you; do not be dismayed, for I am your God.  I will strengthen you and help you; I will uphold you with my righteous hand." Isaiah 41:10

# 7  AND THEN THERE WERE TWO…CITY ATTORNEY ADAM ALBRITTON AND COMMISSIONER ANTONIUS BARNES PLEAD GUILTY; MAYOR ANDERSON AND JAMES FINCH INDICTED AGAIN IN THE SECOND SUPERSEDING INCICTMENT NOVEMBER 16, 2021

October 1, 2021

October first.  Over a year has passed since I was indicted, and the same ominous cloud looms over our lives without an end in sight.  I get up each morning, thankful for Buddy's ever-present morning kisses and paws in my face to get me out of bed by 7 a.m. to take him for his walk, then an hour spent reading the daily devotion and scriptures from *JESUS CALLING,* a book given to me by Julie Higby, the administrative assistant to the City Commission and City Manager when I was Mayor of Lynn Haven.

After Adam Albritton, the City Attorney, pleaded guilty last week, all is quiet as we wait for the government prosecutors to pursue their second superseding indictment (the third indictment against me and the second against James) in this case.  James and I have spoken several times over the last week, but there is really nothing to do except wait…wait to see if there are new charges, if charges have been dropped, if defendants have been added, or if the prosecutors have tried, for the third time , to write an indictment based on the lies of those who actually committed the crimes, complete with a narrative based on posts from Facebook, photographs and videos from the news media, and statements from city employees, temporary workers from during the aftermath of Hurricane Michael, and some recorded statements from individuals incarcerated as far away as Tennessee, who apparently worked for ECS and Mickey White.  Many of the witnesses were interviewed months and even years after actual events;

many employees despised the female Mayor who took office in 2015 and brought about change and progress in the City of Lynn Haven, exposing years of mismanagement of enterprise funds, shaking up an established way of doing things by an eighty-year old Mayor Walt Kelley, who had been in place for almost twenty years, and two City Managers who just did not like assertive, opinionated women like the Mayor, Joel Schubert, and Michael White.

Both James and I wanted to be witnesses for this third grand jury to be convened in this case, even with our attorneys advising against. We believed at this point we had nothing to gain by being silent, with the prosecutor only telling the grand jurors his narrative of lies, we wanted an opportunity to answer questions and to call out the prosecutors on what we believe has been blatant misconduct on their part in what "evidence" they have presented, left out, or misconstrued in the worse possible light in order to gain a conviction rather than find the truth. We had heard rumors that the grand jury might be convened in Pensacola rather than Tallahassee this time, and we did not know what day or days they would meet; our next hearing before Judge Mark Walker was October 26th, over three weeks from now, and so we presumed that whatever the next action to be taken by the prosecution is, will have to take place within the next two weeks as far as another superseding indictment.

My hope is for a trial date to be set for late November or early December, and that this nightmare could be over before Christmas. The thought of another Christmas like last year is unbearable; my Mom spent her last Christmas holiday in complete anguish, listening to the news media and wondering if her daughter would spend the rest of her life in federal prison. Three short months later she died; the stress and grief she had endured because of what happened to me was more than she could bear.

I sent more photographs and information to the attorneys this morning, documenting the days after Michael White resigned as City Manager, using the date stamped photographs on my phone to create the timeline of events which we will be using as evidence in the trial...evidence to show that I was the whistleblower in this case, not Vickie Gainer, not Sheriff Ford, and not even my friend and fellow Commissioner, Judy Tinder. The news media portrayed Commissioner Tinder as having found the "wrongdoing" in Lynn Haven as she made a motion for a forensic audit after I went to her to tell her of what I had found. Because I had been silent at the Commission meetings regarding the investigation and had answered "no comment" to the media when they asked questions about it, at Sheriff Tommy Ford's request, this fueled the fire of public opinion against me even more. Judy Tinder has been my friend for almost thirty years, and while she did call for a forensic audit after Michael White's arrest and resignation, she will also be the first to say that I am the one who told her what happened, the financial information I had found about ECS, literally by accident, and that I had gone to the Sheriff with the information. I have wished at least a thousand times that I had ignored him and called a press conference, telling the world what I had discovered in Lynn Haven, but I did as Tommy Ford asked, and made "no comment about the ongoing investigation." I trusted the Sheriff.

Why Sheriff Tommy Ford has stood silent about how this investigation started, with his pious expression, standing with the U.S. Attorney, the FBI investigators and entourage from Tallahassee, soaking up the spotlight of the media live announcements as I was removed from office, my life and reputation destroyed, is the question I long to ask him in person someday. The question will be a rhetorical one. I already know the answer. The Bay County Sheriff's Office is a corrupt organization; he and the corrupt investigators led by Major Jimmy Stanford, did what Derwin White directed them to do. .

I am anxious again today, feeling as though I cannot breathe. I need to talk with my Mom. I need for this to be over. Dear Lord, help me to remember that you are in control, not them. Tomorrow is my granddaughter's birthday party; she will be twelve years old and texted me last night at 10:36 p.m. wanting to know if I would be there; "absolutely" I replied. "Yay!" her text message answered. I sent her "The Bird Woman Song" from Mary Poppins, on YouTube, the lullaby I have sung to her hundreds of times since she was only weeks old. No reply. But I am sure she listened. I will go over to their house tomorrow to help get ready for the party, trying to do as I have promised myself; I will not think of the indictment or what is happening to me for the next two hours. I will enjoy these two hours with my granddaughter, soaking up each minute, watching her laugh, play with her friends in the flag football game that is planned, remembering how blessed I am to be a MiMi. They cannot take that away from me.

*When you pass through the waters, I will be with you; and when you pass through the rivers, they will not sweep over you. When you walk through the fire, you will not be burned; the flames will not set you ablaze. Isaiah 43:2*

## October 3, 2021

The Bishop led mass this morning, and his topic was marriage and family. I listened intently to his aging voice, the love of Christ so evident in his kind face. Forgiveness is what I am working on in my journey of faith, and I find it the most challenging concept right now. I have always been a forgiving person, always a peacemaker, looking for ways to find reconciliation, but now I find myself fighting a battle with bitterness, a desire for revenge, and although difficult to admit, on many days I find myself filled with hatred for those who have brought this upon me, and each day is a battle with depression, anxiety, literally a battle to keep my sanity. I am incarcerated by my own fears, my hatred of them, of what they have done to my life, my ability to function and to love my family. I blame them for my mother's untimely death, for the unrest in my home, for the complete exhaustion I feel after just about any activity or social event that I try to be a part of. As the bread of life from the eucharist melted upon my tongue I returned to my seat, and then quickly got up, went out a side door of the church, and walked quickly to my car. There I sat and cried, sobs wracking my chest until I could not cry anymore. After a few minutes, I drove to the beach, and ate lunch with my daughter, son-in-law and two granddaughters, keeping my sunglasses on, listening to the ocean, and trying to soak in another precious hour with those two little girls who had no idea what Mimi was going through. Always feeling as though this could be borrowed time, time which I would wish for later if things did not go well at trial.

After reading through the many recent Discovery documents finally given to our defense team, we realized that U.S. Attorney Keefe, Assistant U.S. Attorneys Coody, Kunz, and Grogan, Sheriff Tommy Ford, his investigators, and the local FBI agent, Larry Borghini who conducted many of the interviews, all of them, had this evidence before I was indicted; they knew I was not guilty of the charges of the property cleanup, World Claim Insurance charges, Erosion Control Specialist fraud, the motorhome and jet trip bribery.... they knew....and yet they went forward with their public corruption narrative, ruining my life, using my title of Mayor to inflame the public, the media, and to get the indictment from the grand jury.

They knew that Derwin White told his nephew, Mickey White, the owner of ECS, to create and forge invoices to the City of Lynn Haven showing a cleanup of my private property of almost $50,000. They knew that I told the World Claim Vice-President, Lauren Brubaker that I could not accept a pro bono contract and that she sent me another one, which I paid in full after my insurance company settled. They also knew that Commissioner Dan Russell, *did* sign a pro bono contract with World Claim, and *did* have his private gated neighborhood cleaned and charged to the City/FEMA, yet he remains protected and unindicted. Why?

They knew that every contract with Phoenix construction was voted on legitimately by the Lynn Haven City Commission and that my signature was on every document and check from the City because I was the Mayor, not because I was doing something shady or illegal. They knew all of this and still went forward, with U.S. Attorney Larry Keefe using public tax dollars to fund his nearly half-million dollar advertising account with Sachs Media of Tallahassee to publicize himself in hopes of remaining the U.S. Attorney retained by President Biden after President Trump lost the election of 2020.

Tonight, I cannot sleep again, and all day today I have been filled with all too familiar anxiety and tightness in my chest, knowing that the prosecutors are working on their second superseding indictment, getting ready to present half-truths, partial evidence, and testimony from those who have pleaded guilty hoping to gain a lesser sentence before another grand jury. How is it possible in the United States of America for a prosecutor to tell only his story to a grand jury? There is no reason for this to be secret anymore. I know they are working to indict me again, as James Finch does. James and I both want to testify in front of the grand jury, and our attorneys tell us this would be the worst thing we could do, that we could possibly be charged with making false statements, or worse. I do not understand why we cannot be present to refute what they are saying, to challenge the grand jury to consider listening to both sides if justice and truth is what they seek rather than just a conviction; this is the United States of America, but because our attorneys are not allowed in the grand jury with us, we are persuaded that it is not in our best interest.

We are still three weeks away from our next meeting with Judge Mark Walker, October 26th, 2021, and the new indictment will have been returned by then, complete with media fanfare. My hope is that the trial could happen before Christmas. That James and I can finally tell our story, show our evidence in a court of law before a jury who is allowed to hear both sides of the story, and if the Lord is willing, they will see what a complete sham, a witch hunt this has been, and our lives will be returned to us.

As I took the Eucharist in mass today, I took the first step in trying to forgive. I confessed to the Lord that I had not forgiven them and asked for His divine protection over my life as I try to be better. Try to love those who have wronged me; for only love and forgiveness from me will allow God to begin to work in their lives to turn this around, to open their eyes and their hearts to what they are doing. I do not love them yet, nor do I forgive them. Forgive me Lord for my weakness. I despise them.

October 10, 2021

Today is the third anniversary of Hurricane Michael, the storm that changed everything…the town, the people, the environment, and literally stole my life. I walked around Sheffield Park this afternoon with Buddy,, watching him enjoy each palm tree, each little rose bush or plant around the pond, and I listened to the laughter of the fifty or so children playing on the playground and riding scooters in a fast circle on the sidewalk which encircles the grassy area near the amphitheater, a view I once took in from the window of the Mayor's office, about twenty-five yards away from where I am standing, in the temporary buildings used by the City since the storm.

Two years ago, I worked so hard to organize a Commemoration Celebration of the storm; the celebration which was attended by none of the County Commissioners, none of the officials from other cities, not the Sheriff, and even the President of Florida Blue cancelled his appearance in which he was to make a fifty-thousand dollar donation to the Hurricane Relief Fund for the City of Lynn Haven residents. The Governor showed up for the afternoon celebration in Panama City to make a speech at Tommy Oliver stadium, but he didn't come to Sheffield Park where in 2018 he cinched the Governor's election by the rally heavily attended by the residents of Lynn Haven, determined to vote just three weeks after Hurricane Michael destroyed everything. There was a reason none of them came…they all knew that U.S. Attorney Larry Keefe, accompanied by the local Sheriff's investigators were about to hand down the first indictment in Lynn Haven in early November; the indictment against City Manager Michael White, David "Mickey White", David Horton, Josh Anderson, and Shannon Rodriguez, the indictment which would name me, the Mayor, as having used taxpayer dollars, reimbursed by FEMA, for cleanup and repairs to my private property. An absolute lie which would begin with the removal of a duly elected Mayor from office.

As I walked around the park, I watched the man who lives in the yellow house on the corner near First Baptist Church, the church where I spent my first Sundays as an infant in the nursery, over six decades ago. He was playing Halloween music, decorating his yard, living his life, not recognizing his former Mayor as I walked my dog around the park. He had placed a big sign on his fence on the day I was arrested and indicted, August 19, 2020…the sign the news reporter stood in front of as she announced to thousands of viewers in Bay County who knew my name, the hundreds and hundreds of students I had taught in the last twenty-five years, that the Mayor had been indicted as part of a conspiracy to steal almost five million dollars from the City she loves. The sign on the fence read, REMOVE MAYOR 'THIEF' ANDERSON.

"I wonder why they aren't having a ceremony today," I asked Buddy, as we continued to walk around the park.

"The entire town was destroyed three years ago today, and not one person killed, not one life lost, but there is no thanksgiving ceremony by the City, no remembrance" I said again, as Buddy continued enjoying the soft grass and the autumn sunshine in Sheffield Park. He wasn't worried because there was no ceremony today. "Just as I should not be," I told myself.

I had come back to Lynn Haven this week to meet my brother and the priest as we moved my Mom's body from the temporary mausoleum at Kent Forest Lawn Funeral Home to her mausoleum at the Lynn Haven Mt. Hope Cemetery on Friday, October 8th. The delivery of her mausoleum had been delayed because of Covid-19, and we had been waiting for closure since her passing on March 28th, over six months earlier. The mausoleum is beautiful, and Father Richard blessed her final resting place with Holy water and prayers, I sang *Amazing Grace,* as I held my brother Roy's hand, and then we were finished. We both sat down on the border of the adjacent grave site, and as I leaned against Roy's shoulder, I took a photograph of the front of the mausoleum, not knowing that it would contain our reflection, as though we were part of the stone. I miss her so much; we were blessed to have her as our mother, and maybe someday I will believe that what has happened to me was not why she died. She was so stressed, so full of grief with each news story, with the ugliness against her daughter; she died suddenly, no opportunity to say goodbye, but as we had always told each other, there were no unspoken words, no regrets, just love between all of us.

And almost like clockwork, on the night before we were to lay Mom to rest for the final time, a news story broke that former Commissioner Antonius Barnes had become the seventh person to plead guilty in the Lynn Haven conspiracy case, agreeing with the Government in his plea deal that he had accepted loans from James Finch as bribes for his votes on the Commission, along with the other government leak to the media that they anticipate another indictment against James Finch and Margo Anderson this month; our attorneys believe this second superseding indictment, the third indictment against me, in little more than a year, and the second against James in six months, will be handed down on Thursday, October 14th. The Government is so sure that they will get a True Bill, and indictment against us beforehand, that they can announce the date.

And so once again James and I wait. We wait to see the new lies, the new web spun by the prosecutors to try and charge us again and charge us in a manner that will not be thrown out as the previous two indictments have been for the most part and once again there will be a gut-wrenching week without sleep, with no peace for us or for our families. Undisturbed, restful sleep is a blessing to those who have not been indicted by the federal government. The government employees who bring this Hell do not miss sleep, nor do they worry about the lives they have ruined when they leave their offices in the afternoon and go home to family, to ball practice with their kids, or to have a glass of wine with colleagues. They are peaceful about their taxpayer supported salaries, their 98% conviction rate, knowing that they can indict almost anyone because the grand jury only hears the story and the evidence they present; most of the time the defendant is not even aware that a grand jury has been convened because it is done in secret.(I certainly didn't know I was about to be indicted in August of 2020, but the local law enforcement and their cronies certainly did from the chatter on social media the week before; hindsight is 20/20 as my grandmother used to say.

Almost anyone they indict will eventually plead guilty because they cannot afford the $200,000 down payment to the trust account for a white-collar criminal attorney; even if a defendant is able to mortgage their house, or sell everything, and are able to make the first down payment, within a few months they cannot afford to continue the thousands of dollars in monthly payments to attorneys.

Former U.S. Congressman and Fox news anchor Trey Gowdy in response to the continued prosecution of former President Donald Trump, said on his Sunday night show recently, that "prosecutors are the most powerful entities of the judicial system, not the judges."

Our experience with the federal prosecutors of the Northern District of Florida was that they were interested in a conviction, not seeking the truth. They were shown evidence in the hearings and in meetings with our attorneys of commission meetings, contracts, videos, unrefuted evidence of our innocence and yet they had no interest. They had witnesses who would lie. They wanted a conviction. Nothing else.

Marco Rubio, in reference to the indictments of former President Trump, recently said, that "if this happened to me, I would have to plead guilty to end it. I would not have had the financial resources to fight a case like this."

The stress causes families to fall apart, marriages to end, health issues, and even death or suicide for some. The Government knows this. That is why they are so angry because James Finch is my friend and is helping me to pay my attorney fees. When my case finally ended in August of 2023, my attorney fees were 1.4 million dollars. During the last month of my case before my co-defendant and I were to go to trial on February 27, 2023, my attorney costs for one month were almost a quarter of a million dollars. I have a master's degree in Language and Literature, and I worked thousands of hours doing research, writing, and helping with my own defense. And even with the hours I worked, the time the lawyers spent working on the case came to 1.4 million dollars. I sold my family home to James Finch, who sold it for 205,000.00; my initial escrow payment to the attorneys was $200,000.00 which quickly evaporated just a few months after I was indicted.

And while there must surely be talented, dedicated court-appointed attorneys out there, those willing to do hundreds, no thousands, of hours of research and work to defend a defendant in federal court, apparently most of them, according to statistics, represent clients who take a plea deal. *According to the PEW RESEARCH CENTER, based on their source, Administrative Office of the U.S. Courts, in fiscal 2018, 90% of clients pleaded guilty, 8% had cases dismissed, and 2% went to trial. Of the 2% who went to trial, 83% were convicted and 17% were acquitted. Nearly 80,000 people were defendants in federal cases in fiscal 2018, but just 2% of them went to trial. Most of the defendants who did go to trial were found guilty, either by a jury or judge. Defendants can waive their right to a jury trial in favor of a bench trial if they wish. But there is even a catch to this in the Federal system. James Finch and I asked for a bench trial because our case was so complex, and even though Chief Judge Mark Walker of the Northern District of Florida agreed to the bench trial, the prosecutors objected and insisted on a jury trial. They were allowed, by law, to make the decision for us. Why? Because they knew the Judge would be able to understand the complexity of the charges and render a fair verdict, which I believe he would have. They were counting on the jury being confused or bored by the complexity, which is why they insisted on a jury trial, in my opinion.

The Government did not count on the long-standing friendship between Lee, James and me, because they were so sure that local law enforcement, news media, the old guard city employees, trolls on social media, and Michael White and the other liars who have pleaded guilty were right and that they had found a female Mayor who would nicely fit the U.S. Attorney's and the Bay County Sheriff's public corruption theme. They did not count on attorneys who would call them out on their overreaching, unlawful tactics. They did not count on a friendship that started in childhood, friendship that never had anything to do with one being the Mayor and the other being a multi-millionaire.

They did not count on the power of the Lord, the same Lord who placed me in the position of Mayor because he knew He could count on me to take care of the people of Lynn Haven after Hurricane Michael. Just like Esther did in the Bible, she stood up to powerful men at risk to herself because she loved her people, a woman for "such a time as this." I do not mean that to sound puffed up, or like self-praise; I am humbled by the fact that I was Mayor of Lynn Haven during the twenty days when it counted. While Michael White, Derwin White, Chris Forehand, Mickey White, and Adam Albritton were signing contracts for millions of dollars to benefit themselves, I was unloading trucks of supplies, working fourteen to eighteen hours each day, making sure that people had the necessities they needed, advocating for my city to state and federal officials, and working to raise over a quarter of a million dollars which was disbursed as it was collected in $1,000.00 checks to families who had lost everything. No matter what happens next, I will always be blessed that my Lord trusted *me* with a twenty-day task that meant everything to so many people.

Seven of the nine who have been indicted so far in the Lynn Haven corruption scandal have pleaded guilty: Michael White, David "Mickey" White, Joshua Anderson, David Horton, Shannon Rodriguez, Adam Albritton and Antonius Barnes. Only two are left. James Finch and Margo Anderson. The prosecutors will not stop. They have evidence that we are not guilty, but they have gone too far. The case is too politically charged, and they cannot admit they were wrong. Former U.S. Attorney Larry Keefe, after losing his appointed position of U.S. Attorney when Biden was elected, was named Homeland Security Czar by the Governor of Florida to control the immigration problem in Florida. The same Larry Keefe who said he had no desire to be involved in politics, certainly had no problem in accepting another government dole job which he thought would put him right in line for a cabinet position or other post if Governor DeSantis had been successful in his bid for Republican nominee for President. Former U.S. Attorney Larry Keefe quietly resigned his position in October 2023 as the Homeland Security Czar for Florida after months of scandal over the Vertol contract with a former client of his private legal firm, for the Martha's Vineyard flight using a secret private email account. His "public corruption" theme which was central to the false charges against me is disgusting hypocrisy. Wherever he is now, he is very quiet and out of the public eye.

James and I have read the 302's (the statements by those who have pled guilty and other witnesses in the investigation). The Government knows who set us up and why they did it. So do we. One of those who set us up is dead (Covid-19), one has pled guilty, and at least one is still unindicted and protected. We are not guilty, and we continued to fight the full weight of the federal government. Below is the text of the third indictment against me, and the second indictment against James Finch, November 16, 2021. Fifteen months have now passed since I was first indicted, and the stress and cruelty of it all is unimaginable as we watch others living their lives, getting ready for the holidays, while a dark cloud looms over our future.

Rita Hodge, the legal assistant for my attorneys Rob Vezina and Tony Bajoczky, was so kind to me during the many hours we spent at their firm, and often even kept my dog Buddy under her desk for the long afternoons we spent in hearings at the federal courthouse. But of all her kind acts, one helped me to survive the entire ordeal. She saw me come into the office one afternoon in tears, filled with despair over my future, and she told me about an attorney she had worked for years before, Mallory Horne. He was the former Speaker of the Florida House and then became President of the Florida Senate, was falsely accused and indicted for crimes he did not commit and was eventually acquitted. Rita told me of the book that Mallory had written, *Indicted,* and suggested to me that it might help me to read it, because of the positive outcome of his case. She did not have a copy, and so I immediately went to Amazon and found that it was out of print. I located the book on e-bay, and I received it several days later, to my delight, a hardcover, autographed copy. I stayed up all night reading the book, mesmerized by how his feelings of despair, anxiety, and fear, were so honestly shared in his story. He lost everything. His home, his wife, his reputation, all gone because of an indictment which was false, and prosecutors, who like ours, were hell-bent on conviction. The book was written in 1986, and I was hoping that maybe there would be a way that I could contact him, speak with him, when after doing some research, I found that he died in 2009. I read his obituary, which spoke of his life well-lived, with no mention of the Hell he had endured at the hands of government prosecutors. I read portions of the book again on days when I became discouraged, and I am thankful that Rita shared his powerful story with me…. a story of courage, fortitude, and victory over his accusers.

Now that Adam Albritton and Commissioner Antonius Barnes had pled guilty, all of our preparations for trial in the fall were put on hold again as we waited to be indicted by the Government for the second time in James' case and the third time in mine. The second superseding indictment was unsealed on November 16, 2021. This was the second time James had been indicted, the third time for me.

The Government would repeat many of the same lies from the first two indictments, but with nuances and changes to previous mistakes they had made. I continue to be amazed that they were able to spew this narrative of lies to the grand jury, to the Court, to the media, and ultimately to the public as though it were true. The fact that all of the charges were dismissed or dropped by the time we were preparing for trial in February of 2023, speaks volumes about the dishonesty with which James and I were indicted. The final charge against us was bribery based on the 666 bribery without a *quid pro quo* which has now been struck down by the Supreme Court. And the motorhome which the Government claimed over and over was not paid for by us, was returned to us because they could not prove that my husband did not pay the first $35,000 down payment in cash as he said he did. They had not looked in all of our accounts when they claimed, "he (my husband) did not have the money to have paid cash." The second $35,000 was paid in December of 2019, with a check for $20,000 and a cash withdrawal made for $15,000 on the same day, at the same bank.

In this indictment, as in the others, the Government had charged me with wire fraud every time Phoenix Construction received a check from the City of Lynn Haven for contracts which had been voted for by the entire Commission with unanimous votes. They also charged me with wire fraud every time Michael White had issued a check to ECS with my facsimile signature on the checks without my knowledge. The lies and omission of explanations to the grand jury of statements made by the prosecutor and the sole witness, FBI agent Borghini which resulted in the indictment of James Finch and me are just unbelievable. The "false information" and "misstatements" presented to the grand jury in the indictments simply because the Government was too lazy to do their research of the Lynn Haven Commission Meeting minutes, the City Charter, and other records is inexcusable. Judge Mark Walker would term them, "reckless and haphazard," but he stopped short of calling them "malicious," in our motions for dismissal based on malicious prosecution.

The first paragraph of the first two indictments changes the "powers" or "authority" of the Mayor of the City of Lynn Haven as the prosecutors realized that Special Agent Borghini had not read the City Charter to find out the powers of the Mayor; Lynn Haven was a city manager form of government, not a strong mayor as they indicated in the original indictment against me, which caused great damage to me in the eyes of the grand jury. Their belief that I supervised the city manager, Michael White, made all of the allegations which Michael White had made against me, such as directing him, pressuring him, or causing him to take certain actions, believable to the members of the grand jury.

In the first indictment against me of August 19, 2020, the government stated in the first paragraph that "the mayor was the head of the city government and supervised the city manager." This was blatantly false. The superseding indictment of March 18, 2021 stated that "the mayor presides at all meetings of the Commission, that the mayor was the official head of the city in certain circumstances." The prosecutors maintained that because they corrected their error from the first indictment, that all was well. Our position was, that if they had not made this statement, the grand jury may not have believed a large portion of the indictment, which hinged on my supervising Michael White's actions.

The second superseding indictment which includes only James and me, it constructed in a completely new manner. The government lists every contract of Phoenix Construction in chronological order from the time that I was elected Mayor in 2015, and then inserts travel dates when my husband and I traveled with James and his wife, with their theory, that each time James won a unanimous vote of the Commission, and I was the last vote, that he bribed me or rewarded me with a trip. Of the nine trips that SA Borghini and Kunz presented against us, only six of them actually included me. We proved by credit card transactions that three of the trips only included my husband, not me. On one of the dates when Borghini said I was in Key West and Miami, I was actually in Potomac, Maryland with my family, which is proven by my credit card transactions. They did the same thing with Commissioner Antonius Barnes, by listing the dates of the checks James had given him as business loans, and showing the dates of Commission meetings in proximity, accusing Barnes of "selling" his vote. The Commission met every two weeks, and so it was actually quite easy for the prosecutors to match travel dates and loan checks with a meetings which fit their purpose.

The government again accused my husband and I of not paying anything for hotels, meals, or travel when we were with James, but we proved with our financial records that we paid for our hotel rooms, expensive meals for the four of us, and that I gambled with my own money in Biloxi, not James'. I even had my own casino card which earned rooms and rewards. We were no different from other couples who were friends; sometimes we paid for dinner and drinks, sometimes James paid. We also demonstrated with financial records that we had been traveling with James for years, long before I became Mayor, including a cruise to Alaska in 2013 where we all flew commercially to Vancouver. James and I did not become friends in 2015 when I was elected Mayor; that friendship began between our families in Lynn Haven in childhood.

# November 16, 2021

# The Second Superseding Indictment

UNITED STATES OF AMERICA

v.

MARGO DEAL ANDERSON
and
JAMES DAVID FINCH

THE GRAND JURY CHARGES:

GENERAL ALLEGATIONS

Except as otherwise indicated, at all times material to this Second Superseding Indictment:

      1.      The City of Lynn Haven was a municipality incorporated under the laws of the State of Florida. The City of Lynn Haven's Charter provided for a City Commission, consisting of a "Mayor-Commissioner," described throughout as the "Mayor," and four Commissioners. The Charter required, among other things, that the Mayor preside at all meetings of the commission, that the Mayor was the official head of the city in certain circumstances, and the Mayor may take

command of the police and fire departments and govern the city by proclamation during the times of grave public danger or emergency, and shall be the judge of what constitutes such danger or emergency. The administrative head of the City government was a City Manager, appointed by the Commission, and subject to the Commission's direction and supervision.

2.　　On April 21, 2015, MARGO DEAL ANDERSON was elected as Mayor of Lynn Haven. ANDERSON ran on a platform that the City had too many employees earning too much money who should be laid off.

3.　　As Mayor of Lynn Haven, ANDERSON sometimes acted as the de facto head of the municipal government and sometimes directed the activities of the City Manager, who was responsible for the day-to-day operations and administrative functions of Lynn Haven. ANDERSON presided over and participated in Lynn Haven City Commission meetings, contributed to the agenda for Commission meetings, and possessed one vote on the Commission equal to each other Commissioner. As the Mayor of Lynn Haven, ANDERSON was an agent of the City of Lynn Haven and had a fiduciary duty to act in the best interests of Lynn Haven and its citizens.

4.　　JAMES DAVID FINCH was the owner of Phoenix construction Services, Inc. ("Phoenix Construction"), JDF Properties, LLC ("JDF Properties"), and James Finch & Associates, Inc., businesses incorporated in the State of Florida, which businesses sought and obtained contracts with the City of Lynn Haven or had other matters before the City.

5.　　Antonius Genzarra Barnes ("Barnes") was a City Commissioner for the City of Lynn Haven between 1996 and April 2019. Barnes was an agent of the City of Lynn Haven and had a fiduciary duty to act in the best interests of Lynn Haven and its citizens.

6.　　On or about April 28, 2015, at a special Commission meeting, ANDERSON WAS SWORN INTO OFFICE AS Mayor of Lynn Haven. Barnes was sworn into office as the Commissioner for Seat 2. That same day, at a regular commission meeting, ANDERSON, Barnes, and the rest of the City Commission voted to award a 17th Street Ditch Stormwater Project ("17th Street project") to FINCH's company, Phoenix construction, in the amount of $335,132.

7.　　On or about August 25, 2015, Lynn Haven issued two

"change orders" for the 17ᵗʰ Street project. Change Order #1 was for $3,720,000, financed by Phoenix Construction at a rate of 2.55% for 20 years for the east side of the ditch. Change Order #2 was for the west side of the ditch in the amount of $1,595,000. Barnes was not present for this vote. ANDERSON voted in favor.

8.    On or about September 8, 2015, Barnes asked FINCH for a "loan" of $8,000. FINCH provided Barnes with a check in the amount of $8,000. Barnes never repaid this "loan."

9.    On or about September 28, 2015, Barnes asked FINCH for another loan of $12,000. FINCH agreed to provide said "loan." FINCH provided Barnes with a check in the amount of $12,000. Barnes never repaid this "loan."

10.    On or about October 27, 2015, at a City Commission meeting, ANDERSON and Barnes voted in favor of three ordinances rezoning properties owned or controlled by FINCH.

11.    On or about October 28, 2015, Barnes asked FINCH for another "loan" of $5,000. FINCH agreed to provide said "loan." FINCH provided Barnes with a check in the amount of $5,000. Barnes never repaid this "loan."

12.    On or about December 25, 2015, through on or about December 27, 2015, ANDERSON traveled on FINCH's private jet to Key West, Florida.

13.    On or about January 16, 2016, Barnes asked FINCH for another "loan" of $10,000. FINCH agreed to provide said "loan." FINCH provided Barnes with a check in the amount of $10,000. Barnes never repaid this "loan."

14.    On or about March 22, 2016, ANDERSON and Barnes voted to sell 287.75 acres of City property at 215 Hatcher Drive to FINCH. The City had been holding the property as a potential site for hurricane debris disposal. FINCH made an unsolicited offer to purchase the property at a price of $1,200 per acre. FINCH tried to avoid any bidding process and the involvement of the City Attorney. The City Manager decided to advertise an invitation to bid with FINCH'S offer as the minimum bid. One other individual placed a bid. FINCH placed a second higher bid of $2,100 an acre or $604,300. ANDERSON signed the deed to the property. ANDERSON later directed the City to dispose of hurricane debris at this property, and the City paid for it to be disposed there, rather than on another City property nearby.

15.    On or about May 25, 2016, ANDERSON traveled on

FINCH's private jet to Key West, Florida.

16.     On or about October 7, 2016, ANDERSON traveled on FINCH's private jet to Biloxi, Mississippi, where FINCH provided ANDERSON with lodging, meals, and entertainment, at a casino.

17.     The Bay County Contractors & Associates, Inc. ("BCCA"), was a Florida not-for-profit corporation. Joseph Adam Albritton was an attorney licensed to practice law in the State of Florida and was BCCA's registered agent. FINCH was a director. FINCH caused BCCA to promote a proposed referendum for a ½ cent sales tax to fund infrastructure projects in Lynn Haven. In November 2016, voters in Bay County, Florida, approved the referendum. The revenue from the tax was to be used for repairs to local roads, sidewalk and stormwater improvements and reducing traffic congestion.

18.     On or about November 14, 2016, Barnes asked FINCH for another "loan" of $2,500. FINCH agreed to provide said "loan." FINCH provided Barnes with a check in the amount of $2,500. Barnes never repaid this "loan."

19.     On or about February 28, 2017, the City Commission considered a modification to the 17th Street project. The City Manager recommended adding $668,000 to a promissory note to FINCH's company, Phoenix construction, for piping on the west side of the street, and to increase the promissory note term to 30 years. Barnes moved to approve these recommendations. Barnes and ANDERSON voted in favor.

20.     On or about March 15, 2017, Barnes asked FINCH for another "loan" of $2,500. FINCH agreed to provide said "loan." FINCH provided Barnes with a check in the amount of $2,500. Barnes never repaid this "loan."

21.     On March 20, 2017, ANDERSON signed, on behalf of Lynn Haven, a promissory note to pay Phoenix construction, FINCH's company, $3.72 million with respect to the 17th Street project. The promissory note was for a period of 30 years and required Lynn Haven to pay interest of 2.55 percent and make monthly payments to Phoenix Construction. In financing the 17th Street project with Phoenix construction, Lynn Haven agreed to pay Phoenix Construction approximately $1.6 million, as interest, in addition to the $3.72 million the City would pay Phoenix construction for its work on the 17th Street project contract.

22.     On May 8, 2017 the City Commission approved a

resolution for a Joint Participation Agreement between the City and the Florida Department of Transportation ("FDOT") to complete work along 17th Street, Barnes seconded, and ANDERSON voted in favor of the resolution.

23.     On June 13, 2017, ANDERSON and the Lynn Haven Commission approved a resolution authorizing the issuance by Lynn Haven of a $3,910,000 municipal revenue bond and a loan agreement to be signed with a financial institution to provide the funding for Lynn Haven to pay for infrastructure work in the City that was to be conducted under a ½ Cent Surtax Design/Build Contract. The term of the loan was for 10 years and the interest rate was 2.18 per cent per annum. ANDERSON signed the resolution and bond loan agreement. On or about June 29, 2017, the City received these funds.

24.     On or about June 26, 2017, the City issued a Request for Qualifications ("RFQ") for a "Design/Build" for ½ Sales Tax Infrastructure Projects to be submitted on or before July 20, 2017.

25.     In or around June 2017, the Lynn Haven City Manager resigned. On or about June 17, 2017, Michael Edward White ("M. White") applied to be City Manager of Lynn Haven. FINCH, ANDERSON's husband, and other contractors (including FINCH's relative) interviewed M. White regarding the City Manager position. The questioning concerned, among other things, whether M. White would be a "friend" to City contractors. On or about July 11, 2017, the City Commission appointed M. White as City Manager.

26.     On or about July 12, 2017, M. White entered into a temporary agreement to be the City Manager of Lynn Haven. The City entered into another agreement with M. White on August 22, 2017. As City Manager, M. White was responsible for the day-to-day operations and administrative functions of Lynn Haven.

27.     On or about July 20, 2017, Phoenix construction submitted a RFQ for the ½ Cent Surtax Design/Build Contract, as did one other contractor.

28.     On or about July 22, 2017, ANDERSON traveled on FINCH's private jet to Key West, Florida.

29.     On or about July 25, 2017, the City Commission considered responses to the RFQ submitted by FINCH's company, Phoenix construction first. Barnes and ANDERSON voted in favor of this motion, which the City

Commission approved.

30.    On August 9, 2017, ANDERSON signed an agreement between Lynn haven and FINCH designating Phoenix construction to be the contractor or vendor for all infrastructure improvement projects that would be conducted in Lynn Haven under a ½ Cent Surtax Design/Build Contract, utilizing proceeds from the ½ cent Bay County sales tax that was to be in effect for ten years. This agreement, negotiated by ANDERSON and FINCH, made Phoenix construction the contractor for numerous multi-million-dollar Lynn Haven infrastructure projects that would not require any further bid procedure for any of the projects related to the agreement. That same date, ANDERSON also approved Task Order #1, under this contract, which contemplated approximately $3.8 million in improvements. Thereafter, meetings were periodically held on City projects at FINCH's office at Phoenix Construction. Thereafter, FINCH often proceeded with projects under ½ Cent Surtax Contract without receiving the City's authorization to proceed.

31.    On or about September 13, 2017, ANDERSON traveled on FINCH'S private jet to Biloxi, Mississippi, where FINCH provided ANDERSON and her spouse with lodging, meals, and entertainment at a casino.

32.    With a check dated October 4, 2017, and deposited on or about October 6, 2017, the City paid Phoenix Construction $2,272,669.87 for phase one of the ½ Cent Surtax project.

33.    With a check dated October 11, 2017, and deposited on or about October 13, 2017, the City paid Phoenix construction $72,000 for phase one of the ½ cent Surtax project.

34.    On or about October 24, 2017, FINCH SENT A LETTER TO City Manage White advising that he had completed phase one of the ½ Cent Surtax project and earned the total amount ($3.8 million) authorized to date. The letter further stated that FINCH's company would proceed with the next phase but not invoice Lynn Haven until the City had obtained a new loan. The amount of the referenced additional work, $1.8 million, was submitted to Lynn Haven by FINCH in an invoice in January 2018. Over City Manager M. White's objection, ANDERSON directed M. White to allow FINCH's company to proceed as requested with the work despite no funding being available, the City not having approved the specific roads that Phoenix construction was paving, and engineering work not having been completed on

many of the roads that Phoenix Construction had purportedly finished its work on. Thereafter, M. White recommended to the City Commission to allow FINCH to proceed with work. The Cit Commission accepted M. White's recommendation and voted to approve his proposal.

35. On or about October 26, 2017, ANDERSON traveled on FINCH's private jet to Key West, Florida.

36. With e check dated November 3, 2017, and deposited on or about November 6, 2017, the City paid Phoenix Construction $1,455,330.13 for phase one of the ½ Cent Surtax project.

37. On or about December 4, 2017, Barnes asked FINCH for another "loan" of $5,000. FINCH agreed to provide said "loan." FINCH provided Barnes with a check in the amount of $5,000. Barnes never repaid this "loan."

38. On December 12, 2017, ANDERSON and the Lynn Haven Commission approved a resolution authorizing the issuance by Lynn Haven of a $6,090,000 municipal revenue bond and a loan agreement to be signed with a financial institution to provide the funding for Lynn Haven to pay for infrastructure work in the City under the a/2 Cent Surtax project that was to be conducted by FINCH's company. The term of the loan was for 10 years and the interest rate was 2.35 per cent per annum. ANDERSON signed the resolution and bond loan agreement.

39. On or about January 4, 2018, the City received the funding form the municipal revenue bond described above in paragraph 38. That same day, on January 4, 2018, FINCH submitted an application to Lynn Haven for payment of $1,850,170.66 for work performed on phase two of the ½ Cent Surtax Contract during approximately a two-month period from November 2017 to December 2017. With a check dated January 4, 2018, and deposited on January 8, 2018, the City paid Phoenix construction $1,850,170.66 for this work.

40. In or around February 2018, FINCH spoke with an individual providing engineering services to the City ("City Engineer") about purchasing the City Engineer's 2006 ITAS Motorhome ("Motorhome"). On or about February 14, 2018, FINCH provided the City Engineer a personal check for $75,000 for the motorhome. The City Engineer used the $75,000 and other funds he possessed to pay off a $105,993.73 loan on the Motorhome.

41. Subsequently, in or around March 2018, ANDERSON's spouse applied for a vehicle title for the Motorhome with the State of Florida, falsely representing that ANDERSON's spouse had purchased the Motorhome directly from the City Engineer for $35,000. The representation of the sale was false because no money had been paid by ANDERSON or ANDERSON's spouse to FINCH or the City Engineer to purchase the Motorhome, FINCH had paid the City Engineer $75,000 for the Motorhome, and FINCH had provided the Motorhome for the benefit of ANDERSON and ANDERSON's spouse without payment of money from them.

42. On or about February 24, 2018, ANDERSON traveled on FINCH's private jet to Biloxi, Mississippi, where FINCH provided ANDERSON and her spouse with lodging, meals, and entertainment, at a casino.

43. On or about June 15, 2018, the City paid an invoice in the amount of $368,202.02 from Phoenix Construction for work on the 17th Street project.

44. In June 2018, FINCH and ANDERSON requested City Manager M. White to proceed with an additional phase of the 17th Street project. M. White told ANDERSON and FINCH that he wanted to put the project on hold as it was going to cost the City a large amount of money to continue the project and the City did not have the money to pay for the project at that time. ANDERSON and FINCH told M. White that FINCH wanted to proceed with the project. ANDERSON pressured M. White to have the City proceed with the project and stated that FINCH would finance the additional approximate $1 million cost of the project. Despite protestations by City Manager M. White that Lynn Haven did not need the additional debt, ANDERSON directed M. White to make it happen.

45. Two other City Commissioners indicated concern about one of FINCH'S projects with the City. ANDERSON and another COMMISSIONER supported FINCH. Barnes' position was unclear to the City Manager. FINCH stated to the City Manager, "Antonius Barnes would dance for me if I wanted him to; he probably wants more money," or words to that effect.

46. On or about July 28, 2018, ANDERSON traveled on FINCH's private jet to Biloxi, Mississippi, where FINCH provided ANDERSON and her spouse with lodging, meals,

and entertainment at a casino.

47.    On August 21, 2018, Lynn Haven advertised for sealed bids from businesses to perform additional work on the 17th Street project. Since FDOT had become a partner with Lynn Haven to provide some of the funding for the project, Lynn Haven was required to solicit bids for the additional work on the 17th Street project and obtain the concurrence of FDOT.

48.    On or about August 22, 2018, ANDERSON traveled on FINCH's private jet to Key West, Florida.

49.    On or about September 12, 2018, ANDERSON approved a task order for $688,276.40 in construction and engineering services to FINCH's company, Phoenix Construction, under the ½ cent Sales Tax Design/Build Contract.

50.    On or about September 20, 2018, three sealed bids for the additional work on the 17th Street project were submitted: one from FINCH's company, one from FINCH's relative, and one from Company A. In the past, these three companies had bid on contracts with public entities, agreeing among themselves that one company would submit the lowest bid on a specific project and the other two companies would submit higher bids. Then, in another public project, a different company would submit the lowest bid. Phoenix Construction's $957,000 bid was determined to be the lowest bid and recommended to be awarded to Phoenix Construction by the Lynn Haven City Engineer. The sealed bid procedure was intended to make it appear as if the award of the additional work for the project was fair and above board, and would receive the concurrence of FDOT, which had signed a Joint Participation Agreement with Lynn Haven in the 17th Street project. FDOT concurred in the award to Phoenix Construction.

51.    On September 25, 2018, ANDERSON proposed at a Commission meeting that the City should change how it obtained legal services. ANDERSON suggested that instead of continuing its longstanding relationship with a law firm and attorney who had provided competent legal services for many years, the City could use an attorney with one year of legal experience who was licensed in another state and currently working for the City as an administrative position, to provide legal services under the supervision of an attorney licensed in Florida and thereby save the City money. ANDERSON stated she had already talked to an attorney about providing that supervision. The City Commission approved the

proposal. In or around September 2018, at ANDERSON's direction, M. white contacted Albritton about providing legal services to the City as the supervising attorney, but he was not interested at that time.

52.     On or about October 8, 2018, ANDERSON declared a local state of emergency for the City in anticipation of Hurricane Michael.

53.     On October 10, 2018, Hurricane Michael caused severe damage to public and private property, public utilities, public buildings, public communications systems, public streets and roads, and public drainage systems within the City of Lynn Haven.

54.     On October 16, 2018, as a result of Hurricane Michael, Lynn Haven adopted a local state of emergency for post disaster relief and planning and approved Hurricane Michael Resolution No. 2018-10-16. In the resolution, Lynn Haven waived the procedures and formalities otherwise required under Florida law to take action to ensure the safety, welfare, and health of the citizens of Lynn Haven, including: entering into contracts; incurring obligation; acquisition and distribution of materials, supplies, and other expenses related to the storm event; appropriation and expenditure of public funds; and the employment of permanent and temporary workers. The resolution delegated emergency powers to the Mayor of Lynn Haven, ANDERSON, or her designee, to discharge the duties and exercise powers for the above-described activities until the local emergency declared had expired and the resolution was rescinded. The Declaration of Emergency was to be automatically renewed every seven days until further action was taken by Lynn Haven.

**55.**     Prior to Hurricane Michael, Lynn Haven contracted with two national disaster relief companies to provide disaster relief services for the City following a hurricane. These companies, referred to as Company C and Company D in this Second Superseding Indictment, provided debris removal services for Lynn Haven after Hurricane Michael, submitted invoices with supporting documentation for their services, and received payment from Lynn Haven, which was reimbursed by the Federal Emergency Management Agency ("FEMA") for the expenses.

**56.**     FEMA is an agency of the United States Department of Homeland Security and is responsible for coordinating the federal government's response to natural and man-made disasters. The primary purpose of FEMA is to coordinate the response to a disaster that has occurred in the United States and that overwhelms the resources of local and state authorities. In addition to on-the-ground support of disaster recovery efforts, FEMA provides state and local governments with experts in specialized fields and the funding for rebuilding efforts for infrastructure. FEMA also provides for the reimbursement of many expenses incurred by local governments in cleaning up and restoration after natural disasters, such as hurricanes.

57.    After Hurricane Michael, on or about October 22, 2018, Albritton entered into a contract with Lynn Haven to be the City Attorney, effective October 15, 2018, for one year. The contract retained Albritton to provide professional legal services and perform other related duties to the City and its employees as specified in the agreement.

58.    Erosion Control Specialists ("ECS") was incorporated in the State of Florida on May 10, 2011. David Mitchelle White ("D. White") was listed as a director of ECS. In a 2018 amended annual report and a 2019 annual report filed with the State of Florida, D. White was listed as a director and Vice President of ECS.

59.    On October 22, 2018 with the knowledge and concurrence of ANDERSON, M. White, on behalf of Lynn Haven, and D.White, as an owner of ECS, signed an agreement for ECS to provide Lynn Haven with "Emergency and Or Exigent Services, Ancillary Construction Services, or Construction Due To The Effects of Hurricane Michael." ANDERSON was present with M. White, D. White, and Albritton when they decided to use ECS for cleanup. The agreement referenced ECS as a "contractor," with the effective date of October 11, 2018. The term of the agreement was for no more than 90 days to perform services for Lynn Haven. As part of the agreement, ECS agreed to provide detailed invoices requesting payment for services accompanied by such documentation or data, including back-up documentation sufficient for reimbursement of expenses by FEMA for Lynn Haven payments to ECS.

60.    On October 23, 2018, as a result of Hurricane Michael, Lynn haven again declared and reinstated a local state of emergency for post disaster relief and planning and entered Hurricane Michael Resolution No. 2018-10-23-002. This Declaration of Emergency contained the same provisions as

the original declaration of emergency and was effective for seven days. The Declaration of Emergency was required to be renewed, or it would automatically expire.

**61.**     On October 23, 2018, D. White and ECS submitted to Lynn Haven a false invoice for hurricane clean-up in the amount of $180,722.75 that claimed work by ECS was done at Lynn Haven park and water plant on eight separate days. The ECS supporting documents submitted to Lynn Haven for this fraudulent invoice included individuals who were in fact working at locations outside Lynn Haven for a different contractor. This invoice, and a separate ECS $44,000 invoice for painting a Lynn Haven building prior to the hurricane, were approved and paid by Lynn Haven as emergency expenditures. On or about October 26, 2018, with the specific approval of ANDERSON, M. White issued a handwritten check in the amount of $224,722.75 to ECS.

62.     Following Hurricane Michael, Lynn Haven received a request from World Claim public adjusters to work with Lynn Haven to assist in documentation and adjustment of its claim with insurance companies with respect to losses that Lynn Haven incurred on October 10, 2018, associated with Hurricane Michael. The City Engineer strongly recommended to the City Manager that Lynn Haven select WorldClaim. The City Engineer advised City Manager M. White than an individual was to receive a percentage of whatever business the individual brought to WorldClaim, and that the individual would split with the City Engineer whatever business was obtained from the City. The City Engineer told M. White that if Lynn Haven selected WorldClaim, the City Engineer would give to M. White some of the money that the City Engineer was receiving from the individual, and M. White, ANDERSON, and a Lynn Haven Commissioner would not be charged any claims fees by WorldClaim to adjust any private insurance claims for those public officials.

63.     On or about October 24, 2018, pursuant to the continuing Declaration of Emergency, and against the advice of City Attorney Albritton, ANDERSON and M. White signed a contract retaining WorldClaim to assist in documentation and adjustment of the City's claim under a primary insurance policy with respect to losses that occurred due to Hurricane Michael. The contract obligated the City to pay a sliding fee scale from 3 to 10 per cent of the net recovery between $0

and $60 million. This contract was entered into without any request for bids or requests for qualifications, incurring a significant financial obligation for the City, in accordance with a local state of emergency resolution that had been extended by the City for seven days the day before the signing of the WorldClaim contract and which emergency resolution was scheduled to, and di, expire six days later.

64. Following Hurricane Michael, M. White directed the City Engineer to obtain a permit for City property on Hatcher Drive to be used for hurricane debris disposal, which property had previously been used for such disposal. On or about October 23, 2018, the City Engineer submitted an application for a permit to the Florida Department of Environmental Protection ("FDEP").

65. On or about October 23, 2018, Individual C contacted M. White. Individual C indicated to M. White that Individual C was going to make sure that FINCH got his share of the City's hurricane cleanup business.

66. On or about October 24, 2018, FINCH's company, JDF Properties submitted to the FDEP a notification of intent to use a general permit for a yard trash disposal facility at 215 Hatcher Drive in Bay County, Florida, which property FINCH had previously purchased through JDF Properties from the City.

67. On or about October 29, 2018, with the knowledge and concurrence of ANDERSON, M. White, on behalf of Lynn Haven, and D. White, owner of ECS, signed an amended agreement for ECS to provide Lynn Haven with "Emergency and Or Exigent Services, Ancillary Construction Services, or Construction Due to The Effects of Hurricane Michael." Notably, the 90-day term provided for in the original agreement was replaced with no deadline; rather, the agreement provided the duration to be "for such time as necessary to perform the services for the project." Additionally, the amended agreement included new specific language advising D. White and ECS that FEMA financial assistance would be used to fund the contract with Lynn Haven, and that ECS would comply with all applicable federal regulations and executive orders, as well as all FEMA policies, procedures, and directives. Under the amended agreement ECS also agreed to provide FEMA with access to its books and records and was further advised of federal program fraud and false statement prohibitions.

68. On or about October 30, 2018, ECS submitted invoice number 1618 to the City in the amount of $202,230.56. On or about November 15, 2018, the City paid this invoice in full with check number 744395 and ANDERSON approved an accounts payable report showing this payment.

69. In late October or early November 2018, Albritton discussed with D. White expanding the work the ECS was performing for Lynn Haven, to include the pick-up of residential trash in Lynn Haven. Albritton drafted a supplemental agreement between Lynn Haven and ECs authorizing ECS to assist Lynn Haven in the removal of residential trash. The effective date of this "task order" was listed as three weeks earlier (October 15, 2018) and the "task order" authorized payment to ECS at a rate of no more than $300.00 per hour, per crew, for removal of trash. The task order stated that it would terminate upon notice by Lynn Haven, but was not to exceed 45 days from the effective date.

70. On or about October 30, 2018, ANDERSON learned that the City Engineer had submitted a permit application to FDEP. ANDERSON directed M. White to withdraw the application stating, "Michael White does not run the City. I run the City" or words to that effect. On October 30, 2018, M. White directed the City Engineer via text message to withdraw the permit application to FDEP for the City's property. The City Engineer complied. Thereafter, M. White directed Albritton to inquire about pricing at alternative locations, and provided a list of approved sites.

71. On October 30, 2018, Albritton provided to City Manager M. White a list of prices for debris disposal for companies that he claimed he had contacted, and advised M. White that Company A provided the lowest price at $4.70 per cubic yard. The City Engineer reported to Albritton that FINCH was upset about not receiving hurricane cleanup business and intended to get the vegetative chips.

72. On or about October 31, 2018, ANDERSON convened a meeting with FINCH, one of the owners of Company A, City Manager M. White, and several other persons at FINCH's personal residence. FINCH had been absent from Lynn Haven for a period of time. At the meeting, ANDERSON praised FINCH and his previous post-hurricane assistance to Lynn Haven. FINCH complained about not receiving any of Lynn Haven's post Hurricane Michael business. FINCH wanted the hurricane debris hauling business flowing to

Company C and Company D pursuant to the contracts established before the hurricane, and for the debris to be deposited at a site owned by FINCH's company, JDF Properties. FINCH wanted the City to put out a new request for qualifications for this work. M. White protested that Company C and Company D had contracts with the City. ANDERSON and FINCH were advised that FEMA would not reimburse the City if that was done. FINCH then sought the disposal of the vegetative debris. The owner of Company A agreed to let FINCH have some of the vegetative debris business, which Company A was to receive by Albritton reporting that Company A as the lowest bidder.

73.     On November 1, 2018, at the direction of ANDERSON, City Manager M. White issued a directive via email to Company C, a debris removal company that was contracted with Lynn Haven to conduct post-Hurricane Michael disaster services and clean-up , to utilize a site owned by FINCH's company, JDF Properties, to dispose of all vegetative debris or chips. Company C, which had been disposing of vegetative debris or chips at another site location, stopped dumping at that site location and commenced disposing all its vegetative debris or chips at FINCH's site. Fees totaling approximately $1 million for the disposal of items by Company C at FINCH's site for the next one-year-period were paid by Lynn Haven. Further, ANDERSON directed M. White to have Albritton assess whether the City could shift its debris pickup and hauling business from Company C and Company D to FINCH.

74.     Following Hurricane Michael, City Manager M. White wanted to put the 17th Street project on old and so informed ANDERSON. Because FINCH was not getting more of the City's hurricane clean-up business, ANDERSON pressured M. White to continue with the project. On November 6, 2018, ANDERSON and the City Commission voted for, and ANDERSON signed, a resolution amending the Joint Participation Agreement with FDOT relating to the 17th Street project stating that the City had agreed to contract for and complete the work as described in the Joint Participation Agreement with FINCH's company. On November 7, 2018, M. white awarded the contract to FINCH' s company and executed a contract for Phoenix Construction to perform an additional amount of work on the 17th Street project in exchange for $957,000. As directed by ANDERSON, this

amount was added to the amount of the March 2017 promissory note that Lynn Haven had signed payable to FINCH, increasing the amount that Lynn Haven agreed to pay FINCH for the project to $5,178,555. In addition, Lynn Haven was required to pay 2.55 percent interest annually to FINCH on the new note amount.

75.     ANDERSON directed City Manager M. White to seek authorization from the State of Florida for Lynn Haven to obtain a new Disaster Debris Management Site ("DDMS") at a property owned by FINCH in Bay County at 215 Hatcher Drive. A DDMS is a temporary staging area for hurricane debris. In a letter dated November 7, 2018, and emailed to FDEP the next day, M. White requested, on behalf of the City, that FDEP provide field authorization for a DDMS at the JDF Properties Disposal Facility in Bay County. M. White requested that FDEP evaluate the request at its "earliest convenience."

76.     On November 8, 2018, M. White and D. White executed an "Exhibit A-Task order 18-001" that ostensibly was an agreement under the Amended Agreement described in paragraph 66 above, authorizing ECS to charge Lynn Haven for residential trash pick-up, including allowing ECS to bill Lynn Haven for residential trash pick-up that had not been performed by ECS during October 2018. On November 9, 2018, Albritton sent an email to City Manager M. White and ANDERSON that the trash pick-up work order did not require approval by the City Commission. The trash pick-up Task Order was not brought for approval by the City Commission.

77.     Following Hurricane Michael, ANDERSON caused the City Manager and D. White to have ECS provide debris removal and repairs to her personal residence and the private residences of her mother and another neighbor. ANDERSON asked D. White to perform work at ANDERSON's house and that of her mother. ANDERSON wanted the trees removed so she could move the Motorhome to and from her property. Under Florida law, the City was not obligated to remove the debris from ANDERSON's property, and the City's director of public works would not have authorized the City to pay for the removal. Several days after ANDERSON' s initial request, on or about November 9, 2018, M. White sent a text message to D. White asking him if he was at ANDERSON's residence, and D. White replied

that he was. ANDERSON's spouse directed ECS personnel what to do. ANDERSON's spouse asked D. White, "you got us on this?" D. White responded, "ya, I got you." Thereafter, ECS spent several days providing services at these residences at ANDERSON's request. The services provided at these three residences, which exceeded the services that M. White agreed to, were subsequently valued by ECS at approximately $48,000, but were billed by ECS to, and paid by, Lynn Haven in invoices that falsely claimed services were provided for public areas in Lynn Haven.

78.　　On or about November 11, 2018, Albritton prepared a memorandum with legal advice regarding shifting debris pickup business from Company C and Company D to FINCH. The memorandum advised that, for the City to be eligible for reimbursement from FEMA, the selection of an additional contractor must be made through a competitive bid process in accordance with federal procurement guidelines. The memorandum further warned that the City risked a protest or a lawsuit if an existing contractor, Company C., was displaced as the primary contractor. Albritton explained his opinions to ANDERSON. Thereafter, FINCH summoned Albritton to FINCH's residence and berated Albritton about his legal advice to the City. Albritton informed FINCH that he did not believe that it was a good idea for the City to fire Company C and Company D and hire FINCH for the debris hauling. FINCH replied, in reference to Albritton, that they had "the wrong guy."

79.　　On or about November 11, 2018, at the direction of ANDERSON, City Manager M. White issued a directive to Company D, a debris removal company that was contracted with Lynn Haven to conduct post-Hurricane Michael debris removal and clean-up, to utilize a site owned by FINCH to dispose of all vegetative debris or chips. Company D, which had been disposing of vegetative debris or chips at another site location, ended dumping at that site location and commenced disposing of all its vegetative debris or chips at FINCH's site. Lynn Haven paid fees totaling more than $1 million for the disposal of items by Company D at FINCH's site.

80.　　Ultimately, FINCH SOLD THE CHIPS DISPOSED AT THE 215 Hatcher Road site for approximately $559, 490. Combined with $2,847,504.80 in disposal fees in debris disposal from Company C and Company D, Finch received approximately $3,406,994.90 which he would not have received had ANDERSON not directed the City Manager to cancel the permit application for the City property and then redirect the City business to FINCH.

81.     On November 12, 2018, a false invoice for hurricane clean-up in the amount of $527,512.65 was submitted to Lynn Haven by D. White and ECS that falsely claimed work by ECS was done at a cemetery and sports complexes during a seven-day period. Instead of doing the work at the locations described, ECS workers conducted debris removal and clean-up at the residence of M. White located in Lynn Haven, his farm located outside of Lynn Haven in Bay County, the residences of ANDERSON, her mother, and a neighbor, and the residence of Albritton and another person. The work on these private residences was concealed and not reported in the invoices, and no supporting documents to the invoice were provided. D. White and ECS subsequently submitted false daily timesheets purporting to show numerous individuals worked 12 hours per day on November 11, 2018. These timesheets were prepared by a conspirator, who also prepared timesheets for the same day for ECS to pay its employees. The payroll timesheets prepared by the conspirator and used to pay ECS employees listed most of the employees as not working on that day.

82.     On or about November 27, 2018, the City Commission, including ANDERSON, voted to approve a preliminary plat and a development order for 50 townhomes on the south side of East 17th Street in Lynn Haven, known as Parkview Townhomes. FINCH's company, James Finch & Associates, Inc., owned the property, which was across 17th Street from Cain Griffin Park. FINCH purchased the property in or around November 2017 for $300,000. On or about July 18, 2019, and August 2021, after making improvements, FINCH sole the property for approximately $2,961,000.

83.     On November 20, 2018, ECS submitted a false invoice (number 1627) for hurricane clean-up in the amount of $135,445.03 to Lynn Haven that falsely claimed trash pick-up was conducted by ECS during a seven-day period starting on November 23, 2018 (the day after Thanksgiving). This invoice was included in the payment of two invoices (numbers 1626 and 1627) to ECS in a Lynn Haven check issued to ECS on November 30, 2018, totaling $433,365.85. On or about November 30, 2018, ANDERSON approved an

accounts payable report showing payment of $433,365.85 to ECS.

84. On or about December 26, 2018, M. White texted D. White that he had a "good job" for ECS per ANDERSON. The proposal involved ECS cleaning 112 miles of side roads in Lynn Haven. ANDERSON planned to steer the contract to FINCH, with a subcontract to ECS.

85. On January 13, 2019, three months after Hurricane Michael, D. White and ECS submitted a false invoice numbered 1634 to Lynn Haven for hurricane clean-up in the amount of $479,020.68. The invoice falsely claimed that ECS conducted trash pick-up during a 13-day period starting the day after New Year's Day. The invoice also falsely claimed that between 11 and 13 crews were used to collect trash daily. The invoice falsely claimed trash pick-up during this period totaling $32,278.68 per day for five days, $38,878.44 per day for seven days, and $45,478.20 for the last day. This invoice was included in the payment of two invoices to ECS in a Lynn Haven check 745499 issued to ECS on January 15, 2019, totaling $895,441.52. On or about January 15, 2019, ANDERSON approved the accounts payable report showing the payment of $895,441.52 to ECS.

86. On January 25, 2019, three months after Hurricane Michael, d. White and ECS submitted a false invoice for hurricane clean-up in the amount of $26,771.24 to Lynn Haven which falsely claimed that ECS conducted trash pick-up during a six-day period. The invoice also falsely claimed that crews were used to collect trash daily. The invoice falsely claimed trash pick-up during this period totaling $38,878.44 per day for four days, $35,578.56 for one day, and $25,678.92 for the last day. This invoice was included in the payment of two invoices to ECS in a Lynn Haven check issued to ECS on January 31, 2019, totaling $433.259.16. On or about January 31, 2019, ANDERSON approved an accounts payable report showing the payment of $433,259.16 to ECS.

87. In sum, ANDERSON signed off on accounts payable reports that included the payment of invoices to ECs totaling approximately $1,782,290.09 between October 26, 2018, and January 31 2019.

88. When ECS invoices were being assembled for submission to FEMA by Lynn Haven for FEMA reimbursement, most of the ECS invoices that had been paid provided no details in support of the requested payments. When directed to provide

supporting documentation for the monies requested and
already paid, D. White submitted false timesheets prepared by
another person. The timesheets were false and fraudulent in
that they included names of individuals who had not worked
at the claimed location, were off that day, worked at other
projects outside Lynn Haven, or had never worked for ECS at
the time of the timesheet. Additionally, in many invoices, the
specific Lynn Haven locations of work claimed to have been
done by ECS were false. These timesheets describing the
attendance of ECS workers were certified by a Lynn Haven
Department Head of Recreation and Parks, as accurate, but
they were not, as the public official well knew.

**89.**     On or about February 8, 2019, a WorldClaim
representative sent ANDERSON an email. Consistent with
ANDERSON's earlier agreement to accept free services if
WorldClaim were awarded City business, in the email the
WorldClaim representative stated that WorldClaim would be
handling ANDERSON's insurance claims "pro bono."
Attached to the email was a contract for services, titled a
"Public Insurance Adjuster Services Agreement"
("Agreement"). The Agreement recited that WorldClaim fee
would be 10% of the claim payments by any insurance
company. But it included an addendum titled 'Addendum to
Standard Agreement" ("Addendum") which stated
"WoldClaim will not be taking a fee on any portion of the
claim for Lee and Margo Anderson." After receiving the
Agreement and Addendum, ANDERSON stated to the
WorldClaim representative, " I can't do that, I could lose my
job." Thereafter, ANDERSON agreed to pay WorldClaim a
reduced fee of 5% for its services and executed a contract.
Subsequently, ANDERSON'S insurance company paid her
$81,125.96 in hurricane-related losses. From this money, and
not including any commission on approximately $23,611.96
of additional funds that ANDERSON's insurance company
paid her before she retained WorldClaim, ANDERSON paid
WorldClaim a reduced fee of $3,646.30. Between June 20,
2019, and July 31, 2020, the City paid WorldClaim
$292,245.01 for its services.

90.     On or about March 17, 2019, M. White was arrested on
charges unrelated to City business. Immediately after the City
Commission suspended M. White, ANDERSON
unsuccessfully sought appointment as acting City Manager.
ANDERSON claimed that she had demonstrated the ability

to run the City on her own after Hurricane Michael. On or about March 26, 2019, M. White resigned as City Manager.

91.    On or about March 26, 2019, ANDERSON traveled on FINCH's private jet to Key West, Florida.

92.    Following M. White's arrest, local law enforcement searched his cellular telephone and discovered evidence of M. White's dealings with D. White. Soon after, on or about April 1, 2019, ANDERSON asked the Bay County Sheriff to investigate M. White and his dealings with ECS. ANDERSON did not disclose to the Sheriff that she had asked ECS to perform work at her residence. ANDERSON later claimed that she made this report to the Sheriff because she had recently realized the amount of money the City had paid ECS.

93.    On or about April 9, 2019, at the behest of an owner of Company A, D. White directed an ECS employee to prepare invoices for ANDERSON's personal residence and the private residences of her mother and another neighbor. The ECS employee prepared the invoices (numbers 1697, 1698, and 1699) as instructed, though the invoice numbers were in sequence with others issued in April 2019, rather than those issued in November 2018, when this work was performed, and properly dated. When D. White reviewed these invoices he stated, "this is not going to work, and instructed the employee to back date the invoices to November 2018. The employee complied. D. White provided the invoices to an owner of company A. An owner of Company A provided them to the City Engineer.

94.    On or about April 12, 2019, the Federal Bureau of Investigation ("FBI") and local law enforcement searched ECS' main office.

95.    On or about April 15, 2019, ANDERSON was re-elected as Mayor of Lynn Haven.

96.    In or around early 2019, a reporter approached ANDERSON after a City Commission meeting and asked if she had received a free motorhome from FINCH. Thereafter, ANDERSON'S spouse appeared at the news station with a document showing the sale price of the Motorhome at approximately $35,000.

97.    On or about April 24, 2019, local law enforcement conducted another search of ECS. That same day, ANDERSON contacted the Bay County Sheriff. ANDERSON stated that she had asked M. White to have

trees removed from her pole barn, which were preventing movement of the Motorhome.

98.    Hurricane Michael caused significant damage to municipal buildings in Lynn Haven, including City Hall and the Police Department building. The damage required the City to rebuild these municipal facilities. On September 24, 2019, the Lynn Haven City Manager reported to the City Commission that City staff were working with legal counsel and FEMA on issuing the first round of a RFQ for architectural design and engineering services for Lynn Haven's rebuild of municipal facilities damaged by Hurricane Michael.

99.    On or about November 6, 2019, an Indictment was returned charging M. White, D. White, and others with conspiring to defraud the City of Lynn Haven related to Hurricane Michael cleanup. That Indictment included allegations that the Lynn Haven Mayor (ANDERSON) received post-hurricane repairs to her private property and the work was paid for by Lynn Haven based upon fraudulent invoices that concealed and did not disclose that work performed for Lynn Haven was instead performed at a number of public officials' private residences and the private residences of a few other individuals, yet billed as work performed at Lynn Haven public properties.

100.    On or about November 18, 2019, FBI agents interviewed ANDERSON. During the interview, ANDERSON falsely claimed that she did not know anything about ECS, that she was not aware of the role of ECS in the hurricane cleanup, and she was first introduced to D. White in December 2018 or January 2019. ANDERSON stated that M. White handled the restoration of services and debris removal while she tended to the needs of the people.

101.    On or about December 30, 2019, approximately 22 months after the transfer of the Motorhome to ANDERSON's husband, ANDERSON's husband issued a $20,000 check to FINCH and withdrew $15,000 in cash.

102.    On January 14, 2020, the Lynn Haven City Commission voted to approve the City Manager to proceed with negotiations and contracts to the top three Architect/Design teams for the Lynn Haven rebuild of municipal facilities. The City Manager began negotiations with three architect firms for the Lynn Haven rebuild of municipal facilities, including designs for the City Hall, Police Department, Commission chambers building, and a sports complex.

103. On or about April 3, 2020, FINCH, through JDF Properties, purchased land at 201 14th Street West, Lynn Haven, for approximately $750,000, for purposes of the municipal rebuild, including designs for the old City Hall, new City Hall, Police Department, commission chambers building, and a sports complex.

104. On or about April 20, 2020, ANDERSON caused the City Manager and Police chief to meet with ANDERSON and FINCH. FINCH wanted a design/build contract for the municipal rebuild at a price of $13,000,000. ANDERSON told the City Manager and Police Chief that she supported FINCH's plan.

105. On or about April 22, 2020, ANDERSON told the Police Chief that she did not trust City employees, that FINCH had advised her since she became Mayor, and that FINCH would stay out of the rebuild process until the architects presented their proposal and then FINCH would show the Commission what he could do.

106. On or about April 30, 2020, FINCH met with the Police chief and discussed the rebuild of the Police Department building. After discussing rebuilding with the architects' plans and having FEMA involved, FINCH stated that he could receive the insurance money that the city was going to obtain and financing the rest of the building costs at 2.5% interest. At the meeting, FINCH had in his possession documents that had notes on them by ANDERSON as Mayor relating to the presentations of three different architects regarding their proposed projects and pricing for City Hall, the Police Department, and renovation of the old City Hall. FINCH told the Police Chief that he would get at least 4 votes from the City Commission on rejecting the architects' plan. When the Police Chief tried to explain that the Emergency Operations Center (EOC) should not be separated from the Police Department, FINCH threatened the Police Chief that if he did not agree with FINCH's plan, the easiest thing to do is for the Sheriff's Office to come in and take over the Police Department at a cost of half the Police Department's budget.

107. On or about May 19, 2020, ANDERSON asked the City Manager to put FINCH on the agenda for an upcoming City Commission meeting. The City Manager was concerned that ANDERSON wanted the City Manager to put FINCH on the agenda, rather than ANDERSON doing it herself.

108. On or about May 26, 2020, FINCH made a presentation at

a City Commission workshop regarding problems he claimed existed with the architects' proposal for the municipal rebuild. FINCH presented his proposal for rebuild of the City at a cost of $15 million, 2% financing, which included the property that FINCH recently purchased at 201 14th Street West in the City. ANDERSON stated at the workshop that FINCH's proposal was a wonderful idea.

109. On or about May 28, 2020, FINCH called the City Manager multiple times complaining that the City Commission had decided to deny his proposal for the Police Department. The City Manager replied that the City Attorney advised that a project over a specific amount had to bit out or it would violate state law. FINCH stated that the architects were going to charge the City $40 million to build the Police Department and City Hall. The City Manager replied that was not accurate.

110. On or about June 8, 2020, ANDERSON called the Police Chief and mentioned giving him a raise. She stated that she wanted to fulfill her promise of making him a highly paid Police Chief. She said she did not want him to ever leave the City and go somewhere else. ANDERSON also told the City Manager that she wanted to do the same thing with the City Manager and her salary. Salary increases for City employees are determined by the City Manager and not the Mayor.

111. On or about June 9, 2020, ANDERSON placed on the City Commission meeting an agenda concerning the planning and construction of municipal facilities, and at the meeting urged re-consideration of FINCH's plan.

112. On or about June 23, 2020, ANDERSON placed on the City Commission meeting an agenda item concerning the City rebuild process. At the City Commission meeting, ANDERSON discussed FINCH's proposal and the architects' proposal, highlighting benefits of a guaranteed maximum price. The City Manager explained such a path may result in loss of FEMA funds. ANDERSON replied that she wanted to use insurance funds because they were not subject to FEMA guidelines and complained about not always receiving good advice from the FEMA consultants. ANDERSON stated she wanted to "get off" this $40 million dollar "ship" and go a different course.

113. On or about July 2, 2020, ANDERSON called the City Manager and discussed FINCH's proposal. The City Manager explained to ANDERSON that she was concerned

about losing FEMA funds. The City Manager reiterated that the City stood to lose in excess of $5 million by doing a design/build project as proposed by FINCH.

114.   On or about July 13, 2020, FINCH made false statements to FBI agents concerning the transfer of the Motorhome to ANDERSON and her husband and provided the FBI agents a purported bill of sale relating to the Motorhome. The bill of sale, dated July 6, 2018, falsely represented that the purchase price was $70,000 "in hand paid half down and half due with 6 percent interest. . .the receipt of which is hereby acknowledged." Contrary to this bill of sale, neither ANDERSON nor ANDERSON's spouse had paid money to FINCH for the Motorhome. Several weeks after July 6, 2018, ANDERSON and her spouse sold another motorhome and deposited $10,000 from the proceeds of that sale into their bank account.

115.   On or about July 14, 2020, ANDERSON placed on the City Commission meeting agenda Item #21 concerning the creation of an Assistant City Manager position.

116.   On or about July 22, 2020, FINCH met with the City Manager and stated the city was dragging its feet on the rebuild. FINCH accused the City Manager of being against him on this project and holding up the process. The City Manager stated she was against leaving $5 million dollars on the table and not following the law. FINCH stated that he had supported the City Manager for her position, but they were now going in two different directions.

117.   On or about July 27, 2020, ANDERSON contacted the City Manager and requested copies of the contracts with the architects for the rebuild projects and the amount of money spent on renting the temporary Police Department and City Hall. The next day, FINCH appeared at the City Commission meeting and had in his possession the City documents that the City Manager had provided by email to ANDERSON.

118.   On or about August 14, 2020, FINCH sent a letter to the City Manager withdrawing his offer to build the new Police Department and offering to sell the land located at 201 14th Street West to the City.

119.   On or about September 11, 2020, FINCH provided ANDERSON's spouse with a check in the amount of $8,000, purportedly as a loan.

120.   Under Florida ethics law, the term "gift" meant that which is accepted by a public official or by another on the official's

behalf, or that which is paid or given to another for or on behalf of the official, directly, indirectly, or for the official's benefit, or by any other means, for which equal or greater consideration is not given within 90 days after receipt. Florida law prohibited public officers from soliciting or accepting gifts which the official knows, or with reasonable care should know, were given to influence a vote or other official action. Florida law further required municipal officials such as ANDERSON to file a Form 9, "Quarterly Gift Disclosure" with the Florida Commission on Ethics if the official accepted a gift valued at more than $100. This Form 9 was required to be filed during the calendar quarter for which the gift was received, and describe the gift, the name and address of the person making the gift, and the date the gift was received. ANDERSON failed to file a Quarterly Gift Disclosure form as required by Florida law from the date of her election as Lynn Haven Mayor in 2015 through June of 2020, despite receiving numerous things of value in excess of $100, including travel, lodging, entertainment, and the Motorhome.

121.    Between or about October 1, 2020, and March 10, 2021, FINCH directly transferred at least approximately $569,116.38 to attorneys representing ANDERSON. There was an initial transfer of $200,000 on or about October 2, 2020, for ANDERSON's legal expenses.

122.    On or about April 27, 2021, a document was recorded with the Clerk of Court for Bay County, Florida. The document purports to be a quit claim deed in which ANDERSON and ANDERSON's spouse convey their interest in real property in Lynn Haven, Florida, their residence at 513 Tennessee Avenue, to FINCH. The document falsely stated that ANDERSON and her spouse had received $200,000 in exchange for the property as of September 4, 2020. The document states that it was executed by ANDERSON and her spouse on September 4, 2020, and the execution was purportedly witnessed by two employees of FINCH's company. On April 26, 2021, at the direction of FINCH, a Phoenix Construction employee caused a notary, also an employee of Phoenix Construction , to execute a certification of the document which falsely indicated that ANDERSON's spouse had appeared before the notary on April 26, 2021, and falsely indicated that ANDERSON's spouse had acknowledged before the notary that the

document was executed on September 4, 2020.

## COUNT ONE
### Conspiracy to Commit Honest Services Wire Fraud
### 18 U.S.C. 1343,1346 &1349

123.   The allegations in paragraphs 1 through 122 of this Second Superseding Indictment are hereby realleged and incorporated by reference as if fully set forth herein.

124.   Between on or about August 1, 2015, and on or about November 16, 2021, in the Northern District of Florida and elsewhere, the defendants,

## MARGO DEAL ANDERSON,
### and
## JAMES DAVID FINCH,

did knowingly and willfully combine, conspire, confederate, and agree together and with other persons to devise a scheme to defraud and deprive the city of Lynn Haven and its citizens of their right to the honest services of ANDERSON, the elected Mayor of Lynn Haven, and Barnes as Commissioner, through bribery or kickbacks and to cause wire communications to be transmitted in interstate and foreign commerce for the purpose of executing such scheme, in violation of Title 18, United States Code, Sections 1343 and 1346.

125.   The manner and means of the conspiracy were that the defendants and conspirators used ANDERSON's public official position as the Mayor of Lynn Haven and Barnes' position as City Commissioner to offer, give, solicit, receive, agree to accept, and accept things of value from FINCH, which were offered and provided by FINCH to ANDERSON and Barnes, in exchange for performing official acts. FINCH offered things of value to ANDERSON and Barnes with the intent that they would be influenced in the performance of official acts.   ANDERSON agreed to accept and did accept things of value from FINCH with the intent that she would be influenced in the performance of official acts related to specific matters, to wit, FINCH's business interests before, including the 17th Street project, projects under the ½ Cent Surtax contract, and City business for hurricane recovery, as specific opportunities arose. Thereafter, ANDERSON used her position as Mayor of Lynn Haven to take official action favorable to FINCH's business interests as specific opportunities arose, which included

voting on measures pending before the Lynn Haven City Commission, signing resolutions, contracts, agreements, and promissory notes, and pressuring and advising City officials to perform specific official acts favorable to FINCH's business interests. ANDERSON agreed to and did perform these official acts in favor of FINCH in exchange for things of value from FINCH.

126.    The defendants and conspirators concealed the nature and the receipt of things of value from FINCH in return for the performance of official acts by, among other things, failing to report the receipt of said things of value, executing false documents, filing false documents with government authorities, and making false statements to law enforcement. All in violation of Title 18, United States Code, Section 1349.

## COUNTS TWO THROUGH FOURTEEN
### Honest Services Fraud Wire Fraud
**18 U.S.C. 1343 & 1346**

127.    The allegations in paragraphs 1-122 of this Second Superseding Indictment are hereby realleged and incorporated by reference as if fully set forth herein.

128.    Between on or about August 1, 2015, and on or about November 16, 2021, in the Northern district of Florida and elsewhere, the defendants,

### MARGO DEAL ANDERSON
and
### JAMES DAVID FINCH,

Did knowingly and willfully devise and intend to devise a scheme to defraud and deprive the City of Lynn haven and its citizens of their right to the honest services of ANDERSON, the elected Mayor of Lynn Haven, and Barnes as elected City Commissioner, through bribery or kickbacks, and to cause wire communications to be transmitted in interstate and foreign commerce for the purpose of executing such scheme.

129.    In particular, FINCH offered things of value to ANDERSON and Barnes with the intent that they would be influenced in the performance of official acts. ANDERSON agreed to accept and did accept things of value from FINCH with the intent that they would be influenced in the performance of official acts. ANDERSON agreed to accept and did accept things of value from FINCH with the intent that she would be influenced in the performance of official acts related to specific matters, to wit, FINCH's business

interests, including the 17th Street project, projects under the ½ Cent Surtax contract, and City business for hurricane recovery, as specific opportunities arose. Thereafter, ANDERSON used her position as Mayor of Lynn Haven to take official action favorable to FINCH's business interests as specific opportunities arose, which included voting on measures pending before the Lynn Haven City Commission, signing resolutions, contracts, agreements, and promissory notes, and pressuring and advising City officials to perform specific official acts favorable to FINCH's business interests. ANDERSON agreed to and did perform these official acts in favor of FINCH in exchange for things of value from FINCH.

130.    On or about the following dates, for the purpose of executing the scheme to defraud the defendants,

MARGO DEAL ANDERSON,

and

JAMES DAVID FINCH,

Knowingly did cause wire communications to be transmitted in interstate and foreign commerce as set forth below:

COUNT TWO
DATE:  11/14/2016
WIRE COMMUNICATION:  Deposit of $2,500 check and related wire
FINCH

COUNT THREE
DATE:  3/15/2017
WIRE COMMUNICATION:  Deposit of $2,500 check and related wire
FINCH

COUNT FOUR
DATE:  10/6/2017
WIRE COMMUNICATION:  Deposit of $2,272,669.87 check and related wire
ANDERSON AND FINCH

COUNT FIVE
DATE:10/13/2017
WIRE COMMUNICATION:  Deposit of $72,000 check and related wire

COUNT SIX
DATE: 10/25/2017

WIRE COMMUNICATION: Email with letter from M. White to
engineering firm regarding the ½ Cent Sales Tax Project
ANDERSON AND FINCH

COUNT SEVEN
DATE: 11/6/2017
WIRE COMMUNICATION: Deposit of 41,455,330.13 check and related
wire
ANDERSON AND FINCH

COUNT EIGHT
DATE: 12/4/2017
WIRE COMMUNICATION: Deposit of $5,000 check and related wire
FINCH

COUNT NINE
DATE: 1/8/2018
WIRE COMMUNICATION: Deposit of $1,850,170.66 and related wire
ANDERSON AND FINCH

COUNT TEN
DATE: 2/16/2018
WIRE COMMUNICATION: Deposit of $75,000 check from FINCH
into the account of the City engineer for the Motorhome and related wire
ANDERSON AND FINCH

COUNT ELEVEN
DATE: 10/30/2018
WIRE COMMUNICATION: Text message from M. white to City
Engineer to cancel permit application
ANDERSON AND FINCH

COUNT TWELVE
DATE: 11/1/2018
WIRE COMMUNICATION: Email from M. White to Company C
directing it to use FINCH's pit
ANDERSON AND FINCH

COUNT THIRTEEN
DATE: 11/8/2018
WIRE COMMUNICATION: Email including letter of M. White to State
of Florida requesting approval for DDMS site for FINCH's property
ANDERSON AND FINCH

COUNT FOURTEEN
DATE: 1/16/2020
WIRE COMMUNICATION: Deposit of $20,000 check on ANDERSON account payable to FINCH and related wire
ANDERSON AND FINCH

In violation of Title 18, United States Code, Sections 1343, 1346, and 2.

COUNT FIFTEEN

131.   The allegations in paragraphs 1 through 122 of this Second Superseding Indictment are hereby realleged and incorporated by reference as if fully set forth herein.

132.   Between on or about February 13, 2018, and on or about February 12, 2019, in the Northern District of Florida , and elsewhere, the defendant,

MARGO DEAL ANDERSON,

being an agent of an organization and agency of the local government, that is, the City of Lynn Haven, Florida, which received in the one-year period beginning February 13, 2018, benefits in excess of $10,000 under a federal program involving grants, contracts, subsidies, loans, guarantees, and other forms of federal assistance, did corruptly accept and agree to accept a thing of value, to wit, a motorhome valued at $5,000 or more, intending to be influenced and rewarded in connection with a business, transaction, or series of transactions of the City of Lynn Haven, Florida.

In violation of Title 18, United States Code, Sections 666(a)(1)(B) and 2.

COUNT SIXTEEN

133.   The allegations in paragraphs 1 through 122 of this Second Superseding Indictment are hereby realleged and incorporated by reference as if fully set forth herein.

134.   Between on or about February 13, 2018, and on or about February 12, 2019, in the Northern District of Florida, and elsewhere, the defendant,

JAMES DAVID FINCH,

did corruptly give, offer, and agree to give a thing of value, to wit, the Motorhome, that was valued at $5,000 or more, to MARGO DEAL ANDERSON and her spouse with the intent to influence and reward MARGO DEAL ANDERSON, an agent of a local government, the City of

Lynn Haven, which received in the one-year period beginning February 13, 2018, benefits in excess of $10,000 under a federal program involving grants, contracts, subsidies, loans, guarantees, and other forms of federal assistance, in connection with a business, transaction, or series of transactions of the City of Lynn Haven, Florida.

In violation of Title 18, United States Code, Sections 666(1)(2) and 2.

## COUNT SEVENTEEN

135.   The allegations in paragraphs 1 through 122 of this Second Superseding Indictment are hereby realleged and incorporated by reference as if fully set forth herein.

136.   Between on or about October 10, 2018, and on or about April 30, 2019, in the Northern District of Florida, and elsewhere the defendant,

## MARGO DEAL ANDERSON

Being an agent of an organization and agency of the local government, that is, the City of Lynn Haven, Florida, which received in the one-year period beginning October 10, 2018, benefits in excess of $10,000 under a federal program involving grants, contracts, subsidies, loans, guarantees, and other forms of federal assistance, did knowingly embezzle, steal, obtain by fraud, without authority convert to the use of a person other than the rightful owner, and intentionally misapply property that was valued at $5,000 or more and under the care, custody, and control of such organization, local government, and agency, to wit, hurricane debris cleanup at the residence of ANDERSON and those of other persons.

In violation of Title 18, United States Code, Sections 666(a)(1)(A) and 2.

## COUNTS EIGHTEEN AND NINETEEN
Wire Fraud, 18, U.S.C. 1343 and 2

137.   The allegations in paragraphs 1 through 122 of this Second Superseding Indictment are hereby realleged and incorporated by reference as if fully set forth herein.

138.   Between on or about October 10, 2018, and on or about July 31, 2020, in the Northern District of Florida and elsewhere, the defendant,

## MARGO DEAL ANDERSON,

did knowingly and willfully devise, and intend to devise, a scheme or schemes to defraud and for obtaining money and property, to wit, cleanup at her residence and that of her mother and neighbor, which was falsely billed to the City by ECS, by means of material false and fraudulent pretenses, representations, and promises, and to cause wire communications to be transmitted in interstate and foreign commerce for the purpose of executing such scheme, and

139. On or about the following dates, for the purpose of executing the scheme to defraud, the defendant,

## MARGO DEAL ANDERSON,

did cause wire communications to be transmitted to interstate and foreign commerce as set forth below:

COUNT
EIGHTEEN
DATE: 11/2/2018
WIRE COMMUNICATION: Text messages between M. White and D. White regarding ANDERSON's property clean-up

COUNT
NINETEEN
DATE: 11/15/2018
WIRE COMMUNICATION: Deposit of $1,288,716.54 check from Lynn Haven to ECS and related wire for payment of false invoice related to services provided at ANDERSON's residence
In violation of Title 18, United States Code, Sections 1343 and 2.

### COUNTS TWENTY THROUGH TWENTY-FOUR
Honest Services Wire Fraud, 18 U.S.C. 1343, 1346 & 2

140. The allegations in paragraphs 1 through 122 of this Second Superseding Indictment are hereby realleged and incorporated by reference as if fully set forth herein.
141. Between on or about October 10, 2018, and on or about July 31, 2020, in the Northern District of Florida and elsewhere, the defendant,
MARGO DEAL ANDERSON,

did knowingly and willfully devise and intend to devise a scheme or schemes to defraud and deprive the City of Lynn Haven and its citizens of their right to the honest services of ANDERSON, the elected Mayor of Lynn Haven, through bribery or kickbacks and to cause wire communications to be transmitted in interstate and foreign commerce for the purpose of executing such scheme. In the course of the scheme, ANDERSON agreed to accept a thing of value from WorldClaim, to wit, WorldClaim's services for the insurance claim related to her residence, and the residence of M. White and a City Commissioner, in exchange for ANDERSON permitting WorldClaim to have the City of Lynn Haven's business.

      142.   On or about the following dates, for the purpose of executing the scheme to defraud, the defendant,

## MARGO DEAL ANDERSON,

did cause wire communications to be transmitted in interstate and foreign commerce as set forth below:

COUNT
TWENTY
DATE: 6/20/2019
WIRE COMMUNICATION:  Deposit of Lynn Haven check to WorldClaim in the amount of $176,109.72 and related wire

COUNT
TWENTY-ONE
DATE: 9/6/2019
WIRE COMMUNICATION:  Deposit of check from ANDERSON's insurance company in the amount of $81,125.96 and related wire

COUNT
TWENTY-TWO
DATE: 9/3/2019
WIRE COMMUNICATION:  Deposit of Lynn Haven check to WorldClaim in the amount of $80,365.72 and related wire

COUNT
TWENTY-THREE
DATE: 12/11/2019
WIRE COMMUNICATION:  Deposit of Lynn Haven check to WorldClaim in the amount of $29,457.25 and related wire

COUNT
TWENTY-FOUR
DATE: 7/31/2020
WIRE COMMUNICATION:  Deposit of Lynn Haven check to WorldClaim in the amount of $6,312.32 and related wire

In violation of title 18, United States Code, Sections 1343, 1346, and **2**.

## COUNT TWENTY-FIVE

143.     The allegations in paragraphs 1 through 122 of this Second Superseding Indictment are hereby realleged and incorporated by reference as if fully set forth herein.

144.     On or about November 18, 2019, in the Northern District of Florida and elsewhere, the defendant,

### MARGO DEAL ANDERSON,

did knowingly and willfully make materially false, fictitious, and fraudulent statements and representations in a matter within the executive branch of the Government of the United States, that is, during a criminal investigation of public corruption involving the City of Lynn Haven conducted by the Federal Bureau of Investigation, the defendant falsely stated that:

a.     ANDERSON was unaware of the role of Erosion Control Specialists (ECS) in the post-Hurricane Michael clean-up of Lynn Haven; and

b.     ANDERSON was first introduced to David "Mickey" White in December 2018 or January 2019, when volunteers were used to clean up various streets designated by Lynn Haven as needing some attention and clean-up.

145.     These statements and representations were false because, as ANDERSON then well knew:

a.     ANDERSON was aware that ECS had been contracted by Lynn Haven to conduct debris removal and repairs in the City of Lynn Haven after Hurricane Michael;

b.     ANDERSON interacted with David "Mickey" White through City Manager Michael White shortly after Hurricane Michael and requested David "Mickey" White to have ECS clean up her private residence.

In violation of Title 18, the United States Code, Section 1001(1)(2).

## COUNT TWENTY-SIX

146.     On or about July 13, 2020, in the Northern District of Florida, the defendant,

### JAMES DAVID FINCH,

did knowingly and willfully make materially false, fictitious, and fraudulent statements, representations, and writings in a matter within the executive branch of the Government of the United States, that is, during a criminal investigation of public corruption involving the City of Lynn Haven conducted by the Federal Bureau of Investigation, the defendant falsely stated that:

   a.     FINCH had sold a 2006 ITAS Motorhome to ANDERSON and her husband for $70,000;

   b.     FINCH presented a false bill of sale dated July 6, 2018 that stated the sale of the Motorhome was $70,000 of which half was paid down and half due to FINCH WITH 6% INTEREST;

   c.     FINCH stated that he sold the Motorhome to ANDERSON and her husband for $70,000 and they had paid him with a check and the difference in cash; and

   147.   These statements and representations were false, and the claimed bill of sale dated July 6, 2018, contained false statements, because, as FINCH then well knew:

   a.     FINCH did not sell the Motorhome to ANDERSON and her husband for $70,000.

   b.     As of July 6, 2018, neither ANDERSON nor ANDERSON's husband had paid $35,000 , or any money at all, for the Motorhome.

   c.     Not until approximately 22 months after the transfer of the Motorhome to ANDERSON and her husband, ANDERSON's husband issued a $20,000 check to FINCH, allegedly in relation to the Motorhome, to conceal the receipt of the Motorhome in or around February 2018, without any payment by ANDERSON or ANDERSON's spouse for said Motorhome.

In violation of title 18, United States Code, Sections 1001(a)(2) & (3).

## CRIMINAL FORFEITURE

The allegations contained in Counts One through Twenty-Four of this Second Superseding Indictment are hereby realleged and incorporated by reference for the purpose of alleging forfeiture. From their engagement in the violations alleged in counts One through Twenty-Four of this Second Superseding Indictment, the defendants,

MARGO DEAL ANDERSON<br>and<br>JAMES DAVID FINCH,

Shall forfeit to the United States pursuant to Title 18, United States Code, Section 981(a)(1)(C), and Title 28, United States Code, Section 2461(c), any and all of the defendants' right, title, and interest in any property, real and personal, constituting, and derived from, proceeds traceable to such offenses, including the following:

    a.      2006 ITAS Motorhome, VIN#4UZACKDC26C@30357

If any of the property described above as being subject to forfeiture, as a result of acts or omissions of the defendants:

    i.   cannot be located upon the exercise of due diligence;

    ii.  has been transferred, sold to, or deposited with a third party;

    iii.  has been placed beyond the jurisdiction of this Court;

    iv. has been substantially diminished in value; or

    v .has been commingled with other property that cannot be subdivided without difficulty,

it is the intent of the United States, pursuant to Title 21, United States Code, Section 853(p), as incorporated by Title 28, United States Code, Section 2461©, to seek forfeiture of any other property of said defendant up to the value of the forfeitable property.

                A TRUE BILL:

                FOREPERSON (name blacked out)

                16 Nov 2021

JASON R. COODY
Acting United States Attorney

STEPHEN M. KUNZ
Assistant United States Attorney

ANDREW J. GROGAN
Assistant United States Attorney

# 8 THE U.S. ATTORNEY'S OFFICE OF THE NORTHERN DISTRICT OF FLORIDA, U.S. ATTORNEY LAWRENCE KEEFE'S PUBLIC CORRUPTION AGENDA, AND ASSISTANT U.S. ATTORNEY STEPHEN KUNZ

### U.S. Attorney Larry Keefe

Larry Keefe was appointed the U.S. Attorney for the Northern District of Florida by President Donald Trump on January 9, 2019, (my birthday), just about the time that the City of Lynn Haven was beginning to get past the initial months following the unprecedented disaster of the Category 5 Hurricane which left a path of destruction across Bay County and the

Panhandle of Florida. He was the former law partner of Congressman Matt Gaetz, and Gaetz lobbied for his appointment to this position. The theme of Keefe's office was to prosecute "public corruption," and the FBI investigation which started in Lynn Haven just three short months after he took office, fell neatly into his lap.

Against all Justice Department policies, he hired the prestigious Sachs Media firm of Tallahassee to promote his agenda and himself, with a budget set at close to a half million dollars for this purpose. Our attorneys made public records requests of these expenditures to the Justice Department, and after months of waiting, and paying almost four thousand dollars for the labor costs or our requests, we have yet to receive all of the documentation.

The *Tallahassee Democrat,* reported:

*Ron Sachs, founder and CEO of Sachs Media Group, applauded Keefe's service.*

*"I've had the privilege of working for two great governors, Reubin Askew and Lawton Chiles, and many other dedicated officials in elected and appointed offices," Sachs said. "But U.S. Attorney Larry Keefe stands out to me as the most dedicated public servant I've ever known for his pure heart and stellar, purposeful pursuit of justice on so many levels."*

*In stark contrast to his predecessors, Keefe's insisted on making his office more transparent and media-friendly. His office had a contract with Sachs' firm for public relations, allowing maximum payments totaling $429,000 over an initial year and four optional years.*

Only one month after I was indicted, Keefe placed an editorial in all major newspapers of the Northern District, tainting any potential jury pool for my trial which was initially set for October 26, 2020. My name was neatly sandwiched between several other public officials who had already pled guilty to crimes or were actually incarcerated for crimes, with no mention that I had entered a "not guilty" plea and was awaiting trial. In the September 19, 2020, editorial, U.S. attorney Keefe states:

*One year ago, when I announced the creation of the Public Trust Unit within the United States Attorney's Office, I described its guiding principle simply: A public office is a sacred trust.*

*Today I can report that this specialized unit of dedicated professionals has succeeded beyond expectations, working to restore integrity, responsibility, and trust to public offices across the 23 counties of the Northern District of Florida. Working in close collaboration and unprecedented cooperation with federal, state, and local partners, the Public Trust unit has relentlessly pursued individuals who abused their public positions for personal benefit and those who sought to illegally influence them.*

*Thanks to the ongoing work of this extraordinary team, the word is getting out across the district that if you violate the public trust, we will find you, and you will pay the price.*

*Even amid the COVID-19 pandemic, members of our public Trust Unit work each day to focus the resources of the Department of Justice on supporting and improving public confidence in the institutions of government and the electoral process on which those institutions are built. In just its first year, this team has:*

*Indicted and prosecuted multiple former elected public officials, including Tallahassee City Commissioner Scott Maddox,* **Lynn Haven Mayor Margo Anderson,** *Holmes County Clerk of Court Kyle Martin Hudson, and Milton Mayor Guy W. Thompson. Allegations against these officials, some of whom were still in office when they were charged, ranged from selling their official votes and embezzlement to fraudulently stealing tax dollars intended for hurricane cleanup and drought assistance.*

*Indicted and prosecuted multiple individuals—including Lynn Haven* **Mayor Margo Anderson** *and the City Manager Michael White, the City Attorney J. Adam Albritton, and the City Parks and Recreation Director—in a scheme to defraud taxpayers of $5 million in funds provided for cleanup after Hurricane Michael.*

*Indicted and prosecuted several active law enforcement and correctional officers on charges ranging from assisting a drug enterprise, to participating in a dogfighting ring, to sexually assaulting a female inmate.*

*Secured sentences of a half-dozen separate Postal Service employees after convictions for stealing mail, including debit cards and checks, from residents of the District.*

*Obtained indictments, guilty pleas, or convictions of multiple individuals on health care fraud charges, including stealing more than $4.8 million from TRI-CARE and over $4.4 million from Medicare and Blue Cross Blue Shield.*

*Our system of government-indeed, the American way of life-rests on a foundation of public trust. The people must believe that the individuals in positions of authority will serve the public interest, working for the betterment of all. Any act that violates this trust threatens to do long-lasting harm to the relationships between the people and the federal, state and local governments that exist to serve them.*

*I have lived in North Florida nearly all my life, and it is clear to me that the overwhelming majority of individuals who serve in public office-elected and appointed—are good and honorable women and men. They dedicate themselves to helping their neighbors and making their communities even better places to live, work, and raise a family.*

*That is what the people expect and deserve.*

*Regrettably, there is always a small number who see public office as a golden ticket to undeserved opportunity. They seek to use their positions for their own illegal benefit or profit, or to corrupt our elections for unseemly purposes. Any private citizens who also try to profit by illegal influence over public officials will be primary targets, too.*

*As our recent indictment in the Lynn Haven hurricane and cleanup fraud case underscores, our Public Trust Unit will continue to stop them and reaffirm the people's trust in their government. When corrupt officials seek to undermine the integrity of our public institutions, we simply cannot-and will not-look the other way.*

*The virus of corruption is one for which we already have the cure: accountability and justice.*

*Lawrence Keefe is the United States Attorney for the Northern District of Florida.*

This "Guest" editorial appeared in the *Panama City News Herald, The Gainesville Sun,* and other major newspapers of the Northern District, within six weeks of my first scheduled trial date, and in some of the newspapers a large color photograph of Keefe also appeared, arms crossed like a safari hunter with his foot on the lion. The editorial must have been written by his publicists, Sachs Media, because they use the same "virus of corruption" theme he used in the press conference on the day I was indicted.

According to an article from *Tampa Bay Times,* by Alex Leary, "President Trump has nominated a former law partner of Rep Matt Gaetz to become U.S. attorney for the Northern District of Florida.

The buzz is the nomination of Larry Keefe, subject to Senate confirmation, has stirred talk in the region, not only because of the connection to Gaetz, a leading Trump supporter on Capitol Hill, but because Keefe contributed to Hillary Clinton's campaign.

"Larry Keefe is widely respected in the legal community in North Florida. He will do a great job for us," Gaetz told the *Tampa Bay Times* in a text message. Asked about his influence on the president, he said, "I try to always help Trump."

Per a White House release, Keefe, "has been a trial lawyer for nearly 32 years during which he has tried criminal and civil cases in federal and state courts. He has led and managed a litigation-based law firm with offices throughout northwest Florida. He is currently a partner at the law firm Keefe Anchors & Gordon.

Gaetz worked at Keefe, Anchor & Gordon for about a decade. He was elected in 2016 in a district that overwhelmingly supported Trump. But Keefe's nomination stalled in the Senate, and only through the lobbying of Matt Gaetz, and lobbyist Brian Ballard, did the appointment go through.

On November 5, 2021, about a week before Acting U.S. Attorney Jason Coody and Assistant U.S. Attorneys Kunz and Grogan would seek the third indictment (second superseding indictment against James Finch and I), Larry Keefe, who had no choice but to resign in February 2021 after Biden was sworn in , moved to another powerful position, even though he had said several times that he "had no interest in running for office".

But, he was appointed the "immigration and safety czar "by Governor Ron DeSantis where he could, according to news reports, engage in performance politics for $125,000 a year, have a fat travel budget to raise his profile across Florida for any potential run for office, while knowing that DeSantis was a heavy favorite for re-election. Social media sites also predicted that Keefe was on the short list to fill the "top cop" FDLE position which became vacant in September of that year, however, that did not happen.

Larry Keefe was the U.S. Attorney responsible for the investigation and indictment which ruined my life. He was shown evidence in January of 2021 by a respected Tallahassee defense team, Jimmy Judkins, Rob Vezina and Tony Bajoczky, with "no hiding of the ball." Instead of listening and considering what was before him, he allowed Assistant U.S. Attorney Stephen Kunz to double-down and push forward for a superseding indictment since the first one was obviously deficient. The 63 charges against me in the first indictment was reduced to 26 charges against me in the superseding indictment because of the "mistakes" they had presented to the grand jury which indicted me in August 2020. Keefe had resigned by the time the March 16, 2021, superseding indictment was returned, but he knew the reputation of Kunz, he had seen the grievous "errors" and "misstatements" they made in charging me, but he chose to turn his head, his pious, politically motivated head, which became involved in a deal which benefitted a former client of his, Vertol, the airline which he, using a secret email account under the name, Clarice Starling, and Governor Ron DeSantis used to fly migrants to Martha's Vineyard...a contract secured according to the *New York Post*, "with language in eight paragraphs sent from Keefe to Montgomerie in the secret emails which later appeared almost verbatim in the proposal sent to the Florida Transportation Dept." This story has been ongoing in Florida newspapers and elsewhere, concerning lawsuits filed as a result.

The hypocrisy is palpable when the U.S. Attorney's theme was "rooting out public corruption", an official who enjoyed "suiting up" and going out with law enforcement according to a Tallahassee news report and photograph of Keefe. He quietly resigned his "czar" position in October of 2023 to volunteer for the Ron DeSantis presidential campaign and after DeSantis withdrew from the race, Keefe has been very much out of the public eye, at least for now:

### The New York Post's, Jesse O'Neill reported on December 28, 2022:

*Ron DeSantis aide Larry Keefe used 'Clarice Starling' alias for migrant flight bid.*

*A top aide to Florida Gov Ron DeSantis used an alias from "Silence of the Lambs" while helping a former client secure a bid to fly asylum seekers from Texas to Martha's Vineyard in September.*

*DeSantis' public safety czar, Larry Keefe, used a private email address under the pseudonym Clarice Starling to help private contractor Vertol Systems Company win the opportunity to operate the state's controversial migrant flight program, WTVJ reported last week.*

*Emails between Keefe—who formally represented Vertol for years in the private sector—and CEO James Montgomerie were not initially turned over in connection with a lawsuit, despite Montgomerie's testimony that his company released "every single" record, according to the report.*

*Vertol had reportedly earned at least $1.5 million to fly dozens of mostly Venezuelan migrants from San Antonio to the Massachusetts Island on September 14th, and for other planned migrant flights to Delaware and Illinois that have so far not materialized, according to the article.*

*Language in eight paragraphs sent from Keefe to Montgomerie in late August ended up nearly verbatim in the proposal Vertol sent to Florida transportation officials on Sept. 2, according to the local station.*

*The clandestine communication was finally released just before Christmas after the Florida Center for Government Accountability sued the state and Vertol to obtain documents related to the migrant relocation efforts.*

*The governor's office had previously said it was "unaware of this email address belonging to Mr. Keefe."*

*"This is the email channel to use," Keefe wrote from his Gmail alias to Montgomerie's AOL account on Aug. 26, as the aviation company was poised to bid on the state's program, according to the Miami Herald.*

*In addition to the email chain, the two men had reportedly called or texted each other 33 times in the days before Florida and Vertol agreed on the principle of a contractual agreement, WTVJ said. The state and the contractor have denied accusations of violating the migrants' civil rights and concealing public records in connection with the political stunt orchestrated by DeSantis, who won reelection in a landslide last month and is rumored to be eyeing a presidential bid.*

*Keefe, a former U.S. attorney in the Trump administration, was hired last year by DeSantis to runs his $12 million migration relocation program, which was approved by the Tallahassee legislature earlier this year, despite the fact Florida has no land border with a foreign country. U.S. Border Patrol in Florida recorded 35,000 interactions with migrants in the 2022 year, mostly people arriving by boat. The latest revelations come as the state and the contractor are accused in lawsuits of violating the Texas migrants' civil rights and concealing public records, allegations they deny.*

*Keefe's "Starling" Gmail address—a reference to the FBI trainee who hunts fictional serial killer Hannibal Lecter in the movie "The Silence of the Lambs" and its sequels— also included the phrase "Heat 19" which was a call sign given to Keefe by a military commander when he served in the private sector, the Herald reported.*

*Neither Keefe nor DeSantis responded to a request for comment from the newspaper.*

This story has quietly been buried, and U.S. Attorney, Lawrence Keefe, who was shown evidence by attorneys in January 2021 that I had been falsely indicted, chose to go forward, as the tactics of Stephen Kunz, his assistant U.S. Attorney of presenting false evidence to a grand jury, would continue.

The utter hypocrisy of U.S. Attorney Larry Keefe, who used a private email account "Clarice Starling" avoiding public records, to assist his former client, Vertol Systems Company, (an aviation company) in obtaining a state contract, is just unbelievable, as he indicted me for "public corruption." I was charged with lying to the FBI Special Agent, Larry Borghini, who lied to the grand jury to indict me, and perjured himself in the evidentiary hearing. Why were neither of them charged with a crime?

## Stephen Kunz, Assistant U.S. Attorney

The first time I had heard of Stephen Kunz was in late December 2019 when I was served a federal subpoena for all of my business and tax records for the previous five years by BCSO Investigators Jimmy Stanford and Jeremy Mathis when they came to the Mayor's office to serve the papers and embarrass me publicly.

When I took the papers to my attorney Ron Johnson's office in Pensacola and we began talking about the recent November 2019 indictment of the Lynn Haven City Manager and others, Ron wrinkled his forehead a bit as though he had remembered something, and then said Kunz's name out loud. "I remember something about him," Ron said. "He's a bit of a bad actor…I think he was in some sort of trouble with the Florida Bar a few years back." We continued working on getting the paperwork ready for me to deliver to the FBI agent, but once I returned home to Lynn Haven I got on the computer and began to research "Stephen Kunz". My efforts were rewarded on the first Google search.

The first story I found was in the *Tallahassee Democrat,* written by reporter Jeffrey Schweers, July 22, 2017:

*Prosecutor in Tallahassee FBI probe was disciplined for misconduct*
*The list of federal prosecutors disciplined for professional misconduct is a short one. And Assistant U.S. Attorney Stephen Kunz is on that list. Kunz is the prosecutor in charge of the grand jury investigation into the City of Tallahassee's redevelopment agency and several key developers. His name is on the two subpoenas issued June 13 asking for reams of public records related to business between the CRA and those developers, some of whom have close ties to city commissioners.*
*Kunz's actions in a kidnapping case nearly 20 years ago that got national attention led to the government dropping charges against a former Valrico couple in their daughter's disappearance.*
*Both the U.S. Magistrate judge and U.S. Middle District judge in the case excoriated Kunz for what they called his vexatious and frivolous prosecution of the parents and lack of evidence. A Justice Department investigation showed his reckless disregard of the rules governing federal prosecutors in charging the parents based on evidence that turned out to be non-existent. His supervisor promised that Kunz would never try another criminal case for him. The Florida Bar admonished him for misconduct. And the Justice Department had to pay $1.9 million to the parents' lawyer,*

the largest sanction of its kind ever levied against the government for mishandling a criminal case. It just shows the lengths to which Kunz will go to get a conviction, said Barry Cohen, who represented the parents of the kidnapped girl.

"He absolutely has no business making decisions that affect the freedom of other citizens," Cohen said in a phone interview Friday. "He's a moral bankrupt. He has no respect for the truth. I am basing my opinion on years of experience with him." Cohen said Kunz should have been fired and prosecuted for lying.

"The truth is he should have been indicted for criminal conduct," Cohen said. "It was transparent. How often do you see the government admit they filed a case in bad faith? The tapes didn't say what he said they said."

Given an opportunity to respond, U.S. Attorney for the Northern District Christopher Canova did not answer questions about Kunz's past conduct or discipline.

"Due to the risk of unfair prejudice, we are limited in what we can say about a particular prosecutor as those statements are likely to be tied to a particular investigation," said Amy Alexander, spokeswoman for the U.S. Attorney. The case also shows how reluctant the Justice Department is to strip a prosecutor of their job.

Kunz joined the U.S. Attorney's office for the Northern District of Florida as an Assistant U.S. Attorney in the Criminal Division in September of 2002. "During his tenure in the Northern District, he has served in several key positions under four U.S. Attorneys, including Anti-Terrorism Coordinator, Senior Litigation Counsel, and Chief of the Criminal Division," Alexander said in an email.

Prior to that Kunz worked as a supervisor in the Middle District of Florida, in Tapa.

Federal prosecutors took over the Sabrina Aisenberg case in 1999, after the Hillsborough County State Attorney decided it didn't have enough evidence to charge the parents despite tape recordings of thousands of secretly recorded conversations of the Aisenbergs in their home.

Federal prosecutors said they solved the case, based on what they said they heard on the recordings, according to a 2010 USA TODAY report on prosecutorial misconduct.

Kunz said they could be heard saying "The baby's dead and buried" and "What if they check the shed?" and "I wish I hadn't harmed her. It was the cocaine."

But those who listened to the tapes couldn't hear what Kunz said was there.

A Washington Post article said U.S. Magistrate Judge Mark Pizzo in 2001 criticized the poor audio on the tapes and called the recordings "a canvas of nebulous conversations: and what police said was on them "baseless and reckless."

After a judge ruled the evidence as inadmissible, the Justice Department withdrew the charges before the case went to trial, USA TODAY reported in 2010 in an article about the Justice Department's poor record of disciplining prosecutorial abuse.

In a 2003 ruling granting the Aisenbergs' lawyer 2.89 million, U.S. District Judge Steven Merryday said he could find no incriminating statements on the tapes, either.

The award was later knocked down on appeal to $1.9 million, Cohen said.

Even Paul Perez, the former U.S. Attorney and Kunz' supervisor, admitted he couldn't hear anything on the tapes, according to the USA TODAY report.

*Perez stripped Kunz of his supervisor position while the OPR investigated his case. He gave Kunz the option of working on civil cases or finding a job somewhere else. Kunz quit after he was reassigned and got the job in Tallahassee.*

*In 2005, the Florida Bar admonished Kunz for his misconduct, summarizing the OPR investigation, the results of which up until then had been sealed.*

*That wasn't the first go-round for Kunz. In 1986, the Fifth District Court of Appeal in Florida issued an opinion very critical of the state prosecutors and grand jury in a case against a judge indicted by the Volusia County grand jury on multiple counts.*

*"This court is concerned about the prosecutor's use of the indictment process in this case to level charges which are fatuous and patently without merit," the three-court panel said.*

*"Furthermore, they said, Kunz's use of the grand jury was "a bit like giving a small boy a loaded pistol without instruction as to when and how it is to be used," a quote of former Chief Justice Warren Burger.*

*"This case reveals the principal weakness of the grand jury system—the propensity of well-intentioned laymen in the hands of an irresponsible prosecutor to be led down any path," the three-judge panel said.*

*The panel also quoted United States Judge William Campbell, who said: "Today, the grand jury is the total captive of the prosecutor who, if he is candid, will concede that he can indict anybody, at any time, for almost anything, before any grand jury."*

And this is the prosecutor who instructed the grand jury and questioned the sole witness, FBI SA Larry Borghini, before the grand jury that indicted me. U.S. Attorney Larry Keefe, in my opinion, is just as responsible as Kunz, because he knew Kunz was working for him, and he should have overseen this process.

And there is more about Kunz.

### Ron Word, in his January 15, 1993, AP News story wrote,

*"In Jacksonville Florida, a former judge charged with receiving pornographic videotapes at his courthouse office committed suicide. Richard Kreidler, a former Duval County circuit judge, apparently shot himself in the head at a condominium where he was staying near Crawfordville, said Sheriff David Harvey. Kreidler, 55, pleaded innocent Monday to a federal indictment charging him with ordering "obscene, lewd, lascivious and filthy motion-picture films" and having them shipped to his office on seven occasions since August 1991.*

*His attorneys said they had warned prosecutors before the charges were filed that "his mental state was such that the ending of his life in this manner was very probable."*

*"It's trite to say, 'we told you so' but we did," the attorneys, William Sheppard, Edward Booth and Elizabeth White said in a statement.*

*They said they believed Kreidler would have been exonerated at trial; Kreidler, and a New York City film distributor, Bean Blossom Ltd., and its president were indicted by a federal grand jury Dec. 17. If convicted, Kreidler faced up to 35 years in prison and*

*$1.75 million in fines. Kriedler was the only subscriber of the video company named in the indictment, and his position as a judge was a factor in the decision to prosecute him, said Assistant U.S. Attorney Stephen Kunz. Kriedler, a Duval County judge for nine years, resigned December 1st. He did not seek re-election to his $80,000 a year post last fall, citing health reasons. On Monday, he told U.S. Magistrate John E. Steele he was under the care of a psychiatrist.*

## According to a November 22, 1994 article from the *Orlando Sentinel*:

*After the suicide of Kreidler, a judicial grievance committee said there was no evidence that Michelle Heldmyer and Stephen Kunz, both assistant U.S. Attorneys, improperly handled the high-profile obscenity case, in which Duval County Judge Richard M. Kreidler killed himself a month after being indicted in December 1992 on federal charges of ordering and receiving obscene videotapes from a New York company at his courthouse office.*

*During the investigation of Kreidler, it was learned that Assistant U.S. Attorney Michelle Heldmyer's husband, Joseph, was on the same subscriber list as Kreidler and had received tapes. A Jacksonville defense lawyer who asked for the inquiry, questioned why the husband was never charged. Sources said the cases were very different, however. For example, Heldmyer cooperated with authorities, destroyed the tapes when questions arose about their legality and did not have the judge's responsibility for hearing obscenity cases.*

I found this case to be even more disgusting to read than what was done to the Aisenbergs. Kriedler was prosecuted because he was a judge, yet the Assistant U.S. Attorney Michelle Heldmyer's husband, who received the same tapes was not charged. Kunz and Heldmyer continued on with their lives, moving on to prosecute others, while Judge Kriedler, age 55, put a bullet through his brain because he was held to a higher standard as a public official.

I know very little about Stephen Kunz, except that he along with several others in the U.S. Attorney's office and the Bay County Sheriff's office have destroyed my life. "It takes a lifetime to build a good reputation, but you can lose it in a minute." Will Rogers was right about that, except he should have added that you don't necessarily have to lose it, someone like Kunz can take it from you with all the power of the Federal government behind him. And we would not have been able to use any of this information about Kunz as part of our defense after documenting false information that Kunz and SA Borghini provided to the Grand Jury.

The grand jury transcript of August 19, 2020, the document released by Judge Mark Walker, reveals that AUSA Stephen Kunz continued his same methodology in achieving the indictment of this Mayor. His sole witness is

SA Lawrence Borghini who answers "correct" to Kunz's barrage of questions more often than he gives any detail, and there are many completely false statements made by the special agent and by the U.S. Attorney which are irrefutable. Their defense at the evidentiary hearing is that they corrected their mistakes in the superseding indictment. The point which for some reason was lost on everyone, including the Court, was that without their false statements and misleading information the first indictment may not have been a true bill. When a grand jury is told that someone has already been indicted and the superseding indictment is simply to add information or defendants, the defendant is already damned before the process begins.

I do know that my attorney Ron Johnson of Pensacola, spoke with Kunz by phone several times in the early months of 2019, asking him if we could provide him with information or meet with him if he had questions about me after my banking and business tax records were subpoenaed, and he continued to refuse, and also to say that I was a "subject" and not a "target" of the investigation. Another lie. The grand jury met in June of 2020 where he presented "evidence" against me, and then in August an indictment was returned against me for 64 counts--more than John Gotti or Al Capone, or even President Donald J. Trump.

Immediately following the evidentiary hearings of December 12th and 13th, 2022, we were told of Kunz's impending retirement on December 31st, which the Government said many times had nothing to do with the defense allegations of malicious and reckless prosecution of this case, referencing Kunz's jaded and malicious past as a prosecutor, and that his retirement was long planned before our evidentiary hearings.

9  MOTIONS TO DISMISS AND TO COMPEL DISCOVERY; THE
FIRST EVIDENTIARY HEARING; THE AFFIDAVIT FOR GAC
PROPERTY IS ACCIDENTALLY RELEASED TO THE MEDIA;
BUDDY, MY RESCUE DOG DIES; THE THIRD SUPERSEDING
INDICTMENT OF OCTOBER 18, 2022; THE SECOND
EVIDENTIARY HEARING; THE TIDE BEGINS TO TURN:  THE
BEACON OF BAY COUNTY AND THE BURNIE THOMPSON
SHOW


December 2, 2021

After the guilty pleas of both City Attorney Adam Albritton and former Commissioner Antonius Barnes, the trial was once again postponed, and all of us once again faced the holiday season with the stress and uncertainty of days filled with researching evidence; James and I worked as many hours as the attorneys, combing through City of Lynn Haven documents, contracts, commission meeting notes, emails, looking for anything and everything which was exculpatory for us, and at the same time, our attorneys were fighting the government, filing motion after motion, just to get the *Brady* information (any information in possession of the government which could be exculpatory to the defendants) due to us by law, and to show cause to Judge Mark Walker why the case should be dismissed altogether.  The following is the motion to dismiss the Second Superseding Indictment which was filed by Guy Lewis and also by my attorneys, on December 2, 2021.  The motion was also made public by Channel 13, WMBB, Panama City, Florida:

## DEFENDANT FINCH'S MOTION TO DISMISS THE SECOND SUPERSEDING INDICTMENT

Defendant James D. Finch by and through undersigned counsel, moves to dismiss the Second Superseding Indictment pursuant to Federal Rule of Criminal Procedure 12.

The Second Superseding Indictment is, once more, a strained attempt to transform unrelated conspiracy allegations into a single, overarching "honest services conspiracy. (1) The allegations, which are incorporated into all 26 Counts of the Second Superseding Indictment, again , describe a series of distinct schemes that properly at best may be charged only as multiple conspiracies in separate acts.

(1) Exactly as before, the government takes these same multitude of "overt acts" and re-incorporates them into each of the substantive counts. So, based on the way the Second Superseding Indictment is now pled, a jury could find that an event occurred unrelated to Finch and was committed by someone other than Finch, and yet convict him of a substantive count.

Since the Court ruled on this issue in August the law on duplicity has Changed. Indeed, the doctrine of duplicity still forbids pleading multiple conspiracies within a single count. Because the government has returned another charging document with the same legal defects, the Second Superseding Indictment should be dismissed. (2)

(2) The severe and undeniable unfair prejudice that has occurred before the Grand Jury cannot be overstated. The Grand Jury that heard this matter has been presented with evidence and a charging document making it appear that Finch is involved in multiple conspiracies that he had absolutely nothing to do with. This fatal legal flaw will be presented to the Court shortly in a distinct motion detailing legal and factual improprieties before the Grand Jury

### I.Procedural Background

On August 18, 2020, a Federal Grand Jury in Tallahassee returned the original, 64 count Indictment, charging Margo Anderson and Adam Albritton with wire fraud conspiracy to violate honest services and with substantive counts of hones services wire fraud. ECF No. 1

On December 31, 2020, Anderson's and Albritton's respective counsel challenged much of the language in the Indictment, arguing multiplicity, confusion, and inaccuracy. ECF Nos. 48, 49, and 50. Following a hearing, the Court ordered the government to "clean up" this initial Indictment, requiring amendments to factual allegations and corrections to multiplicitous counts. The Court further dismissed two counts as insufficiently pled. ECF No. 60.

On March 16, 2021, the Grand Jury returned a 41-count Superseding Indictment adding James Finch and former Lynn Haven City Commissioner Antonius Barnes. ECF No. 64. Unfortunately, the Superseding Indictment incorporated much of the same confusing legally flawed, inaccurate language from the initial Indictment.

The Superseding Indictment charged Anderson, Albritton, Finch, and Barnes with a single conspiracy count for engaging in honest services fraud, alleging violations of 18 U.S.C. 1343 an, 1346, and 1349. The "Manner and Means" section of Count 1 covered a period 66 months and included over 100 paragraphs. It was broken down into 9 subheadings—each containing different facts of the alleged "overall" conspiracy of honest services fraud. Each section involved a different set of facts, people, circumstances and time frame. Thematically, the charging language attempted to first describe a fraud associated with post-hurricane cleanup and involving a fraudulent invoicing scheme between Erosion Control Specialist ("ECS") and Michael White, the City of Lynn Haven's former City Manager. The allegations eventually transformed into an attempt to criminalize repeated complaints by Finch about the high cost of proposed construction projects.

On June 7, 2021, Anderson's and Finch's counsel challenged Count 1 of the Superseding Indictment, arguing that it violated the well-settled doctrine of duplicity. After oral argument over multiple days and careful consideration by the Court, the Court dismissed Count 1 of the Superseding Indictment on August 19, 2021. ECF No 185. Following the dismissal of Count 1, and with leave of Court, the government wanted "to take another stab at Count –at the conspiracy allegations" and figure out "how to charge them in light of the Court's ruling," for the third time in this case.

On November 16, 2021, a Federal Grand Jury in Pensacola returned a 26-count Second Superseding Indictment against Anderson and Finch. ECF No. 2014. Incredibly, the Second Superseding Indictment contains the same allegations of an overarching honest services fraud count involving the same five "projects," (3) and then reincorporating each and every allegation into Counts 1-26.

(3) In its Order dismissing Count 1 of the Superseding Indictment, the Court divided the allegations into five "projects": 17th Street, ECS, Debris Disposal, World Claim, and Rebuild. ECF No. 185 at 3.

## II. Multiple and Alleged Conspiracies

The Second Superseding Indictment alleges that Anderson and Finch participated in separate and distinct schemes in violation of the honest services statute designed to defraud the City of Lynn Haven and its citizens.

Rather than attempting to parse out each conspiracy contained in the Second Superseding Indictment yet again, (4) we respectfully direct the Court's attention to two separate "projects" that are alleged in the Second Superseding Indictment that are unconnected to Finch.

(4) We incorporate by reference the Court's previous discussions and ruling and our original Motion to Dismiss. ECF Nos. 149, 164, and 185.

## A. The ECS Conspiracy

The events alleged in paragraphs 59, 61, 67, 68, 76, 77, 81, 83, 84,(5) 85, 86, 87, 88, 92, 93, 94, and 97, involve the fraudulent billing scheme concocted by the owner of ECS (David "Mickey" White), the former Lynn Haven City Manager (Michael White), and others (The "ECS Conspiracy"). ECS was a company that performed debris removal and trash pickup services in the City of Lynn Haven after Hurricane Michael. (6) As part of the scheme ECS submitted false invoices to and received payment from the City.(7) Some of the services invoiced to and paid by the City were allegedly performed by ECS for City Officials.

(5) Paragraph 84 is the only paragraph of the Second Superseding Indictment that contains "ECS" and "Finch." Aside from the fact that this paragraph is wholly unsupported by any document, report, or 302 provided to the defense over the last eight months, the paragraph still fails to allege or prove interdependence.

(6) ECS was incorporated in 2011 by David "Mickey" White and was not licensed in Florida to do contracting, electrical, or plumbing activities, and held no business licenses within the State of Florida. After Hurricane Michael devastated the City of Lynn Haven, David "Mickey" White, Michael White, and others, including the former City Attorney and other unindicted public and law enforcement officials used ECS's services for their personal benefit and at the expense of the City. Unindicted conspirators carefully orchestrated work between vetted and contracted disaster relief companies and ECS. Indeed, there is no allegation or combination of allegations indicating that Finch had knowledge of or acted in concert with the common goals of David "Mickey White, Michael White, or any unindicted conspirator. See Also *United States vs. Michael White,* Case NO. 5:19-cr78 (N.D. Fla), ECS Nos. 65, 66, 70, 71, 75, 76, 83, 83, 105, 106; *United States v Adam Albritton,* Case No. 5:20-CR-28 (N.D. Fla), ECF Nos 196,197; *United States v. Antonius Barnes,* Case No. 5:21-CR-31 (N.D. Fla.), ECF 12, 13.

It is undisputed that the ECS Conspiracy as alleged does not involve Finch. There are no allegations that Finch or his companies worked with ECS. There are no allegations that Finch knew of or participated in the ECS Conspiracy.(8)

(7) Per the Second Superseding Indictment, Finch had no knowledge of or role in the contracts or invoices involving ECS. Most, if not all of the work ECS performed for the City was at the knowledge and direction of former City Manager Michael White. The false invoices were prepared and submitted by ECS and David "Mickey" White, many at the direction of Michael White. The Second Superseding Indictment even alleges that the "owner of Company A" instructed David "Mickey" White to "prepare" invoices for work allegedly performed at Anderson's residence. Nothing within the ECS conspiracy allegations contained in paragraphs 59, 61, 67, 68, 76, 77, 81, 83, 85, 86, 87, 88, 92, 93, 94 and 97 involves Finch or is required to ensure the success of the alleged conspiracy allegations against Finch.

(8) Indeed, the allegations claim that this conspiracy was allegedly hatched, on or about October 9, 2018, after Hurricane Michael. As this plan was hatched, James Finch was in a coma in the hospital in Jacksonville, Florida, having suffered a debilitating stroke. Finch was completely unaware of a hurricane hitting Lynn Haven and the magnitude of damage to the city until he was being driven back to his hometown on or about October 30, 2018.

## B. World Claim Insurance

Likewise, paragraphs 62, 63, and 89 involve the same alleged illegal insurance scheme (the "WorldClaim Conspiracy"). WorldClaim contracted to perform public adjustment work for the City and allegedly offered to perform public adjustment work at no cost to City officials, including Anderson (9). Again, there are no allegations against Finch.

(9) As alleged in the second superseding indictment, Anderson refused WorldClaim's offer of "pro bono" services, stating "I can't do that, I could lose my job." ECS No. 214 at 89. Anderson paid WorldClaim a negotiated, five percent fee. *Id.*

Indeed, this Court has previously held that the ECS and WorldClaim "projects" are separate conspiracies. ECF NO. 185 at 6. Nothing has changed in the allegations that would support a different holding or conclusion.

## III. Standard of Review

Duplicitous counts impermissibly charge "two or more 'separate and distinct' offenses." *United States v Schlei,* 122F.3d944,977 (11th Cir. 1997). The problems with a duplicitous count are threefold: "(1) A jury may convict a defendant without unanimously agreeing on the same offense; (2) A defendant may be prejudiced in a subsequent double jeopardy defense; and (3) A court may have difficulty determining the admissibility of evidence." *Id.; see also United States v. Kamalu,* No. 06-4956, 298 Fed. App'x ;1104,1108n.4(6th Cir.1988).

Charging multiple conspiracies in a single count is impermissibly duplicitous. *See, e.g. United States v. Urbanik,* 801 F.2d 692, 695, (4th Cir.1986) ("It is improper to charge a single conspiracy when multiple conspiracies exist. . ."); *United States v. Allmendinger,* No. 3:10-CR-248, 2011 WL 1157554, at (E.D. Va., March 2011) ("It is unquestioned than an indictment cannot charge two conspiracies in a single count."); *United States v. Berlin, 707 F. Supp.* 832,836 (E.D.Va. 1989) ("There is no doubt that an indictment cannot charge two conspiracies in a single count."); *accord United States v. Trainor,* 477 F.3d24, 31 (1st Cir. 2007) ("A claim that the government improperly has characterized a series of allegedly unlawful transactions as a single enterprise can implicate. . .the doctrine of 'duplicity'—the joining of two or more distinct offenses in a single count of an indictment…");*United States v Alexander,* 736 F. Supp.968, 994-95 (D.Minn1990) ("Defendants argue that Count I fails to charge a single conspiracy and that, on its face, it demonstrates the charging of at least two, and as many as eight, separate conspiracies. If that is indeed the case, the indictment is duplicitous on its face. . .").

Although a single conspiracy may consist of an agreement to commit multiple offenses, a single conspiracy count is impermissibly duplicitous when, rather than alleging multiple objects, it alleges multiple conspiracies. As established by the many cases that have condemned the charging of multiple conspiracies within a single count, the government is not permitted to circumvent the doctrine of duplicity by cobbling together unrelated schemes into one count and labeling the charge as a single conspiracy.

To determine whether the Second Superseding Indictment charges one conspiracy, this Court must ask whether there is "an 'interdependence' among the alleged co-conspirators." *United States v Toler,* 144 F.3d 1423, 1426 (11th Cir. 1998). The questions are whether Defendants "act[ed] *in concert* to further a common goal" and whether their "combined efforts" through the different sub-schemes "were…required to ensure the success of the venture." *United States v. Chandler,* 388 F.3d 796, 811 (11th Circ. 2004) (emphasis in original). To guide this analysis, this Court also looks to "(1) whether a common goal existed; (2) the nature of the underlying scheme; and (3) the overlap of participants." *United States v. Richardson,* 532 F.3d 1279, 1284 (11th Cir.2008). And this Court must apply the common goal element broadly because "'common' means 'similar' or 'substantially the same' rather than 'shared' or 'coordinate.'" *United States v. Holt, 777 F.3d 1234, 1263 11th Cir 2015) (*quoting *Richardson,* 532 F.3d at 1285).

An application of the relevant factors to the allegations that are incorporated into every Count within the Second Superseding Indictment demonstrates that the government, once again, has not pleaded (and cannot prove) one overarching conspiracy among the Defendants.

## IV. The Multiple Conspiracy Allegations

The factual allegations underlying the Second Superseding Indictment show that it charges multiple distinct schemes to violate different theories of the honest services statute. Critically missing from the allegations that ostensibly support the existence of "one" conspiracy are allegations that the various schemes shared a common purpose, depended on each other for their own success, were of a like or even similar nature, or had a substantial overlap in membership. Instead, the government has *again* alleged distinct and freestanding allegations of schemes that existed independently of one another, and therefore, if anything, constitute separate conspiracies.

### A.   No Common Purpose

There is no common objective that unites the various "projects" under the umbrella of a single conspiracy. *See Alexander,* 736 F. Supp. At 995 (explaining that when complex multiple-object conspiracies are alleged in a single count, "[t}he linchpin for such a charge to be properly pleaded is the existence of a single common objective"). Instead, as set forth in the Second Superseding Indictment, and as previously found by this Court, each of the alleged "projects" involved their own discrete objectives(s):

Contracts Conspiracy—An alleged bribery scheme to acquire infrastructure contracts for the benefit of Finch's companies.

ECS Conspiracy—Multiple schemes involving false invoices to acquire money and services at the expense of the City. Part of the alleged scheme involved wasteful spending, false invoices, and the payment of kickbacks.

Post-Hurricane Debris Disposal Conspiracy—Multiple schemes involving logistics (pricing, justification, and directives) for the disposal of vegetative debris to acquire money and/or services at the expense of the City. This alleged bribery scheme also includes allegations of seeking and obtaining DDMS approval from the State of Florida.

World Claim Conspiracy—An alleged insurance scheme involving public adjustment work for the City and offers to perform public adjustment work at no cost to certain City officials.

Rebuild Conspiracy—An alleged political conspiracy involving disagreements and different opinions regarding the rebuilding of public buildings and the high costs associated with proposed plans.

The government may attempt to argue, yet again, that each "project" was directed toward "defraud[ing} and depriv[ing} the City of Lynn Haven and its citizens of their right to honest services" of Anderson. But the totality of the allegations fails to establish a commonality of purpose. The government must do more than allege a general conspiratorial purpose between the defendants.

## B. Absence of Interdependence

Even if the allegations sufficiently allege a common purpose, which they do not, the allegations are duplicitous (alleging multiple conspiracies) because the Second Superseding Indictment fails to allege sufficient interdependence among the alleged co-conspirators. *See United States v. Woodard,* 459 F.3d 1078 (11th Cir. 2006) (A single conspiracy requires "an interdependence among the alleged co-conspirators") (citing *United States v. Chandler,* 388 F.3d 796, 811 (11th Cir. 2004); *United States v. Harrison,* 942 F.2d 751, 756 (10th Cir 1991) (internal quotation marks omitted) (explaining that interdependence is the "principal concern" in distinguishing between single and multiple conspiracies); *United States v. Smith,* 86 F.3d 1154 (4th Cir. June 4, 1996) (unpublished) (internal quotation marks omitted); *United States v. Hadeed,* No. 1:08-CV-461, 2009 WL 1657539, at *10 (E.D. Va. June 12, 2009) ("One conspiracy requires "interdependence among the alleged co-conspirators'....")

That is, even if the alleged purpose of defrauding the City and its citizens is a sufficient conspiratorial objective, a single conspiracy has not been charged because Defendants were not doing so collectively. *See First Fin. Sav. Bank, Inc. v Am. Bankers of Fla., Inc.,* No. 88-33-CIV-5-H, 1990 WL 302790 at *3(E.D.N.C. Apr. 17, 1990) ("the existence of a common goal, standing alone, will not suffice to show a single conspiracy" but must be "combined with evidence of interdependence between and among the alleged co-conspirators"); *United States v. Carnagie,* 533 F.3d 1231, 1239 (10th Cir.2008) ("This common goal, however, is not by itself enough to establish interdependence: 'What is required is a *shared,* single criminal objective, not just similar or parallel objectives between similarly situated people.") (quoting *United States v. Evans,* 970 F.2d 663, 671 (10th Cir. 1992*).* "Interdependence is established when the activities of the alleged co-conspirators in one aspect of the charged scheme are necessary or advantageous to the success of the activities of co-conspirators in another aspect of the charged scheme or the success of the venture as a whole." *United States v. Steward,* 256 F.3d231, 250 (4th Cir.2001).

As alleged in the Second Superseding Indictment, the various "projects" operated independently, and the success of one "project" did not affect another or even increase the probability that another "project" would succeed. For instance, the alleged acquisition of the 17th Street and ½ cent sales tax contracts have no bearing on the alleged schemes involving ECS or the World Claim events, and vice versa. Based on the Second Superseding Indictment's own allegations, the alleged schemes were not subparts of some greater, overarching conspiracy. The alleged "projects" rise and fall entirely on their own terms, and the government cannot prove (and the Second Superseding Indictment does not even allege) otherwise.

## C. Distinct Nature, Time and Membership

The conspiracies are uniquely distinct in nature, time and membership, as detailed above. Indeed, the Second Superseding Indictment contains no allegations that Anderson and Finch collectively participated in or were even aware of the alleged efforts of (1) convicted felons Michael White and David "Mickey" White., (2) one another, or (3) the unindicted "conspirators" or "others" to defraud the City and its citizens. The overarching honest services conspiracy allegations are legally and factually defective on its face and should be dismissed.

## V. The Appropriate Remedy: Dismissal

In general, the Court has discretion to fashion appropriate relief "according to the particular harm or harms to be avoided" in a particular case. *United States v. Sturdivant,* 244 F. 3d 71, 79 (2nd Cir. 2001). "Where an indictment or information contains a duplicitous count, the property remedy is to dismiss the count or to require the United States to elect which offense it desires to pursue." *United States v. Pleasant,* 125 F. Supp. 2d173, 176 (E.E. Va. 2000); *see also United States v. Aguilar,* 756 F.2d 1418, 1423 (9th Cir.1985); *United States v. Roy,* No. 11-CR-109, 2012 WL 47768 at *5 (D.Vt.Jan.9, 2012); *United States v. Bachman,* 164 F. Supp. 898, 900 (D.D.C. 1958) ("[I]f there are two or more separate and distinct offenses charged in one count, the indictment becomes subject to a motion to dismiss.").

Again, Finch does not believe that it is appropriate to ask the Court itself to reformulate the indictment into multiple offenses because such separate offenses have not been presented to or charged by a grand jury. Any effort by the government or even asking the Court to unilaterally rewrite the indictment by dividing it into multiple conspiracy counts or by electing one conspiracy and striking allegations of the others would unconstitutionally invade the province of the grand jury. (10)

(10) The same Fifth Amendment arguments and concerns apply to Counts 2026 of the Second Superseding Indictment because the 122 paragraphs of general allegations containing the multiple conspiracies are incorporated and realleged into each count.

*See Stirone v. United States,* 361 U.S. 212, 218-19 (1960) ("The Right to have the grand jury make the charge on its own judgment is a substantial right which cannot be taken awai with or without court amendment"); *accord United States v. Lentz,* 524 F.3e 501, 511 (4th Cir. 2008) ("[T}he 'court cannot permit a defendant to be tried on charges that are not made in the indictment against him'") quoting *Stirone,* 361 U.S. at 217); *United States v. Randall,* 171 F.3d 195,203 (4th Cir. 1999) ("[O]nly the grand jury may broaden or alter the charges in the indictment.").

The fact that the Second Superseding Indictment contains multiple conspiracy allegations that ultimately cannot be joined under Federal Rule of Criminal Procedure 8, however, provides further reason to dismiss the whole indictment rather than to order an alternative form of relief. *See e.g. United States v. Marlinga,* No. CRIM 04-80372, 2005 WL 513494, at *7 (E.D. Mich. Feb. 28, 2005) (finding single count charging multiple conspiracies to be "duplicitous," and concluding that "[b}ecause of the Court's finding that misjoinder has occurred [under Rule 8] …a single superceding [sic} indictment charging two conspiracies is not appropriate. Separate indictments is the only solution").

*United States v. Marlinga,* No. CRIM 04-80372, 2005 WL 513494 (E.E. Mich. Feb. 28, 2005), though not binding authority, provides a useful comparison and wise guidance. In *Marlinaga,* two defendants were charged in a single conspiracy count with conspiracy to deprive citizens of a right to honest services where the defendants allegedly offered to make and accept campaign contributions to a prosecutor running for Congress, in exchange for certain prosecutorial acts in two pending court cases. *Id.* at *4. Thus, the court determined that count one was duplicitous. *Id.* With respect to remedies, the court first recognized that a jury instruction would be an unsatisfactory remedy where the defect in the indictment is recognized in advance of trial and the indictment is "duplicitous on its face." *Id.* at *6.

The duplicity cannot be chalked up in this case as a harmless pleading defect or remedied by a curative jury instruction at trial. Indeed, leaving the multiple conspiracies alleged in the Second Superseding Indictment, even as separate counts, would run afoul of the standards for proper joinder under Rule 8. (11) Under the circumstances, dismissal of the whole indictment is the only remedy that will ensure compliance with the mandatory pleading requirements of Rule 8. And, even if misjoinder were not an insurmountable problem for the government, the indictment should be dismissed because the risk of trial prejudice is too severe. (12).

11. Because the Second Superseding Indictment alleges multiple conspiracies "the general rule" that "defendants charged in the same criminal conspiracy should be tried together," *United States v. Reavis,* 48 F.3d 763, 767 (4th Cir. 1995), does not apply. Instead, under Rule 8(b), the

alleged offenses must be "unified by some substantial identity of facts or participants" or "arise out of a common plan or scheme." *United States v. Porter,* 821 F.23 968, 972 (4th Cir. 1987). Thus, while multiple conspiracies may be alleged against multiple defendants in the same indictment, "the fact [that] two conspiracies 'are of a similar character or involve one or more common participants' is not enough. Even if there are some common participants, generally similar objectives and common confidential informants, multiple conspiracies must have a common goal or purpose to be joined under Rule 8(b)" *United States v. Greenfield,* No. 01-CR-401, 2001 WL 1230538 at *3-4 (S.D.N.Y. Oct. 16, 2001) (quoting *United States v Lech,* 161 F.R.D. 255, 256(S.D.N.Y. 1995) (Sotomayor,J.) (other internal citations omitted).

12. Even if dismissal were not otherwise required, it is the only remedy that will protect Finch from substantial trial prejudice (including potential violation of his constitutional rights). In this case, trial prejudice will inevitably result if the jury is asked to consider any of the counts as charged. First, there is a substantial risk of "prejudicial spillover" of evidence from one conspiracy into another. For example, evidence of the World Claim and ECS Conspiracies will be admitted against Finch even though the Superseding Indictment contains no allegations that Finch was aware of, involved in, or participated in those distinct and unrelated conspiracies.

Because this issue has been raised before trial, a mere jury instruction would not be appropriate. As one District Judge explained after concluding that a charged conspiracy count was duplicitous:

**{T}his court chooses to heed the time-honored adage that "an ounce of prevention is worth a pound of cure." This is particularly true, whereas here, the preservation of defendants' Fifth and Sixth Amendment rights hangs in the balance. In light of the potential infringement of these rights if this court chose to roll the dice and preserve the confusion of the [duplicitous count] until a jury instruction at the end of trial, the Ninth Circuit's observation concerning the timing of duplicity objections is particularly instructive: "A duplicity objection can easily be made before trial because a duplicity claim is directed at the face of the indictment and not at the evidence presented at trial."** *United States v Hardy* 762 F. Supp 1403, 1410 (D. Hawaii 1991); *Marlinga,* 2005 WL 513494 at *6 (Acknowledging that Count One of the Indictment is duplicitous prior to trial but failing to cure the duplicity until the jury instruction state, would leave Defendant open to the very prejudices the Court can prevent. Hoping that a jury instruction will remedy a problem that can clearly be solved now, makes no sense.")

## V.    Conclusion

As previously indicated, the Court previously ordered the government to "clean up" the initial Indictment. The Court required amendments to factual allegations and corrections to multiplicitous counts. The Court dismissed two counts as insufficiently pled. *See* ECF No. 60. The Court further has dismissed Count 2, which attempted to charge an offense clearly on its face outside the statute of limitations. ECF No. 121. Three months ago, the Court dismissed the same legally flawed allegations and conspiracy count that the government returned on November 16, 2021. ECF No. 185. The Court could not have been clearer in its ruling.

The government bears the responsibility of authoring the charging document. That responsibility carries with it a burden commensurate with the awesome power to investigate and prosecute on behalf of the United States. In this case, the sovereign no longer is entitled to the "benefit of the doubt" regarding drafting errors, mistakes, and decisions to disregard the Court's prior rulings.

For the reasons stated above, the Second Superseding Indictment should be dismissed as duplicitous.

## LOCAL RULE 7.1(K) REQUEST FOR HEARING

Pursuant to Local Rule 7.1(K), Defendant James D Finch respectfully requests that the Court set this matter for hearing because oral argument would assist the Court in resolving the issues raised in this Motion to Dismiss. The undersigned estimates that the defense would need approximately 30 minutes for argument.

Respectfully submitted,

Guy A. Lewis
Jeffrey Forman
Counsel for Defendant,
James D. Finch

**Throughout the agonizing years of this case, my attorneys, Rob Vezina and Tony Bajoczky, worked closely with Guy Lewis and Jeffrey Forman, and as each motion, argument, or rebuttal was filed, Rob and Tony would file on the same day on behalf of me, as James and I were committed to proving our innocence, and our defense strategies were aligned.**

Judge Mark Walker did grant the hearing requested by Guy Lewis, but the hearing did not occur until the end of March, and did not last thirty minutes, but rather *several days*, stretching into the first week of April of 2022. For those not familiar with the federal court system, after each motion is filed, such as this one, the government has at least seven days, sometimes more, to respond, and then after the government responds, the defense has yet another time period in which to rebut or respond to the government's response. With each motion filed, the days become weeks, and the weeks become months, dragging by in agonizingly slow motion for the defendants and for their families.

This motion to dismiss was filed just before the Christmas holidays, and so the response we even slower than usual. Prosecutors responded on January 21, 2022, and the news media immediately published their response; **Channel 13, WMBB Panama City's Brady Calhoun, reported:**

*Federal prosecutors have responded to arguments from the two remaining defendants in the Lynn Haven corruption trial.*

*James Finch, the owner of Phoenix Construction, and Margo Anderson, the former mayor of Lynn Haven, are accused of fraud and bribery in connection to several city projects both before and after Hurricane Michael.*

*Six other individuals, including the former city manager, city attorney, and leisure services coordinator have pleaded guilty in the case. And, a former city commissioner, Antonious Barnes, pleaded guilty in a separate matter but, according to prosecutors, plans to testify that Finch bribed him.* (**During the first evidentiary hearing of March 2022, Barnes testified that the prosecutors coerced him into the plea deal, and that Finch never bribed him. Barnes remained steadfast in this testimony and said during the first trial of James Finch that he never sold his vote, that Finch did not bribe him.**)

*Finch and Anderson contend that prosecutors allowed an FBI agent to lie during testimony to the grand jury, that much of the facts presented by prosecutors are wrong, and that prosecutors have repeatedly failed to provide important evidence to the defendants that exonerate their clients.*

*They also said that an investigator on the case was "involved in deeply troubling corruption." And they took aim at the prosecutor on the case by citing serious misconduct on a case from the 1990s and arguing that his actions during this investigation have been similarly unethical.*

*They hope these arguments will be enough to get the entire case thrown out.*

*In their response, prosecutors argue that none of these concerns are legally valid or are the basis for throwing out any count in the case, much less the entire case.*

*First, they minimize the role and actions of the local investigator and the FBI agent.* **(The local investigator is Major Jimmy Stanford of the Bay County Sheriff's Office who admitted under oath in the hearing to accepting** a motorcycle as a gift from Derwin White, and that Derwin White paid for his sister's funeral. **The FBI Agent referred to is Larry Borghini, whose many false statements to the grand jury along with those of Assistant U.S. Attorney Stephen Kunz, are excused here by the government.)**

*"This was clearly not knowingly false testimony," prosecutors wrote. "It is mistaken testimony or some indication that the case agent overlooked something."*

*They describe the allegations against the local investigator as "unconfirmed, sometimes hearsay at one or more levels, and-or already disproven allegations of misconduct against a law enforcement officer," they wrote. They add that he, "was present for some interviews conducted by the FBI but was never expected to be a government witness in this case."*

**Major Jimmy Stanford was the lead investigator for Sheriff Tommy Ford's "public corruption" case; this is false information.**

*They also state that "defendants have articulated no basis how any allegation of misconduct against (REDACTED) make it less likely that Defendant Finch paid bribes to Defendant Anderson,…or that Defendant Finch lied to the FBI about the Motorhome transaction."*

**The redacted name here is the contracted City Engineer, Chris Forehand, who had his hands in virtually every part of the corruption, as evidence has shown. His name was redacted at the time of this filing by the government.**

*The defense states that prosecutors violated Judge Mark Walker's ruling by filing a grand conspiracy charge again even though Walker previously threw that charge out. Prosecutors say that the new indictment does not try to prove a grand conspiracy.*

*While arguing that the legal claims of the defense, prosecutors reiterated their case against Finch and Anderson.*

**Here, the prosecutors once again state their allegations as fact, and Channel 13 is more than happy to print the allegations again. One of the most disturbing aspects of being a defendant in a federal case is the manner in which the government prosecutors state allegations against the defendant in a narrative as though it is true, and in the months, and in our case, years, of pre-trial motions, they continue to repeat their narrative and defendants must watch in silence as their lives are destroyed, over and over again, as they wait for their day in court. And then at the very end, they always state: "defendants are presumed innocent."**

*"Defendant Anderson pressured City officials with respect to Defendant Finch's projects (say, by steering $3.4 million of hurricane recovery business to him" they wrote. "And overruled the city manager about the conduct of Defendant Finch's projects, that Defendant Anderson took many benefits from Defendant Finch and they covered up the nature of the largest one (the motorhome)."*

*This was an expensive deal for the city, they added.*

*"The City could have sold the debris to the company across the street for*

*approximately $500,000 just as Defendant Finch later did, and had Defendant Anderson not so intervened to benefit Defendant Finch, the taxpayers would have been $3.4 million better off" they wrote.*

*They claim that Finch and his legal team have lied several times as the case headed to trial, including whether or not he would participate in a grand jury session, about his contact with Lynn Haven officials after he was ordered to stay away from them, and about whether or not he shared the discovery in the case with other individuals.*

*Although it is redacted, a portion of the filing suggests that Finch or one of his attorneys gave discovery material to GAC Contractors and that the FBI found the material when they raided GAC offices in August of 2021. GAC has at times been connected to the corruption case, but no charges have been filed against anyone who worked for or owned the company.*

This paragraph from the prosecutor's argument would become laughable when just a few months later, in August of 2022, the Affidavit for the Search of GAC (included in this chapter) was accidentally unsealed by the government and the *Panama City News Herald,* as well as WMBB Channel 13, published it, revealing widespread corruption, not only by GAC, but by many Bay County and State officials.

*The motorhome comes up again several times with prosecutors noting that Anderson was seen driving it around town and referred to it as "our" motorhome.*

We could not believe that the government apparently relied on testimony from someone who said they saw me driving a forty-foot motorhome around town, like maybe I used it to go to the post office or the grocery store.

*"The Andersons paid Defendant Finch $20,000 by check (and perhaps $15,000 in cash withdrawn) 22 months after receiving the motorhome and only after individuals were indicted in the related case and the FBI interviewed Defendant Anderson about her involvement with ECS," they wrote.*

Now the government begins to rewrite their story, saying *something* was paid for the motorhome instead of the original statement by Stephen Kunz, the assistant U.S. Attorney who stated in the press conference that I was "given a 106,000 motorhome." The government after seizing my husband's property, placed a value of $57,400 on the motor home; the $106,000 that Kunz originally claimed was the amount the Chris Forehand still owed the bank on the 12 - year- old motorhome in 2018. Eventually, the government would admit they had not checked all of our bank accounts, and we had the funds in our account to have paid cash for the initial down payment on the motorhome, and they returned the motorhome to us.

*They added that money seems to have come from hurricane insurance settlements.*

Another totally disingenuous statement by them; we received over 80,000 dollars in September 2019 from our insurance company as settlement for hurricane damage to our home. Our home was mortgage free, and if we had used the "insurance money" to go on an extended vacation instead of repairs to our home, to pay off the motorhome, or to give it to our favorite charity, we were under no obligation to use that money for any purpose other than whatever we wished to use it for, even though the prosecutors tried to portray everything about us in the worst possible light.

*A hearing in the case is scheduled for late February.*

*WMBB Channel 13-TV Panama City, Florida:*

Brady Calhoun would follow with another story on February 17, 2022, entitled, ***"Evidentiary hearing could impact Lynn Haven corruption case."***

*The Lynn Haven corruption defendants are rapidly heading for a showdown that could decide the fate of the case.*

*James Finch, the owner of Phoenix Construction, and Margo Anderson, the former mayor of Lynn Haven, are accused of fraud and bribery in connection to several city projects both before and after Hurricane Michael.*

*Six other individuals, including the former city manager, city attorney, and leisure services coordinator have pleaded guilty in the case. And, a former city commissioner, Antonious Barnes, pleaded guilty in a separate matter, but, according to prosecutors, plans to testify that Finch bribed him.*

*During a Thursday hearing, Judge Mark Walker said he was prepared to rule on several key issues in the case. Anderson and Finch's attorneys are asking the judge to unseal transcripts from the secret grand jury proceedings. They contend that prosecutors allowed an FBI agent to lie during testimony to the grand jury, that much of the facts presented by prosecutors are wrong, and that prosecutors repeatedly failed to provide important evidence to the grand jury that exonerates their clients.*

*They also said than an investigator on the case was "involved in deeply troubling corruption." And they took aim at a prosecutor on the case by citing serious misconduct on a case from the 1990's and arguing that his actions during this investigation have been similarly unethical.*

*They hope these arguments will be enough to get the entire case thrown out. Walker's first ruling on these issues is set for next week and the judge indicated that ruling would likely then lead to both an evidentiary hearing and a hearing on legal issues in the case.*

*Guy Lewis, Finch's attorney, said he plans to call the FBI agent to testify during the evidentiary hearing. However, he and the defense attorneys for Anderson stopped short of requesting that the prosecutors themselves testify and defend their decisions.*

*Judge Mark Walker said it was vital to know if either Anthony Bajoczky, Jr., Anderson's attorney, or prosecutor Andrew J. Grogan would be called as witnesses in these hearings. If they were that would require him to determine if they were credible witnesses and since both of them once worked as his law clerks, he would have to recuse himself from the case.*

*Walker explained that judges across the country deal with attorneys who they have once worked with or for.*

*"But there is a huge difference between having somebody appear in front of me and make a legal argument versus having somebody who is going to be examined, or their credibility is questioned and I have to weigh their credibility as a witness," Walker said. "But if I've got to judge the credibility…as a fact witness with Mr. Grogan or Mr. Bajoczky that I am unwilling to do."*

*After getting reassurances from both sides that it was unlikely the attorneys would be called as witnesses, Walker moved forward.*

*A ruling on how much grand jury information will be disclosed is expected next week. A hearing on several matters is set for March 8. A tentative date for the trial was set for April 2022.*

The evidentiary hearing surprised everyone in attendance, including the attorneys, at how much testimony Judge Mark Walker allowed, and the hearing was the beginning of a turning point in public perception of the case; two citizen journalists, Jodi Moore and Gerri "GAP" Parker, *The Beacon of Bay County,* attended the first day of the hearing, and then reported on it live, from the courthouse steps, incredulous at what they had heard. Burnie Thompson, of *The Burnie Thompson Show,* attended the second day of the hearing and every day thereafter, and began reporting on the hearing live. James and I are both grateful for all three of them, who after attending the hearing, were filled with questions, with curiosity, and they began a pursuit of the truth, reporting everything they found in a very public way, at their own peril. Because of their reporting, the tide of public opinion began to turn, and I began to feel my first glimmer of hope that this story could have a happy ending.

**The Beacon of Bay County**
**By Jodi Christine Moore**                    **April 2, 2022**
I have heard that people are criticizing the defense's case, saying that the lawyers are "trying to blame a dead man." I want you all to know none of this gives me any pleasure. Not a single decent person wants to "speak ill of the dead." I am completely empathetic to Derwin White's family and their wish to preserve his reputation, which they now feel has been trampled on by Anderson and Finch's lawyers. I will say, however, that if you carefully read what took me so long to write, the defense is presenting evidence of what they're alleging. There is the testimony of Mickey White and Major Jimmy Stanford, who each answered questions under oath in a Federal court under threat of perjury. This is not to be taken lightly. I have not said this before, but I'll reveal it now: the defense stated to the court

Thursday that Derwin White was also the target of FBI prosecution and would have been arrested if he had not died before his arrest could take place. That doesn't mean Derwin was guilty, of course, just like Anderson and Finch are innocent till proven guilty, but it does mean the prosecution had evidence of a crime if they were going to arrest him. Mr. Lewis is a top-notch and experienced lawyer with a national reputation, and I don't think he and the legal team would say that with no evidence to back it up. The prosecution did not refute that claim in court on Thursday either, so this has to be part of the unsealed grand jury papers, unless the defense has other substantial confirmation from a different source.

I'm just the messenger here and I am making no judgements about the guilt or innocence of any part. All of what I have stated and will state in the future will be reflected in the complete court transcripts from last Thursday and I am sure they are public record if anyone wants to request them. The hearing itself was public so I can imagine the court records would be as well. Further, since there is another hearing Monday at 1:30 p.m. EST at the Federal Courthouse in Tallahassee, I invite all of you who want to see first hand to drive over and get a front row seat to the testimony. Make your own judgement when you view all the facts. Until that time comes, you have no standing to make a judgement call in this case in my opinion. You're only speculating.

I want justice done no matter what. I think Anderson and Finch have every right to pursue a vigorous defense and seek the truth. Wouldn't you if you were in their shoes? I would. I would use every tool at my disposal and fight going to prison if I knew I were innocent.


The Burnie Thompson Show                    April 6, 2022
By Burnie Thompson

Back at the federal courthouse in Tallahassee figuring things out in the evidentiary hearing for developer James Finch and former Lynn Haven Mayor Margo Anderson.

Don't be shocked if this entire case against these two gets dismissed before trial.

I expect Chief Judge Mark Walker to take it under advisement after today's proceedings and then issue a ruling later on the motion to dismiss with prejudice.

Odds are still that it's heading to trial. But, I'm saying don't be shocked otherwise.

    I'll explain why later.


The Beacon of Bay County Florida
By Jodi Christine Moore                 April 8, 2022

Lynn Haven: Shared from WMBB: This is Brady Calhoun's report from last Wednesday's (4/6) hearing at the Federal Courthouse in Tallahassee in the Anderson/Finch case. I will be writing up my own report after conferring with Gap Parker who has her own notes from the hearings. The Burnie Thompson Show was also there at the courthouse Wednesday and Burnie devoted his Thursday night show to this topic. Frank Sewell shared the (more than) an hour-long show to the Beacon page already if anyone wants to hear what Burnie has to say about this case.

    There is a lot, lot more that Calhoun has not reported or has glossed over. Regarding Margo Deal Anderson, he seemed to imply, in my opinion, that ECS did free work AT Anderson's property. Anderson states storm debris was never cleaned up ON her property after Hurricane Michael. It was cleaned up on an easement next to her property that was not her responsibility to clean up. Anderson says she can prove what she says and the defense claims the prosecution has known for months the truth about the claim about the easement.

    The defense claims, and has evidence, that Anderson also honestly told World Claim Insurance that she could not accept pro bono work when it was offered.

    Federal agent Borghini also stated that when Anderson flew on Finch's plane, that had a value of nearly $40,000. The defense says that Florida statute says flights on such planes by a public official have the same value as flights on commercial airlines, and therefore there is no way the flights were worth tens of thousands of dollars.

    Calhoun also left out of his story that at the beginning of Wednesday's hearing Major Jimmy Stanford had reported to the court that he reviewed his records and now remembers that Derwin White paid for his (Stanford's) sister's funeral after Stanford initially denied it on the first day of the hearing.

    Just like Burnie Thompson showed his viewers Thursday night, there are pages and pages of notes from the hearing to go through. I have only reported a few things here. More is to come.

WMBB-TV Channel 13                     April 6, 2022
By Brady Calhoun
TALLAHASSEE : LYNN HAVEN DEFENDANTS ATTACK
INDICTMENT, INVESTIGATORS

A three-day hearing in the Lynn Haven corruption case that a federal judge described as extraordinary, concluded Wednesday in Tallahassee.

Defense attorneys for former Lynn Haven Mayor Margo Anderson and James Finch, the owner of Phoenix Construction, continued to attack the bribery and fraud charges against them.

The attorneys took issue with actions by investigators, statements to the grand jury, and the actions of one witness, former prosecutor Greg Wilson.

They alleged that Wilson was used as an informant by the FBI and used to get information about the defense in violation of attorney-client privilege. It is a claim that FBI Agent Lawrence Borghini denied on the stand Wednesday.

But, in another extraordinary moment, Borghini, the lead investigator on the case, testified that he was unaware federal prosecutors had called Finch, and Derwin White, the co-owner of GAC Construction, the quote, 'goal' of the investigation.

Prosecutors made the statement to a grand jury in June of 2020. But in July of 2020 Borghini told Finch he was only a witness.

It is "pretty important that the lead investigator of a federal agency…did not know that Mr. Finch was a target," Judge Mark Walker said later in the hearing.

In another unique moment, Borghini testified that Wilson, a former prosecutor, came to him with information about alleged corruption at the State Attorney's Office. Borghini said he took all of Wilson's information and filed it away for a possible future investigation into the office.

However, that investigation never moved forward, he said. The defense also brought up an "untrue" claim Wilson had made that Finch had hired a private investigator to record who was coming and going from the FBI office in Panama City and the Bay County Sheriff's Office in Lynn Haven.

Borghini did not answer as to whether or not he believed that claim but did say he never investigated the issue further.

Guy Lewis, Finch's attorney, took issue with Borghini's handling of the matter. He noted that Borghini never made Wilson fill out a form that said he waived his rights before talking to the FBI. Borghini countered that Wilson, an attorney, and former law enforcement officer was well aware of his rights. He added that he believed Wilson had filled out the form on the same day while in the custody of the Bay County Sheriff's Office.

Lewis also said that Borghini's reports in the case sat idle, and in some cases were not properly filed for nearly two years.

What impact these issues will have on the case is unclear. The defense is hoping Walker will agree that prosecutors were reckless and perhaps even malicious and that they violated the law and their clients' rights multiple times during the investigation. If he agrees he could throw the entire case out with prejudice.

However, Walker said multiple times that he was allowing the defense to investigate the usually secret and sealed grand jury process in order to "preserve the record" for future appeals. Walker also suggested multiple times that attorneys should not look to his comments during the proceeding for any indication of what he actually thought about the issues in the case.

**The Beacon of Bay County**
**By Autumn Miller    (Attorney)**                              **April 8, 2022**

Some questions that I have that have not been addressed in relation to the federal corruption investigation, especially in light of Major Stanford's clear conflict of interest yet continuing participation in the investigation: What are the terms of any Task Force Agreement(s) between the Department of Justice and the BCSO? Are there special terms within the Task Force Agreements relating to sharing or disbursement of funds from seized/forfeited property (monies, vehicles, personal property, real property, businesses and corporate/business property, etc.)? Has the BCSO applied to receive any forfeiture proceeds under the Equitable Sharing Program, if so, how many requests and for how much in relation to this investigation? What is the total potential financial interest of BCSO in this case? Were/have any civil or criminal forfeiture proceedings taken place? Are any civil forfeiture proceedings still possible or pending? Has any property been forfeited pursuant to negotiated pleas? How much property is seized and held pending the outcome of the case in hope/expectation that the court will order forfeiture of seized property? What is the financial interest of the Federal Government Agencies involved in investigating this case? Did the timing of when the Federal Government became involved (some cases are still only being prosecuted in State Court) coincide with any discovery/disclosure that large properties and funds might be subject to seizure/forfeiture? What, if any agencies, offices, businesses (In example law enforcement equipment store owner), or non-profits (501c3) that regularly receive payments purchases or contributions from **BCSO (under permissible use of ESP funds) are led by family or "friends" of those investigating or are led by "enemies/rivals/competitors of those investigated?**

The questions asked by Autumn Miller in the post above are important ones, especially the one concerning non-profits which "regularly receive contributions from BCSO and are led by family or friends of those investigating? The Gulf Coast Children's Advocacy Center (GCCAC), awarded GAC Contractors $729K on April 8, 2019, seven days after I went to Sheriff Tommy Ford with evidence of fraud by ECS in Lynn Haven. Then, on May 27, 2020, AshBritt Environmental donated $625K that was earmarked for GAC Contractors who was awarded that $625K on that same day. Sheriff Tommy Ford was an officer of the Board in 2019, (Member at Large), and 2020 (Treasurer). The Chief Executive Officer is Lori Allen, who is the daughter of Maj. Jimmy Stanford of the Bay County Sheriff's Department, who led the investigation against James Finch and Margo Anderson.

**The Beacon of Bay County**                                    **April 13, 2022**
**By Jodi Christine Moore**
  "As promised, here is my synopsis of BCSO Major Jimmy Stanford's testimony from 3/31/22:
  Stanford told the court when he was called to testify at the hearing he had been with BCSO for 26 years and a Major for 5 years. Michael White was discussed, and the fact that as City Manager he got a gun issued by the City, as well as blue lights and a badge. Mr. Stanford denied knowledge of the vehicle lights. He told the court that he had sat in more than a dozen interviews with witnesses in the corruption case along with FBI Special Agent Borghini. He said if he took notes in those interviews they would have been transcribed into a report and he was not asked to save those notes, so he had none. This is significant because in an FBI investigation, investigators (and the defense considers Stanford to be an investigator in the case) are supposed to keep their notes and provide those along with the "302s," which are the official records submitted in such cases. Stanford stated at that time his opinion to Mr. Lewis (James Finch's defense lawyer) that there is "a witch hunt to make me look like a dirty cop."
  The defense stated, and Jimmy Stanford did not deny, that at one time Stanford and Derwin White were "best friends." They met after a murder investigation and, as it turns out, did not live far from each other. Stanford said his uncle was friends with Derwin too.
  The defense stated that Stanford received (from Derwin) part of a

downpayment on a house; cash; gifts and services; that Derwin paid for Stanford's sister's funeral; and free work was done by GAC or ECS (Mickey White's company) at Stanford's home. Stanford denied almost all of this, saying he paid or offered to pay Mickey White for services performed and says if Mickey White testified any differently, Mickey is lying. He says one day Mickey White just showed up at his house and started demo on some concrete on a job that needed to be done but Stanford had not asked him to come. Stanford admits to receiving a "used" motorcycle from Derwin White as a birthday gift but says he himself thought it was "too much" and returned the bike to Derwin. The bike went back and forth between the two of them and eventually Stanford kept the motorcycle. Stanford also said one of his sons bought an older truck from GAC. (At a later court date, last Wednesday, 4/2/22, Stanford amended his testimony for the court to state that he checked his records and now remembers that Derwin White did indeed pay for his sister's funeral. No amount was given.)

Mr. Lewis stated that Derwin White was one of the main targets of the FBI investigation and was going to be arrested, and therefore it was a huge conflict of interest for Stanford, as a close friend of Derwin's, to be a lead investigator on the case for BCSO. Stanford says that at the time of the FBI investigation into Derwin, he and Derwin were no longer friends, and in fact, were "mortal enemies." Derwin fell out with Stanford when SAO Attorney Greg Wilson (another very good friend of Derwin's) was arrested in another case. Stanford testified against Wilson. Derwin was very unhappy with Stanford about that. Stanford told the defense that he did not pass along any information about the FBI investigation to Derwin White, and he also did not think he needed to recuse himself from the investigation even though he and Derwin had been such close friends. Stanford stated the was "an honest police officer" and he did not see that there was a conflict of interest.

Stanford denied that Margo Deal Anderson was a "whistleblower" in the case regarding Michael White and ECS. He stated that the investigation into White and ECS started right after Michael White was arrested for domestic violence in March of 2019 and some suspicious activity was seen on Michael White's phone. Mr. Lewis pointed out that Margo Anderson went with Lynn Haven Police Chief Ramie to BCSO on 4/1/29 with evidence of corruption in the City, and a warrant for Michael White's phone was not obtained until 4/10/19.

Regarding Greg Wilson, Mr. Lewis of the defense team stated that Agent Borghini went to Greg Wilson for information in the case and

Wilson was cooperating with the FBI. (In fact, Mr. Lewis characterizes Greg Wilson as an informant and agent of the FBI, even though in later testimony, Agent Borghini denied this. He says Wilson would call him up and they would meet but denies formalizing this arrangement.) Greg Wilson (and Derwin) thought Wilson had been "set up" by Stanford. After Wilson had to leave the State Attorney's Office (SAO) following his arrest, he took a job with Derwin's company, GAC. Stanford testified he did not "set up" Wilson and also denied ever telling Borghini to not trust Wilson, which is an allegation that was made.

When asked, Stanford agreed that a police officer cannot talk to a defendant without his/her lawyer present.

Mr. Lewis made reference to the 2 identical sets of invoices ECS had made up months after the work they billed for what was supposedly done. In those invoices were records of work supposedly done at Anderson's home and her mother's home (work that Anderson denies was done and that she says she can prove was also not her property.) The significance of the invoices as it pertains to Stanford is that the defense is asking how Derwin knew "the FBI was coming." How did he know to tell his nephew Mickey to make up the "false" invoices? (Mickey claims they are not false, but he and his staff wrote them from memory, months after the work was supposedly performed.) Stanford testified he doesn't know how Derwin got the information about the FBI coming to ECS because he says he and Derwin were not friends by then. Derwin and Mickey knew the FBI was coming, but they did not realize the "raid" on the ECS offices would be the very next day after the invoices were created and Derwin received them, in April of 2019. That's why one set of invoices was found in the trash. (I have also been told the invoice numbers were "sequential," which would not be realistic for work that was actually performed in real time.)

As for my opinion: I would agree that friends can give each other gifts, although I've never had a friend give me a motorcycle! Derwin was apparently known for giving gifts and being very generous. The implication of the defense, of course, is that Stanford was "bought and paid for." (My words.) The defense also is maintaining that someone in the BCSO close to the FBI investigation was leaking information, especially leaking it to Derwin White, and the defense is pointing the finger at Stanford, who denies it. The implication of the Derwin White/Stanford relationship is that Derwin had a copy (and a lawyer in the State Attorney's Office, Wilson) who were in his corner. The defense is making the case that if Derwin needed something taken care of legally, he could call on Stanford, Wilson, or both, and

Derwin returned the favor with services, gifts, and money. I don't know what really happened. Only Stanford truly knows, because Derwin can no longer tell us. But I personally think it was very improper of Stanford to be part of the FBI investigation in any capacity considering his past close relationship with Derwin, whether they were friends or enemies at the time in question.
Next up: My report of the hearing from 4/6/22. Bear with me.

After the hearing was over, the defense and the prosecution submitted arguments and rebuttals to the Court, and the process was endless. After almost two years of stress and fighting the government, I was no longer the same person I had been before the August 2020 indictment, and my attorneys, Rob Vezina and Tony Bajoczky, often listened to my tears, to my angry, impatient venting of my frustration, so uncharacteristic of the person I had been before this happened. And yet, through it all, they believed in my innocence, they remained steadfast, they kept our ship on course, and along with Guy Lewis and Jeffrey Forman, continued to whittle down the case of 64 charges against me and almost thirty against James Finch, until in the end, we only faced conspiracy and bribery, two charges, based on the "666" wink and a nod bribery charge, which our attorneys argued vehemently on our behalf; Supreme Court in May of 2024, ruled against prosecutors using this type of charge in May of 2024, just a little over a year too late for me.

April 21, 2022

Today is the seventh anniversary of the day I was elected the Mayor of Lynn Haven, Florida, according to my Facebook memories…April 21, 2015.
And today has been a battle with attorneys…mine. How can I have the energy to fight the Government and my own attorneys at the same time? I just feel exhausted and defeated. I received the "working rough draft" of our supplemental brief in support of motions to dismiss, yesterday afternoon at approximately 4:30 p.m. eastern time. But only because I had written an email request the day before asking for it. And Tony Bajoczky, one of my attorneys, was reluctant to send me the draft. I wanted to see how far along we were in the process since the brief is due to the court tomorrow, April 22,2022, following the evidentiary hearing we had just been through.
I made breakfast for my husband, then sat down and read the rough

draft one more time before going to the computer to start working on additions or ideas for the brief that I wanted to make sure we included. As I turned on the computer, an email popped up from 1:59 a.m. this morning in which Tony was writing to Rob Vezina, my other attorney, to tell him he thought we would need two more business days, or until Tuesday, April 26th to finish the brief.

I was livid. After teaching English at the high school and college level for thirty years, I had seen more research papers than I care to remember which had been assigned in January of a semester, and then the day before the paper was due in May, watching students frantically trying to finish on time. This is what I envision has happened over the last two weeks. The hearing was April 6, 2022, and the first brief from the defense was due tomorrow, April 22, 2022. That is sixteen days, and no matter what is said, I cannot be convinced that this brief has been the central focus of the last two weeks. I believe it was drafted beginning early yesterday morning, and now the weekend is here, one attorney has his email shut down with an "out of town' email responder to whoever writes, and the other attorney is not answering his phone.

I called James Finch, my co-defendant, and read the email to him. He was as outraged by the delay as I was, and I told him I was going to call Rob. James said, "they probably didn't start working on it until yesterday," which was of course my immediate thought, even though I knew this was not true.

I call Rob, and he answers. I speak in anger, I use terrible language, and he remains calm and deliberate in his answers which only make me angrier. I use an example of information Tony did not present at the hearing two weeks ago, and I tell him that waiting until the last minute to prepare is how mistakes and omissions are made. He then calmly tells me that maybe we should get together next week sometime and talk, and if I have lost confidence in them perhaps I need different attorneys. At this point I am no longer able to have a coherent conversation. I apologize for my language, do not apologize for what I said, and then once again, I am reduced to rubble. Tears. Humiliated in front of another man who has control of my life. The one who will either be able to gain my freedom for me through his legal expertise, or the one who will lose the case and my life in the process. And now I have pissed him off or hurt his feelings to the point he apparently no longer wants to represent me. All I wanted was to express how resentful I was feeling at being left out of the decision to put my life on hold again, because of what I felt was unpreparedness on their part. For some reason I was unable to do that. After angrily crying for the next few minutes, I picked up my phone and sent a text message to Rob, who is one of the gentlest, kind men I have ever known:

*Words spoken in anger are never of any meaning. I hope to someday be the person I once was. The teacher that students loved because she never raised her voice, never blamed or berated others for those things for which they had no control.*

*If I have not completely destroyed our attorney-client relationship, I sincerely ask for your forgiveness for the way I spoke to you just now, and I can promise you that, with the Lord's help it will not happen again.*

*I find myself living from one court date to the next, and sometimes even adding another twenty-four hours seems an eternity.*

*I have a difficult time not being involved in the process and maybe that is unusual for a client; I don't know because this is not a path I have ever been on.*

*I am seeing a therapist, I seek the Lord's face every morning of my life, but it seems I continue a downward spiral in being the Mom, the grandmother, the wife, and the friend I have always been as this situation slowly takes away my joy and my life, hour by hour, day by day.*

*I will try to be better; you and Tony are a large part of my hope for having a future. Again, I am sincerely sorry, and I wish I could take back the phone call I made, but I can't."*

I then looked again at the email thread from early this morning:

From: Tony Bajoczky
To:    Rob Vezina
"We should talk in the morning. I propose we move for an extension to Monday/Tuesday. I can have a product to file by Friday lunch. We're at 46 pages. Will balloon to 50 before we're done. I'm sure we can edit it down and make it more user friendly with a little more time.
Talked to Jeffrey around 1230. He's a little ahead of us but supportive of the proposal. (Jeffrey is one of my co-defendant, James Finch's attorneys)

Then at 11:56 a.m. today Tony forwarded the above email to me with a separate email to me:
"Margo,
We are asking for an extension until Tuesday (2 additional business days) to file the supplemental brief. There are a lot of facts and law and issue. You and James can direct blame to me, but we will be better off with the extra days."

I answered at 1:41 after having yelled at Rob on the phone and then apologizing to him:

"Tony,
I sent you the email with some of my thoughts about the brief, but I sent it before I saw your email about the extension.

If you can use the information in the brief that I see as important, I hope that you will, and I will send you any additional thoughts that I have. As I told Rob, I am probably more involved in the process than I should be, or maybe I am not, because I have never experienced this path before. I don't know how involved other clients are with their own defense.

I was very unhappy that an extension was done without talking about it first, and I also expressed that to Rob. I didn't see your email from around 2 this morning until a little while ago because it was in the email thread and didn't show up as a new mail, but you did say that we needed to talk this morning.

I tried to call you as well, before I called Rob, but you didn't answer, and as far as blame goes, there is no blame, just a missed deadline, which in the grand scheme of things doesn't make a lot of difference, the delay just seemed bigger than it was today. I just want my life back, and in retrospect, looking back, if the trial had happened when I wanted it to in March of 2021, we would have had none of the information we have now; the process just seems endless, and some days, like today, just seem unbearable.

I have apologized to Rob for the way I spoke, and he was gracious and kind in response, the way the person I used to be spoke in every conversation I had with anyone, friend or stranger.

As you progress with more information or versions of the draft, I would be interested in reading, and when you have the final draft, I am happy to be an additional set of eyes for typos or for substantive or other factors."

Sincerely,
Margo"


I called James and told him how horrible I was on the phone to Rob and then how I had texted him an apology because I felt so terrible.

"I have eaten so many shit sandwiches in my life that I have gotten used to it," he said.

His voice sounded flat, dejected, and not full of humor like it usually did when he was talking about the attributes, or lack of them, possessed by attorneys. James does not like attorneys.

"Well, we are not going to get used to eating them anymore," I answered. "This is going to be over with soon, and we will have our lives back."

He did not have an enthusiastic reply, and we ended the conversation.

Buddy, my dog, was curled in a ball on the bed, miserable, as he listened to me cry and rail against the world to my long-suffering husband, Lee. Lee finally got up and said he was going to run some errands and get a hot dog for lunch. I think he just needed to escape my day of emotional outburst…certainly not his first rodeo in three years of listening to all of this, and I thanked God that he was still here, still with me through the Hell that no one who has not been indicted by the Federal Government can possibly imagine. The toll it takes on each day of your life, the pressure on marriage, on finances, on every part of daily life that one sees as normal. Nothing is normal, nor can it ever be again. Ever.

Because we have filed for an extension for our brief, I am more than certain that the prosecutors will now do the same, further delaying the Court's ruling, but I have got to get a grip on the time factor. This month has been three years since Derwin White and the other thugs with law enforcement, elected officials and others started their campaign to take down the Mayor of Lynn Haven. Three years is a very long time to endure attacks from the media, and to live under a dread of fear and uncertainty; it is also plenty of time to wallow in self-pity, to allow circumstances to control one's life instead of faith.

Today has been a day of defeat; but tomorrow will be better because I will make sure it is. I will try to trust the attorneys to do their jobs, I will keep my eyes on the Lord, and I will not allow the evil that brought this on my life to have any more of the days that God has promised me were mine on this earth.

"Thank you, Jesus, for one more day. Thank you for forgiving me of my sins. Let me be more like you tomorrow, especially when I am speaking with the attorneys."

**The Beacon of Bay County Florida**
**By Jodi Christine Moore**　　　　　　　　**May 16, 2022**

**BAY COUNTY/LYNN HAVEN: This is from a story the *Panama City News Herald* published online on Friday and the piece, in part, discusses Major Jimmy Stanford of BCSO. Stanford has been accused of corruption by James Finch's defense team, and he admits to accepting a motorcycle and payment of his sister's funeral from**

Derwin White. Major Stanford denies being a "dirty cop" and is still employed with BCSO. Sheriff Tommy Ford says he can't comment on the situation because of a court order. What court order is that? Can he produce it? The hearings in Tallahassee at the Federal Courthouse when Stanford testified were open to the public and not secret. The prosecution in the Margo Deal Anderson and James Finch case has until next week to present its response to the federal court.

*(The article Jodi Moore refers to is the online edition of the Panama City News Herald, by Tom McLaughlin, May 13, 2022.)*


The Burnie Thompson Show
By Burnie Thompson                    May 17, 2022

Tonight is the deadline for federal prosecutors to file their brief in the Lynn Haven corruption case.

It's in response to the briefs filed by former Mayor Margo Anderson and developer James Finch regarding the evidentiary hearing in early April.

Judge Mark Walker will issue a ruling on the Defendants' motion to dismiss with prejudice after the Defendants file a final rebuttal no later than May 24, 2022.

The Court will base its decision on whether or not
(1) The FBI violated the Defendants' 6th Amendment right to attorney-client privilege;
(2) The FBI and federal prosecutor Stephen Kunz willfully and repeatedly misled the Grand Juries in order to obtain indictments;
(3) Investigators and prosecutors withheld evidence that could be exculpatory.

From what I saw at the evidentiary hearings, the evidence does not support the charges against Anderson and Finch.

The prosecution is rattled because Judge Walker ordered the Grand Jury transcripts and investigation notes to be provided to the Defense.

This happens less than 1% of the time. But EVERY Defendant deserves to see what investigators and prosecutors tell the Grand Jury, which is composed of ordinary people with no legal training.

You'd think the investigators and prosecutors would be proud of their findings and testimony.

But they're not. Instead, they're pissed. And that's

understandable because there are many false statements to the Grand Jury and discrepancies in the investigators' notes.

Now here's my opinion (keep in mind that I only know what I've seen. There's much more to learn if it goes to trial):

1.  The prosecutors and investigators don't look happy or confident. In fact, I don't think that they want to go to trial where they'll have to answer tough questions under oath to a federal judge and jury.

2.  I think it's more likely than not that Judge Mark Walker will dismiss the case with prejudice. Prosecutors already have had several bites at the superseding indictment apple.

3.  Though the Prosecution has the power to appeal a dismissal with prejudice, I don't think they will. At this point, I think they'd MUCH rather avoid putting investigators and others under cross-examination and just blame the Judge and powerful defense attorneys if it gets thrown out.

4.  There's no doubt Lynn Haven residents were victims of public corruption. Those who did it have pleaded guilty.

5.  There seems to be much more to this story.


May 17, 2022

As Burnie Thompson was doing a show and posting about the document which James Finch and I were waiting to receive from the prosecutors, I was in such a dark, emotionally drained place, that I wrote a letter, pouring out my heart to my "accusers," knowing it would never be delivered. I wrote it anyway:

Dear Acting U.S. Attorney for the Northern District of Florida Coody, Assistant U.S. Prosecutor Kunz, and Assistant U.S. Prosecutor Grogan, Former U.S. Attorney Larry Keefe, FBI Agents Borghini and Rojas, Sheriff Tommy Ford, Major Jimmy Stanford, and the other investigators who falsely accused and indicted me beginning on August 19, 2020:

Although you will not receive this letter, since I cannot speak with you directly, I am writing to you this evening, and this letter will become part of the book I am writing, slowly, painstakingly, as slowly and painstakingly as this case of over three years continues to loom like a dark cloud over my life, the life of my co-defendant, James Finch, and our families.

Today is the day you are to file your brief in response to the evidentiary hearing of March 31, April 4th and April 6th, 2022, and the brief filed by the Defense on April 26th, 2022. The time is now 6:02 p.m., May 17th, and all of the federal offices in Tallahassee are closed; the brief is not filed. The defendants have looked for it all day today, because the contents of your argument as well as the contents of ours will determine how we will live the rest of our lives. Once again, your office will wait until the last hour to file, either out of arrogance, (for both the Court and the defendants) or perhaps just another example of the incompetence of how the U.S. Attorney's office of the Northern District operates.

Once again, I am paralyzed and unable to go about any meaningful tasks because you are in my head, as is former U.S. Attorney Larry Keefe, now in the position of Florida's security "czar", for after the comments he made as he was leaving office about " staying active in Tallahassee", I feel sure he is in contact with your office, but I could be wrong.

I will be up, as will my co-defendant, James Finch, until midnight, waiting to see what new version of deceit you have to offer. What I believe right now is that you probably finished writing this document days ago, and it is lying on one of your legal clerk's desks, with instructions to file it at 11:59 eastern time. But again, I could be wrong, and the three of you might be in your office, completely convinced of our guilt, working diligently until the last moment to make sure your brief is perfect, stellar, worded to convict us. But I really do not believe that. Because in the two years since you destroyed my life, I have come to know all of you. I listened to the press conference for which you drove to my hometown. Grandstanding with the corrupt Bay County Sheriff, making sure that I could never hold my head up again in the town where I was born, taught school, went to church, and lived my life. You meticulously planned the press conference of August 19, 2020, to be on the one-year anniversary of Mr. Keefe's establishment of the public corruption unit, and the taking down of Lynn Haven's Mayor fit your agenda perfectly. You let me sit extra hours in the jail cell in Jacksonville, so that at the very hour I was in front of the judge listening to the 64 charges being read against me, you were gloating and standing in front of the press and the people of Bay County who used to love me, to trust me, and were ready to elect me to a higher office according to the polls.

So, as I am waiting this evening to read whatever argument you are preparing for Judge Walker to convince him that I masterminded the theft of five million dollars from my hometown, I would like to tell *you* what you have taken from me.

You have taken my ability to sleep. I have not slept in peace for over three years now, since the day I discovered what Michael White had done and went to the person I trusted for help…Sheriff Tommy Ford. Sleep is a precious thing; without it one's health quickly begins to deteriorate, as mine has, and aging begins to come upon one quickly, almost as though time begins to move forward without one's permission. When I look at myself in the mirror, I no longer recognize the person I see there; I no longer see the energetic, health-conscious person I was, but a face covered in a rash I cannot explain, a weight gain of over twenty-five pounds due to a thyroid issue, deep lines which were not in my face three years ago, and tired swollen eyes which no longer sparkle with joy, but are sad, and defeated.

You have taken the life of my Mom, my beautiful Mom, who I believe would still be with us if not for you. On Palm Sunday, March 28, 2021, she suffered a sudden, massive heart attack. She had never had any heart issues. She had literally grieved herself to death, listening week after week to the local news media calling her daughter a thief, seeing video of our homes in the nightly news over and over, with the FBI agents surrounding the property, seizing our motorhome from beneath the pole barn on our property, and accusing the "mayor's mother of having her property cleaned and charged to the city." She was humiliated, heart-broken, and embarrassed in the hometown where she was loved and respected by everyone; and her beautiful soul could no longer bear the pain. I know you were aware of her death because you follow my social media page so closely, and the "secret tapes," recordings made of my conversations over months with Lynn Haven Police Chief Ricky Ramie, were suddenly released to us by email on the day of her funeral, another calculated and cruel tactic to try and terrorize me further. As we left Kent Forest Lawn funeral home, an escort of Bay Count Sheriff's Office deputies sped along beside us, stopping traffic, flashing blue lights, something we had not requested. I asked the funeral director to tell them they were not needed for my Mom's last journey from the church to the cemetery. She would not have wanted them there, and neither did we. We drove without the escort to her resting place. One small victory.

You have taken joy from my marriage of twenty-three years to Lee Anderson; a three tour Vietnam Veteran, a 100 % disabled veteran; our ability to travel, to socialize with friends, to book and perform musical concerts, to interact with our children and their social circles without embarrassing them, just to relax with each other, cooking, laughing, having a glass of wine, all of this has been taken from us. Our marriage has suffered because of financial loss, loss of sleep, stress over legal decisions, arguments that seem to happen with more and more frequency, and health conditions related to stress.

You have taken away the pride and confidence my daughter and my granddaughters had in me; my daughter, an attorney, had just taken a new position a few months before I was arrested; she had to go in and explain to her boss that her mother, the Mayor of a Florida City, had just been suspended by the Governor and indicted with 64 federal charges; my daughter had to explain to my two little granddaughters why their Mimi was on the news not only in the Panama City area, but in Jacksonville where they live, all over the state of Florida and nationally as the Mayor who had stolen five million dollars in the aftermath of Hurricane Michael and had been suspended by Governor Ron DeSantis. My daughter and granddaughters had been on local television and radio stations in Jacksonville, collecting supplies after Hurricane Michael in 2018 in their very successful efforts to fill several box trucks with supplies for the victims of Lynn Haven, the hometown where my daughter had grown up, graduated from high school, and was well-known and loved by hundreds of friends. She no longer feels comfortable, safe, or welcome to go there.

You have taken away my ability to teach a class at one of the universities in Jacksonville as I had planned to do or to volunteer at my granddaughter's school, because a background check would reveal that I have been indicted by the federal government; you have taken away my ability to continue my professional career as a singer and musician, because anyone who googles my name as an entertainer also sees that I am the infamous Mayor of the City of Lynn Haven.

You have taken away my ability to protect myself; as the former Mayor of a city, the one who came forward with evidence of fraud and theft against those who have now pled guilty or who have been given immunity, I am no longer allowed to have my concealed weapon permit or to keep firearms in my home because of the conditions of pre-trial release. I have been afraid of personal harm ever since the day I went to Sheriff Ford. I was offered no protection. I have no protection now, and these same admitted felons are walking about free, awaiting sentencing, knowing that I am the one who found what they were doing and turned them in.

You have taken away my hope for the future. The looming cloud of darkness and foreboding placed upon one's life cannot be described by those who have not experienced such a thing. But I believe that you and those who worked with you to bring this evil into my life are well-aware of the suffering, the fear, the hopelessness, it brings, and I believe you thrive on this sense of power, power which I have come to believe is sociopathic, if not sadistic in nature, held close to the chests of you entrenched in government positions with no fear of reprisal. I have lost the deep and abiding respect I have had my entire life for law enforcement. When I see someone in a uniform now, I cannot breathe, my chest tightens, and all I can think of is being chained in a cell without windows or explanation for hours without knowing what charges had been brought against me, while Mr. Keefe was a hundred miles away in my hometown, grandstanding with Mr. Kunz, FBI Agent Rojas, and Sheriff Ford in front of the media, as my life of sixty-four years was taken away in just one sixty minute news conference, on August 19, 2020.

And finally, you have done that thing that cannot be repaired, cannot be restored, or given back. You have destroyed my good name. I have lived a good and decent life, I was a revered teacher, a well-known musical performer, and a very well-loved and respected Mayor by the people of my town.  I cannot go back there to live now.  It is too painful.  The "world's most beautiful beaches," the place which has always been beautiful to me is now filled with only ugliness…ugly memories of the non-stop media destruction of me in front of my family, friends and neighbors, all who watched in horror as it happened, with most too afraid to say anything publicly to try and help me.  Now after over three years, with the evidence that has finally come to light, literally hundreds are speaking out and changing their minds about what really happened.  But it is too late.  Not only is my home, built by my grandparents now gone because of legal fees, but all of those intangible things also built in Bay County by three generations of my family before me are now no longer mine.

And they will never be mine again.

June 14, 2022

After two months of both sides filing arguments after the evidentiary hearing, Judge Mark Walker issued a ruling, and Channel 13 WMBB's headline that evening was, *"Judge Rules Lynn Haven Corruption Case Will Go to Trial."*

Reporter Brady Calhoun wrote, *"Judge Mark Walker ruled Tuesday that most of the counts against the former mayor of Lynn Haven and a local business leader will stand and the corruption case will go to trial.  Although it has been postponed multiple times in the past, the trial for Margo Anderson, the former mayor, and James Finch, the owner of Phoenix Construction is currently set for June 27, 2022.*

*Six others, including former City Manager Mike White and former City Attorney Adam Albritton have already pleaded guilty in the case and are awaiting sentencing.  A seventh defendant, former City Commissioner Antonius Barnes, pleaded guilty in a separate case but is now prepared to testify that Finch bribed him.*

*Finch and Anderson's attorneys sought to have the entire case thrown out with prejudice.*

*In an April 27th motion, Anderson and Finch accused prosecutors, witnesses, and investigators of violating the law and the judge's orders during the investigation and the run-up to the trial.*

*Prosecutors responded on May 17th in a 216-page document that is still sealed from the public.*

*Regardless, Walker does not mention the various accusations against law enforcement, prosecutors or other individuals in the case.*

*Walker threw out Count 1, a conspiracy charge that tied Finch and Anderson to five conspiracies involving city work before and after Hurricane Michael.*

*Walker labeled those conspiracies as :*

**17th Street:** *Finch allegedly bribed Anderson and City Commissioner Antonious Barnes to support his projects with the City of Lynn Haven.  In addition, Finch obtained one of those projects, the 17th Street project, through a bid-rigging agreement with other* *companies.*

**ECS:** *Erosion Control Specialists (ECS) allegedly bribed City Manager Michael White, Anderson, and City Attorney Adam Albritton and received hurricane cleanup and trash pickup contracts in return. ECS also submitted false invoices and, when those invoices were paid, allegedly paid kickbacks to Albritton.*

**Debris Disposal:** *Unbeknownst to the City, a company that employed Albritton directed city contractors to use that company's property to dispose of debris. After a meeting with Anderson, Finch, White, and the owner of the other company, Anderson directed two other companies to dispose of debris at one of Finch's properties. Anderson also allegedly vetoed White's plan to designate city-owned property as a disposal site and secured state government support for a plan to use Finch's site. At the same time, Anderson allegedly accepted things of value from Finch.*

**World Claim:** *World Claim, a public adjusting firm; approached a contract engineer with the city for help in getting a city contract for hurricane claims. WorldClaim offered the engineer a percentage of whatever they recovered. The engineer, in turn, approached Anderson and White, offering free services from WorldClaim. Anderson and White signed an agreement with World Claim using Anderson's post-hurricane emergency powers. WorldClaim, in turn, allegedly provided them free or reduced services.*

**Rebuild:** *After Hurricane Michael, the City had to rebuild many of its facilities. Finch allegedly bribed Anderson for inside information and to exert pressure on city officials to aid Finch in obtaining the rebuild project at a significantly higher cost than the City would pay through its already-planned rebuild project.*

*Collectively, 25 counts against Finch and Anderson involving bribery and fraud remain. Walker did not dismiss Count 1 with prejudice which means prosecutors could, once again, get an indictment on this charge.*

*"An indictment's primary purpose is to "inform the defendant of the nature of the accusation against him." Russell v. United States, 369 U.S. 749,767 (1962)," Walker wrote. "While the vast majority of counts fulfill that purpose, Count 1 again fails to do so. And so this Court must again dismiss it."*

*A statement was posted by Anderson on News 13's Facebook page Tuesday afternoon. The statement, which is from her attorney,* **W. Robert Vezina, III,** *says Anderson is ready to defend herself:*

**"On Monday, the court granted the motions of Margo Anderson and James Finch to dismiss the conspiracy count of the second superseding indictment. That count charged both Anderson and Finch with conspiracy to commit honest services wire fraud.**

**This is the second time the Court has dismissed the conspiracy count as being infirm. In September of last year, the conspiracy count in the first superseding indictment was dismissed. In Monday's order**

*the Court said that 'Count 1 falls short because it leaves the charged conspiracy's scope ambiguous, combining an open-ended list of matters within the conspiracy with dozens of paragraphs of allegations unrelated to the matters specifically enumerated on the list. Thus, Count 1 does not fairly inform defendants of the charges against which they must defend.'*

*As was the case in 2021, the dismissal is without prejudice so the government could decide to seek a third superseding indictment from a grand jury. The court has granted (at least in part) four motions to dismiss in this case. If the government decides to move forward with a revamped indictment against Ms. Anderson that is cognizable, Ms. Anderson is prepared to defend herself in every regard at trial."*

*W. Robert Vezina*
*Defense Counsel for Margo Anderson*

Once again, the trial was delayed and did not take place in June of 2022, as our attorneys filed new motions including a motion to sever the ECS and World Claim charges, asking for separate trials for James Finch and me, a motion in which we were all in agreement. We also decided to ask for a bench trial rather than a jury trial because of the complexity of the case and the intense media coverage and publicity, believing we would have a better chance of acquittal with Judge Mark Walker hearing the evidence and deciding our guilt or innocence than we would have with a jury.

On June 25th, WMBB-Channel 13 reported the following:

**Prosecutors, defendants say they are ready for Lynn Haven corruption trial: by: S. Brady Calhoun**

*Lynn Haven, Fla (WMBB) – The trial for two defendants in the Lynn Haven corruption case is getting closer and could go forward as soon as August.*

*Former Lynn Haven Mayor Margo Anderson and James Finch, the owner of Phoenix Construction, are facing fraud and bribery projects over several city projects before and after Hurricane Michael.*

*During a status conference on Friday, Judge Mark Walker and attorneys for both sides agreed to confer on trial dates and meet again on July 7. That means the case could conceivably go to trial as soon as August.*

*In a previous ruling, Walker threw out one of the charges in the indictment but during the hearing prosecutors said they will not move forward with a new indictment and will instead take the rest of the charges to trial.*

*However, a jury may never hear the case. Finch's attorney, Guy Lewis, asked Walker to consider having a bench trial. That means Walker will be both judge and jury at trial and decide if Finch is guilty in the case.*

*"As we're considering and trying to get a trial date our clients are actually anxious to move forward as quickly as possible," Lewis said. He added that Finch, 72, is getting ready to undergo some "very serious procedures," and that a bench trial may be a better situation.*

*Lewis suggested that an August or September trial, which could last as long as three weeks, would have to build in "days off" multiple times while Finch dealt with these medical procedures.*

*In order for that to happen prosecutors have to agree to a bench trial. Prosecutors Stephen Kunz said his team would consider it but that they were not ready to make a decision on the issue Friday.*

*The judge and the attorneys also discussed a separate order in the case that was issued by Walker but has been sealed from the public. Kunz said prosecutors would provide Walker with sections of the order that they would like to remain redacted. The defense, who is asking that the order be unsealed, will be offered a chance to respond before Walker unseals the order with any redactions.*

*"There is some disclosure of specific grand jury testimony," Kunz said, the prosecutors hope will remain hidden from the public.*

*However, the defense argued that most, if not all of that testimony, was revealed to the public during a three-day evidentiary hearing in March. The defense is also asking that a large motion from prosecutors in the case also be unsealed.*

The Beacon of Bay County
By Jodi Christine Moore                    June 25, 2022

**LYNN HAVEN:** Shared from WMBB: This story by Mr. Calhoun mostly gets it right but does not highlight how important it is that Count 1, the superseding conspiracy indictment, will not be charged again. That is a big win for the defense! That was the charge that held the other charges together. I effect, the prosecution is admitting they cannot prove conspiracy between Margo Deal Anderson and James Finch! I'm personally surprised Judge Walker did not throw out the case entirely after we all saw the prosecutorial misconduct in this case. I also don't really know why the prosecution doesn't drop charges altogether when their case against these two has pretty much fallen apart. I guess they are hoping one or two charges will stick somehow and they can claim victory. At any rate, I'm hoping that these cases will **FINALLY GO TO TRIAL IN** August or early September, if the charges aren't dropped entirely (which is unlikely at this point, but still possible.) I also want to see the court papers the defense wants all of us to see but that the **PROSECUTION** doesn't want us to see!

Margo Deal Anderson                                    June 30, 2022
(my Facebook post)

Jay Trumbull said in his debate tonight for the Florida Senate seat:
"We saw the Mayor of Lynn Haven be accessible yet we still got
hoodwinked." What a self-righteous statement.
If not for the corrupt investigation and indictment I would have been
the one debating, you tonight. And I would have won.
This is not over yet; you showed your cards too soon.

The Beacon of Bay County Florida
By Jodi Christine Moore                                 July 7, 2022

Lynn Haven:  7/7/22 at 3 PM
    Gap Parker and I just listened in to the telephonic hearing for the
Margo Deal Anderson/Finch corruption case.  The prosecution is
insisting upon a jury trial even though the defense had requested a
bench trial before the judge.  Therefore, the trial dates are still
undetermined but will hopefully be this fall sometime.  All the
lawyers for the defense and prosecution are talking about scheduling
and a proposed schedule will be presented Monday.  The now-
unredacted and now-unsealed ruling from Judge Walker (when he
declined to dismiss charges) will be available tomorrow but with one
name redacted.  I wonder who THAT could be?  I think we will likely
be able to figure it out.

The Beacon of Bay County Florida
By Jodi Christine Moore                                 July 15, 2022

Lynn Haven:  Here are the charges against Margo Deal Anderson
and James Finch in the Lynn Haven corruption case.  Since Count 1,
the superseding indictment, was thrown out and apparently won't be
charged again, Anderson has 20 counts against her and Finch has 15.
I and others do not see how this all holds together without Count 1,
(which charged Anderson and Finch with conspiracy), but the

prosecution is apparently determined to take this to court in the hope that something sticks. The jury trial date is currently set for November 28, 2022. There will be other motions and court actions before that date in order to prepare for trial, as noted in the judge's order setting the schedule.

As we waited for the decision on a motion filed by our attorneys on the severing of charges which were against only me (WorldClaim and ECS conspiracies)from those against both James and me , just when it seemed that after all of the bombshells that could possibly be dropped had fallen, August of 2022 brought the accidental unsealing of the **Affidavit for a Search Warrant against Gulf Asphalt Corporation (GAC)** which had been signed just five days after the death of Derwin White, July 31, 2021. The government had withheld the most damning *Brady* evidence of all, after signing a document just a month before, informing Judge Walker and the defense that they had produced, to the best of their knowledge, all *Brady* material to the defense. The entire affidavit was available for download by the public on Channel 13-ABC affiliate in Panama City, Florida, and the story broke in *The Panama City News Herald, as follows:*

### FBI: Company led by ex-Florida House speaker bilked 'millions' for Hurricane Michael Cleanup.

**Tom McLaughlin**
**The News Herald**
**August 11, 2022**

*PANAMA CITY—GAC Contractors, a local company whose top executives include former House Speaker Allan Bense, bilked "millions of dollars" from local governments in 2018 when it was contracted to clean up debris caused by Hurricane Michael, newly released court documents from an ongoing federal investigation show.*

*The company's top executives, including Bense and its late CEO Derwin White, commanded its crews to visit work sites with equipment but not perform any work, and then billed Bay County, the school district and other government municipalities, federal investigators allege in an affidavit filed with a search warrant carried out last year at the company's headquarters.*

*Federal law enforcement authorities, in the affidavit, said that Bense and White ordered GAC's workers to clean up their own homes or properties and that of other top public officials, including state Sen. George Gainer, Lynn Haven City Attorney Adam Albritton's house and Bay County School Superintendent Bill Husfelt, among others.*

*Bense is not charged in connection with the federal investigation of GAC Contractors. White has since died. Bense, who was the company's managing partner, is the company's chairman.*

*Bense did not immediately return a phone call seeking comment.*

*The allegations against GAC Contractors surfaced in the affidavit that was unsealed Monday in federal court. The affidavit was written by FBI agent Lawrence Borghini. The search warrant was executed August 5, 2021, court records show.*

*The criminal allegations raised in the affidavit expand the scope of possible corruption in Bay County following Hurricane Michael far beyond the borders of Lynn Haven, where five city officials and four local businesspeople previously have been charged with federal crimes.*

*The 45-page document quotes a director of operations for a national debris removal company as saying, "Bay County was more corrupt" than either New Jersey or New Orleans—locations where he previously had done work following hurricanes.*

*The search warrant itself called for government review of any and all records, documents and supporting documentation relating to owner account expenditures and accounting entries for Derwin White and Allan Bense. It calls for the seizure of information pertaining to credit card loans, lines of credit, expenditures made on behalf of used by or at the direction of Derwin White, Allan Bense or Steven Clements. It also seeks any and all records relating to entities owned or controlled by White, Bense or Clements.*

*The U.S. Attorney's Office and Bay County Sheriff Tommy Ford declined to comment on the status of the investigation of GAC.*

*Bense who served in the Florida House of Representatives from 1998 to 2006 and as House Speaker between 2004-06, has been a managing partner of GAC Contractors, alongside Derwin White, since 1996. This year he is listed by the Florida Division of Corporations as the company's chairman.*

*Through April of 2019, Bense was listed as GAC Contractors president. He became chairman when White assumed the title of president, according to Division of Corporations documents.*

*Prior to Hurricane Michael, GAC pre-positioned equipment throughout Bay County, and after the storm passed the School District executed an emergency plan and utilized GAC, along with some other contractors, to clean up hurricane debris, make repairs and assess damage, the affidavit said.*

*In the aftermath of the hurricane, GAC crews "would receive their assignments each day from Derwin White or Allan Bense, whichever one had attended the morning meeting at the operations center that day," the affidavit said.*

*"Both of them would instruct the crews to report to the school sites but not to do any work," the affidavit states.*

*GAC also brought at least one piece of equipment to each site at which its crews were doing nothing.*

*"The GAC crews were being sent to the schools because GAC had a contract with Bay District Schools and their presence was necessary to give the appearance that GAC was doing work at the schools," the FBI agent wrote. "The GAC crews did this for about a month."*

*Work that was being done at the school sites, the affidavit states, was performed by subcontractors such as Erosion Control Specialist, whose owner, David White, has been previously indicted as part of a scheme to steal millions from the city of Lynn Haven. David White, Derwin White's nephew, has pleaded guilty in the case.*

*Bay County and the School District were billed for equipment brought to job sites but never used, the affidavit said, citing testimony of a former GAC foreman who worked road and site work projects. The witness testified that GAC Vice President Steven Clements instructed him to "bring as much equipment as he had access to" to the school jobs.*

*"He said it didn't matter if the equipment was used or not. Clements was going to charge the jobs with 10 of everything," the affidavit said. "In most cases (the foreman) did not have 10 of everything to bring to the jobs and a lot of equipment charged to the jobs was not even needed."*

*While the GAC crews were supposed to be working for Bay District Schools, they were actually removing debris from Derwin White's house, Derwin White's farm, Clements' house, Bense's house, previously indicted Lynn Haven City Attorney Adam Albritton's house and others, the affidavit said, paraphrasing testimony of another former GAC employee. That employee said he worked one weekend at Gainer's home "cleaning up debris" and he had been informed GAC crews had cleared debris at Bay County School Superintendent Bill Husfelt's house as well.*

*"It was to GAC's benefit to perform such work for local public officials and government employees, who were either witting or unwitting, for future favorable treatment and lucrative contracts," Borghini wrote. "Many, if not all, of the costs associated with providing those benefits were billed to jobs and projects that GAC had ongoing at the time the benefits were conveyed.*

*One of the charges Albritton faced when he was indicted in 2020 was for accepting work done at his home as a form of bribe. Lynn Haven Mayor Margo Anderson, indicted alongside Albritton, faces an identical charge. She maintains her innocence.*

*GAC crews were instructed to remove debris from the home of Don Churchwell, an employee of the Panama City Public Works Department, according to the affidavit. A footnote in the affidavit states that at the time the work was done "GAC had a number of road projects in Panama City Beach" as well as contracts for construction of city buildings.*

*One of the former GAC employees told the FBI he spent some days removing debris at GAC Contractors headquarters and when that job was complete, he traveled to the homes of GAC employees to help there. When the employee and his crew were sent to his own home to do work, Clements ordered him to bill the school district for the cost.*

*Assistant County Manager Joel Schubert told the FBI that hurricane damage to his home was so severe that for a period of time he and his family could not live at the residence.*

*Schubert said he asked Derwin White for the names of local contractors who did tree work and White told him he would "put him on the list" for work to be done by GAC, the affidavit said. White did not provide him a price for work or the names of the subcontractors.*

*A few days later, the affidavit said, Schubert was contacted by someone who told him work was being done at his residence. He arrived to find enough debris removal had been completed to allow him access to his driveway, so he told the GAC crew on site that they could leave.*

*For months after the work was done, Schubert said he touched base with White, either in person or by text, to inquire as to the status of his bill. Having not received one as of April 2019, he went to the bank, obtained a cashier's check for $3,000 and dropped if off at GAC with a note offering to pay the balance if additional money was needed.*

*On April 22, according to the affidavit, Schubert received an email from GAC with an invoice for $3,000 attached. When he again inquired about the bill and whether more might be due, he was told, "As far as I know there is no other charges."*

*A review of a GAC bill sent to the county, signed by Clements, the vice president, sought payment of $9,613 for the work done at Schubert's residence, according to the FBI affidavit.*

I find it more than interesting that Joel Schubert, after many months, bought a cashier's check for $3,000 without having an invoice on April 4, 2019, after the word was out that I had been to the Sheriff with the fraud I had found in Lynn Haven. There was a flurry of activity in Bay County in that month. Joel Schubert was never charged for having his property cleaned by GAC, and he and his boss, County Manager Bob Majka, along with School Superintendent Bill Husfelt, were all given television time by WMBB Channel 13, ABC affiliate in Panama City to explain themselves and to refute what was written by SA Borghini in the affidavit; apparently that was all they had to do to prove their innocence because they were never charged with any crimes. I remain the only elected official in Bay County who was indicted, and I did not do a damn thing except discover fraud and take it to the Sheriff, who we believe, based on information and evidence, was involved himself.

### Sen. George Gainer

*The affidavit states that in 2016, Gainer, who had spent 18 years as a Bay County Commissioners was elected the state senate. In August of that same year, Derwin White and Gainer went into business together at Yellow Jackets LLC. In September of 2016, following Gainer's purchase of a condominium in Tallahassee, White sent a GAC superintendent to the state capital to remodel Gainer's unit. He instructed the employee "to charge all his supplies to complete the remodel to other active GAC jobs."*

*According to testimony provided by a former GAC employee, Derwin White had a large generator installed at Gainer's home following Hurricane Michael. The search warrant executed at GAC in 2021 sought all records the company had related to Gainer.*

### Adam Albritton

*As noted in his indictment, Albritton was hired to work as the attorney for the city of Lynn Haven without informing city officials that he was also employed by Derwin White and GAC.*

*Just days after Hurricane Michael, Albritton informed Lynn Haven City Manager Michael White, no relation to Derwin White or David White, that he had solicited six companies for tipping fees for disposal of the city's "reduced vegetation debris." According to the FBI affidavit, he told White that GAC had provided the lowest price for the tipping fees and presented "the most economical solution" for debris removal.*

*"Investigation revealed the businesses Albritton claimed to have contacted had never been contacted or Albritton's listed prices were not accurate" for them, Borghini wrote.*

*Albritton also told Michael White that any contractors hauling debris for the city should pay the Gac price for vegetative debris disposal.*

*Lynn Haven*

*The affidavit states that in November of 2018, Derwin White took Michael White to one of several Bay County automobile dealerships owned by Gainer.*

*Derwin White, arranged with George Gainer for payment of $18,561 for a 2016 Hyundai Tucson for Michael White, the affidavit states. "The vehicle was added to a GAC account and subsequently paid for with a GAC check."*

*In January of 2019, the city of Lynn Haven requested bids for the construction of temporary facilities to house its city hall and police department. GAC submitted the only bid for the project.*

*Two other companies, ECS and Phoenix Construction," both submitted letters saying they were unable to bid on the project due to limited resources and an extensive work schedule," Borghini wrote.*

*James Finch, the owner of Phoenix Construction, has, like David White, been charged with crimes committed as part of the Lynn Haven corruption scandal. Finch maintains his innocence and his case has been scheduled for trial in November.*

*Lynn Haven unanimously approved the GAC contract and as of August 2021, when the search warrant at GAC Contractors was served, GAC had been paid $623,508 under terms of the contract for the city projects.*

*"After a search warrant was executed at (David White's) ECS, Michael White wrote a personal check for the vehicle that was deposited in Derwin White's personal account," the application for the search warrant said.*

**The raid on ECS was April 12, 2019, eleven days after I went as the whistleblower to the Sheriff; here, another of the conspirators, Michael White, raced to pay for something he had received from GAC, a car, as a bribe for the fraud that was taking place.**

*Michael White was indicted alongside David White and three others in the Lynn Haven corruption case.*

## Ashbritt and Crowder Gulf

*Before Hurricane Michael, Bay County had pre-negotiated debris removal contracts with Ashbritt and Crowder Gulf, two large national providers, as a hedge against hurricane damage. Following the storm, Derwin White went to the county and local municipalities "seeking to secure hurricane clean up business."*

*Informed by emergency management and government officials that he would have to deal with Ashbritt and Crowder Gulf, the affidavit said, White went to both.*

*"Crowder Gulf's director of operations told the FBI that White contacted him after the hurricane and asked if Crowder Gulf needed help (implying he had connections). He said if they would cut him in he would help them," Borghini wrote.*

*"Derwin White wanted to get paid to do nothing."*

*The affidavit states White attempted to have Crowder Gulf pay GAC a percentage of revenues based on the volume of cubic yards of hurricane debris collected. He also wanted to get paid a percentage to facilitate a site or get Crowder Gulf work.*

*"Crowder Gulf did not need Derwin White's influence with local public officials or connections to conduct their cleanup operations," the affidavit said. "Thereafter, Crowder Gulf had nothing to do with Derwin White or GAC."*

*While Crowder Gulf refused to deal with White, Ashbritt chose to contract with GAC. The affidavit said some portion of the work performed at the homes of local government employees, and paid for by Bay County taxpayers, was performed by GAC and billed through Ashbritt.*

*Ashbritt also negotiated contracts with smaller Bay County municipalities like Springfield and Callaway that had not, like the county itself, pre-negotiated emergency contracts.*

*"The debris collected by Ashbritt was brought to sites owned by, or that had been secured by, Derwin White for reduction. The reduced debris was then transported to sites for final disposal owned by Derwin White and GAC," the affidavit said.*

*"Derwin White and GAC made millions of dollars in fees from operations of sites, while Bay County and other municipalities paid an artificial disposal rate that had not been properly bid out," Borghini wrote*

*County taxpayers wound up paying hundreds of thousands of dollars in excess vegetative debris disposal fees, he added. The Crowder Gulf director of operations told Borghini that in his career "he had never seen anything like Bay County."*

*"He had worked cleanup operations following Hurricane Sandy in New Jersey and Hurricane Katrina in New Orleans and a number of other disasters over the years," Borghini wrote. "Bay County was more corrupt than any of those places."*

When I was made aware of this article in the *News Herald* in August of 2022 I was physically sick when I read it, and then in the days after, as I watched in silence as we were preparing for trial, I became angry…angry at the level of corruption that had gone on in Bay County, angry that the Government had sealed the affidavit for a year, and angry that James Finch and I would probably never have seen it, clear *Brady* material, without the document being accidentally unsealed by the Government through their own incompetence. I wanted to shake the author of the article's hand, even though he had certainly written his fair share of inflammatory articles about me as the corruption scandal stayed in the headlines for months, and then years.  Hurricane Michael made landfall on October 10, 2018; it is now 2024, and the northwest Florida "protection racket" has allowed the statute of limitations to run out on charging these people with all of the evidence they carried out of GAC in boxes, and according to them at the evidentiary hearing in 2022, still in boxes.  The FBI's possession of the evidence still in boxes, was a fact on which the federal Judge made comment during our hearings.

The following paragraphs are taken from the forty-five page Affidavit written by SA Lawrence Borghini in the matter of the search of GAC Contractors, Inc.  Because of the length of the affidavit, I have excluded some portions of it but have numbered the paragraphs as they are numbered in the actual document; the entire document was filed in federal court in Tallahassee and the document was also available for download to the public by WMBB-Channel 13, Panama City, Florida.  The document still remains on WMBB's site, was the source of the document we presented in the evidentiary hearing, and is the source used here:

3. Special Agent Borghini wrote, "I am familiar with the facts and circumstances surrounding this investigation, both from my own investigative activities and from information obtained from law enforcement officers and others with personal knowledge of the facts.  Those facts necessary to establish probable cause are included in this affidavit.  This affidavit is intended to show only that there is sufficient probable cause for the requested warrant and does not set forth all of my knowledge about this matter.  For the reasons set forth below, I believe there is probable cause to believe evidence relating to violations of Title 18 U.S.C. 1343, Wire Fraud, and Title 18, U.S.C. 1349, Conspiracy to violate Section 1343, are located at the location described in Attachment A.

4. Under 18, U.S.C., "Whoever, having devised or intending to devise any scheme or artifice to defraud , or for obtaining money or property by means of false or fraudulent pretenses, representations, or promises, transmits or causes to be transmitted by means of wire…communication in interstate or foreign commerce…for the purpose of executing such scheme or artifice, shall be fined under this title or imprisoned not more than twenty years, or both."

5. GAC Contractors, Inc., is a Florida corporation with a registered address of 4116 Highway 231 N, Panama City, Florida 32404 (hereinafter referred to as GAC).  GAC is a general contractor specializing in road sitework and building construction in Northwest Florida.  GAC is owned

and operated by Allan Bense and Derwin White, the latter of whom is recently deceased.

**The raid on GAC took place five days after Derwin White passed away from Covid, July 31, 2021. Allan Bense was said to have cleaned out his office of "personal effects" after the raid was over; even after the affidavit story broke on August 11, 2022, once the initial news coverage was over, and it was limited, short coverage, Bense's name was not mentioned again. The story simply went away in Bay County, as though it never happened...except as evidence in our hearing of December 2022, as we once again filed a motion for dismissal of the entire case.**

9. Bay District Schools (hereafter BDS) is headquartered in Panama City, Florida and is responsible for the operation of forty-two public schools located throughout Bay County, Florida. Every school in the district as well as the BDS administration building was damaged by Hurricane Michael and required some type of debris cleanup, emergency maintenance, and/or repair.

10. Throughout the years, GAC has been awarded a number of BDS projects that include the construction of new schools, specialty buildings, athletic facilities and a stadium. BDS holds a continuing contract with GAC for specific small maintenance and construction tasks. The contract contains exact line-item costs to perform specific tasks. When services are needed, the BDS Facilities Department would contact GAC and provide them with the scope of work to be performed. GAC would submit a proposal based on the line item prices in their contract. The proposal would then be approved by BDS' Executive Director for Facilities and a purchase order generated based on the proposal. Once the work was completed, GAC would submit an invoice. The BDS Executive Director for Facilities and /or the Facilities Project Manager would confirm that the work had been completed to satisfaction and approve the invoice for payment. The BDS Finance Department would pay the invoice(s) after matching it to the purchase order.

11. Prior to Hurricane Michael, GAC arranged to preposition GAC equipment at various locations throughout Bay County. After Hurricane Michael passed, BDS executed their emergency plan and utilized GAC, as well as some other contractors, to clean up hurricane debris, make repairs, and help assess the damage to BDS facilities.

12. On November 13, 2018, GAC prepared and submitted invoice number 31144 to BDS for Hurricane Michael 2018 clean-up for a period ending on October 31, 2018, in the amount of $1,418,481.48. Attached to the invoice was a sheet listing each BDS school location at which GAC had performed cleanup work, the date, and an amount for each school location. The amount on that sheet totaled $1,418,481.48. A second sheet was

attached to the invoice that detailed the cumulative value for each category of labor, equipment and materials in a single line item for all the school locations that totaled $1,418,481.48. The GAC invoice and attachments did not list the names of the employees that had worked at the BDS locations or the equipment that had been used at the location. The GAC invoice was approved for payment and the funds paid by BDS to GAC on December 21, 2018.

13. On December 11, 2018, Leon Walters, BDS Director of Facilities, sent an email to Steven Clements, Project Engineer/Manager at GAC. (Clemens has since been promoted to Vice President of the Civil Division at GAC.) The email state the following: "Since we have an invoice for 1.4 million for cleanup, I think GAC is doing a good job billing the district. The board approved our FEMA consultant today and we have a meeting with them next Wednesday. I would like to have their input for the proper billing structure to ensure FEMA reimbursement. I am thinking using the continuing contract is going to be our best option and avoid the three bids we have been told FEMA is going to be looking for. Sent from my iPhone.

14. On February 8, 2019, BDS' consultant, Hagerty Consulting, advised Leon Walters that a number of items were needed for the submission of BDS' Category A debris project to FEMA for reimbursement. Leon Walters contacted Steven Clements by email and requested that GAC provide the needed backup documentation for the billings that BDS had received from GAC.

16. On February 27, 2019, GAC prepared and submitted a second round of invoices for each of the BDS school locations for hurricane debris cleanup and removal for the period October, November and December 2018 totaling $1,047,041.02. It appears to be for work not billed on the previous invoice. Unlike the first invoice GAC submitted to BDS, GAC generated an invoice for each location. Leon Walters approved the invoices, and GAC was paid with BDS check number 175117 dated March 15, 2019.

17. On April 12, 2019, a search warrant was executed at the business offices of Erosion Control Specialist (hereafter "ECS") by law enforcement.

**SA Borghini does not mention here that "law enforcement" is the Bay County Sheriff's office.**

ECS was one of the subcontractors that GAC had used for hurricane debris cleanup and removal at the BDS school locations. An investigation had been initiated after invoices the City of Lynn Haven received and paid to ECS for hurricane Michael cleanup came into question.

**SA Borghini does not mention here that the Mayor of Lynn Haven, me, brought the information to law enforcement, BCSO, only that it "came into question".**

A subsequent investigation revealed that ECS had submitted invoices to the

City of Lynn Haven and had been paid for work they had not performed. During the time period October 14-22, 2018, ECS claimed they had employees working at the City of Lynn Haven when in fact the ECS employees were actually working at Bay High School and Springfield Elementary School for GAC.

18. On June 13, 2019, Leon Walters emailed Steven Clements and Derwin White. Walters' email stated the following: "Steven, we are still struggling with invoices in a format FEMA will be able to grant reimbursement to our district. Also still need the load tickets. From reading the Hagerty summary we are going to need another sit-down with your team. Sent from my iPhone. Derwin White responded: "Steven, let's get together in the morning and address. Thanks, Derwin. Lee, I will handle. Derwin. Sent from my iPhone.

19. On June 21, 2019, GAC provided various documents and records to BDS that purport the GAC invoices for hurricane debris cleanup and removal.

20. On December 4, 2019, Hagerty Consulting reached out again to Leon Walters and requested another in person meeting with GAC via email stating: "Hi Lee, can we reach out to GAC again to discuss their Debris invoices? Attached is the RFI we have to try to figure out how they got to their numbers in the absence of other documentation. Hagerty Consulting was attempting to identify the GAC employees who had worked at, and what equipment had been used, at the various BDS school locations. Hagerty Consulting was also requesting how the debris disposal rates charged to BDS by GAC had been derived. Subsequent emails between Leon Walters and Steven Clements show that the matter remained unresolved as of March 2020.

**When Hagerty Consulting reached out to Leon Walters again on December 4th, 2019, above, the first indictment for FEMA fraud had just been unsealed against Michael White, Mickey White, David Horton, Josh Anderson, and Shannon Rodriguez. Mickey White and Michael White had pled guilty and were talking; there was a general panic about this time apparently from the school district to the County, as well as other cities.**

21.On March 5, 2020, Ryan Sweat, a former equipment operator in underground utilities for GAC, was interviewed. Sweat advised that prior to Hurricane Michael, he had been directed to preposition various pieces of GAC equipment through Bay County. Each GAC equipment operator was thereafter assigned a piece of equipment that they were supposed to report to after the hurricane passed and start clearing roads.

22. After the hurricane passed, Sweat reported to the piece of equipment he had been assigned to and found it missing. Sweat went to Derwin White's house and found two pieces of GAC equipment located there.

Derwin White and Steven Clements' properties had been cleared of hurricane debris and the equipment was parked there.

23. Derwin White told Sweat to take one of the tractors and clear a certain church parking lot. After he was done there, Sweat was to clear the roads to Jenks Middle School and leave the tractor at Jenks Middle School. The next day, Sweat was sent to Front Beach Road where he had been instructed to pick up a tractor and clear the roads back to Rosenwald High School where he left that tractor. The day after that, Sweat was instructed to pick up a tractor at the GAC yard and clear the roads to Rutherford High School where he left that tractor. Sweat spent three days moving equipment and leaving it at school properties.

24. Sweat stated that GAC had a contract with BDS and GAC crews were sent to the BDS school locations throughout Bay County. The GAC crews were instructed to report to the schools but did not do any work there. Instead, what Sweat believed to be FEMA personnel did the work at the schools. The personnel were easy to identify because they were not GAC employees and all wearing similar clothing. The FEMA personnel that Sweat referred to were actually subcontractors GAC had hired and were paying such as ECS. The GAC foreman on site would record the GAC crews' hours on paper timesheets. They only worked until approximately 3:00 PM each day because of the curfew in place. At first, only about fifteen (15) people a day reported to GAC for work. It took about two weeks to fill the GAC crews with 4-5 employees. Sweat stated they were paid $550 a week which was much less than the hourly pay he had been making on GAC jobs. GAC employees had been told that they were going to get paid the FEMA rate for twelve (12) hours each day. The crews were advised that GAC was going to be working 12-hour days, 7 days a week.

25. The GAC crews worked from 6:00 AM to 3:30 PM each day. They **watched** the subcontractors do the cleanup work at the schools. The GAC crews were being sent to the schools because GAC had a contract with BDS and their presence was necessary to give the **appearance** that GAC was doing work at the schools. The GAC crews did this for about a month.

26. The GAC crews would receive their assignments each day from **Derwin White** or **Allan Bense,** whichever one had attended the morning meetings at the operations center that day. Both of them would instruct the crews to report to the school sites but not to do any work. GAC also had at least one piece of equipment at each school site (loader, skid steer, mini excavator). The superintendents overseeing the work on Sweat's jobs were Tim Brown and Reggie Sewell. Both are very loyal to GAC because of the "hookups" they receive from Derwin White (trips, use of Derwin White's boats and motorhomes, use of GAC equipment, etc.). After about a month, Sweat was transitioned back to GAC's Highway 98 project and did not report to any more BDS locations.

27. Sweat stated that during the time GAC crews were supposed to be working for BDS, they actually did hurricane cleanup work at Derwin White's house, Derwin White's farm on John Pitts Road, Steven Clement' house, Allan Bense's house, Adam Albritton's (the city attorney for Lynn Haven and GAC attorney) house and others. One weekend, Sweat worked at State Senator George Gainer's house on Beach Drive in Panama City cleaning up debris. Sweat also heard that some crews worked at BDS Superintendent Bill Husfelt's house. Sweat stated that with regard to reporting the crews' hours working at these houses, the GAC superintendent assigned to oversee the task, told them not to worry about it, that he would take care of it. The work at each of the locations was mostly hurricane debris cleanup and tarping of roofs.

**When the affidavit was accidentally released and the story was in the local newspaper as well as the local television stations, Superintendent William Husfelt was given time on television by Channel 13 to give a lengthy denial of property cleanup, but the billing issues with GAC were not addressed nor were the allegations of property cleanup and repair to the homes of other school district officials. Husfelt suddenly retired over a year before the scheduled election, "to spend more time with his family." He was never charged with a crime, and if he was questioned by local law enforcement or the FBI, my co-defendant, James Finch and I were not given a copy of any such interview. Apparently law enforcement, the FBI nor FEMA (Homeland Security) had any curiosity whatsoever to question him or the other school district officials. George Gainer also denied having had his property cleaned by GAC, which was ultimately billed to the school district and then submitted to FEMA. He also denied the renovations at no charge to his Tallahassee condominium by GAC.**

28. Sweat also stated that after the hurricane, Derwin White had three large generators at his house. One of the generators was carried to and hooked up at George Gainer's house. Sweat was not sure where the third generator went to, however, GAC crews were constantly delivering fuel to the generators.

30. On August 28, 2020, Adam Usery, a former GAC foreman working on road and site work projects, was interviewed. Usery supervised a crew of three plus himself performing site work from the dirt up to asphalt. On October 11, 2018, Usery went to GAC's main office and reported to Derwin White. Usery thereafter worked at GAC's office for approximately three days running an excavator.

31. In addition to himself, Usery supervised three employees during that period of time. The hours Usery and his crew were working were recorded on paper timesheets. The timesheets were turned into Steven Clements.

The timesheets captured the name of the employees, hours they worked, and what the employee did. Usery recorded the time as having been worked at GAC's main office. After cleaning up GAC's office location, Usery and his crew went to GAC employees' houses to help clean up their residences.

32. Usery advised that GAC crews worked on cleaning up his residence. The GAC crews spent 3 to 4 days working at his residence. A John Deere loader and four dump trucks were used to clean Usery's residence. The dump trucks were from Cedar Creek Trucking and described as a red dump truck, a black dump truck, blue dump truck and a red/white dump truck. When Usery asked about recording the time spent working on GAC employee residences, GAC superintendent Reggie Sewell instructed Usery to charge the time to BDS (Bay District Schools).

33. Usery stated that he received direction from Steven Clements on where he and his crew were being assigned. Clements told Usery to bring as much equipment as he had access to, to the jobs. Clements stated it did not matter whether the equipment was used or not, Clements was going to charge the jobs with ten of everything. In most cases, Usery did not have ten of everything to even bring to the jobs and a lot of the equipment charged to the jobs was not even needed to complete the job. This was done on hurricane cleanup work for the BDS and Bay County jobs.

34. When Usery and his crew, as well as other GAC crews, were sent to BDS school locations, they would stand around and do nothing. Other crews (sub-contractors) had been hired by GAC and were working at the sites. The equipment that Usery and his crew brought to the sites was not used. A number of times, Usery and his crew were instructed to leave the BDS sites and work on personal residences. The time worked and equipment used on residences were charged to the BDS.

35. One of the residences that Usery and his crew worked on was located off of Baldwin Road. Usery was not sure who's house it was but they spent a day working there. GAC superintendent Reggie Sewell was the one sending Usery to the various locations. Sewell would send Usery a pin drop on Usery's GAC issued work phone with the location he was to go to. Usery advised that his GAC work phone would have on it the locations he was sent to, as well as pictures of the locations they worked at. Usery recalls cleaning a number of other personal residences. Usery specifically recalls being sent to Churchwell's house in Lynn Haven. He and GAC crews spent a week to a week and a half cleaning up Churchwell's property. After recording his time and the times of his crew, Usery was instructed by Reggie Sewell to have the time reflect that they had worked on a BDS job. Usery advised that they used paper timesheets to record hours worked until the Verizon network got back up and GAC could go back to using their GAC issued iPads to record hours worked. Don Churchwell works for the

City of Panama City Beach Public Works Department in the Utilities Department. GAC had a number of road projects in Panama City Beach as well as contracts with the City of Panama City Beach for the construction of a number of city buildings (Public Works Building, Police Department, City Hall). A check of the Bay County Property Appraiser's website reveals that Don Churchwell owns a residence located on Delaware Avenue in Lynn Haven, Florida. A Google Maps satellite image pre-Hurricane Michael shows the ½ acre lot was heavily wooded and satellite photos post-hurricane shows virtually all the trees on the property are gone.

36. Usery also stated that he was sent to three different BDS schools where they stood around before being sent to work on residences. After completing work on the residences, Usery and his crew were sent back to BDS schools where, once again, they stood around. Usery and his crew were not allowed to go back to the project they were working on prior to the hurricane. Usery advised that Steven Clements was adding various pieces of equipment to the jobs that Usery and his crew were being sent to even though the equipment was not physically present at the job sites. Steven Clements was billing for equipment that was not on the job sites. Steven Clements was also instructing Matt Sauls and Sam Bass to do the same thing. Steven Clements was having them pad the invoices.

37. Usery advised that in GAC's office, there were mailboxes in which paperwork for GAC jobs, subcontractors and vendors was placed in. One of those mailboxes in GAC was marked ECS. After David "Mickey" White was arrested, ECS' mailbox was removed.

38. In December 2018, Usery was hurt on the job and left working for GAC. After leaving GAC, Usery turned in his GAC phone that contained his contacts, text messages and pictures on it. In the course of his duties, Usery kept a green notebook in his work truck. Usery used the green notebook to record everything he and his crew did each day. The notebook had in it the places he worked after the hurricane as well as other jobs. Usery advised that the green notebooks were kept by the crew foremen and retained by GAC.

39. Doug Lee was the Executive Director of Operations for BDS. On October 10, 2018, Doug Lee sent Derwin White the following text message: "Derwin this is Doug Lee down the street. I have several trees laying on my house with no chain saw available. Do you have any capabilities of helping me just get it off my house?"

40. On November 15, 2018, Doug Lee sent the following iMessage to Stevie Clements: "Stevie, this is Doug Lee, what were the 3 guys names that helped you that day at my house? I think one was QV? Clements responded: "You are very welcome and let me know if you need anything in the future!" Doug Lee than asked: "If I wanted to get something to them in the future what would be the best way?" A check of the Bay

County Property Appraiser's website reveals that Douglas Lee owns a residence located at High Point Road in Panama City, Florida. A Google Maps satellite image pre–Hurricane Michael shows the 1/3 of an acre lot was heavily wooded and satellite photos post-hurricane show virtually all the trees on the property were gone.

41. Steven Clements eventually responded to Doug Lee with the GAC employee names and their home addresses. Clements provided the names of Tim Bell, JQ Leverette and Walter McDonald to Doug Lee.

42. During the investigation of ECS, a Federal Grand Jury subpoena was issued to GAC for any and all records relating to work performed by ECS. One of the documents that GAC provided was a typed summary sheet listing the names of the employees and subcontractors that had worked at Bay High School. On 10/23/2018 through 10/25/2018, Adam Usery was listed as a foreman and Tim Bell was listed as a laborer as having worked at Bay High School. Even though the Federal Grand Jury subpoena served on GAC requested timesheets, the raw timesheets and documents used to prepare the summary were not provided to the Government by GAC in response to the subpoena.

**Connection to Senator George Gainer**

43. In 2016, after eighteen years as a Bay County Commissioner, George Gainer ran unopposed and was elected to the Florida State Senate. On September 1, 2016, Gainer purchased a condominium located at 300 South Duval Street, Unit 2108, in Tallahassee, Florida. In 2016, Derwin White sent GAC superintendent Scott Joiner to Tallahassee to remodel Senator Gainer's unit. Joiner spent two weeks working on Gainer's condo unit. Joiner had been instructed by Derwin White to charge his time and all supplies needed to complete the remodel to other active GAC jobs which Joiner did.

44. On August 25, 2016, Derwin White and George Gainer filed Articles of Organization for a Florida Limited Liability Company for Yellow Jackets, LLC with a principal office located at 4116 Highway 231 North, Panama City, Florida.

**City of Lynn Haven Investigation**

**Paragraphs 45 – 54 are repetitive of information from previous chapters concerning Lynn Haven. One sentence of interest in paragraph 52, is "a number of contracts that Lynn Haven had entered into came into question after finding text messages between Michael White and Mickey White and it was determined that Lynn Haven paid ECS in excess of $5 million dollars. The FBI and Bay County Sheriff's Office initiated a joint investigation." Again, SA Borghini does not mention that the investigation started two days after the Mayor of Lynn Haven, me, went to Sheriff Tommy Ford as the whistleblower.**

55. On November 16, 2020, Antonius Barnes (Barnes) was interviewed. Barnes was a long time Lynn Haven City Commissioner. Barnes stated that Derwin White was a friend of his and had helped Barnes out in the past. Barnes advised that Derwin White had improved Barnes driveway with milled asphalt. Barnes was not charged by GAC for the work. After the hurricane, Barnes stated that Derwin White helped him out by cleaning Barnes' property of hurricane debris. Again, Barnes was not charged for the work. Barnes' house was severely damaged by Hurricane Michael. GAC made repairs to Barnes' house which Barnes claimed he paid for. A google maps satellite image pre-Hurricane Michael shows the 3/4 of an acre lot was wooded and satellite photos post-hurricane show the trees on the property were gone and Barnes' pool enclosure removed.

56. With regard to Phoenix Construction owner James Finch, Barnes admitted to receiving $45,000 in cash payments from Finch. Barnes claimed that the monies were loans to his insurance business. When questioned regarding the execution of any note(s) between Barnes and Finch documenting the loan(s) and /or terms, Barnes stated he had not executed any such documents and was not able to provide any details of the loan such as an interest rate or repayment terms. Barnes further stated that he had not made any payments to Finch or attempts to repay the monies back to Finch.

57. During Barnes' tenure and in the course of his duties as a Lynn Haven City Commissioner, Barnes regularly voted on matters and advanced the business interests of both GAC and Phoenix Construction.

58. In March 2021, a superseding indictment was returned adding former Lynn Haven City Commissioner Antonius Barnes and Phoenix Construction owner James Finch to the Anderson and Albritton indictment for their participation in the conspiracy, wire fraud and honest services fraud, and related offenses. All four defendants are awaiting trial.

**James Finch was acquitted at his second trial in October of 2023. My case was resolved in February 2023 as described in Chapter 10, former Lynn Haven City Commissioner Antonius Barnes' case was resolved in June 2023 when he was sentenced to 45 days in federal prison, one year of probation, and $40,000 in restitution. The Government was angry with Barnes because he refused to lie and say that James Finch bribed him.**

## Bay County and Ashbritt, Inc.

61. Ashbritt, Inc. and Crowder Gulf are two of the large national providers in the disaster response and recovery industry with pre-negotiated contracts with Bay County. In response to Hurricane Michael, Bay County activated both companies and they responded. In addition to having their

own company resources, Ashbritt and Crowder Gulf have subcontractors who are available to respond based on the magnitude of the damage and the size of the area affected.

62. Due to the devastating effects of Hurricane Michael, such as the loss of everyday utilities such as electrical power, water and communication networks, and sever damage to property, many local employers and businesses were looking for ways to continue operations and derive revenues. Derwin White went to Bay County officials as well as the local governments attempting to secure hurricane cleanup work. Derwin White was advised by Emergency Management personnel and government officials that he would have to deal with the national companies holding the pre-negotiated contracts. Derwin White approached both Ashbritt and Crowder Gulf.

63. Your affiant (**SA Borghini)** has interviewed Crowder Gulf's Director of Operations. He has stated that Derwin White contacted him after the hurricane and asked if Crowder Gulf needed help (implying that he had connections). Derwin White stated that he was willing to assist/help Crowder Gulf if they would cut him in. Derwin White wanted to get paid a percentage of Crowder Gulf's revenues off the volume of cubic yards of hurricane debris. Derwin White also wanted to get paid a percentage to facilitate a site or get Crowder Gulf work. In other words, Derwin White wanted to get paid to do nothing. Crowder Gulf already had pre-negotiated contracts with set prices within Bay County and the equipment and subcontracts to handle the work. Crowder Gulf did not need Derwin White's influence with local public officials or connections to conduct their cleanup operations. Thereafter, Crowder Gulf had nothing to do with Derwin White or GAC. Crowder Gulf's Director of Operations further advised that in his career, he had never seen anything like Bay County. He had worked clean-up operations following Hurricane Sandy in New Jersey, Hurricane Katrina in New Orleans, and a number of other major disasters over the years. Bay County was more corrupt than any of those places.

64. Your affiant's investigation has revealed that Ashbritt did partner with Derwin White and GAC. In addition to using GAC as a subcontractor on many of its services, Ashbritt used GAC sites for debris management, reduction and disposal. The disposal of vegetative debris and rate charge by Ashbritt were in accordance with the direction that Lynn Haven City Attorney Albritton provided in paragraph #49.

**Adam Albritton, unbeknownst to the City of Lynn Haven, was also the attorney for Derwin White and GAC. He was charged as co-defendant in the indictment with me, which originally charged me with 64 counts and being part of the conspiracy in Lynn Haven. Albritton was receiving $10,000 weekly kickbacks from Mickey White of ECS for his work on contracts which benefited ECS. Mickey**

**White is the nephew of Derwin White.**

65. In November 2018, the price that Ashbritt was charging for the vegetative debris disposal was questioned by Bay County after some owners of other debris disposal sites in Bay County came forward and challenged Ashbritt's rate and the selection of GAC's site. Albritton wrote a justification email for the artificial $4.70 rate being charged and the selection of GAC's disposal site. In his email, Albritton once again misrepresented his contact with pit owners and the prices he received. Albritton's "Justification email" was sent to Derwin White who forwarded it to Matt Gierden, a Senior Vice President at Ashbritt. The email was used by Matt Gierden to respond to Bay County defending the price and selection of GAC's site.

66. The debris collected by AshBritt was brought to sites owned by, or that had been secured by Derwin White for reduction. The reduced debris was then transported to sites for final disposal owned by Derwin White and GAC. Many of the smaller cities with Bay County such as Callaway and Springfield did not have pre-negotiated contracts with disaster recovery companies. Ashbritt was able to secure contracts for these cities as well as securing half of the debris removal for the City of Lynn Haven. Dewin White and GAC made millions of dollars in fees from the operation of these sites while Bay County and other municipalities paid an artificial disposal rate that had not been properly bid out and subsequently concealed by the actions of Albritton, Derwin White and Matt Gierden, thereby costing the taxpayers hundreds of thousands of dollars in excess vegetative debris disposal fees.

**The most interesting point about this affidavit for me is that it was executed on August 3, 2021, three days *after* Derwin White passed away from Covid, and the raid on GAC took place on August 5, 2021. Allan Bense is the co-owner of the company and according to the affidavit was at the meetings taking place described in this affidavit, yet he is not mentioned; the former Speaker of the House is not referred to in the bulk of the document; instead of saying Derwin White and Allan Bense, owners of GAC made millions, SA Borghini just says, Derwin White and GAC. Why? None of the officials of Bay County, the State, Ashbritt, or elected officials were charged after the raid on GAC; the only elected official indicted and arrested was me, the Mayor of Lynn Haven, all 64 charges against me were dropped except for "conspiracy and bribery" with James Finch; James Finch, my co-defendant was in the hospital in a coma after suffering a stroke, for the month of October when all of the corruption was taking place, yet he was charged as well. I was the whistleblower who pissed off Derwin White when I went to Sheriff Tommy Ford with the fraud James Finch, and I had found as described earlier. The BCSO**

planted evidence on April 12th at the raid on ECS owned by Mickey White, Derwin's nephew; the good old boys of Bay County made an example of me and continued with their business as usual in the Panhandle… 'business" which I, and many others believe continues to this day, leaving destroyed lives behind.

67. As previously stated above in paragraphs 39-41, on October 10, 2018, Doug Lee sent Derwin White a text message stating that he had several trees laying on his house with no chain saw available. On November 15, 2018, Doug Lee contacted Steven Clements requesting the names of the three (3) guys that helped out that day at his house. Clement responded, "You are very welcome and let me know if you need anything in the future!" Doug Lee than asked, "If I wanted to get something to them in the future what would be the best way." Steven Clements responded to Doug Lee with the GAC employee names of Tim Bell, JQ Leverette and Walter McDonald.

68. On November 14, 2018, Ashbritt issued invoice number 1810-004 to Bay County for debris cleanup services for the period October 11-31, 2018, in the amount of $393,995.61. The invoice listed a Quantity, Period, Description, Unit, Unit Price and Total for each line item displayed on the invoice. Some of the line items listed on the invoice included charges for Project Managers, Supervisors, Operators, Laborer, Skid Steer, Chainsaw, etc. The single line-item entries displayed the cumulative amounts for the period for those categories covered by the invoice. An excel spreadsheet was attached to the invoice that provided the daily itemized detail for each line item displayed on Ashbritt invoice number 1810-004.

69. The spreadsheet provided additional detail regarding the charges on the invoice to include a ticket number, location, employee name and line-item description. The line items can be referenced back to an Ashbritt numbered ticket titled "Time and Materials Log." The Ashbritt Time and Materials Logs are preprint forms that contain sections for the recording of a date, personnel, start time, end time, hours worked, equipment/vehicles and materials. Information on the logs were filled out by hand and signed and dated by an Ashbritt Representative and Subcontractor representative. The very bottom of the log has a comments section which was used to describe the work that was complete and gave a location.

70. Contained within the excel spreadsheet is a ticket number 6012. A copy of the ticket was obtained by a Federal Grand Jury Subpoena issued to Ashbritt and is stamped with bates number AB-GJ-14479. The Time and Materials Log lists the names Walter McDonald, Tim Bell and JQ in the personnel section of the log. In the equipment section, a front-end loader, two chainsaws and a pickup truck are listed. Each item was billed for eleven hours at the scheduled rates for a total charge to Bay County of $3,405.98. The Time and Materials Log was handwritten showing the

subcontractor as GAC and signed by Steven Clements. The work was performed on October 11, 2018, on "High Point Road and side streets." The log does not list, nor is it signed by an Ashbritt Representative. See paragraphs #39-41 above.

71. A check of the Bay County Property Appraiser's website revealed that Douglas Lee owns a residence located at 7934 High Point Road in Panama City, Florida, on one-third of an acre of land. A Google Maps satellite image pre-Hurricane Michael shows Doug Lee's lot was heavily wooded and satellite photos post-hurricane show virtually all the trees on the property having been removed.

**Doug Lee was the Executive Director of Operations for Bay District Schools; there is evidence in this affidavit and in his text messages that he had his property cleaned by GAC, charged to Bay District Schools and ultimately to FEMA. Why was he not indicted? Another rhetorical question.**

72. Joel Schubert is the Assistant County Manager for Bay County. Schubert's residence was badly damaged from Hurricane Michael. Schubert's residence is on Wildridge Road on four acres of land with a number of trees on the property. Schubert and his family were not able to stay at their residence because of the hurricane damage and had to relocate.

73. During and after the hurricane, Schubert was working at the emergency operations center (EOC) every day. After approximately two weeks, Schubert asked Derwin White for the names of some local contractors that do tree work that he could hire to remove some trees that were blocking his driveway and his ability to access his residence. Derwin White responded that he would have GAC handle it and would "put him on the list." Schubert asked Derwin White to give him a price for the work. Derwin White did not give Schubert a price nor provide him with the names of any subcontractors.

74. A few days later Schubert was alerted there was work going on at his residence. Schubert was eventually able to catch a GAC worker at his residence and told him to stop working because they had cleared enough of the driveway so that Schubert could get in and out of his property. Schubert was not there when work was being done but estimated that one or two GAC workers had worked on and off on his driveway for 2 or 3 days maximum and had used an excavator.

75. Schubert thereafter contacted Derwin White several times in person and by text messaging requesting a bill for the work GAC had done at his residence. On December 12, 2018, Schubert texted Derwin White, "need a bill for the tree work when y'all get a chance." On March 13, 2019, Schubert texted Derwin White, "Still owe you some money for the house." On April 4, 2019, Schubert went to his bank and purchased a cashier's check payable to GAC Contractors in the amount of $3,000. On April 9,

2019, Schubert took the check to GAC with a letter attached that stated, "please accept the $3,000 for tree services at 1616 Wildridge Road and advise of any additional payment necessary." Schubert then texted Derwin White "Dropped a cashier's check off for $3,000 for the work y'all already did. Let me know if there is still a balance."

**Incredibly, Schubert bought a cashier's check on April 4, 2019, the day that the investigators from the Bay County Sheriff's Office started their investigation and began questioning the employees of the City of Lynn Haven, three days after I went to Sheriff Tommy Ford to show him that I had found evidence of possible fraud in the City of Lynn Haven. Vickie Gainer was hired by Joel Schubert when he was the City Manager of Lynn Haven in 2016. Vickie Gainer wrote a letter to FEMA on this same day, April 4, 2019, trying to justify an emergency contract with Erosion Control Specialist, owned by Mickey White.**

76. On April 22, 2019, Schubert received an email from GAC with an invoice for $3,000 attached. Schubert responded, "I never received a bill, and I based the $3,000 on two or three days of work at $1,000 a day per conversation with DW. Please let me know if there was any other/additional work done and any remaining balance that is due." GAC responded, "Here is a copy of the invoice that I sent you. As far as I know there is no other charges."

77. A review of Ashbritt's invoice number 1810-004 excel spreadsheet shows work being done on Wildridge Road on ticket numbers 6126, 6135, 6136 and 6144. A copy of the Time and Materials Log for ticket number 6126 dated 10/26/2018, lists the names of three workers in the personnel section and a front-end loader, skid steer, mini excavator, pickup truck and chainsaw in the equipment section. The workers were billed for ten hours while the equipment was billed for a variety of hours at the scheduled rates. A copy of the Time and Materials Log for ticket number 6135 dated 10/27/2018, lists the names of three workers in the personnel section and a pickup truck and chainsaw in the equipment section. The workers and equipment were billed for six and a half hours at the scheduled rates. A copy of the Time and Materials Log for ticket number 6136 dated 10/27/2018, lists the names of three workers in the personnel section and a skid steer, mini excavator, pickup truck and chainsaw in the equipment section. The workers were billed for ten hours, and the equipment were billed for eight hours at the scheduled rates. A copy of the Time and Materials Log for ticket number 6144 dated 10/29/2018, lists the names of three workers in the personnel section and a skid steer, mini excavator, pickup truck and chainsaw in the equipment section. The workers and the equipment were billed for ten hours at the scheduled rates. The four tickets produced a total charge to Bay County of $9,613.48. The Time and

Materials Logs were handwritten showing the subcontractor as GAC and were signed by Steven Clements. All the tickets were signed by an Ashbritt representative.

78.  Based upon all of the above information and investigation, your affiant believes that the work performed by GAC on October 11, 2018, and October 26, 27, and 29, 2018 and billed through Ashbritt to and paid by Bay County, was actually performed at the personal residences of local government employees. *Derwin White's statement that there was a list being maintained and with statements* from *former GAC employees stating that they were sent to a number of personal residences and that documents were generated for such work,* leads to the logical conclusion that more records exist. GAC produced a number of billings over an extended period of time thereby confirming the existence of such records.

79.  Based on my training and experience, it was to GAC's benefit to perform such work for local public officials and government employees, who were either witting or unwitting, for future favorable treatment and lucrative contracts. Your affiant believes that many, if not all, of the costs associated with providing these benefits were billed to jobs and projects that GAC had ongoing at the time that the benefits were conveyed. Your affiant is aware that criminal organizations engaged in illegal activity use various means to conceal their activities and a search of the "PREMISES" as described in Attachment A, for the things described in Attachment B, will provide evidence for further discovery of violations of federal statute.

The Affidavit states that Derwin White made a statement that there was *a list being maintained* in paragraph 78 above. The boxes of evidence that were removed from GAC are still in Government custody and the contents have never been revealed. Derwin White's "statement" referred to by Borghini, was never given to the defense as part of the *Brady* material discovery if it was a written statement; we believe that Derwin White was given immunity and was a witness for the Government. The list of names that he was maintaining would be interesting to know; it would also be interesting if the list of jobs and projects includes more than just property cleanup after Hurricane Michael. Maybe the list includes construction projects, homes, swimming pools, painting, and landscaping. Mickey White stated in his FBI interview that Derwin was paying for these types of amenities for BCSO Major Jimmy Stanford, and for BCSO Deputy Mickey Vestal, and Stanford admitted to some of them in federal court. Derwin White told James Finch, after I was indicted, that Sheriff Tommy Ford had his property cleaned by county employees. We have no evidence to prove this is true, unless of course the Sheriff is on Derwin's "list", but if it is true, maybe there are Bay County or

GAC employees who will come forward during civil litigation. But for now, the boxes of sealed materials seized from GAC, owned by Derwin White and Allan Bense, remain in the custody of the Government. One has to wonder why the Government waited until five days *after* Derwin White's death to raid the premises of GAC; one theory is that the "list" and other incriminating evidence was destroyed.

The summer of 2022 was hot and humid, and I felt as listless and worn out from fighting the U.S. Government as the flowers looked that I was watering in my front yard. James Finch and I were living our lives waiting on the filing of one motion to the next, one trial date set and then changed, and from one news story in Bay County about us, to the next, as we had been coined, "the Bonnie and Clyde" of Lynn Haven.

As the summer began to come to an end, and fall was in the air, I was to suffer another extraordinary loss. I had rescued a scruffy little dog, a Yorkie mix, who had been abandoned after Hurricane Michael, and he had been a loyal companion, a source of strength to me both in the aftermath of the storm as well as through all of the hell that was to follow. I had lost my mom just after James was indicted in March of 2021, and now I would lose my sweet Buddy.

## August 23, 2022 "Buddy"

Today is one week since I lost Buddy. I have prayed each day for peace, for comfort, and have just sobbed my heartache to the Lord. I have cried several times today, and tonight while I was cooking I kept looking at the spot on the back of the couch in the den where he liked to lie on his blanket to watch me in the kitchen, be close to Lee as he watched tv, and also where he also had birds eye view of the front door, and the back yard area through the den windows. When I made up the bed this morning, I kept waiting for him to come running around the corner to our bedroom, to run up his little stairs and jump in the middle of the covers to play our "make up the bed game". He would jump up in the middle of the pillows while I tried to smooth the comforter, or we would play with his treat or bone that he had brought to challenge me with. Growling, eyes sparkling, he would playfully bite at my hands as I pretended to steal the treat, finally taking it to a far corner of the bed, holding it between his paws, and watching me as he chewed it.

Buddy didn't play when I first got him. He didn't know how. But he liked to be held, as I quickly learned. He had been left in a crate in the Wal-

Mart parking lot of Lynn Haven, Florida, on October 10, 2018, where he survived Hurricane Michael, a Category Five hurricane that destroyed the town, nearly drowning in his own crate, left without food or water until he was rescued by Ramona, the director of the Lynn Haven Animal Shelter.

I met Buddy on November 7th, 2018, when Ramona brought him over to Sheffield Park, where the City, the police, and the fire departments had set up temporary trailers and tents to run the City. He was nothing but hair and bones, but he licked me in the face and his soft brown eyes had me at hello.

The first night we had Buddy, we opened a door to the garage, and he bolted like a streak and was gone. There were no streetlights since the storm, debris was piled ten and twelve feet high on the sides of the streets, and as quickly as he had come into my life, Buddy was gone. I chased him, running and screaming his name in the dark, in my pajamas, barefoot, feeling broken glass and debris beneath my feet. I ran until I could run no more, but he was simply gone. He was silky, black and invisible in the dark terrible night in the aftermath of Hurricane Michael. Lee got on his motorcycle and took off looking for him. I was walking the streets, calling the little dog who had only known me a few hours, crying, thinking I would never see him again. A few minutes later, I saw the headlight of Lee's Harley, and he yelled at me, "I've got him," and Buddy was back in my arms, after riding home on a Harley in Lee's lap, looking as though riding on a motorcycle was the most natural thing in the world.

I sank to my knees in the middle of the road in relief, knowing that I had already "bought in" to this relationship with a tiny little dog who would soon own my heart. Lee said he had found him around the corner in the driveway where some children were playing, just hanging out.

I petted him and held him close, set a bowl of water and the floor, and he drank greedily. He would not eat anything though. I had a little red blanket from a play I had done at the school where I taught, Bozeman, High School, that had the *Wizard of Oz* embroidered on it. I laid the blanket on the foot of our bed and Buddy curled up on it and went to sleep. He looked just like Toto, and he had literally come out of a cyclone. At around 5:30 a.m. he was standing in my face, and then he began licking my face, telling me he was ready to go outside. I had sworn when I retired from teaching a year earlier, that I would never be out of bed before 8:00 a.m. again. Buddy was an early bird, and so would I be for the next three and a half years as he became my morning routine, walking at a fast pace, leading me along the streets of Lynn haven as we both dodged trash and debris of unbelievable proportions left by the storm.

Within weeks, Buddy was famous. Everyone in Lynn Haven knew his story. We were inseparable. He rode with me on the golf cart throughout the town as I visited residents handing out water, blankets, food supplies, bringing information and trying to answer their many questions about the progress the town was making. He sat in my lap during FEMA meetings and he met Ben Carson, Congressman Kevin McCarthy, Senator Bill Nelson, Governor Rick Scott, and numerous national news media personalities in the aftermath of the storm. Channel 7, the local NBC news station did a special on Buddy and be became known as the vice-mayor of Lynn Haven. He was a symbol of resilience, survival, and optimism.

He rode with me in the Lynn Haven Christmas Parade two months after the storm, he helped me hand out Christmas presents to children, and he now moved from the foot of the bed and slept curled up between Lee and I on his own pillow, helping to calm my anxiety in what I perceived to be the worst of times. I began to realize that I had not rescued him; he had rescued me.

Over the course of the next three- and one-half years, Buddy would be with me through the terrible days when the corruption scandal began in Lynn Haven, and as my anxiety grew, I would hold him and pet him until I am sure he thought I would rub all of the fur from his back, but he was content to be in my lap. On August 19, 2020, he was thrown into a bathroom at my house by the FBI agents who raided my home, and he barked and scratched frantically at the door as they took me away. He was waiting for me that night when I finally returned home after the most devastating day of my life. He loved to go on long walks, he loved riding in the car, and he especially loved riding on the golf cart, his ears flying back in the wind, taking in all that he saw. He chased squirrels, he smelled every flower, he followed me from room to room of our house all day, sat in my lap while I worked at the computer and hid bones in the far corners of my closet. He loved to be brushed, would come running if I picked up his brush and called him, and then would lie on his back with all four feet in the air while I laughed out loud, brushing his beautiful soft hair as he posed in every position possible, sometimes falling asleep and snoring he loved it so much.

If he knew I was going somewhere he would leap into the air, almost waist high, wanting to go. When I said, "Buddy gets to go" he was ecstatic, chasing his tail in circles and standing on two legs so that I could pick him up. If I was going to the grocery store or somewhere he couldn't go, I would tell him to stay with "Dad", and he would immediately go and sit next to Lee, or in Lee's lap until I returned. He hated to be left alone, and if we both had to leave, for a doctor's appointment or if we went out to dinner, I would tell him, "Buddy stay," and he would retreat to our bedroom with a hurt expression, looking back at us.

But when we returned, he would bark loudly, scolding us for leaving him, running about the house, joyously jumping from one couch to another, while we petted and loved him.

Buddy taught me so many things. Courage. Resilience. Unconditional love and trust. Last year when he was diagnosed with kidney failure, after spending four days in an emergency hospital on IV fluids, I carried him to the car and told Lee that the veterinarians said that he would not survive. I had hated leaving him there, but they had called me several times a day to tell me progress, but I knew how afraid he must be. As I left, they gave me medications as well as a bag of fluids with a terrible looking needle, with instructions on how to place fluid under his skin as a kind of dialysis; I could not stand to do it, and so started taking him to the vet every other day for subcutaneous fluids. Sometimes he cried and sometimes he acted as though it didn't bother him at all, but after several weeks of fluids, coaxing him to take anti-nausea medicine, placing prescription cream to increase his appetite inside one of ears, cooking chicken and rice, and actually laying my hands on him and praying for his healing, he started to respond. I have had him for more than a year longer than I was supposed to; for over fourteen months, he was completely healthy, without treatment, and I declared to everyone who asked about him that the Lord had healed him. The veterinarians had no explanation; his creatinine, and other blood work was still terrible. Buddy was running and walking with me, sometimes two or three miles each day. He was a miracle in my life, convincing me that God indeed answers prayers, that we only need to have faith.

When he suddenly took a turn for the worse about three weeks ago, I took him for a blood screen. His creatinine levels (kidney numbers) were over 9. They were between 3 and 4 when I was told he wasn't going to make it a year before. My heart sank. The vet said we would flush his system with 200 ml of subcutaneous fluids each day for a week and see what happened. He responded well, and began to eat and drink water, and I thought he was improving. We went in at the end of the week for the blood screen, and he began to shake and cry when we went into the vet's office. He was afraid. My heart was broken. He had improved only minimally.

I took him home and just held him for a while. The vet had suggested we continue the fluids and see if he improved any more. He had become more fearful each time we went in for fluids or a test, and his tiny little frame would just tremble. I told Lee that I was going to stop treatment. I was not going to subject him to any more fear or any more needles; I grieved and questioned myself if I made the right decision about this, but the sadness and pain in Buddy's eyes told me he was ready, that he was tired, and very sick. He ate for the first two or three days after we stopped the fluids, mostly vanilla ice cream. He would eat a little chicken and rice, and the final time he ate was a little hamburger and gravy, which he later threw up.

Nine days later, on August 15, 2022, almost four years after Buddy became part of our lives, I called the vet and scheduled to bring Buddy in for euthanasia. He had thrown up, not eaten in three days, had continuous diarrhea and no longer wanted to go outside for his morning walk, the favorite time of his day. He would wag his tail weakly but showed no enthusiasm for moving or getting up. On the night before I called the vet, he drank water like he had not had water in days, and then immediately threw it up, his tiny little body wracked with dry heaves.

I scheduled the appointment for the next day at 10:00 a.m. and the vet asked no questions. She knew how sick he was. I then called and scheduled a private cremation at a pet crematorium and cemetery. Buddy was lying on the bed in my room as I scheduled the appointments and I felt like a traitor, like I was giving up on my sweet little guy. I took a quilt out of the closet, a hundred-year-old quilt sewn by my great-grandmother, Cora Stafford, that Buddy liked to curl up on. I took it outside on our front lawn, beneath the two giant oak trees, and Buddy and I laid down on the quilt together, enjoying the sun, and a surprisingly cool breeze that was blowing for an August afternoon. I told him how much I loved him, that I would never forget him, and that I hoped he understood what I was doing. I told him I would see him when I got to heaven, and that I would look for him there. That night, just after midnight, I heard him get up and I followed him into another part of the house where he continued to be sick. I cleaned him up and placed the quilt on the couch in the living room to make it easier for him to get down if he needed to than from our bed. I didn't sleep anymore, and just petted him, talking to him, dreading for the morning to come. I had spoken to my brother, Roy, earlier, who is a doctor, and he told me that a person with Buddy's creatinine numbers would be in a coma; that Buddy was very sick, in pain, and although it was a terrible decision to have to make, that I was doing the right thing for Buddy.

Lee drove me to the veterinarian's office at ten minutes till ten, and they had a room ready for us. It just didn't go the way I had thought it would. They had blankets on the table for him, and I had brought his own blanket for him to lie on, but he was trembling, because he knew where he was. Lee and I both went into the room and waited for the veterinarian to come in. A technician came in and said she had a sedative shot for him first. Lee and I had petted him, and he had actually stopped trembling and laid down on his blanket while we petted him. When she gave him the sedative shot, he cried out, and it just broke my heart in two. Lee told me he just could not stay any longer. He loved Buddy as much as I did. The veterinarian told me the shot was a sedative strong enough for a forty-pound dog, and Buddy weighed just under seven pounds. He immediately began to fall asleep, as we petted him, and the veterinarian picked him up and said she would be back that she was going to go to place the IV. I stopped her and said no, that I was staying with Buddy. Lee told Buddy goodbye and left to go and wait for me. They went to go and get the IV equipment while I stayed with Buddy and kept petting him and talking to him. His eyes became glassy, and his mouth was open because the muscles had relaxed, and as they began to prepare his leg for the IV, I asked her if he was asleep, and she said no, that he was just heavily sedated. I leaned down and softly sang, "Somewhere Over the Rainbow," close to his face, petting him, tears rolling down my face.

They could not place the IV because his leg was too tiny, and he was so dehydrated and so they called another technician in to help her place it in his hip. I continued to talk to him and pet him, praying for him, not knowing if he was feeling pain from the IV or if he was confused. They told me later that he had very little awareness at that point, but I was still worried that he was confused or afraid. Before I knew it, they told me he was gone. I cried uncontrollably and stayed there a few more minutes before wrapping Buddy in his blanket and carrying him to the car where Lee was waiting.

We took him home and I laid him in the blanket on the bed, and just sat beside him, feeling so empty, wondering if I had done the right thing, should I have given him another day or two to just see if he would naturally pass away in his sleep. Lee assured me that I had done the right thing, but I could not find comfort, could not find peace.

While most people might not understand what I did next, I had to do it. I had heard if you left a dog for the veterinarians to transport to the crematoriums that there was no assurance that your dog was cremated alone, or if the ashes were really those of your dog. I know he was gone, and I know it sounds crazy, but Buddy had been thrown away once in his life, he had been the most special dog of my life, and I was determined I would see him through. Lee drove me to the crematorium, and I carried my sweet Buddy inside, and waited while he was cremated. I placed him myself in the blanket lined cardboard tray they provided, arranged his soft little body gently, and watched as they took him and placed him in the crematory. I waited for the 45 minutes it took, watched as they removed his ashes, and then they placed them in a small rosewood box, sealed it up and returned it to me. The images of this experience will be with me for a very long time, but I am not sorry for staying with him, I could not have left him there alone.

Lee helped me in the car, and I cried uncontrollably all the way home. I placed the little box on the night table in our room, placed his collar on top, and began to feel a sense of peace that he was home now, and that he was no longer in pain. Without Buddy, I would not have gotten out of bed for the last three years while the government indictment and preparations for trial have destroyed virtually everything in my life. Because of Buddy, I got up each morning to take him for his 6:30 a.m. walk, he would curl up beside me while I said my morning prayers and read my devotional, and then I was able to stay up and function, to do whatever I had to do to get through one more day.

Buddy was a gift to me from God; a special little dog filled with grit, a will to survive, a heart full of love, and eyes which could look deeply into your soul. He came into our lives for a season, for "such a time as this". He has seen me through the death of my precious Mom, and he was a special comfort to her as well. He has been a source of comfort and companionship to Lee through illness and surgery, always ready to hang out and take a nap, snuggling close, knowing that Lee needed him too, and he was always filled with joy when our grandchildren were in the house. He loved children, and when they would spend the night, he would sleep with them, watching over them while they slept.

We had only lived in Jacksonville for two years when Buddy died, but Buddy knew everyone in our neighborhood, stopping to speak to all of the other dogs we passed as we walked, wagging his little tail, sometimes walking throwing his little front feet out like a show dog at the international dog show instead of the yorkie, maltese, and cairn terrier mix the vets have speculated him to be. He has listened to me pray so much in the mornings when we walked, I was sure he would think his name was Jesus instead of Buddy. I sang to him sometimes when he became so sick, singing "How Much is that Doggie in the Window," or "Somewhere Over the Rainbow," just as I had sung to him as he was sedated and began to fall asleep last week for the last time. His fur was so soft that I petted him and put my face close to his.

Many would say I should not have stayed with him while he died, that I should not have tortured myself by watching the process of cremation; but I could not have been anywhere else. He was alone when I met him, thrown away by his previous owners and left to die in a storm; I was determined he would not be alone when we parted. The night after he died, I awoke after having a dream so real, I was sure I was awake. In the dream, Buddy ran into my arms, joyful, healthy, chasing his tail and licking my face; he was only in my arms for a few seconds, but I felt his soft fur, saw joy in his eyes, and then suddenly I woke up. I knew he was alright, safe, and healthy again, that his precious little spirit was no longer here, but safe, with the Lord.

Rest in peace my sweet Buddy; you are never forgotten, never far from our hearts. *"Are not two sparrows sold for a copper coin? And not one of them falls to the ground apart from your Father's will."* Matthew 10:29

September 26, 2022

Attorney Guy Lewis filed a motion for Order to Show Cause and Third Motion to Compel after the Affidavit for the Search of GAC was mistakenly made public by the Government in August. We were livid that this document had been hidden from the defense for over a year, and the following is the motion, with redactions which was filed, leading to the second evidentiary hearing of our case, which would be held in December 2022. Although this motion was filed on behalf of James Finch, my attorneys filed the same motion on my behalf as they worked closely with Guy Lewis and Jeffrey Forman:

## Defendant Finch's Redacted Motion for
## ORDER TO SHOW CAUSE AND THIRD MOTION TO COMPEL

Defendant Finch respectfully moves for an order to show cause why this case should not be dismissed due to the government's continued, repeat failures to comply with *Brady* obligations under the Court's Discovery Order. Alternatively, Finch moves for appropriate sanctions, along with an order compelling the government to produce materials, stating:

For over two years, there has been a wholesale failure on the part of the government to comply with the letter and spirit of the Court's Orders and case law requiring the disclosure of *Brady, Giglio* and *Napue* information to the defense. (2)

(1) **Pursuant to Local Rule 5.5(D), Defendant Finch files this redacted version of his Motion for Order to Show Cause and Third Motion to Compel, which was filed under seal on September 26, 2022. Finch has redacted quotations and direct references to material that is subject to the Protective Order, ECF No. 174.**

(2) *Brady v. Maryland*, **373 U.S. 83 (1963),** *Giglio v. United States*, **405 U.S. 150 (1972), and** *Napue v. Illinois*, **360 U.S. 264 (1959).**

On March 31, 2021, the government provided a written response to Finch's request for Rule 16 discovery. The government represented that "the United States does not have information or material at this time which may be favorable to the defendants on the issues of guilt or punishment," citing *Brady v. Maryland* and *United States v. Augurs*. The government also took the position that defense discovery requests may include information to which the defense is "not entitled" and information that may or may not exist. Letter from AUSA Kunz to Defense Counsel, 13 (March 31, 2021) (attached as Exhibit A) ("Finally, if your discovery letter includes requests for information to which you are not entitled to Fed. R. Cr. Pr. 16, Local Rule 26.2, or the pre-trial order of the court, please be advised that the failure of the United States to respond directly to those requests not encompassed by the federal discovery rules should not be construed as any representation as to the non-existence of any requested information.").

On May 14, 2021, Finch responded, seeking specific clarification as to the information that may or may not "exist." We also identified several individuals who were interviewed by state and federal agents, requesting those reports. Many of these witnesses were involved in the Lynn Haven contracting process, participated in City government, or were contextually identified in the Indictment and Superseding Indictment. This information was not provided by the government in its initial discovery response. (3)

(3) The government's April 1, 2021, production included witness statements from only Defendant Margo Anderson, Adam Albritton, Finch, and former Lynn Haven City Commissioner Antonius Barnes. The July 19, 2021, production included 53 reports of witness statements, nearly all of which were prepared and available before the Superseding Indictment. Much of the information that was provided contained classic *Brady*, *Giglio*, and *Napue* material. Witness statements contradicted each other. Many of the reports contradicted fundamental theories of specific allegations in the Indictment.

Even after the defense specifically identified Brady material, the material was not willingly produced. Instead, the government pressed for an all-encompassing protective order on the basis that the defendants were improperly disclosing discovery material. When challenged to support this allegation, the government altered its argument, requesting the Court enter an overly restrictive protective order without precedent or justifiable cause. It was a clear attempt to control defense's access to materials to which the defense was entitled. (4)

(4) As demonstrated herein the government is yet again improperly withholding discovery, including *Brady* material, on the cusp of trial.

This Court rejected the government's overreach, summarily denying the government's attempt to unfairly restrict our review of discovery. ECF No. 174 (rejecting the government's request to "retroactively impose restrictions on documents it has already produced" and holding "that the provision limiting Defendants to reviewing witness material at their counsel's office is overly restrictive").

After repeated requests by the defense, on July 19, 2021, the government's second wave of discovery was produced (well *after* the discovery deadlines had passed). This production demonstrated that the government's March 31, 2021, written representation that it was *not* in possession of additional **Brady** material was manifestly untrue.

## A. First Motion to Compel

During the time the government was supposed to be repairing the legal and factual flaws in the Superseding Indictment, Finch's counsel continued to try to resolve without Court intervention discovery disputes relating to Brady issues, sealed pleadings, and redacted 302's. Unsuccessful in our attempts, on October 22, 2021, Finch was forced to file his first Motion to Compel the production of redacted 302s and sealed pleadings. ECF No. 200. Finch's motion detailed a history of the government's discovery violations, including the government's misrepresentation on March 31, 2021, that it was not in possession of additional *Brady* material.

On November 9, 2021, the Court granted Finch's Motion to Compel over the government's objection and express representation that the redacted material was not *Brady*. ECF No. 221. The unredacted material was produced on November 12, 2021. A review of that unredacted material was both startling and disturbing, unequivocally demonstrating that the government's representations of "not *Brady*" were false. (5)

> **(5)** For example, the suppressed material contained direct evidence of law enforcement corruption, false testimony before the Grand Jury, and actual evidence of innocence. See e.g., ECF Nos. 228 at 12-13, 229 (government witnesses Michael White and David "Mickey" White revealing substantial misconduct by government witnesses). The suppressed reports directly implicated co-case agent Major Jimmy Stanford of the Bay County Sheriff's Office in serious criminal conduct—much of which occurred while investigating this very case. See ECF No. 274 at 11-13, 16-20.

On November 16, 2021, the government suggested that its decision to suppress this critical information was driven by its lack of "confidence in [our] ability to control [Finch}." The government further criticized the Court, stating "that the Court directed production without reviewing the redacted material or making a determination the material is *Brady*." See ECF No. 228 at Ex. F.

## B. Second Motion to Compel

Armed with these unredacted revelations and evidence that the government solicited false testimony, the defense filed a Motion to Dismiss the Second Superseding Indictment, which alternatively requested production of all Grand Jury transcripts, agents' notes and reports. ECF No. 228. In response, the government characterized the redacted statements, which originated from the government's own cooperating witnesses, as "not *Brady*." ECF No. 238. The government's position that such information was "not *Brady*" was both legally and factually unsupportable. The Court ordered immediate production of all Grand Jury transcripts, agent reports, and notes by March 1, 2022, and set the matter for an evidentiary hearing. ECF No 256.

Unfortunately, the government utterly failed to comply with this Court Order of Production as well. Instead, it disregarded the Court's instructions in the most flagrant fashion. (6) Rather than complying or seeking an extension, the government made:

**Seven** late productions between March 4, 2022, and 8:24 a.m. on March 31, 2022;

**One** late production *during* the evidentiary hearing; and

**Three** late productions *after* the evidentiary hearing's conclusion.
As presented during the three-day evidentiary hearing and Defendant's Post-Hearing Briefing, the government's multiple March 1 – April 13, 2022, late productions contained significant *Brady* material. (7) Each late production constituted a violation of this Court's Orders.

(6)　The government never sought an extension of the Court's Order of Production. See Fed. R. Crim P. 16(d) ("At any time the court may, for good cause, deny, restrict, or defer discovery.") Failure to comply with Rule 16 may result in prohibition of the introduction of the undisclosed evidence or entry of an "order that is just under the circumstances." *Id.* at 16(d)(2).

(7)　For example, multiple reports of Samantha Lind, which were withheld, were extraordinarily disturbing because they described the manufacturing of evidence against Anderson. ECF No. 274 at 21. Likewise, Borghini hid his notes from an interview with Denise "DeDe" Rowan (with counsel present) that directly contradicted the testimony of the government's cooperating witnesses, Michael White and Chris Forehand. *Id.* at 32-34. The Court later rejected the government's insinuation that some of the late produced material was not Brady simply because it believed Defendants are guilty. ECF No. 294 (concluding the government's position was "nonsense").

In the June 13, 2022, Order, the Court rejected several of the government's arguments and characterizations of the withheld materials and described the government's conduct as "fall[ing] well short of best practices." ECF No. 294. Ultimately, the Court declined to conclude that the government acted in bad faith or that Defendants were sufficiently prejudiced to warrant dismissal. But the government was ordered to file a notice stating that, to the best of its knowledge, all outstanding reports had been produced. Id. at 11-12. On July 1, 2022, the government submitted notice that it had fully complied with the Court's February 22, 2022, Order. ECF No 303.

We now know this notice and the representation to the Court were yet again untrue.

## C. **Third Motion to Compel**

On August 11, 2022, the media reported on an unsealed warrant affidavit signed by former FBI Special Agent Borghini that was used to obtain and acquire three search warrants on properties owned and controlled by GAC Contractors, Inc. ("GAC"). (8)

    (8) Prior to March 2022, GAC was co-owned by Former Speaker of the Florida House of Representatives Allan Bense and Lynn Haven contractor Derwin White. GAC and Derwin White, along with Ashbritt, were actively involved in orchestrating all post-hurricane Michael debris disposal in Lynn Haven. The government's charging documents, of course, would have one believe that Margo Anderson and James Finch were the wizards behind the curtain, despite overwhelming evidence to the contrary, including Finch's being in Jacksonville recuperating from a serious, debilitating stroke.

After the warrant documents were unsealed and widely reported on by the media, the government sought an order re-sealing the materials.

Considering the Court's orders and admonitions regarding the government's repeated failure to comply with its discovery obligations, it was disturbing to read Borghini's warrant affidavit, which clearly contained *Brady* and *Giglio* information that was not produced to Defendants Finch and Anderson. Borghini's sworn statements within the warrant affidavit are factually inconsistent with the government theories in this case. In addition, several statements directly contradict Borghini's testimony before the Grand Juries. (9) We also believe that the affidavit would have constituted a statement of the witness that should have been produced consistent with Brady, Giglio, and the Court's February 22, 2022, Order as Borghini testified at the evidentiary hearing on the Motions to Dismiss.

On August 26, 2022, we sought an explanation as to why the

government failed to produce the warrant and the affidavit (10) We also requested a copy of any and all materials obtained as a result of the FBI's August 5, 2021, search warrants because the warrants permitted the FBI to search for and seize, among other things, "any and all records and documents relating to James Finch, Phoenix construction, or entity owned by or controlled by James Finch or Phoenix construction" as well as "any and all documents relating to Ashbritt." (11).

(9) Borghini was the only witness presented to each and every Grand Jury to secure the return of these complicated, convoluted indictments.

(10) *See United States v. Search Warrant,* Case Nos. 5-21-mj-00078, 5-21-mj00079; 5:21-mj-00080 (N.D. Fla.)

(11) As further described herein, the FBI's receipts for property seized in case numbers 5:21-mj-00078, 5:21-mj-00079, and 5:21-mj-00080 list a series of thumb drives, computers, phones, and other items. Although overly generic in their description, some items bear the description of material that is likely relevant to the allegations and circumstances surrounding the post-hurricane debris disposal, which is part of the Count One conspiracy allegations regarding Finch's so-called "Business Interests."

On August 29, 2022, the government responded:

**Regarding materials seized at GAC, we have not completed our review of it but will produce any material we identify as relevant. In the meantime, you are welcome to inspect it at the FBI office in Panama City and copy any particular document you identify as relevant. We think this is necessary given what the Court described as Mr. Finch's "irresistible urge to share discovery materials in direct violation of . . .Court's orders." We are happy to reconsider that procedure if you provide sufficient assurance that Mr. Finch has not otherwise violated the protective order.**

However, because the Court previously rejected the government's prior attempts at limiting the review of discovery, ECF No. 174, Defendant Finch respectfully rejected the government's offer to review all documents at the FBI office in Panama City. We again asked the government to confirm whether the government is opposed or unopposed to providing the defendants with access to all the material seized pursuant to the GAC search warrant. We also asked the government to provide a copy of the Order in which, the government claimed, the Court found Finch to have an "irresistible urge to share discovery materials in direct violation of . .

.Court's orders.") (12)

(12) The defense does not have possession of or access to any Order containing this alleged quote from the Court. In the event the government is quoting from a sealed or *ex parte* pleading, ECF Nos. 276 or 322, Defendant Finch respectfully requests that the pleading be produced now that the government has quoted from it and is attempting to use the Court's findings, allegedly concluding that Finch has an "irresistible urge to share discovery in direct violation of . . .Court's orders." With the greatest deference to the Court, we are simply skeptical that the Court reached this conclusion apparently *ex parte* without adversarial due process.

On September 6, 2022, the government responded, "As we said, the GAC search materials are available for your inspection and copying at FBI headquarters in Panama City. . .Should you choose to file a motion to compel production in some other form, you may represent that we oppose that request for relief." Notably, the government ignored Finch's request for and/or refused to provide the order or document in which the government claimed the Court made statements or findings about Defendant Finch.

On August 26, 2022, we also informed the government that we had information and reason to believe that Borghini interviewed several witnesses or potential witnesses and did not generate an FBI 302 or notes of the interview. We believe the information was not transcribed because it was exculpatory to Defendants Finch and/or Anderson.

Unfortunately, within weeks of trial's beginning, we are once more in the untenable position of seeking Court intervention in the production of Court-ordered discovery. Specifically, the defense is seeking Court-ordered discovery regarding all witnesses interviewed by the FBI and Bay County Sheriff's Office in relation to this case and the search of GAC's properties.

## II. ARGUMENT

At the August 13, 2021, hearing on Defendants' Motions to Dismiss the Superseding Indictment, the Court inquired about the number of conspiracies that were alleged in the indictment. Hr'gTr. At 6:4-7:21 (Aug. 13,2021). Specifically, the Court rightly questioned the government as to the identity of the "hub or the rim" as it relates to the government's conspiracy theories. *Id. The limited and incomplete discovery paints a partial picture of answers to the Court's questions. Most certainly, portions of the discovery also reveal who is **NOT***
the hub, rim, or spokes to this alleged conspiracy: James Finch.

The limited and incomplete discovery produced by the government in this case demonstrates that Derwin White was the "hub" of the conspiracies surrounding post-hurricane cleanup. Ashbritt is undoubtedly a "spoke" or "rim" as it agreed to allow White to direct and control the debris disposal in Lynn Haven. And, Chris Forehand, with his connections and control of Tetra Tech, is also a "spoke" or "rim." To disprove the government's allegations against Finch and to prove the government's grossly inadequate, sloppy, and misleading investigation, we are requesting the Court compel production of the material seized from GAC in that it relates to the unindicted "hub," "spokes," and "rim" of corruption in Lynn Haven related to the post-Hurricane Michael debris disposal.

## A. GAC, Derwin White, and Ashbritt, Inc.

GAC is a Florida corporation specializing in road, sitework, and building construction in North Florida. Prior to its sale in March 2022, GAC was co-owned and operated by Derwin White, who is recently deceased. Crowder Gulf and Ashbritt, Inc. ("Ashbritt"), are two large national providers in the disaster response and recovery industry with pre-negotiated contracts within Bay County, including with the City of Lynn Haven. In response to Hurricane Michael, Lynn Haven and surrounding counties and municipalities activated Crowder Gulf and Ashbritt to perform post-hurricane services.

According to the Borghini affidavit in support of the GAC search At the direction of Anderson,. . .Company C, which had been disposing of vegetative debris or chips at another site location, implying that he had connections in Lynn Haven, and asked if Crowder Gulf needed help. Derwin White stated that he was willing to assist Crowder Gulf if it would cut him in on a percentage of its revenues and to facilitate a debris disposal site. Crowder Gulf did not need Derwin White and had nothing to do with Derwin White or GAC. However, Ashbritt did partner with Derwin White and GAC.

Ashbritt used GAC as a subcontractor on many services and used GAC sites for debris management, reduction, and disposal. According to Borghini THREE LINES REDACTED *United States v. Search Warrant,* Case nos. 5:21-mj-00078; 5:21-mj-00079; 5:21-mj-00080, ECF No. 2 (emphasis added). This portion of Borghini's sworn statement is wholly inconsistent with Borghini's (further directly inconsistent with the government's theory in this case—that **Anderson directed that all debris be transported to Finch's site for final disposal. (13)**

(13)    See ECF No. 214 P 14 ("ANDERSON later directed the City

to dispose of hurricane debris at [Finch's] property, and the City paid for it to be disposed there, rather than on another City property nearby"); *id* P 73 ("[*stopped dumping at that site* location and *commenced disposing all* its vegetative debris or chips at [Finch's site) (emphasis added); *id* P 79 ("At the direction of Anderson. . .Company D, which had been disposing of vegetative debris or chips at another site location, *ended dumping at that site* location and *commenced disposing all* its vegetative debris or chips at FINCH's site")(emphasis added).

Derwin White's and Ashbritt's control of the debris disposal process, however, would not have been possible without their coordinating efforts with Forehand and Tetra Tech, the company that was selected by former Lynn Haven City Manager Michael White as its FEMA monitor. Among several generic entries, the FBI listed "REDACTED" among the items it seized from GAC.

## B.   Chris Forehand and Tetra Tech

Forehand is presumably a principal witness against Finch's purchase and sale of a motor home to Defendant Anderson's husband. Aside from the tenuous allegations surrounding the motorhome transaction, Forehand's involvement and influence permeate several other aspects of the alleged honest services fraud within the City of Lynn Haven. Indeed, Forehand's reach and influence also extended to areas of the post-hurricane clean up.

The government's own reports implicate Forehand as essential to bribing the former City Manager, Michael White, to award a FEMA monitoring contract to Tetra Tech. Michael White stated (REDACTED). See Michael White 302 (Dec. 11, 2019) Exhibit B. In reality, Forehand illegally caused Michael White to alter the selection committee's scoring to award a FEMA monitoring contract for personal financial gain. Again, this evidence directly contradicts the government narrative that Anderson and Finch controlled this illegal conduct.

Former City Attorney Adam Albritton has stated that (REDACTED). See Albritton 302 (Sept 10, 2021), Exhibit C. But Lynn Haven did not have a contract in place for FEMA consulting and was looking to negotiate a contract for assistance with FEMA reimbursement. *Id.* Michael White and Forehand wanted to (REDACTED), BUT Albritton advised it was against federal law. *Id.* After further discussion, Forehand provided Albritton with (REDACTED). *Id.*

Albritton recalled a meeting between Michael White, Jay Moody, (14) and Forehand where Michael White informed Forehand that (REDACTED). *Id.*

After further discussion, Forehand provided Albritton with (REDACTED). Forehand asked to have a private meeting with Michael White but Albritton witnessed Michael White and Forehand engaged in a discussion about (REDACTED). *Id.* Albritton allegedly heard Forehand say to Michael White, (REDACTED). After their conversation, Michael White advised that Lynn Haven (REDACTED). Thereafter, Michael White, Kelli Battistini, and Vicky Gainer changed their ranking so that Tetra Tech was the highest ranked and awarded the contract. (15)

(14) Moody was the outside auditor for the City of Lynn Haven.

(15) Vickey Gainer (Who is Lynn Haven's current City Manager after having worked with former City Manager Michael White during his reign of corruption) and Kelly Battistini were on the selection committee with Michael White. *See* Michael White 302 (Dec. 12, 2019), Exhibit D. They were (REDACTED) that the city wanted to use Tetra Tech based on Forehand's recommendation. *Id.* The committee members' score sheets reflect scores that (REDACTED).

In December 2018, Forehand sent a text to Albritton regarding the Tetra Tech contract, stating "REDACTED". (16*) Id.* Forehand also boasted to Albritton that "REDACTED".

(16) Forehand has also used "redacted" references when committing illicit activity. For instance, in December 2017, after Michael White was hired as the City Manager, Forehand (REDACTED). Ex. D. Forehand told Michael White he was (REDACTED). and this was a "REDACTED*) Id.*

Forehand and his partner, Jim Slonina, started Panhandle Engineering Disaster Services ("PEDS") on October 23, 2018, days following Hurricane Michael. See Jim Slonina 302 (July 22, 2020), Exhibit E; Chris Forehand 302 (Aug 23, 2019), Exhibit F. Tetra Tech hired PEDS as a subcontractor to assist with their debris- monitoring operations. Ex. E. A percentage of the Tetra Tech monitors doing the work were employees of PEDS. *Id.*

Forehand was financially benefiting from every aspect of post-hurricane recovery efforts. He was getting kickbacks from claims adjusters after bribing City Manager Michael White. He was a subcontractor for Tetra Tech after bribing City Manager Michael White. He was also working as the Lynn Haven City Engineer, preparing plans and demolition documents and conducting contract negotiations and permit review.

As unindicted corporate actors and individual witnesses for the government, GAC's, Ashbritt's, Tetra Tech's, and Forehand's conduct relates to Lynn Haven debris disposal. Their agreements and relationships with each other and with the government are clearly subject to discovery. *Strickler v Greene,* 527 U.S. 263, 283 n 21 (1999) *("Brady's* disclosure requirements extend to materials that, whatever their other characteristics, may be used to impeach a witness.").

### III. Impermissible and Unreasonable Control Over the Access and Review of Court-Ordered Discovery.

Derwin White's, GAC's, Ashbritt's, Forehand's, and Tetra Tech's collective conduct is truly at the heart of this case. Borghini's affidavit about the relationship, agreements, and communications between Derwin White, GAC, and Ashbritt are inconsistent with the government's theories and indictments in this case. Thus, the government's former lead case agent and his sworn statements and reports are subject to discovery and rigorous cross-examination. In sum, his affidavit should have been produced over a year ago. See *Giglio v. United States,* 405 U.S. 150 (19720 (the government is constitutionally obligated to produce to the defense information that would tend to impeach a government witness). (17)

> (17) The government has previously disclosed that Borghini submitted false testimony to at least one Grand Jury. ECF No. 228 at 10. In truth, the defense proved Borghini perjured himself multiple times over multiple presentations. *See* ECF No. 294 at 21-22 (finding Borghini's testimony regarding FEMA funding "appeared" to be false [] and the Government knew or should have known); *id.* at 34 ("The Government concedes that Borghini's 'testimony was not accurate'"); *id.* (conceding that at least one of Borghini's Grand Jury exhibits contained false information).

Additionally, the August 2021 GAC search warrants permitted the seizure of "any and all records and documents relating to James Finch, Phoenix Construction, or entity owned by or controlled by James Finch or Phoenix Construction" as well as "any and all documents relating to Ashbritt." Despite the pendency of this case, the government claims it has not completed its review of the seized documents. (18) In other words, the government has been sitting on volumes of relevant discovery for over a year and has neither produced nor offered Defendants access to the material until the media discovered the unsealed pleadings. Rather than owning up to its suppression and attempted cover up, the government tries to put the toothpaste back in the tube and reseal the warrants and affidavits. (19)

(18) The search warrant affidavit was apparently sworn to on August 3, 2021, and then executed on August 5, 2021.
(19) As indicated above, the unsealed warrant and affidavit received widespread media attention. The government provided neither Finch nor Anderson with any information regarding the warrant or the critical affidavit, though apparently the affidavit was executed on August 3, 2021. *See United States v. Search Warrant*, Case Nos. 5:21-mj-00078; 5:21-mj00079; 5:21-mj-00080 (N.D. Fla.) at ECF No. 2.

Defendant Finch requested production of the warrant and the affidavit on August 26, 2022, 15 days after they were disclosed through the press. Like with previous discovery, the government offered restricted access. Of course, restricted access comes at an unreasonable and unduly prejudicial cost. The government will allow access to the discovery only if defense counsel endures the cost and inconvenience of traveling hundreds of miles from their office during the weeks and days leading up to trial, while the defense is working hard to comply with every filing deadline as outlined by the Court. If the government's army of FBI agents have yet to complete their review of the seized GAC material within a year, how is it reasonable to force the defendants to complete their review within weeks or days before trial? The government's position is pure gamesmanship, and its offer was made in bad faith.

## IV. The government continues to withhold witness statements.

Sanctions, including dismissal of the Second Superseding Indictment with prejudice for deliberate, flagrant, repeat violations of Court Orders and intentional suppression of *Brady* information, are appropriate under the Court's supervisory authority. See generally ECF no. 274 at 34-40 (citing *United States v. Chapman*, 524 F.3d 1073 (9th Cir. 2008) ("The failure to produce documents and to record what had or had not been disclosed, along with the affirmative misrepresentations to the court of full compliance, support the district court's finding of 'flagrant' prosecutorial misconduct even if the documents themselves were not intentionally withheld from the defense.")).

During preparation for the November trial date, the defense team discovered several individuals were interviewed by Borghini, providing exculpatory testimony. The government has not produced either notes or

FBI 302s of those interviews. Specifically, Borghini contacted and interviewed Harold Parker, a pilot who works for Finch. Yet, no notes or 302's were produced. Borghini also contacted and spoke with Hulon E. Walsingham, an employee and surveyor with Country Wide Surveying, Inc., which was hired by Lee Anderson in August 2020 to confirm the boundary lines of the Andersons' former home in Lynn Haven. Again, the government has not produced any notes or the reports of this exculpatory interview despite the witness's having rejected the corruption theory suggested by the interviewing FBI agent.

Additionally, following the release of the GAC search warrants, Allen Byrd, the owner of Byrd Enterprises & Land Development, Inc., filed a lawsuit against GAC. *See Byrd Enters. & Land Dev., Inc. v. GAC* Contractors, *Inc.,* Case NO.22000841CA (Fla. 14th Cir.). In his verified complaint seeking monetary damages and a declaratory judgment related to GAC's and Derwin White's manipulation of the post-hurricane debris disposal, Byrd swears under the penalty of perjury that he "was interviewed by the FBI at the Bay County Sheriff's Office along with Jimmy Stanford." (20)

> (20) The defense need not detail nor repeat the obvious relevance of BCSO Major Jimmy Stanford's relationship to this case and his admission to destroying interview notes. See ECF no. 274 at 11-13, 16-20.

Incredibly, the government identified Byrd and other material witnesses, such as Commissioner Rodney Friend, as potential witnesses, listing them on the "No Contact List." What purpose does it serve to include potential witness names on a "No Contact List" but withhold witness reports and notes against the Court's Orders?

The government's "less than laudable" conduct regarding discovery is flagrant. There is no justifiable excuse. The government cannot plausibly or legally claim that it was without knowledge of these interviews. In fact, the government is "deemed to have knowledge of and access to anything in the possession, custody, or control of any federal agency participating in the same investigation of the defendant." *United States v. Bryan*, 868 F.2d 1032, 1036 (9th Cir. 1989); *see also Carey v. Duckworth*, 738 F.2d 875, 878 (7th Cir. 1984) ("A prosecutor's office cannot get around *Brady* by keeping itself in ignorance, or by compartmentalizing information about different aspects of a case."). And, to the extent that any government agencies or actors, through their own flagrant misconduct, failed to make known exculpatory information, the flagrant nature of such conduct will be imputed to the prosecution team. *United States v. Bundy*, 968 F.3d 1019, 1037 (9th Cir. 2020).

Indeed, courts have recognized that a prosecutor's reckless disregard of *Brady* and other discovery obligations can constitute "flagrant" misconduct, particularly where, as here, the government tries to hide its mistakes and refuses to acknowledge its errors. See, *e.g., United States v. Kojayan*, 8F.3d 1315, 1322-23 (9th Cir. 1993) (government's discovery violations, misleading statements, and failure to accept responsibility for its wrongdoing constituted "flagrant" misconduct); *United States v. Fitzgerald*, 615 F. Supp 2d 1156, 1159-60 (S.D. Cal. 2009) (discovery log to keep track of what had been disclosed to the defense); see also *Bundy*, 968 F.3d at 1043 (affirming the district court's dismissal of an indictment with prejudice, explaining that such a result was appropriately within the range of reasonable and appropriate remedies).

WHEREFORE, Defendant James D. Finch respectfully moves for the entry of an order requiring the government to show cause why its conduct should not be considered flagrant, bad faith, and as warranting additional sanctions, including dismissal, and additionally, compelling the disclosure of the material seized from GAC Contractors, and other such relief as the Court deems just and proper.

Respectfully submitted,

Guy A. Lewis
Jeffrey M. Forman

The Beacon of Bay County would report on the motion to compel filed by Guy Lewis as follows, breaking it down for readers in Bay County:

**The Beacon of Bay County Florida**
**By Jodie Christine Moore**          **September 26, 2022**

**Dear Beaconers: This document sent to Judge Walker by the defense in this case is going to blow you away. Wow. I received these papers today regarding the Anderson/Finch case. This was filed today by Mr. Finch's lawyer, Guy Lewis. I have not even had time to process all this myself, but I wanted to go ahead and put this out there. I've heard the Burnie Thompson Show is going to talk about this tonight so you should also tune in to see what he has to say. Keep in mind that this is filed by the defense, but it is based**

upon fact and evidence seen by the defense. It names Derwin White, Mickey White, Adam Albritton, Allan Bense, Chris Forehand, Vickie Gainer, Jimmy Stanford, and more.

The defense begins by stating that despite repeated attempts to receive discovery and exculpatory material from the prosecution, the prosecution/government has STILL not complied with the court's directive. In one instance, the defense requested records from the prosecution regarding the raid on GAC, which occurred not long after Derwin White passed away. The prosecution basically told the defense, "We haven't had time to review everything. You can go down to the FBI office in Panama City and see what you can find and make copies." There are likely hundreds of individual documents. It seems to me that this is a way for the prosecution to stick it to the defense and drive up the lawyer fees that are surely already upwards of a million dollars each.

On page 6, the defense alleges that Major Jimmy Stanford (still an employee under Sheriff Tommy Ford at BCSO) engaged in "serious criminal conduct" himself, all while he was engaged as an investigator in the corruption case! The defense maintains that this information was contained in documents hidden from them by the prosecutors. The defense accuses the prosecution of doing this multiple times: withholding evidence that contradicts the narrative of the prosecution and says there is evidence and witness statements that contradict each other. The defense also states that it has evidence that the FBI interviewed witnesses, but there are no field notes or 302 files to show what happened in those interviews.

On page 8, the defense ties Former House Speaker Allan Bense to GAC and Derwin White, as co-owners of GAC, and alleges both were "actively involved in orchestrating" the post Michael debris disposal, which is alleged in a lawsuit filed by Mr. Byrd as fraudulent and corrupt. There is evidence to this effect as shown on Burnie Thompson's show and in court filings.

On page 14, the defense states FBI Agent Borghini gave a sworn statement inconsistent with his grand jury testimony that was used to secure indictments against Anderson and Finch. Bear in mind that Mr. Borghini was the ONLY witness called to testify at the grand jury, with the exception of perhaps one other witness. The entire case hinges on Mr. Borghini's investigation. If he isn't credible, is the case credible?

On pages 15 and 16, the document talks about Chris Forehand, the Lynn Haven City Engineer and VP of Panhandle Engineering. This section talks about him "bribing" then-City Manager Michael White per "the government's own reports." After Hurricane Michael, on

October 23, 2018, Chris Forehand started a company called "PEDS" (Panhandle Engineering Disaster Services.) The allegation is that Forehand pressured/bribed Michael White to hire Tetra Tech (a debris monitoring service that was supposed to ensure that the debris was being picked up as claimed) and these documents state that PEDS employees were subcontracted to work for Tetra Tech! Not all the Tetra Tech employees were also PEDS employees, but a significant percentage were. So, the defense is claiming that Forehand was not only earning money through Panhandle Engineering as the Lynn Haven City Engineer, days after the storm he formed PEDS, then talked Michael White into hiring Tetra Tech, and then he subcontracted PEDS employees to Tetra Tech and he was raking in the cash from all directions. The defense also says that Michael White, Kelly Battistini, and current City Manager Vicki Gainer (on the selection committee) changed the score sheets so that Tetra Tech would get the contract. (See pages 15, 16, and 17.) The defense accuses Forehand of engaging in bribery and accepting kickbacks. The defense alleges Derwin White, GAC, Chris Forehand, and Tetra Tech are all at the heart of the corruption in Lynn Haven, as well as Michael White, the former City Manager—not James Finch and Margo Deal Anderson.

## THE THIRD SUPERSEDING INDICTMENT

October 18, 2022

The following indictment was sought as James Finch and I were preparing to go to trial the last week in November of 2022. We were exhausted, frustrated, and ready to put our story and our evidence in front of the Court and in front of the jury.

The Court had granted our motion to sever the counts which were solely against me from the counts which involved both James and me, and this action by the Court, if you will pardon my use of the vernacular, "pissed off" the Government. They waited until we had begun submitting our motions *in limine*, preparing for trial, learned as much of our trial strategy as possible, and then at the last possible moment notified the Court and the Defense that they were going to seek another indictment against us…the fourth indictment against me and the third against James. Even though Judge Walker had warned them that they would not get unlimited "bites at the apple" it certainly looked as though they were going to get a huge bite of this one. The Government's "new and improved" indictment was much more streamlined than previous ones, but misleading to the eye. They had incorporated their conspiracy charge into Count One, and then focused on a new strategy of no "honest services charges" which really "pissed me off" because the honest service charges were the charges which were used to remove me from office. I was now facing just two charges: 1 count of conspiracy with James and accepting a bribe from James (the motorhome), and James was now charged with one count of conspiracy with me, bribing me with a motorhome, accepting Lee's check to pay for the motorhome, and lying to the FBI about a bill of sale for the motorhome. Sixty-four charges against me had now dwindled to two charges. The Government's new strategy would be to list all of the Federal program assistance received from the Federal government during the time I was Mayor until the time I was arrested, and this would be used as a basis for turning the motorhome charge into a straight bribery charge (known as a 666 charge if one can believe that symbolic number) and would not require a *quid pro quo* as the "denying of honest services" charges did. The government listed two pages of federal grants received by the City before and after Hurricane Michael, hell-bent on tying this money in some way to a motorhome purchased by my husband from James Finch. In May of 2024, the Supreme Court would rule against these 666 charges, based on what prosecutors referred to as "a wink and a nod"; the last charge against me, for which I was scheduled to stand trial in February of 2023 would have been dismissed, but the Supreme Court was a year too late.

There were seven charges against me which had been severed by the Court which the Government had dropped from this indictment. The attorneys believed if James and I were acquitted in this trial, that the Government would surely realize that I was not involved in any conspiracy and not indict me again for the other charges which had been severed, and for which we had shown evidence in the evidentiary hearing were false, but we were to learn that we were wrong.

Three weeks before our trial date of February 27, 2023, the Government would demonstrate once again the full power of the United States Government against Margo Anderson. But I get ahead of myself again.

The Government's new and improved third superseding indictment is as follows; their first indictment against me had contained sixty-four charges, and *they had now dropped all but two charges*. At this point, most of my hometown, even the media, had begun to change their minds about the legitimacy of the federal charges against me. This would be the fourth indictment against me, the third against James Finch.

Of particular interest to me is that the government, in this fourth indictment against me, has changed, for *the third time*, their definition of the duties and authority of the Mayor of Lynn Haven in the first paragraph.

UNITED STATES OF AMERICA
v.
MARGO DEAL ANDERSON
And
JAMES DAVID FINCH

### THIRD SUPERSEDING INDICTMENT
Case No. 5:20cr28-MW/MJF

THE GRAND JURY CHARGES:

### INTRODUCTION

Except as otherwise indicated, at all times material to this Third Superseding Indictment:

1. The City of Lynn Haven ("City") was a municipality incorporated under the laws of the State of Florida and was a political subdivision within the State. The City's Charter provided for a City Commission, consisting of a "Mayor-Commissioner" (hereinafter "Mayor"), and four Commissioners. The Charter required, among other things, that the Mayor preside at all meetings of the commission, and that the Mayor was the official head of the City in certain circumstances. The administrative head of the City government was a City Manager, who was appointed by the City Commission, and subject to the City Commission's direction and supervision. The Charter provided that the Mayor may govern the city by proclamation during times of grave public danger or emergency, and shall be the judge of what constitutes such danger or emergency.

2. Between on or about September 16, 2016 and on or about June 18, 2020, the City received benefits in excess of $10,000 under a federal program involving a grant, contract, subsidy, loan, guarantee, insurance, and other form of Federal assistance including:

a. On or about September 16, 2016, the City received $78,537.00 in Federal financial assistance for the City's emergency operations center.

b.    On or about May 1, 2017, the City received $10,200 in Federal financial assistance for law enforcement equipment.

c.    On or about February 15, 2018, the City received $30,000 in Federal financial assistance for shore stabilization.

d.    On or about May 7, 2019, the City received $232,264.60 in Federal financial assistance to acquire property, remove debris, and restore the property to open space.

e.    On or about June 6, 2019, the City received $4,999,306.43 in Federal financial assistance for hurricane relief.

f.    On or about October 17, 2019, the City received $1,673,126.73 in Federal financial assistance for hurricane relief.

g.    On or about October 18, 2019, the City received $107,914.95 in Federal financial assistance for hurricane relief.

h.    On or about March 6, 2020, the City received $26,100.95 in Federal financial assistance for hurricane relief.

i.    On or about March 6, 2020, the City received $36,441.68 in federal financial assistance for hurricane relief.

j.    On or about March 19, 2020, the City received $3,600,000 in Federal financial assistance for hurricane relief.

k.    On or about April 21, 2020, the City received $4,666,761.47 in Federal financial assistance for hurricane relief.

l.    On or about May 12, 2020, the City received $3,229,351.23 in Federal financial assistance for hurricane relief.

m.    On or about June 15, 2020, the City received $27,248.48 in federal financial assistance for hurricane relief.

n.    On or about June 15, 2020, the City received $48,091.87 in Federal financial assistance for hurricane relief.

o.    On or about June 18, 2020, the city received $68,59.16 in Federal financial assistance for hurricane relief.

p.    On or about June 18, 2020, the City received $249,965.32 in Federal financial assistance for hurricane relief.

3.    On April 28, 2015, MARGO DEAL ANDERSON became Mayor of the City. As Mayor, ANDERSON acted on behalf of, and was an agent of, the City.

4.    JAMES DAVID FINCH was the owner of Phoenix construction Services, Inc. ("Phoenix Construction"), JDF Properties, LLC ("JDF Properties"), and James Finch & Associates, Inc., businesses incorporated in the State of Florida.

5.    Antonius Genzarra Barnes ("Barnes") was a City Commissioner for the City of Lynn Haven between 1996 and April 2019. As a Commissioner, Barnes acted on behalf of, and was an agent of, the City. Between on or about September 28, 2015, and on or about December 4, 2017, JAMES DAVID FINCH provided money to

Commissioner Barnes totaling $37,000. Between on or about September 28, 2015, and on or about April 2019, Commissioner Barnes voted in favor of FINCH'S matters before the City Commission.

6. Between on or about September 16, 2015, and on or about August 2020, MARGO DEAL ANDERSON acted in favor of JAMES DAVID FINCH's matters before the City of Lynn Haven. These matters included a project to improve the 17th Street ditch, a contract to use sales tax funds for road and sidewalk improvements, disposal of debris in the City from the impact of Hurricane Michael in October 2018, and the rebuilding of City municipal facilities damaged by Hurricane Michael. Such action by ANDERSON included City Commission votes and pressuring, advising, and influencing City officials to conduct City business in a manner favorable to FINCH.

7. Between in or around December 2015, and on or about August 18, 2020, on numerous occasions, JAMES DAVID FINCH provided travel on a private jet to and lodging at the Florida Keys and Biloxi, Mississippi, to MARGO DEAL ANDERSON and the spouse of ANDERSON. On or about February 14, 2018, FINCH paid $75j,000 for a 2006 ITAS Motorhome and subsequently caused the transfer of its legal title to the spouse of ANDERSON for the benefit and enjoyment of ANDERSON. ANDERSON and her spouse paid no money to FINCH for this Motorhome until December 2019, shortly after ANDERSON was interviewed by agents of the Federal Bureau of Investigation, ANDERSON was alleged to have directed the City Manager to have a City Manager (government typo) clean up Hurricane Michael debris at her property, and ANDERSON and FINCH were each served with legal process compelling production of documents regarding their financial relationship.

## COUNT ONE
## Conspiracy to Commit Bribery
## 18 U.S.C 371 & 666

8. The allegations in paragraphs 1 through 7 of this Third Superseding Indictment are hereby realleged and incorporated by reference as if fully set forth herein.

### Objects of the conspiracy

9. From on or about September 16, 2015, up to and including on or

about April 27, 2021, in the Northern District of Florida and elsewhere, the defendants,

MARGO DEAL ANDERSON
And
JAMES DAVID FINCH,

Did knowingly and willfully combine, conspire, confederate, and agree together and with others to commit offenses against the United States, namely,

a. Being an agent of the City , which received in a one year period benefits in excess of $10,000 under a Federal program involving a grant, contract, subsidy, loan, guarantee, insurance, or other form of Federal assistance, as described in paragraph 2 above, for MARGO DEAL ANDERSON to knowingly and corruptly solicit and demand for the benefit of any person, and accept and agree to accept, anything of value from any person, intending to be influenced and rewarded in connection with any business, transaction, and series of transactions of the City, involving anything of value of $5,000 or more, in violation of Title 18, United States Code, Section 666(a)(1)(B); and

b. For JAMES DAVID FINCH to knowingly and corruptly give, offer, and agree to give anything of value to any person, with intent to influence and reward an agent of the City, which received in a one year period benefits in excess of $10,000 under a Federal program involving a grant, contract, subsidy, loan, guarantee, insurance, or other form of Federal assistance, as described in paragraph 2 above, in connection with any business, transaction, and series of transactions of the City involving anything of value of $5,000 or more, in violation of Title 18, United States Code, Section 666(a)(2).

Purposes of the Conspiracy

10. It was a purpose of the conspiracy for MARGO DEAL ANDERSON and Barnes to enrich themselves with money and other things of value and agree to accept things of value from JAMES DAVID FINCH intending to be influenced and rewarded in connection with any business, transaction, and series of transactions of the City in a manner favorable to FINCH.

11. It was also a purpose of the conspiracy for MARGO DEAL ANDERSON, Barnes, and JAMES DAVID FINCH to hide, conceal, and cover up the nature and scope of the dealings between themselves.

556

## The Manner and Means of the Conspiracy

12. The manner and means by which the conspirators achieved and attempted to achieve the objects of the conspiracy included, but were not limited to the following:

a. It was part of the conspiracy that between on or about September 28, 2015, and on or about December 4, 2017, JAMES DAVID FINCH provided several checks to Barnes totaling $37,000.

b. It was further part of the conspiracy that Barnes performed actions as a Lynn Haven City Commissioner for the benefit of FINCH, including voting on matters before the City Commission.

c. It was further part of the conspiracy that FINCH provided MARGO DEAL ANDERSON and the spouse of ANDERSON with travel to the Florida Keys and Biloxi, Mississippi, and a 2006 ITAS Motorhome.

d. It was further part of the conspiracy that ANDERSON performed actions as Mayor of Lynn Haven for the benefit of FINCH, including voting on the City Commission and pressuring and advising City officials to take action favorable to FINCH on certain matters, including the 17th Street ditch project, a ½ Sales Tax Contract, hurricane debris disposal, and the rebuilding of municipal facilities damaged by Hurricane Michael.

e. It was further part of the conspiracy that defendants and conspirators concealed the nature and the receipt of things of value from FINCH in return for conducting City business favorable to FINCH by, among other things, failing to report the receipt of said things of value, executing and using false documents, and making false statements to law enforcement.

## Overt Acts

13. In furtherance of this conspiracy, and to effect the illegal objects thereof, the following overt acts, among others, were committed in the Northern District of Florida, and elsewhere:

a. On or about September 28, 2015, Barnes asked JAMES DAVID FINCH for money. FINCH agreed and provided Barnes with a check in the amount of $12,000 which included the word "loan" in the memo portion of the check. Barnes never repaid this money to FINCH.

b. On or about October 28, 2015, Barnes asked FINCH for more money. FINCH agreed and provided Barnes with a check in the amount of $5,000 which included the word "loan" in the memo portion of the check. Barnes never repaid this money to FINCH.

c. On or about January 26, 2016, Barnes asked FINCH for more money. FINCH agreed and provided Barnes with a check in the amount of $10,000 which included the word "loan" in the memo portion of the check. Barnes never repaid this money to FINCH.

d.    On or about November 14, 2016, Barnes asked FINCH for more money. FINCH agreed and provided Barnes with a check in the amount of $2,500. Barnes never repaid this money to FINCH.

e.    On or about March 15, 2017, Barnes asked FINCH for more money. FINCH agreed and provided Barnes with a check in the amount of $2,500. Barnes never repaid this money to FINCH.

f.    In or around October 2017, MARGO DEAL ANDERSON pressured the City Manager to allow FINCH's company to proceed on a contract to use sales tax funds for road and sidewalk improvements.

g.    On or about December 4, 2017, Barnes asked FINCH for more money. FINCH agreed and provided Barnes with a check in the amount of $5,000 which included the word "loan" in the memo portion of the check. Barnes never repaid this money to FINCH.

h.    On or about February 14, 2018, FINCH paid $75,000 to an individual for a 2006 ITAS Motorhome. Subsequently, FINCH caused its transfer to the spouse of ANDERSON for the benefit and enjoyment of ANDERSON.

i.    In or around June 2018, ANDERSON pressured the City Manager to have the City proceed with an additional phase of the 17th Street project.

j.    On or about October 30, 2018, ANDERSON learned that the Lynn Haven City Engineer had submitted a permit application for the disposal of vegetative hurricane debris at City property. ANDERSON directed the City Manager to withdraw the application.

k.    On or about October 31, 2018, ANDERSON directed the City Manager to have the City assess whether the City could shift its debris pickup and hauling business from preexisting contractors to FINCH'S company.

l.    On or about November 1, 2018, ANDERSON directed the City Manager to dispose of the City's vegetative hurricane debris at FINCH's company's property.

m.    On or about December 30, 2019, approximately 22 months after the transfer of the Motorhome to ANDERSON's husband, a check was issued in the amount of $20,000 from ANDERSON's husband, a check was issued in the amount of $20,000 from ANDERSON'S bank account to FINCH and there was a $15,000 cash withdrawal from ANDERSON's bank account.

**This is the final payment Lee made on the motor home of $35,000.00.**

The government finally acknowledges it, but the date is December 31, 2019. James and Lee had always done their transactions in cash and the Naval Federal Credit Union did not have 35,000.00 on hand. Therefore, Lee wrote a check for 20,000.00 after withdrawing the $15,000 the credit union had on hand. Assistant U.S. Attorney Stephen Kunz knew about this transaction on the day of the press conference in Panama City when he told the world that I had received a free motorhome from James Finch. He is an evil liar.

    n.    On or about July 13, 2020, FINCH provided FBI agents with a purported bill of sale relating to the Motorhome. The bill of sale, dated July 6, 2018, falsely represented that the purchase price of the Motorhome was $70,000 "in hand paid half down and half due with 6 percent interest. the receipt of which is hereby acknowledged." The bill of sale was false because neither ANDERSON nor her spouse had paid $35,000 for the Motorhome as of July 6, 2018.

All in violation of Title 18, United States Code, Section 371.

COUNT TWO
Bribery (Finch)
18 U.S.C. 666(a)(2)

14.    The allegations in paragraphs 1, 2, 4, 5, 12a, 12b, paragraphs 13a through 13e, and paragraph 13g of this Third Superseding Indictment are hereby realleged and incorporated by reference as if fully set forth herein.

15.    On or about December 4, 2017, in the Northern district of Florida, and elsewhere, the defendant,

JAMES DAVID FINCH,

did corruptly give, offer, and agree to give a thing of value, to wit, a check in the amount of $5,000, that was valued at $5,000 or more, to Antonius Genzarra Barnes with the intent to influence and reward Antonius Genzarra Barnes, an agent of a local government, the City of Lynn Haven, which received in the one-year period beginning on or about May 1, 2017, benefits in excess of $10,000 under a federal program involving grants, contracts, subsidies, loans, guarantees, and other forms of federal assistance, as described in paragraphs 2b and 2c in connection with a business, transaction, or series of transactions of the city of Lynn Haven, Florida, as described in paragraph 5 and 12b.

In violation of Title 18, United States Code, Sections 666(1)(2) and 2.

COUNT THREE
Bribery (Finch)
18 U.S.C. 666(a)(2)

16. The allegations in paragraphs 1 through 4, 6, and 7, 11, 12c through 12e, 13f, and paragraphs 13h through 13n, of this Third Superseding Indictment are hereby realleged and incorporated by reference as if fully set forth herein.

17. On or about February 14, 2018, in the Northern District of Florida, and elsewhere, the defendant,

JAMES DAVID FINCH,

did corruptly give, offer, and agree to give a thing of value, to wit, a 2006 ITAS, that was valued at 45,000 or more, to MARGO DEAL ANDERSON and her spouse with the intent to influence and reward MARGO DEAL ANDERSON, an agent of a local government, the City of Lynn Haven, which received in the one-year period beginning on or about May 1, 201, benefits in excess of $10,000 under a federal program involving grants, contracts, subsidies, loans, guarantees, and other forms of federal assistance, as described in paragraphs 2b and 2c, in connection with a business, transaction, or series of transactions of the City of Lynn Haven, Florida, as described in paragraphs 1 through 4, 6 and 7, 12c, 12d, 13f, and 13i through 13l.

In violation of Title 18, United States Code, Sections 666(a)(2) and 2.

COUNT FOUR
Bribery (Anderson)
18 U.S.C. 666(a)(1)(B)

18. The allegations in paragraphs 1 through 4, 6, and 7, 11, 12c through 12e, 13f, and paragraphs 13h through 13n, of this Third Superseding Indictment are hereby realleged and incorporated by reference as if fully set forth herein.

19. On or about February 14, 2018, in the Northern District of Florida, and elsewhere, the defendant,

MARGO DEAL ANDERSON

being an agent of an organization and agency of a local government, that is, the City of Lynn Haven, Florida, which received in the one-year period beginning on or about May 1, 2017, benefits in excess of $10,000 under a federal program involving grants, contracts, subsidies, loans, guarantees, and other forms of federal assistance, as described in paragraph 2b and 2c, did corruptly accept and agree to accept a thing of value, to wit, a 2006

ITAS Motorhome, valued at $5,000 or more, intending to be influenced and rewarded in connection with a business, transaction, or series of transactions of the City of Lynn Haven, Florida, as described in paragraphs 1 through 4, 6 and 7, 12c, 12d, 13f, and 13i through 13l.

In violation of Title 18, United States Code, Sections 666(a)(1)(B) and 2.

## COUNT FIVE
### Knowing and Willful False Statement
### To the Federal Bureau of Investigation (Finch)
### 18 U.S.C. 1001(a)(2) & (3)

20. The allegations in paragraphs 1 through 7, and paragraphs 10 through 13 of this Third Superseding Indictment are hereby realleged and incorporated by reference as if fully set forth herein.
21. On or about July 13, 2020, in the Northern District of Florida, the defendant,

## JAMES DAVID FINCH,

did knowingly and willfully make materially false, fictitious, and fraudulent statements, representations, and writings in a matter within the executive branch of the Government of the United States, that is, during a criminal investigation of public corruption involving the City of Lynn Haven conducted by the Federal Bureau of Investigation, the defendant falsely stated that:

a. FINCH had sold a 2006 ITAS Motorhome to MARGO DEAL ANDERSON's husband for a purchase price of $70,000;

b. FINCH presented a bill of sale dated July 6, 2018 which stated the sale of the Motorhome was for $70,000, of which half was paid down and half due to FINCH with 6% interest;

22. These statements and representations and representations were false, and the claimed bill of sale dated July 6, 2018, contained false statements, because, as FINCH then well knew:

a. FINCH did not sell the Motorhome to ANDERSON and-or her husband for $70,000 but FINCH paid for it and caused it to be transferred to ANDERSON's husband for ANDERSON's benefit and enjoyment without receiving payment of money for the Motorhome from ANDERSON or her husband.

b. As of July 6, 2018, neither ANDERSON nor ANDERSON'S husband had paid "half down," that is, $35,000 for the Motorhome; and not until approximately 22 months after the transfer of the Motorhome to ANDERSON and her husband, did ANDERSON's husband issue a $20,000 check to FINCH, allegedly in relation to the

Motorhome, to conceal the nature of the receipt of the Motorhome in or around February 2018, without payment of money by ANDERSON or ANDERSON's spouse for said Motorhome.

In violation of Title 18, United States Code, Sections 1001(a)(2) & (3).

## CRIMINAL FORFEITURE

The allegations contained in Counts One through Four of this Third Superseding Indictment are hereby realleged and incorporated by reference for the purpose of alleging forfeiture. From their engagement in the violations alleged in Counts One through Four of this Third Superseding Indictment, the defendants,

MARGO DEAL ANDERSON
and
JAMES DAVID FINCH,

Shall forfeit to the United States, pursuant to Title 18, United States Code, Section 981(a)(1)(C), and Title 28, United States code, Section 2461(c), any and all of the defendants' right, title, and interest in any property, real and personal, constituting, and derived from, proceeds traceable to such offenses, including the following:

a.    2006 ITAS Motorhome, Vin#4uzackdc26cw30357.

If any of the property described above as being subject to forfeiture, as a result of acts or omissions of the defendants:

i.cannot be located upon the exercise of due diligence;
ii.has been transferred, sold to, or deposited with a third party;
iii.has been placed beyond the jurisdiction of this Court;
iv.has been substantially diminished in value; or
v.has been commingled with other property that cannot be sub-divided without difficulty,

it is the intent of the United states, pursuant to Title 21, United States Code, Section 853(p), as incorporated by Title 28, United States Code, Section 2461©, to seek forfeiture of any other property of said defendant up to the value of the forfeitable property.

A TRUE BILL
(BLACKED OUT NAME)
FOREPERSON

October 18, 2022

JASON R. COODY
United States Attorney

Stephen M. Kunz
Assistant United States Attorney

Andrew J. Grogan
Assistant United States Attorney

Justin M. Keen
Assistant United States Attorney

*The U.S. Attorney's office has a new player, Assistant U.S. Attorney Justin Keen, in the mix with this indictment; we have noticed that Kunz has not been talking on the last few status calls with the Court, and James made the comment that they have "benched" him. I used a worse description; I said, "maybe they have neutered the lying bastard." *Even David railed against his enemies in Psalm 109, so hopefully the Lord will forgive me too.*

We were not far off; Kunz retired December 31, 2022, just after the evidentiary hearings of December 12th and 13th in which we were attempting to prove vindictive and malicious prosecution and listing the "bad actors" responsible for such.

Judge Mark Walker had set trial for November 28, 2022, but after the information which was exposed in the affidavit the government had withheld from the defense for over a year, the attorneys filed a motion for another evidentiary hearing before trial.

James and I were hopeful that the evidentiary hearings of December 12th and 13th, 2022, would finally convince the Court to dismiss the remaining charges against us, particularly because of the unsealing (by mistake) of an Affidavit for a Search warrant by the Government which led to the printing of the entire affidavit in *The Panama City News Herald* as well as a broadcast by WMBB Channel 13 the ABC affiliate in Panama City Florida which placed a copy of the affidavit on their website for public download, which was our source as defendants after the Government quickly moved to have it sealed again, and then later it would again be unsealed. The affidavit was particularly damning to the prosecutors because of the government's statement on July 1, 2022 that they had produced all documents containing *Brady* information to the defense, which as shown in the Third Motion to Compel, was clearly not true. The affidavit was a searing document naming officials far and wide, including former Speaker of the House Allan Bense and GAC as having "bilked" the county out of millions.

## The Second Evidentiary Hearing
## December 12th and December 13th, 2022

The tide continued to turn and public opinion changed rapidly concerning the validity of the case against us, most notably because of Burnie Thompson of *The Burnie Thompson Show,* and two women who would later become my friends, citizen journalists, Jodi Moore and Gerri Parker, of *The Beacon of Bay County* who attended, along with Burnie Thompson, both evidentiary hearings and the two trials to follow, as well as my plea and sentencing hearings.

The fact that all but two of the original 64 charges against me, had been dropped or dismissed in the Third Superseding Indictment, and all but three dropped against James Finch, became a topic for Burnie Thompson's nightly podcasts, and *The Beacon of Bay County* social media page was filled with excoriating descriptions of the evidentiary hearings. For the first time in three years, James and I could hold our heads up in our hometown of Lynn Haven, Florida and look people in the eye. A large number of people began to speak out; it was all a lie, and public outcry was growing.

The Judge did not dismiss the final charges against James Finch and me, and the trial was set for February 27, 2023; both of us were surprised, as well as disappointed, as the fourth holiday season under the dark cloud of the government would continue for me, the third for James. The holidays are incredibly difficult to face knowing that the entire future may be taken away; Christmas has always been my favorite time of year, and my depression and feelings of hopelessness grew. James was battling liver cancer and radiation treatments while also battling the federal government. Sometimes I could not pray at all, and instead would just weep and pray the rosary, or just say the name of Jesus aloud, sobbing my fears to the Lord.

We did not understand with all of the evidence we had presented of what we believed to go beyond reckless and haphazard behaviors of the Government and the local BCSO investigators; we believed their actions were deliberate and malicious, and we also believed their actions were criminal. Judge Mark Walker saw it differently. I have included some of the Burnie Thompson's posts below as well as the Beacon of Bay County coverage of the evidentiary hearings of December 12 and 13, 2022, here. I chose not to include any of WMBB's coverage of the evidentiary hearings because they, for the most part, just regurgitated the prosecutors' false allegations against us. For those who would like to read all of the coverage surrounding the case, simply search "Lynn Haven Florida Corruption Case" and you will have many perspectives to compare. Burnie Thompson, Jodi Moore and Gap Parker, were the only positive news sources surrounding our case, even when "the tide turned" and everyone could see what really happened. I will forever thank God for them; I am reminded of Edmund Burke's quote, "The only thing necessary for the triumph of evil is for good men to do nothing."

Through all of what happened to me as a public official, I never received one phone call or word of compassion or encouragement from the elected officials of Bay County that I considered my colleagues. And even when all but two of the sixty-four charges against me were dropped, still, silence.

I kept hoping that I would arrive at the Tallahassee Federal Courthouse to crowds holding signs that read, "Free Mayor Anderson," similar to John Grisham's novel, *A Time to Kill*, when crowds surrounded the courthouse shouting, "Free Carl Lee," but when I arrived at the courthouse there was only silence. The only elected official who stood up for me was Commissioner Judy Tinder, a woman of courage and strength. She was at the hearings, and she was at my sentencing, a silent pillar of support; and her letters of encouragement buoyed me up on my worst days sitting in a federal prison for thirty days, questioning every belief I had ever based my life upon.

**The Burnie Thompson Show**
**Burnie Thompson**                                      **November 23, 2022**


**For the first time, WMBB-TV didn't include a link for you to read the Lynn Haven defendant's motion. They don't want you to see it.**

**And no wonder. Developer James Finch says the Bay County Sheriff's Office was conspiring with late contractor Derwin White to set up former Lynn Haven Mayor Margo Anderson.**

**Finch gets to prove his explosive claims at an evidentiary hearing on Dec 12 & 13 with documents and testimony.**

**Prosecutors pleaded with the Judge not to allow Finch to put the Sheriff's Office and the FBI on the witness stand.**

**They also denied having exculpatory evidence but a few months ago the year-old search warrant affidavit for GAC Contractors proved that the FBI told a different judge that Bay County was more corrupt than New Jersey and New Orleans. That affidavit has since been sealed**

again.

They gave names of local officials, and Mayor Anderson was not among them. Days after Derwin White died, the Sheriff and the FBI raided GAC Contractors. Nearly a year-and-a-half later, they say that they haven't had time to review the evidence.

Instead, they've sat on a treasure trove of evidence waiting for the statute of limitations to expire on their friends in high office while focusing on the persecution of Mayor Anderson instead.

On December 12, the Sheriff's Office has a chance to prove they've honestly been working to clean up public corruption. They don't want to, but they have to.

WMBB-TV has been doing PR for the Sheriff's Office. They have quite a quid pro quo relationship. Let's just say, it's a family affair. Now WMBB-TV won't even link the motions.

Back on Aug 19, 2020, the Sheriff joined the FBI and U.S. Attorney at a big TV press conference promising to clean up public corruption in Bay County. We were very excited.

They started by charging Mayor Anderson on 64 counts. There was a whole lot of peacocking and chest-thumping in front of the TV cameras.

Now prosecutors themselves have dropped all but two counts against Mayor Anderson. They no longer stand by their previous shocking allegations.

I wonder if prosecutors will drop the entire case before Dec. 12, when the Sheriff's Office is scheduled to go under oath in front of the federal judge? That would save a tremendous amount of transparency.

Meanwhile, local government officials who extended Hurricane cleanup and inflated prices to line their own pockets are endorsed by Sheriff Ford and get swooning coverage by WMBB-TV.

The Beacon of Bay County

Gap Parker                                November 25, 2022

LYNN HAVEN: As the time approaches for the evidentiary hearing in the Margo Deal Anderson James Finch case, in a few weeks, starting December 12, it will be interesting to see how this turns out. The Burnie Thompson Show seems to think there won't be an evidentiary hearing. But, for that to happen, I think that the prosecution would have to drop ALL the charges against the two defendants. The evidentiary hearing was filed before the current superseding indictment, before the trial date was set for February, so the two proceedings are somewhat independent of each other. Up to this point, I'm not aware that Judge Walker put any restrictions on who could be subpoenaed and called to testify at this hearing. That may happen at a later date.

So far, if the defense is tipping its hand with the last court filing, it looks like the lawyers are planning to focus at least part of the hearing on law enforcement: BCSO and Lynn Haven Police Chief Ramie. I would also expect that perhaps City Manager Vickie Gainer, former City Manager Michael White, and City Engineer Chris Forehand may be called to the stand. There may be others as well—if there IS a hearing.

As Burnie Thompson says, this is the prosecutions', chance to bring their A-game and show all of us that this is a righteous case. Will they?

The Burnie Thompson Show
Burnie Thompson                            December 13, 2022

Federal Judge Mark Walker told Lynn Haven Defendants Margo Anderson and James Finch to submit a list of "bad actors" and "bad acts for possible sanctions at today's evidentiary hearing.

The Defendants showed evidence of false statements to grand juries, targeted and selective investigations, planted evidence, and a coerced witness plea deal.

Judge Walker has already rebuked the investigators and prosecutors as unprofessional, haphazard, and reckless earlier this year.

Defendants have accused FBI Agent Larry Borghini of misleading Grand Juries in order to obtain indictments as well as ignoring significant evidence that shows other people directed hurricane clean-up fraud rather than Anderson and Finch.

Defendants say that Major Jimmy Stanford tipped off late contractor Derwin White about a 2019 search warrant raid of the ECS office that led to owner Mickey White planting a fake invoice in order to set up then-Mayor Margo Anderson.

Today prosecutors agreed that ECS never cleared hurricane debris at Mayor Anderson's property after all.

That was the initial charge that led to the removal of the duly elected Mayor of Lynn Haven in 2020. She resigned soon after the big TV press conference announcing her arrest.

Former Mayor Anderson maintains that she blew the whistle to Sheriff Tommy Ford on April 1, 2019, that ECS had fraudulently billed the City of Lynn Haven for $5 million.

Then Sheriff Ford assigned Major Stanford to lead his Public Trust Unit to support the FBI's crackdown on public corruption throughout Bay County.

So far, the effort has been unfruitful despite a 2021 FBI affidavit for a search warrant on GAC contractors in which Special Agent Borghini told another judge that Bay County was more corrupt than New Jersey or New Orleans. The narrative named different officials and presented a story that contradicts the several indictments against Anderson and Finch.

Judge Walker is considering what sanctions, if any, to impose on the government's case against Anderson and Finch.

The legal standard to dismiss a criminal case entirely before the trial is extraordinarily high. Judge Walker said that the Court is obligated to exhaust lower sanctions first.
Anderson was indicted in August 2020 on 64 counts. The Court threw out most of them, and then the Prosecutors recently dropped another 25.

She is now facing two counts, and Finch is charged with four.

The trial is set for the end of February.

More to follow...

The Burnie Thompson Show
By Burnie Thompson                    December 20, 2022

Things WMBB-TV won't tell you about last week's evidentiary hearing:

1.  The Judge told the Defendants to file a list of "bad actors" and their "bad acts" as he considers possible sanctions against investigators and prosecutors.

2.  Judge Mark Walker reviewed Mayor Margo Anderson's property lines and said, "The land survey shows it's not Anderson's property." Even if there were no easement, this accusation was false from the outset. Sheriff Tommy Ford and the FBI agent knew this information but pressed on with the charge resulting I the removal of Anderson as mayor.

3.  City Manager Vickie Gainer lied to the FBI when she told them that Commissioner Judy Tinder voted against James Finch on several occasions because of poor performance. On the witness stand, Gainer admitted that it was untrue. Gainer told the Judge it was just a mistake. (Vickie Gainer is the one who counts the votes and writes the meeting minutes.)

4.  Before James Finch was indicted in 2021, City Manager Vickie Gainer deprived him of business to which he was entitled by denying his lowest bids and telling City-contracted engineer Chris Forehand not to do any business with Finch. Essentially, Vickie Gainer used her position to vindictively cancel Finch.

5.  Judge Walker asked the lead prosecutor, "Is there any doubt that there are a bunch of bad actors robbing the community blind? Is that even—is that even in dispute?" Prosecutor Andrew Grogan responded, "I think there's a lot of corruption

there, Your Honor." Grogan specifically mentioned the School District and the County. WMBB falsely reported Grogan saying, "There WAS a lot of corruption there." By not including context, WMBB implied that there was a lot of corruption in Lynn Haven until they cleaned it up. This is worse than sloppy reporting; it's an absolute lie.

6.   As Judge Walker saw more proof that the FBI ignored tons of evidence indicating that the late contractor Derwin White (not Anderson or Finch) directed massive fraud throughout Bay County, he asked the prosecutor, "Since when did the FBI start putting corruption in boxes?" In other words, investigators have been ignoring the real criminals and severing lines that would show conspiracy and racketeering throughout the entire county, not just in Lynn Haven. Stunned, the Judge said, "That's not how investigations work!"

WMBB's coordinated propaganda to cover up massive local corruption is journalistic malpractice, if not criminal.

Are they just incompetent or on the take?

The Burnie Thompson Show
By Burnie Thompson                    December 22, 2022

Here's what really happened at today's emergency hearing in the Lynn Haven Corruption case.

Federal Judge Mark Walke said that he needed to clarify last week's testimony from a former City Commissioner.

At issue was the testimony from Antonius Barnes that he felt coerced into MAKING A FALSE STATEMENT in exchange for a plea deal for lying on a bank loan application.

Barnes' plea deal involved two things: Admitting that he made a false statement on a bank loan application and testifying against developer James Finch in the separate Lynn Haven corruption case.

Despite continuing reports from WMBB that Barnes had previously confessed to taking bribes in exchange for the plea deal, that never happened. Barnes has always maintained that Finch never bribed him. Barnes pled guilty to only one charge: Lying on a bank loan application.

Barnes clarified to Judge Walker that he should have been more specific at last week's evidentiary hearing. He explained that he felt "overwhelmed" to cooperate with prosecutors because his teacher's pension was at stake.

If Barnes had pled guilty to taking bribes, he would've lost his pension. So he agreed to testify against Finch in the separate case if prosecutors only charged him with the bank loan violation, which would not affect his pension.

Therefore, his pension is not on the line, as WMBB reports.

Barnes has been consistent from the outset. He will indeed take the witness stand for the prosecution if the case goes to trial, and he can continue to say that he never sold his vote to Finch as a bribe without losing his unrelated plea deal.

All parties were satisfied.

1. Barnes is satisfied that he keeps his plea for the bank loan violation in exchange for taking the witness stand during the separate Lynn Haven case if it goes to trial.
2. Prosecutors are satisfied that Assistant U.S. Attorney Stephen Kunz was not accused of coercing Barnes into a plea deal in exchange for a false statement.
3. Defendants are satisfied that Barnes can continue giving consistent testimony that Finch never bribed him without fear of losing his plea deal.

WMBB's reporting of Barnes is fraught with actual malice, the legal standard for defamation against a public figure.

Reporter Brady Calhoun was in the courtroom and has an obligation to tell the story accurately and with context. Instead, WMBB continues to knowingly disparage Barnes' reputation by falsely reporting that he had pled guilty for selling his vote to Finch as a bribe.

Barnes' attorney explained that he left last week's evidentiary hearing before his client took that stand for a legitimate reason. Judge Walker made it clear that was indeed the case and showed respect and affinity for Barnes' attorney.

Furthermore, Judge Walker said that today's emergency hearing would be unnecessary had Barnes' attorney been present during his testimony last week. The Judge wanted Barnes to have proper representation while clarifying his testimony regarding the plea deal.

Barnes' sentencing date was moved to the end of March.

The Burnie Thompson Show
By Burnie Thompson                    December 31, 2022

"The bottom line is that residents of Lynn Haven had their most popular mayor removed in 2020 based on a fatally flawed indictment riddled with false allegations."

Assistant U.S. Attorney Stephen Kunz filed for retirement after federal Judge Mark Walker signaled at the Dec. 13 evidentiary hearing that he's considering issuing sanctions against him in the Lynn Haven corruption case.

In August 2020, then-U.S. Attorney Larry Keefe held a grandiose press conference announcing 64 counts against Lynn Haven Mayor Margo Anderson.

Since then, 62 counts have been thrown out, and Judge Walker is now considering dismissing the final two counts based on vindictive prosecution.

The video of Keefe promising to hold government officials accountable for secretly steering contracts to their friends is priceless now that his private email and its contents have been discovered.

Keefe had to resign as U.S. Attorney after Joe Biden took office.

Kunz has been the lead prosecutor in the crumbling case against the Lynn Haven Mayor from the outset.

Federal Judge Mark Walker rebuked the investigators and prosecutors earlier this year as "unprofessional, haphazard, and reckless."

On Dec. 13, Judge Walker told the Defense to submit a list of "bad actors" and "bad acts" as he reviews: evidence of multiple false statements to multiple grand juries, continual withholding of exculpatory evidence in violation of the Court's deadline, Sixth Amendment violations (attorney/client privilege), planting of evidence, selective and incompetent investigation, vindictive prosecution, perjury during the March evidentiary hearing, and more.

Judge Walker has also expressed deep concern over the multiple iterations of the original indictment. (Margo Anderson is facing her fourth superseding indictment on the final two counts).

In a very rare twist last year, Judge Walker released the grand jury transcripts and investigation notes to the defense. He also released the FBI investigation notes.

That was the turning point that revealed shocking misconduct by investigators and prosecutors. This long and winding case is finally nearing its crescendo.

The trial is scheduled for Feb. 28, but it probably will be postponed as the defense needs at least six weeks to review evidence seized from GAC Contractors a year-and-a-half ago. It likely contains even more exculpatory evidence.

The FBI and the Bay County Sheriff's "Public Trust Unit" have been sitting on the treasure trove of evidence for so long that Judge Walker was surprised. He said that he didn't realize the FBI was putting "corruption in boxes."

"That's not how investigations work," Judge Walker told the prosecutors during the Dec. 13 evidentiary hearing. He wondered why they only focus on Margo Anderson and James Finch.

"Is there any doubt there's bad actors robbing the county blind?" Judge Walker asked.

The GAC search warrant was obtained in August 2021 after the FBI presented an affidavit saying that Bay County is more corrupt than New Jersey and New Orleans. They named Allan Bense, George Gainer, and Bill Husfelt.

The bottom line is that residents of Lynn Haven had their most popular mayor removed in 2020 based on a fatally flawed indictment riddled with false allegations.

Meanwhile, all the king's horses and all the king's men allow the real criminals to continue "robbing the county blind."

December 30, 2022

"Burnie T"

We drove from Jacksonville to Lynn Haven yesterday to pick up our new rescue dog.

I said I would never have another dog...just four months ago when I had my heart ripped out as I took Buddy to the vet for euthanasia. I have cried more days about that tiny little dog than I can count; some days crying gut-wrenching cries, missing the unconditional love of Buddy, who was taken away by illness as quickly as he had arrived in the aftermath of Hurricane Michael.

But Ramona Bibbs, the director of the Lynn Haven Animal Shelter, saw a post I made on Halloween night 2022 on Facebook, a post about how I missed Buddy, how he loved helping me answer the door and greet the trick-or-treaters, how empty my house was without him. She sent me a photo of a white Maltese/Yorkie mix that she had rescued and said, "Would you like to have him? He could keep you company."

It was such an unexpected message. Because of the conditions of release, I was not permitted to contact City of Lynn Haven employees, but of course Ramona did not know this, and quite frankly, I was so taken by the photos of the dog, and caught off-guard, that I didn't even think about it until much later.

I wrote Ramona back and thanked her for her compassion, for thinking of me and for offering the little dog to me. But I told her I just couldn't think of replacing Buddy. The thought of bringing another dog into

Buddy's house just broke my heart, made me feel disloyal. She told me that she understood, but that she would hold onto him a little longer to see if I changed my mind. She took him home with her from the shelter and rescued him herself. Ramona has always seemed like an angel to me. As Mayor, I visited the shelter often, just to see the dogs and other animals she had, ranging from chickens, goats, litters of kittens, ferrets, and birds. If an animal was abandoned, Ramona made it her mission to save it. On the day after the hurricane, she came to the area where the City had set up in the parking lot of Southerland funeral Home with a baby goat in her arms, looking for milk for it. Ramona took care of Lynn Haven's abandoned animals with a passion that went far beyond the job description of Animal Shelter Director.

I wrote on November 7th on Facebook messenger: "Ramona, he is beautiful. You are so sweet to offer. I am traveling so much right now for the next 90 days or so and the trial is scheduled for February 27th and will probably last three weeks. The case has a possibility of being thrown out before Christmas. His face looks a lot like Buddy. It would not be fair to take him right now because we are back and forth with lawyers in Tallahassee, etc. I wouldn't want to leave him alone and board him so much. If you still have him in January, and this trial by some miracle is dismissed I would love to have him. But if you find a good home for him then that's what should happen. I felt a tug at my heart when I saw the photo of him. Like when I held Buddy the first time. If you are not too attached to him after the first of the year maybe all of this will be over, and I could take him. I love you. Thank you for thinking of me."

Ramona answered just seconds later on messenger, saying, "I will hold him for you. He is at my home."

"He looks so much like Buddy," I wrote. His little eyes are soft brown. I will let you know if anything changes about the trial. If a good home comes along for him before I am free of all of this, please do what is best for the sweet little boy. If not, and you still have him, I will love him just like I did Buddy. God bless."

"You know, he gets so happy when you say are you, my Buddy?" Ramona wrote. "So, we have been calling him Mr. Buddy. He will be waiting for you." "Always praying for you," wrote Ramona.

"Thank you," I wrote. "This has been so hard. I think it is finally coming to an end soon. I am not afraid. Love you. You lifted my heart today. Take care, and I will keep you updated."

"Keep your head up," Ramona wrote. "God is with you."

As the days went by, I found myself looking at the photo of the dog she sent me, which she said she had named Mr. Buddy. I could not stop thinking about him. I wrote Ramona another private message and told her that I had a hearing coming up in December, was traveling quite a bit back and forth to Tallahassee and Lynn Haven to work on the case and would possibly have a month-long Federal trial in February with no idea what the results would be. The unthinkable thing was that I might be found guilty in a jury trial and sentenced to prison.

On December 21st, I wrote, "Hope you have a very Merry Christmas. The little white dog is still on my heart. If you haven't found a home for him yet and I can get through all of this mess, I would love to have him. I don't know what is going to happen yet; it will probably be mid- January before we know if the case is dismissed or if it is going to trial. If you have found a home for your Mr. Buddy, or if you are attached to him, I completely understand. I wish I could take him now, but it would not be fair to him while we are dealing with hearings, attorney appointments in Tallahassee and possibly a trial. He looks so sweet, so much like Buddy. Merry Christmas. Thank you for all you do for the animals that have been thrown away. You are an angel."

Ramona replied, "Oh, Margo. Buddy is waiting for you."

I answered, "hopefully this will be over soon and I can have him. Love and blessings to you and your family for this Christmas season."

Ramona said, "Seems like this is going the right way. From what Jodie and Burnie have been putting out, it sounds very promising that this will be over soon. Besides, there are others running around scared. So much that they are making really stupid decisions and mistakes. Hopefully in the end those will be punished for what they did."

"I just want the truth to be told so that I can have my life back. It has taken a huge toll on my family. I believe it will be over soon. Nothing can ever be the same for us again, but I look forward to brighter days. Take care and I hope to see you soon to give another fur baby a home. I miss Buddy so much; he was such a blessing in my life. I would not have made it through the last three years without him," I wrote back.

Lee's son, had rented a house for thirty-five people in October, hoping that our entire family could fly to Park City, Utah, and stay together the week of Christmas, for skiing, riding snow mobiles, and what all of us began to refer to as "the Griswold Family Christmas." I did not think I would be allowed to travel that far because of the conditions of release (similar to probation) which would not even allow me to travel from Jacksonville to Lynn Haven unless I received permission from my pre-trial officer. But I decided to ask. And like an unexpected blessing from Heaven, she replied the very next day and told me the travel had been approved. The thought of actually getting on an airplane and leaving the state of Florida for Christmas seemed like a dream after three years of traveling nowhere. The thought of a noisy, bustling Christmas with our family, fourteen grandchildren in the same house, seemed like just the distraction we needed from the depression, the ominous cloud of the federal charges which hung over our lives, never leaving our thoughts.

The night before the trip, December 20th, I sat on the edge of my bed, looking at the beautiful little mahogany box on the desk which contained Buddy's ashes, with his tiny collar on top. I cried and prayed out loud, "Jesus, please heal my heart. Take away the pain. I know that he was just a dog, but I know he was precious to you, and no matter how crazy anyone thinks I am, I still feel him close to me, still love him."

I sat for a long time just letting God's spirit surround me and comfort me, and I asked for a sign, if I should take on another rescue dog, let my grief go, and try to help another little throw away.

The next morning as we were loading the rest of our bags and getting ready to drive to my daughter's house where we would all meet and ride to the Orlando airport together, I found a package on the front porch. As I opened it, I realized it was a framed piece of art; as I tore the paper and packing away, a beautiful oil painting of Buddy appeared. The card was from our dear friends, Eddie and Cyndi Mercer, wishing us a Merry Christmas. The painting, to me, arriving as it did, was Buddy's approval for me to adopt the little rescue dog, "Mr. Buddy," and I said, through my tears, "Oh Lee, let's tell Ramona we will take him." He had tears in his eyes and shook his head in approval.

I messaged Ramona from the Orlando airport at 11:44 am as we were waiting for our boarding call. "My husband Lee said we will come over right after our next hearing in January and pick him up. He said I need him. My heart is so broken. If that's ok, I will call you in about a week to see if you still have him and pick him up. I know my Buddy will be glad I am rescuing another Buddy. I love you Ramona. If I have to go to trial my family will keep him for me."

She answered immediately, "That will be great."

"Are you sure you are not attached to him?" I asked. He is so adorable I don't want to take him from you if you love him. But if not, Lee and I will probably come over sometime around December 29th. I will call first. I think Buddy will approve," I wrote.

"Although I love all dogs, no I am not attached to Buddy. I am a big dog person," wrote Ramona.

"Awesome "I texted back. Will get over there as soon next week as possible, lots going on. Tell him his new momma already loves him."
"I have been, and will," she said

And that was that. Ramona brought "Mr. Buddy" to my mom's former house on Tennessee Avenue on the morning of December 29th, which happened to be mine and Lee's 21st wedding anniversary. As she got out of the car with the beautiful little white Yorkie/Maltese mix in her arms, I burst into tears and hugged her, thanking her for saving him for me. She said he had some problems, and that he was a difficult rescue. She said she had kept him because she didn't want to give him to just anyone. His owners had abandoned him to the shelter after having him for two years, deciding that they wanted to get a larger breed dog. His little face looked so sad; he knew he had been thrown away.

Ramona had brought him in a crate with a pillow, and she also brought his little bed with him…a bed that he refused to leave for the first few days unless we picked him up.

As we tried to think of a name for him, (because I could not call him Buddy, as Ramona had named him), we thought of names that would sound similar to Buddy so as not to confuse him. And then I thought of the perfect name, "Burnie." Burnie Thompson had done as he had promised me he would; he had searched for the truth, he looked at the evidence, and he finally believed me. I loved the idea of naming this sweet little dog after a person like Burnie Thompson; a man of courage and conviction, but also a man who is humble. Burnie had trusted law enforcement in Bay County, much in the same way that I had. He was a Captain in the United States Air Force, possessed advanced academic degrees, and was fired from a major radio station because he reported the truth based on his evidence and his belief in honest journalism. Burnie was a perfect name.

Over the next months as I went through a plea hearing, a sentencing hearing, and a thirty-day sentence in federal prison, the small white dog was a source of strength and peace for me, something to hold on to when I did not think I would survive. Animals are a blessing from the Lord, and I praise Him for making sure this little dog found his way to me. I needed him.

# 10 AND THEN THERE WAS ONE: THE GUILTY PLEA OF MARGO ANDERSON, THE FIRST TRIAL OF JAMES FINCH, THE SENTENCING OF THE MAYOR AND THE 2ND TRIAL OF JAMES FINCH

On February 9th, 2023, I stopped by Rob Vezina's office to drop off some materials for trial exhibits to Tony on my way to Lynn Haven to work with my co-defendant James Finch on our trial preparation, and we were planning to visit the FBI office with one of our attorneys to view the Discovery from the GAC raid from July of 2021. We had been denied access to the discovery materials unless we came to the Panama City office of the FBI to look through and copy the materials we wanted with our attorney present as well as the FBI. The trial was only sixteen days away; Judge Mark Walker had ruled against dismissal of the case after the evidentiary hearing before Christmas. James and I, as well as our attorneys had been hopeful for dismissal after all the evidence of corruption and false information that had been presented against us, but the Judge used words he had used before, stating that the bar was high for dismissal, and although we had come close, that the bar had not been reached. The trial was going forward, and as frightening as sitting before a jury who could determine freedom or prison for the rest of our lives, we were both resolute, we were innocent, and we were ready to go forward after years of fighting the full weight of the United States Government vs. Margo Deal Anderson and James David Finch.

But the visit turned took a bit of a surprising turn when both Rob and Tony came into the conference room and asked if they could speak to me alone without Lee (who was sitting with me) in the room. They said I could share with him later what we talked about if I chose to do so, but they wanted to talk to me privately first.

Lee had our new rescue dog, Burnie, in his lap, and he stood up and said he would take the dog for a walk. I had an ominous feeling as Tony closed the conference room door behind him.

"The government has contacted us and said they have a reverse proffer which they would like to present to us," said Tony.

"What is that?" I asked.

"It means they have some additional information which they want to share with us, and I am assuming because of this information, they will possibly offer you some type of deal," Tony said.

I felt my chest tighten, the familiar sensation of pressure and not being able to breathe when anxiety sets in. My first reaction was a negative one.

"No,", I said. "Absolutely not."

Rob and Tony were quiet as I felt my eyes filling with tears, and then as I took a breath, I asked them more about what kind of information they were talking about that the prosecutors were claiming to have. They didn't know, but they thought it would be worthwhile meeting with them, if for nothing else to find out what the information was.

We had been hearing rumors for a couple of weeks that the prosecutors had convened another grand jury against James, although it seemed that nothing had come from that, and we were all completely absorbed with preparing for the trial which was now just three weeks away, February 27th.

They both asked me if there was anything I could think of that for whatever reason we had not talked about, anything about the case that I could think of that the Government would have that for some reason we had overlooked. I reassured them that I had told them everything, that everything I had told them was absolutely the truth, and that whatever new "evidence" the Government might have was not about me.

After some discussion, I agreed to meet with them, and Tony made a phone call to set it up with the prosecutors. The meeting time was set for Thursday at 2 pm, and I felt sick. Something was not right. I had no good feelings about meeting with the "devil." We called Lee back in and I shared with him what we had talked about, and in a few minutes we were continuing on to Lynn Haven.

Rob and Tony stressed to me how very important it was that the news does not leak out to anyone that the Government had asked for a meeting with us, but there was no way I was keeping anything from James. We had been through Hell and back fighting the lies and the travesty of what the FBI, the BCSO, Derwin White, and the prosecutors had done to us, and I called him immediately as soon as we were on the road out of Tallahassee. He was as shocked by it as I was, and we talked about what else they could have come up with against us now, just three weeks before trial. He agreed with me that meeting with them was not a bad idea, a sort of fishing expedition on our part.

All day Wednesday I wondered what the meeting would entail, and no matter how much I prayed, talked it out with Lee, spent time talking with James, I could find no peace. These people had ruined my life; I did not trust them. I could think of nothing good that could possibly come with meeting with them.

We drove back to Tallahassee on Thursday and Rob had his driver pick us up for the drive over to the Federal Courthouse. As we waited outside their office, we were given nametags, and I noticed looking through the glass window where the receptionist was sitting that Senator Rick Scott had an office there. I did not realize that the U.S. Senator was housed in the Federal Courthouse in Tallahassee.

Assistant U.S. Attorney Justin Keene met us at the door, and we followed him into a rather large expansive area, down a hall, and into a conference room with a long table and large windows looking out over Tallahassee on one side. Assistant U.S. Attorney Andrew Grogan was already seated at one end of the table, and I don't remember if he said anything or not, but I don't think he did. After a brief exchange of cordiality between the attorneys, Keen got right down to business. He had been the apparent replacement for Stephen Kunz who had suddenly retired in December after the two days of the second evidentiary hearing. Keen had been doing most of the talking at the hearing, when the prosecutors spoke at all.

I did not take very many notes, but I had brough a notepad and pen with me in case I needed somewhere to look beside their faces. As he began to speak, I found myself looking directly at him, and I knew my face probably did not hide any of the anger, the outrage I felt, just sitting in the same room with the prosecutors.

He spoke very calmly, his voice smooth, as he began with what was not quite an apology, but almost, for how the "case had been handled to this point" and while "he could not change what had transpired before, he was hoping that we could go forward in a different way." That is a paraphrase of what I remember, but I believe I captured it well. He then said something to the effect that they wanted to offer a reverse proffer, in essence a plea deal, and he also referred to the fact that he did not understand why this had not been approached earlier. Again, a paraphrase on my part, but again, the essence of what he said.

I immediately turned my stare from his face and wrote the word NO! in huge letters on my notepad, which Rob, sitting next to me covered with his hand. There were probably cameras in the ceiling in this office of the Government.

He then launched into his offer of my agreeing to plead guilty to the false statement charge from the first indictment, the statement I made to the FBI agent at the interview the night before their indictment was unsealed against Michael White and the others, November 18, 2019. The statement was concerning when I met David "Mickey" White. I had said I met him in December of 2018 or January 2019, when I was leading the volunteer cleanup of Lynn Haven's streets, and Mickey was cooking hot dogs and hamburgers with other employees in the park for the volunteers.

The reason it was so important to their narrative for me to "admit" that I met Mickey in October of 2018, is this is when Michael White, not me, signed the contract with ECS. Michael 's interview in his plea deal states that I was present when the contract was signed, that I had full knowledge of the ECS activities, etc. This was totally untrue, but because Michael White had said it as part of his plea deal, they wove it into the first indictment against me.

In exchange for my taking the "false statement plea deal" the Government would drop all other charges against me, not indict me again, and they would return the infamous motorhome which they now realized we had evidence to prove we had the money on hand to pay for it when Special Agent Lawrence Borghini and AUSA Stephen Kunz told the Grand Jury that indicted me that we did not.

Keen's monolog continued, as I stared at him with absolute disgust. He spoke of how juries were "unpredictable" and while I might be acquitted, I might not, and even if I were acquitted at the upcoming trial on February 27th, that they intended to go forward afterward with another indictment on the previously severed charges against me, the World Claim and the ECS schemes. Keen told me that the guidelines for the false statement sentencing would be 0-6 months considering that I had no record, and that the Government would also ask for a two-point reduction for my "showing remorse" by taking the plea. He then went on to say if I were found guilty of conspiracy or bribery charges in either the upcoming trial or in the next indictment for the severed World Claim and ECS schemes, that the sentencing guidelines could be from 151-188 months. I glared at him as he smoothly went through this carefully prepared speech, pretending it was not extortion, presenting the offer as though it were a favor to me, when without me in the upcoming trials, their witnesses who had already perjured themselves in the evidentiary hearing would not be necessary. Without me, the trial against my co-defendant became much smaller, something they could win or lose without the public exposure and media coverage again of the newly retired Assistant U.S. Attorney Stephen Kunz, newly retired FBI Agent Borghini, Sheriff Tommy Ford, City Manager Vickie Gainer, Lynn Haven Police Chief Ricky Ramie, Major Jimmy Stanford of the BCSO, Chris Forehand, Commissioner Dan Russell; all of these testimonies would never be heard without me in the trial; if they could sufficiently frighten me about the odds of winning two back to back jury trials in Federal Court with a full acquittal, they were home free.

At this point he asked Grogan to share with us the new "discovery" or information they had, and they hinted that they were going to pursue their allegation that James had continued to have contact with witnesses on the no contact list, and he alluded to the Government's intent to go forward with another indictment against me after the February 27th trial concluded, regardless of the result. He looked intently at his notes and made absolutely no eye contact with me.

"What a coward you are," I thought as I continued to stare at him, wishing I could say to him exactly what I was thinking. I had promised both attorneys that I would not say one single word in the meeting. They didn't trust the Government either.

Keen then told us he did not expect an answer today, that we should take the weekend to talk about it and discuss our decision, but that they would like to know something by Monday afternoon, February 13th. I was now feeling physically sick to my stomach, and stood up when the attorneys did, not speaking to the prosecutors, and walking out of the office with Rob and Tony by my side.

We rode back to the office in absolute silence, and as we walked in, Rob went and got a bottle of bourbon and asked if I would like some. I asked for a double without ice.

The next part of the conversation was when I realized that I would have to plead guilty. I didn't say it out loud, but the unspoken words hung over the room like a dark cloud, as Rob set three glasses on the table and poured the straight bourbon. Lee did not have any because he would be driving us home.

Rob and Tony pointed out to me that the Government, if they pursued the ECS charges, which we all believed now they would, had several witnesses who were willing to swear that I met Mickey White in October, that I knew about the ECS contract, that I was aware of the amount of money that Lynn Haven was paying them. Michael White, David "Mickey" White, Adam Albritton David Horton, and Josh Anderson. All had pleaded guilty and had been awaiting sentencing for over two years. They would say anything at this point to lessen their sentences, with nothing to lose and everything to gain; the same witnesses who had lied in their 302 interviews to help the Government with their investigation and eventual indictment of me just nine months after they were indicted themselves. The government had waited three years after their indictment to sentence them; they were waiting for me to go to trial before their "witnesses would be sentenced," and their sentences would depend upon the "assistance" they gave to the government.

Who would the jury believe? The mayor, or five or more witnesses for the government, all swearing that I knew about Mickey White and the ECS contract. And in addition to the witnesses awaiting sentencing, Chris Forehand had been given immunity by the Government, and we believed that possibly Vickie Gainer and Ricky Ramie had also been given immunity based on the completely "rogue" testimony that Ramie, in particular, had given after the evidentiary hearing was complete. We knew that Vickie Gainer had lied, both in her 302 interviews and also during her testimony, and she had told me from the beginning of the investigation that "she couldn't discuss anything with me because she was a 'witness,' and was being asked to provide information to FBI SA Borghini.

I began to cry, for the first time that day, in utter disbelief and frustration. Such a feeling of hopelessness, despair, and anger as I had never experienced just enveloped my soul. I knew at that moment, although I was going home to "think about it" that my fight was over. I had won, in that they were so afraid of my testimony, my evidence, and so afraid to bring their own witnesses against me in the trial, that they would just come after me again if I were acquitted. But I had also lost. I did not have the money to continue fighting them for another year, maybe two, over another indictment, even though I believed our evidence had every chance in the world of convincing a jury I was innocent. But I was 68 years old at the time of the offered plea, and even five years in prison would separate me from my 77-year-old husband into his eighties, I would not be able to be part of my children and grandchildren's lives any longer; the risk was too great. I had everything to lose; all the prosecutors wanted was a "win," and they had unlimited resources to continue prosecuting me for as long as I had the means and the will to fight them. They were too angry and too humiliated by our defense to walk away at this point; to coin Guy Lewis' words from the beginning, "they were hell-bent to prosecute James Finch and me."

I had Lee drive us back to Lynn Haven instead of to Jacksonville, and I had several conversations with James, with Lee, with my family, and with the attorneys. We waited until Tuesday to let the Government know anything. I wasn't ready on Monday.

## The Guilty Plea of Mayor Anderson

We had a hearing with the Judge before everything was finalized and my attorneys asked if I could plead less than a guilty plea; something known as an Alford plea or a no lo contendere plea, in a criminal prosecution by which a defendant accepts conviction as though a guilty plea had been entered but does not admit guilt.

The Judge actually issued an order stating that he would accept such a plea and Channel 13-WMBB quickly reported the story before I had even signed the paperwork thanks to the prosecutors letting them know:

*WMBB Lynn Haven, FL: After two years of fighting, the former mayor of Lynn Haven is expected to plead to a single charge of misleading the FBI. The exact statute being used to charge Ms. Anderson is not known at this time. The plea hearing is scheduled to take place Thursday afternoon in Tallahassee.*

*As part of the deal, Anderson will not have to admit guilt of any crime, according to Judge Mark Walker. Walker entered an order in the case Wednesday announcing that he would allow Anderson to make that plea in his courtroom.*

*Walker is allowing Anderson to enter either an Alford plea or a nolo contendere plea. An Alford plea is one where the defendant does not admit guilt but does acknowledge that the prosecution has enough to obtain a guilty verdict at trial. A nolo contendere plea is one where the defendant neither admits nor denies guilt but is willing to accept the punishment. A no-lo contendere plea can only be entered with the Judge's permission, which Judge Walker gave on Wednesday.*

*Anderson will still face the punishment for that single crime regardless of her plea. The plea deal looks to be a massive win for Anderson who at one time faced 64 felony charges in the case. Sources close to the investigation tell News 13 that Anderson is facing up to six months in prison, but Walker could give her no prison time at all."*

*News 13 called the U.S. Attorney's Office on Wednesday morning and asked about the alleged agreement with Anderson.*

*The U.S. Attorney's office immediately emailed us an information document stating that Anderson willfully made "false, fictitious and fraudulent statements and representations," during the criminal investigation of public corruption and fraud by the FBI...*

*The document is signed by three federal prosecutors but is not signed by Anderson. If this deal is finalized, it appears Anderson will have gone from facing 64 charges to pleading guilty to a single charge."*

When I returned on February 16, the attorneys had asked me that morning to come to their office as early as possible, noon if I could. The drive from Lynn Haven is about two and a half hours plus there is a time change from central to eastern time zones, making it even more difficult to get there quickly. They would not tell me why.

Once I got there, I realized the problem; the Government would not accept the no lo contendere or Alford plea and would only sign the deal if I pleaded a straight guilty plea, which also included the words that I "intentionally lied" to the FBI agent. There were other items they wanted in the statement which we did not agree to which were left out. The Statement of Facts accompanying my plea of guilty read as follows:

## STATEMENT OF FACTS

The Defendant, MARGO DEAL ANDERSON, admits that if this case were to proceed to trial the government could prove the following beyond a reasonable doubt.

1. Beginning in March 2019, the Federal Bureau of Investigation ("FBI") was investigating allegations of fraud involving the City of Lynn Haven, Florida ("City") concerning Erosion Control Specialists ("ECS") and its owner, David "Mickey" White,

2. In an interview with two FBI agents on the evening of November 18, 2019, ANDERSON stated that ANDERSON first met David "Mickey" White in December 2018 or January 2019, when volunteers were used to clean up various streets in the City.

3. In truth and in fact, ANDERSON knew that she had met David "Mickey" White through City Manager Michael White shortly after Hurricane Michael.

4. ANDERSON's statement to the FBI was material to its on-going criminal investigation, which was a matter within the jurisdiction of an agency of the federal government.

18 U.S.C. & 1001—False Statement to a Federal Agency

The elements of this offense are:

1) The Defendant made the statement, as charged;
2) The statement was false;
3) The falsity concerned a material matter;
4) The Defendant acted willfully, knowing that the statement was false; and
5) The false statement was made or used for a matter within the jurisdiction of a department or agency of the United States.

The document was signed by U.S. Attorney Jason Coody, Justin Keen, my attorneys, and there was a blank space for my name.

*As I read the part about, "admitting that if the case proceeds the Government could prove beyond a reasonable doubt…" I realized that was definitely true, because they had Michael White, Mickey White, Adam Albritton, and others who would swear that I had met Mickey White in October, even though the 302 interviews of Adam Albritton do not include my name at the crucial meetings when the decisions were made. But they had all lied to this point hoping for lesser sentences, and if I had gone to trial, they would have been willing to lie again. Albritton received no prison time, and Mickey and Michael White each received 42 months, well below the minimum sentencing guidelines. As difficult as it was, I had made the right decision. What I learned about the Government prosecutors, at least during the long ordeal of our case, is that they do not mind *lies if the lies verify the narrative of their indictment.*


When we arrived at the Federal Courthouse, my brother, Roy Deal was there, his face filled with emotion and concern for me as my eyes met his; my brother and I have always been close, and as all of this transpired, I often thought of how horrible it must be to watch someone you love going through such a travesty. I would have been devastated to see him going through something like I was experiencing. I smiled my bravest smile at him as we went to our seats. My husband Lee was with me, and I saw the owners of Beacon of Bay County online news, Jodie Moore and Gerri Parker were there, as well as Burnie Thompson, journalist of the Burnie Thompson Show. Brady Calhoun from Channel Thirteen News, ABC, of Panama City was also present.

Before the proceedings began, Rob Vezina, my attorney, brought the plea agreement over for me to sign, handing me his pen. I sat and held the pen for what seemed like an eternity. I just could not put the pen to the paper. I thought back to the day over forty years ago when I was about to sign the final divorce papers between my daughter's father and me.

"It's only a signature," I told myself. "You have made the decision, who cares what anyone says, what anyone thinks, they are government thugs, they don't matter."

I looked at Rob directly in the eyes for a long moment, and I realized he knew the pain and emotions I was experiencing. He knew my soul was in complete turmoil. I had often told Rob during the three years of this fight that he reminded me of my favorite literary character, Atticus Finch, the attorney in *To Kill a Mockingbird.* He was soft-spoken, but deliberate, formidable in the courtroom with his cross-examination during the evidentiary hearings, and kind to me during what were some of the worst moments of my life, when I did not always deserve his kindness. I was terrified, fighting for my life, and I often interjected my opinions and advice when I should have been quiet; he endured many emotional and angry tirades from me yet still remained not only my attorney, but my friend. Rob's wife, as well as another attorney from their firm had come to sit in the audience for support. No one was happy about this ending; not even the Government. They looked like absolute fools for the way this case had been handled, and they knew it. But they also knew they did not want me in the upcoming trial which had now been moved to March 13, 2023, instead of February 27, 2023, as had been scheduled.

Even if I had been convicted in that trial, which we all did not think would have happened, they did not want their witnesses exposed, and they did not want the jury to hear my testimony. No one had heard my story, not even the Judge. Only the story woven by AUSA Stephen Kunz, and

FBI Agent Lawrence Borghini had been told. And that is how they wanted it to stay. They did not drop 64 charges because they felt sorry for me and wanted to do the right thing. If that was the case, they would have done it nearly three years ago when they were shown evidence that the entire case was based on faulty evidence, lies, no evidence, and social media posts recorded as fact by investigators.

I do not remember everything about the hearing, except that I remember Judge Mark Walker seemed empathetic; he took his time explaining everything he legally had to explain, read maximum sentencing guidelines as well as made comments about the recommended sentencing guidelines, and made a point of telling me several times, that should I enter the guilty plea, that he, and he alone could decide the sentence. He also asked me more than once if I understood that.

Throughout the entire nightmare of this case, the only anchor in the storm, the only bastion of fairness, the only glimmer of hope that I had that at some point there would be justice in some form for me, was the fact that I was assigned Chief Judge Mark Walker. I read everything I could find out about him. The most encouraging fact I found was that he had been a public defender before he was a Judge. Not a prosecutor. A defender of those who had been accused.

He spoke directly to me, made sure I understood what I was saying, and I assured him that I understood completely what I was doing. My only hope was that he had read between the lines and knew that I had wanted to plead to Alford or no lo contendere plea that he had ordered was acceptable. He had to know that the Government had refused. The same way the Government had refused me a bench trial over a year ago when I requested one. I waived my rights, asked for a bench trial, the Judge agreed, and the prosecutors denied that request. The reason? Just as they stated to me in the meeting, "juries are unpredictable". They knew that this Judge would be able to discern facts in such a complicated case much more easily than a jury; basically, what the prosecutors admitted when they denied us a bench trial was that they did not trust Judge Walker. They thought they had a better chance at conviction with a jury.

Within what seemed a very short time, my plea was entered, and before we left the courtroom, a probation officer came over and handed me a thick packet of paperwork saying, "here's a little homework for you to fill out before you meet for your interview with probation." I did not look at it until later, but it took me almost a week to completely fill it out before meeting with the probation officer in Panama City on February 28th for the pre-sentencing interview. (This was something else I did not know about before pleading guilty)

Brady Calhoun asked me if I wanted to make a statement for Channel 13, and my attorneys and I walked past him as though he was not there. I believe that News Director Tom Lewis and Station Manager Terry Cole of Channel 13 played an integral role in the investigation which ultimately led to my indictment and removal from office, and their role will hopefully lead to successful civil litigation against them personally and the WMBB affiliate of ABC in Panama City, Florida, in the future.

## The Motorhome

The next few days were horrible. I did not want to see anyone, talk with anyone, or even leave the house. I felt sick inside; after almost three years of fighting the Government's lies, the evidentiary hearings, preparing for trial, and then to end this by taking a plea deal…I felt like a coward, weak, forced to my knees by the heavy hand of the prosecutors of the Northern District of Florida.

I needed something to fight about, and so I chose the motorhome. The attorneys felt that it might be many weeks before we got it back, possibly even after sentencing scheduled for May 5, over two months away. Every bit of strength I had left inside me rose up and said, "no!" The motorhome was part of the deal I had agreed to, they had dropped those charges after discovering that at the time they said we had no funds to pay for it, we did, and I wanted the damn thing back. I was sure it was probably not worth anything after sitting in some outdoor storage facility for three years exposed to heat and cold, but that didn't matter to me anymore. I wanted it back, and I wanted the entire county to see what the Bay County Sheriff's Department lied about and stole from us. And so, I started to email the attorneys.

On February 22, 2023, just six days after my guilty plea, I sent the following email to Tony and Rob:

*What are the next steps to get Lee's motorhome back? Is there a contact that the Government is going to provide, do we have to go somewhere to get it, or do they bring it back?*

*My thinking is that we need to make a formal request of the Government so that if we do not have it back by May 5th, we can let the Court know.*

*They have had it for 31 months. I have honored my part of the plea deal; they need to take care of this.*

*Thanks; hope you both are having a blessed Ash Wednesday*

### On March 1, 2023, Tony Bajoczky replied:

*I inquired about the time frame for the return of the motorhome. I have not received a response but will let you know when I do.*

*I am sure I have annoyed you but want to emphasize again. Be careful about complying with your conditions of pretrial release. There has been ongoing allegations that*

*James violated (or was violating) his conditions of release, but probation finally acted on it. There is a hearing set for tomorrow to determine whether he violated the conditions, and if so the repercussions.*

*Tb*

(This hearing found that James had not violated his conditions of release, and the Government even had wrong who the witness was that he had supposedly spoken with. This was brought about by a phone call and a lie from the present City Manager of the City of Lynn Haven, Vickie Gainer., who we believe was given a deal or immunity by the Government.; we know that her interviews with the FBI contain false statements, and there is no reason for her to have made the false statements if she were not involved in the kickbacks or corruption with Michael White.)

### On March 2, 2023, I sent the following email to Tony and Rob:

*Lee called me and said he got a tag for the motorhome and has air compressor, filters, diesel fuel, batteries and assistance to help him with it, if someone from the Government will contact him.*

*Margo*

### On March 2, 2023, I sent the following email to Tony and Rob:

*Would one of you please let me know the results of today's hearing? I am worried about James. Thank you.*

*Margo*

### On March 2, 2023, Tony Bajoczky replied:

*He will be fine. He's not going to jail.*

### On March 6, 2023, I sent the following email to Tony and Rob:

*Any word from Grogan or others about the motorhome? Lee is still in Lynn Haven and since it has now been three weeks was hoping to at least be given some information concerning a timeline before he drives back home.*

*He hired an attorney at Ausley over two years ago who filed the papers on our behalf as required by the Government in the process of the return of seized property, and so I am assuming the government employees in charge of that still have the filing we made, on time.*

*That cost Lee over 3K if I recall; I am not criticizing you or Rob about this, but my thinking is that they need to be reminded frequently. It is not a priority for them, but they made it part of the plea deal.*

*They continue to prove they are slow to honor their word. Gorgan filing a paper means nothing if he doesn't follow up on it. It could sit on another government employee's desk for a long time.*

*If you could give him (Grogan) another gentle reminder I would appreciate it on behalf of Lee. The motorhome is symbolic in many ways and it would help Lee to regain a little self-esteem back in the community where he has been humiliated.*

*Hope your Monday is going well other than an annoying email from me.*

*Margo*

### On March 7, 2023, Tony Bajoczky wrote:

*I have not received an update. Tomorrow will be 1 week since Grogan said he would get us an estimate. I will remind him this evening if we don't hear anything today.*

### On March 8, 2023, Tony Bajoczky wrote:

*From Grogan:*

*"According to USMS, the motorhome is stored in Montgomery, Alabama. USMS has contacted the storage facility and will schedule a date/time next week for the release to Mr. Anderson."* The USMS is the United States Marshals Service.

### On March 10, 2023, I wrote:

*The Federal Marshall contacted Lee today and he has made arrangements to go to Montgomery to pick up the motorhome on Monday. I wanted to thank you for following up with Grogan and getting this done. Lee looked happy today for the first time in a long time. The motorhome was symbolic in many ways, but they humiliated and lied about my husband in the community where he knew everyone. Today went a long way in repairing damage. Even if it is totally destroyed inside from not being plugged in and maintained and is not usable, at least the Government won't have it anymore.*

*Thanks, so much,*

*Margo*

## MARCH 13, 2023      The First Trial of James Finch

This is the first day of James' trial. I am not there to show support for the friend who has paid over 1.4 million as of today in legal fees on my behalf. When I agreed to the guilty plea, the conditions of release went back to the original terms of no contact between James and me. This makes absolutely no sense when one considers the fact that we have discussed every aspect of this case, read every single document, and know the testimony of every witness, government or defense. There is literally nothing we could discuss between us at this point that has not been discussed.

Lee is on his way to Montgomery, Alabama today to pick up the motorhome the Government seized (stole) from us on August 19, 2020, when I was indicted and arrested. As soon as he gets the motor home to Lynn Haven, he will spend the night, and then travel to Tallahassee on

Tuesday morning to be with James through the rest of the week, to support his friend.

My news of the trial has come today from my attorney Rob Vezina and from Burnie Thompson's live broadcasts and Tweets from the Federal Courthouse.

Rob Vezina texted me late this afternoon:

"Openings reflect the gov is putting on a very "simple" case; Remarkably, Keen said in opening that James and Antonius Barnes were not "friends." No clue how gov could have failed to know the history. Guy crammed this down their throat and had slides of Antonius Barnes' denials of influence and ending with Borghini's "I believe you."

Gov put Schubert on to establish ????I think the jury must be wondering why: James never tried to improperly influence him; James generous to the City where he was born and raised, no question James loves the City, etc. I think the gov wanted to set the state that Joel wanted to get away from you because you tried to exert too much influence, but Guy saw this coming and successfully objected. I had to leave while Guy was in midst of Joel's cross. Michael is next and I'm assuming he'll be first up tomorrow."

I replied to Rob:

"Thank you so much for the update. Joel went to the county because he was going through a custody battle with his ex, needed more money, and the county paid significantly more with better retirement and benefits. Also, the job was not so political and precarious where one could be dismissed without reason with 3 votes from the Commission. If he said anything different it was simply not true."

Rob:

"He said it was a better opportunity, less political and more stable commission. After he was pushed he said ya'll's relationship had deteriorated and that was a factor. Also said you and James asked him to stay based on his performance history."

I replied:

"I appreciate the update. Hard not to be there after three years of this but sounds pretty weak on their part so far. Good news."

Rob:

"yep"

*WMBB Channel 13-Panama City reported on the mistrial in their March 18, 2023 news headline, "Mistrial declared in Finch bribery case."*

*A Lynn Haven businessman fought the federal government to a draw Thursday.*

*After three days of trial and about 9 hours of deliberations jurors in the James finch bribery trial announced that they were deadlocked on both charges. Finch, the owner of Phoenix Construction, is accused of conspiracy and bribery over $45,000 in payments he made to Antonius Barnes, a former Lynn Haven City Commissioner.*

Jurors split, in large part, over the testimony of Barnes and another key witness, Mike White, the former city manager for the city of Lynn Haven. White claimed that Finch told him privately that he had bribed Barnes and that he was not worried about an upcoming vote on a Phoenix project with the city because Barnes would, "dance if I told him to." White did nothing about this statement at the time but after he was arrested in a multi-million dollar scheme involving city funds after Hurricane Michael he agreed to tell the FBI everything he knew about corruption in the city.

Prosecutors pointed out during the trial that while White might not seem credible but he had no way of knowing that investigators would find actual bank records showing $45,000 in payments from Finch to Barnes.

However, Finch and Barnes both maintained that they are innocent, and the money was simply a loan between friends to help Barnes start an insurance agency. During the trial, Finch's defense team pointed out that the votes on city contracts were all vetted by city staff and always approved by a unanimous vote of the commission. Finch did not need to bribe Barnes, the defense argued.

Judge Mark Walker met with the jurors privately after he declared a mistrial and got comments from them that he relayed to the court. Walker said the jurors were evenly split and that some of them did not understand some of the particulars of the case. They said that while the prosecutors and the defense attorneys clearly knew the case very well that information did not always come through to them.

Jurors said they wanted to hear from Finch's secretary, or anyone else, who might have known about the payments.

"What was that person told?" Walker said.

He added that the jurors did not think White or Barnes "were very credible."

While deliberating, jurors asked for more information about Barnes' plea agreement. Prosecutors argued that Barnes was lying to them on the stand after he took a plea agreement on a bank fraud charge. The plea agreement states that Barnes would testify that Finch bribed him. However, when the time came, Barnes refused to do so testifying that he did not sell his vote.

The jurors were split into two camps with one agreeing with the defense that it did not make sense for Finch, who has an incredibly successful construction business that deals in large contracts across the country to bother to bribe Barnes.

The other camp said, "You don't give a commissioner $45,000 if you don't want something," Walker recalled. "Common sense says it's a bribe."

The jurors also took issue with White's demeanor during his testimony. Whie repeatedly looked at the jurors while talking. When Guy Lewis, Finch's attorney, brought up how unnatural White was acting, the witness said prosecutors told him jurors want the witness to look at them.

These jurors apparently disagreed.

"They didn't love Mr. White looking at them," Walker said.

And in a moment of levity after a long day, Walker noted that the jurors were amused that Lewis scolded White for looking at the jury and then he did that very same thing for the next 10 minutes.

*Finch and Lewis declined to comment outside of the courtroom. Walker and the attorneys scheduled a retrial in the case for May 16. A request for comment from federal prosecutors remains unanswered.*

Burnie Thompson of *The Burnie Thompson Show* gave an update after the day's proceedings from in front of the federal courthouse in Tallahassee and concluded promising to write and post more later that evening on his show. (His voice seemed to be failing him, probably from broadcasting so much over the past few days with updates on the trial.)

Burnie shared that the prosecution has a new document which was introduced late on Thursday, and reviewed by the defense on Friday, March 10th, in which Government witness, former City Manager Michael White, has once again added/changed his testimony, and this time will put forward the notion that James Finch has used some type of racial slur/description in regard to co-defendant Antonius Barnes. Apparently, Judge Walker was not pleased with this and said that he would allow the document but that it would open the door for the defense to cross examine Michael White with the text messages containing racial slurs which the prosecution had asked to be suppressed before. (This is my understanding of what Burnie reported, of course I am learning about the trial from those in attendance since I am in Jacksonville, making sure there are no accusations of contact between James and myself.)

Months later, James and I would talk about both of the trials and his thoughts about them.

"When Barnes testified in the first trial, he was asked if I bribed him, and he answered no," James said. "Barnes is the only witness in the case who was videotaped during his interview with the FBI, and Agent Borghini told Barnes how much he appreciated him coming by, and that he found that Barnes had been more than truthful in his answers to questions."

James added, "Barnes even asked the agent if there was anything else he needed to do."

Borghini, on the video tape which James and I had both received as part of the discovery from the Government, replies to Barnes, "if we need anything else we will let you know."

James had several character witnesses at the first trial, including Harold Bazzel, the Bay County Clerk of 31 years, Guy Tunnel, former Lynn Haven Police Chief for 15 years, former Bay County Sheriff for 12 years, and then he was appointed Commissioner of FDLE, Jack Prescott, the General Manager for International Paper Company in Panama City, and his longtime friend, Willie B. Carpenter. All of the witnesses spoke of James' integrity, his reputation as a contractor, his charitable work in the community, and, in the case of Willie B. Carpenter, who is African-American, a witness who spoke of their long friendship, of James' visits to his home to "eat collard greens," which refuted Michael White's testimony that James used racist language in referring to Commissioner Barnes, who is also African American.

"The government has dropped the conspiracy charge against me three times," said James, "and then after the mistrial, they continued to try and get met to plead guilty before the second trial. They even suggested that I plead guilty to "misprision" which requires active concealment of a known felony rather than simple failure to report it."

"I could not believe the government wanted me to plead guilty of misprision, when you and I were the only ones who *did* report the crime that we saw. I told them that they should plead guilty to misprision since *they* knew that Kunz and the FBI Agent Borghini had lied to the grand jury and did not prosecute them," added James.

I have second-guessed myself many times today, wondering if I should have stayed the course, gone to trial, but as I have posted on social media, "it is well with my soul." I truly believe that God opened the door for me to walk through, and in faith, I did so. If I were sitting next to James at the table as a defendant, the jury would be considering the possibility that he bribed two officials instead of one, and the Government would have the shiny objects they have used to inflame the public through the media: the trips on James' jet, and the alleged bribe of the motorhome. If I had gone to trial, we would have offered significant evidence of how I paid my way for every flight on the plane, which is why I did not report the trips as "gifts" to the ethics board, and we obviously offered significant evidence that Lee paid for the motorhome at the evidentiary hearing, or they would not have given it back. But even if both James and I had been acquitted at this trial, the trial of February 27, 2023, the prosecutors were quite clear that they intended to indict me again as soon as the trial was over on the ECS and World Claim conspiracies, and with the number of guilty government witnesses willing to testify against me, the odds were probably 50/50 at best for an acquittal, and a conviction, as they stated in our meeting for the plea deal, would mean they would ask for 150-188 months in prison for me. I would have been over 80 years old when released, if I lived that long.

I now despise the Government of the country I have cherished and believed in my entire life. The only reason that I stand for the National Anthem and say the Pledge Allegiance to the flag is in honor of the veterans of this country. Period. There is no justice, no honor in the federal judicial system. None. I never broke my oath of office as Mayor of the City of Lynn Haven. The FBI agent, Lawrence Borghini, who accused me of lying, making the false statement for which I pleaded guilty, lied to the grand jury himself, as did Assistant U.S. Attorney Stephen Kunz, to get the indictment. They are both now retired, collecting pensions paid for by my tax money and yours, and because of the plea deal I accepted, he, nor any of the other corrupt law enforcement who were part of this investigation will be cross-examined at trial, because now there will be no trial for me, only a sentencing date. The government did not call their own investigators as witnesses in the trial against the remaining defendant, James Finch, because they are liars, not credible.

Where is justice? This is the reason they made a deal with me. Certainly not because it was for my benefit or because they had compassion or care that I was wrongly charged; they dropped the remaining two charges against me, conspiracy and bribery with James Finch, and went to the tried and true "false statement to the FBI" to save face. They got the conviction against the elected official they needed for their public corruption case in Bay County Florida, and with all other charges dropped, Assistant U.S. Attorney Stephen Kunz, Special Agent Lawrence Borghini, Sheriff Tommy Ford, BCSO Investigators Jimmy Stanford, Jeremy Mathis and Aubrey Chance, Lynn Haven Police Chief Ricky Ramie, Lynn Haven City Manager Vicky Gainer, Lynn Haven City Attorney Adam Albritton, and City Engineer Chris Forehand (immunized from testimony by the Government) are all off the proverbial "hook". They will not be called on to give testimony in my trial; evidence will not be presented that I was the "whistleblower," that I was "set-up" with fake invoices, that I was targeted because Derwin White was angry that I discovered what they were doing, angry that I was honest, not able to be controlled or to be bought. They wanted me out of the way. The indictment against me was so large in scope, so egregious, so shocking, that I wondered if in the beginning my closest friends, my teaching colleagues of decades, or even my own family questioned my innocence, although all of them say they never doubted me.

*"No one is charged with 64 federal counts who is innocent. The FBI has a 98% conviction rate; how could they be wrong? She must have done something."* This was the chatter, the talk in my hometown of Lynn Haven and all over Bay County. Not one elected official, not one Mayor in Bay County called me to see if I was alright, to offer to help, or just to say, "I am sorry this is happening to you." They were either terrified of what was coming next, guilty of some misstep in the chaos and the aftermath of Hurricane Michael, they had made themselves, or they just didn't care enough to reach out. I was told that one County Commissioner said that it was what I deserved, that I "had tried to move ahead too quickly," thought that "I was entitled after the visit by President Trump", that I had been "too vocal about the lack of Congressional action after the storm," that I ruffled "too many feathers."

The second in command under Sheriff Tommy Ford, Joel Heape, told a local journalist that I was now taken care of…that I would either plead guilty right away or spend the rest of my life in prison. There were also rumors and comments on social media that I might commit suicide. The "boys" thought I was weak, that I would break under such pressure. But they were not prepared for what happened. They were not prepared that James Finch, the multi-millionaire who grew up dirt poor in Lynn Haven, and had known me since childhood, would stand by me. They were not prepared for a friendship like his that would take on the full measure of the United States Government and pay my attorney's costs of more than a million dollars. And no matter what happens now, they lose, not us, because their corruption, their way of "doing business" is finally exposed.

Maybe the citizens of Bay County and all over the Panhandle of Florida will stand up to them now. If not, this will keep happening to other innocent people who get in their way; if they can do this to me, to James, if they are left in power, they can do it to anyone…and they will.

The question most people ask me now that the case is over, concerns the importance of the date on which I first met David "Mickey" White, "the crime", the false statement I made to the FBI for which I have now pleaded guilty. I stated to the FBI agents who showed up at my house at night, unexpectedly, the night before Michael White was indicted in November of 2019, that I first met Mickey White in either December of 2018 or January 2019 when I was organizing a volunteer group "Street by Street" to clean up remaining debris in Lynn Haven, and to clear the blocked culverts causing flooding in the neighborhoods. I remembered Mickey White being in Sheffield Park cooking hamburgers and hot dogs for the volunteers, and someone introducing me to him at that time. I had no idea why the FBI agent was asking me when I met Mickey White or why it was important at the time the question was asked, and I had no attorney present with me. Like General Flynn, I spoke to them because I had nothing to hide. I spoke the truth; the only problem was that the truth did not match up with their primary government witness' story, City Manager Michael White, who was doing everything in his power to not go to prison.

What I would later find out was that Michael White, as part of his plea deal to "tell the government everything he knew, tell them the truth" told the FBI agent that I was present and was part of the conspiracy to hire Erosion Control Specialist (ECS) when the contract was signed. Michael White lied to them; he and Mickey White are the only two signatures on the contract, the contract drafted by attorney Adam Albritton. The contract was signed in October of 2018, and this is why it is so important to the Government for me to say that October 2018 is when I met Mickey White, not December 2018 or January 2019, otherwise, their conspiracy theory is out the window.

The Government can now continue with their "theory" that I agreed for ECS to have the contract in return for the alleged property cleanup and repairs for me, my Mom, and a neighbor. A property cleanup that was disproven at the evidentiary hearing of December 12th and 13th of 2022, when my attorneys presented the property survey demonstrating that what was cleaned was a City stormwater easement, and photographs of my son-in-law and his friends from Jacksonville cleaning debris from my property and that of my Mom over a month earlier than when Michael White and ECS cleaned the city-owned easement. Michael White's and Mickey White's testimonies that I was involved are part of their deal for a lesser sentence; they were each sentenced to 42 months of incarceration for embezzling millions of dollars from the City of Lynn Haven, below the minimum sentencing guidelines. And now the Government can say they have another conviction. The Mayor of Lynn Haven pleaded guilty to making a false statement to the FBI. Not stealing any money. Not taking part in any conspiracy. Not taking bribes from contractors. Just making a false statement to the FBI agents who came to her home, by surprise, at night. The same FBI agent who made false statements to the grand jury which originally indicted her and who quickly retired after the first evidentiary hearing with his benefits and his reputation intact. His false statements were called "misstatements" or "mistakes" which were not intentional due to his shoddy investigation when he did not even bother to read the Lynn Haven City Charter or Lynn Haven Commission minutes, both documents which are public record, and which disproved his "misstatements"

I will not be allowed to own a firearm again, nor will I be able to vote again. I am now a convicted felon. But I still won. And they know it.

## The Sentencing of Mayor Anderson

After the plea hearing before Judge Mark Walker, a sentencing hearing was scheduled for June 10, 2023; no one thought that I would be sentenced to any time in a federal prison, but the hearing took a downward turn, with the prosecutors putting on almost a mini-trial, bringing case law from a case which had been decided by Judge Walker of a corrupt police officer, and pushing for me to receive a period of incarceration, as they reminded the Judge that he had sentenced the police officer to many months in prison. I read a statement at the hearing, and my attorneys had also submitted dozens of letters of support from my family and friends, a portfolio of my life's work as a teacher, my charitable and community work, and awards and recognition I had received over sixty-eight years of a life well-lived. As I described earlier in the book, my attorney stated that the reason there was not a room full of people there to support me was that because of all of the media attention on the case, people had seen what had happened to me, were afraid of the FBI, afraid of retribution. This statement sent the Judge into a tirade which lasted several minutes in which he ended by calling the FBI the "premiere law enforcement agency in the world" and stating that "it was a disgrace the things that were being said in Washington D.C. about the agency." He then took a recess, came back and sentenced me to thirty days in federal prison, a year of probation, and 100 hours of community service. Before he sentenced me, he made a statement that his remarks before he took the recess had no bearing on the sentence he was about to impose. My attorney, Tony Bajoczky, was devastated that I was sentenced to prison, even for thirty days, but I assured him it was not his fault; the prosecutors put on a mini-trial at what was supposed to be a sentencing hearing; I will always be grateful to him for defending me, for listening to me pour out my heart, listening to me cry, and standing with me as I was sentenced. The prosecutors of the Northern District, led by Jason Coody, were angry that I had fought them for so long, angry that they had been embarrassed over and over again during the three years of our legal battle. Andrew Grogan, Justin Keene, Jason Coody, and Stephen Kunz; prosecutors who sought conviction over truth. That is their legacy.

I was ordered to self-surrender to the federal marshal in Tallahassee on July 10, 2023, to begin the thirty days. He did not sentence me to any fines or financial retribution because he did not believe the property cleanup charges against me, based on the evidence he had seen, and despite the slanted media reporting stating that I was the Mayor who had stolen 5 million dollars from FEMA, I was never charged with theft by the Government, because there was no evidence nor testimony. On the contrary, while Michael White and the others were stealing from the City of Lynn Haven, I personally raised over $250,000.00 in hurricane relief funds that was distributed to the residents in $1,000 grants. This was never mentioned by the Government to the court, and Judge Walker knew nothing of it, until I read it in my statement to the Court before I was sentenced.

I was devastated at the thought of thirty days in a federal prison, but even that experience turned into something I did not expect. I wrote a book while in prison, which is now available on Amazon, entitled, *Campers: Thirty Days in the Marianna Federal Correctional Institution Satellite Camp,* which tells the stories of women I met there, the daily dreariness of the federal prison routine, harsh and cruel sentences of 10, 20, and even 30 years for non-violent crimes committed by women, many who went to trial rather than accept a plea deal. They were then punished with sentences that separated them from their families, their small children for years, or even decades. The book, which is very different from this one, is a rare look from an insider's view of the life of an inmate in federal prison; the narrative is raw, filled with the hostility and anger I felt as an innocent woman sentenced to thirty days in prison for a crime I did not commit, yet ashamed to admit I was there for only thirty days when my cellmate was serving thirty years. The book is a recounting of how approximately 200 incarcerated women manage to live their lives, visit with their children and families on weekends, and still find moments of joy, all the while subjected to the prison's routines, terrible food, illness, poor sanitary conditions, daily work routines from mopping floors, working in the laundry or food services as they are paid literally pennies on the dollar for their labor, with most of it applied to fines imposed upon them by the Government. I was not assigned a job while I was incarcerated because the government employees there could not process my paperwork that quickly; therefore, I spent my hours there listening to their stories and writing a daily journal, hoping that my story might be used for grand jury reform, for prison reform, especially for young mothers with children at home, and elderly women in their seventies, still with twenty years to go for non-violent, financial crimes in most cases, with many first-time offenders. The book is a snapshot of thirty days inside a federal prison camp: thirty days of anger, fear, boredom, surviving a Covid outbreak, and ultimately learning a new walk of faith, forgiveness, and hope.

## The Second Trial of James Finch    October 2, 2023

After the trial of March 13, 2021, ended in a hung jury, to the disbelief of James, his family, and attorneys, the prosecutors were going to try the case again. As I have said before, they were hell-bent for a conviction, first against me, and now, James, who would go through the stress of another trial on a single "666" bribery charge, the "wink and a nod" with no quid pro quo needed, which a year after my guilty plea and James' acquittal, has now been struck down by the Supreme Court and neither of us should have ever been charged, as our attorneys had argued to no avail. The chief witness for the prosecution, former Commissioner Antonius Barnes, continued to stand by his testimony that he was not bribed, yet the Government continued to prosecute the case.

James wanted the second trial to be scheduled as soon as possible. Those who have not been through a federal indictment with months of stress, expense, sleeplessness, depression and uncertainty for the future, cannot understand this, but the defendants reach a point, as both of us had, when we just wanted it over. And the prosecutors know this. They break defendants financially, emotionally, and physically, as they continue their prosecution with unlimited resources and government witnesses all to willing to lie to shorten their own prison sentences.

At this point, James and his attorney, Guy Lewis, would have irreconcilable differences when James discovered that Guy had postponed the trial until the end of the summer without conferring with him. James made the decision to change his defense team, and he and Guy Lewis, after two years of battling the government, parted company.

James hired a long-time friend, Indianapolis attorney Jim Voyles and his partner Jennifer Lukemeyer as his new defense team, and a hearing was held before Judge Walker to set the new trial date with the new attorneys.

### WMBB-Channel 13-ABC affiliate in Panama City, Florida reported on this change as follows:

*It will now be at least another five months until anyone in Lynn Haven gets closure on one aspect of that city's federal corruption case.*

*James Finch, the owner of Phoenix Construction, is charged with conspiracy and bribery over $45,000 in payments he made to then Lynn Haven City Commissioner Antonius Barnes. Finch and Barnes say the money was a business loan.*

*While eight other defendants in the case pled guilty and some have been sentenced to prison, Finch is still fighting.*

*Over two years of legal maneuvers, Finch and his attorney, Guy Lewis, whittled the case against him down to two charges. They went to trial in March of 2023, but the jury could not reach a verdict and a mistrial was declared.*

*Despite these successes, Finch said earlier this month that he was firing Lewis and hiring a new attorney—James Voyles Jr. Finch said he was unhappy that a May retrial was postponed without his knowledge to July. He added that he also knew changing his attorney would likely mean the trial would be postponed again.*

*On Friday, Judge Mark Walker expressed his displeasure with how Voyles and federal prosecutors worked with his office to postpone the case.*

*"Let me make it plain, that's my call, not the lawyer's call," Walker said. "Ya'll don't get to get with my courtroom deputy and rearrange my calendar."*

*He also took issue with the presumption that a continuance would be granted because a new lawyer was hired.*

*"Just because somebody wants to hire a new lawyer…doesn't mean they get to hire one lawyer, fire another, and grant their own continuance," Walker said. "That is not, nor has that ever been the law."*

*In the end, though, Walker granted the continuance and accepted Voyles onto the case. He set the new trial for October 2. He also said he wanted to make it clear that he was not granting a motion for Lewis to leave the case because of any issue related to the South Florida attorney's performance.*

*The judge noted that Lewis had been able to convince him to reveal Grand Jury transcripts, nearly convinced him to drop the case, gotten multiple charges dropped, and took the case to a mistrial. Walker then expressed his own admiration for Lewis's work on the case.*

*"His performance has been extraordinary," Walker said. "You are an extraordinary lawyer, and your work on this case should be put into some sort of publication for students at the law school down the hill from me to study. You are a credit to the profession."*

After Judge Walker said that he thought a book about this case would make its way down the hill for students at the law school to study, I thought to myself, I hope *my* book will make it to the law school down the hill that the Judge referred to (FSU in Tallahassee) for the students to read; U.S. Attorney Stephen Kunz, who lied to the grand jury in order to get an indictment against me, and then James, was a teacher there at one time, and possibly still is.

The prosecutors again listed both me and my husband, Lee, as "witnesses" on the Government witness list, which meant that we could neither attend the second trial until after all the witnesses had been called, nor could we have contact with James until that time.

After my release from the thirty days in the Marianna, Florida Federal prison camp on August 8, 2023, James' new team of lawyers did meet with me. We talked about my friendship with James and also about matters pertaining to the case as they prepared for trial. I was so worried for James, and I was extremely depressed, not feeling well, having had Covid with no treatment while being incarcerated, and just humiliated beyond words at having just spent a month in a federal prison. All I could do was pray for him, that the Lord would deliver him, and he would be acquitted.

On the last day of the trial, I was finally permitted to attend, and Lee and I sat together in the same federal courtroom where I had pled guilty and had been sentenced, waiting to hear the closing arguments and then the decision of the jury, which was to my great joy, acquittal of James Finch!

Months after the trial, I sat with James to ask him about the second trial because I wanted to include his perspective about the trial instead of just including a transcript or summary in my story.

"I had several character witnesses in the first trial," James said. "Harold Bazzel, who was the Bay County Clerk of Court for thirty-one years, Guy Tunnel, who had been the City of Lynn Haven Police Chief for fifteen years, Bay County Sheriff for 12 years, and then was appointed as the Commissioner of the Florida Department of Law Enforcement (FDLE), Jack Prescott, the General Manager of International Paper Company, and Willie B. Carpenter, a dear friend of many years."

"Willie B. was questioned in the first trial about his friendship with me."

"Did you ever go to Mr. Finch's house?" asked the prosecutor.

"He mostly came to my house," answered Willie B. "I had a better cook than him, and James loved the collard greens."

"Willie B. had also talked about the dangers of the 17th Street ditch, and how James had fixed the problem by piping and covering the ditch which had been there for over fifty years."

"People wrecked their cars, and several people died in that ditch when it was filled with water; I turned my car over in it myself one night," said Willie B.

The prosecutor then wanted to know what the circumstances were for Willie B.'s car to have gone into the ditch that night.

"I'd rather not talk about that," smiled Willie B. Willie B. is black, and his friendship with James was a genuine friendship of many years. Michael White had accused James of calling Antonius Barnes the "n" word in his testimony, trying to make it appear that James is a racist, which he is not.

"The prosecutors had cross-examined the witnesses in the first trial and we were now told that if I called the character witnesses again in the second trial, that instead of them just "staying in the box" of the single bribery charge against me in regard to the business loans I gave to Antonius Barnes, that they would be able to go outside of that box and question the witnesses about their knowledge of my friendship with you, the trips on the plane, the motorhome, and other information that would perhaps influence the jury against me. We decided not to call the character witnesses," said James.

"As the trial began, one morning I woke up the hotel room about 3 a.m. and I could not go back to sleep," James continued.

I thought to myself, "they are not bringing the guy I was supposed to have bribed as a witness. He is not on the witness list, and they did not accept his guilty plea for bribery, but instead, for not disclosing to a federal lending institution that he had another loan. Even the witness from the lending institution was not sure if Barnes legally had to disclose information about a personal loan, so Barnes should not have been charged with that."

"How in the hell is this happening in the United States of America," James said to himself. "Why in the hell did the judge not throw this case out when he read the grand jury transcript and knew that the prosecutor lied to the grand jury to get the indictments in the first place?"

James said he thought about the indictment, about Kunz telling the grand jury that I was floating on his yacht in Florida Keys in the weeks after the hurricane, when he had sold the boat in June of 2018.

"How in the hell can that be in the indictment with all the resources the federal government had. They never checked."

"Only two people spoke to the grand jury: Assistant U.S. Attorney Stephen Kunz and FBI Agent Borghini. The same SOB that is prosecuting me, Kunz, was responsible for the lies presented to the grand jury in the Aisenberg case. He indicted them for murdering their baby based on tapes that did not say what he said they said. The case was dropped by the prosecutors, but just like me and Margo, their lives were ruined. How is he allowed to do this thirty years later using the same tactics?"

"After the colloquy came out on Kunz in our evidentiary hearing somebody gave him one of those "Joe Biden" letters telling him he was done, because he and the FBI agent resigned," James added.

"Those bastards tried everything to get me to plead guilty right up to the trial," continued James. "I had my lawyers tell them that monkeys would jump out of my ass before I pleaded guilty, maybe gorillas."

"The morning of my trial they were pissed off and wanted to convict me of something. They called Chris Forehand to the stand and asked him about his immunity letter."

"Why are you asking him about that," the Judge inquired. "Where are you going with this?"

"We are just trying to take the sting out of this before the defense questions him" replied the prosecutor.

Judge Walker then replied, "I am getting dumber by the minute. Where are we going here?"

Voyles, my defense attorney stated, "We weren't planning on asking him anything about immunity."

As Voyles stood to cross examine Forehand, he said, "Mr. Forehand, we know that you got immunity for crimes you committed or something you did that was illegal, is that right?"

Forehand answered, "Yes."

Voyles then followed with, "What do you know about James Finch bribing Commissioner Barnes?"

Forehand answered, "Nothing."

Voyles finished with, "No further questions."

"After the government called the new FBI Agent Crecelius for questions, my attorneys followed up with questions of their own," recalled James. "They asked him if there was another FBI agent on the case before him, and they also asked him if he knew why the other agent (Borghini) was no longer on the case, to which he replied that he was now the acting agent."

"Do you know if Antonius Barnes is in Lynn Haven?" asked Voyles. He was pointing out to the jury that the prosecutors were not calling Barnes as a witness, the man I was supposed to have bribed.

"In other words, you know how to find him and get him here," continued my attorney.

The prosecutors then objected with, "The defense knew how to get him here."

Voyles and Lukemeyer, my attorneys, shit a brick, leaping to their feet and shouting, "Objection!"

The Judge called them up for a sidebar; the prosecutors were trying for another mistrial, and it didn't work," said James. "They were trying to shift the burden of proof to the defense."

"While the jury was out, they sent a note to the Judge with two questions, and the Judge had the jury called back in. They asked the Judge if Barnes had received immunity or if the charges against Barnes had been dropped," James said.

Judge Walker told the jury "I can't answer these questions. You are going to have to decide on this case based on the evidence you have seen if he is guilty or not."

James smiled, "The jury went out and they were not gone very long before returning with a verdict of not guilty."

I was in the courtroom when the verdict was returned, "Not guilty."

I was so relieved for James. As with me, they had tried to take away his life, and they had failed. Judge Walker came down to where James was sitting and shook his hand, congratulating him. As I walked toward the hallway with my attorney, Rob Vezina, I could see Judge Walker standing in the doorway, and I asked Rob if I could speak to him. Rob walked over and got Judge Walker's attention, and I walked to him, stuck out my hand, and said," I just wanted to say hello." Judge Walker recognized me, smiled warmly, and took my hand.

"Are you doing ok?" he asked.

"I'm doing great," I answered, and smiled back at him.

And with that, he turned to someone else who asked him something, and I walked out of the courtroom with Rob. I had accomplished what I wanted to do. I wanted the Judge to know that I was not broken, that I was still standing, despite all that had happened to me. What I really wanted was for him to know that I was innocent, that I was not the person the prosecutors had portrayed me as being. I am regretful that he was never able to hear my story at trial, but not regretful that I did not go to trial. I could not have won with five or six of the government witnesses testifying against me, as I know they had been doing all along, and would do again in front of a jury. Whether the jury would have believed my story or theirs would have been a toss-up, risking the rest of my life. The odds would not have been good. I felt something inside me rise up, part of the old me that was outspoken, courageous, and not weak or afraid as I had felt for so many months. I am glad that I spoke to the Judge; I will never understand why he did not dismiss our case with all of the evidence we presented, especially the grand jury transcripts that he read for himself. As I have said before, Judge Mark Walker was the only glimmer of fairness in the entire federal court system that I encountered. Maybe he did not want to risk being overturned by the higher court if he dismissed the case; I even speculated that maybe he was fearful of the prosecutors as well; they went after my attorneys at one point in the case, trying to disqualify them, questioning their integrity. I will never understand all that happened in the years of complete turmoil surrounding our case, but I do believe that all things work together for good for those who love the Lord, as the scripture says. My story is not over, and neither is James'.

WMBB-Channel 13 of Panama City, the television station which had persecuted us, along with the Bay County Sheriff's Office and the Government prosecutors, after three years of maligning both James and I in the worst possible light, reported on his acquittal. The story was lackluster, and it had no celebratory tone, but at least it was mostly factual, something new for their slanted reporting which had served the prosecutors and the BCSO from the beginning: Station Manager Terry Cole, News Director Tom Lewis and Anchor Amy Hoyt, were all part of the Bay County Sheriff's Office narrative for almost three years, and even sent text messages offering to interview me, at the worst possible moments of the case. Even on this fantastic day when James Finch was acquitted, the headline of their story did not say "acquitted" just that a verdict had been reached:

*TALLAHASSEE, Fla. (WMBB) A jury in a federal bribery trial asked two questions of Judge Mark Walker during their deliberations Thursday.*

*They wanted to know why Antonius Barnes, the man who was accused of taking bribes from business owner James Finch, did not testify, and they wanted to know if he had an immunity deal.*

*Federal prosecutors accused Finch, the owner of Phoenix Construction, of bribing Barnes, a former Lynn Haven city commissioner, with $45,000 in checks over several years. Barnes and Finch maintained that the money was a business loan.*

*Barnes eventually took a plea deal in the case and agreed to cooperate with the government. But at the first trial, he refused to testify that the money was a bribe saying only that it was a business loan from an old friend. The trial ended in a hung jury.*

*During a second trial this week, prosecutors declined to call Barnes. The defense did not call him either and in closing arguments, Finch's defense attorney, Jennifer Lukemeyer, asked the jury to consider that the man who should have been a key witness in the case never took the stand.*

*When the jury returned to Walker with that specific question about Barnes, he told them he could not explain the issue to them. Walker said that the jury could only consider the evidence presented to them at the trial and that they could not use any other evidence or an explanation by the judge to make their decision.*

*A few minutes later they came back with a not guilty verdict.*

*After the verdict, Walker spoke with the jurors in private about their decision and he relayed back to the attorneys that the fact that Barnes did not testify was the key factor in their decision.*

*Outside the courtroom, Finch celebrated with his supporters and promised retribution against some of the people who he believed worked against him.*

*"I've got a few lawsuits to file," Finch said. "I've got to prove that I was right and who was wrong. And there were some of them that have been wrong over here that have been totally wrong. That will come out starting tomorrow."*

"Do not judge me by my successes, judge me by how many times I fell down and got back up again."

Nelson Mandela

# EPILOG

I was the Mayor of the City of Lynn Haven from 2015 until August 2020, when following suspension from office by Governor Ron DeSantis after I was indicted, I resigned on that same day. Before becoming Mayor of the beautiful little coastal town of Lynn Haven, Florida, nestled in the Panhandle of Florida, I taught high school English, Drama, and Journalism, and I am also an accomplished musician and professional singer, best-known for Tribute Concerts featuring the music of Patsy Cline, Loretta Lynn, and Tammy Wynette. I look forward to just living my life again now and finding peace and strength with my faith in the same Lord who carried me through this nightmare, opened the door to my freedom, and truly delivered me from evil.

I also hope to find a way to help others who have been falsely accused, caught in the web of the Federal Grand Jury system, with seemingly no way out. I was a member of the League of Cities of Florida, as well as a member of the Board of Mayors before I was suspended from office by Governor DeSantis. I hope for an opportunity to speak to other elected officials in Florida and other states through the League of Cities, to share my story, to educate others how they must be vigilant and protect themselves from city employees, from law enforcement, and other officials in their municipalities who may not share their political views or who may harbor resentment or jealousy of their political success.

I will seek opportunities to speak to Congress, and elsewhere, to use my voice and my belief in justice to tell of this travesty to anyone who will listen, in hopes of making a difference, in working to abolish or reform the present Federal Grand Jury system that is used in only two countries in the world.... the United States and Liberia. The very institution which was put in place to protect and to provide advocacy for the citizens of this country has somehow gone awry. Every defendant should have access to his grand jury transcripts, to know what evidence was presented against him in secret by the prosecutors. Without our grand jury transcripts, James Finch and I would not have had the information we needed for our successful defense. How many rogue prosecutors have broken the very law they are supposed to uphold, by seeking convictions instead of the truth? How many have used their great powers for self-serving purposes, for "lawfare" and political interference, and destroying lives, families, careers, and hope for far too many individuals who have committed no crime, have no resources to defend themselves, and so plead guilty, and in some cases, end their lives in suicide because the pressure and the pain is too horrific to endure. James Finch was indicted because he was a multi-millionaire, a self-made man who came from abject poverty; he was targeted because of jealousy, set up by a fellow contractor who was angry with the me and with James because we discovered fraud, and I turned the information over to law enforcement.

I believe I was indicted because after the storm, I was a rising political star, a voice for the people, and a woman who could not be controlled by the local good old boys of the Florida Panhandle, "The Redneck Riviera" who have a political machine, smoothly run and controlled by a small group of powerful men. They destroyed my life, thinking I was out of the way, never counting on the fact that my lifelong friend, James Finch, would stand beside me, with his millions of dollars to pay for my defense and his, and expose the corrupt Sheriff, Lynn Haven Police Chief, investigators, FBI agents, U.S. Attorney, and Assistant U.S. Attorneys who were not counting on the exposure and the court battle which was coming from the Anderson/Finch defense team.

May God continue to bless America, and my prayer is that justice finds every corrupt, and reckless person of the United States Justice Department, particularly those prosecutors of the Northern District of Florida, U.S. Attorney Larry Keefe, and assistant U.S. Attorneys, Coody, Keen, and Grogan, who brought this indictment of "public corruption', so intent on a conviction that they refused to look for the truth, even when evidence they were provided by the defense proved they were wrong; for them, a "win" was all that mattered, with no regard for the collateral damage they left behind. Nelson Mandela, as he walked out of prison where he had been unjustly sentenced for decades said, "As I walked out the door toward the gate that would lead to my freedom, I knew if I didn't leave my bitterness and hatred behind, I would still be in prison."

As for Assistant United States Attorney Stephen Kunz and FBI Special Agent Lawrence Borghini, both who provided false evidence and statements to the Grand Jury, Sheriff Tommy Ford who targeted me, the respected Mayor of the City of Lynn Haven when I came to him for help, Major Jimmy Stanford and the other corrupt investigators of the Bay County Florida Sheriff's Office, Lynn Haven Police Chief Ricky Ramie who lied to the FBI in his interviews and in the evidentiary hearing, City Manager Vickie Gainer, and City Engineer Chris Forehand, both who gave false information to investigators to protect themselves, I will never be able to comprehend the cruelty of their actions, their having no remorse for the pain and devastation they brought to my life, to the life of James Finch, and to our families.

Derwin White and GAC , with the teaming agreement signed by Allan Bense with AshBritt, were "paid" over 16 million dollars in debris hauling and disposal, by AshBritt, after Michael White, as part of a deal with Derwin, fired CERES, to assure a bigger cut for Derwin *and* AshBritt; his nephew, Mickey White, along with City Manager, Michael White, defrauded the City of Lynn Haven for almost five million dollars. Derwin White passed away in July 2021. Allan Bense nor anyone from AshBritt were charged with crimes. City Manager Michael White and ECS owner Mickey White were each sentenced to 42 months, below the minimum guidelines, City Attorney Adam Albritton was sentenced to probation, and Josh Anderson and David Horton were sentenced to home confinement and probation.

Since the time of my indictment there has been a growing list of elected and appointed officials in Bay County Florida who have retired early to "spend more time with family," or who decided to not seek re-election to office. In April 2019, the same month I went to Sheriff Tommy Ford, according to the Florida Business website, Allan Bense moved from his position with GAC as President to "Chairman" and Derwin White became the President.. Gulf Alsphalt, GAC, the company of Allan Bense and the late Derwin White, has since been sold.

Martin Luther King, Jr. said, "Injustice anywhere is a threat to justice everywhere."

Until the people of the Panhandle of Florida stand up against this, the good old boy cartel and the elected officials they own will continue enjoying cocktails and a good laugh about how they prevailed one more time over some rising star, idealistic politician who thought she could change things, could make a difference, as they watch another sunset over the beautiful turquoise waves of the Emerald Coast. They are not worried. Their boy, Sheriff Tommy Ford and the U.S. Attorney of the Northern District of Florida got their token elected official for their public corruption crusade.... the female Mayor with the audacity to think she could challenge the incumbent Congressman, Neil Dunn, criticizing his weak actions and lack of visibility after Category 5 storm Hurricane Michael decimated the area, and then she walked down the street of her city, shoulder to shoulder with President Donald Trump, who brought needed help and visibility to the devastation in the Panhandle. They made sure the local newspaper, *The Panama City News Herald,* did not publish even a single photograph of the President of the United States and the Lynn Haven Mayor. The former editor of *The Panama City News Herald,* Mike Cazalas, is now employed by the State Attorney of the 14th Judicial Circuit, Larry Basford.

**Do not miss the journey of faith of former Mayor Margo Anderson, in her new book,**

CAMPERS: *Thirty Days in the Marianna Federal Correctional Institution Satellite Camp*

*by Margo Anderson*

The Mayor's story continues with a recounting of her sentence of thirty days in a minimum security federal prison camp to which the Federal Judge sentenced her, the stories of women she met there, the daily dreariness of the federal prison routine, harsh and cruel sentences of 10, 20, and even 30 years for non-violent crimes committed by women, many who went to trial rather than accept a plea deal and then were punished with sentences that separated them from their families, their small children for years, or even decades. Margo Anderson's story is a rare look from an insider's view of the life of an inmate in federal prison; the narrative is raw, filled with the hostility and anger of an innocent woman sentenced to thirty days in prison for a crime she did not commit, yet ashamed to admit she was there for only thirty days when her cellmate was serving thirty years. Her story is one of anger, fear, boredom, surviving a Covid outbreak, and ultimately, learning a new walk of faith, forgiveness, and hope for the future.

**To view a four-part interview recorded before a live audience with former Mayor Margo Anderson, as well as other interviews with her and news coverage regarding this case:**

**YouTube Channel,
"The Burnie Thompson Show"**

*For attorneys, defendants, or media who would like to review the publicly filed motions, arguments, transcripts and orders of this case: the Federal Courthouse, Tallahassee Florida, Case 5:20-cr-00028-MW-MJF.*

Made in the USA
Columbia, SC
27 November 2024

47725929R00350